The Editor

SIDNEY E. BERGER is Professor of English and Communications at Simmons College. He was for many years Head of Special Collections at the University of California, Riverside. His many publications include *The Design of Bibliographies: Observations, References and Examples* and *Medieval English Drama: An Annotated Bibliography of Recent Criticism.*

W. W. NORTON & COMPANY, INC.
Also Publishes

Mark Twain

PUDD'NHEAD WILSON and THOSE EXTRAORDINARY TWINS

AUTHORITATIVE TEXTS

TEXTUAL INTRODUCTION

TABLES OF VARIANTS

CRITICISM

SECOND EDITION

Edited by

SIDNEY E. BERGER

SIMMONS COLLEGE

W · W · NORTON & COMPANY · *New York* · *London*

W. W. Norton & Company has been independent since its founding in 1923, when William Warder and Mary D. Herter Norton first published lectures delivered at the People's Institute, the adult education division of New York City's Cooper Union. The Nortons soon expanded their program beyond the Institute, publishing books by celebrated academics from America and abroad. By mid-century, the two major pillars of Norton's publishing program—trade books and college texts—were firmly established. In the 1950s, the Norton family transferred control of the company to its employees, and today—with a staff of four hundred and a comparable number of trade, college, and professional titles published each year—W. W. Norton & Company stands as the largest and oldest publishing house owned wholly by its employees.

Every effort has been made to contact the copyright holders of each selection. Rights holders of any selections not credited should contact W. W. Norton & Company, Inc., 500 Fifth Avenue, New York, NY 10110, for a correction to be made in the next printing of our work.

Manufacturing by the Courier Companies—Westford Division.
Book design by Antonina Krass.
Production Manager: Benjamin Reynolds.

Library of Congress Cataloging-in-Publication Data

Twain, Mark, 1835–1910.
Pudd'nhead Wilson; and, Those extraordinary twins : authoritative texts, textual introduction and tables of variants, criticism / Mark Twain; edited by Sidney E. Berger.—2nd ed.
    p. cm.—(A Norton critical edition)
Includes bibliographical references.

ISBN 0-393-92535-8 (pbk.)

1. Twain, Mark, 1835–1910. Puddn'head Wilson. 2. Twain, Mark, 1835–1910. Those extraordinary twins. 3. Infants switched at birth—Fiction. 4. Imposters and imposture—Fiction. 5. Passing (Identity)—Fiction. 6. Trials (Murder)—Fiction. 7. Conjoined twins—Fiction. 8. Race relations—Fiction. 9. Missouri—Fiction. I. Twain, Mark, 1835–1910. Those extraordinary twins. II. Berger, Sidney E. III. Title. IV. Series.

PS1317.B4 2004
813'.4—dc22

2004054770

W. W. Norton & Company, Inc., 500 Fifth Avenue, New York, N. Y. 10110
www.wwnorton.com

W. W. Norton & Company Ltd., Castle House, 75/76 Wells Street,
London W1T 3QT

1 2 3 4 5 6 7 8 9 0

MARK TWAIN

Bequeathed us
In perpetuity
Himself, a
National park
Of the mind
With a river
Draining him,
Down which
Millions,
Alone,
Together,
Drift on a
Raft as if
It were the
Ark away
From the world.

—Ernest Kroll

Contents

Preface to the First Edition

When Mark Twain began the composition of what he then called "Those Extraordinary Twins"—some time in 1892—he was fifty-seven years old. He had reached a moment of desperation in his life. His past successes (*The Innocents Abroad* [1869], *Roughing It* [1872], *Tom Sawyer* [1876], *The Prince and the Pauper* [1882], *The Adventures of Huckleberry Finn* [1884], and *A Connecticut Yankee in King Arthur's Court* [1889]) had been followed by three years of what every author fears: literary stagnation—despite his writing of *The American Claimant* (1892), which he must have known was far from being in the same class as his earlier masterpieces.

His desperation came from many sources, not the least of which would have been his own recognition of the low quality of his work. It also came from his precarious financial position. He was sinking a fortune in the Paige typesetting machine, a fantastical creature doomed to failure; and his own publishing house, Charles L. Webster & Company, was—like him—going bankrupt. He was in urgent need of money. He was also traveling with Olivia, his wife, vainly trying to find a spa which would cure her of her ailment. (She suffered from syncope, a fainting disease.) And his extensive travel would have made him hungry for one thing a writer needs as much as he or she needs inspiration: time.

This desperation can be seen in his writing of the *Claimant* and his feverish work on *Tom Sawyer Abroad* and the early version of *Those Extraordinary Twins*, all works of dubious literary merit. It can be seen too in his numerous lecture trips, and in his experimentation with dramatized performances of his novels.

The initial conception of the tale—about which he writes in the opening passages of *Those Extraordinary Twins* (preceding Chapter 1)—was that it would be a farce based on the antics and activities of Siamese twins, "a human creature that had two heads, two necks, four arms, and one body, with a single pair of legs attached." (See *Those Extraordinary Twins*, "Emendations of the Copy-Text, Substantives," 130.24–26.) The humor involved here is from Clemens's desperation—from a writer whose imagination had paled with his shaking self-esteem, with his preoccupation with his financial affairs and his wife's health, and with fatigue. That he should introduce

David Wilson into the story was a stroke of luck, perhaps, or possibly a stroke of genius. With the introduction of Wilson, Tom Driscoll and Roxana easily followed, and the story "changed itself from a farce to a tragedy while I was going along with it," Twain says. When he recognized the inappropriateness of a murder in a farce, when he realized that he had two stories and not one, he "pulled one of the stories out by the roots, and left the other one—a kind of literary Caesarean operation." This accounts for the existence of two tales in this volume.

Several things from the author's life influenced his writing of these stories. He had seen Siamese twins on exhibit in 1891. He had been interested in fingerprinting as a means of identification at least as early as 1883 in "A Dying Man's Confession" (Chapter 31) of *Life on the Mississippi,* and he had gotten specific details of fingerprinting from Sir Francis Galton's book *Finger Prints* (London, 1892). The topics of slavery and miscegenation (the interbreeding of races) had been with him since his childhood. From his earliest days on the Virginia City *Territorial Enterprise*—as early as 1863—when he adopted the pen name Mark Twain, his own identity had taken on at least two public faces: the humorist writer and the serious reporter. As Frederick Anderson points out, "Identical twins are an obvious and graphic symbol of divided identity and Clemens' preoccupation with them appeared early and was persistent thereafter. In 1869 he had published an account of the 'Personal Habits of the Siamese Twins'—twins possessing many habits and characteristics later to be assigned to the twins, Luigi and Angelo. . . ." And he was influenced by his observations of the social evils in his society stemming from humankind's baseness—a baseness that allowed slavery and its inhumanity to come into being. Finally, Twain's home town of Hannibal must have served as his model for Dawson's Landing—the name coming from J. D. Dawson, who ran a school in Hannibal. Twain attended this school, which also served as a model for Dobbin's school in *Tom Sawyer.*

Mark Twain is generally considered a humorist, but his humor throughout this novel—like the idyllic nature of Dawson's Landing—is only on the surface. In *Pudd'nhead Wilson* the humor residual from the excised farce is not the guffawing type; it makes one grin and grimace at the same time. The potential humor from the dialect of the slaves ("'He tuck'n dissenhurrit him.' He licked his chops with relish after the stately word. Roxy struggled with it a moment, then gave it up and said—'Dissen*whiched* him?'") is undercut by the overall picture we get of slavery and the level of education allowed the slave. This is underscored in the change of babies—another plot element that could yield humor but ultimately yields a grim situation, with Tom cursing his heritage, and the rightful heir subjected to the pitiful life of a slave. The last words of the story ("the creditors sold him down the river")—emanating as they do from the exchange of babies—make the reader shudder, for we know what that terrible phrase "down the river" means. We have seen Roxy utter it in complete despair (at the end of Chapter 16), and we hear her horror story when she returns from down the river two chapters later.

The humor on the surface that surrounds David Wilson—with his ignominious name and treatment far below what his education, intelligence, and profession deserve—this humor points up the stupidity of all the residents of Dawson's Landing, a pessimistic though perhaps justifiable commentary on the common man. Even Pudd'nhead's own maxims, with their wry humor and satire, make us grimace at how bitter our existence must be, how foolish we all are, how insignificant humankind is. And the humor in the duel, both for its participants and its observers, is not terribly funny. The seconds get shot. Roxy, observing from afar, gets the skin of her nose shot off. What we have in the duel is Twain's broad criticism of an entire code of conduct represented by the First Families of Virginia—an antiquated code in a depressingly corrupt South with its fading, outdated aristocracy.

Part of Twain's attempt to depict the plight of the innocent Negro slave and the corruption of the southern system almost backfires: the murderer, the derelict, the primary source of evil is Tom, who is really Valet de Chambre. Roxy, when she is disturbed at her son's cowardice at his refusal to fight a duel, says of him, "Ain't nigger enough in him to show in his finger-nails, en dat takes mighty little—yit dey's enough to paint his soul." She even says to Tom, ". . . here you is, a slinkin' outen a duel en disgracin' our whole line like a ornery low-down hound! Yes, it's de nigger in you!" The phrase "our whole line" ostensibly refers to the Essex blood in him, but her final statement redirects our thinking. From the mouth of a character whom we respect we hear that cowardice is a racial matter. Both the southern aristocracy and the black race suffer here.

For the present edition all versions of the text on which Mark Twain might have worked have been collated, the variations tabulated, and the copy-text emended so as to produce an authoritative version of the novels. So much revision and outside intervention (in the form of typists, compositors, and editors) took place between the first penning of the story (in the Berg Manuscript) and the final printed texts (the serialized version and the English and American first editions) that I have deemed it proper to show the reader, first, where the base texts (the Morgan and Berg Manuscripts) have been emended, and, second, what variants exist in these versions that were not used for emendation. Explanations for all categories of editorial selection will be found in the Textual Introduction. The tabular matter includes

Emendations of the Copy-Text (Accidentals and Substantives) and Rejected Variants (Substantives). No table of Rejected Variants (Accidentals) has been included, for it would have been many pages long and would have shown little more than the vagaries of the styles of the printing houses that published the stories. To have included the rejected accidentals (mostly not the author's) in the listing of Rejected Variants would have buried important rejected readings in a long list of unimportant nonauthorial ones. What may seem to be peculiarities or inconsistencies in punctuation, spelling, or paragraphing are the author's own.

The criticism, arranged chronologically, covers a wide range of approaches—thematic, character study, plot and structure evaluation, humorous and serious elements, literary quality, genre, dialogue, the social and moral commentary of the novel, the entertainment value of the story, the flaws in the novel's construction, and so on. I have not included two "standard" essays on the text (Daniel Morley McKeithan's "The Morgan Manuscript of Mark Twain's *Pudd'nhead Wilson*" and Anne P. Wigger's "The Composition of Mark Twain's *Pudd'nhead Wilson* and *Those Extraordinary Twins*: Chronology and Development"—both cited in the Bibliography) because much of these writers' findings are covered in my own Textual Introduction. However, these two pieces have excellent materials not covered in any of the criticism in this volume and ought to be consulted by those wishing to know how the novels evolved.

The illustrations accompanying the text are selected from those in the first American edition (Hartford, Conn.: American Publishing Company, 1894). They have been reduced to about 60 percent of their original size, and a few have been slightly cropped. The artists are C. H. Warren and F. M. Senior; their initials or names can occasionally be seen in the illustrations.

I gratefully acknowledge Greg Bentley, Elyse Blankley, Robert Fitch, Paul J. B. Graham, Mary Hicks, Donna Holt, Carlton Holte, Alice Jurish, Timothy Lulofs, Jeff Meyn, Donald Peri, and Jeannie Rossi for their assistance at various stages of production.

I would also like to thank the people at the J. Pierpont Morgan Library, the Berg Collection of the New York Public Library, and the Mark Twain Papers at the Bancroft Library for making their manuscripts and archives available to me. Thanks are due also to Frederick Anderson and Professors Paul Baender, Warner Barnes, O M Brack, James M. Cox, and G. Thomas Tanselle for their help and encouragement, and to John W. N. Francis, Emily Garlin, and Cynthia Carr of W. W. Norton & Company for their assistance.

Finally, special thanks to Karen J. Ford for her strong coffee and careful proofreading.

SIDNEY E. BERGER

Preface to the Second Edition

Since the publication of the first edition of the Norton Critical Edition of Mark Twain's *Pudd'nhead Wilson* and *Those Extraordinary Twins* in 1980, interest in the novel has continued to grow. Part of its appeal has to do with the fact that Twain has remained a central figure in the canon of American letters, and when scholars, filmmakers, or lecturers talk about Mark Twain's accomplishments, they generally mention his three greatest literary achievements: *Tom Sawyer*, *Huckleberry Finn*, and *Pudd'nhead Wilson*.

Additionally, the basic story of *Pudd'nhead Wilson* concerns issues that remain central to American politics and interests: miscegenation, race relations, slavery, and so forth.

On top of this, *Pudd'nhead Wilson* is simply a wonderful story, despite its melodrama and, to us, predictable conclusion with the use of fingerprints to solve the crime. As many have pointed out, such a crime-fighting tool was fairly new in Twain's day, the Francis Galton book on fingerprints having been published only a year or so before the novel began appearing serially in the pages of *The Century Magazine* (December 1893). But it is like the perpetual interest in any good piece of literature. Theatergoers know that Hamlet is going to die and that Oedipus will blind himself. But they return century after century for the thrill of the performance.

Pudd'nhead Wilson is also popular in schools for a number of reasons. First, it addresses head-on—maybe for the first time in literature—the issues of miscegenation and slavery. So it can be used in literature and history classes as a way to reveal cultural interests in the middle and at the end of the nineteenth century. Second, it is funny, not just in the "Calendar" entries at the opening of each chapter but also in its plot, characterization, and satire. That the humor is sardonic or grim does not detract from its ability to amuse. Third, it plays on stereotypes that are easily penetrated and finely created. Also, it is simply a fascinating story—a murder mystery (always a popular genre) with twists, hidden identities, a duel, a clearly delineated sense of good versus evil, character assassination, victory in the face of great odds, crime and punishment, humorous (if forced) dialogue, witty observations, and much more. And it is all packaged by Mark Twain, one of the great raconteurs of American letters, who could really tell a story!

It is no wonder that the tale has maintained its popularity for more than a hundred years.

Pudd'nhead Wilson should not be consumed by itself. The linked text *Those Extraordinary Twins* is so interconnected with *Pudd'nhead Wilson* that to understand one, one must read both. There are shared characters, shared plot elements, and shared themes. In fact, when Mark Twain began writing what eventually turned out to be *Pudd'n-head Wilson*, he first titled it *Those Extraordinary Twins*, thinking he would write a farce about incompatible Siamese twins. He saw the possibilities for humor in, for example, a teetotaler twin getting drunk when his connected brother went on a binge but stayed sober.

To reinforce the dictum that these should be read together, one must know that at a late stage of the works' development, in the 633½-page Morgan Manuscript, the two tales were still linked as one. When Mark Twain saw the problem of having them together—a farce within a "tragedy"—he did his "literary Caesarean operation" and pulled *Those Extraordinary Twins* from the belly of *Pudd'nhead Wilson*. It is for this reason that Norton has agreed to print both in its Critical Edition.

Those Extraordinary Twins is instructive, as well, because it presents the author's own statements about writing in general and writing these two pieces specifically. We don't often get an author's views on the process of composition, and though Mark Twain writes somewhat tongue in check here, it is nonetheless instructive to see his take on how the two pieces were conceived and born.

There are many signs that interest in *Pudd'nhead Wilson* is not waning, either in the scholarly world or in the public at large. Sales of the book are steady and have been since the first Norton Critical Edition came out twenty-four years ago. The text continues to be taught in classes in the humanities at the secondary and college level. And scholarship on the book persists. In 1990, for instance, a whole volume of essays was published on the novel: *Mark Twain's* Pudd'nhead Wilson: *Race, Conflict, and Culture* (ed. Susan Gillman and Forrest G. Robinson [Durham and London: Duke University Press]; three of the essays in the present edition are taken from this book). The dozen essays in the Gillman and Robinson collection are joined by dozens of others in the academic press.

As I wrote this [in June 2003], I conducted an Internet search on the title *Pudd'nhead Wilson* and got 10,200 hits. A search on the title *Those Extraordinary Twins* turned up 39,000 hits.

For the general public, an hour-and-a-half dramatization of the text, created in 1983, premiered on PBS's *American Playhouse* on January 24, 1984 (and was later issued in video), directed by Alan Bridges and part of the Mark Twain Library Collection. *Mark Twain: A Musical Biography* was released in video in 1992. A&E aired its video biography *Mark Twain* in 1995. In 1996 the video *Mark Twain* in the Famous Author series was released. April of 1999 saw the release of Hal Holbrook's video *Mark Twain Tonight*.

On April 29, 2002, TBE (To Be Equal) reported on a version of *Pudd'nhead Wilson* adapted for the stage and reinterpreted somewhat by the playwright Charles Smith. The play, based on the novel, opened in New York on May 15 at the Lucille Lortel theater, in Greenwich Village. The play was staged by The Acting Company, a New York–based repertory theater company that performs throughout the country each year to bring plays, both classical and modern, to communities large and small.

January 2002 saw the premiere of Ken Burns's *Mark Twain*. In April 2003 PBS began airing its three-part documentary *Race—The Power of an Illusion,* in which *Pudd'nhead Wilson* is quoted.

Since its publication in book form in 1894, *Pudd'nhead Wilson* has become a classic, much cited, often assigned, and yielding many rewards.

Because of copyright restrictions, five long passages from the manuscript had to be presented in brief summary in the first Norton Critical Edition. Since then, copyright no longer applies and these passages have been supplied in full in the present edition. Some of the old articles have been dropped in favor of seven new ones, reflecting recent scholarship on the text. (And many more of the marginal illustrations from the first American edition [Hartford: American Publishing Company, 1894] have been added to the present edition.)

I have been teaching *Pudd'nhead Wilson*—and rereading it—for the last quarter century, and I am still thrilled by it. It yields new fruits with each dip into its text.

Along with my repeated thanks to those who assisted me in the production of the first edition, I would like to add for this new version notes of thanks to Christine Nelson at the J. Pierpont Morgan Library, and to Carol Bemis, Brian B. Baker, Marian Johnson, and Kurt Wildermuth of W. W. Norton & Company. Cheryl Kohen, Iris O'Donnell, Erin Rook, and Danielle Sweeney have helped brilliantly in the proofreading of this new edition. And a Simmons Fund for Research Grant from Simmons College in Boston assisted me in the proofreading of the text. Finally, my deepest appreciation to Michèle V. Cloonan, without whom the present volume could not have blossomed.

End-of-Line Hyphenation in This Volume

The following table clarifies all ambiguous end-of-line hyphenations in the Twain texts in this volume. The left column shows the page and line number (including lines in the text and in the calendar entries) of the reading in question, and the right column shows how the compound ought to be styled.

3.4	steamboat	103.17	finger-prints
4.1	half-moon	106.32	footsteps
11.1	finger-prints	116.43	finger-marks
15.16	baby-gowns	117.19	knife-handle
21.14	overstepped	117.29	blood-stained
21.25	body-guard	117.32	finger-prints
22.27	canoe-bottom	117.34	finger-prints
27.43	good-natured	131.11	million-voiced
28.12	everybody	139.5	table-room
33.26	four-handed	143.9	freethinkers
36.38	June-bug	145.9	cobwebby
37.9	wash-tub	148.12	nowdays
37.13	bar'footed	151.37	freethinking
43.35	to-night	152.26	back-breaking
52.40	good-naturedly	173.20	Hartwort
54.15	finger-mark	181.21	mouthpiece
62.12	fire-boys	181.45	turn-out
73.31	battle-ground	182.10	extra-temperance
75.10	re-make	190.11	re-wrote
76.1	low-down	207, col. 2.43	freethinkers
76.32	a-cussin'	208, col. 2.31	freethinkers
76.35	a-standin'	209, col. 2.60	to-night's
84.44	rag-tag	210, col. 2.48	news-boys
89.15	back-alley	211, col. 1.41	long-drawn
92.41	woodyard	211, col. 1.55	eyelids
100.18	room-door	211, col. 2.4	to-day
102.15	everybody	211, col. 2.19	shame-facedly
102.21	finger-prints	212, col. 1.51	fellow-citizens

In most editions of this novel the title is given as *The Tragedy of Pudd'nhead Wilson*. But on the first page of the Morgan Manuscript, in Mark Twain's own hand, the title is simply *Pudd'nhead Wilson, A Tale*. Whether the work is a tragedy and in what sense it is are topics of debate among scholars. For the present edition the simple title *Pudd'nhead Wilson, A Tale* is adopted.

Similarly, the simple title *Those Extraordinary Twins* is used here, though the title page of the first printed edition (American Publishing Company, 1894) says: And the Comedy/THOSE EXTRAORDINARY TWINS. The words "The Tragedy of" and "And the Comedy" are printed in very small type, and seem to be more descriptive than titular.

The Text of
PUDD'NHEAD WILSON
A TALE

There is no character, howsoever good and fine, but it can be destroyed by ridicule, howsoever poor and witless. Observe the ass, for instance: his character is about perfect, he is the choicest spirit among all the humbler animals, yet see what ridicule has brought him to. Instead of feeling complimented when we are called an ass, we are left in doubt.

—PUDD'NHEAD WILSON'S CALENDAR.

A Whisper to the Reader

A person who is ignorant of legal matters is always liable to make mistakes when he tries to photograph a court scene with his pen; and so, I was not willing to let the law-chapters in this book go to press without first subjecting them to rigid and exhausting revision and correction by a trained barrister—if that is what they are called. These chapters are right, now, in every detail, for they were re-written under the immediate eye of William Hicks, who studied law part of a while in southwest Missouri thirty-five years ago and then came over here to Florence for his health and is still helping for exercise and board in Maccaroni and Vermicelli's horse-feed shed which is up the back alley as you turn around the corner out of the Piazza del Duomo just beyond the house where that stone that Dante used to sit on six hundred years ago is let into the wall when he let on to be watching them build Giotto's Campanile and yet always got tired looking as soon as Beatrice passed along on her way to get a chunk of chestnut-cake to defend herself with in case of a Ghibelline outbreak before she got to school, at the same old stand where they sell the same old cake to this day and it is just as light and good as it was then,

1

too, and this is not flattery, far from it. He was a little rusty on his law, but he rubbed up for this book, and those two or three legal chapters are right and straight, now. He told me so himself.

Given under my hand this second day of January, 1893, at the Villa Viviani, village of Settignano, three miles back of Florence, on the hills—the same certainly affording the most charming view to be found on this planet, and with it the most dream-like and enchanting sunsets to be found in any planet or even in any solar system—and given, too, in the swell room of the house, with the busts of Cerretani senators and other grandees of this line looking approvingly down upon me as they used to look down upon Dante, and mutely asking me to adopt them into my family, which I do with pleasure, for my remotest ancestors are but spring chickens compared with these robed and stately antiques, and it will be a great and satisfying lift for me, that six hundred years will.

MARK TWAIN.

Chapter 1

Tell the truth or trump—but get the trick.
—PUDD'NHEAD WILSON'S CALENDAR.

The scene of this chronicle is the town of Dawson's Landing, on the Missouri side of the Mississippi, half a day's journey, per steamboat, below St. Louis.

In 1830 it was a snug little collection of modest one- and two-story frame dwellings whose whitewashed exteriors were almost concealed from sight by climbing tangles of rose vines, honeysuckles and morning-glories. Each of these pretty homes had a garden in front fenced with white palings and opulently stocked with hollyhocks, marigolds, touch-me-nots, prince's feathers and other old-fashioned flowers; while on the window-sills of the houses stood wooden boxes containing moss-rose plants, and terra cotta pots in which grew a breed of geranium whose spread of intensely red blossoms accented the prevailing pink tint of the rose-clad house-front like an explosion of flame. When there was room on the ledge outside of the pots and boxes for a cat, the cat was there—in sunny weather—stretched at full length, asleep and blissful, with her furry belly to the sun and a paw curved over her nose. Then that home was complete, and its contentment and peace were made manifest to the world by this symbol, whose testimony is infallible. A home without a cat—and a well fed, well petted, and properly revered cat—may be a perfect home, perhaps, but how can it prove title?

All along the streets, on both sides, at the outer edge of the brick sidewalks, stood locust trees, with trunks protected by wooden boxing, and these furnished shade for summer and a sweet fragrance in spring when the clusters of buds came forth. The main street, one block back from the river, and running parallel with it, was the sole business street. It was six blocks long, and in each block two or three brick stores three stories high towered above interjected bunches of little frame shops. Swinging signs creaked in the wind, the street's whole length. The candy-striped pole which indicates nobility proud and ancient, along the palace-bordered canals of Venice, indicated merely the humble barber shop along the main street of Dawson's Landing. On a chief corner stood a lofty unpainted pole wreathed from top to bottom with tin pots and pans and cups, the chief tin-monger's noisy notice to the world (when the wind blew) that his shop was on hand for business at that corner.

The hamlet's front was washed by the clear waters of the great river; its body stretched itself rearward up a gentle incline; its most rearward border fringed itself out and scattered its houses about the base line of the hills; the hills rose high, enclosing the town in a half-moon curve, clothed with forests from foot to summit.

Steamboats passed up and down every hour or so. Those belonging to the little Cairo line and the little Memphis line always stopped; the big Orleans liners stopped for hails only, or to land passengers or freight; and this was the case also with the great flotilla of "transients." These latter came out of a dozen rivers—the Illinois, the Missouri, the Upper Mississippi, the Ohio, the Monongahela, the Tennessee, the Red river, the White river, and so on; and were bound every whither and stocked with every imaginable comfort or neces-

sity which the Mississippi's communities could want, from the frosty Falls of St. Anthony down through nine climates to torrid New Orleans.

Dawson's Landing was a slave-holding town, with a rich slave-worked grain and pork country back of it. The town was sleepy, and comfortable, and contented. It was fifty years old, and was growing slowly—very slowly, in fact, but still it was growing.

The chief citizen was York Leicester Driscoll, about forty years old, Judge of the county court. He was very proud of his old Virginian ancestry, and in his hospitalities and his rather formal and stately manners he kept up its traditions. He was fine, and just, and generous. To be a gentleman—a gentleman without stain or blemish—was his only religion, and to it he was always faithful. He was respected, esteemed, and beloved by all the community. He was well off, and was gradually adding to his store.

He and his wife were very nearly happy, but not quite, for they had no children. The longing for the treasure of a child had grown stronger and stronger as the years slipped away, but the blessing never came—and was never to come.

With this pair lived the Judge's widowed sister, Mrs. Rachel Pratt, and she also was childless—childless, and sorrowful for that reason, and not to be comforted. The women were good and commonplace people, and did their duty and had their reward in clear consciences and the community's approbation. They were Presbyterians, the Judge was a free-thinker.

Pembroke Howard, lawyer and bachelor, aged about forty, was another old Virginian grandee with proved descent from the First Families. He was a fine, brave, majestic creature, a gentleman according to the nicest requirements of the Virginian rule, a devoted Presbyterian, an authority on the "code," and a man always courteously ready to stand up before you in the field if any act or word of his had seemed doubtful or suspicious to you, and explain it with any weapon you might prefer, from brad-awls to artillery. He was very popular with the people, and was the Judge's dearest friend.

Then there was Colonel Cecil Burleigh Essex, another F.F.V. of formidable calibre—however, with him we have no concern.

Percy Northumberland Driscoll, brother to the Judge, and younger than he by five years, was a married man, and had had children around his hearthstone; but they were attacked in detail by measles, croup and scarlet fever, and this had given the doctor a chance with his effective antediluvian methods; so the cradles were empty. He was a prosperous man, with a good head for speculations, and his fortune was growing. On the first of February, 1830, two boy babes were born in his house: one to him, the other to one of his slave girls, Roxana by name. Roxana was twenty years old. She was up and around the same day, with her hands full, for she was tending both babies.

Mrs. Percy Driscoll died within the week. Roxy remained in charge of the children. She had her own way, for Mr. Driscoll soon absorbed himself in his speculations and left her to her own devices.

In that same month of February Dawson's Landing gained a new citizen. This was Mr. David Wilson, a young fellow of Scotch parentage. He had wandered to this remote region from his birth-place in the interior of the State of New York, to seek his fortune. He was twenty-five years old, college-bred, and had finished a post-college course in an eastern law school a couple of years before.

He was a homely, freckled, sandy-haired young fellow, with an intelligent blue eye that had frankness and comeradeship in it and a covert twinkle of a pleasant sort. But for an unfortunate remark of his, he would no doubt have entered at once upon a successful career at Dawson's Landing. But he made his fatal remark the first day he spent in the village, and it "gauged" him. He had just made the acquaintance of a group of citizens when an invisible dog began to yelp and snarl and howl and make himself very comprehensibly disagreeable, whereupon young Wilson said, much as one who is thinking aloud—

"I wish I owned half of that dog."

"Why?" somebody asked.

"Because, I would kill my half."

The group searched his face with curiosity, with anxiety even, but found no light there, no expression that they could read. They fell away from him as from something uncanny, and went into privacy to discuss him. One said—

" 'Pears to be a fool."

" 'Pears?" said another. "*Is,* I reckon you better say."

"Said he wished he owned *half* of the dog, the idiot," said a third. "What did he reckon would become of the other half if he killed his half? Do you reckon he thought it would live?"

"Why, he must have thought it, unless he *is* the downrightest fool in the world; because if he hadn't thought that, he would have wanted to own the whole dog, knowing that if he killed his half and the other half died, he would be responsible for that half, just the same as if he had killed that half instead of his own. Don't it look that way to you, gents?"

"Yes, it does. If he owned one half of the general dog, it would be so; if he owned one end of the dog and another person owned the other end, it would be so, just the same; particularly in the first case, because if you kill one half of a general dog, there ain't any man that can tell whose half it was, but if he owned one end of the dog, maybe he could kill his end of it and—"

"No, he couldn't, either; he couldn't and not be responsible if the other end died, which it would. In my opinion the man ain't in his right mind."

"In my opinion he hain't *got* any mind."

No. 3 said—

"Well, he's a lummux, anyway."

"That's what he is," said No. 4, "he's a labrick—just a Simon-pure labrick, if ever there was one."

"Yes, sir, he's a dam fool, that's the way I put him up," said No. 5. "Anybody can think different that wants to, but those are my sentiments."

"I'm with you, gentlemen," said No. 6. "Perfect jackass—yes, and it ain't going too far to say he is a pudd'nhead. If he ain't a pudd'nhead, I ain't no judge, that's all."

Mr. Wilson stood elected. The incident was told all over the town, and gravely discussed by everybody. Within a week he had lost his first name; Pudd'nhead took its place. In time he came to be liked, and well liked, too; but by that time the nickname had got well stuck on, and it stayed. That first day's verdict made him a fool, and he was not able to get it set aside, or even modified. The nickname soon ceased to carry any harsh or unfriendly feeling with it, but it held its place, and was to continue to hold its place for twenty long years.

Chapter 2

Adam was but human—this explains it all. He did not want the apple for the apple's sake, he only wanted it because it was forbidden. The mistake was in not forbidding the serpent; then he would have eaten the serpent.

—PUDD'NHEAD WILSON'S CALENDAR.

Pudd'nhead Wilson had a trifle of money when he arrived, and he bought a small house on the extreme western verge of the town. Between it and Judge Driscoll's house there was only a grassy yard, with a paling fence dividing the properties in the middle. He hired a small office down in the town and hung out a tin sign with these words on it:

DAVID WILSON
ATTORNEY AND COUNSELOR AT LAW.
SURVEYING, CONVEYANCING, ETC.

But his deadly remark had ruined his chance—at least in the law. No clients came. He took down his sign, after a while, and put it up on his own house with the law features knocked out of it. It offered his services now in the humble capacities of land surveyor and expert accountant. Now and then he got a job of surveying to do, and now and then a merchant got him to straighten out his books. With Scotch patience and pluck he resolved to live down his reputation and work his way into the legal field yet. Poor fellow, he could not

foresee that it was going to take him such a weary long time to do it.

He had a rich abundance of idle

time, but it never hung heavy on his hands, for he interested himself
in every new thing that was born into the universe of ideas, and studied it and experimented upon it at his house. One of his pet fads was
palmistry. To another one he gave no name, neither would he explain
to anybody what its purpose was, but merely said it was an amusement. In fact he had found that his fads added to his reputation as a
pudd'nhead; therefore he was growing chary of being too commu-
nicative about them. The fad without a name was one which dealt
with people's finger-marks. He carried in his coat pocket a shallow
box with grooves in it, and in the grooves strips of glass five inches
long and three inches wide. Along the lower edge of each strip was
pasted a slip of white paper. He asked people to pass their hands
through their hair, (thus collecting upon them a thin coating of the
natural oil,) and then make a thumb-mark on a glass strip, following
it with the mark of the ball of each finger in succession. Under this
row of faint grease-prints he would write a record on the strip of
white paper—thus:

"JOHN SMITH, *right hand*"—

and add the day of the month and the year, then take Smith's left
hand on another glass strip, and add name and date and the words
"left hand." The strips were now returned to the grooved box, and
took their place among what Wilson called his "records."

He often studied his records, examining and poring over them with
absorbing interest until far into the night; but what he found there—
if he found anything—he revealed to no one. Sometimes he copied
on paper the involved and delicate pattern left by the ball of a finger,
and then vastly enlarged it with a pantagraph so that he could examine its web of curving lines with ease and convenience.

One sweltering afternoon—it was the first day of July, 1830—he
was at work over a set of tangled account books in his work-room,
which looked westward over a stretch of vacant lots, when a conversation outside disturbed him. It was carried on in yells, which
showed that the people engaged in it were not close together:

"Say, Roxy, how does yo' baby come on?" This from the distant
voice.

"Fust rate; how does *you* come on, Jasper?" This yell was from
close by.

"Oh, I's middlin'; hain't got noth'n to complain of. I's gwyne to
come a-court'n you bime by, Roxy."

"*You* is, you black mud-cat! Yah-yah-yah! I got sump'n better to do
den 'sociat'n wid niggers as black as you is. Is ole Miss Cooper's
Nancy done give you de mitten?" Roxy followed this sally with
another discharge of care-free laughter.

"You's jealous, Roxy, dat's what's de matter
wid *you*, you huzzy—yah-yah-yah! Dat's de
time I got you!"

"Oh, yes, *you* got me, hain't you. 'Clah to
goodness if dat conceit o' yo'n strikes in,
Jasper, it gwyne to kill you, sho'. If you
b'longed to me I'd sell you down de river 'fo'
you git too fur gone. Fust time I runs acrost
yo' marster, I's gwyne to tell him so."

This idle and aimless jabber went on and
on, both parties enjoying the friendly duel and
each well satisfied with his own share of the
wit exchanged—for wit they considered it.

Wilson stepped to the window to observe
the combatants; he could not work while
their chatter continued. Over in the vacant lots was Jasper, young,
coal-black and of magnificent build, sitting on a wheelbarrow in the
pelting sun—at work, supposably, whereas he was in fact only
preparing for it by taking an hour's rest before beginning. In front of
Wilson's porch stood Roxy, with a local hand-made baby-wagon, in
which sat her two charges—one at each end and facing each other.
From Roxy's manner of speech, a stranger would have expected her
to be black, but she was not. Only one-sixteenth of her was black,
and that sixteenth did not show. She was of majestic form and
stature, her attitudes were imposing and statuesque, and her gestures and movements distinguished by a noble and stately grace. Her
complexion was very fair, with the rosy glow of vigorous health in the
cheeks, her face was full of character and expression, her eyes were
brown and liquid, and she had a heavy suit of fine soft hair which
was also brown, but the fact was not apparent because her head was
bound about with a checkered handkerchief and the hair was concealed under it. Her face was shapely, intelligent, and comely—even
beautiful. She had an easy, independent carriage—when she was
among her own caste—and a high and "sassy" way, withal; but of
course she was meek and humble enough where white people were.

To all intents and purposes Roxy was as white as anybody, but the
one-sixteenth of her which was black out-voted the other fifteen
parts and made her a negro. She was a slave, and salable as such. Her
child was thirty-one parts white, and he, too, was a slave, and by a
fiction of law and custom a negro. He had blue eyes and flaxen curls,
like his white comrade, but even the father of the white child was
able to tell the children apart—little as he had commerce with
them—by their clothes: for the white babe wore ruffled soft muslin
and a coral necklace, while the other wore merely a coarse tow-linen
shirt which barely reached to its knees, and no jewelry.

The white child's name was Thomas à Becket Driscoll, the other's name was Valet de Chambre: no surname—slaves hadn't the privilege. Roxana had heard that phrase somewhere, the fine sound of it had pleased her ear, and as she had supposed it was a name, she loaded it onto her darling. It soon got shortened to "Chambers," of course.

Wilson knew Roxy by sight, and when the duel of wit began to play out, he stepped outside to gather in a record or two. Jasper went to work energetically, at once—perceiving that his leisure was observed. Wilson inspected the children and asked—

"How old are they, Roxy?"

"Bofe de same age, sir—five months. Bawn de fust o' Febuary."

"They're handsome little chaps. One's just as handsome as the other, too."

A delighted smile exposed the girl's white teeth, and she said:

"Bless yo' soul, Misto Wilson, it's pow'ful nice o' you to say dat, caze one of 'em ain't on'y a nigger. Mighty prime little nigger, I allays says, but dat's caze it's mine, o' course."

"How do you tell them apart, Roxy, when they haven't any clothes on?"

Roxy laughed a laugh proportioned to her size, and said:

"Oh, I kin tell 'em 'part, Misto Wilson, but I bet Marse Percy couldn't, not to save his life."

Wilson chatted along for a while, and presently got Roxy's finger-prints for his collection—right hand and left—on a couple of his glass strips; then labeled and dated them, and took the "records" of both children, and labeled and dated them also.

Two months later, on the third of September, he took this trio of finger-marks again. He liked to have a "series"—two or three "tak-ings" at intervals during the period of childhood, these to be followed by others at intervals of several years.

The next day—that is to say, on the fourth of September,—some-thing occurred which profoundly impressed Roxana. Mr. Driscoll missed another small sum of money—which is a way of saying that this was not a new thing, but had happened before. In truth it had happened three times before. Driscoll's patience was exhausted. He was a fairly humane man, toward slaves and other animals; he was an exceedingly humane man toward the erring of his own race. Theft he could not abide, and plainly there was a thief in his house. Nec-essarily the thief must be one of his negroes. Sharp measures must be taken. He called his servants before him. There were three of these, besides Roxy: a man, a woman, and a boy twelve years old. They were not related. Mr. Driscoll said:

"You have all been warned before. It has done no good. This time I will teach you a lesson. I will sell the thief. Which of you is the guilty one?"

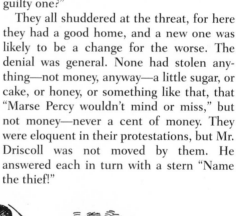

They all shuddered at the threat, for here they had a good home, and a new one was likely to be a change for the worse. The denial was general. None had stolen any-thing—not money, anyway—a little sugar, or cake, or honey, or something like that, that "Marse Percy wouldn't mind or miss," but not money—never a cent of money. They were eloquent in their protestations, but Mr. Driscoll was not moved by them. He answered each in turn with a stern "Name the thief!"

The truth was, all were guilty but Roxana; she suspected that the others were guilty, but she did not know them to be so. She was horrified to think how near she had come to being guilty herself; she had been saved in the nick of time by a revival in the colored Methodist church a fortnight before, at which time and place she "got religion." The very next day after that gracious experience, while her change of style was fresh upon her and she was vain of her purified condition, her master left a couple of dollars lying unprotected on his desk, and she happened upon that temptation when she was polishing around with a dust-rag. She looked at the money a while with a steadily rising resentment, then she burst out with—

"Dad blame dat revival, I wisht it had a ben put off till tomorrow!"

Then she covered the tempter with a book, and another member of the kitchen cabinet got it. She made this sacrifice as a matter of religious etiquette; as a thing necessary just now, but by no means to be wrested into a precedent; no, a week or two would limber up her piety, then she would be rational again, and the next two dollars that got left out in the cold would find a comforter—and she could name the comforter.

Was she bad? Was she worse than the general run of her race? No. They had an unfair show in the battle of life, and they held it no sin to take military advantage of the enemy—in a small way; in a small way, but not in a large one. They would smouch provisions from the pantry whenever they got a chance; or a brass thimble, or a cake of wax, or an emery-bag, or a paper of needles, or a silver spoon, or a dollar bill, or small articles of clothing, or any other property of light value; and so far were they from considering such reprisals sinful, that they would go to church and shout and pray their loudest and sincerest with their plunder in their pockets. A farm smoke-house had to be kept heavily padlocked, for even the colored deacon himself could not resist a ham when Providence showed him in a dream, or otherwise, where such a thing hung lonesome and longed for some one to love. But with a hundred hanging before him the deacon would not take two—that is, on the same night. On frosty nights the humane negro prowler would warm the end of a plank and put it up under the cold claws of chickens roosting in a tree; a drowsy hen would step onto the comfortable board, softly clucking her gratitude, and the prowler would dump her into his bag, and later into his stomach, perfectly sure that in taking this trifle from the man who daily robbed him of an inestimable treasure—his liberty—he was not committing any sin that God would remember against him in the Last Great Day.

"Name the thief!"

For the fourth time Mr. Driscoll had said it, and always in the same hard tone. And now he added these words of awful import:

"I give you one minute"—he took out his watch—"if at the end of that time you have not confessed, I will not only sell all four of you, *but*—I will sell you DOWN THE RIVER!"

It was equivalent to condemning them to hell! No Missouri negro doubted this. Roxy reeled in her tracks and the color vanished out of her face; the others dropped to their knees as if they had been shot; tears gushed from their eyes, their supplicating hands went up, and three answers came in the one instant:

"I done it!"

"I done it!"

"I done it!—have mercy, marster—Lord have mercy on us po' niggers!"

"Very good," said the master, putting up his watch, "I will sell you *here*, though you don't deserve it. You ought to be sold down the river."

The culprits flung themselves prone, in an ecstasy of gratitude, and kissed his feet, declaring that they would never forget his goodness and never cease to pray for him as long as they lived. They were sincere, for like a god he had stretched forth his mighty hand and closed the gates of hell against them. He knew, himself, that he had done a noble and gracious thing, and he was privately well pleased with his magnanimity; and that night he set the incident down in his diary, so that his son might read it in after years and be thereby moved to deeds of gentleness and humanity himself.

Chapter 3

*Whoever has lived long enough to find out what life is, knows how
deep a debt of gratitude we owe to Adam, the first great benefactor of
our race. He brought death into the world.*
                              —PUDD'NHEAD WILSON'S CALENDAR.

Percy Driscoll slept well the night he saved his house-minions
from going down the river, but no wink of sleep visited Roxy's eyes.
A profound terror had taken possession of her. Her child could grow
up and be sold down the river! The thought crazed her with horror.
If she dozed, and lost herself for a moment, the next moment she was
on her feet and flying to her child's cradle to see if it was still there.
Then she would gather it to her heart and pour out her love upon it
in a frenzy of kisses, moaning, crying, and saying "Dey shant, oh, dey
shan't!—yo' po' mammy will kill you fust!"

Once, when she was tucking it back in its cradle again, the other
child nestled in its sleep and attracted her attention. She went and
stood over it a long time, communing with herself:

"What has my po' baby done, dat he couldn't have yo' luck? He
hain't done nuth'n. God was good to you; why warn't He good to him?
Dey can't sell *you* down de river. I hates yo' pappy; he ain't got no
heart—for niggers he haint, anyways. I hates him, en I could kill
him!" She paused a while, thinking; then she burst into wild sobbings
again, and turned away, saying, "Oh, I got to kill my chile, dey ain't
no yuther way,—killin' *him* wouldn't save de chile fum goin' down de
river. Oh, I got to do it, yo' po' mammy's got to kill you to save you,
honey"—she gathered her baby to her bosom, now, and began to
smother it with caresses—"Mammy's got to kill you,—how *kin* I do
it! But yo' mammy ain't gwyne to desert you,—no, no; *dah*, don't
cry—she gwyne *wid* you, she gwyne to kill herself, too. Come along,
honey, come along wid Mammy; we gwyne to jump in de river, den
de troubles o' dis worl' is all over—dey don't sell po' niggers down de
river over *yonder*."

She started toward the door, crooning to the child and hushing it;
midway she stopped, suddenly. She had caught sight of her new Sunday gown—a cheap curtain-calico thing, a conflagration of gaudy
colors and fantastic figures. She surveyed it wistfully, longingly.

"Hain't ever wore it yit," she said, "en it's jist lovely." Then she nodded her head in response to a pleasant idea, and added, "No, I ain't
gwyne to be fished out, wid everybody lookin' at me, in dis misable
ole linsey-woolsey."

She put down the child and made the change. She looked in the
glass and was astonished at her beauty. She resolved to make her
death-toilet perfect. She took off her handkerchief-turban and
dressed her glossy wealth of hair "like white folks;" she added some

odds and ends of rather lurid ribbon and a spray of atrocious artificial flowers; finally, she threw over her shoulders a fluffy thing called
a "cloud" in that day, which was of a blazing red complexion. Then
she was ready for the tomb.

She gathered up her baby once more: but when her eye fell upon
its miserably short little gray tow-linen shirt and noted the contrast
between its pauper shabbiness and her own volcanic irruption of
infernal splendors, her mother-heart was touched, and she was
ashamed.

"No, dolling, mammy ain't gwyne to treat you so. De angels is
gwyne to 'mire you jist as much as dey does yo' mammy. Ain't gwyne
to have 'em putt'n dey han's up 'fo' dey eyes en sayin' to David en
Goliah en dem yuther prophets, Dat chile is dress' too indelicate fo'
dis place."

By this time she had stripped off the shirt. Now she clothed the
naked little creature in one of Thomas à Becket's snowy long baby-
gowns, with its bright blue bows and dainty flummery of ruffles.

"Dah—now you's fixed." She propped the child in a chair and
stood off to inspect it. Straightway her eyes began to widen with
astonishment and admiration, and she clapped her hands and cried
out, "Why, it do beat all!—I *never* knowed you
was so lovely. Marse Tommy ain't a bit put-
tier—not a single bit."

She stepped over and glanced at the other
infant; she flung a glance back at her own;
then one more at the heir of the house. Now
a strange light dawned in her eyes, and in a
moment she was lost in thought. She seemed
in a trance; when she came out of it she muttered, "When I 'uz a-washin' 'em in de tub,
yistiddy, his own pappy asked me which of
'em was his'n."

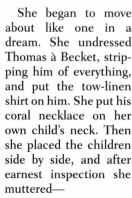

She began to move
about like one in a
dream. She undressed
Thomas à Becket, strip-
ping him of everything,
and put the tow-linen
shirt on him. She put his
coral necklace on her
own child's neck. Then
she placed the children
side by side, and after
earnest inspection she
muttered—

"Now who would b'lieve clo'es could do de like o' dat? Dog my cats if it ain't all *I* kin do to tell t'other fum which, let alone his pappy."

She put her cub in Tommy's elegant cradle and said—

"You's young Marse *Tom* fum dis out, en I got to practice and git used to 'memberin' to call you dat, honey, or I's gwyne to make a mistake some time en git us bofe into trouble. Dah—now you lay still en don't fret no mo', Marse Tom—oh, thank de good Lord in heaven, you's saved, you's saved!—dey ain't no man kin ever sell mammy's po' little honey down de river now!"

She put the heir of the house in her own child's unpainted pine cradle, and said, contemplating its slumbering form uneasily—

"I's sorry for you, honey; I's sorry, God knows I is,—but what *kin* I do, what *could* I do? Yo' pappy would sell him to somebody, some time, en den he'd go down de river, sho', en I couldn't, couldn't, *couldn't* stan' it."

She flung herself on her bed, and began to think and toss, toss and think. By and by she sat suddenly upright, for a comforting thought had flown through her worried mind—

" 'Tain't no sin—*white* folks has done it! It ain't no sin, glory to goodness it ain't no sin! *Dey*'s done it—yes, en dey was de biggest quality in de whole bilin', too—*Kings!*"

She began to muse; she was trying to gather out of her memory the dim particulars of some tale she had heard some time or other. At last she said—

"Now I's got it; now I 'member. It was dat ole nigger preacher dat tole it, de time he come over here fum Illinois en preached in de nigger church. He said dey ain't nobody kin save his own self—can't do it by faith, can't do it by works, can't do it no way at all. Free grace is de *on'y* way, en dat don't come fum nobody but jis' de Lord; en *He* kin give it to anybody He please, saint or sinner—*He* don't k'yer. He do jis' as He's a mineter. He s'lect out anybody dat suit Him, en put another one in his place, en make de fust one happy forever en leave t'other one to burn wid Satan. De preacher said it was jist like dey done in Englan' one time, long time ago. De queen she lef' her baby layin' aroun' one day, en went out callin'; en one o' de niggers roun' 'bout de place dat was mos' white, she come in en see de chile layin' aroun', en tuck en put her own chile's clo'es on de queen's chile, en put de queen's chile's clo'es on her own chile, en den lef' her own chile layin' aroun' en tuck en toted de queen's chile home to de nigger quarter, en nobody ever foun' it out, en her chile was de king, bimeby, en sole de queen's chile down de river one time when dey had to settle up de estate. Dah, now—  de preacher said it his own self, en it ain't no sin, caze white folks done it. *Dey* done it—yes, *dey* done it; en not on'y jis' common white folks, nuther, but de biggest quality dey is in de whole bilin'. Oh, I's *so* glad I 'member 'bout dat!"

She got up light-hearted and happy, and went to the cradles and spent what was left of the night "practicing." She would give her own child a light pat and say, humbly, "Lay still, Marse Tom," then give the real Tom a pat and say with severity, "Lay *still*, Chambers!—does you want me to take sump'n *to* you?"

As she progressed with her practice, she was surprised to see how steadily and surely the awe which had kept her tongue reverent and her manner humble toward her young master was transferring itself to her speech and manner toward the usurper, and how similarly handy she was becoming in transferring her motherly curtness of speech and peremptoriness of manner to the unlucky heir of the ancient house of Driscoll.

She took occasional rests from practicing, and absorbed herself in calculating her chances.

"Dey'll sell dese niggers to-day fo' stealin' de money, den dey'll buy some mo' dat don't know de chillen—so *dat's* all right. When I takes de chillen out to git de air, de minute I's roun' de corner I's gwyne to gaum dey mouths all aroun' wid jam, den dey can't *nobody* notice dey's changed. Yes, I gwineter do dat till I's safe, if it takes a year.

"Dey ain't but one man dat I's afeard of, en dat's dat Pudd'nhead Wilson. Dey calls him a pudd'nhead, en says he's a fool. My lan', dat man ain't no mo' fool den I is! He's de smartes' man in dis town, less'n it's Jedge Driscoll, or maybe Pem. Howard. Blame dat man, he worries me wid dem ornery glasses o' his'n; *I* b'lieve he's a witch. But nemmine, I's gwyne to happen aroun' dah one o' dese days en let on dat I reckon he wants to print de chillen's fingers agin; en if *he* don't notice dey's changed, I boun' dey ain't nobody gwyne to notice it, en den I's safe, sho'. But I reckon I'll tote along a hoss-shoe to keep off de witch-work."

The new negroes gave Roxy no trouble, of course. The master gave her none, for one of his speculations was in jeopardy, and his mind was so occupied that he hardly saw the children when he looked at them, and all Roxy had to do was to get them both into a gale of laughter when he came about; then their faces were mainly cavities exposing gums, and he was gone again before the spasm passed and the little creatures resumed a human aspect.

Within a few days the fate of the speculation became so dubious that Mr. Percy went away with his brother the Judge to see what could be done with it. It was a land speculation, as usual, and it had gotten complicated with a lawsuit. The men were gone seven weeks. Before they got back Roxy had paid her visit to Wilson, and was satisfied. Wilson took the finger-prints, labeled them with the names and with the date—October the first—put them carefully away, and continued his chat with Roxy, who seemed very anxious that he should admire the great advance in flesh and beauty which the babies had made since he took their finger-prints a month before. He complimented their improvement to her contentment; and as they were without any disguise of jam or other stain, she trembled all the while and was miserably frightened lest at any moment he—

But he didn't. He discovered nothing; and she went home jubilant, and dropped all concern about this matter permanently out of her mind.

Chapter 4

Adam and Eve had many advantages, but the principal one was, that they escaped teething.
—PUDD'NHEAD WILSON'S CALENDAR.

There is this trouble about special providences—namely, there is so often a doubt as to which party was intended to be the beneficiary. In the case of the children, the bears and the prophet, the bears got more real satisfaction out of the episode than the prophet did, because they got the children.
—PUDD'NHEAD WILSON'S CALENDAR.

This history must henceforth accommodate itself to the change which Roxana has consummated, and call the real heir "Chambers" and the usurping little slave "Thomas à Becket"—shortening this latter name to "Tom," for daily use, as the people about him did.

"Tom" was a bad baby, from the very beginning of his usurpation. He would cry for nothing; he would burst into storms of devilish temper without notice, and let go scream after scream and squall after squall, then climax the thing with "holding his breath"— that frightful specialty of the teething nursling, in the throes of which the creature exhausts its lungs, then is convulsed with noiseless squirmings and twistings and kickings in the effort to get its breath, while the lips turn blue and the mouth stands wide and rigid, offering for inspection one wee tooth set in the lower rim of a hoop of red gums; and when the appalling stillness has endured until one is sure the lost breath will never return, a nurse comes flying and dashes water in the child's face, and—presto! the lungs fill, and instantly discharge a shriek, or a yell, or a howl which bursts

the listening ear and surprises the owner of it into saying words which would not go well with a halo if he had one. The baby Tom would claw anybody who came within reach of his nails, and pound anybody he could reach with his rattle. He would scream for water until he got it, and then throw cup and all on the floor and scream for more. He was indulged in all his caprices, howsoever troublesome and exasperating they might be; he was allowed to eat anything he wanted, particularly things that would give him the stomach ache.

When he got to be old enough to begin to toddle about, and say broken words, and get an idea of what his hands were for, he was a more consummate pest than ever. Roxy got no rest while he was awake. He would call for anything and everything he saw, simply saying "Awnt it!" (want it), which was a command. When it was brought, he said, in a frenzy, and motioning it away with his hands, "Don't awnt it! don't awnt it!" and the moment it was gone he set up frantic yells of "Awnt it! awnt it! awnt it!" and Roxy had to give wings to her heels to get that thing back to him again before he could get time to carry out his intention of going into convulsions about it.

What he preferred above all other things was the tongs. This was because his "father" had forbidden him to have them lest he break windows and furniture with them. The moment Roxy's back was turned he would toddle to the presence of the tongs and say, "Like it!" and cock his eye to one side to see if Roxy was observing; then, "Awnt it!" and cock his eye again; then, "Hab it!" with another furtive glance; and finally, "Take it!"—and the prize was his. The next moment the heavy implement was raised aloft; the next, there was a crash and a squall, and the cat was off, on three legs, to meet an engagement; Roxy would arrive just as the lamp or a window went to irremediable smash.

Tom got all the petting, Chambers got none. Tom got all the delicacies, Chambers got mush and milk, and clabber without sugar. In consequence, Tom was a sickly child and Chambers wasn't. Tom was "fractious," as Roxy called it, and overbearing, Chambers was meek and docile.

With all her splendid common sense and practical every-day ability, Roxy was a doting fool of a mother. She was this toward her child—and she was also more than this: by the fiction created by herself, he was become her master; the necessity of recognizing this relation outwardly and of perfecting herself in the forms required to express the recognition, had moved her to such diligence and faithfulness in practicing these forms that this exercise soon concreted itself into habit; it became automatic and unconscious; then a natural result followed: deceptions intended solely for others gradually grew practically into self-deceptions as well; the mock reverence became real reverence, the mock obsequiousness real obsequiousness, the mock homage real homage; the little counterfeit rift of separation between imitation-slave and imitation-master widened and widened, and became an abyss, and a very real one—and on one side of it stood Roxy, the dupe of her own deceptions, and on the other stood her child, no longer a usurper to her, but her accepted and recognized master.

He was her darling, her master, and her deity, all in one, and in her worship of him she forgot who she was and what he had been.

In babyhood Tom cuffed and banged and scratched Chambers unrebuked, and Chambers early learned that between meekly bearing it and resenting it the advantage all lay with the former policy. The few times that his persecutions had moved him beyond control and made him fight back had cost him very dear at headquarters; not at the hands of Roxy, for if she ever went beyond scolding him sharply for "fogitt'n who his young marster was," she at least never extended her punishment beyond a box on the ear. No, Percy Driscoll was the person. He told Chambers that under no provocation whatever was he privileged to lift his hand against his little master. Chambers overstepped the line three times, and got three such convincing canings from the man who was his father and didn't know it, that he took Tom's cruelties in all humility after that, and made no more experiments.

Outside of the house the two boys were together, all through their boyhood. Chambers was strong beyond his years, and a good fighter; strong because he was coarsely fed and hard worked about the house, and a good fighter because Tom

furnished him plenty of practice—on white boys whom he hated and was afraid of. Chambers was his constant bodyguard, to and from school; he was present on the play-ground at recess to protect his charge. He fought himself into such a formidable reputation, by and by, that Tom could have changed clothes with him, and "ridden in peace," like Sir Kay in Launcelot's armor.

He was good at games of skill, too. Tom staked him with marbles to play "keeps" with, and then took all the winnings away from him. In the winter season Chambers was on hand, in Tom's worn-out clothes, with "holy" red mittens, and "holy" shoes, and pants "holy" at the knees and seat, to drag a sled up the hill for Tom, warmly clad, to ride down on; but he never got a ride himself. He built snow men and snow fortifications under Tom's direction. He was Tom's patient target when Tom wanted to do some snow-balling, but the target couldn't fire back. Chambers carried Tom's skates to the river and strapped them on him, then trotted around after him on the ice, so as to be on hand when wanted; but he wasn't ever asked to try the skates himself.

In summer the pet pastime of the boys of Dawson's Landing was to steal apples, peaches and melons from the farmers' fruit wag-ons,—mainly on account of the risk they ran of getting their heads laid open with the butt of the farmer's whip. Tom was a distinguished adept at these thefts—by proxy. Chambers did his stealing, and got the peach stones, apple cores and melon rhinds for his share.

Tom always made Chambers go in swimming with him, and stay by him as a protection. When Tom had had enough, he would slip out and tie knots in Chambers's shirt, dip the knots in the water to make them hard to undo, then dress himself and sit by and laugh while the naked shiverer tugged at the stubborn knots with his teeth.

Tom did his humble comrade these various ill turns partly out of native viciousness, and partly because he hated him for his superi-orities of physique and pluck, and for his manifold clevernesses. Tom couldn't dive, for it gave him splitting headaches. Chambers could dive without inconvenience, and was fond of doing it. He excited so much admiration, one day, among a crowd of white boys, by throw-ing back-summersaults from the stern of a canoe that it wearied Tom's spirit, and at last he shoved the canoe underneath Chambers while he was in the air—so he came down on his head in the canoe-bottom; and while he lay unconscious several of Tom's ancient adver-saries saw that their long-desired opportunity was come, and they gave the false heir such a drubbing that with Chambers's best help he was hardly able to drag himself home afterward.

When the boys were fifteen and upwards, Tom was "showing off" in the river one day, when he was taken with a cramp, and shouted for help. It was a common trick with the boys—particularly if a stranger was present—to pretend a cramp and howl for help; then when the stranger came tearing hand-over-hand to the rescue, the howler would go on struggling and howling till he was close at hand, then replace the howl with a sarcastic smile and swim blandly away, while the town-boys assailed the dupe with a volley of jeers and laughter. Tom had never tried this joke as yet, but was supposed to be trying it now, so the boys held warily back; but Chambers believed his master was in earnest, therefore he swam out and arrived in time, unfortunately, and saved his life.

This was the last feather. Tom had managed to endure everything else, but to have to remain publicly and permanently under such an obligation as this to a nigger, and to this nigger of all niggers—this was too much. He heaped insults upon Chambers for "pretending" to think he was in earnest in calling for help, and said that anybody but a blockheaded nigger would have known he was funning and left him alone.

Tom's enemies were in strong force here, so they came out with their opinions quite freely. They laughed at him, and called him coward, liar, sneak, and other sorts of pet names, and told him they meant to call Chambers by a new name after this, and make it common in the town—"Tom Driscoll's Nigger-pappy"—to signify that he had had a second birth into this life, and that Chambers was the author of his new being. Tom grew frantic under these taunts, and shouted—

"Knock their heads off, Chambers! knock their heads off! What do you stand there with your hands in your pockets for?"

Chambers expostulated, and said—

"But Marse Tom, dey's too many of 'em—dey's—"

"Do you hear me?"

"Please, Marse Tom, don't make me! Dey's so many of 'em dat—"

Tom sprang at him and drove his pocket knife into him two or three times before the boys could snatch him away and give the wounded lad a chance to escape. He was considerably hurt, but not seriously. If the blade had been a little longer his career would have ended there.

Tom had long ago taught Roxy "her place." It had been many a day, now, since she had ventured a caress or a fondling epithet in his quarter. Such things, from a "nigger," were repulsive to him, and she had been warned to keep her distance and remember who she was. She saw her darling gradually cease from being her son, she saw *that* detail perish utterly; all that was left was master—master, pure and simple, and it was not a gentle mastership, either. She saw herself sink from the sublime height of motherhood to the sombre deeps of

unmodified slavery. The abyss of separation between her and her boy was complete. She was merely his chattel, now, his convenience, his dog, his cringing and helpless slave, the humble and unresisting victim of his capricious temper and vicious nature.

Sometimes she could not go to sleep, even when worn out with fatigue, because her rage boiled so high over the day's experiences with her boy. She would mumble and mutter to herself—

"He struck me, en I warn't no way to blame—struck me in de face, right before folks. En he's allays callin' me nigger wench, en hussy, en all dem mean names, when I's doin' de very bes' I kin. O, Lord, I done so much for him—I lift' him away up to whar he is—en dis is what I git for it."

Sometimes when some outrage of peculiar offensiveness stung her to the heart, she would plan schemes of vengeance, and revel in the fancied spectacle of his exposure to the world as an impostor and a slave; but in the midst of these joys fear would strike her: she had made him too strong; she could prove nothing, and—heavens, she might get sold down the river for her pains! So her schemes always went for nothing, and she laid them aside in impotent rage against the fates, and against herself for playing the fool on that fatal September day in not providing herself with a witness for use in the day when such a thing might be needed for the appeasing of her vengeance-hungry heart.

And yet the moment Tom happened to be good to her, and kind—and this occurred every now and then—all her sore places were healed and she was happy; happy and proud, for this was her son, her nigger son, lording it among the whites and securely avenging their crimes against her race.

There were two grand funerals in Dawson's Landing that fall—the fall of 1845. One was that of Colonel Cecil Burleigh Essex, the other that of Percy Driscoll.

On his death-bed Driscoll set Roxy free and delivered his idolized ostensible son solemnly into the keeping of his brother the Judge and his wife. Those childless people were glad to get him. Childless people are not difficult to please.

Judge Driscoll had gone privately to his brother, a month before, and bought Chambers. He had heard that Tom had been trying to get his father to sell the boy down the river, and he wanted to prevent the scandal—for public sentiment did not approve of that way of treating family servants for light cause or for no cause.

Percy Driscoll had worn himself out in trying to save his great speculative landed estate, and had died without succeeding. He was hardly in his grave before the boom collapsed and left his hitherto envied young devil of an heir a pauper. But that was nothing; his uncle told him he should be his heir and have all his fortune when he died; so Tom was comforted.

Roxy had no home, now; so she resolved to go around and say good-bye to her friends and then clear out and see the world—that is to say, she would go chambermaiding on a steamboat, the darling ambition of her race and sex.

Her last call was on the black giant, Jasper. She found him chopping Pudd'nhead Wilson's winter provision of wood.

Wilson was chatting with him when Roxy arrived. He asked her how she could bear to go off chambermaiding and leave her boys; and chaffingly offered to copy off a series of their finger-prints, reaching up to their twelfth year, for her to remember them by; but she sobered in a moment, wondering if he suspected anything; then she said she believed she didn't want them. Wilson said to himself, "The drop of black blood in her is superstitious; she thinks there's some deviltry, some witch-business, about my glass mystery somewhere; she used to come here with an old horseshoe in her hand; it could have been an accident, but I doubt it."

Chapter 5

Training is everything. The peach was once a bitter almond; cauliflower is nothing but cabbage with a college education.
                        —PUDD'NHEAD WILSON'S CALENDAR.

Remark of Dr. Baldwin's, concerning upstarts: We don't care to eat toadstools that think they are truffles.
                        —PUDD'NHEAD WILSON'S CALENDAR.

Mrs. York Driscoll enjoyed two years of bliss with that prize, Tom; bliss that was troubled a little at times, it is true, but bliss nevertheless; then she died, and her husband and his childless sister, Mrs. Pratt, continued the bliss-business at the old stand. Tom was petted

and indulged and spoiled to his entire content—or nearly that. This went on till he was nineteen, then he was sent to Yale. He went handsomely equipped with "conditions," but otherwise he was not an object of distinction there. He remained at Yale two years, and then threw up the struggle. He came home with his manners a good deal improved; he had lost his surliness and brusqueness, and was rather pleasantly soft and smooth, now; he was furtively, and sometimes openly, ironical of speech, and given to gently touching people on the raw, but he did it with a good-natured semi-conscious air that carried it off safely and kept him from getting into trouble. He was as indolent as ever, and showed no very strenuous desire to hunt up an occupation. People argued from this that he preferred to be supported by his uncle until his uncle's shoes should become vacant. He brought back one or two new habits with him, one of which he rather openly practiced—tippling—but concealed another, which was gambling. It would not do to gamble where his uncle could hear of it; he knew that quite well.

Tom's eastern polish was not popular among the young people. They could have endured it, perhaps, if Tom had stopped there; but he wore gloves, and that they couldn't stand, and wouldn't; so he was mainly without society. He brought home with him a suit of clothes of such exquisite style and cut and fashion—eastern fashion, city fashion—that it filled everybody with anguish and was regarded as a peculiarly wanton affront. He enjoyed the feeling which he was exciting, and paraded the town serene and happy all day; but the young fellows set a tailor to work that night, and when Tom started out on his parade next morning he found the old deformed negro bellringer straddling along in his wake tricked out in a flamboyant curtain-calico exaggeration of his finery, and imitating his fancy eastern graces as well as he could.

Tom surrendered, and after that clothed himself in the local fashion. But the dull country town was tiresome to him, since his acquaintanceship with livelier regions, and it grew daily more and more so. He began to make little trips to St. Louis for refreshment. There he found companionship to suit him, and pleasures to his taste, along with more freedom, in some particulars, than he could have at home. So, during the next two years his visits to the city grew in frequency and his tarryings there grew steadily longer in duration.

He was getting into deep waters. He was taking chances, privately, which might get him into trouble some day—in fact, *did*.

Judge Driscoll had retired from the Bench and from all business activities in 1850, and had now been comfortably idle three years. He was President of the Freethinkers' Society, and Pudd'nhead Wilson was the other member. The Society's weekly discussions were now the old lawyer's main interest in life. Pudd'nhead was still toiling in obscurity at the bottom of the ladder, under the blight of that unlucky remark which he had let fall twenty-three years before about the dog.

Judge Driscoll was his friend, and claimed that he had a mind above the average, but that was regarded as one of the Judge's whims, and it failed to modify the public opinion. Or, rather, that was one of the reasons why it failed, but there was another and better one. If the Judge had stopped with bare assertion, it would have had a good deal of effect; but he made the mistake of trying to prove his position. For some years Wilson had been privately at work on a whimsical almanac, for his amusement—a calendar, with a little dab of ostensible philosophy, usually in ironical form, appended to each date; and the Judge thought that these quips and fancies of Wilson's were neatly turned and cute; so he carried a handful of them around, one day, and read them to some of the chief citizens. But irony was not for those people; their mental vision was not focussed for it. They read those playful trifles in the solidest earnest, and decided without hesitancy that if there had ever been any doubt that Dave Wilson was a pudd'nhead—which there hadn't—this revelation removed that doubt for good and all. That is just the way, in this world; an enemy can partly ruin a man, but it takes a good-natured injudicious

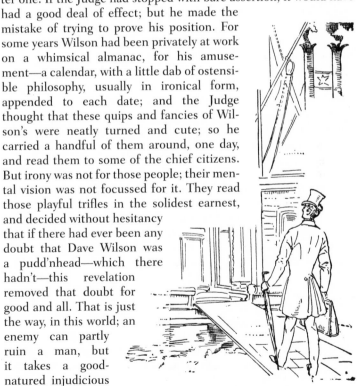

friend to complete the thing and make it perfect. After this the Judge felt tenderer than ever toward Wilson, and surer than ever that his calendar had merit.

Judge Driscoll could be a freethinker and still hold his place in society because he was the person of most consequence in the community, and therefore could venture to go his own way and follow out his own notions. The other member of his pet organization was allowed the like liberty because he was a cipher in the estimation of the public, and nobody attached any importance to what he thought or did. He was liked, he was welcome enough all around, but he simply didn't count for anything.

The widow Cooper—affectionately called "aunt Patsy" by everybody—lived in a snug and comely cottage with her daughter Rowena, who was nineteen, romantic, amiable, and very pretty, but otherwise of no consequence. Rowena had a couple of young brothers—also of no consequence.

The widow had a large spare room which she let to a lodger, with board, when she could find one, but this room had been empty for a year now, to her sorrow. Her income was only sufficient for the family support, and she needed the lodging-money for trifling luxuries. But now, at last, on a flaming June day, she found herself happy; her tedious wait was ended; her year-worn advertisement had been answered; and not by a village applicant, oh, no!—this letter was from away off yonder in the dim great world to the North: it was from St. Louis. She sat on her porch gazing out with unseeing eyes upon the shining reaches of the mighty Mississippi, her thoughts steeped in her good fortune. Indeed it was specially good fortune, for she was to have two lodgers instead of one.

She had read the letter to the family, and Rowena had danced away to see to the cleaning and airing of the room by the slave woman Nancy, and the boys had rushed abroad in the town to spread the great news, for it was matter of public interest, and the public would wonder and not be pleased if not informed. Presently Rowena returned, all aflush with joyous excitement, and begged for a re-reading of the letter. It was framed thus:

> HONORED MADAM: My brother and I have seen your advertisement, by chance, and beg leave to take the room you offer. We are twenty-four years of age and twins. We are Italians by birth, but have lived long in the various countries of Europe, and several years in the United States. Our names are Luigi and Angelo Cappello. You desire but one guest; but dear Madam, if you will allow us to pay for two, we will not incommode you. We shall be down Thursday.

"Italians! How romantic! Just think, ma—there's never been one in this town, and everybody will be dying to see them, and they're all *ours!* Think of that!"

"Yes, I reckon they'll make a grand stir."

"Oh, indeed they will. The whole town will be on its head! Think—they've been in Europe and everywhere! There's never been a traveler in this town before. Ma, I shouldn't wonder if they've seen kings!"

"Well, a body can't tell; but they'll make stir enough, without that."

"Yes, that's of course. Luigi—Angelo. They're lovely names; and so grand and foreign—not like Jones and Robinson and such. Thursday they are coming, and this is only Tuesday; it's a cruel long time to wait. Here comes Judge Driscoll in at the gate. He's heard about it. I'll go and open the door."

The judge was full of congratulations and curiosity. The letter was read and discussed. Soon Justice Robinson arrived with more congratulations, and there was a new reading and a new discussion. This was the beginning. Neighbor after neighbor, of both sexes, followed, and the procession drifted in and out all day and evening and all Wednesday and Thursday. The letter was read and re-read until it was nearly worn out; everybody admired its courtly and gracious tone, and smooth and practiced style, everybody was sympathetic and excited, and the Coopers were steeped in happiness all the while.

The boats were very uncertain, in low water, in those primitive times. This time the Thursday boat had not arrived at ten at night—so the people had waited at the landing all day for nothing; they were driven to their homes by a heavy storm without having had a view of the illustrious foreigners.

Eleven o'clock came; then twelve, and the Cooper house was the only one in the town that still had lights burning. The rain and thunder were booming yet, and the anxious family were still waiting, still hoping. At last there was a knock on the door and the family jumped to open it. Two negro men entered, each carrying a trunk, and proceeded up stairs toward the guest room. Then entered the twins—the handsomest, the best dressed, the most distinguished-looking pair of young fellows the West had ever seen. One was a little fairer than the other, but otherwise they were exact duplicates.

Chapter 6

Let us endeavor so to live that when we come to die even the under-taker will be sorry.

        —PUDD'NHEAD WILSON'S CALENDAR.

Habit is habit, and not to be flung out of the window by any man, but coaxed down-stairs a step at a time.

        —PUDD'NHEAD WILSON'S CALENDAR.

At breakfast in the morning the twins' charm of manner and easy and polished bearing made speedy conquest of the family's good graces. All constraint and formality quickly disappeared, and the

friendliest feeling succeeded. Aunt Patsy called them by their Christian names almost from the beginning. She was full of the keenest curiosity about them, and showed it; they responded by talking about themselves, which pleased her greatly. It presently appeared that in their early youth they had known poverty and hardship. As the talk wandered along the old lady watched for the right place to drop in a question or two concerning that matter, and when she found it she said to the blonde twin, who was now doing the biographies in his turn while the brunette one rested—

"If it ain't asking what I ought not to ask, Mr. Angelo, how did you come to be so friendless and in such trouble when you were little? Do you mind telling? But don't, if you do."

"Oh, we don't mind it at all, madam; in our case it was merely misfortune, and nobody's fault. Our parents were well-to-do, there in Italy, and we were their only child. We were of the old Florentine nobility"—

Rowena's heart gave a great bound, her nostrils expanded, and a fine light played in her eyes—"and when the war broke out my father was on the losing side and had to fly for his life. His estates were confiscated, his personal property seized, and there we were, in Germany, strangers, friendless, and in fact paupers. My brother and I were ten years old, and well educated for that age, very studious, very fond of our books, and well grounded in the German, French, Spanish and English languages. Also, we were marvelous musical prodigies—if you will allow me to say it, it being only the truth.

"Our father survived his misfortunes only a month, our mother soon followed him, and we were alone in the world. Our parents could have made themselves comfortable by exhibiting us as a show, and they had many and large offers; but the thought revolted their pride, and they said they would starve and die first. But what they wouldn't consent to do we had to do without the formality of consent. We were seized for the debts occasioned by their illness and their funerals, and placed among the attractions of a cheap museum in Berlin to earn the liquidation money. It took us two years to get out of that slavery. We traveled all about Germany, receiving no wages, and not even our keep. We had to exhibit for nothing, and beg our bread.

"Well, madam, the rest is not of much consequence. When we escaped from that slavery at twelve years of age, we were in some respects men. Experience had taught us some valuable things; among others, how to take care of ourselves, how to avoid and defeat sharks and sharpers, and how to conduct our own business for our own profit and without other people's help. We traveled everywhere—years and years—picking up smatterings of strange tongues, familiarizing ourselves with strange sights and strange customs, accumulating an education of a wide and varied and curious sort. It was a pleasant life. We went to Venice—to London, Paris, Russia, India, China, Japan—"

At this point Nancy the slave woman thrust her head in at the door and exclaimed:

"Ole Missus, de house is plum jam full o' people, en dey's jes' a spilin' to see de gen'lmen!" She indicated the twins with a nod of her head, and tucked it back out of sight again.

It was a proud occasion for the widow, and she promised herself high satisfaction in showing off her fine foreign birds before her neighbors and friends—simple folk who had hardly ever seen a foreigner of any kind, and never one of any distinction or style. Yet her feeling was moderate indeed, when contrasted with Rowena's. Rowena was in the clouds, she walked on air; this was to be the greatest day, the most romantic episode in the colorless history of that dull country town, she was to be familiarly near the source of its glory and feel the full flood of it pour over her and about her, the other girls could only gaze and envy, not partake.

The widow was ready, Rowena was ready, so also were the foreigners.

The party moved along the hall, the Twins in advance, and entered the open parlor door, whence issued a low hum of conversation. The Twins took a position near the door, the widow stood at Luigi's side, Rowena stood beside Angelo, and the march-past and the introductions began. The widow was all smiles and contentment. She received the procession and passed it on to Rowena.

"Good-mornin' Sister Cooper"—hand-shake.

"Good-morning, Brother Higgins—Count Luigi Cappello, Mr. Higgins"—hand-shake, followed by a devouring stare and "I'm glad to see ye," on the part of Higgins, and a courteous inclination of the head and a pleasant "Most happy!" on the part of Count Luigi.

"Good-mornin', Rowena"—handshake.

"Good-morning, Mr. Higgins—present you to Count Angelo Cappello." Handshake, admiring stare, "Glad to see ye,"—courteous nod, smily "Most happy!" and Higgins passes on.

None of these visitors was at ease, but being honest people, they didn't pretend to be. None of them had ever seen a person bearing a title of nobility before, and none had been expecting to see one now, consequently the title came upon them as a kind of pile-driving surprise and caught them unprepared. A few tried to rise to the emergency, and got out an awkward My Lord, or Your Lordship, or something of the sort, but the great majority were overwhelmed by the unaccustomed word and its dim and awful associations with gilded courts and stately ceremony and anointed kingship, so they only fumbled through the handshake, and passed on, speechless. Now and then, as happens at all receptions, everywhere, a more than ordinarily friendly soul blocked the procession and kept it waiting while he inquired how the brothers liked the village, and how long they were going to stay, and if their families were well, and dragged in the weather, and hoped it would get cooler soon, and all that sort of thing, so as to be able to say, when they got home, "I had quite a long talk with them;" but nobody did or said anything of a regrettable kind, and so the great affair went through to the end in a creditable and satisfactory fashion.

General conversation followed, and the twins drifted about from group to group, talking easily and fluently, and winning approval, compelling admiration, and achieving favor from all. The widow followed their conquering march with a proud eye, and every now and then Rowena said to herself with deep satisfaction, "And to think, they are ours—all ours!"

There were no idle moments for mother or daughter. Eager inquires concerning the Twins were pouring into their enchanted ears all the time; each was the constant centre of a group of breathless listeners; each recognized that she knew now for the first time the real meaning

of that great word Glory, and perceived the
stupendous value of it, and understood why
men in all ages had been willing to throw away
meaner happinesses, treasure, life itself, to
get a taste of its sublime and supreme joy.
Napoleon and all his kind stood accounted
for—and justified.

When Rowena had at last done all her duty
by the people in the parlor, she went up stairs
to satisfy the longings of an overflow meeting
there, for the parlor was not big enough to
hold all the comers. Again she was besieged by
eager questioners and again she swam in sun-
set seas of glory. When the forenoon was
nearly gone, she recognized with a pang that
this most splendid episode of her life was
almost over, that nothing could prolong it, that nothing quite its equal
could ever fall to her fortune again. But never mind, it was sufficient
unto itself, the grand occasion had moved on an ascending scale from
the start, and was a noble and memorable success. If the twins could
but do some crowning act, now, to climax it, something unusual,
something startling, something to concentrate upon themselves the
company's loftiest admiration, something in the nature of an electric
surprise—

Here a prodigious slam-banging broke out below, and everybody
rushed down to see. It was the twins knocking out a classic four-
handed piece on the piano, in great style. Rowena was satisfied; satisfied down to the bottom of her heart.

The young strangers were kept long at the piano. The villagers
were astonished and enchanted with the magnificence of their performance, and could not bear to have them stop. All the music that
they had ever heard before seemed spiritless prentice-work and barren of grace or charm when compared with these intoxicating floods
of melodious sound. They realized that for once in their lives they
were hearing masters.

Chapter 7

One of the most striking differences between a cat and a lie is that a cat has only nine lives.
            —PUDD'NHEAD WILSON'S CALENDAR.

The company broke up reluctantly, and drifted toward their several homes, chatting with vivacity, and all agreeing that it would be many a long day before Dawson's Landing would see the equal of this one again. The Twins had accepted several invitations while the reception was in progress, and had also volunteered to play some duets at an amateur entertainment for the benefit of a local charity. Society was eager to receive them to its bosom. Judge Driscoll had the good fortune to secure them for an immediate drive, and to be the first to display them in public. They entered his buggy with him and were paraded down the main street, everybody flocking to the windows and sidewalks to see.

The Judge showed the strangers the new graveyard, and the jail, and where the richest man lived, and the Freemasons' hall, and the Methodist church, and the Presbyterian church, and where the Baptist church was going to be when they got some money to build it with, and showed them the town hall and the slaughter-house, and got out the independent fire company in uniform and had them put out an imaginary fire; then he let them inspect the muskets of the militia company, and poured out an exhaustless stream of enthusiasm over all these splendors, and seemed very well satisfied with the responses he got, for the Twins admired his admiration and paid him back the

best they could, though they could have done better if some fifteen or sixteen hundred thousand previous experiences of this sort in various countries had not already rubbed off a considerable part of the novelty of it.

The Judge laid himself hospitably out to make them have a good time, and if there was a defect anywhere it was not his fault. He told them a good many humorous anecdotes, and always forgot the nub, but they were always able to furnish it, for these yarns were of a pretty early vintage, and they had had many a rejuvenating pull at them before. And he told them all about his several dignities, and how he had held this and that and the other place of honor or profit, and had once been to the legislature, and was now president of the Society of Freethinkers. He said the society had been in existence four years and already had two members, and was firmly established. He would call for the brothers in the evening if they would like to attend a meeting of it.

Accordingly he called for them, and on the way he told them all about Pudd'nhead Wilson, in order that they might get a favorable impression of him in advance and be prepared to like him. This scheme succeeded—the favorable impression was achieved. Later it was confirmed and solidified when Wilson proposed that out of courtesy to the strangers the usual topics be put aside and the hour be devoted to conversation upon ordinary subjects and the cultivation of friendly relations and good-fellowship,—a proposition which was put to vote and carried.

The hour passed quickly away in lively talk, and when it was ended the lonesome and neglected Wilson was richer by two friends than he had been when it began. He invited the Twins to look in at his lodgings, presently, after disposing of an intervening engagement, and they accepted with pleasure.

Toward the middle of the evening they found themselves on the road to his house. Pudd'nhead was at home waiting for them and putting in his time puzzling over a thing which had come under his notice that morning. The matter was this. He happened to be up very early—at dawn, in fact; and he crossed the hall which divided his cottage through the centre and entered a room to get something there. The window of the room had no curtains, for that side of the house had long been unoccupied, and through this window he caught sight

of something which surprised and interested him. It was a young woman—a young woman where properly no young woman belonged; for she was in Judge Driscoll's house, and in the bedroom over the Judge's private study or sitting room. This was young Tom Driscoll's bedroom. He and the Judge, the Judge's widowed sister Mrs. Pratt, and three negro servants were the only people who belonged in the house. Who, then, might this young lady be? The two houses were separated by an ordinary yard, with a low fence running back through its middle from the street in front to the lane in the rear. The distance was not great, and Wilson was able to see the girl very well, the window shades of the room she was in being up, and the window also. The girl had on a neat and trim summer dress patterned in broad stripes of pink and white, and her bonnet was equipped with a pink veil. She was practicing steps, gaits and attitudes, apparently; she was doing the thing gracefully, and was very much absorbed in her work. Who could she be, and how came she to be in young Tom Driscoll's room?

Wilson had quickly chosen a position from which he could watch the girl without running much risk of being seen by her, and he remained there hoping she would raise her veil and betray her face. But she disappointed him. After a matter of twenty minutes she disappeared, and although he stayed at his post half an hour longer, she came no more.

Toward noon he dropped in at the Judge's and talked with Mrs. Pratt about the great event of the day, the levèe of the distinguished foreigners at Aunt Patsy Cooper's. He asked after her nephew Tom, and she said he was on his way home, and that she was expecting him to arrive a little before night; and added that she and the Judge were gratified to gather from his letters that he was conducting himself very nicely and creditably—at which Wilson winked to himself privately. Wilson did not ask if there was a new-comer in the house, but he asked questions that would have brought light-throwing answers as to that matter if Mrs. Pratt had had any light to throw; so he went away satisfied that he knew of things that were going on in her house of which she herself was not aware.

He was now waiting for the Twins, and still puzzling over the problem of who that girl might be, and how she happened to be in that young fellow's room at day-break in the morning.

Chapter 8

The holy passion of Friendship is of so sweet and steady and loyal and enduring a nature that it will last through a whole lifetime if not asked to lend money.

—PUDD'NHEAD WILSON'S CALENDAR.

Consider well the proportions of things. It is better to be a young June-bug than an old bird of paradise.

—PUDD'NHEAD WILSON'S CALENDAR.

It is necessary, now, to hunt up Roxy.

At the time she was set free and went away chambermaiding, she was thirty-five. She got a berth as second chambermaid on a Cincinnati boat in the New Orleans trade, the "Grand Mogul." A couple of trips made her wonted and easy-going at the work, and infatuated her with the stir and adventure and independence of steamboat life. Then she was promoted and became head chambermaid. She was a favorite with the officers, and exceedingly proud of their joking and friendly ways with her.

During eight years she served three parts of the year on that boat, and the winters on a Vicksburg packet. But now for two months she had had rheumatism in her arms, and was obliged to let the wash-tub alone. So she resigned. But she was well fixed—rich, as she would have described it; for she had lived a steady life, and had banked four dollars every month in New Orleans as a provision for her old age. She said in the start that she had "put shoes on one bar'footed nigger to tromple on her with," and that one mistake like that was enough: she would be independent of the human race thenceforth forever-more if hard work and economy could accomplish it.

When the boat touched the levee at New Orleans she bade good-bye to her comrades on the Grand Mogul and moved her kit ashore.

But she was back in an hour. The bank had gone to smash and carried her four hundred dollars with it. She was a pauper, and home-less. Also disabled bodily, at least for the present. The officers were full of sympathy for her in her trouble, and made up a little purse for her. She resolved to go to her birth-place; she had friends there among the negroes, and the unfortunate always help the unfortunate, she was well aware of that; those lowly comrades of her youth would not let her starve.

She took the little local packet at Cairo, and now she was on the home-stretch. Time had worn away her bitterness against her son, and she was able to think of him with serenity. She put the vile side of him out of her mind, and dwelt only on recollections of his occa-sional acts of kindness to her. She gilded and otherwise decorated these, and made them very pleasant to contemplate. She began to long to see him. She would go and fawn upon him, slave-like—for this would have to be her attitude, of course—and maybe she would find that time had modified him, and that he would be glad to see his long forgotten old nurse and treat her gently. That would be lovely; that would make her forget her woes and her poverty.

Her poverty! That thought inspired her to add another castle to her dream: Maybe he would help her; maybe he would give her a trifle now and then—maybe a dollar, once a month, say; any little thing like that would help, oh, ever so much.

By the time she reached Dawson's Landing she was her old self again; her blues were gone, she was in high feather. She would get along, surely; there were many kitchens where the servants would share their meals with her, and also steal sugar and apples and other dainties for her to carry home—or give her a chance to pilfer them herself, which would answer just as well. And there was the church. She was a more rabid and devoted Methodist than ever, and her piety was no sham, but was strong and sincere. Yes, with plenty of creature comforts and her old place in the amen corner in her possession again, she would be perfectly happy and at peace thenceforward to the end.

She went to Judge Driscoll's kitchen first of all. She was received there in great form and with vast enthusiasm. Her wonderful travels, and the strange countries she had seen and the adventures she had had, made her a marvel and a heroine of romance. The negroes hung enchanted upon the great story of her experiences, interrupting her all along with eager questions, with laughter, exclamations of delight and expressions of applause; and she was obliged to confess to herself that if there was anything better in this world than steamboating, it was the glory to be got by telling about it. The audience loaded her stomach with their dinners and then stole the pantry bare to load up her basket.

Tom was in St. Louis. The servants said he had spent the best part of his time there during the previous two years. Roxy came every day, and had many talks about the family and its affairs. Once she asked why Tom was away so much. The ostensible "Chambers" said:

"De fac' is, ole marster kin git along better when young marster's away den he kin when he's in de town; yes, en he love him better, too;

so he gives him fifty dollahs a month—"

"No, is dat so? Chambers, you's a jokin', ain't you?"

"'Clah to goodness I ain't, mammy; Marse Tom tole me so, his own self. But nemmine, t'ain't enough."

"My lan', what de reason t'ain't enough?"

"Well, I's gwyne to tell you, if you gimme a chanst, mammy. De reason it ain't enough is becase Marse Tom gambles."

Roxy threw up her hands in astonishment, and Chambers went on—

"Ole marse found it out, becase he had to pay two hundred dollahs for Marse Tom's gamblin' debts, en dat's true, mammy, jes' as dead certain as you's bawn."

"Two—hund'd—dollahs! Why, what is you talkin' 'bout? Two—hund'd—dollahs. Sakes alive, it's mos' enough to buy a tol-lable good second-hand nigger wid. En you ain't lyin', honey?—you wouldn't lie to yo' ole mammy?"

"It's Gawd's own truth, jes' as I tell you—two hunderd dollahs—I wisht I may never stir outen my tracks if it ain't so. En, oh, my lan', ole Marse was jes' a hoppin! he was bilin' mad, I tell you! He tuck'n dissenhurrit him."

He licked his chops with relish after that stately word. Roxy strug-gled with it a moment, then gave it up and said—

"Dissen*whiched* him?"

"Dissenhurrit him."

"What's dat? What do it mean?"

"Means he busted de will."

"Bus-ted de will! He wouldn't *ever* treat him so! Take it back, you misable imitation nigger dat I bore in sorrow en tribbilation."

Roxy's pet castle—an occasional dollar from Tom's pocket—was tumbling to ruin before her eyes. She could not abide such a disaster as that; she couldn't endure the thought of it. Her remark amused Chambers:

"Yah-yah-yah! jes' listen to dat! If I's imitation, what is you? Bofe of us is imitation *white*—dat's what we is—en pow'full good imita-tion, too—Yah-yah-yah!—we don't 'mount to noth'n as imitation *nig-gers*; en as for—"

"Shet up yo' foolin', 'fo' I knock you side de head, en tell me 'bout de will. Tell me t'ain't busted—do, honey, en I'll never fogit you."

"Well, *t'ain't*—caze dey's a new one made, en Marse Tom's all right agin. But what is you in sich a sweat 'bout it for, mammy? T'ain't none o' your business I don't reckon."

"Tain't none o' my business? Whose business is it den, I'd like to know? Was I his mother tell he was fifteen years old, or wusn't I?—you answer me dat. En you speck I could see him turned out po' en ornery on de worl' en never care noth'n 'bout it? I reckon if you'd ever ben a mother yo'self, Vallet de Chambers, you wouldn't talk sich foolishness as dat."

"Well, den, old Marse forgive him en fixed up de will agin—do dat satisfy you?"

Yes, she was satisfied, now, and quite happy and sentimental over it. She kept coming daily, and at last she was told that Tom had come home. She began to tremble with emotion, and straightway sent to beg him to let his "po' ole nigger mammy have jes' one sight of him en die for joy."

Tom was stretched at his lazy ease on a sofa when Chambers brought the petition. Time had not modified his ancient detestation of the humble drudge and protector of his boyhood; it was still bitter and uncompromising. He sat up and bent a severe gaze upon the fair face of the young fellow whose name he was unconsciously using and whose family rights he was enjoying. He maintained the gaze until the victim of it had become satisfactorily pallid with terror, then he said—

"What does the old rip want with me?"

The petition was meekly repeated.

"Who gave you permission to come and disturb me with the social attentions of niggers?"

Tom had risen. The other young man was trembling, now, visibly. He saw what was coming, and bent his head sideways and put up his left arm to shield it. Tom rained cuffs upon the head and its shield, saying no word; the victim received each blow with a beseeching "Please, Marse Tom!—oh, please, Marse Tom!" Seven blows—then Tom said, "Face the door—March!" He followed behind with one, two, three solid kicks. The last one helped the pure-white slave over the door-sill, and he limped away mopping his eyes with his old ragged sleeve. Tom shouted after him, "Send her in!"

Then he flung himself panting on the sofa again and rasped out the remark, "He arrived just at the right moment; I was full to the brim with bitter thinkings, and nobody to take it out of. How refreshing it was!—I feel better."

Tom's mother entered, now, closing the door behind her, and approached her son with all the wheedling and supplicating servilities that fear and interest can impart to the words and attitudes of the born slave. She stopped a yard from her boy and made two or three admiring exclamations over his manly stature and general handsomeness, and Tom put an arm under his head and hoisted a leg over the sofa-back in order to look properly indifferent.

"My lan', how you is growed, honey! 'Clah to goodness I wouldn't a knowed you, Marse Tom! 'deed I wouldn't! Look at me good; does you 'member ole Roxy?—does you know yo' ole nigger mammy, honey? Well, now, I kin lay down en die in peace, caze I's seed—"

"Cut it short, damn it, cut it short! What is it you want?"

"You heah dat? Jes' de same old Marse Tom, allays so gay and funnin' wid de ole mammy. I 'uz jes' as shore—"

"Cut it short, I tell you, and get along! What do you want?"

This was a bitter disappointment. Roxy had for so many days nourished and fondled and petted her notion that Tom would be glad to see his old nurse and would make her proud and happy to the marrow with a cordial word or two, that it took two rebuffs to convince her that he was not funning and that her beautiful dream was a fond and foolish vanity, a shabby and pitiful mistake. She was hurt to the heart, and so ashamed that for a moment she did not quite know what to do or how to act. Then her breast began to heave, the tears came, and in her forlornness she was moved to try that other dream of hers—an appeal to her boy's charity; and so, upon the impulse, and without reflection, she offered her supplication—

"Oh, Marse Tom, de po' ole mammy is in sich hard luck, dese days; en she's kinder crippled in de arms en can't work, en if you could gimme a dollah—on'y jes' one little dol—"

Tom was on his feet so suddenly that the supplicant was startled into a jump herself.

"A dollar!—give you a dollar! I've a notion to strangle you! Is *that* your errand here? Clear out! and be quick about it!"

Roxy backed slowly toward the door. When she was half-way she stopped, and said, mournfully—

"Marse Tom, I nussed you when you was a little baby, en I raised you all by myself tell you was most a young man; en now you is young en rich en I is po' en gitt'n ole, en I come heah b'lievin' dat you would he'p de ole mammy 'long down de little road dat's lef' twix her en de grave, en—"

Tom relished this tune less than any that had preceded it, for it began to wake up a sort of echo in his conscience; so he interrupted and said with decision, though without asperity, that he was not in a situation to help her, and wasn't going to do it.

"Ain't you ever gwyne to he'p me, Marse Tom?"

"No! Now go away and don't bother me any more."

Roxy's head was down, in an attitude of humility. But now the fires of her old wrongs flamed up in her breast and began to burn fiercely. She raised her head slowly, till it was well up, and at the same time her great frame unconsciously assumed an erect and masterful attitude, with all the majesty and grace of her vanished youth in it. She raised her finger and punctuated with it:

"You has said de word. You has had yo' chance, en you has trompled it under yo' foot. When you git another one, you'll git down on yo' knees en *beg* for it!"

A cold chill went to Tom's heart, he didn't know why; for he did not reflect that such words, from such an incongruous source, and so solemnly delivered, could not easily fail of that effect. However, he did the natural thing: he replied with bluster and mockery:

"*You'll* give me a chance—*you*! Perhaps I'd better get down on my knees now! But in case I don't—just for argument's sake—what's going to happen, pray?"

"Dis is what is gwyne to happen. I's gywne as straight to yo' uncle as I kin walk, en tell him every las' thing I knows about you."

Tom's cheek blenched, and she saw it. Disturbing thoughts began to chase each other through his head. "How can she know? And yet she must have found out—she looks it. I've had the will back only three months and am already deep in debt again and moving heaven and earth to save myself from exposure and destruction, with a reasonably fair show of getting the thing covered up if I'm let alone, and now this fiend has gone and found me out somehow or other. I wonder how much she knows. Oh, oh, oh, it's enough to break a body's heart! But I've got to humor her—there's no other way."

Then he worked up a rather sickly sample of a gay laugh and a hollow chipperness of manner, and said—

"Well, well, Roxy dear, old friends like you and me mustn't quarrel. Here's your dollar—now tell me what you know."

He held out the wild-cat bill, she stood as she was, and made no movement. It was her turn to scorn persuasive foolery, now, and she did not waste it. She said, with a grim implacability in voice and manner which made Tom almost realize that even a former slave can remember for ten minutes insults and injuries returned for compliments and flatteries received, and can also enjoy taking revenge for them when the opportunity offers—

"What does I know? I'll tell you what I knows. I knows enough to bust dat will to flinders—en more, mind you, *more*!"

Tom was aghast.

"More?" he said. "What do you call more? Where's there any room for more?"

Roxy laughed a mocking laugh, and said scoffingly, with a toss of her head, and her hands on her hips—

"Yes!—oh, I reckon! '*Cose* you'd like to know—wid yo' po' little ole rag dollah. What you reckon I's gywne to tell *you*, for?—you ain't got no money. I's gwyne to tell yo' uncle—en I'll do it dis minute, too—he'll gimme *five* dollahs for de news, en mighty glad, too."

She swung herself around disdainfully, and started away. Tom was in a panic. He seized her skirts and implored her to wait. She turned and said, loftily—

"Look-a-here, what was it I tole you?"

"You—you—I don't remember anything. What was it you told me?"

"I tole you dat de next time I give you a chance you'd git down on yo' knees en beg for it."

Tom was stupefied for a moment. He was panting with excitement. Then he said—

"Oh, Roxy, you wouldn't require your young master to do such a horrible thing. You can't mean it."

"I'll let you know mighty quick whether I means it or not! You call me names, en as good as spit on me when I comes here po' en ornery en 'umble, to praise you for bein' growed up so fine en handsome, en tell you how I used to nuss you en tend you en watch you when you was sick en you hadn't no mother but me in de whole worl', en beg you to give de po' ole nigger a dollah for to git her sum'n to eat, en you call me names—*names*, dad blame you! Yassir, I gives you jes' one chance mo', and dat's *now*, en it las' on'y a half a second—you hear?"

Tom slumped to his knees and began to beg, saying—

"You see I'm begging, and it's honest begging, too! Now tell me, Roxy, tell me."

The heir of two centuries of unatoned insult and outrage looked down on him and seemed to drink in deep draughts of satisfaction. Then she said—

"Fine nice young white gen'lman kneelin' down to a nigger wench! I's wanted to see dat jes' once befo' I's called. Now, Gabrel, blow de hawn, I's ready . . . . . . Git up!"

Tom did it. He said, humbly—

"Now Roxy, don't punish me any more. I deserved what I've got, but be good and let me off with that. Don't go to uncle. Tell me—I'll give you the five dollars."

"Yes, I bet you will; en you won't stop dah, nuther. But I ain't gwyne to tell you here—"

"Good gracious, no!"

"Is you feared o' de ha'nted house?"

"N-no."

"Well, den, you come to de ha'nted house 'bout ten or 'leven to-night, en climb up de ladder, caze de star-steps is broke down, en you'll fine me. I's a roostin' in de ha'nted house becaze I can't 'ford to roos' nowher's else." She started toward the door, but stopped and said "Gimme de dollah bill!" He gave it to her. She examined it and said, "Hm—like enough de bank's busted." She started again, but halted again. "Has you got any whisky?"

"Yes, a little."

"Fetch it!"

He ran to his room overhead and brought down a bottle which was two-thirds full. She tilted it up and took a drink. Her eyes sparkled with satisfaction, and she tucked the bottle under her shawl, saying,—

"It's prime—I'll take it along."

Tom humbly held the door for her, and she marched out as grim and erect as a grenadier.

Chapter 9

Why is it that we rejoice at birth and grieve at a funeral? It is because we are not the person involved.

—PUDD'NHEAD WILSON'S CALENDAR.

It is easy to find fault, if one has that disposition. There was once a man who, not being able to find any other fault with his coal, complained that there were too many prehistoric toads in it.

—PUDD'NHEAD WILSON'S CALENDAR.

Tom flung himself on the sofa, and put his throbbing head in his hands and rested his elbows on his knees. He rocked himself back and forth and moaned.

"I've knelt to a nigger wench!" he muttered. "I thought I had struck the deepest deeps of degradation before, but oh, dear, it was nothing to this. . . . . . . Well, there is one consolation, such as it is—I've struck bottom this time; there's nothing lower."

But that was a hasty conclusion.

At ten that night he climbed the ladder in the haunted house, pale, weak, and wretched. Roxy was standing in the door of one of the rooms, waiting, for she had heard him.

This was a two-story log house which had acquired the reputation a few years before of being haunted, and that was the end of its usefulness. Nobody would live in it afterward or go near it by night, and most people even gave it a wide berth in the daytime. As it had no competition, it was called *the*

haunted house. It was getting crazy and ruinous, now, from long neglect. It stood three hundred yards beyond Pudd'nhead Wilson's
house, with nothing between but vacancy. It was the last house in
the town at that end.

Tom followed Roxy into the room. She had a pile of clean straw in
the corner for a bed, some cheap but well-kept clothing was hanging
on the wall, there was a tin lantern freckling the floor with little spots
of light, and there were various soap and candle boxes scattered
about, which served for chairs. The two sat down. Roxy said—

"Now, den. I'll tell you straight off, en I'll begin to k'leck de money
later on; I ain't in no hurry. What does you reckon I's gwyne to tell you?"

"Well, you—you—oh, Roxy, don't make it too hard for me! Come
right out and tell me you've found out somehow what a shape I'm in
on account of dissipation and foolishness."

"Disposition en foolishness! *No* sir, dat ain't it. Dat jist ain't noth'n
at all, 'longside o' what *I* knows."

Tom stared at her, and said—

"Why—Roxy, what do you mean?"

She rose, and gloomed above him like a fate.

"I mean dis—en it's de Lord's truth. You ain't no more kin to ole
Marse Driscoll den I is!—*dat's* what I mean!" and her eyes flamed
with triumph.

"What!"

"Yassir, en *dat* ain't all! You is a *nigger!*—*bawn* a nigger en a *slave!*—
en you's a nigger en a slave dis minute; en if I opens my mouf, ole
Marse Driscoll 'll sell you down de river befo' you is two days older
den what you is now!"

"It's a thundering lie, you miserable old blatherskite!"

"It ain't no lie, nuther. It's jes' de truth, en noth'n *but* de truth, so
he'p me. Yassir—you's my *son*—"

"You devil!—"

—"en dat po' boy dat you's been a kickin' en a cuffin' to-day is Percy
Driscoll's son en yo' *marster*—"

"You beast!"

—"en *his* name's Tom Driscoll en *yo'* name's Vallet de Chambers,
en you ain't *got* no fambly name, becaze niggers don't *have* 'em!"

Tom sprang up and seized a billet of wood and raised it; but his
mother only laughed at him and said—

"Set down, you pup! Does you think you kin sk'yer me? It ain't in
you, nor de likes of you. I reckon you'd shoot me in de back, maybe,
if you got a chance, for dat's jist yo' style, *I* knows you, thoo en thoo—
but I don't mind gitt'n killed, becaze all dis is down in writin', en it's
in safe hands, too, en de man dat's got it knows whah to look for de
right man when I gits killed. Oh, bless yo' soul, if you puts yo' mother
up for as big a fool as *you* is, you's pow'ful mistaken, I kin tell you!

Now den, you set still en behave yo'self; en don't you git up agin till I tell you!"

Tom fretted and chafed a while in a whirlwind of disorganizing sensations and emotions, and finally said with something like settled conviction—

"The whole thing is moonshine—now, then, go ahead and do your worst; I'm done with you."

Roxy made no answer. She took the lantern and started toward the door. Tom was in a cold panic in a moment.

"Come back, come back!" he wailed. "I didn't mean it, Roxy, I take it all back, and I'll never say it again! Please come back, Roxy!"

The woman stood a moment, then she said gravely—

"Dah's one thing you's got to stop, Vallet de Chambers. You can't call me *Roxy*, same as if you was my equal. Chillen don't speak to dey mammies like dat. You'll call me Ma or mammy, dat's what you'll call me—leastways when dey ain't nobody aroun'. *Say* it!"

It cost Tom a struggle, but he got it out.

"Dat's all right. Don't you ever fogit it agin, if you knows what's good for you. Now, den, you has said you wouldn't ever call it lies en moonshine agin. I'll tell you dis, for a warnin': if you ever does say it agin it's de *las'* time you'll ever say it to me; I'll tramp as straight to de Judge as I kin walk, en tell him who you is en *prove* it. Does you b'lieve me when I says dat?"

"Oh," groaned Tom, "I more than believe it, I *know* it."

Roxy knew her conquest was complete. She could have proven nothing to anybody, and her threat about the writings was a lie; but she knew the person she was dealing with, and had made both statements without any doubts as to the effect they would produce.

She went and sat down on her candle-box, and the pride and pomp of her victorious attitude made it a throne. She said—

"Now, den, Chambers, we's gwyne to talk business, en dey ain't gwyne to be no mo' foolishness. In de fust place, you gits fifty dollahs a month; you's gwyne to han' over half of it to yo' ma. Plank it out!"

But Tom had only six dollars in the world. He gave her that, and promised to start fair on next month's pension.

"Chambers, how much is you in debt?"

Tom shuddered, and said—

"Nearly three hundred dollars."

"How is you gwyne to pay it?"

Tom groaned out—

"Oh, I don't know—don't ask me such awful questions."

But she stuck to her point until she wearied a confession out of him: he had been prowling about in disguise, stealing small valuables from private houses; in fact had made a good deal of a raid on his fellow villagers a fortnight before, when he was supposed to be in St. Louis; but he doubted if he had sent away enough stuff to realize the required amount, and was afraid to make a further venture in the present excited state of the town. His mother approved of his conduct, and offered to help, but this frightened him. He tremblingly ventured to say that if she would retire from the town he should feel better and safer, and could hold his head higher—and was going on to make an argument, but she interrupted and surprised him pleasantly by saying she was ready, it didn't make any difference to her where she stayed, so that she got her share of the pension regularly. She said she would not go far, and would call at the haunted house once a month for her money. Then she said—

"I don't hate you so much now, but I've hated you a many a year—and anybody would. Didn't I change you off en give you a good fambly en a good name, en made you a white genl'man en rich, wid store clothes on—en what did I git for it? You despised me all de time; en was allays sayin' mean hard things to me befo' folks, en wouldn't ever let me fogit I's a nigger—en—en—"

She fell to sobbing, and broke down. Tom said—

"But you know, I didn't know you were my mother—and besides —"

"Well, nemmine 'bout dat, now—let it go. I's gwyne to fogit it." Then she added fiercely, "En don't you ever make me remember it agin, or you'll be sorry, *I* tell you."

When they were parting, Tom said, in the most persuasive way he could command—

"Ma, would you mind telling me who was my father?"

He had supposed he was asking an embarrassing question. He was mistaken. Roxy drew herself up, with a proud toss of her head, and said:

"Does I mine tellin' you? No, dat I don't! You ain't got no 'casion to be shame' o' yo' father, *I* kin tell you. He was de highest quality in dis whole town—Ole Virginny stock, Fust Famblies, he was. Jes' as good stock as de Driscolls en de Howards, de bes' day dey ever seed." She put on a still prouder air, if possible, and added impressively, "Does you 'member Cunnel Cecil Burleigh Essex dat died de same year yo' young Marse Tom Driscoll's pappy died, en all de Masons en Odd Fellers en churches turned out en give him de bigges' funeral dis town ever seed? Dat's de man."

Under the inspiration of her soaring complacency the departed graces of her earlier days returned to her, and her bearing took to itself a dignity and state that might have passed for queenly if her surroundings had been a little more in keeping with it.

"Dey ain't another nigger in dis town dat's as high-bawn as you is.

Now, den, go 'long! En jes' you hold yo' head up as high as you want
to—you has de right, en dat I kin swah."

Chapter 10

*All say "How hard it is that we have to die"—a strange complaint to
come from the mouths of people who have had to live.*
                              —PUDD'NHEAD WILSON'S CALENDAR.

When angry, count four; when very angry, swear.
                              —PUDD'NHEAD WILSON'S CALENDAR.

Every now and then, after Tom went to bed, he had sudden wakings
out of his sleep, and his first thought was, "O, joy, it was all a dream!"
Then he laid himself heavily down again, with a groan and the muttered words, "A nigger!—I am a nigger!—oh, I wish I was dead!"

He woke at dawn with one more repetition of this horror, and then

he resolved to meddle no more with that treacherous sleep. He began
to think. Sufficiently bitter thinkings they were. They wandered
along something after this fashion:

"Why were niggers *and* whites made? What crime did the uncreated first nigger commit that the curse of birth was decreed for
him? And why is this awful difference made between white and
black?. . . . . . How hard the nigger's fate seems, this morning!—yet
until last night such a thought never entered my head."

He sighed and groaned an hour or more away. Then "Chambers"
came humbly in to say that breakfast was nearly ready. "Tom"
blushed scarlet to see this aristocratic white youth cringe to him, a
nigger, and call him "Young marster." He said, roughly—

"Get out of my sight!" and when the youth was gone, he muttered,
"He has done me no harm, poor wretch, but he is an eyesore to me,
now, for he is Driscoll the young gentleman, and I am a—oh, I wish
I was dead!"

.   .   .

A gigantic irruption like that of Krakatoa a few years ago, with the accompanying earthquakes, tidal waves and clouds of volcanic dust, changes the face of the surrounding landscape beyong recognition, bringing down the high lands, elevating the low, making fair lakes where deserts had been, and deserts where green prairies had smiled before. The tremendous catastrophe which had befallen Tom had changed his moral landscape in much the same way. Some of his low places he found lifted to ideals, some of his ideals had sunk to the valleys, and lay there with the sackcloth and ashes of pumice stone and sulphur on their ruined heads.

For days he wandered in lonely places thinking, thinking, thinking—trying to get his bearings. It was new work. If he met a friend he found that the habit of a lifetime had in some mysterious way vanished—his arm hung limp instead of involuntarily extending the hand for a shake. It was the "nigger" in him asserting its humility, and he blushed and was abashed. And the "nigger" in him was surprised when the white friend put out his hand for a shake with him. He found the "nigger" in him involuntarily giving the road, on the sidewalk, to the white rowdy and loafer. When Rowena, the dearest thing his heart knew, the idol of his secret worship, invited him in, the "nigger" in him made an embarrassed excuse and was afraid to enter and sit with the dread white folks on equal terms. The "nigger" in him went shrinking and skulking here and there and yonder, and fancying it saw suspicion and maybe detection in all faces, tones and gestures. So strange and uncharacteristic was Tom's conduct that people noticed it and turned to look after him when he passed on; and when he glanced back—as he could not help doing, in spite of his best resistance—and caught that puzzled expression in a person's face, it gave him a sick feeling, and he took himself out of view as quickly as he could. He presently came to have a hunted sense and a hunted look, and then he fled away to the hilltops and the solitudes. He said to himself that the curse of Ham was upon him.

He dreaded his meals; the "nigger" in him was ashamed to sit at the white folks' table, and feared discovery all the time; and once when Judge Driscoll said, "What's the matter with you?—you look as meek as a nigger," he felt as secret murderers are said to feel when the accuser says "Thou art the man!" Tom said he was not well, and left the table.

His ostensible "aunt's" solicitudes and endearments were become a terror to him, and he avoided them.

And all the time, hatred of his ostensible "uncle" was steadily growing in his heart; for he said to himself, "He is white; and I am his chattel, his property, his goods, and he can sell me, just as he could his dog."

For as much as a week after this, Tom imagined that his character had undergone a pretty radical change. But that was because he did not know himself.

In several ways his opinions were totally changed, and would never go back to what they were before, but the main structure of his character was not changed, and could not be changed. One or two very important features of it were altered, and in time effects would result from this, if opportunity offered; effects of a quite serious nature, too. Under the influence of a great mental and moral upheaval his character and habits had taken on the appearance of complete change, but after a while with the subsidence of the storm both began to settle toward their former places. He dropped gradually back into his old frivolous and easy-going ways, and conditions of feeling, and manner of speech, and no familiar of his could have detected anything in him that differentiated him from the weak and careless Tom of other days.

The theft-raid which he had made upon the village turned out better than he had ventured to hope. It produced the sum necessary to pay his gaming-debts, and saved him from exposure to his uncle and another smashing of the will.

He and his mother learned to like each other fairly well. She couldn't love him, as yet, because there "warn't nothing *to* him," as she expressed it, but her nature needed something or somebody to rule over, and he was better than nothing. Her strong character and aggressive and commanding ways compelled Tom's admiration in spite of the fact that he got more illustrations of them than he needed for his comfort. However, as a rule, her conversation was made up of racy tattle about the privacies of the chief families of the town (for she went harvesting among their kitchens every time she came to the village), and Tom enjoyed this. It was just in his line. She always collected her half of his pension punctually, and he was always at the haunted house to have a chat with her on these occasions. Every now and then she paid him a visit there on between-days also.

Occasionally he would run up to St. Louis for a few weeks, and at last temptation caught him again. He won a lot of money, but lost it, and with it a deal more besides, which he promised to raise as soon as possible.

For this purpose he projected a new raid on his town. He never meddled with any other town, for he was afraid to venture into houses whose ins and outs he did not know, and the habits of whose households he was not acquainted with. He arrived at the haunted house in disguise on the Wednesday before the advent of the Twins,—after writing his aunt Pratt that he would not arrive until two days later—and lay in hiding there with his mother until toward daylight Friday morning, when he went to his uncle's house and entered by the back way with his own key and slipped up to his room, where he could have the use of mirror and toilet articles. He had a suit of girl's clothes with him in a bundle as a disguise for his raid, and was wearing a suit of his mother's clothing, with black gloves and veil. By dawn he was tricked out for his raid, but he caught a glimpse of Pudd'nhead Wilson through the window over the way and knew that Pudd'nhead had caught a glimpse of him. So he entertained Wilson with some airs and graces and attitudes for a while, then stepped out of sight and resumed the other disguise, and by and by went down and out the back way and started downtown to reconnoitre the scene of his intended labors.

But he was ill at ease. He had changed back to Roxy's dress, with the stoop of age added to the disguise, so that Wilson would not bother himself about a humble old woman leaving a neighbor's house by the back way in the early morning, in case he was still spying. But supposing Wilson had seen him leave, and had thought it suspicious, and had also followed him? The thought made Tom cold. He gave up the raid for the day, and hurried back to the haunted house by the obscurest route he knew. His mother was gone; but she came back, by and by, with the news of the grand reception at Patsy Cooper's, and soon persuaded him that the opportunity was like a special providence it was so inviting and perfect. So he went raiding, after all,

and made a nice success of it while everybody was gone to Patsy Cooper's. Success gave him nerve; and even actual intrepidity; insomuch, indeed, that after he had conveyed his harvest to his mother in a back alley, he went to the reception himself, and added several of the valuables of that house to his takings.

After this long digression we have now

arrived, once more, at the point where Pudd'nhead Wilson, while waiting for the arrival of the Twins on that same Friday evening, sat puzzling over the strange apparition of that morning—a girl in young Tom Driscoll's bedroom; fretting, and guessing, and puzzling over it, and wondering who the shameless creature might be.

Chapter 11

There are three infallible ways of pleasing an author, and the three form a rising scale of compliment: 1, to tell him you have read one of his books; 2, to tell him you have read all of his books; 3, to ask him to let you read the manuscript of his forthcoming book. No. 1 admits you to his respect; No. 2 admits you to his admiration; No. 3 carries you clear into his heart.
—PUDD'NHEAD WILSON'S CALENDAR.

As to the Adjective: when in doubt, strike it out.
—PUDD'NHEAD WILSON'S CALENDAR.

The twins arrived presently, and talk began. It flowed along chattily and sociably, and under its influence the new friendship gathered ease and strength. Wilson got out his Calendar, by request, and read a passage or two from it, which the Twins praised quite cordially. This pleased the author so much that he complied gladly when they asked him to lend them a batch of the work to read at home. In the course of their wide travels they had found out that there are three sure ways of pleasing an author; they were now working the best of the three.

There was an interruption, now. Young Tom Driscoll appeared, and joined the party. He pretended to be seeing the distinguished strangers for the first time when they rose to shake hands; but this was only a blind, as he had already had a glimpse of them at the reception while robbing the house. The Twins made mental note that

he was smooth-faced and rather handsome, and smooth and undulatory in his movements—graceful, in fact. Angelo thought he had a good eye, Luigi thought there was something veiled and sly about it. Angelo thought he had a pleasant free-and-easy way of talking, Luigi thought it was more so than was agreeable. Angelo thought he was a sufficiently nice young man, Luigi reserved his decision. Tom's first contribution to the conversation was a question which he had put to Wilson a hundred times before. It was always cheerily and good-naturedly put, and always inflicted a little pang, for it touched a secret sore; but this time the pang was sharp, since strangers were present:

"Well, how does the law come on? Had a case yet?"

Wilson bit his lip, but answered, "No—not yet," with as much indifference as he could assume. Judge Driscoll had generously left the law feature out of the Wilson biography which he had furnished to the Twins. Young Tom laughed pleasantly and said—

"Wilson's a lawyer, gentlemen, but he doesn't practice now."

The sarcasm bit, but Wilson kept himself under control, and said, without passion—

"I don't practice, it is true. It is true that I have never had a case, and have had to earn a poor living for twenty years as an expert accountant in a town where I can't get hold of a set of books to untangle as often as I should like. But it is also true that I did fit myself well for the practice of the law. By the time I was your age, Tom, I had chosen a profession and was soon competent to enter upon it." Tom winced. "I never got a chance to try my hand at it, and I may never get a chance; and yet if I ever do get it I shall be found ready, for I have kept up my law-studies all these years."

"That's it—that's good grit! I like to see it. I've a notion to throw all my business your way. My business and your law-practice ought to make a pretty gay team, Dave," and the young fellow laughed again.

"If you will throw—" Wilson had thought of the girl in Tom's bedroom, and was going to say, "If you will throw the surreptitious and disreputable part of your business my way, it may amount to something," but thought better of it and said, "However, this matter doesn't fit well in a general conversation."

"All right, we'll change the subject—I guess you were about to give me another dig, anyway, so I'm willing to change. How's the Awful Mystery flourishing these days? Wilson's got a scheme for driving plain window-glass out of the market by decorating it with greasy finger-marks and getting rich by selling it at famine prices to the crowned heads over in Europe to outfit their palaces with. Fetch it out, Dave."

Wilson brought three of his glass strips and said:

"I get the subject to pass the fingers of his right hand through his hair, so as to get a little coating of the natural oil on them, and then press the balls of them on the glass. A fine and delicate print of the lines in the skin results, and is permanent if it doesn't come in contact with something able to rub it off. You begin, Tom."

"Why, I think you took my finger-marks once or twice before."

"Yes, but you were a little boy, the last time, only about twelve years old."

"That's so. Of course I've changed entirely since then, and variety is what the crowned heads want, I guess."

He passed his fingers through his crop of short hair and pressed them one at a time on the glass. Angelo made a print of his fingers on another glass, and Luigi followed with the third. Wilson marked the glasses with names and date and put them away. Tom gave one of his little laughs and said—

"I thought I wouldn't say anything, but if variety is what you are after, you have wasted a piece of glass. The hand-print of one twin is the same as the hand-print of the fellow-twin."

"Well, it's done, now, and I like to have them both, anyway," said Wilson, returning to his place.

"But look here, Dave," said Tom, "you used to tell people's fortunes, too, when you took their finger-marks. Dave's just an all-around genius, a genius of the first water, gentlemen, a great scientist running to seed here in this village, a prophet with the kind of honor that prophets generally get at home—for here they don't give shucks for his scientifics, and they call his skull a notion-factory—hey, Dave, ain't it so?—but never mind, he'll make his mark some day—finger-mark, you know, he-he! But really, you want to let him take a shy at your palms once, it's worth twice the price of admission or your money's returned at the door. Why, he'll read your wrinkles as easy as a book, and not only tell you fifty or sixty things that's going to happen to you, but fifty or sixty thousand that ain't. Come, Dave, show the gentlemen what an inspired Jack-at-all-science we've got in this town and don't know it."

Wilson winced under this nagging and not very courteous chaff, and the Twins suffered with him and for him. They rightly judged, now, that the best way to relieve him would be to take the thing in earnest and treat it with respect, ignoring Tom's rather overdone raillery; so Luigi said:

"We have seen something of palmistry in our wanderings, and know very well what astonishing things it can do. If it isn't a science, and one of the greatest of them, too, I don't know what its other name ought to be. In the Orient—"

Tom looked surprised and incredulous. He said—

"That jugglery a science? But really, you ain't serious, are you?"

"Yes, entirely so. Four years ago we had our hands read out to us as if our palms had been covered with print."

"Well, do you mean to say there was actually anything in it?" asked Tom, his incredulity beginning to weaken a little.

"There was this much in it," said Angelo; "what was told us of our characters was minutely exact—we could not have bettered it ourselves. Next, two or three memorable things that had happened to us were laid bare—things which no one present but ourselves could have known about."

"Why, it's rank sorcery!" exclaimed Tom, who was now becoming very much interested. "And how did they make out with what was going to happen to you in the future?"

"On the whole, quite fairly," said Luigi. "Two or three of the most striking things foretold have happened since; much the most striking one of all happened within that same year. Some of the minor prophecies have come true; some of the minor and some of the major ones have not been fulfilled yet, and of course may never be—still, I should be more surprised if they failed to arrive than if they didn't."

Tom was entirely sobered, and profoundly impressed. He said, apologetically—

"Dave, I wasn't meaning to belittle that science, I was only chaffing—chattering, I reckon I better say. I wish you would look at their palms. Come, won't you?"

"Why, certainly, if you want me to, but you know I've had no chance to become an expert, and don't claim to be one. When a past event is somewhat prominently recorded in the palm, I can generally detect that, but minor ones often escape me—not always, of course, but often—but I haven't much confidence in myself when it comes to reading the future. I am talking as if palmistry was a daily study with me, but that is not so. I haven't examined half a dozen hands in the last half a dozen years; you see, the people got to joking about it, and I stopped to let the talk die down. I'll tell you what we'll do, Count Luigi: I'll make a try at your past, and if I have any success there—no, on the whole I'll let the future alone; that's really the affair of an expert."

He took Luigi's hand. Tom said—

"Wait—don't look yet, Dave! Count Luigi, here's paper and pencil. Set down that thing that you said was the most striking one that was foretold to you and happened less than a year afterwards, and give it to me so I can see if Dave finds it in your hand."

Luigi wrote a line privately, and folded up the piece of paper and handed it to Tom, saying—

"I'll tell you when to look at it, if he finds it."

Wilson began to study Luigi's palm, tracing life lines, heart lines, head lines, and so on, and noting carefully their relations with the cobweb of finer and more delicate marks and lines that enmeshed them on all sides; he felt of the fleshy cushion at the base of the thumb, and noted its shape; he felt of the fleshy side of the hand between the wrist and the base of the little finger, and noted its shape also; he pains-takingly examined the fingers, observing their form, proportions and natural manner of disposing themselves when in repose. All this process was watched by the three spectators with absorbing interest, their heads bent together over Luigi's palm and nobody disturbing the stillness with a word. Wilson now entered upon a close survey of the palm again, and his revelations began.

He mapped out Luigi's character and disposition, his tastes, aversions, proclivities, ambitions and eccentricities in a way which sometimes made Luigi wince and the others laugh, but both Twins declared that the chart was artistically drawn and was correct.

Next, Wilson took up Luigi's history. He proceeded cautiously and with hesitation, now, moving his finger slowly along the great lines of the palm, and now and then halting it at a "star" or some such landmark and examining that neighborhood minutely. He proclaimed one or two past events, Luigi confirmed his correctness, and the search went on. Presently Wilson glanced up suddenly with a surprised expression—

"Here is record of an incident which you would perhaps not wish me to—"

"Bring it out," said Luigi, good-naturedly, "I promise you it shan't embarrass me."

But Wilson still hesitated, and did not seem quite to know what to do. Then he said—

"I think it is too delicate a matter to—to—. I believe I would rather write it or whisper it to you, and let you decide for yourself whether you want it talked out or not."

"That will answer," said Luigi; "write it."

Wilson wrote something on a slip of paper and handed it to Luigi, who read it to himself and said to Tom—

"Unfold your slip and read it, Mr. Driscoll."

Tom read:

"It was prophesied that I would kill a man. It came true before the year was out." Tom added, "Great Scott!"

Luigi handed Wilson's paper to Tom and said—

"Now read this one."

Tom read.

"You have killed some one—but whether man, woman or child, I do not make out." "Caesar's ghost!" commented Tom, with astonishment. "It beats anything that was ever heard of! Why, a man's own

hand is his deadliest enemy! Just think of that—a man's own hand keeps a record of the deepest and fatalest secrets of his life, and is treacherously ready to expose him to any black-magic stranger that comes along. But what do you let a person look at your hand for, with that awful thing printed in it?"

"Oh," said Luigi reposefully, "I don't mind it. I killed the man for good reasons, and I don't regret it."

"What were the reasons?"

"Well, he needed killing."

"I'll tell you why he did it, since he won't say himself," said Angelo warmly. "He did it to save my life—that's what he did it for. So it was a noble act, and not a thing to be hid in the dark."

"So it was, so it was," said Wilson; "to do such a thing to save a brother's life is a great and fine action."

"Now come," said Luigi, "it is very pleasant to hear you say these things, but for unselfishness, or heroism, or magnanimity, the circumstance won't stand scrutiny. You overlook one detail: suppose I hadn't saved Angelo's life, what would have become of mine? If I had let the man kill him, wouldn't he have killed me, too? I saved my own life, you see."

"Yes, that is your way of talking," said Angelo, "but I know you, and I don't believe you thought of yourself at all. I keep that weapon yet that Luigi killed the man with, and I'll show it to you some time. That incident makes it interesting, and it had a history before it came into Luigi's hands which adds to its interest. It was given to Luigi by a great Indian prince, the Gaikowar of Baroda, and it had been in his family two or three centuries. It killed a good many disagreeable people who troubled that hearthstone at one time and another. It isn't much to look at, except that it isn't shaped like other knives, or dirks, or whatever it may be called—here, I'll draw it for you." He took a sheet of paper and made a rapid sketch. "There it is—a broad and murderous blade, with edges like a razor for sharpness. The devices engraved on it are the ciphers or names of its long line of possessors—I had Luigi's name added in Roman letters, myself, with our coat of arms, as you see. You notice what a curious handle the thing has. It is solid ivory, polished like a mirror, and is four or five inches long—round, and as thick as a large man's wrist, with the end squared off flat, for your thumb to rest on; for you grasp it, with your thumb resting on the blunt end—so—and lift it aloft and strike downwards. The Gaikowar showed us how the thing was done when he gave it to Luigi, and before that night was ended Luigi had used the knife and the Gaikowar was a man short by reason of it. The sheath is magnificently ornamented with gems of great value. You will find the sheath more worth looking at than the knife itself, of course."

Tom said to himself:

"It's lucky I came here; I would have sold that knife for a song; I supposed the jewels were glass."

"But go on—don't stop," said Wilson. "Our curiosity is up, now, to hear about the homicide. Tell us about that."

"Well, briefly, the knife was to blame for that, all around. A native servant slipped into our room in the palace in the night, to kill us and steal that knife on account of the fortune encrusted on its sheath, without a doubt. Luigi had it under his pillow; we were in bed together. There was a dim night-light burning. I was asleep, but Luigi was awake, and he thought he detected a vague form nearing the bed. He slipped the knife out of the sheath, and was ready and unembarrassed by hampering bed-clothes, for the weather was hot and we hadn't any. Suddenly that native rose at the bedside and bent over me with his right hand lifted and a dirk in it aimed at my throat, but Luigi grabbed his wrist, pulled him downward and drove his own knife into the man's neck. That is the whole story."

Wilson and Tom drew deep breaths, and after some general chat about the tragedy, Pudd'nhead said, taking Tom's hand—

"Now Tom, I've never had a look at your palms, as it happens; perhaps you've got some little questionable privacies that need—hel-lo!"

Tom had snatched away his hand, and was looking a good deal confused.

"Why, he's blushing!" said Luigi.

Tom darted an ugly look at him and said, sharply—

"Well, if I am, it ain't because I'm a murderer!" Luigi's dark face flushed, but before he could speak or move, Tom added with anxious haste, "Oh, I beg a thousand pardons, I didn't mean that, it was out before I thought, and I'm very, very sorry—you must forgive me!"

Wilson came to the rescue, and smoothed things down as well as he could; and in fact was entirely successful as far as the Twins were concerned, for they felt sorrier for the affront put upon him by his guest's outburst of ill manners than for the insult offered to Luigi; but the success was not so pronounced with the offender. Tom tried to seem at his ease, and he went through the motions fairly well, but at bottom he felt resentful toward all the three witnesses of his exhibition—in fact he felt so annoyed at them for having witnessed it and noticed it that he almost forgot to feel annoyed at himself for placing it before them. However, something presently happened which made him almost comfortable, and brought him nearly back to a state of charity and friendliness. This was a little spat between the Twins; not much of a spat, but still a spat; and before they got far with it they were in a decided condition of irritation with each other. Tom was charmed; so pleased, indeed, that he cautiously did what he could to increase the irritation while pretending to be actuated by more respectable motives. By his help the fire got warmed up to the blazing point, and he might have had the happiness of seeing the flames show up, in another moment, but for the interruption of a knock on the door—an interruption which fretted him as much as it gratified Wilson. Wilson opened the door.

The visitor was a good-natured, ignorant, energetic, middle-aged Irishman named John Buckstone, who was a great politician in a small way, and always took a large share in public matters of every sort. One of the town's chief excitements just now, was over the matter of rum. There was a strong rum party and a strong anti-rum party. Buckstone was training with the rum party, and he had been sent to hunt up the Twins and invite them to attend a mass meeting of that faction. He delivered his errand and said the clans were already gathering in the big hall over the market house. Luigi accepted the invitation cordially, Angelo less cordially, since he disliked crowds, and did not drink the powerful intoxicants of America. In fact, he was even a teetotaler sometimes—when it was judicious to be one.

The Twins left with Buckstone, and Tom Driscoll joined company with them uninvited.

In the distance one could see a long wavering line of torches drifting down the main street, and could hear the throbbing of the bass drum, the clash of cymbals, the squeaking of a fife or two, and the faint roar of remote hurrahs. The tail end of this procession was climbing the market house stairs when the Twins arrived in its neighborhood; when they reached the hall it was full of people, torches, smoke, noise and enthusiasm. They were conducted to the platform by Buckstone,—Tom Driscoll still following—and were delivered to the chairman in the midst of a prodigious

explosion of welcome. When the noise had moderated a little, the chair proposed that "our illustrious guests be at once elected, by complimentary acclamation, to membership in our ever glorious organization, the paradise of the free and the perdition of the slave."

This eloquent discharge opened the flood-gates of enthusiasm again, and the election was carried with thundering unanimity. Then arose a storm of cries:

"Wet them down! wet them down! give them a drink!"

Glasses of whisky were handed to the Twins. Luigi waved his aloft, then brought it to his lips, but Angelo set his down. There was another storm of cries—

"What's the matter with the other one?" "What is the blonde one going back on us for?" "Explain! Explain!"

The chairman inquired, and then reported—

"We have made an unfortunate mistake, gentlemen. I find that the Count Angelo Cappello is opposed to our creed—is a teetotaler, in fact, and was not intending to apply for membership with us. He desires that we reconsider the vote by which he was elected. What is the pleasure of the house?"

There was a general burst of laughter, plentifully accented with whistlings and cat-calls, but the energetic use of the gavel presently restored something like order. Then a man spoke from the crowd and said that while he was very sorry that the mistake had been made, it would not be possible to rectify it at the present meeting. According to the bye-laws it must go over to the next regular meeting for action. He would not offer a motion, as none was required. He desired to apologize to the gentleman in the name of the house, and begged to assure him that as far as it might lie in the power of the Sons of Liberty, his temporary membership in the order would be made pleasant to him.

This speech was received with great applause, mixed with cries of—

"That's the talk!" "He's a good fellow, anyway, if he *is* a teetotaler!" "Drink his health!" "Give him a rouser, and no heel-taps!"

Glasses were handed around, and everybody on the platform drank Angelo's health, while the house bellowed forth in song:

> "For he's a jolly good fel-low,
> For he's a jolly good fel-low,
> For he's a jolly good fe-el-low—
> Which nobody can deny."

Tom Driscoll drank. It was his second glass, for he had drunk Angelo's the moment that Angelo had set it down. The two drinks made him very merry—almost idiotically so—and he began to take a most lively and prominent part in the proceedings, particularly in the music and cat-calls and side-remarks.

The chairman was still standing at the front, the Twins at his side. The extraordinarily close resemblance of the brothers to each other suggested a witticism to Tom Driscoll, and just as the Chairman began a speech he skipped forward and said with an air of tipsy confidence to the audience—

"Boys, I move that he keeps still and lets this human philopena[1] snip you out a speech."

The descriptive aptness of the phrase caught the house, and a mighty burst of laughter followed.

Luigi's southern blood leaped to the boiling-point in a moment under the sharp humiliation of this insult delivered in the presence of four hundred strangers. It was not in the young man's nature to let the matter pass, or to delay the squaring of the account. He took a couple of strides and halted behind the unsuspecting joker. Then he drew back and delivered a kick of such titanic vigor that it lifted Tom clear over the footlights and landed him on the heads of the front row of the Sons of Liberty.

Even a sober person does not like to have a human being emptied on him when he is not doing any harm; a person who is not sober cannot endure such an attention at all. The nest of Sons of Liberty that Driscoll landed in had not a sober bird in it; in fact there was probably not an entirely sober one in the auditorium. Driscoll was promptly and indignantly flung onto the heads of Sons in the next row, and these Sons passed him on toward the rear, and then immediately began to pummel the front-row Sons who had passed him to them. This course was strictly followed by bench after bench as Driscoll traveled in his tumultuous and airy flight toward the door; so he left behind him an ever lengthening wake of raging and plunging and fighting and swearing humanity. Down went group after group of torches, and presently, above the deafening clatter of the gavel, roar of angry voices and crash of succumbing benches, rose the paralyzing cry of

"FIRE!"

The fighting ceased instantly; the cursings ceased; for one distinctly defined moment there was a dead hush, a motionless calm, where the tempest had been; then with one impulse the multitude awoke to life and energy again, and went surging and struggling and swaying, this way and that, its outer edges melting away through windows and doors and gradually lessening the pressure and relieving the mass.

The fire-boys were never on hand so suddenly before; for there was no distance to go, this time, their quarters being in the rear end of the market house. There was an engine company and a hook and lad-

---

1. See "Textual Notes" to *Pudd'nhead Wilson*, 61.6, herein.

der company. Half of each was composed of rummies and the other half of anti-rummies, after the moral and political share-and-share-alike fashion of the frontier town of the period. Enough anti-rummies were loafing in quarters to man the engine and the ladders. In two minutes they had their red shirts and helmets on—they never stirred officially in unofficial costume—and as the mass meeting overhead smashed through the long row of windows and poured out upon the roof of the arcade, the deliverers were ready for them with a powerful stream of water which washed some of them off the roof and nearly drowned the rest. But water was preferable to fire, and still the stampede from the windows continued, and still the pitiless drenchings assailed it until the building was empty; then the fire-boys mounted to the hall and flooded it with water enough to anni-hilate forty times as much fire as there was there: for a village fire company does not often get a chance to show off, and so when it does get a chance it makes the most of it. Such citizens of that village as were of a thoughtful and judicious temperament did not insure against fire, they insured against the fire-company.

Chapter 12

Courage is resistance to fear, mastery of fear—not absence of fear. Except a creature be part coward it is not a compliment to say it is brave, it is merely a loose misapplication of the word. Consider the flea!—incomparably the bravest of all the creatures of God, if igno-rance of fear were courage. Whether you are asleep or awake he will attack you, caring nothing for the fact that in bulk and strength you are to him as are the massed armies of the earth to a sucking child; he lives both day and night and all days and nights in the very lap of peril and the immediate presence of death, and yet is no more afraid than is the man who walks the streets of a city that was threatened by an earthquake ten centuries before. When we speak of Clive, Nelson and Putnam as men who "didn't know what fear was," we ought always to add the flea—and put him at the head of the procession.
—PUDD'NHEAD WILSON'S CALENDAR.

Judge Driscoll was in bed and asleep by ten o'clock on Friday night, and he was up and gone a-fishing before daylight in the morning with his friend Pembroke Howard. These two had been boys together in Virginia when that State still ranked as the chief and most imposing member of the Union, and they still coupled the proud and affectionate adjective "old" with her name when they spoke of her. In Missouri a recognized superiority attached to any person who hailed from Old Virginia; and this superiority was exalted to supremacy when a person of such nativity could also prove descent from the First Families of that great commonwealth. The Howards and Driscolls were of this aristocracy. In their eyes it was a nobility. It had its unwritten laws, and they were as clearly defined and as strict as any that could be found among the printed statutes of the land. The F.F.V. was born a gentleman; his highest duty in life was to watch over that great inheritance and keep it unsmirched. He must keep his honor spotless. Those laws were his chart; his course was marked out on it; if he swerved from it by so much as half a point of the compass it meant shipwreck to his honor; that is to say, degradation from his rank as a gentleman. These laws required certain things of him which his religion might forbid: then his religion must yield—the laws could not be relaxed to accommodate religion or anything else. Honor stood first; and the laws defined what it was and wherein it differed, in certain details, from honor as defined by church creeds and by the social laws and customs of some of the minor divisions of the globe that had got crowded out when the sacred boundaries of Virginia were staked out.

If Judge Driscoll was the recognized first citizen of Dawson's Landing, Pembroke Howard was easily its recognized second citizen. He was called "the great lawyer"—an earned title. He and Driscoll were of the same age—a year or two past sixty.

Although Driscoll was a free-thinker and Howard a strong and determined Presbyterian, their warm intimacy suffered no impairment in consequence. They were men whose opinions were their own property and not subject to revision and amendment, suggestion or criticism, by anybody, even their friends.

The day's fishing finished, they came floating down stream in their skiff, talking national politics and other high matters, and presently met a skiff coming up from town, with a man in it who said:

"I reckon you

know one of the new Twins gave your nephew a kicking last night, Judge?"

"Did *what*?"

"Gave him a kicking."

The old Judge's lips paled and his eyes began to flame. He choked with anger for a moment, then he got out what he was trying to say—

"Well—well—go on! Give me the details."

The man did it. At the finish, the Judge was silent a minute, turning over in his mind the shameful picture of Tom's flight over the footlights, then he said, as if musing aloud—

"Hm—I don't understand it. I was asleep at home. He didn't wake me. Thought he was competent to manage his affair without my help, I reckon." His face lit up with pride and pleasure at that thought, and he said with a cheery complacency, "I like that—it's the true old blood—hey, Pembroke?"

Howard smiled an iron smile and nodded his head approvingly. Then the news-bringer spoke again—

"But Tom beat the twin on the trial."

The Judge looked at the man wonderingly, and said—

"The trial? What trial?"

"Why, Tom had him up before Judge Robinson for assault and battery."

The old man shrank suddenly together like one who has received a death-stroke. Howard sprang for him as he sank forward in a swoon, and took him in his arms, and bedded him on his back in the boat. He sprinkled water in his face, and said to the startled visitor—

"Go, now—don't let him come to and find you here. You see what an effect your heedless speech has had; you ought to have been more considerate than to blurt out such a cruel piece of slander as that."

"I'm right down sorry I did it, now, Mr. Howard, and I wouldn't have done it if I had thought; but it ain't a slander, it's perfectly true, just as I told him."

He rowed away. Presently the old Judge came out of his faint and looked up piteously into the sympathetic face that was bent over him.

"Say it ain't true, Pembroke, tell me it ain't true!" he said, in a weak voice.

There was nothing weak in the deep organ-tones that responded—

"You know it's a lie as well as I do, old friend. He is of the best blood of the Old Dominion."

"God bless you for saying it!" said the old gentleman fervently. "Ah, Pembroke, it was such a blow!"

Howard stayed by his friend, and saw him home, and entered the house with him. It was dark, and past supper time, but the Judge was not thinking of supper, he was eager to hear the slander refuted from headquarters, and as eager to have Howard hear it, too. Tom was sent for, and he came immediately. He was bruised and lame, and was not a happy-looking object. His uncle made him sit down, and said—

"We have been hearing about your adventure, Tom, with a handsome lie added to it for embellishment. Now pulverize that lie to dust! What measures have you taken? How does the thing stand?"

Tom answered guilelessly: "It don't stand at all; it's all over. I had him up in court and beat him. Pudd'nhead Wilson defended him—first case he ever had, and lost it. The judge fined the miserable hound five dollars for the assault."

Howard and the Judge sprang to their feet with the opening sentence—why, neither knew; then they stood gazing vacantly at each other. Howard stood a moment, then sat mournfully down without saying anything. The Judge's wrath began to kindle, and he burst out—

"You cur! you scum! you vermin! Do you mean to tell me that blood of my race has suffered a blow and crawled to a court of law about it? Answer me!"

Tom's head drooped, and he answered with an eloquent silence. His uncle stared at him with a mixed expression of amazement and shame and incredulity that was sorrowful to see. At last he said—

"Which of the twins was it?"

"Count Luigi."

"You have challenged him?"

"N-no," hesitated Tom, turning pale.

"You will challenge him to-night. Howard will carry it."

Tom began to turn sick, and to show it. He turned his hat round and round in his hand, his uncle glowering blacker and blacker upon

him as the heavy seconds drifted by; then at last he began to stammer, and said, piteously—

"Oh, please don't ask me to do it, uncle! I never could. He is a murderous devil. I-I'm afraid of him!"

Old Driscoll's mouth opened and closed three times before he could get it to perform its office; then he stormed out—

"A coward in my family! A Driscoll a coward! Oh, what have I done to deserve this infamy!" He tottered to his secretary in the corner repeating that lament again and again in heart-breaking tones, and got out of a drawer a paper, which he slowly tore to bits scattering the bits absently in his track as he walked up and down the room, still grieving and lamenting. At last he said—

"There it is, shreds and fragments once more—my will. Once more you have forced me to disinherit you, you base son of a most noble father! Leave my sight! Go—before I spit on you!"

The young man did not tarry. Then the Judge turned to Howard:

"You will be my second, old friend?"

"Of course."

"There is pen and paper. Draft the cartel, and lose no time."

"The Count shall have it in his hands in fifteen minutes," said Howard.

Tom was very heavy-hearted. His appetite was gone with his property and his self-respect. He went out the back way and wandered down the obscure lane, grieving, and wondering if any course of future conduct, however discreet and carefully perfected and watched over, could win back his uncle's favor and persuade him to reconstruct once more that generous will which had just gone to ruin before his eyes. He finally concluded that it could. He said to himself that he had accomplished this sort of triumph once already, and that what had been done once could be done again. He would set about it. He would bend every energy to the task, and he would score that triumph once more, cost what it might to his convenience, limit as it might his frivolous and liberty-loving life.

"To begin," he said to himself, "I'll square up with the proceeds of my raid, and then gambling has got to be stopped—and stopped short off. It's the worst vice I've got—from my standpoint, anyway, because it's the one he can most easily find out, through the impatience of my creditors. He thought it expensive to have to pay two hundred dollars to them for me once. Expensive—*that!* Why, it cost me the whole of his fortune—but of course he never thought of that; some people can't think of any but their own side of a case. If he had known how deep I am in, now, the will would have gone to pot without waiting for a duel to help. Three hundred dollars! It's a pile! But he'll never hear of it, I'm thankful to say. The minute I've cleared it off, I'm safe; and I'll never touch a card again. Anyway I won't while he lives, I make oath to that. I'm entering on my last reform—I know it—yes, and I'll win; but after that, if I ever slip again I'm gone."

Chapter 13

When I reflect upon the number of disagreeable people who I know have gone to a better world, I am moved to lead a different life.
—PUDD'NHEAD WILSON'S CALENDAR.

OCTOBER. *This is one of the peculiarly dangerous months to specu-late in stocks in. The others are July, January, September, April, November, May, March, June, December, August, and February.*
—PUDD'NHEAD WILSON'S CALENDAR.

Thus mournfully communing with himself Tom moped along the lane past Pudd'nhead Wilson's house, and still on and on, between fences enclosing vacant country on each hand, till he neared the haunted house, then he came moping back again, with many sighs and heavy with trouble. He sorely wanted cheerful company. Rowena! His heart gave a bound at the thought, but the next thought quieted it—the detested Twins would be there.

He was on the inhabited side of Wilson's house, and now as he approached it he noticed that the sitting-room was lighted. This would do; others made him feel unwelcome sometimes, but Wilson never failed in courtesy toward him, and a kindly courtesy does at least save one's feelings, even if it is not professing to stand for a welcome. Wilson heard footsteps at his threshold, then the clearing of a throat.

"It's that fickle-tempered, dissipated young goose—poor devil, he finds friends pretty scarce to-day, likely, after the disgrace of carrying a personal-assault case into a law-court."

A dejected knock. "Come in!"

Tom entered and drooped into a chair, without saying anything. Wilson said, kindly—

"Why, my boy, you look desolate. Don't take it so hard. Try and forget you have been kicked."

"Oh, dear," said Tom, wretchedly, "it's not that, Pudd'nhead—it's not that. It's a thousand times worse than that—oh, yes, a million times worse."

"Why, Tom, what do you mean? Has Rowena—"

"Flung me? No, but the old man has."

Wilson said to himself, "Aha!" and thought of the mysterious girl in the bed-room. "The Driscolls have been making discoveries!" Then he said aloud, gravely:

"Tom, there are some kinds of dissipation which—"

"Oh, shucks, this hasn't got anything to do with dissipation. He wanted me to challenge that derned Italian savage, and I wouldn't do it."

"Yes, of course he would do that," said Wilson in a meditative matter-of-course way; "but the thing that puzzled me, was, why he didn't look to that last night, for one thing, and why he let you carry such a matter into a court of law at all, either before the duel or after it. It's no place for it. It was not like him. I couldn't understand it. How did it happen?"

"It happened because he didn't know anything about it. He was asleep when I got home last night."

"And you didn't wake him? Tom, is that possible?"

Tom was not getting much comfort here. He fidgeted a moment, then said:

"I didn't choose to tell him—that's all. He was going a-fishing before dawn, with Pembroke Howard, and if I got the Twins into the common calaboose,—and I thought sure I could—I never dreamed of their slipping out on a paltry fine for such an outrageous offense— well, once in the calaboose they would be disgraced, and uncle wouldn't want any duels with that sort of characters, and wouldn't allow any."

"Tom, I am ashamed of you! I don't see how you could treat your good old uncle so. I am a better friend of his than you are; for if I had known the circumstances I would have kept that case out of court until I got word to him and let him have a gentleman's chance."

"You would?" exclaimed Tom, with lively surprise. "And it your first case! and you know perfectly well there never would have *been* any case if he had got that chance, don't you? and you'd have finished your days a pauper nobody, instead of being an actually launched and recognized lawyer to-day. And you would really have done that, would you?"

"Certainly."

Tom looked at him a moment or two, then shook his head sorrowfully and said—

"I believe you—upon my word I do. I don't know why I do, but I do. Pudd'nhead Wilson, I think you're the biggest fool I ever saw."

"Thank you."

"Don't mention it."

"Well, he has been requiring you to fight the Italian and you have refused. You degenerate remnant of an honorable line! I'm thoroughly ashamed of you, Tom!"

"Oh, that's nothing! I don't care for anything, now that the will's torn up again."

"Tom, tell me squarely—didn't he find any fault with you for anything but those two things—carrying the case into court and refusing to fight?"

He watched the young fellow's face narrowly, but it was entirely reposeful, and so also was the voice that answered:

"No, he didn't find any other fault with me. If he had had any to find, he would have begun yesterday, for he was just in the humor for it. He drove that jack-pair around town and showed them the sights, and when he came home he couldn't find his father's old silver watch that don't keep time and he thinks so much of, and couldn't remember what he did with it three or four days ago when he saw it last; and so when I arrived he was all in a sweat about it, and when I suggested that it probably wasn't lost but stolen, it put him in a regular passion and he said I was a fool—which convinced me, without any trouble, that that was just what he was afraid *had* happened, himself, but did not want to believe it, because lost things stand a better chance of being found again than stolen ones."

"Whe-ew!" whistled Wilson; "score another on the list."

"Another what?"

"Another theft!"

"Theft?"

"Yes, theft. That watch isn't lost, it's stolen. There's been another raid on the town—and just the same old mysterious sort of thing that has happened once before, as you remember."

"You don't mean it!"

"It's as sure as you are born! Have you missed anything yourself?"

"No. That is, I did miss a silver pencil case that aunt Mary Pratt gave me last birth-day—"

"You'll find it's stolen—that's what you'll find."

"No, I shan't; for when I suggested theft about the watch and got such a rap, I went and examined my room, and the pencil-case was missing, but it was only mislaid, and I found it again."

"You are sure you missed nothing else?"

"Well, nothing of consequence. I missed a small plain gold ring worth two or three dollars, but that will turn up. I'll look again."

"In my opinion you'll not find it. There's been a raid, I tell you. Come *in!*"

Mr. Justice Robinson entered, followed by Buckstone and the town constable, Jim Blake. They sat down, and after some wandering and aimless weather-conversation, Wilson said—

"By the way, we've just added another to the list of thefts, maybe two. Judge Driscoll's old silver watch is gone, and Tom here has missed a gold ring."

"Well, it is a bad business," said the Justice, "and gets worse the further it goes. The Hankses, the Dobsons, the Pilligrews, the Ortons, the Grangers, the Hales, the Fullers, the Holcombs, in fact everybody that lives around about Patsy Cooper's has been robbed of little things like trinkets and teaspoons and such-like small valuables that are easily carried off. It's perfectly plain that the thief took advantage of the reception at Patsy Cooper's, when all the neighbors were in her house and all their niggers hanging around her fence for a look at the show, to raid the vacant houses undisturbed. Patsy is miserable about it; miserable on account of the neighbors, and particularly miserable on account of her foreigners, of course; so miserable on their account that she hasn't any room to worry about her own little losses."

"It's the same old raider," said Wilson, "I suppose there isn't any doubt about that."

"Constable Blake doesn't think so."

"No, you're wrong there," said Blake, "the other times it was a man; there was plenty of signs of that, as we know, in the profession, though we never got hands on him; but this time it's a woman."

Wilson thought of the mysterious girl, straight off. She was always in his mind, now. But she failed him again. Blake continued:

"She's a stoop-shouldered old woman with a covered basket on her arm in a black veil dressed in mourning. I saw her going aboard the ferry-boat yesterday. Lives in Illinois, I reckon; but I don't care where she lives, I'm going to get her—she can make herself sure of that."

"What makes you think she's the thief?"

"Well, there ain't any other, for one thing; and for another, some of the nigger draymen that happened to be driving along saw her coming out or going into houses and told me so—and it just happens that they was *robbed* houses, every time."

It was granted that this was plenty good enough circumstantial evidence. A pensive silence followed, which lasted for some moments, then Wilson said—

"There's one good thing, anyway. She can't either pawn or sell Count Luigi's costly Indian dagger."

"My!" said Tom; "is *that* gone?"

"Yes."

"Well, that was a haul! But why can't she pawn it or sell it?"

"Because when the Twins went home from the Sons of Liberty meeting last night, news of the raid was sifting in from everywhere and Aunt Patsy was in distress to know if they had lost anything. They found that the dagger was gone, and they notified the police and pawnbrokers everywhere. It was a great haul, yes, but the old woman won't get anything out of it, because she'll get caught."

"Did they offer a reward?" asked Buckstone.

"Yes—five hundred dollars for the knife, and five hundred more for the thief."

"What a leather-headed idea!" exclaimed the constable. "The thief dasn't go near them, nor send anybody. Whoever goes is going to get himself nabbed, for there ain't any pawnbroker that's going to lose the chance to—"

If anybody had noticed Tom's face at that time, the gray-green color of it might have provoked curiosity; but nobody did. He said to himself, "I'm gone! I never can square up; the rest of the plunder won't pawn or sell for half of the bill. Oh, I know it—I'm gone, I'm gone—and this time it's for good. Oh, this is awful—I don't know what to do, nor which way to turn!"

"Softly, softly," said Wilson to Blake, "I planned their scheme for them at midnight last night, and it was all finished up ship shape by two this morning. They'll get their dagger back, and then I'll explain to you how the thing was done."

There were strong signs of a general curiosity, and Buckstone said—

"Well, you have whetted us up pretty sharp, Wilson, and I'm free to say that if you don't mind telling us in confidence—"

"Oh, I'd as soon tell as not, Buckstone, but as long as the Twins and I agreed to say nothing about it, we must let it stand so. But you can take my word for it you won't be kept waiting three days. Somebody will apply for that reward pretty promptly, and I'll show you the thief and the dagger both very soon afterward."

The Constable was disappointed, and also perplexed. He said—

"It may all be—yes, and I hope it will, but I'm blamed if I can see my way through it. It's too many for yours truly."

The subject seemed about talked out. Nobody seemed to have anything further to offer. After a silence the justice of the peace informed Wilson that he and Buckstone and the constable had come as a committee, on the part of the Democratic party, to ask him to run for mayor—for the little town was about to become a city and the first charter election was approaching. It was the first attention which Wilson had ever received at the hands of any party; it was a sufficiently humble one, but it was a recognition of his début into the town's life and activities at last; it was a step upward, and he was deeply gratified. He accepted, and the committee departed, followed by young Tom.

Chapter 14

The true southern watermelon is a boon apart, and not to be mentioned with commoner things. It is chief of this world's luxuries, king by the grace of God over all the fruits of the earth. When one has tasted it, he knows what the angels eat. It was not a southern watermelon that Eve took: we know it because she repented.
—PUDD'NHEAD WILSON'S CALENDAR.

About the time that Wilson was bowing the committee out, Pembroke Howard was entering the next house to report. He found the old Judge sitting grim and straight in his chair, waiting.

"Well, Howard—the news?"

"The best in the world."

"Accepts, does he?" and the light of battle gleamed joyously in the Judge's eye.

"Accepts? Why, he jumped at it."

"Did, did he? Now that's fine—that's very fine. I like that. When is it to be?"

"Now! Straight off! To-night! An admirable fellow—admirable!"

"Admirable? He's a darling! Why, it's an honor as well as a pleasure to stand up before such a man. Come—off with you! Go and arrange everything—and give him my heartiest compliments. A rare fellow, indeed; an admirable fellow, as you have said!"

Howard hurried away, saying—

"I'll have him in the vacant stretch between Wilson's and the haunted house within the hour, and I'll bring my own pistols."

Judge Driscoll began to walk the floor in a state of pleased excitement; but presently he stopped, and began to think—began to think of Tom. Twice he moved toward the secretary, and twice he turned away again; but finally he said—

"This may be my last night in the world—I must not take the chance. He is worthless and unworthy, but it is largely my fault. He was entrusted to me by my brother on his dying bed, and I have indulged him to his hurt, instead of training him up severely and making a man of him. I have violated my trust, and I must not add the sin of desertion to that. I have forgiven him once, already, and would subject him to a long and hard trial before forgiving him again, if I could live; but I must not run that risk. No, I must restore the will. But if I survive the duel I will hide it away and he will not know, and I will not tell him until he reforms and I see that his reformation is going to be permanent."

He re-drew the will, and his ostensible

nephew was heir to a fortune again. As he was finishing his task, Tom, wearied with another brooding tramp, entered the house and went tip-toeing past the sitting-room door. He glanced in, and hurried on, for the sight of his uncle had nothing but terrors for him to-night. But his uncle was writing! That was unusual at this late hour. What could he be writing? A chill anxiety settled down upon Tom's heart. Did that writing concern him? He was afraid so. He reflected that when ill luck begins, it does not come in sprinkles, but in showers. He said he would get a glimpse of that document or know the reason why. He heard someone coming, and stepped out of sight and hearing. It was Pembroke Howard. What could be hatching?

Howard said, with great satisfaction—

"Everything's right and ready. He's gone to the battle-ground with his second and the surgeon—also with his brother. I've arranged it all with Wilson—Wilson's his second. We are to have three shots apiece."

"Good! How is the moon?"

"Bright as day, nearly. Perfect for the distance—fifteen yards. No wind—not a breath; hot and still."

"All good; all first-rate. Here, Pembroke, read this, and witness it."

Pembroke read and witnessed the will, then gave the old man's hand a hearty shake and said—

"Now that's right, York—but I knew you would do it. You couldn't leave that poor chap to fight along without means or profession, with certain defeat before him, and I knew you wouldn't, for his father's sake if not for his own."

"For his dead father's sake I couldn't, I know; for poor Percy—but you know what Percy was to me. But mind—Tom is not to know of this unless I fall to-night."

"I understand. I'll keep the secret."

The Judge put the will away, and the two started for the battle-ground. In another minute the will was in Tom's hands. His misery vanished, his feelings underwent a tremendous revulsion. He put the will carefully back in its place and spread his mouth and swung his hat once, twice, three times around his head, in imitation of three rousing huzzas, no sound issuing from his lips. He fell to communing with himself excitedly and joyously, but every now and then he let off another volley of dumb hurrahs.

He said to himself: "I've got the fortune again, but I'll not let on that I know about it. And this time I'm going to hang on to it. I take no more risks. I'll gamble no more, I'll drink no more, because—well, because I'll not go where there is any of that sort of thing going on, again. It's the sure way, and the only sure way; I might have thought of that sooner—well, yes, if I had wanted to. But now—dear me, I've had a bad scare this time, and I'll take no more chances. Not a single chance more. Land! I persuaded myself this evening that I could fetch him around without any great amount of effort, but I've been getting more and more heavy-hearted and doubtful straight along, ever since. If he tells me about this thing, all right; but if he doesn't, I shan't let on. I—well, I'd like to tell Pudd'nhead Wilson, but—no, I'll think about that; perhaps I won't." He whirled off another dead huzza, and said, "I'm reformed, and this time I'll stay so, sure!"

He was about to close with a final grand silent demonstration, when he suddenly recollected that Wilson had put it out of his power to pawn or sell the Indian knife, and that he was once more in awful peril of exposure by his creditors for that reason. His joy collapsed utterly, and he turned away and moped toward the door moaning and lamenting over the bitterness of his luck. He dragged himself upstairs, and brooded in his room a long time, disconsolate and forlorn, with Luigi's Indian knife for a text. At last he sighed and said:

"When I supposed these stones were glass and this ivory bone, the thing hadn't any interest for me because it hadn't any value and couldn't help me out of my trouble. But now—why, now it is full of interest; yes, and of a sort to break a body's heart. It's a bag of gold that has turned to dirt and ashes in my hands. It could save me, and save me so easily, and yet I've got to go to ruin. It's like drowning with a life-preserver in my reach. All the hard luck comes to me and all the good luck goes to other people—Pudd'nhead Wilson, for instance; even his career has got a sort of a little start at last, and what has he done to deserve it, I should like to know? Yes, he has opened his own road, but he isn't content with that, but must block mine. It's a sordid, selfish world, and I wish I was out of it." He allowed the light of the candle to play upon the jewels of the sheath, but the flashings and sparklings had no charm for his eye, they were only just so many pangs to his heart. "I must not say anything to Roxy about this thing," he said, "she is too daring. She would be for digging these stones out and selling them, and then—why, she would be arrested and the stones traced, and then—" The thought made him quake, and he hid the knife away, trembling all over and glancing furtively about, like a criminal who fancies that the accuser is already at hand.

Should he try to sleep? Oh, no, sleep was not for him; his trouble was too haunting, too afflicting for that. He must have somebody to mourn with. He would carry his despair to Roxy.

He had heard several distant gun shots, but that sort of thing was not uncommon, and they had made no impression upon him. He went out at the back door, and turned westward. He passed Wilson's house and proceeded along the lane, and presently saw several figures approaching Wilson's place through the vacant lots. These were the duelists returning from the fight; he thought he recognized them, but as he had no desire for white people's company he stooped down behind the fence until they were out of his way.

Roxy was feeling fine. She said:

"Whah was you, child? Warn't you in it?"

"In what?"

"In de duel."

"Duel? Has there been a duel?"

"'Cose dey has. De ole Jedge has been havin' a duel wid one o' dem Twins."

"Great Scott!" Then he added to himself, "That's what made him re-make the will; he thought he might get killed, and it softened him toward me. And that's what he and Howard were so busy about. . . . . . . Oh, dear, if the Twin had only killed him, I should be out of my—"

"What is you mumblin' 'bout, Chambers? Whah was you? Didn't you know dey was gwyne to be a duel?"

"No, I didn't. The old man tried to get me to fight one with Count Luigi, but he didn't succeed; so I reckon he concluded to patch up the family honor himself."

He laughed at the idea, and went rambling on with a detailed account of his talk with the Judge, and how shocked and ashamed the Judge was to find that he had a coward in his family. He glanced up at last, and got a shock himself. Roxana's bosom was heaving with suppressed passion, and she was glowering down upon him with measureless contempt written in her face.

"En you refuse' to fight a man dat kicked you, 'stid o' jumpin' at de chance! En you ain't got no mo' feelin' den to come en tell me, dat fetched sich a po' low-down ornery rabbit into de worl'! Pah! it make me sick! It's de nigger in you, dat's what it is. Thirty-one parts o' you is white, en on'y one part nigger, en dat po' little one part is yo' *soul*. 'Tain't wuth savin'; 'tain't wuth totin' out on a shovel en tho'in' in de gutter. You has disgraced yo' birth. What would yo' pa think o' you? It's enough to make him turn in his grave."

The last three sentences stung Tom into a fury, and he said to himself that if his father were only alive and in reach of assassination his mother would soon find that he had a very clear notion of the size of his indebtedness to that man and was willing to pay it up in full, and would do it, too, even at risk of his life; but he kept his thought to himself; that was safest, in his mother's present state.

"What ever has 'come o' yo' Essex blood? Dat's what I can't under-stan'. En it ain't only jist Essex blood dat's in you, not by a long sight—'deed it ain't! My great-great-great-gran'father en yo' great-great-great-great-gran'father was ole Cap'n John Smith, de highes' blood dat Ole Virginny ever turned out; en *his* great-great-gran'-mother or somers along back dah, was Pocahontas de Injun queen, en her husbun' was a nigger king outen Africa—en yit here you is, a slinkin' outen a duel en disgracin' our whole line like a ornery low-down hound! Yes, it's de nigger in you!"

She sat down on her candle-box and fell into a reverie. Tom did not disturb her; he sometimes lacked prudence, but it was not in cir-cumstances of this kind. Roxana's storm went gradually down, but it died hard, and even when it seemed to be quite gone it would now and then break out in a distant rumble, so to speak, in the form of muttered ejaculations. One of these was, "Ain't nigger enough in him to show in his finger-nails, en dat takes mighty little—yit dey's enough to paint his soul."

Presently she muttered, "Yassir, enough to paint a whole thimble-ful of 'em." At last her rumblings ceased altogether and her counte-nance began to clear—a welcome sign to Tom, who had learned her moods and knew she was on the threshold of good-humor, now. He noticed that from time to time she unconsciously carried her finger to the end of her nose. He looked closer and said—

"Why, mammy, the end of your nose is skinned. How did that come?"

She sent out the sort of whole-hearted peal of laughter which God has vouchsafed in its perfection to none but the happy angels in heaven and the bruised and broken black slave on the earth, and said:

"Dad fetch dat duel, I ben in it myself."

"Gracious! did a bullet do that?"

"Yassir, you bet it did!"

"Well, I declare! Why, how did that happen?"

"Happen dis-away. I 'uz a sett'n here kinder dozin' in de dark, en *che-bang!* goes a gun, right out dah. I skips along out towards t'other end o' de house to see what's gwyne on, en stops by de ole winder on de side towards Pudd'nhead Wilson's house dat ain't got no sash in it—but dey ain't none of 'em got any sashes, fur as dat's concerned—en I stood dah in de dark en look out, en dah in de moonlight, right down under me 'uz one o' de Twins a-cussin'—not much, but jist a-cussin' soft,—it 'uz de brown one dat 'uz cussin', caze he 'uz hit in de shoulder. En Doctor Claypool he 'uz a workin' at him, en Pudd'nhead Wilson he 'uz a he'pin, en ole Jedge Driscoll en Pem. Howard 'uz a-standin' out yonder a little piece waitin' for 'em to git ready agin. En toreckly dey squared off en give de word, en *bang-bang* went de pis-tols, en de twin he say 'Ouch!'—hit him on de han' dis time—en I hear dat same bullet go '*spat!*' agin de logs under de winder; en de nex' time dey shoot, de twin say 'Ouch!' agin, en I done it too, caze de bullet glance' on his cheek bone en skip up here en glance on de side o' de winder en whiz right acrost my face en tuck de hide off'n my nose—why, if I'd a ben jist a inch or a inch en a half furder, 'twould a tuck de whole nose en disfigger' me. Here's de bullet; I hunted her up."

"Did you stand there all the time?"

"Dat's a question to ask, ain't it! What else would I do? Does I git a chance to see a duel every day?"

"Why, you were right in range! Weren't you afraid?"

The woman gave a sniff of scorn.

"'Fraid! De Smith-Pocahontases ain't 'fraid o' nothin', let alone bullets."

"They've got pluck enough, I suppose; what they lack is judgment. *I* wouldn't have stood there."

"Nobody's accusin' you!"

"Did anybody else get hurt?"

"Yes, we all got hit 'cep' de blon' twin en de doctor en de seconds. De Jedge didn't git hurt, but I hear Pudd'nhead say de bullet snip some o' his ha'r off."

"'George!" said Tom to himself, "to come so near being out of my trouble, and miss it by an inch. O, dear, dear, he'll live to find me out and sell me to some nigger-trader yet—yes, and he would do it in a minute." Then he said aloud, in a grave tone—

"Mother, we are in an awful fix."

Roxana caught her breath with a spasm, and said—

"Chile! What you hit a body so sudden for, like dat? What's ben en gone en happen'?"

"Well, there's one thing I didn't tell you. When I wouldn't fight, he tore up the will again, and—"

Roxana's face turned a dead white, and she said—

"Now you's *done!*—done forever! Dat's de end. Bofe un us is gwyne to starve to—"

"Wait and hear me through, can't you! I reckon that when he

resolved to fight, himself, he thought he might get killed and not have a chance to forgive me any more in this life, so he made the will again, and I've seen it and it's all right. But—"

"Oh, thank goodness, den we's safe agin!—safe! en so what did you want to come here en talk sich dreadful—"

"Hold *on*, I tell you, and let me finish. The swag I gathered won't half square me up, and the first thing we know my creditors—well, you know what'll happen."

Roxana dropped her chin and told her son to leave her alone—she must think this matter out. Presently she said, impressively:

"You got to go mighty keerful now, I tell you! En here's what you got to do. He didn't git killed, en if you gives him de least reason, he'll bust de will agin, en dat's de *las'* time, now you hear me! So—you's got to show him what you kin do in de nex' few days. You's got to be pison good, en let him see it; you got to do everything dat'll make him b'lieve in you, en you got to sweeten aroun' ole Aunt Pratt, too—she's pow'ful strong wid de Jedge, en de bes' frien' you got. Nex', you'll go 'long away to Sent Louis, en dat'll *keep* him in yo' favor. Den you go en make a bargain wid dem people. You tell 'em he ain't gwyne to live long—en dat's de fac', too—en tell 'em you'll pay 'em intrust, en big intrust, too—ten per—what you call it?"

"Ten per cent a month?"

"Dat's it. Den you take en sell yo' truck aroun', a little at a time, en pay de intrust. How long will it las'?"

"I think there's enough to pay the interest five or six months."

"Den you's all right. If he don't die in six months, dat don't make no diff'rence—Providence 'll provide. You's gwyne to be safe—if you behaves." She bent an austere eye on him and added, "En you *is* gwyne to behave—does you know dat?"

He laughed and said he was going to try, anyway. She did not unbend. She said gravely—

"Tryin' ain't de thing. You's gwyne to *do* it. You ain't gwyne to steal a pin—caze it ain't safe no mo'; en you ain't gwyne into no bad comp'ny—not even once, you understand; en you ain't gwyne to drink a drap—nary a single drap; en you ain't gwyne to gamble one single gamble—not one! Dis ain't what you's gwyne to *try* to do, it's what you's gwyne to *do*. En I'll tell you how I knows it. Dis is how. I's gwyne to foller along to Sent Louis my own self; en you's gwyne to come to me every day o' yo' life, en I'll look you over; en if you fails in one single one o' dem things—jist *once*—I take my oath I'll come straight down to dis town en tell de Jedge you is a nigger en a slave— en *prove* it!" She paused, to let her words sink home. Then she added: "Chambers, does you b'lieve me when I say dat?"

Tom was sober enough now. There was no levity in his voice when he answered:

"Yes, mother. I know, now, that I am reformed—and permanently. Permanently—and beyond the reach of any human temptation."

"Den g'long home en begin!"

Chapter 15

Nothing so needs reforming as other people's habits.
—PUDD'NHEAD WILSON'S CALENDAR.

*Behold, the fool saith, "Put not all thine eggs in the one basket"—which is but a manner of saying, "Scatter your money and your attention"; but the wise man saith, "Put all your eggs in the one basket and—*WATCH THAT BASKET.*"*
—PUDD'NHEAD WILSON'S CALENDAR.

What a time of it Dawson's Landing was having! All its life it had been asleep, but now it hardly got a chance for a nod, so swiftly did big events and crashing surprises come along in one another's wake: Friday morning, first glimpse of Real Nobility, also grand reception at Aunt Patsy Cooper's, also great robber-raid; Friday evening, dramatic kicking of the heir of the chief citizen in presence of four hundred people; Saturday morning, emergence as practising lawyer of the long-submerged Pudd'nhead Wilson; Saturday night, duel between chief citizen and titled stranger.

The people took more pride in the duel than in all the other events put together, perhaps. It was a glory to their town to have such a thing happen there. In their eyes the principals had reached the summit of human honor. Everybody paid homage to their names; their praises were in all mouths. Even the duelists' subordinates came in for a handsome share of the public approbation: wherefore Pudd'nhead Wilson was suddenly become a man of consequence. When asked to run for the mayoralty Saturday night he was risking defeat, but Sunday morning found him a made man and his success assured.

The twins were prodigiously great, now; the town took them to its bosom with enthusiasm. Day after day, and night after night, they went dining and visiting from house to house, making friends, enlarging and solidifying their popularity, and charming and surprising all with their musical prodigies, and now and then heightening the effects with samples of what they could do in other directions, out of their stock of rare and curious accomplishments. They were so pleased that they gave the regulation thirty days' notice, the required preparation for citizenship, and resolved to finish their days in this pleasant place. That was the climax. The delighted community rose as one man and applauded; and when the twins were asked to stand for seats in the forthcoming aldermanic board, and consented, the public contentment was rounded and complete.

Tom Driscoll was not happy over these things; they sunk deep, and hurt all the way down. He hated the one twin for kicking him, and the other one for being the kicker's brother.

Now and then the people wondered why nothing was heard of the raider, or of the stolen knife or the other plunder, but nobody was able to throw any light on that matter. Nearly a week had drifted by, and still the thing remained a vexed mystery.

On Saturday, Constable Blake and Pudd'nhead Wilson met on the street, and Tom Driscoll joined them in time to open their conversation for them. He said to Blake—

"You are not looking well, Blake, you seem to be annoyed about something. Has anything gone wrong in the detective business? I believe you fairly and justifiably claim to have a pretty good reputation in that line, isn't it so?"—which made Blake feel good, and look it; but Tom added, "for a country detective"—which made Blake feel the other way, and not only look it but betray it in his voice—

"Yes, sir, I *have* got a reputation, and it's as good as anybody's in the profession, too, country or no country."

"Oh, I beg pardon, I didn't mean any offence. What I started out to ask, was, only about the old woman that raided the town—the stoop-shouldered old woman, you know, that you said you were going to catch—and I knew you would, too, because you have the reputation of never boasting, and—well, you—you've caught the old woman?"

"Damn the old woman!"

"Why, sho! you don't mean to say you haven't caught her?"

"No, I haven't caught her. If anybody could have caught her, I could; but nobody couldn't, I don't care who he is."

"I am sorry, real sorry—for your sake; because when it gets around that a detective has expressed himself so confidently, and then—"

"Don't you worry, that's all—don't you worry; and as for the town, the town needn't worry, either. She's my meat—make yourself easy about that. I'm on her track; I've got clews that—"

"That's good! Now if you could get an old veteran detective down from St. Louis to help you find out what the clews mean, and where they lead to, and then—"

"I'm plenty veteran enough myself, and I don't need anybody's help. I'll have her inside of a we—inside of a month. That I'll swear to!"

Tom said, carelessly—

"I suppose that will answer—yes, that will answer. But I reckon she is pretty old, and old people don't often outlive the cautious pace of the professional detective when he has got his clews together and is out on his still-hunt."

Blake's dull face flushed, under this gibe, but before he could set his retort in order Tom had turned to Wilson and was saying, with placid indifference of manner and voice—

"Who got the reward, Pudd'nhead?"

Wilson winced slightly, and saw that his own turn was come.

"What reward?"

"Why, the reward for the thief, and the other one for the knife."

Wilson answered—and rather uncomfortably, to judge by his hesitating fashion of delivering himself—

"Well, the—well, in fact nobody has claimed it yet."

Tom seemed surprised.

"Why, is that so?"

Wilson showed a trifle of irritation when he replied—

"Yes, it's so. And what of it?"

"Oh, nothing. Only I thought you had struck out a new idea and invented a scheme that was going to revolutionize the time-worn and ineffectual methods of the—" He stopped, and turned to Blake, who was happy, now that another had taken his place on the gridiron: "Blake, didn't you understand him to intimate that it wouldn't be necessary for you to hunt the old woman down?"

"B'George, he said he'd have thief and swag both inside of three days—he did, by hokey! and that's just about a week ago. Why, I said at the time, that no thief and no thief's pal was going to try to pawn or sell a thing where he knowed the pawn-broker could get both rewards by taking *him* into camp *with* the swag. It was the blessedest idea that ever *I* struck!"

"You'd change your mind," said Wilson, with irritated bluntness, "if you knew the entire scheme instead of only part of it."

"Well," said the constable, pensively, "I had the idea that it wouldn't work, and up to now I'm right, anyway."

"Very well, then, let it stand at that, and give it a further show. It has worked at least as well as your own methods, you perceive."

The constable hadn't anything handy to hit back with, so he discharged a discontented sniff and said nothing.

After the night that Wilson had partly revealed his scheme at his house, Tom had tried for several days to guess out the secret of the rest of it, but had failed. Then it occurred to him to give Roxana's smarter head a chance at it. He made up a supposititious case and laid it before her. She thought it over, and delivered her verdict upon it. Tom said to himself, "She's hit it, sure!" He thought he would test that verdict, now, and watch Wilson's face; so he said, reflectively—

"Wilson, you're not a fool—a fact of recent discovery. Whatever your scheme was, it had sense in it, Blake's opinion to the contrary notwithstanding. I don't ask you to reveal it, but I will suppose a case—a case which will answer as a starting point for the real thing I'm going to come at, and that's all I want. You offered five hundred dollars for the knife, and five hundred for the thief. We will suppose, for argument's sake, that the first reward is *advertised*, and the second offered by *private letter* to the pawnbrokers and—"

Blake slapped his thigh and cried out—

"By Jackson he's got you, Pudd'nhead! Now why couldn't I or *any* fool have thought of that?"

Wilson said to himself, "Anybody with a reasonably good head would have thought of it. I am not surprised that Blake didn't detect it, I am only surprised that Tom did. There is more to him than I supposed." He said nothing aloud, and Tom went on:

"Very well. The thief would not suspect that there was a trap, and he would bring or send the knife and say he bought it for a song, or found it in the road, or something like that, and try to collect the reward, and be arrested—wouldn't he?"

"Yes," said Wilson.

"I think so," said Tom. "There can't be any doubt of it. Have you ever seen that knife?"

"No."

"Has any friend of yours?"

"Not that I know of."

"Well, I begin to think I understand why your scheme failed."

"What do you mean, Tom?—What are you driving at?" asked Wilson with a dawning sense of discomfort.

"Why, that there *isn't* any such knife."

"Look here, Wilson," said Blake, "Tom Driscoll's right, for a thousand dollars—if I had it."

Wilson's blood warmed a little, and he wondered if he had been played upon by those strangers—it certainly had something of that look. But what could they gain by it? He threw out that suggestion. Tom replied:

"Gain? Oh, nothing that you would value, maybe. But they are strangers making their way in a new community. Is it nothing to them to appear as pets of an Oriental prince—at no expense? Is it nothing to them to be able to dazzle this poor little town with thousand-dollar rewards—at no expense? Wilson, there isn't any such knife, or your scheme would have fetched it to light. Or if there is any such knife they've got it yet. I believe, myself, that they've seen such a knife, for Angelo pictured it out with his pencil too swiftly and handily for him to have been inventing it; and of course I can't swear that they've never had it; but this I'll go bail for—if they had it when they came to this town, they've got it yet."

Blake said,—

"It looks mighty reasonable, the way Tom puts it—it most certainly does."

Tom responded—turning to leave—

"You find the old woman, Blake, and if she can't furnish the knife, go and search the Twins!"

Tom sauntered away. Wilson felt a good deal depressed. He hardly knew what to think. He was loth to withdraw his faith from the Twins, and was resolved not to do it on the present indecisive evidence; but—well, he would think—and then decide how to act.

"Blake, what do you think of this matter?"

"Well, Pudd'nhead, I'm bound to say I put it up the way Tom does. They hadn't the knife; or if they had it they've got it yet."

The men parted. Wilson said to himself:

"I believe they had it; if it had been stolen, the scheme would have restored it, that is certain. And so I believe they've got it yet."

Tom had had no purpose in his mind when he encountered those two men. When he began his talk he hoped to be able to gall them a little and get a trifle of malicious entertainment out of it. But when he left, he left in great spirits, for he perceived that just by pure luck and no troublesome labor, he had accomplished several delightful things: he had touched both men on a raw spot and seen them squirm; he had modified Wilson's sweetness for the Twins with one small bitter taste that he wouldn't be able to get out of his mouth right away; and—best of all—he had taken the hated Twins down a peg with the community; for Blake would gossip around freely, after the manner of detectives, and within a week the town would be laughing at them in its sleeve for offering a gaudy reward for a bauble which they either never possessed or hadn't lost. Tom was very well satisfied with himself.

Tom's behavior at home had been perfect during the entire week. His uncle and aunt had seen nothing like it before. They could find no fault with him anywhere.

On Saturday evening he said to the Judge—

"I've had something preying on my mind, uncle, and as I am going away and might never see you again, I can't bear it any longer. I made you believe I was afraid to fight that Italian adventurer. I had to get out of it on some pretext or other, and maybe I chose badly, being taken unawares, but no honorable person could consent to meet him in the field, knowing what I knew about him."

"Indeed? What was that?"

"Count Luigi is a confessed assassin."

"Incredible!"

"It is perfectly true. Wilson detected it in his hand, by palmistry, and charged him with it and cornered him up so close that he had to confess; but both Twins begged us on their knees to keep the secret, and swore they would lead straight lives here; and it was all so pitiful that we gave our word of honor never to expose them while they kept that promise. You would have done it yourself, uncle."

"You are right, my boy, I would. A man's secret is still his own property, and sacred, when it has been surprised out of him like that. You did well, and I am proud of you." Then he added, mournfully, "But I wish I could have been saved the shame of meeting an assassin on the field of honor."

"It couldn't be helped, uncle. If I had known you were going to challenge him I should have felt obliged to sacrifice my pledged word in order to stop it, but Wilson couldn't be expected to do otherwise than keep silent."

"Oh, no, Wilson did right, and is in no way to blame. Tom, Tom, you have lifted a heavy load from my heart; I was stung to the very soul when I seemed to have discovered that I had a coward in my family."

"You may imagine what it cost *me* to assume such a part, uncle."

"Oh, I know it, poor boy, I know it. And I can understand how much it has cost you to remain under that unjust stigma to this time. But it is all right, now, and no harm is done. You have restored my comfort of mind, and with it your own; and both of us had suffered enough."

The old man sat a while plunged in thought; then he looked up with a satisfied light in his eye, and said: "That this assassin should have put the affront upon me of letting me meet him on the field of honor as if he were a gentleman is a matter which I will presently settle—but not now. I will not shoot him until after election. I see a way to ruin them both before; I will attend to that first. Neither of them shall be elected, that I promise. You are sure that the fact that he is an assassin has not got abroad?"

"Perfectly certain of it, sir."

"It will be a good card. I will fling a hint at it from the stump on the polling-day. It will sweep the ground from under both of them."

"There's not a doubt of it. It will finish them."

"That and outside work among the voters will, to a certainty. I want you to come down here by and by and work privately among the rag-tag and bobtail. You shall spend money among them; I will furnish it."

Another point scored against the detested Twins! Really it was a great day for Tom. He was encouraged to chance a parting shot, now, at the same target, and did it—

"You know that wonderful Indian knife that the Twins have been making such a to-do about? Well, there's no track or trace of it yet; so the town is beginning to sneer and gossip and laugh. Half the people believe they never had any such knife, the other half believe they had it and have got it still. I've heard twenty people talking like that to-day."

Yes, Tom's blemishless week had restored him to the favor of his aunt and uncle.

His mother was satisfied with him, too. Privately, she believed she was coming to love him, but she did not say so. She told him to go along to St. Louis, now, and she would get ready and follow. Then she smashed her whisky bottle and said—

"Dah, now! I's a gwyne to make you walk as straight as a string, Chambers, en so I's boun' you ain't gwyne to git no bad example out o' yo' mammy. I tole you you couldn't go into no bad comp'ny. Well, you's gwyne into my comp'ny, en I's gwyne to fill de bill. Now, den, trot along, trot along!"

Tom went aboard one of the big transient boats that night with his heavy satchel of miscellaneous plunder, and slept the sleep of the unjust, which is serener and sounder than the other kind, as we know by the hanging-eve history of a million rascals. But when he got up in the morning, luck was against him again. A brother-thief had robbed him while he slept, and gone ashore at some intermediate landing.

Chapter 16

If you pick up a starving dog and make him prosperous, he will not bite you. This is the principal difference between a dog and a man.
—PUDD'NHEAD WILSON'S CALENDAR.

We know all about the habits of the ant, we know all about the habits of the bee, but we know nothing at all about the habits of the oyster. It seems almost certain that we have been choosing the wrong time for studying the oyster.
—PUDD'NHEAD WILSON'S CALENDAR.

When Roxana arrived, she found her son in such despair and misery that her heart was touched and her motherhood rose up strong in her. He was ruined past hope, now; his destruction would be immediate and sure, and he would be an outcast and friendless.— That was reason enough for a mother to love a child; so she loved him, and told him so. It made him wince, secretly—for she was a "nigger." That he was one himself was far from reconciling him to that despised race.

Roxana poured out endearments upon him, to which he responded uncomfortably, but as well as he could. And she tried to comfort him, but that was not possible. These intimacies quickly became horrible to him, and within the hour he began to try to get up courage enough to tell her so, and require that they be discontinued or very considerably modified. But he was afraid of her; and besides, there came a lull, now, for she had begun to think. She was trying to invent a saving plan. Finally she started up and said she had found a way out. Tom was almost suffocated by the joy of this sudden good news. Roxana said—

"Here is de plan, en she'll win, sure. I is a nigger, en nobody ain't gwyne to doubt it dat hears me talk. I's wuth six hund'd dollahs. Take en sell me en pay off dese gamblers."

Tom was dazed. He was not sure he had heard aright. He was dumb for a moment; then he said:

"Do you mean that you would be sold into slavery to save me?"

"Ain't you my chile? En does you know anything dat a mother won't do for her chile? Dey ain't nothin' a white mother won't do for her chile. Who made 'em so? De Lord done it. En who made de niggers? De Lord made 'em. In de inside, mothers is all de same. De good Lord He made 'em so. I's gwyne to be sole into slavery, en in a year you's gwyne to buy yo' ole mammy free agin. I'll show you how. Dat's de plan."

Tom's hopes began to rise, and his spirits along with them. He said—

"It's lovely of you, mammy—it's just—"

"Say it agin! En keep on sayin' it! It's all de pay a body kin want in dis worl', en it's mo' den enough. Laws bless you honey, when I's slavin' aroun' en dey 'buses me, if I knows you's asayin' dat, 'way off yonder somers, it'll heal up all de sore places, en I kin stan' 'em."

"I *do* say it again, mammy, and I'll keep on saying it, too. But how am I going to sell you?—you're free, you know."

"Much diffrence dat make! White folks ain't particklar. De law kin sell me now, if dey tell me to leave de State in six months en I don't go. You draw up a paper—bill o' sale—en put it 'way off yonder, down in de middle o' Kaintuck somers, en sign some names to it, en say you'll sell me cheap caze you's hard up; you'll fine you ain't gwyne to have no trouble. You take me up de country a piece, en sell me on a farm—dem people ain't gwyne to ask no questions, if I's a bargain."

Tom forged a bill of sale and sold his mother to an Arkansas cotton planter for a trifle over six hundred dollars. He did not want to commit this treachery, but luck threw the man in his way, and this saved him the necessity of going up country to hunt up a purchaser, with the added risk of having to answer a lot of questions, whereas this planter was so pleased with Roxy that he asked next to none at all. Besides, the planter insisted that Roxy wouldn't know where she was, at first, and that by the time she found out she would already have become contented. And Tom argued with himself that it was an immense advantage for Roxy to have a master who was so pleased with her as this planter manifestly was. In almost no time his flowing reasonings carried him to the point of even half believing he was doing Roxy a splendid surreptitious service in selling her "down the river." And then he kept diligently saying to himself all the time, "It's for only a year—in a year I buy her free again; she'll keep that in mind, and it'll reconcile her." Yes, the little deception could do no harm, and everything would come out right and pleasant in the end, anyway. By agreement, the conversation in Roxy's presence was all about the man's "up-country" farm, and how pleasant a place it was, and how happy the slaves were, there; so poor Roxy was entirely deceived; and easily, for she was not dreaming that her own son could be guilty of treason to a mother who, in voluntarily going into slavery—slavery of any kind, mild or severe, or of any duration, brief or long—was making a sacrifice for him compared with which death would have been a poor and commonplace one. She lavished tears and loving caresses upon him, privately, and then went away with her owner; went away broken-hearted, and yet proud of what she was doing and glad that it was in her power to do it.

Tom squared his accounts, and resolved to keep to the very letter of his reform, and never put that will in jeopardy again. He had three hundred dollars left. According to his mother's plan, he was to put that safely away, and add her half of his pension to it monthly. In one year this fund would buy her free again.

For a whole week he was not able to sleep well, so much the villainy which he had played upon his trusting mother preyed upon his rag of a conscience; but after that he began to get comfortable again and was presently able to sleep like any other miscreant.

The boat bore Roxy away from St. Louis at four in the afternoon, and she stood on the lower guard abaft the paddle-box and watched Tom through a blur of tears until he melted into the throng of people and disappeared; then she looked no more, but sat there on a coil of cable crying, till far into the night. When she went to her foul steerage bunk at last, between the clashing engines, it was not to sleep, but only to wait for the morning; and waiting, grieve.

It had been imagined that she "would not know," and would think she was traveling up stream. She!—why, she had been steamboating for years. At dawn she got up and went listlessly and sat down on the cable-coil again. She passed many a snag whose "break" could have

told her a thing to break her heart, for it showed
a current moving in the same direction that the
boat was going; but her thoughts were elsewhere,
and she did not notice. But at last the roar of a
bigger and nearer break than usual brought her
out of her torpor, and she looked up and her practised eye fell upon that tell-tale rush of water. For
one moment her petrified gaze fixed itself there.
Then her head dropped upon her breast and she
said—

"Oh, de good Lord God have mercy on po' sinful me—*I's sole down de river!*"

Chapter 17

*Even popularity can be overdone. In Rome, along at first, you are full
of regrets that Michelangelo died; but by and by you only regret that
you didn't see him do it.*

—PUDD'NHEAD WILSON'S CALENDAR.

*July 4. Statistics show that we lose more fools on this day than in all
the other days of the year put together. This proves, by the number left
in stock, that one Fourth of July per year is now inadequate, the country has grown so.*

—PUDD'NHEAD WILSON'S CALENDAR.

The summer weeks dragged by, and then the political campaign
opened—opened in pretty warm fashion, and waxed hotter and hotter daily. The twins threw themselves into it with their whole heart,
for their self-love was engaged. Their popularity, so general at first,
had suffered afterward; mainly because they had been *too* popular,
and so a natural reaction had followed. Besides, it had been diligently
whispered around that it was curious—indeed, *very* curious—that
that wonderful knife of theirs did not turn up—*if* it was so valuable,
or *if* it had ever existed. And with the whisperings went chucklings

and nudgings and winks, and such things have an effect. The twins considered that success in the election would reinstate them, and that defeat would work them irreparable damage. Therefore they worked hard, but not harder than Judge Driscoll and Tom worked against them in the closing days of the canvass. Tom's conduct had remained so letter-perfect during two whole months, now, that his uncle not only trusted him with money with which to persuade voters, but trusted him to go and get it himself out of the safe in the private sitting-room.

The closing speech of the campaign was made by Judge Driscoll, and he made it against both of the foreigners. It was disastrously effective. He poured out rivers of ridicule upon them, and forced the big mass-meeting to laugh and applaud. He scoffed at them as adventures, mountebanks, side-show riff-raff, dime-museum freaks; he assailed their showy titles with measureless derision; he said they were back-alley barbers disguised as nobilities, peanut pedlers masquerading as gentlemen, organ-grinders bereft of their brother-monkey. At last he stopped and stood still. He waited until the place had become absolutely silent and expectant, then he delivered his deadliest shot; delivered it with ice-cold seriousness and deliberation, with a significant emphasis upon the closing words: he said he believed that the reward offered for the lost knife was humbug and buncombe, and that its owner would know where to find it whenever he should have occasion *to assassinate somebody*.

Then he stepped from the stand, leaving a startled and impressive hush behind him instead of the customary explosion of cheers and party cries.

The strange remark flew far and wide over the town and made an extraordinary sensation. Everybody was asking, "What could he mean by that?" And everybody went on asking that question, but in vain; for the Judge only said he knew what he was talking about, and stopped there; Tom said he hadn't any idea what his uncle meant, and Wilson, whenever he was asked what he thought it meant, parried the question by asking the questioner what *he* thought it meant.

Wilson was elected, the twins were defeated—crushed, in fact, and left forlorn and substantially friendless. Tom went back to St. Louis happy.

Dawson's Landing had a week of repose, now, and it needed it. But it was in an expectant state, for the air was full of rumors of a new duel. Judge Driscoll's election labors had prostrated him, but it was said that as soon as he was well enough to entertain a challenge he would get one from Count Luigi.

The brothers withdrew entirely from society, and nursed their humiliation in privacy. They avoided the people, and went out for exercise only late at night, when the streets were deserted.

Chapter 18

*Gratitude and treachery are merely the two extremities of the same
procession. You have seen all of it that is worth staying for when the
band and the gaudy officials have gone by.*
—PUDD'NHEAD WILSON'S CALENDAR.

*THANKSGIVING DAY. Let all give humble, hearty, and sincere thanks,
now, but the turkeys. In the island of Fiji they do not use turkeys; they
use plumbers. It does not become you and me to sneer at Fiji.*
—PUDD'NHEAD WILSON'S CALENDAR.

The Friday after the election was a rainy one in St. Louis. It rained
all day long, and rained hard, apparently trying its best to wash that
soot-blackened town white, but of course not succeeding. Toward
midnight Tom Driscoll arrived at his lodgings from the theatre in the
heavy downpour, and closed his umbrella and let himself in; but
when he would have shut the door, he found that there was another
person entering—doubtless another lodger; this person closed the
door and tramped up stairs behind Tom. Tom found his door in the
dark, and entered it and turned up the gas. When he faced about,
lightly whistling, he saw the back of a man. The man was closing and
locking his door for him. His whistle faded out and he felt uneasy.
The man turned around, a wreck of shabby old clothes sodden with
rain and all a-drip, and showed a black face under an old slouch hat.
Tom was frightened. He tried to order the man out, but the words
refused to come, and the other man got the start. He said, in a low
voice—

"Keep still—I's yo' mother!"

Tom sunk in a heap on a chair, and gasped out—

"It was mean of me, and base—I know it; but I meant it for the
best, I did indeed—I can swear it."

Roxana stood a while looking mutely down on him while he
writhed in shame and went on incoherently babbling self-accusations mixed with pitiful attempts at explanation and palliation of his
crime; then she seated herself and took off her hat, and her unkempt
masses of long brown hair tumbled down about her shoulders.

"It ain't no fault o' yo'n dat dat ain't gray," she said, sadly, noticing
the hair.

"I know it, I know it! I'm a scoundrel. But I swear I meant for the
best. It was a mistake, of course, but I thought it was for the best, I
truly did."

Roxy began to cry softly, and presently words began to find their
way out between her sobs. They were uttered lamentingly, rather
than angrily—

"Sell a pusson down de river—*down de river!*—for de bes'! I
wouldn't treat a dog so! I is all broke down en wore out, now, en so I

reckon it ain't in me to storm aroun' no mo', like I used to when I 'uz trompled on en 'bused. I don't know—but maybe it's so. Leastways, I's suffered so much dat mournin' seem to come mo' handy to me now den stormin'.'"

These words should have touched Tom Driscoll, but if they did, that effect was obliterated by a stronger one—one which removed the heavy weight of fear which lay upon him, and gave his crushed spirit a most grateful rebound and filled all his small soul with a deep sense of relief. But he kept prudently still, and ventured no comment. There was a voiceless interval of some duration, now, in which no sounds were heard but the beating of the rain upon the panes, the sighing and complaining of the winds, and now and then a muffled sob from Roxana. The sobs became more and more infrequent, and at last ceased. Then the refugee began to talk again:

"Shet down dat light a little. More. More yit. A pusson dat is hunted don't like de light. Dah—dat'll do. I kin see whah you is, en dat's enough. I's gwyne to tell you de tale, en cut it jes' as short as I kin, en den I'll tell you what you's got to do. Dat man dat bought me ain't a bad man, he's good enough, as planters goes; en if he could a had his way I'd a ben a house servant in his fambly en ben comfortable; but his wife she was a Yank, en not right down good lookin', en she riz up agin me straight off; so den dey sent me out to de quarter mongst de common fiel' han's. Dat woman warn't satisfied, even wid dat, but she worked up de overseer agin me, she 'uz dat jealous en hateful; so de overseer he had me out befo' day in de mawnins en worked me de whole long day as long as dey 'uz any light to see by; en many's de lashin' I got becaze I couldn't come up to de work o' de stronges'. Dat overseer 'uz a Yank, too, outen New Englan', en anybody down South kin tell you what dat mean. *Dey* knows how to work a nigger to death, en dey knows how to whale 'em, too—whale 'em till dey backs is welted like a washboard. 'Long at fust my marster say de good word for me to de overseer, but dat 'uz bad for me; for de mistis she fine it out, en arter dat I jist ketched it at every turn—dey warn't no mercy for me no mo'.'"

Tom's heart was fired—with fury against the planter's wife; and he said to himself, "But for that meddlesome fool, everything would have gone all right." He added a deep and bitter curse against her.

The expression of this sentiment was fiercely written in his face, and stood thus revealed to Roxana by a white glare of lightning which turned the sombre dusk of the room into dazzling day at that moment. She was pleased—pleased and grateful; for did not that expression show that her child was capable of grieving for his mother's wrongs and of feeling resentment toward her persecutors?—a thing which she had been doubting. But her flash of happiness was only a flash, and went out again and left her spirit dark; for she said to herself, "He sole me down de river—he can't feel for a body long; dis'll pass en go." Then she took up her tale again:

"'Bout ten days ago I 'uz sayin' to myself dat I couldn't las' many mo' weeks, I 'uz so wore out wid de awful work en de lashins, en so down-hearted en misable. En I didn't care no mo', nuther—life warn't wuth noth'n to me if I got to go on like dat. Well, when a body is in a frame o' mine like dat, what do a body care what a body do? Dey was a little sickly nigger wench 'bout ten year ole dat 'uz good to me, en hadn't no mammy, po' thing, en I loved her en she loved me; en she come out whah I 'uz workin', en she had a roasted tater, en tried to slip it to me—robbin' herself, you see, caze she knowed de overseer didn't gimme enough to eat—en he ketched her at it, en give her a lick acrost de back wid his stick which 'uz as thick as a broom-han'le, en she drop' screamin' on de groun', en squirmin' en wallerin' aroun' in de dust like a spider dat's got crippled. I couldn't stan' it. All de hell-fire dat 'uz ever in my heart flame' up, en I snatch de stick outen his han' en laid him flat. He laid dah moanin' en cussin', en all out of his head, you know, en de niggers 'uz plum skyerd to death. Dey gethered 'roun' him to he'p him, en I jumped on his hoss en took out for de river as tight as I could go. I knowed what dey would do wid me. Soon as he got well he would start in en work me to death if marster let him; en if dey didn't do dat dey'd sell me furder down de river, en dat's de same thing. So I 'lowed to drown myself en git out o' my troubles. It 'uz gitt'n towards dark. I 'uz at de river in two minutes. Den I see a canoe, en I says dey ain't no use to drown myself tell I got to; so I ties de hoss in de edge o' de timber en shove out down de river, keepin' in under de shelter o' de bluff bank en prayin' for de dark to shet down quick. I had a pow'ful good start, caze de big house 'uz three mile back fum de river en on'y de work mules to ride dah on, en on'y niggers to ride 'em, en *dey* warn't gwyne to hurry—dey'd gimme all de chance dey could. Befo' a body could go to de house en back it would be long pas' dark, en dey couldn't track de hoss en fine out which way I went tell mawnin', en de niggers would tell 'em all de lies dey could 'bout it.

"Well, de dark come, en I went on a spinnin' down de river. I paddled mo'n two hours, den I warn't worried no mo'; so I quit paddlin', en floated down de current, considerin' what I 'uz gwyne to do if I didn't have to drown myself. I made up some plans, en floated along, turnin' 'em over in my mine. Well, when it 'uz a little pas' midnight, as I reckoned, en I had come fifteen or twenty mile, I see de lights o' a steamboat layin' at de bank, whah dey warn't no town en no wood-yard, en putty soon I ketched de shape o' de chimbly-tops agin de stars, en de good gracious me, I most jumped out o' my skin for joy! It 'uz de Gran' Mogul—I 'uz chambermaid on her for eight seasons in de Cincinnati en Orleans trade. I slid 'long pas'—don't see nobody

stirrin' nowhah—hear 'em a hammerin' away in de engine room, den
I knowed what de matter was—some o' de machinery's broke. I got
asho' below de boat en turn' de canoe loose, den I goes 'long up, en
dey 'uz jes' one plank out, en I step 'board de boat. It 'uz pow'ful hot;
deckhan's en roustabouts 'uz sprawled roun' asleep on de fo'cas'l, de
second mate, Jim Bangs, he sot dah on de bitts wid his head down,
asleep—caze dat's de way de second mate stan' de cap'n's watch!—
en de ole watchman, Billy Hatch, he 'uz a noddin' on de compan-
ionway;—en I knowed 'em all; en lan', but dey did look good! I says
to myself, I wisht old marster'd come along *now* en try to take me—
bless yo' heart, I's 'mong frien's, I is. So I tromped right along 'mongst
'em, en went up on de biler deck en 'way back aft to de ladies' cabin
guard, en sot down dah in de same cheer dat I'd sot in mos' a hund'd
million times, I reckon; en it 'uz jist home agin, I tell you!

"In 'bout an hour I heard de ready-bell jingle, en den de racket
begin. Putty soon I hear de gong strike. 'Set her back on de outside,'
I says to myself—'I reckon I knows dat music!' I hear de gong agin.
'Come ahead on de inside,' I says. Gong agin. 'Stop de outside.' Gong
agin. 'Come ahead on de outside—now we's pinted for Sent Louis,
en I's outer de woods en ain't got to drown myself, at all.' I knowed
de Mogul 'uz in de Sent Louis trade now, you see. It 'uz jes' fair day
light when we passed our plantation, en I seed a gang o' niggers en
white folks huntin' up en down de sho', en troublin' deyselves a good
deal 'bout me, but I warn't troublin' myself none 'bout dem.

"'Bout dat time Sally Jackson, dat used to be my second chambermaid en 'uz head chambermaid now, she come out on de guard en
'uz pow'ful glad to see me, en so 'uz all de officers; en I tole 'em I'd
got kidnapped en sole down de river, en dey made me up twenty dollahs en give it to me, en Sally she rigged me out wid good clo'es, en
when I got here I went straight to whah you used to was, en den I
come to dis house en dey say you's away but 'spected back every day;
so I didn't dast to go down de river to Dawson's, caze I might miss
you.

"Well, las' Monday I 'uz pass'n by one o' dem places in Fourth street
whah dey sticks up runaway-nigger bills en he'ps to ketch 'em, en I
seed my marster! I mos' flopped down on de groun', I felt so gone.
He had his back to me, en 'uz talkin' to de man en givin' him some
bills—nigger-bills, I reckon, en I's de nigger. He's offerin' a reward—
dat's it. Ain't I right, don't you reckon?"

Tom had been gradually sinking into a state of ghastly terror, and
he said to himself, now, "I'm lost, no matter what turn things take!
This man has said to me that he thinks there was something suspicious about that sale. He said he had a letter from a passenger on the
Grand Mogul saying that Roxy came here on that boat and that
everybody on board knew all about the case; so he says that her com-

ing here instead of flying to a free State looks bad for me, and that if I don't find her for him, and that pretty soon, he will make trouble for me. I never believed that story; I couldn't believe she would be so dead to all motherly instincts as to come here, knowing the risk she would run of getting me into irremediable trouble. And after all, here she is! And I stupidly swore I would help him find her, thinking it was a perfectly safe thing to promise. If I venture to deliver her up, she— she—but how can I help myself? I've got to do that or pay the money, and where's the money to come from? I—I—well, I should think that if he would swear to treat her kindly hereafter—and she says, herself, that he is a good man—and if he would swear to never allow her to be overworked, or ill fed, or—"

A flash of lightning exposed Tom's pallid face drawn and rigid with these worrying thoughts. Roxana spoke up sharply, now, and there was apprehension in her voice—

"Turn up dat light! I want to see yo' face better. Dah, now—lemme look at you. Chambers, you's as white as yo' shirt! Has you seen dat man? Has he ben to see you?"

"Ye-s."

"When?"

"Monday noon."

"Monday noon! Was he on my track?"

"He—well, he thought he was. That is, he hoped he was. This is the bill you saw." He took it out of his pocket.

"Read it to me!"

She was panting with excitement, and there was a dusky glow in her eyes that Tom could not translate with certainty, but there seemed to be something threatening about it. The handbill had the usual rude wood-cut of a turbaned negro woman running, with the customary bundle on a stick over her shoulder, and the heading, in bold type, "*$100 Reward.*" Tom read the bill aloud—at least the part that described Roxana and named the master and his St. Louis address and the address of the Fourth-street agency; but he left out the item that applicants for the reward might also apply to Mr. Thomas Driscoll.

"Gimme de bill!"

Tom had folded it and was putting it in his pocket. He felt a chilly streak creeping down his back, but said, as carelessly as he could—

"The bill? Why, it isn't any use to you, you can't read it. What do you want with it?"

"Gimme de bill!" Tom gave it to her, but with a reluctance which he could not entirely disguise. "Did you read it *all* to me?"

"Certainly I did."

"Hole up yo' han' en swah to it."

Tom did it. Roxana put the bill carefully away in her pocket, with her eyes fixed upon Tom's face all the while, then she said—

"You's lyin'!"

"What would I want to lie about it for?"

"I don't know—but you is. Dat's my opinion, anyways. But nemmine 'bout dat. When I seed dat man, I 'uz dat s'kyerd dat I could scasely wobble home. Den I give a nigger man a dollah for dese clo'es, en I ain't ben in a house sence, night ner day, till now. I blacked my face en laid hid in de cellar of a ole house dat's burnt down, daytimes, en robbed de sugar hogsheads en grain sacks on de wharf, nights, to git somethin' to eat, en never dast to try to buy noth'n; en I's mos' starved. En I never dast to come near dis place till dis rainy night, when dey ain't no people roun', scasely. But tonight I ben a stannin' in de dark alley ever sence night come, waitin' for you to go by. En here I is."

She fell to thinking. Presently she said—

"You seed dat man at noon, las' Monday?"

"Yes."

"I seed him de middle o' dat arternoon. He hunted you up, didn't he?"

"Yes."

"Did he give you de bill dat time?"

"No, he hadn't got it printed, yet."

Roxana darted a suspicious glance at him.

"Did you he'p him fix up de bill?"

Tom cursed himself for making that stupid blunder, and tried to rectify it by saying he remembered, now, that it *was* at noon Monday that the man gave him the bill. Roxana said—

"You's lyin' agin, sho'." Then she straightened up and raised her finger:

"Now, den! I's gwyne to ast you a question, en I wants to know how you's gwyne to git aroun' it. You knowed he 'uz arter me; en if you run off, 'stid o' stayin' here to he'p him, he'd know dey 'uz somethin' wrong 'bout dis business, en den he would inquire 'bout you, en dat would take him to yo' uncle, en yo' uncle would read de bill en see dat you ben sellin' a free nigger down de river, en you know *him* I reckon! He'd tar up de will en kick you outen de house. Now, den, you answer me dis question: hain't you tole dat man dat I would be sho' to come here, en den you would fix it so he could set a trap en ketch me?"

Tom recognized that neither lies nor arguments could help him any longer—he was in a vise, with the screw turned on, and out of it there was no budging. His face began to take on an ugly look, and presently he said, with a snarl—

"Well, what could I do? You see, yourself, that I was in his grip and couldn't get out."

Roxy scorched him with a scornful gaze a while, then she said—

"What could you do? You could be Judas to yo' own mother to save yo' wuthless hide! Would anybody b'lieve it? No—a dog couldn't! You is de low-downest orneriest hound dat was ever pup'd into dis worl'—en I's 'sponsible for it!"—and she spat on him.

He made no effort to resent this. Roxy reflected a moment, then she said—

"Now I'll tell you what you's gwyne to do. You's gwyne to give dat man de money dat you's got laid up, en make him wait till you kin go to de Jedge en git de res' en buy me free agin."

"Thunder! what are you thinking of? Go and ask him for three hundred dollars and odd? What would I tell him I want with it, pray?"

Roxy's answer was delivered in a serene and level voice—

"You'll tell him you's sole me to pay yo' gamblin' debts, en dat you lied to me en was a villain, en dat I 'quires you to git dat money en buy me back agin."

"Why, you've gone stark mad! He would tear the will to shreds in a minute—don't you know that?"

"Yes, I does."

"Then you don't believe I'm idiot enough to go to him, do you?"

"I don't b'lieve nothin' 'bout it—I *knows* you's a-goin'. I knows it becaze you knows dat if you don't raise dat money I'll go to him myself, en den he'll sell *you* down de river en you kin see how you like it!"

Tom rose, trembling and excited, and there was an evil light in his eye. He strode to the door and said he must get out of this suffocating place for a moment and clear his brain in the fresh air so that he could determine what to do. The door wouldn't open. Roxy smiled grimly, and said—

"I's got de key, honey—set down. You needn't cle'r up yo' brain none to fine out what you gwyne to do—*I* knows what you's gwyne to do." Tom sat down and began to pass his hands through his hair with a helpless and desperate air. Roxy said, "Is dat man in dis house?"

Tom glanced up with a surprised expression, and asked—

"What gave you such an idea?"

"You done it. Gwyne out to cle'r yo' brain! In de fust place you ain't got none to cle'r, en in de second place yo' ornery eye tole on you. You's de low-downest hound dat ever—but I done tole you dat, befo'. Now den, dis is Friday. You kin fix it up wid dat man, en tell him you's gwyne away to git de res' o' de money, en dat you'll be back wid it nex' Tuesday, or maybe Wednesday. You understan'?"

Tom answered sullenly—

"Yes."

"En when you gits de new bill o' sale dat sells me to my own self, take en send it in de mail to Mr. Pudd'nhead Wilson, en write on de back dat he's to keep it tell I come. You understan'?"

"Yes."

"Dat's all, den. Take yo' umbereller, en put on yo' hat."

"Why?"

"Becaze you's gwyne to see me home to de wharf. You see dis knife? I's toted it aroun' sence de day I seed dat man en bought dese clo'es en it. If he ketched me, I 'uz gwyne to kill myself wid it. Now start along, en go sof', en lead de way; en if you gives a sign in dis house, or if anybody comes up to you in de street, I's gwyne to jam it into you. Chambers, does you b'lieve me when I says dat?"

"It's no use to bother me with that question. I know your word's good."

"Yes, it's diffrent fum yo'n! Shet de light out en move along—here's de key."

They were not followed. Tom trembled every time a late straggler brushed by them on the street, and half expected to feel the cold steel in his back. Roxy was right at his heels and always in reach. After tramping a mile they reached a wide vacancy on the deserted wharves, and in this dark and rainy desert they parted.

As Tom trudged home, his mind was full of dreary thoughts and wild plans; but at last he said to himself, wearily—

"There is but the one way out. I must follow her plan. But with a variation—I will not ask for the money and ruin myself, I will *rob* the old skinflint."

Chapter 19

Few things are harder to put up with than the annoyance of a good example.

—PUDD'NHEAD WILSON'S CALENDAR.

It were not best that we should all think alike; it is difference of opinion that makes horse-races.

—PUDD'NHEAD WILSON'S CALENDAR.

Dawson's Landing was comfortably finishing its season of dull repose and waiting patiently for the duel. Count Luigi was waiting, too; but not patiently, rumor said. Sunday came, and Luigi insisted on having his challenge conveyed. Wilson carried it. Judge Driscoll declined to fight with an assassin—"that is," he added, significantly, "in the field of honor."

Elsewhere, of course, he would be ready. Wilson tried to convince him that if he had been present himself when Angelo told about the homicide committed by Luigi, he would not have considered the act discreditable to Luigi; but the obstinate old man was not to be moved.

Wilson went back to his principal and reported the failure of his mission. Luigi was incensed, and asked how it could be that the old gentleman, who was by no means dull-witted, held his trifling nephew's evidence and inferences to be of more value than Wilson's. But Wilson laughed, and said—

"That is quite simple; that is easily explicable. I am not his doll—his baby—his infatuation: his nephew is. The Judge and his late wife never had any children. The Judge and his wife were past middle age when this treasure fell into their lap. One must make allowances for a parental instinct that has been starving for twenty-five or thirty years. It is famished, it is crazed with hunger by that time, and will be entirely satisfied with anything that comes handy; its taste is atrophied, it can't tell mud-cat from shad. A devil born to a young couple is measurably recognizable by them as a devil before long, but a devil adopted by an old couple is an angel to them, and remains so, through thick and thin. Tom is this old man's angel; he is infatuated with him. Tom can persuade him into things which other people can't—not all things, I don't mean that, but a good many—particularly one class of things: the things that create or abolish personal partialities or prejudices in the old man's mind. The old man liked both of you. Tom conceived a hatred for you. That was enough; it turned the old man around at once. The oldest and strongest friendship must go to the ground when one of these late-adopted darlings throws a brick at it."

"It's a curious philosophy," said Luigi.

"It ain't a philosophy at all,—it's a fact. And there is something pathetic and beautiful about it, too. I think there is nothing more pathetic than to see one of these poor old childless couples taking a menagerie of yelping little worthless dogs to their hearts; and then adding some cursing and squawking parrots and a jackass-voiced macaw; and next a couple of hundred screeching song-birds; and presently some fetid guinea-pigs and rabbits, and a howling colony of cats. It is all a groping and ignorant effort to construct out of base metal and brass filings, so to speak, something to take the place of that golden treasure denied them by Nature, a child. But this is a digression. The unwritten law of this region requires you to kill Judge

Driscoll on sight, and he and the community will expect that attention at your hands—though of course your own death by his bullet
will answer every purpose. Look out for him! Are you heeled—that
is, fixed?"

"Yes; he shall have his opportunity. If he attacks me I will respond."

As Wilson was leaving, he said—

"The Judge is still a little used up by his campaign work, and will
not get out for a day or so, but when he does get out you want to be
on the alert."

About eleven at night the twins went out for exercise, and started
on a long stroll in the veiled moonlight.

Tom Driscoll had landed at Hackett's Store, two miles below Dawson's, just about half an hour earlier, the only passenger for that
lonely spot, and had walked up the shore road and entered Judge
Driscoll's house without having encountered any one, either on the
road or under the roof.

He pulled down his window-blinds and lighted his candle. He laid
off his coat and hat, and began his preparations. He unlocked his
trunk and got his suit of girl's clothes out from under the male attire
in it, and laid it by. Then he blacked his face with a burnt cork and
put the cork in his pocket. His plan was, to slip down to his uncle's
private sitting room below, pass into the bedroom, steal the safe-key
from the old gentleman's clothes, and then go back and rob the safe.
He took up his candle to start. His courage and confidence were
high, up to this point, but both began to waver a little, now. Suppose
he should make a noise, by some accident, and get caught—say in
the act of opening the safe? Perhaps it would be well to go armed.
He took the Indian knife from its hiding place, and felt a pleasant
return of his waning courage. He slipped stealthily down the narrow
stair, his hair rising and his pulses halting at the slightest creak.
When he was half way down he was disturbed to perceive that the
landing below was touched by a faint glow of light. What could that
mean? Was his uncle still up? No, that was not likely; he must have
left his night-taper there when he went to bed. Tom crept on down,
pausing at every step to listen. He found the door standing open, and
glanced in. What he saw pleased him beyond measure. His uncle was
asleep on the sofa. On a small table at the head of the sofa a lamp
was burning low, and by it stood the old man's small tin cash-box,
closed. Near the box was a pile of bank notes and a piece of paper
covered with figures in pencil. The safe-door was not open. Evidently
the sleeper had wearied himself with work upon his finances, and
was taking a rest.

Tom set his candle on the stairs, and began to make his way toward
the pile of notes, stooping low as he went. When he was passing his
uncle, the old man stirred in his sleep and Tom stopped instantly—

stopped, and softly drew the knife from its sheath, with his heart thumping and his eyes fastened upon his benefactor's face. After a moment or two he ventured forward again—one step—reached for his prize, and seized it, dropping the knife-sheath. Then he felt the old man's strong grip upon him, and a wild cry of "Help! help!" rang in his ear. Without hesitation he drove the knife home—and was free. Some of the notes escaped from his left hand and fell in the blood on the floor. He dropped the knife and snatched them up and started to fly; transferred them to his left hand and seized the knife again, in his fright and confusion, but remembered himself and flung it from him, as being a dangerous witness to carry away with him.

He jumped for the stair-foot, and closed the door behind him; and as he snatched his candle and fled upward, the stillness of the night was broken by the sound of urgent footsteps approaching the house. In another moment he was in his room, and the Twins were standing aghast over the body of the murdered man!

Tom put on his coat, buttoned his hat under it, threw on his suit of girl's clothes, dropped the veil, blew out his light, locked the room-door by which he had just entered, taking the key, passed through his other door into the back hall, locked that door and kept the key, then worked his way along in the dark and descended the back stairs. He was not expecting to meet anybody, for all interest was centred in the other part of the house, now; his calculation proved correct. By the time he was passing through the back yard, Mrs. Pratt, her servants, and a dozen half dressed neighbors had joined the Twins and the dead, and accessions were still arriving at the front door.

As Tom, quaking as with a palsy, passed out at the gate three women came flying from the house on the opposite side of the lane. They rushed by him and in at the gate, asking him

what the trouble was, there, but not waiting for an answer. Tom said to himself, "Those old maids waited to dress—they did the same thing the night Stevens's house burned down next door." In a few minutes he was in the haunted house. He lighted a candle, and took off his girl-clothes. There was blood on him all down his left side, and his right hand was red with the stains of the blood-soaked notes which he had crushed in it; but otherwise he was free from this sort of evidence. He cleansed his hand on the straw, and cleaned most of the smut from his face. Then he burned his male and female attire to ashes, scattered the ashes, and put on a disguise proper for a tramp. He blew out his light, went below, and was soon loafing down the river road, with the intent to borrow and use one of Roxy's devices. He found a canoe and paddled off down stream, setting the canoe adrift as dawn approached, and making his way by land to the next village, where he kept out of sight till a transient steamer came along, and then took deck passage for St. Louis. He was ill at ease until Dawson's Landing was behind him; then he said to himself, "All the detectives on earth couldn't trace me now; there's not a vestige of a clew left in the world; that homicide will take its place with the permanent mysteries, and people won't get done trying to guess out the secret of it for fifty years."

In St. Louis, next morning, he read this brief telegram in the papers—dated at Dawson's Landing:

"Judge Driscoll, an old and respected citizen, was assassinated here about mid-night by a profligate Italian nobleman or barber on account of a quarrel growing out of the recent election. The assassin will probably be lynched."

"One of the twins!" soliloquised Tom; "how lucky! It is the knife that has done him this grace. We never know when fortune is trying to favor us. I actually cursed Pudd'nhead Wilson in my heart for putting it out of my power to sell that knife. I take it back, now."

Tom was now rich and independent. He arranged with the planter, and mailed to Wilson the new bill of sale which sold Roxana to herself; then he telegraphed his aunt Pratt:

"Have seen the awful news in the papers and am almost prostrated with grief. Shall start by packet to-day. Try to bear up till I come."

When Wilson reached the house of mourning and had gathered such details as Mrs. Pratt and the rest of the crowd could tell him, he took command, as mayor, and gave orders that nothing should be touched, but everything left as it was until Justice Robinson should arrive and take the proper measures as coroner. He cleared everybody out of the room but the Twins and himself. The sheriff soon arrived and took the Twins away to jail. Wilson told them to keep heart, and promised to do his best in their defence when the case should come to trail. Justice Robinson came presently, and with him Constable Blake. They examined the room thoroughly. They found the knife and the sheath. Wilson noticed that there were fingerprints on the knife-handle. That pleased him, for the Twins had required the earliest comers to make a scrutiny of their hands and clothes, and neither these people nor Wilson himself had found any blood-stains upon them. Could there be a possibility that the Twins had spoken the truth when they said they found the man dead when they ran into the house in answer to the cry for help? He thought of

that mysterious girl, at once. But this was not the sort of work for a girl to be engaged in. No matter; Tom Driscoll's room must be examined.

After the coroner's jury had viewed the body and its surroundings, Wilson suggested a search up stairs, and he went along. The jury forced an entrance to Tom's room, but found nothing, of course.

The coroner's jury found that the homicide was committed by Luigi, and that Angelo was accessory to it.

The town was bitter against the unfortunates, and for the first few days after the murder they were in constant danger of being lynched. The grand jury presently indicted Luigi for murder in the first degree, and Angelo as accessory before the fact. The Twins were transferred from the city jail to the county prison to await trial.

Wilson examined the finger-marks on the knife handle, and said to himself, "Neither of the Twins made those marks." Then manifestly there was another person concerned, either in his own interest or as hired assassin.

But who could it be? That, he must try to find out. The safe was not open, the cash-box was closed, and had three thousand dollars in it. Then robbery was not the motive, and revenge was. Where had the murdered man an enemy except Luigi? There was but that one person in the world with a deep grudge against him.

The mysterious girl! The girl was a great trial to Wilson. If the motive had been robbery, the girl might answer, but there wasn't any girl that would want to take this old man's life for revenge. He had no quarrels with girls; he was a gentleman.

Wilson had perfect tracings of the finger-marks of the knife handle; and among his glass records he had a great array of the finger-prints of women and girls, collected during the last fifteen or eighteen years, but he scanned them in vain, they successfully withstood every test; among them were no duplicates of the prints on the knife.

The presence of the knife on the stage of the murder was a worrying circumstance for Wilson. A week previously he had as good as admitted to himself that he believed Luigi had possessed such a knife and that he still possessed it notwithstanding his pretence that it had been stolen. And now here was the knife, and with it the Twins. Half the town had said the Twins were hum-bugging when they claimed that they had lost their knife, and now these people were joyful, and said "I told you so!"

If their finger-prints had been on the handle—but it was useless to bother any further about that; the finger-prints on the handle were *not* theirs—that he knew, perfectly.

Wilson refused to suspect Tom; for, firstly, Tom couldn't murder anybody—he hadn't character enough; secondly, if he could murder a person he wouldn't select his doting benefactor and nearest relative; thirdly, self-interest was in the way; for while the uncle lived, Tom was sure of a free support and a chance to get the destroyed will revived again, but with the uncle gone, that chance was gone, too. It was true the will had really been revived, as was now discovered, but Tom could not have been aware of it, or he would have spoken of it, in his native talky unsecretive way. Finally, Tom was in St. Louis when the murder was done, and got the news out of the morning journals, as was shown by his telegram to his aunt. These speculations were unemphasized sensations rather than articulated thoughts, for Wilson would have laughed at the idea of seriously connecting Tom with the murder.

Wilson regarded the case of the Twins as desperate—in fact, about hopeless. For he argued that if a confederate was not found, an enlightened Missouri jury would hang them, sure; if a confederate was found, that would not improve the matter, but simply furnish one more person for the sheriff to hang. Nothing could save the Twins but the discovery of a person who did the murder on his sole personal account—an undertaking which had all the aspect of the impossible. Still, the person who made the finger-prints must be sought. The Twins might have no case *with* him, but they certainly would have none without him.

So Wilson mooned around, thinking, thinking, guessing, guessing, day and night, and arriving nowhere. Whenever he ran across a girl or a woman he was not acquainted with, he got her finger-prints, on one pretext or another; and they always cost him a sigh when he got home, for they never tallied with the finger-marks on the knife handle.

As to the mysterious girl, Tom swore he knew no such girl, and did not remember ever seeing a girl wearing a dress like the one described by Wilson. He admitted that he did not always lock his room, and that sometimes the servants forgot to lock the house doors; still, in his opinion the girl must have made but few visits or she would have been discovered. When Wilson tried to connect her with the stealing-raid, and thought she might have been the old woman's confederate, if not the very thief herself disguised as an old woman, Tom seemed struck, and also much interested, and said he would keep a sharp eye out for this person or persons, although he was afraid that she or they would be too smart to venture again into a town where everybody would now be on the watch for a good while to come.

Everybody was pitying Tom, he looked so quiet and sorrowful, and seemed to feel his great loss so deeply. He was playing a part, but it was not all a part. The picture of his alleged uncle, as he had last seen him, was before him in the dark pretty frequently, when he was awake, and called again in his dreams, when he was asleep. He wouldn't go into the room where the tragedy had happened. This charmed the doting Mrs. Pratt, who "realized now, as she had never done before," she said, what a sensitive and delicate nature her darling had, and how he adored his poor uncle.

Chapter 20

Even the clearest and most perfect circumstantial evidence is likely to be at fault, after all, and therefore ought to be received with great caution. Take the case of any pencil, sharpened by any woman: if you have witnesses, you will find she did it with a knife; but if you take simply the aspect of the pencil, you will say she did it with her teeth.
—PUDD'NHEAD WILSON'S CALENDAR.

The weeks dragged along, no friend visiting the jailed Twins but their counsel and Aunt Patsy Cooper, and the day of trial came at last—the heaviest day in Wilson's life, for with all his tireless diligence he had discovered no sign or trace of the missing confederate. "Confederate" was the term he had long ago privately accepted for that person—not as being unquestionably the right term, but as being at least possibly the right one, though he was never able to understand why the Twins didn't vanish and escape, as the confederate had done, instead of remaining by the murdered man and getting caught there.

The court house was crowded, of course, and would remain so to the finish, for not only in the town itself, but in the country for miles around the trial was the one topic of conversation among the people. Mrs. Pratt, in deep mourning, and Tom with a weed on his hat, had seats near Pembroke Howard the public prosecutor, and back of them sat a great array of friends of the family. The Twins had but one friend present to keep their counsel in countenance, their poor old sorrowing landlady. She sat near Wilson, and looked her friendliest. In the "nigger corner" sat Chambers; also Roxy, with good clothes on and her bill of sale in her pocket. It was her most precious possession, and she never parted with it, day or night. Tom had allowed her thirty-five dollars a month ever since he came into his property, and had said that he and she ought to be grateful to the Twins for making them rich; but had roused such a temper in her by this speech that he did not repeat the argument afterward. She said the old Judge had treated her child a thousand times better than he deserved, and had never done her an unkindness in his life; so she hated these outlandish devils for killing him and shouldn't ever sleep satisfied till she saw them hanged for it. She was here to watch the trial, now, and was going to lift up just one "hooraw" over it if the County Judge put her in jail a year for it. She gave her turbaned head a toss and said, "When dat verdic' comes, I's gwyne to lif' dat *roof*, now, I *tell* you."

Pembroke Howard briefly sketched the State's case. He said he would show by a chain of circumstantial evidence without break or fault in it anywhere, that the principal prisoner at the bar committed the murder; that the motive was partly revenge, and partly a desire to take his own life out of jeopardy, and that his brother, by his presence, was a consenting accessory to the crime; a crime which was the basest known to the calendar of human misdeeds—assassination; that it was conceived by the blackest of hearts and consummated by the cowardliest of hands; a crime which had broken a loving sister's heart, blighted the happiness of a young nephew who was as dear as a son, brought inconsolable grief to many friends, and sorrow and loss to the whole community. The utmost penalty of the outraged law would be exacted, and upon the accused, now present at the bar, that penalty would unquestionably be executed. He would reserve further remark until his closing speech.

He was strongly moved, and so also was the whole house; Mrs. Pratt and several other women were weeping when he sat down, and many an eye that was full of hate was riveted upon the unhappy prisoners.

Witness after witness was called by the State, and questioned at length; but the cross-questioning was brief: Wilson knew they could furnish nothing valuable for his side. People were sorry for Pudd'nhead; his budding career would get hurt by this trial.

Several witnesses swore they heard Judge Driscoll say in his public speech that the Twins would be able to find their lost knife again when they needed it to assassinate somebody with. This was not news, but now it was seen to have been sorrowfully prophetic, and a profound sensation quivered through the hushed court room when those dismal words were repeated.

The public prosecutor rose and said that it was within his knowledge, through a conversation held with Judge Driscoll on the last day of his life, that counsel for the defence had brought him a challenge from the person charged at this bar with murder; that he had refused to fight with a confessed assassin—"that is, on the field of honor," but had added significantly, that he would be ready for him elsewhere. Presumably the person here charged with murder was warned that he must kill or be killed the first time he should meet Judge Driscoll. If counsel for the defence chose to let the statement stand so, he would not call him to the witness stand. Mr. Wilson said he would offer no denial. [Murmurs, in the house—"It is getting worse and worse for Wilson's case."]

Mrs. Pratt testified that she heard no outcry, and did not know what woke her up, unless it was the sound of rapid footsteps approaching the front door. She jumped up and ran out in the hall just as she was, and heard the footsteps flying up the front steps and then following behind her as she ran to the sitting room. There she found the accused standing over her murdered brother—[Here she broke

down and sobbed. Sensation in the court.] Resuming, she said the persons entering behind her were Mr. Rogers and Mr. Buckstone.

Cross-examined by Wilson, she said the Twins proclaimed their innocence; declared that they had been taking a walk, and had hurried to the house in response to a cry for help which was so loud and strong that they had heard it at a considerable distance; that they begged her and the gentlemen just mentioned to examine their hands and clothes—which was done, and no blood stains found.

Confirmatory evidence followed, from Rogers and Buckstone.

The finding of the knife was verified, the advertisement minutely describing it and offering a reward for it was put in evidence, and its exact correspondence with that description proven. Then followed a few minor details, and the case for the State was closed.

Wilson said that he had three witnesses, the Misses Clarkson, who would testify that they met a veiled young woman leaving Judge Driscoll's premises by the back gate a few minutes after the cries for help were heard, and that their evidence, taken with certain circumstantial evidence which he would call the court's attention to would in his opinion convince the court that there was still one person concerned in this crime who had not yet been found, and also that a stay of proceedings ought to be granted, in justice to his clients, until that person should be discovered. As it was late, he would ask leave to defer the examination of his three witnesses until the next morning.

The crowd poured out of the place and went flocking away in excited groups and couples, talking the events of the session over with vivacity and consuming interest, and everybody seemed to have had a satisfactory and enjoyable day except the accused, their counsel, and their old-lady friend. There was no cheer among these, and no substantial hope.

In parting with the Twins Aunt Patsy did attempt a good-night with a gay pretence of hope and cheer in it, but broke down without finishing.

Absolutely secure as Tom considered himself to be, the opening solemnities of the trial had nevertheless oppressed him with a vague uneasiness, his being a nature sensitive to even the smallest alarms; but from the moment that the poverty and weakness of Wilson's case lay exposed to the court, he was comfortable once more, even jubilant. He left the court-room sarcastically sorry for Wilson. "The Clarksons met an unknown woman in the back lane," he said to himself—"*that* is his case! I'll give him a century to find her in—a couple of them if he likes. A woman who doesn't exist any longer, and the clothes that gave her her sex burnt up and the ashes thrown away—oh, certainly, he'll find *her* easy enough!" This reflection set him to admiring, for the hundredth time, the shrewd ingenuities by which he had insured himself against detection—more, against even suspicion.

"Nearly always in cases like this there is some little detail or other overlooked, some wee little track or trace left behind, and detection follows; but here there's not even the faintest suggestion of a trace left. No more than a bird leaves when it flies through the air—yes, through the night, you may say. The man that can track a bird through the air in the dark and find that bird is the man to track me out and find the Judge's assassin—no other need apply. And that is the job that has been laid out for poor Pudd'nhead Wilson, of all people in the world! Lord, it will be pathetically funny to see him grubbing and groping after that woman that don't exist, and the right person sitting under his very nose all the time!" The more he thought the situation over, the more the humor of it struck him. Finally he said, "I'll never let him hear the last of that woman. Every time I catch him in company, to his dying day, I'll ask him in the guileless affectionate way that used to gravel him so when I inquired how his unborn law-business was coming along, 'Got on her track yet—hey, Pudd'nhead?'" He wanted to laugh, but that would not have answered; there were people about, and he was mourning for his uncle. He made up his mind that it would be good entertainment to look in on Wilson that night and watch him worry over his barren law-case and goad him with an exasperating word or two of sympathy and commiseration now and then.

Wilson wanted no supper, he had no appetite. He got out all the finger-prints of girls and women in his collection of records and pored gloomily over them an hour or more, trying to convince himself that that troublesome girl's marks were there somewhere and had been overlooked. But it was not so. He drew back his chair, clasped his hands over his head, and gave himself up to dull and arid musings.

Tom Driscoll dropped in, an hour after dark, and said with a pleasant laugh as he took a seat—

"Hello, we've gone back to the amusements of our days of neglect and obscurity for consolation, have we?" and he took up one of the glass strips and held it against the light to inspect it. "Come, cheer up, old man, there's no use in losing your grip and going back to this child's play merely because this big sun-spot is drifting across your shiny new disk. It'll pass, and you'll be all right again"—and he laid the glass down. "Did you think you could win always?"

"Oh, no," said Wilson, with a sigh, "I didn't expect that, but I can't believe Luigi killed your uncle, and I feel very sorry for him. It makes me blue. And you would feel as I do, Tom, if you were not prejudiced against those young fellows."

"I don't know about that," and Tom's countenance darkened, for his memory reverted to his kicking; "I owe them no good will, considering the brunette one's treatment of me that night. Prejudice or no prejudice, Pudd'nhead, I don't like them, and when they get their deserts you're not going to find me sitting on the mourners' bench."

He took up another strip of glass, and exclaimed—

"Why, here's old Roxy's label! Are you going to ornament the royal palaces with nigger paw-marks, too? By the date here, I was seven months old when this was done, and she was nursing me and her little nigger cub. There's a line straight across her thumb-print. How comes that?" and Tom held out the piece of glass to Wilson.

"That is common," said the bored man, wearily. "Scar of a cut or a scratch, usually"—and he took the strip of glass indifferently and raised it toward the lamp.

All the blood sunk suddenly out of his face; his hand quaked, and he gazed at the polished surface before him with the glassy stare of a corpse.

"Great Heavens, what's the matter with you, Wilson? Are you going to faint?"

Tom sprang for a glass of water and offered it, but Wilson shrank shuddering from him and said—

"No, no!—Take it away!" His breast was rising and falling, and he moved his head about in a dull and wandering way, like a person who has been stunned. Presently he said, "I shall feel better when I get to bed; I have been overwrought to-day; yes, and overworked for many days."

"Then I'll leave you and let you get to your rest. Good night, old man." But as Tom went out he couldn't deny himself a small parting gibe: "Don't take it so hard; a body can't win every time; you'll hang somebody yet."

Wilson muttered to himself, "It is no lie to say I am sorry I have to begin with you, miserable dog though you are!"

He braced himself up with a glass of cold whisky and went to work again. He did not compare the new finger-marks unintentionally left by Tom a few minutes before on Roxy's glass with the tracings of the marks left on the knife handle, there being no need of that—for his trained eye—but busied himself with another matter, muttering from time to time, "Idiot that I was! Nothing but a *girl* would do me—a man in girl's clothes never occurred to me." First, he hunted out the plate containing the finger-prints made by Tom when he was twelve years old, and laid it by itself; then he brought forth the marks made by Tom's baby fingers when he was a suckling of seven months, and placed these two plates with the one containing this subject's newly (and unconsciously) made record.

"Now the series is complete," he said with satisfaction, and sat down to inspect these things and enjoy them.

But his enjoyment was brief. He stared a considerable time at the three strips, and seemed stupefied with astonishment. At last he put them down and said, "I can't make it out at all—hang it, the baby's don't tally with the others!"

He walked the floor for half an hour puzzling over his enigma, then he hunted out two other glass plates.

He sat down and puzzled over these things a good while, but kept muttering, "It's no use; I can't understand it. They don't tally right, and yet I'll swear the names and dates are right, and so of course they *ought* to tally. I never labeled one of these things carelessly in my life. There is a most extraordinary mystery here."

He was tired out, now, and his brains were beginning to clog. He said he would sleep himself fresh, and then see what he could do with this riddle. He slept through a troubled and unrestful hour, then unconsciousness began to shred away and presently he rose drowsily to a sitting posture. "Now what was that dream?" he said, trying to recall it; "What was that dream?—it seemed to unravel that puz—"

He landed in the middle of the floor at a bound, without finishing the sentence, and ran and turned up his light and seized his "records." He took a single swift glance at them and cried out—

"It's so! Heavens, what a revelation! And for twenty-three years no man has ever suspected it!"

Chapter 21

He is useless on top of the ground; he ought to be under it, inspiring the cabbages.
—PUDD'NHEAD WILSON'S CALENDAR.

April 1. This is the day upon which we are reminded of what we are on the other three hundred and sixty-four.
—PUDD'NHEAD WILSON'S CALENDAR.

Wilson put on enough clothes for business purposes, and went to work under a high pressure of steam. He was awake all over. All sense of weariness had been swept away by the invigorating refreshment of the great and hopeful discovery which he had made. He made fine and accurate reproductions of a number of his "records," and then enlarged them on a scale of ten to one with his pantograph. He did these pantograph enlargements on sheets of white cardboard, and made each individual line of the bewildering maze of whorls or curves or loops which constituted the "pattern" of a "record" stand out bold and black by reinforcing it with ink. To the untrained eye the collection of delicate originals made by the human finger on the glass plates looked about alike; but when enlarged ten times, they resembled the markings of a block of wood that has been sawed across the grain, and the dullest eye could detect at a glance, and at a distance of many feet, that no two of the patterns were alike. When Wilson had at last finished his tedious and difficult work, he arranged its results according to a plan in which a progressive order and sequence was a principal feature, then he added to the batch several pantograph enlargements which he had made from time to time in bygone years.

The night was spent and the day well advanced, now. By the time he had snatched a trifle of breakfast it was nine o'clock and the court was ready to begin its sitting. He was in his place twelve minutes later, with his "records."

Tom Driscoll caught a slight glimpse of the records and nudged his nearest friend and said, with a wink, "Pudd'nhead's got a rare eye to business—thinks that as long as he can't win his case, it's at least a noble good chance to advertise his palace-window decorations without any expense." Wilson was informed that his witnesses had been delayed, but would arrive presently; but he rose and said he should probably not have occasion to make use of their testimony. [An amused murmur ran through the

room—"It's a clean back-down! he gives up without hitting a lick!"]
Wilson continued—

"I have other testimony,—and better." [This compelled interest,
and evoked murmurs of surprise that had a detectible ingredient
of disappointment in them.] "If I seem to be springing this evidence upon the court, I offer as my justification for this, that I did
not discover its existence until late last night, and have been
engaged in examining and classifying it ever since until half an
hour ago. I shall offer it presently; but first I wish to say a few preliminary words.

"May it please the court, the claim given the front place, the claim
most persistently urged, the claim most strenuously and I may even
say, aggressively and defiantly insisted upon by the prosecution, is
this—that the person whose hand left the blood-stained finger-prints
upon the handle of the Indian knife is the person who committed the
murder." Wilson paused, during several moments, to give impressiveness to what he was about to say, and then added, tranquilly, *"We
grant that claim."*

It was an electrical surprise. No one was prepared for such an
admission. A buzz of astonishment rose on all sides, and people were
heard to intimate that the overworked lawyer had lost his mind. Even
the veteran Judge, accustomed as he was to legal ambushes and
masked batteries in criminal procedure, was not sure that his ears
were not deceiving him, and asked counsel what it was he had said.
Howard's impassive face betrayed no sign, but his attitude and bearing lost something of their careless confidence for a moment. Wilson resumed:

"We not only grant that claim, but we welcome it and strongly
endorse it. Leaving that matter for the present, we will now proceed
to consider other points in the case which we propose to establish by
evidence, and shall include that one in the chain, in its proper place."

He had made up his mind to try a few hardy guesses, in mapping
out his theory of the origin and motive of the murder—guesses
designed to fill up gaps in it—guesses which could help if they hit,
and would probably do no harm if they didn't.

"To my mind, certain circumstances of the case before the court
seem to suggest a motive for the homicide quite different from the
one insisted on by the State. It is my conviction that the motive was
not revenge, but robbery. It has been urged that the presence of the
accused brothers in that fatal room, just after notification that one
of them must take the life of Judge Driscoll or lose his own the
moment the parties should meet, clearly signifies that the natural
instinct of self-preservation moved my clients to go there secretly and
save Count Luigi by destroying his adversary.

"Then why did they stay there, after the deed was done? Mrs. Pratt had time, although she did not hear the cry for help, but woke up some moments later, to run to that room—and there she found these men standing, and making no effort to escape. If they were guilty, they ought to have been running out of the house at the same time that she was running to that room. If they had had such a strong instinct toward self-preservation as to move them to kill that unarmed man, what had become of it now, when it should have been more alert than ever? Would any of us have remained there? Let us not slander our intelligence to that degree.

"Much stress has been laid upon the fact that the accused offered a very large reward for the knife with which this murder was done; that no thief came forward to claim that extraordinary reward; that the latter fact was good circumstantial evidence that the claim that the knife had been stolen was a vanity and a fraud; that these details taken in connection with the memorable and apparently prophetic speech of the deceased concerning that knife and the final discovery of that very knife in the fatal room where no living person was found present with the slaughtered man but the owner of the knife and his brother, form an indestructible chain of evidence which fixes the crime upon those unfortunate strangers.

"But I shall presently ask to be sworn, and shall testify that there was a large reward offered for the *thief*, also; that it was offered secretly and not advertised; that this fact was indiscreetly mentioned—or at least tacitly admitted—in what was supposed to be safe circumstances, but may *not* have been. The thief may have been present himself." [Tom Driscoll had been looking at the speaker, but dropped his eyes at this point.] "In that case he would retain the knife in his possession, not daring to offer it for sale, or for pledge in a pawn shop." [There was a nodding of heads among the audience by way of admission that this was not a bad stroke.] "I shall prove to the satisfaction of the jury that there *was* a person in Judge Driscoll's room several minutes before the accused entered it." [This produced a strong sensation; the last drowsy-head in the court room roused up, now, and made preparation to listen.] "If it shall seem necessary, I will prove by the Misses Clarkson that they met a veiled person— ostensibly a woman—coming out of the back gate a few minutes after the cry for help was heard. This person was not a woman, but a man dressed in woman's clothes." Another sensation. Wilson had his eye on Tom when he hazarded this guess, to see what effect it would produce. He was satisfied with the result, and said to himself, "It was a success—he's hit!"

"The object of that person in that house was robbery, not murder. It is true that the safe was not open, but there was an ordinary tin cash-box on the table with three thousand dollars in it. It is easily supposable that the thief was concealed in the house; that he knew of this box, and of its owner's habit of counting its contents and arranging his accounts at night—if he had that habit, which I do not assert, of course; that he tried to take the box while its owner slept, but made a noise and was seized, and had to use the knife to save himself from capture; and that he fled without his booty because he heard help coming.

"I have now done with my theory, and will proceed to the evidences by which I propose to try to prove its soundness." Wilson took up several of his strips of glass. When the audience recognized these familiar mementoes of Pudd'nhead's old-time childish "puttering" and folly, the tense and funereal interest vanished out of their faces and the house burst into volleys of relieving and refreshing laughter, and Tom chirked up and joined in the fun himself; but Wilson was apparently not disturbed. He arranged his records on the table before him, and said—

"I beg the indulgence of the court while I make a few remarks in explanation of some evidence which I am about to introduce, and which I shall presently ask to be allowed to verify under oath on the witness stand. Every human being carries with him from his cradle to his grave certain physical marks which do not change their character, and by which he can always be identified—and that without shade of doubt or question. These marks are his signature, his physiological autograph, so to speak, and this autograph cannot be counterfeited, nor can he disguise it or hide it away, nor can it become illegible by the wear and the mutations of time. This signature is not his face—age can change that beyond recognition; it is not his hair, for that can fall out; it is not his height, for duplicates of that exist; it is not his form, for duplicates of that exist, also, whereas this signature is each man's very own—there is no duplicate of it among the swarming populations of the globe!" [The audience were interested once more.]

"This autograph consists of the delicate lines or corrugations with which Nature marks the insides of the hands and the soles of the feet. If you will look at the balls of your fingers—you that have very sharp eyesight—you will observe that these dainty, curving lines lie close together, like those that indicate the borders of oceans in maps, and that they form various clearly defined patterns, such as arches, circles, long curves, whorls, etc., and that these patterns differ on the different fingers." [Every man in the room had his hand up to the light, now, and his head canted to one side, and was minutely scrutinizing the balls of his fingers; there were whispered ejaculations of, 'Why, it's so—I never noticed that before!'] "The patterns on the right hand are not the same as those on the left." [Ejaculations of 'Why, that's so, too!'] "Taken finger for finger, your patterns differ from your neighbor's." [Comparisons were made, all over the house—even the judge and jury were absorbed in this curious work.] "The patterns of a twin's right hand are not the same as those on his left. One twin's patterns are never the same as his fellow-twin's patterns—the jury will find that the patterns upon the finger-balls of the accused follow this rule."—[An examination of the Twins' hands was begun at once.] "You have often heard of twins who were so exactly alike that when dressed alike their own parents could not tell them apart. Yet there was never a twin born into this world that did not carry from birth to death a sure identifier in this mysterious and marvelous natal autograph. That once known to you, his fellow-twin could never personate him and deceive you."

Wilson stopped, and stood silent. Inattention dies a quick and sure death when a speaker does that. The stillness gives warning that something is coming. All palms and finger-balls went down, now, all slouching forms straightened, all heads came up, all eyes were fastened upon Wilson's face. He waited yet one, two, three moments, to let his pause complete and perfect its spell upon the house; then, when through the profound hush he could hear the ticking of the clock on the wall, he put out his hand and took the Indian knife by the blade and held it aloft where all could see the sinister spots upon its ivory handle; then he said, in a level and passionless voice—

"Upon this haft stands the assassin's natal autograph, written in the blood of that helpless and unoffending old man who loved you and whom you all loved. There is but one man in the whole earth whose hand can duplicate that crimson sign"—he paused and raised his eyes to the pendulum swinging back and forth—"and please God we will produce that man in this room before the clock strikes noon!"

Stunned, distraught, unconscious of its own movement, the house half rose, as if expecting to see the murderer appear at the door, and a breeze of muttered ejaculations swept the place. "Order in the court!—sit down!" This from the sheriff. He was obeyed, and quiet reigned again. Wilson stole a glance at Tom, and said to himself, "He is flying signals of distress, now; even people who despise him are pitying him; they think this is a hard ordeal for a young fellow who has lost his benefactor by so cruel a stroke—and they are right." He resumed his speech:

"For more than twenty years I have amused my compulsory leisure with collecting these curious physical signatures in this town. At my house I have hundreds upon hundreds of them. Each and every one is labeled with name and date; not labeled the next day or even the next hour, but in the very minute that the impression was taken. When I go upon the witness stand I will repeat under oath the things which I am now saying. I have the finger-prints of the court, the sheriff, and every member of the jury. There is hardly a person in this room, white or black, whose natal signature I cannot produce, and not one of them can so disguise himself that I cannot pick him out from a multitude of his fellow creatures and unerringly identify him by his hands. And if he and I should live to be a hundred I could still do it!" [The interest of the audience was steadily deepening, now.]

"I have studied some of these signatures so much that I know them as well as the bank cashier knows the autograph of his oldest customer. While I turn my back, now, I beg that several persons will be so good as to pass their fingers through their hair and then press them upon one of the panes of the window near the jury, and that among them the accused may set *their* finger-marks. Also, I beg that these experimenters, or others, will set their finger-marks upon another pane, and add again the marks of the accused, but not placing them in the same order or relation to the other signatures as before—for, by one chance in a million, a person might happen upon the right marks by pure guesswork, *once*, therefore I wish to be tested twice."

He turned his back, and the two panes were quickly covered with delicately-lined oval spots, but visible only to such persons as could get a dark background for them,—the foliage of a tree, outside, for instance. Then, upon call, Wilson went to the window, made his examination, and said—

"This is Count Luigi's right hand; this one, three signatures below, is his left. Here is Count Angelo's right; down here is his left. Now for the other pane: here and here are Count Luigi's, here and here are his brother's." He faced about. "Am I right?"

A deafening explosion of applause was the answer. The Bench said—

"This certainly approaches the miraculous!"

Wilson turned to the window again and remarked, pointing with his finger—

"This is the signature of Mr. Justice Robinson." [Applause.] "This, of Constable Blake." [Applause.] "This, of John Mason, juryman." [Applause.] "This, of the sheriff." [Applause.] "I cannot name the others, but I have them all at home, named and dated, and could identify them all by my finger-print records."

He moved to his place through a storm of applause—which the sheriff stopped, and also made the people sit down, for they were all standing, and struggling to see, of course. Court, jury, sheriff and everybody had been too absorbed in observing Wilson's performance to attend to the audience earlier.

"Now then," said Wilson, "I have here the natal autographs of two children—thrown up to ten times the natural size by the pantograph, so that any one who can see at all can tell the markings apart at a glance. We will call the children A and B. Here are A's finger-marks, taken at the age of five months. Here they are again, taken at seven months." [Tom started.] "They are alike, you see. Here are *B*'s at five months, and also at seven months. They, too, exactly copy each other, but the patterns are quite different from *A*'s, you observe. I shall refer to these again presently, but we will turn them face down, now.

"Here, thrown up ten sizes, are the natal autographs of the two persons who are here before you accused of murdering Judge Driscoll. I made these pantograph copies last night, and will so swear when I go upon the witness stand. I ask the jury to compare them with the finger-marks of the accused upon the window panes, and tell the court if they are the same."

He passed a powerful magnifying glass to the foreman.

One jury man after another took the cardboard and the glass and made the comparison. Then the foreman said to the Judge—

"Your honor, we are all agreed that they are identical."

Wilson said to the foreman—

"Please turn that cardboard face down, and take this one and compare it searchingly, by the magnifier, with the fatal signature upon the knife-handle, and report your finding to the court."

Again the jury made minute examination, and again reported—

"We find them to be exactly identical, your honor."

Wilson turned toward the counsel for the prosecution, and there was a clearly recognizable note of warning in his voice when he said—

"May it please the court, the State has claimed, strenuously and persistently, that the blood-stained finger-prints upon that knife handle were left there by the assassin of Judge Driscoll. You have heard us grant that claim, and welcome it." He turned to the jury: "Compare the finger-prints of the accused with the finger-prints left by the assassin—and report."

The comparison began. As it proceeded, all movement and all sound ceased, and the deep silence of an absorbed and waiting suspense settled upon the house; and when at last the words came—

"They do not even resemble," a thunder-crash of applause followed and the house sprang to its feet, but was quickly repressed by official force and brought to order again. Tom was altering his position every few minutes, now, but none of his changes brought repose nor any small trifle of comfort. When the house's attention was become fixed once more, Wilson said gravely, indicating the Twins with a gesture—

"These men are innocent—I have no further concern with them." [Another outbreak of applause began, but was promptly checked.] "We will now proceed to find the guilty." [Tom's eyes were starting from their sockets—yes, it was a cruel day for the bereaved youth, everybody thought.] "We will return to the infant autographs of *A* and *B*. I will ask the jury to take these large pantograph facsimilies of *A*'s, marked five months and seven months. Do they tally?"

The foreman responded—

"Perfectly."

"Now examine this pantograph, taken at eight months, and also marked *A*. Does it tally with the other two?"

The surprised response was—

"No—they differ widely!"

"You are quite right. Now take these two pantographs of *B*'s autograph, marked five months and seven months. Do they tally with each other?"

"Yes—perfectly."

"Take this third pantograph marked '*B*, eight months.' Does it tally with *B*'s other two?"

"By no means!"

"Do you know how to account for those strange discrepancies? I will tell you. For a purpose unknown to us, but probably a selfish one, somebody changed those children in the cradle."

This produced a vast sensation, naturally; Roxana was astonished at this admirable guess, but not disturbed by it. To guess the exchange was one thing, to guess who did it quite another. Pudd'nhead Wilson could do wonderful things, no doubt, but he couldn't do impossible ones. Safe? She was perfectly safe. She smiled privately.

"Between the ages of seven months and eight months those children were changed in the cradle"—he made one of his effect-collecting pauses, and added—"and the person who did it is in this house!"

Roxy's pulses stood still! The house was thrilled as with an electric shock, and the people half rose, as if to seek a glimpse of the person who had made that exchange. Tom was growing limp; the life seemed oozing out of him. Wilson resumed:

"*A* was put into *B*'s cradle in the nursery; *B* was transferred to the kitchen, and became a negro and a slave"—[Sensation—confusion

of angry ejaculations]—"but within a quarter of an hour he will stand before you white and free!" [Burst of applause, checked by the officers.] "From seven months onward until now, *A* has still been a usurper, and in my finger-records he bears *B*'s name. Here is his pantograph, at the age of twelve. Compare it with the assassin's signature upon the knife handle. Do they tally?"

The foreman answered—

"To the minutest detail!"

Wilson said, solemnly—

"The murderer of your friend and mine—York Driscoll, of the generous hand and the kindly spirit—sits among you. Valet de Chambre,

negro and slave—falsely called Thomas à Becket Driscoll—make upon the window the finger-prints that will hang you!"

Tom turned his ashen face imploringly toward the speaker, made some impotent movements with his white lips, then slid limp and lifeless to the floor.

Wilson broke the awed silence with the words—

"There is no need. He has confessed."

Roxy flung herself upon her knees, covered her face with her hands, and out through her sobs the words struggled—

"De Lord have mercy on me, po' misable sinner dat I is!"

The clock struck twelve.

The court rose; the new prisoner, handcuffed, was removed.

Conclusion

It is often the case that the man who can't tell a lie thinks he is the best judge of one.
— PUDD'NHEAD WILSON'S CALENDAR.

October 12, the Discovery. It was wonderful to find America, but it would have been more wonderful to miss it.
— PUDD'NHEAD WILSON'S CALENDAR.

The town sat up all night to discuss the amazing events of the day and swap guesses as to when Tom's trial would begin. Troop after troop of citizens came to serenade Wilson, and require a speech, and shout themselves hoarse over every sentence that fell from his lips—for all his sentences were golden, now, all were marvelous. His long fight against hard luck and prejudice was ended; he was a made man for good.

And as each of these roaring gangs of enthusiasts marched away, some remorseful member of it was quite sure to raise his voice and say—

"And this is the man the likes of us have called a pudd'nhead for more than twenty years. He has resigned from that position, friends."

"Yes, but it isn't vacant—we're elected."

The Twins were heroes of romance, now, and with rehabilitated reputations. But they were weary of Western adventure, and straightway retired to Europe.

Roxy's heart was broken. The young fellow upon whom she had inflicted twenty-three years of slavery continued the false heir's pension of thirty-five dollars a month to her, but her hurts were too deep for money to heal; the spirit in her eye was quenched, her martial bearing departed with it, and the voice of her laughter ceased in the land. In her church and its affairs she found her only solace.

The real heir suddenly found himself rich and free, but in a most

embarrassing situation. He could neither read nor write, and his speech was the basest dialect of the negro quarter. His gait, his attitudes, his gestures, his bearing, his laugh—all were vulgar and uncouth; his manners were the manners of a slave. Money and fine clothes could not mend these defects or cover them up, they only made them the more glaring and the more pathetic. The poor fellow could not endure the terrors of the white man's parlor, and felt at home and at peace nowhere but in the kitchen. The family pew was a misery to him, yet he could nevermore enter into the solacing refuge of the "nigger gallery"—that was closed to him for good and all. But we cannot follow his curious fate further—that would be a long story.

The false heir made a full confession and was sentenced to imprisonment for life. But now a complication came up. The Percy Driscoll estate was in such a crippled shape when its owner died that it could pay only sixty per cent of its great indebtedness, and was settled at that rate. But the creditors came forward, now, and complained that inasmuch as through an error for which *they* were in no way to blame the false heir was not inventoried at that time with the rest of the property, great wrong and loss had thereby been inflicted upon them. They rightly claimed that "Tom" was lawfully their property and had been so for eight years; that they had already lost sufficiently in being deprived of his services during that long period, and ought not to be required to add anything to that loss; that if he had been delivered up to them in the first place, they would have sold him and he could not have murdered Judge Driscoll, therefore it was not he that had really committed the murder, the guilt lay with the erroneous inventory. Everybody saw that there was reason in this. Everybody granted that if "Tom" were white and free it would be unquestionably right to punish him—it would be no loss to anybody; but to shut up a valuable slave for life—that was quite another matter.

As soon as the Governor understood the case, he pardoned Tom at once, and the creditors sold him down the river.

The Text of
THOSE EXTRAORDINARY
TWINS

A man who is not born with the novel-writing gift has a troublesome time of it when he tries to build a novel. I know this from experience. He has no clear idea of his story; in fact he has no story. He merely has some people in his mind, and an incident or two, also a locality. He knows these people, he knows the selected locality, and he trusts that he can plunge those people into those incidents with interesting results. So he goes to work. To write a novel? No—that is a thought which comes later; in the beginning he is only proposing to tell a little tale; a very little tale; a six-page tale. But as it is a tale which he is not acquainted with, and can only find out what it is by listening as it goes along telling itself, it is more than apt to go on and on and on till it spreads itself into a book. I know about this, because it has happened to me so many times.

And I have noticed another thing: that as the short tale grows into the long tale, the original intention (or motif) is apt to get abolished and find itself superseded by a quite different one. It was so in the case of a magazine sketch which I once started to write—a funny and fantastic sketch about a prince and a pauper; it presently assumed a grave cast of its own accord, and in that new shape spread itself out into a book. Much the same thing happened with "Pudd'nhead Wilson." I had a sufficiently hard time with that tale, because it changed itself from a farce to a tragedy while I was going along with it,—a most embarrassing circumstance. But what was a great deal worse was, that it was not one story, but two stories tangled together; and they obstructed and interrupted each other at every turn and created no end of confusion and annoyance. I could not offer the book for publication, for I was afraid it would unseat the reader's reason, I did not know what was the matter with it, for I had not noticed, as yet, that it was two stories in one. It took me months to make that discovery. I carried the manuscript back and forth across the Atlantic two or three times, and read it and studied over it on shipboard; and at last I saw where the difficulty lay. I had no further trouble. I pulled one of the stories out by the roots, and left the other one—a kind of literary Cæsarean operation.

Would the reader care to know something about the story which I pulled out? He has been told many a time how the born-and-trained novelist works; won't he let me round and complete his knowledge by telling him how the jack-leg does it?

Originally the story was called "Those Extraordinary Twins." I meant to make it very short. I had seen a picture of a youthful Italian "freak"—or "freaks"—which was—or which were—on exhibition in our cities—a combination consisting of two heads and four arms joined to a single body and a single pair of legs—and I thought I would write an extravagantly fantastic little story with this freak of nature for hero—or heroes—a silly young Miss for heroine, and two old ladies and two boys for the minor parts. I lavishly elaborated these people and their doings, of course. But the tale kept spreading along and spreading along, and other people got to intruding themselves and taking up more and more room with their talk and their affairs. Among them came a stranger named Pudd'nhead Wilson, and a woman named Roxana; and presently the doings of these two pushed up into prominence a young fellow named Tom Driscoll, whose proper place was away in the obscure background. Before the book was half finished those three were taking things almost entirely into their own hands and working the whole tale as a private venture of their own—a tale which they had nothing at all to do with, by rights.

When the book was finished and I came to look around to see what had become of the team I had originally started out with—Aunt Patsy Cooper, Aunt Betsy Hale, the two boys, and Rowena the light-weight heroine—they were nowhere to be seen; they had disappeared from the story some time or other. I hunted about and found them—found them stranded, idle, forgotten, and permanently useless. It was very awkward. It was awkward all around, but more particularly in the case of Rowena, because there was a lovematch on, between her and one of the twins that constituted the freak, and I had worked it up to a blistering heat and thrown in a quite dramatic love-quarrel, wherein Rowena scathingly denounced her betrothed for getting drunk, and scoffed at his explanation of how it had happened, and wouldn't listen to it, and had driven him from her in the usual "forever" way; and now here she sat crying and broken-hearted; for she had found that he had spoken only the truth; that it was not he, but the other half of the freak that had drunk the liquor that made him drunk; that her half was a prohibitionist and had never drunk a drop in his life, and although tight as a brick three days in the week, was wholly innocent of blame; and indeed, when sober, was constantly doing all he could to reform his brother, the other half, who never got any satisfaction out of drinking, anyway, because liquor never affected him. Yes, here she was, stranded with that deep injustice of hers torturing her poor torn heart.

I didn't know what to do with her. I was as sorry for her as anybody could be, but the campaign was over, the book was finished, she was sidetracked, and there was no possible way of crowding her in, anywhere. I could not leave her there, of course; it would not do. After spreading her out so, and making such a to-do over her affairs, it would be absolutely necessary to account to the reader for her. I thought and thought and studied and studied; but I arrived at nothing. I finally saw plainly that there was really no way but one—I must simply give her the grand bounce. It grieved me to do it, for after associating with her so much I had come to kind of like her after a fashion, notwithstanding she was such an ass and said such stupid, irritating things and was so nauseatingly sentimental. Still it had to be done. So at the top of Chapter XVII. I put a "Calendar" remark concerning July the Fourth, and began the chapter with this statistic:

"Rowena went out in the back yard

after supper to see the fireworks and fell down the well and got drowned."

It seemed abrupt, but I thought maybe the reader wouldn't notice it, because I changed the subject right away to something else. Anyway it loosened up Rowena from where she was stuck and got her out of the way, and that was the main thing. It seemed a prompt good way of weeding out people that had got stalled, and a plenty good enough way for those others; so I hunted up the two boys and said "they went out back one night to stone the cat and fell down the well and got drowned." Next I searched around and found old Aunt Patsy Cooper and Aunt Betsy Hale where they were aground, and said "they went out back one night to visit the sick and fell down the well and got drowned." I was going to drown some of the others, but I gave up the idea, partly because I believed that if I kept that up it

would arouse attention, and perhaps sympathy with those people, and partly because it was not a large well and would not hold any more anyway.

Still the story was unsatisfactory. Here was a set of new characters who were become inordinately prominent and who persisted in remaining so to the end; and back yonder was an older set who made a large noise and a great to-do for a little while and then suddenly played out utterly and fell down the well. There was a radical defect somewhere, and I must search it out and cure it.

The defect turned out to be the one already spoken of—two stories in one, a farce and a tragedy. So I pulled out the farce and left the tragedy. This left the original team in, but only as mere names, not as characters. Their prominence was wholly gone; they were not even worth drowning; so I removed that detail. Also I took those twins apart and made two separate men of them. They had no occasion to have foreign names now, but it was too much trouble to remove them all through, so I left them christened as they were and made no explanation.

The Suppressed Farce

Chapter 1

The conglomerate twins were brought on the stage in Chapter I. of the original extravaganza. Aunt Patsy Cooper has received their letter applying for board and lodging, and Rowena, her daughter, insane with joy, is begging for a hearing of it:

"Well, set down then, and be quiet a minute and don't fly around so; it fairly makes me tired to see you. It starts off so: 'Honored Madam'—"

"I like that, ma, don't you? It shows they're high-bred."

"Yes, I noticed that when I first read it. 'My brother and I have seen your advertisement, by chance, in a copy of your local journal—'"

"It's so beautiful and smooth, ma—don't you think so?"

"Yes, seems so to me—'and beg leave to take the room you offer. We are twenty-four years of age, and twins—'"

"Twins! How sweet! I do hope they are handsome, and I just know they are! Don't you hope they are, ma?"

"Land, I ain't particular. 'We are Italians by birth—'"

"It's so romantic! Just think—there's never been one in this town, and everybody will want to see them, and they're all *ours*! Think of that!"

"—'but have lived long in the various countries of Europe, and several years in the United States.'"

"Oh, just think what wonders they've seen, ma! Won't it be good to hear them talk?"

"I reckon so; yes, I reckon so. 'Our names are Luigi and Angelo Cappello—'"

"Beautiful, perfectly beautiful! Not like Jones and Robinson and those horrible names."

"'You desire but one guest, but dear Madam, if you will allow us to pay for two we will not discommode you. We will sleep together in the same bed. We have always been used to this, and prefer it.' And then he goes on to say they will be down Thursday."

"And this is Tuesday—I don't know how I'm ever going to wait, ma! The time does drag along so, and I'm so dying to see them! Which of them do you reckon is the tallest, ma?"

"How do you s'pose I can tell, child? Mostly they are the same size—twins are."

"Well, then, which do you reckon is the best looking?"

"Goodness knows—I don't."

"I think Angelo is; it's the prettiest name, anyway. Don't you think it's a sweet name, ma?"

"Yes, it's well enough. I'd like both of them better if I knew the way to pronounce them—the Eyetalian way, I mean. The Missouri way and the Eyetalian way is different, I judge."

"May be—yes. It's Luigi that writes the letter. What do you reckon is the reason Angelo didn't write it?"

"Why, how can I tell? What's the difference who writes it, so long as it's done?"

"Oh, I hope it wasn't because he is sick! You don't think he is sick, do you, ma?"

"Sick your granny; what's to make him sick?"

"Oh, there's never any telling. Those foreigners with that kind of names are so delicate, and of course that kind of names are not suited to our climate—you wouldn't expect it."

[And so-on and so-on, no end. The time drags along; Thursday comes; the boat arrives in a pouring storm toward midnight.]

At last there was a knock on the door and the family jumped to open it. Two negro men entered, each carrying a trunk, and proceeded up stairs toward the guest room. Then followed a stupefying apparition—a double-headed human creature with four arms, one body, and a single pair of legs!

It—or they, as you please—bowed with elaborate foreign formality, but the Coopers could not respond, immediately; they were paralyzed. At this moment there came from the rear of the group a fervent ejaculation—"My lan'!"—followed by a crash of crockery, and the slave wench Nancy stood petrified and staring, with a tray of wrecked tea things at her feet. The incident broke the spell, and brought the family to consciousness. The beautiful heads of the new comer bowed again, and one of them said with easy grace and dignity—

"I crave the honor, Madam and Miss, to introduce to you my brother, Count Luigi Cappello," (the other head bowed,) "and myself—Count Angelo, and at the same time offer sincere apologies for the lateness of our coming, which was unavoidable;" and both heads bowed again.

The poor old lady was in a whirl of amazement and confusion, but she managed to stammer out—

"I'm sure I'm glad to make your acquaintance, sir—I mean, gentlemen. As for the delay, it is nothing, don't mention it. This is my

daughter Rowena, sir—gentlemen. Please step into the parlor and sit down and have a bite and sup; you are dreadful wet and must be uncomfortable—both of you, I mean."

But to the old lady's relief they courteously excused themselves, saying it would be wrong to keep the family out of their beds longer; then each head bowed in turn and uttered a friendly good night, and the singular figure moved away in the wake of Rowena's small brothers, who bore candles, and disappeared up the stairs.

The widow tottered into the parlor and sank into a chair with a gasp, and Rowena followed, tongue-tied and dazed. The two sat silent in the throbbing summer heat, unconscious of the million-voiced music of the mosquitoes, unconscious of the roaring gale, the lashing and thrashing of the rain along the windows and the roof, the white glare of the lightnings, the tumultuous booming and bellowing of the thunder, conscious of nothing but that prodigy, that uncanny apparition that had come and gone so suddenly—that weird strange thing that was so soft spoken and so gentle of manner, and yet had shaken them up like an earthquake with the shock of its grewsome aspect. At last a cold little shudder quivered along down the widow's meagre frame and she said in a weak voice—

"Ugh, it was awful—just the mere look of that phillipena!"[1]

Rowena did not answer. Her faculties were still caked, she had not yet found her voice. Presently the widow said, a little resentfully—

"Always been *used* to sleeping together—in fact, *prefer* it. And I was thinking it was to accommodate me. I thought it was very good of them, whereas a person situated as that young man is—"

1. See "Textual Notes" to *Pudd'nhead Wilson*, 61.6, herein.

"Ma, you oughtn't to begin by getting up a prejudice against him. I'm sure he is good hearted and means well. Both of his faces show it."

"I'm not so certain about that. The one on the left—I mean the one on *its* left—hasn't near as good a face, in my opinion, as its brother."

"That's Luigi."

"Yes, Luigi; anyway it's the dark-skinned one; the one that was west of his brother when they stood in the door. Up to all kinds of mischief and disobedience when he was a boy, I'll be bound. I lay his mother had trouble to lay her hand on him when she wanted him. But the one on the right is as good as gold, I can see that."

"That's Angelo."

"Yes, Angelo, I reckon, though I can't tell t'other from which by their names, yet awhile. But it's the right-hand one—the blonde one. He has such kind blue eyes, and curly copper hair and fresh complexion—"

"And such a noble face!—oh, it *is* a noble face, ma, just royal, you may say! And beautiful—deary me, how beautiful! But both are that; the dark one's as beautiful as a picture. There's no such wonderful faces and hand-some heads in this town—none that even begin. And such hands!—especially Angelo's—so shapely and—"

"Stuff, how could you tell which they belonged to?—they had gloves on."

"Why, didn't I see them take off their hats?"

"That don't signify. They might have taken off each other's hats. Nobody could tell. There was just a wormy squirming of arms in the air—seemed to be a couple of dozen of them, all writhing at once, and it just made me dizzy to see them go."

"Why, ma, I hadn't any difficulty. There's two arms on each shoulder—"

"There, now. One arm on each shoulder belongs to each of the creatures, don't it? For a person to have two arms on one shoulder wouldn't do him any good, would it? Of course not. Each has an arm on each shoulder. Now then, you tell me which of them belongs to which, if you can. *They* don't know, themselves—they just work whichever arm comes handy. Of course they do; especially if they are in a hurry and can't stop to think which belongs to which."

The mother seemed to have the rights of the argument, so the daughter abandoned the struggle. Presently the widow rose with a yawn and said—

"Poor thing, I hope it won't catch cold; it was powerful wet, just drenched, you may say. I hope it has left its boots outside, so they can be dried." Then she gave a little start, and looked perplexed. "Now I remember I heard one of them ask Joe to call him at half after seven,—I think it was the one on the left—no, it was the one to the east of the other one—but I didn't hear the other one say anything. I wonder if he wants to be called, too. Do you reckon it's too late to ask?"

"Why, ma, it's not necessary. Calling one is calling both. If one gets up, the other's *got* to."

"Sho, of course; I never thought of that. Well, come along, maybe we can get some sleep, but I don't know, I'm so shook up with what we've been through."

The stranger had made an impression on the boys, too. They had a word of talk as they were getting to bed. Henry, the gentle, the humane, said—

"I feel ever so sorry for it, don't you, Joe?"

But Joe was a boy of this world, active, enterprising, and had a theatrical side to him.

"Sorry? Why how you talk! It can't stir a step without attracting attention. It's just grand!"

Henry said, reproachfully—

"Instead of pitying it, Joe, you talk as if—"

"Talk as if *what*? I know one thing mighty certain: if you can fix me so I can eat for two and only have to stub toes for one, I ain't going to fool away no such chance just for sentiment."

The Twins were wet and tired, and they proceeded to undress without any preliminary remarks. The abundance of sleeves made the partnership coat hard to get off, for it was like skinning a tarantula, but it came at last, after much tugging and perspiring. The mutual vest followed. Then the brothers stood up before the glass, and each took off his own cravat and collar. The collars were of the standing kind, and came high up under the ears, like the sides of a wheelbarrow, as required by the fashion of the day. The cravats were as broad as a bank bill, with fringed ends which stood far out to right and left like the wings of a dragon-fly, and this also was strictly in accordance with the fashion of the time. Each cravat, as to color, was in perfect taste, so far as its owner's complexion was concerned—a delicate pink, in the case of the blonde brother, a violent scarlet in the case of the brunette—but as a combination they broke all the laws of taste known to civilization. Nothing more fiendish and irreconcilable than those shrieking and blaspheming colors could have been contrived. The wet boots gave no end of trouble—to Luigi. When they were off at last, Angelo said, with bitterness—

"I wish you wouldn't wear such tight boots, they hurt my feet."

Luigi answered with indifference—

"My friend, when I am in command of our body, I choose my apparel according to my own convenience, as I have remarked more than several times already. When you are in command, I beg you will do as you please."

Angelo was hurt, and the tears came into his eyes. There was gentle reproach in his voice, but not anger, when he replied:

"Luigi, I often consult your wishes, but you never consult mine. When I am in command I treat you as a guest; I try to make you feel at home; when you are in command you treat me as an intruder, you make me feel unwelcome. It embarrasses me cruelly in company, for I can see that people notice it and comment on it."

"Oh, damn the people," responded the brother languidly, and with the air of one who is tired of the subject.

A slight shudder shook the frame of Angelo, but he said nothing and the conversation ceased. Each buttoned his own share of the night shirt in silence; then Luigi, with Paine's "Age of Reason" in his hand, sat down in one chair and put his feet in another and lit his pipe, while Angelo took his "Whole Duty of Man," and both began to read. Angelo presently began to cough; his coughing increased and became mixed with gaspings for breath, and he was finally obliged to make an appeal to his brother's humanity:

"Luigi, if you would only smoke a little milder tobacco I am sure I could learn not to mind it in time, but this is so strong, and the pipe is so rank that—"

"Angelo, I wouldn't be such a baby! I have learned to smoke in a week, and the trouble is already over with me; if you would try, you could learn, too, and then you would stop spoiling my comfort with your everlasting complaints."

"Ah, brother, that is a strong word—everlasting—and isn't quite fair. I only complain when I suffocate; you know I don't complain when we are in the open air."

"Well, anyway, you could learn to smoke, yourself."

"But my *principles*, Luigi, you forget my principles. You would not have me do a thing which I regard as a sin?"

"Oh, d-bosh!"

The conversation ceased again, for Angelo was sick and discouraged and strangling; but after some time he closed his book and asked Luigi to sing "From Greenland's Icy Mountains" with him, but he would not, and when he tried to sing by himself Luigi did his best to drown his plaintive tenor with a rude and rollicking song delivered in a thundering bass.

After the singing there was silence, and neither brother was happy. Before blowing the light out Luigi swallowed half a tumbler of whisky, and Angelo, whose sensitive organization could not endure intoxicants of any kind, took a pill to keep it from giving him the headache.

Chapter 2

The family sat in the breakfast room waiting for the Twins to come down. The widow was quiet, the daughter was all alive with happy excitement. She said—

"Ah, they're a boon, ma, just a boon! don't you think so?"

"Laws, I hope so, I don't know."

"Why, ma, yes you do. They're so fine, and handsome, and high-bred, and polite, so every way superior to our gawks here in this village; why, they'll make life different from what it was—so humdrum and commonplace, you know—oh, you may be sure they're full of accomplishments, and knowledge of the world, and all that, that will be an immense advantage to society here. Don't you think so, ma?"

"Mercy on me, how should I know, and I've hardly set eyes on them, yet." After a pause, she added, "They made considerable noise after they went up."

"Noise? Why, ma, they were singing! And it was beautiful, too."

"Oh, it was well enough, but too mixed-up, seemed to me."

"Now, ma, honor bright, did you ever hear 'Greenland's Icy Mountains' sung sweeter—now did you?"

"If it had been sung by itself, it would have been uncommon sweet, I don't deny it; but what they wanted to mix it up with 'Old Bob Ridley' for, I can't make out. Why, they don't go together, at all. They are not of the same nature. 'Bob Ridley' is a common rackety slam-bang secular song, one of the rippingest and rantingest and noisiest there is. I am no judge of music, and I don't claim it, but in my opinion nobody can make those two songs go together right."

"Why, ma, I thought—"

"It don't make any difference what you thought, it can't be done. They tried it, and to my mind it was a failure. I never heard such a crazy uproar; seemed to me, sometimes, the roof would come off; and as for the cats—well, I've lived a many a year, and seen cats aggravated in more ways than one, but I've never seen cats take on the way they took on last night."

"Well, I don't think that that goes for anything, ma, because it is the nature of cats that any sound that is unusual—"

"Unusual! You may well call it so. Now if they are going to sing duets every night, I do hope they will both sing the same tune at the same time, for in my opinion a duet that is made up of two different tunes is a mistake; especially when the tunes ain't any kin to one another, that way."

"But ma, I think it must be a foreign custom; and it must be right, too, and the best way, because they have had every opportunity to know what is right, and it don't stand to reason that with their education they would do anything but what the highest musical authorities have sanctioned. You can't help but admit that, ma."

The argument was formidably strong; the

old lady could not find any way around it; so, after thinking it over a while she gave in with a sigh of discontent, and admitted that the daughter's position was probably correct. Being vanquished, she had no mind to continue the topic at that disadvantage, and was about to seek a change when a change came of itself. A footstep was heard on the stairs, and she said—

"There—he's coming!"

"*They*, ma—you ought to say *they*—it's nearer right."

The new lodger, rather shoutingly dressed but looking superbly handsome, stepped with courtly carriage into the trim little breakfast room and put out all his cordial arms at once, like one of those pocket knives with a multiplicity of blades, and shook hands with the whole family simultaneously. He was so easy and pleasant and hearty that all embarrassment presently thawed away and disappeared, and a cheery feeling of friendliness and comradeship took its place. He—or preferably they—were asked to occupy the seat of honor at the foot of the table. They consented with thanks, and carved the beef steak with one set of their hands while they distributed it at the same time with the other set.

"Will you have coffee, gentlemen, or tea?"

"Coffee for Luigi, if you please, madam, tea for me."

"Cream and sugar?"

"For me, yes, madam; Luigi takes his coffee black. Our natures differ a good deal from each other, and our tastes also."

The first time the negro girl Nancy appeared in the door and saw the two heads turned in opposite directions and both talking at once, then saw the commingling arms feed potatoes into one mouth and coffee into the other at the same time, she had to pause and pull herself out of a faintness that came over her; but after that she held her grip and was able to wait on the table with fair courage.

Conversation fell naturally into the customary grooves. It was a little jerky, at first, because none of the family could get smoothly through a sentence without a wobble in it here and a break there, caused by some new surprise in the way of attitude or gesture on the part of the twins. The weather suffered the most. The weather was all finished up and disposed of, as a subject, before the simple Missourians had gotten sufficiently wonted to the spectacle of one body feeding two heads to feel composed and reconciled in the presence of so bizarre a miracle. And even after everybody's mind became tranquilized there was still one slight distraction left: the hand that picked up a biscuit carried it to the wrong head, as often as any other way, and the wrong mouth devoured it. This was a puzzling thing, and marred the talk a little. It bothered the widow to such a degree that she presently dropped out of the conversation without knowing it, and fell to watching, and guessing, and talking to herself:

"Now that hand is going to take that coffee to—no, it's gone to the other mouth; I can't understand it; and now, here is the dark-complected hand with a potatoe on its fork, I'll see what goes with it—there, the light-complected head's got it, as sure as I live!" Finally Rowena said—

"Ma, what is the matter with you? Are you dreaming about something?"

The old lady came to herself, and blushed; then she explained with the first random thing that came into her mind:

"I saw Mr. Angelo take up Mr. Luigi's coffee, and I thought maybe he—shan't I give *you* a cup, Mr. Angelo?"

"Oh, no, madam, I am very much obliged, but I never drink coffee, much as I would like to. You did see me take up Luigi's cup, it is true, but if you noticed, I did not carry it to my mouth, but to his."

"Y-es, I thought you did. Did you mean to?"

"How?"

The widow was a little embarrassed again. She said:

"I don't know but what I'm foolish, and you mustn't mind; but you see, he got the coffee I was expecting to see you drink, and you got a potatoe that I thought he was going to get. So, I thought it might be a mistake all around, and everybody getting what wasn't intended for him."

Both twins laughed, and Luigi said—

"Dear madam, there wasn't any mistake. We are always helping each other that way. It is a great economy for us both; it saves time and labor. We have a system of signs which nobody can notice or understand but ourselves. If I am using both my hands and want some coffee, I make the sign and Angelo furnishes it to me; and you saw that when he needed a potatoe I delivered it."

"How convenient!"

"Yes, and often of the extremest value. Take these Mississippi boats, for instance. They are always overcrowded. There is table-room for only half of the passengers, therefore they have to set a second table for the second half. The stewards rush both parties, they give them no time to eat a satisfying meal, both divisions leave the table hungry. It isn't so with us. Angelo books himself for the one table, I book myself for the other. Neither of us eats anything at the other's table, but just simply works—works. Thus, you see, there are four hands to feed Angelo, and the same four to feed me. Each of us eats two meals."

The old lady was dazed with admiration, and kept saying, "It is *perfectly* wonderful, perfectly wonderful!" and the boy Joe licked his chops enviously but said nothing—at least aloud.

"Yes," continued Luigi, "our construction may have its disadvantages—in fact, *has*—but it also has its compensations, of one sort and another. Take travel, for instance. Travel is enormously expensive, in all countries; we have been obliged to do a vast deal of it—come, Angelo, don't put any more sugar in your tea, I'm just over one indigestion and don't want another right away—been obliged to do a deal of it, as I was saying. Well, we always travel as one person, since we occupy but one seat, so we save half the fare."

"How romantic!" interjected Rowena, with effusion.

"Yes, my dear young lady, and how practical, too, and economical. In Europe, beds in the hotels are not charged with the board, but separately—another saving, for we stood to our rights and paid for the one bed only. The landlords often insisted that as both of us occupied the bed we ought—"

"No, they didn't," said Angelo. "They did it only twice, and in both cases it was a double bed—a rare thing in Europe—and the double bed gave them some excuse. Be fair to the landlords; twice doesn't constitute 'often'."

"Well, that depends—that depends. I knew a man who fell down a well twice. He said he didn't mind the first time, but he thought the second time was once too often. Have I misused that word, Mrs. Cooper?"

"To tell the truth, I was afraid you had, but it seems to look, now, like you hadn't." She stopped, and was evidently struggling with the difficult problem a moment, then she added in the tone of one who is convinced without being converted, "It seems so, but I can't somehow tell why."

Rowena thought Luigi's retort was wonderfully quick and bright, and she remarked to herself with satisfaction that there wasn't any young native of Dawson's Landing that could have risen to the occasion like that. Luigi detected the applause in her face, and expressed his pleasure and his thanks with his eyes, and so eloquently withal, that the girl was proud and pleased, and hung out the delicate sign of it on her cheeks.

Luigi went on, with animation:

"Both of us get a bath for one ticket, theatre seat for one ticket, pew-rent is on the same basis, but at peep-shows we pay double."

"We have much to be thankful for," said Angelo, impressively, with a reverent light in his eye and a reminiscent tone in his voice, "we have been greatly blessed. As a rule, what one of us has lacked, the other, by the bounty of Providence, has been able to supply. My brother is hardy, I am not; he is very masculine, assertive, aggressive, I am much less so. I am subject to illnesses, he is never ill. I cannot abide medicines, and cannot take them, but he has no prejudice against them, and—"

"Why, goodness gracious," interrupted the widow, "when you are sick, does he take the medicine for you?"

"Always, madam."

"Well, I never heard such a thing in my life! I think it's beautiful of you."

"Oh, madam, it's nothing, don't mention it, it's really nothing at all."

"But I say it's beautiful, and I stick to it!" cried the widow, with a speaking moisture in her eye. "A well brother to take the medicine for his poor sick brother—I wish I had such a son," and she glanced reproachfully at her boys. "I declare I'll never rest till I've shook you by the hand," and she scrambled out of her chair in a fever of generous enthusiasm, and made for the twins, blind with her tears, and began to shake. The boy Joe corrected her:

"You're shaking the wrong one, ma."

This flurried her, but she made a swift change and went on shaking.

"Got the wrong one again, ma," said the boy.

"Oh, shut up, can't you!" said the widow, embarrassed and irritated. "Give me *all* your hands, I want to shake them all; for I know you are both just as good as you can be."

It was a victorious thought, a master-stroke of diplomacy, though that never occurred to her and she cared nothing for diplomacy. She shook the four hands in turn cordially, and went back to her place in a state of high and fine exaltation that made her look young and handsome.

"Indeed I owe everything to Luigi," said Angelo, affectionately. "But for him I could not have survived our boyhood days, when we were friendless and poor—ah, so poor! We lived from hand to mouth—lived on the coarse fare of unwilling charity, and for weeks and weeks together not a morsel of food passed my lips, for its character revolted me and I could not eat it. But for Luigi I should have died. He ate for us both."

"How noble!" sighed Rowena.

"Do you hear that?" said the widow, severely, to her boys. "Let it be an example to you—I mean you, Joe."

Joe gave his head a barely perceptible disparaging toss and said—

"Et for both. It ain't anything—I'd a done it."

"Hush, if you haven't got any better manners than that. You don't see the point at all. It wasn't good food."

"I don't care—it was food, and I'd a et it if it was rotten."

"Shame! Such language! Can't you understand? They were starving—actually starving—and he ate for both, and—"

"Shucks! you gimme a chance and I'll—"

"There, now—close your head! and don't you open it again till you're asked."

[Angelo goes on and tells how his parents the Count and Countess had to fly from Florence for political reasons, and died poor in Berlin bereft of their great property by confiscation; and how he and Luigi had to travel with a freak-show during two years and suffer semi-starvation.]

"That hateful black bread! but I seldom ate anything during that time, that was poor Luigi's affair—"

"I'll never *Mister* him again!" cried the widow, with strong emotion, "he's Luigi to me, from this out!"

"Thank you a thousand times, madam, a thousand times! though in truth I don't deserve it."

"Ah, Luigi is always the fortunate one when honors are showering," said Angelo, plaintively, "now what have I done, Mrs. Cooper, that you leave me out? Come, you must strain a point in my favor."

"Call you Angelo? Why, certainly I will; what are you thinking of! In the case of twins, why—"

"But ma, you're breaking up the story—do let him go on."

"You keep still, Rowena Cooper, and he can go on all the better, I reckon. One interruption don't hurt, it's two that makes the trouble."

"But you've added one, now, and that is three."

"Rowena! I will not allow you to talk back at me when you have got nothing rational to say."

Chapter 3

[After breakfast the whole village crowded in, and there was a grand reception in honor of the twins; and at the close of it the gifted "freak" captured everybody's admiration by sitting down at the piano and knocking out a classic four-handed piece in great style. Then the Judge took it—or them—driving in his buggy and showed off his village.]

All along the streets the people crowded the windows and stared at the amazing twins. Troops of small boys flocked after the buggy, excited and yelling. At first the dogs showed no interest. They thought they merely saw three men in a buggy—a matter of no consequence; but when they found out the facts of the case, they altered their opinion pretty radically, and joined the boys, expressing their minds as they came. Other dogs got interested; indeed all the dogs. It was a spirited sight to see them come leaping fences, tearing around corners, swarming out of every by-street and alley. The noise they made was something beyond belief—or praise. They did not seem to be moved by malice, but only by prejudice, the common human prejudice against lack of conformity. If the Twins turned their heads, they broke and fled in every direction, but stopped at a safe distance and faced about, and then formed and came on again as soon as the strangers showed them their back. Negroes and farmers' wives took to the woods when the buggy came upon them suddenly, and altogether the drive was pleasant and animated, and a refreshment all around.

[It was a long and lively drive. Angelo was a Methodist, Luigi was a Freethinker. The Judge was very proud of his Freethinker Society, which was flourishing along in a most prosperous way and already had two members—himself and the obscure and neglected Pudd'nhead Wilson. It was to meet that evening, and he invited Luigi to join; a thing which Luigi was glad to do, partly because it would please himself, and partly because it would gravel Angelo.]

They had now arrived at the widow's gate, and the excursion was ended. The Twins politely expressed their obligations for the pleasant outing which had been afforded them; to which the Judge bowed his thanks, and then said he would now go and arrange for the freethinkers' meeting, and would call for Count Luigi in the evening.

"For you, also, dear sir," he added, hastily, turning to Angelo and bowing. "In addressing myself particularly to your brother, I was not meaning to leave you out. It was an unintentional rudeness, I assure you, and due wholly to accident—accident and preoccupation. I beg you to forgive me."

His quick eye had seen the sensitive blood mount into Angelo's face, betraying the wound that had been inflicted. The sting of the slight had gone deep, but the apology was so prompt, and so evidently sincere, that the hurt was almost immediately healed, and a forgiving smile testified to the kindly Judge that all was well again.

Concealed behind Angelo's modest and unassuming exterior, and unsuspected by any but his intimates, was a lofty pride, a pride of almost abnormal proportions, indeed, and this rendered him ever the prey of slights, and although they were almost always imaginary ones, they hurt none the less on that account. By ill fortune Judge

Driscoll had happened to touch his sorest point, *i.e.,* his conviction that his brother's presence was welcomer everywhere than his own; that he was often invited, out of mere courtesy, where only his brother was wanted, and that in the majority of cases he would not be included in an invitation if he could be left out without offence. A sensitive nature like this is necessarily subject to moods; moods which traverse the whole gamut of feeling; moods which know all the climes of emotion, from the sunny heights of joy to the black abysses of despair. At times, in his seasons of deepest depression, Angelo almost wished that he and his brother might become segregated from each other and be separate individuals, like other men. But of course

as soon as his mind cleared and these dis-eased imaginings passed away, he shuddered at the repulsive thought, and earnestly prayed that it might visit him no more. To be separate, and as other men are! How awk-ward it would seem; how unendurable. What would he do with his hands, his arms? How would his legs feel? How odd, and strange, and grotesque every action, attitude, move-ment, gesture would be. To sleep by himself, eat by himself, walk by himself—how lonely, how unspeakably lonely! No, no, any fate but that. In every way and from every point, the idea was revolting.

This was of course natural; to have felt otherwise would have been unnatural. He had known no life but the combined one; he had been familiar with it from his birth; he was not able to conceive of any other as being agreeable, or even bearable. To him, in the privacy of his secret thoughts, all other men were monsters, deformities; and during three-fourths of his life their aspect had filled him with what promised to be an unconquerable aver-sion. But at eighteen his eye began to take note of female beauty, and, little by little, undefined longings grew up in his heart under whose softening influences the old stubborn aversion gradually diminished, and finally disappeared. Men were still monstrosities to him, still deformities, and in his sober moments he had no desire to be like them, but their strange and unsocial and uncanny construction was no longer offensive to him.

This had been a hard day for him, physically and mentally. He had been called in the morning before he had quite slept off the effects of the liquor which Luigi had drunk; and so, for the first half hour had had the seedy feeling, the languor, the brooding depression, the cobwebby mouth and druggy taste that come of dissipation, and are so ill a preparation for bodily or intellectual activities; the long and violent strain of the reception had followed; and this had been followed, in turn, by the dreary sight-seeing, the Judge's wearying explanations and laudations of the sights, and the stupefying clamor of the dogs. As a congruous conclusion, a fitting end, his feelings had been hurt, a slight had been put upon him. He would have been glad to forego dinner, and betake himself to rest and sleep, but he held his peace and said no word, for he knew his brother. Luigi was fresh, unweary, full of life, spirit, energy, he would have scoffed at the idea of wasting valuable time on a bed or a sofa, and would have refused permission.

Chapter 4

Rowena was dining out, Joe and Harry were belated at play, there were but three chairs and four persons that noon, at the home dinner table—the Twins, the widow, and her chum, Aunt Betsy Hale. The widow soon perceived that Angelo's spirits were as low as Luigi's were high, and also that he had a jaded look. Her motherly solicitude was aroused, and she tried to get him interested in the talk and win him to a happier frame of mind, but the cloud of sadness remained on his countenance. Luigi lent his help, too. He used a form and a phrase which he was always accustomed to employ in these circumstances. He gave his brother an affectionate slap on the shoulder and said, encouragingly—

"Cheer up, the worst is yet to come!"

But this did no good. It never did. If anything, it made the matter worse, as a rule, because it irritated Angelo. This made it a favorite with Luigi. By and by the widow said—

"Angelo, you are tired, you've overdone yourself. You go right to bed, after dinner, and get a good nap and a rest, then you'll be all right."

"Indeed I would give anything if I could do that, madam."

"And what's to hender, I'd like to know? Land, the room's yours, to do what you please with! The idea that you can't do what you like with your own!"

"But, you see, there's one prime essential—an essential of the very first importance—which isn't my own."

"What is that?"

"My body."

The old ladies looked puzzled, and Aunt Betsy Hale said—

"Why, bless your heart, how is that?"

"It's my brother's."

"Your brother's! I don't quite understand. I supposed it belonged to both of you."

"So it does. But not to both at the same time."

"That is mighty curious; I don't see how it can be. I shouldn't think it could be managed that way."

"Oh, it's a good enough arrangement, and goes very well—in fact it wouldn't do to have it otherwise. I find that the Teetotalers and the Anti-Teetotalers, hire the use of the same hall for their meetings. Both parties don't use it at the same time, do they?"

"You bet they don't!" said both old ladies in a breath.

"And moreover," said Aunt Betsy, "the Freethinkers and the Babtist Bible class use the same room over the market-house, but you can take my word for it they don't mush-up together and use it at the same time."

"Very well," said Angelo, "you understand it now. And it stands to reason that the arrangement couldn't be improved. I'll prove it to you. If our legs tried to obey two wills, how could we ever get anywhere? I would start one way, Luigi would start another, at the same moment—the result would be a standstill, wouldn't it?"

"As sure as you are born! Now ain't that wonderful! A body would never have thought of it."

"We should always be arguing and fussing and disputing over the merest trifles. We should lose worlds of time, for we couldn't go down stairs or up, couldn't go to bed, couldn't rise, couldn't wash, couldn't dress, couldn't stand up, couldn't sit down, couldn't even cross our legs without calling a meeting first, and explaining the case, and passing resolutions, and getting consent. It wouldn't ever do—now would it?"

"Do? Why, it would wear a person out in a week! Did you ever hear anything like it, Patsy Cooper?"

"Oh, you'll find there's more than one thing about them that ain't commonplace," said the widow, with the complacent air of a person with a property right in a novelty that is under admiring scrutiny.

"Well, now, how ever do you manage it? I don't mind saying I'm suffering to know."

"He who made us," said Angelo, reverently, "and with us this difficulty, also provided a way out of it. By a mysterious law of our being, each of us has utter and indisputable command of our body a week at a time, turn and turn about."

"Well, I never! Now ain't that beautiful!"

"Yes, it is beautiful and infinitely wise and just. The week ends every Saturday at midnight to the minute, to the second, to the last shade and fraction of a second, infallibly, unerringly, and in that instant the one brother's power over the body vanishes and the other brother takes possession, asleep or awake."

"How marvelous are His ways, and past finding out!"

Luigi said—

"So exactly to the instant does the change come, that during our stay in many of the great cities of the world, the public clocks were regulated by it; and as hundreds of thousands of private clocks and watches were set and corrected in accordance with the public clocks, we really furnished the standard time for the entire city."

"Don't tell me that He don't do miracles any more! Blowing down the walls of Jericho with rams' horns warn't as difficult, in my opinion."

"And that is not all," said Angelo. "A thing that is even more marvelous, perhaps, is the fact that the change takes note of longitude and fits itself to the meridian we are on. Luigi is in command this week. Now, if on Saturday night at a moment before midnight we could fly in an instant to a point fifteen degrees west of here, he would hold possession of the power another hour, for the change observes *local* time and no other."

Betsy Hale was deeply impressed, and said with solemnity—

"Patsy Cooper, for *de*tail it lays over the Passage of the Red Sea."

"No, I shouldn't go as far as that," said Aunt Patsy, "but if you're a mind to say Sodom and Gomorrah, I am with you, Betsy Hale."

"I am agreeable, then, though I do think I was right, and I believe parson Maltby would say the same. Well, now, there's another thing. Suppose one of you wants to borrow the legs a minute from the one that's got them, could he let him?"

"Yes, but we hardly ever do that. There were disagreeable results, several times, and so we very seldom ask or grant the privilege, now-days, and we never even think of such a thing unless the case is extremely urgent. Besides, a week's possession at a time seems so little that we can't bear to spare a minute of it. People who have the use of their legs all the time never think of what a blessing it is, of course. It never occurs to them; it's just their natural ordinary con-dition, and so it does not excite them at all. But when I wake up, on Sunday morning, and it's my week and I feel the power all through me, oh, such a wave of exultation and thanksgiving goes surging over me, and I want to shout 'I can walk! I can walk!' Madam, do you ever, at your uprising, want to shout 'I can walk! I can walk!' "

"No, you poor unfortunate cretur, but I'll never get out of my bed again without *doing* it! Laws, to think I've had this unspeakable bless-ing all my long life and never had the grace to thank the good Lord that gave it to me!"

Tears stood in the eyes of both the old ladies, and the widow said, softly—

"Betsy Hale, we have learnt something, you and me."

The conversation now drifted wide, but by and by floated back once more to that admired detail, the rigid and beautiful impartial-ity with which the possession of power had been distributed between the Twins. Aunt Betsy saw in it a far finer justice than human law exhibits in related cases. She said—

"In my opinion it ain't right now, and never has been right, the way a twin born a quarter of a minute sooner than the other one gets all the land and grandeurs and nobilities in the old countries and his brother has to go bare and be a nobody. Which of you was born first?"

Angelo's head was resting against Luigi's; weariness had overcome him, and for the past five minutes he had been peacefully sleeping. The old ladies had dropped their voices to a lulling drone, to help him steal the rest his brother wouldn't take him up stairs to get. Luigi lis-tened a moment to Angelo's regular breathing, then said in a voice barely audible:

"We were both born at the same time, but I am six months older than he is."

"For the land's sake!—"

"'Sh! don't wake him up; he wouldn't like my telling this. It has always been kept secret till now."

"But how in the world can it be? If you were both born at the same time, how can one of you be older than the other?"

"It is very simple, and I assure you it is true. I was born with a full crop of hair, he was as bald as an egg for six months. I could walk six months before he could make a step. I finished teething six months ahead of him. I began to take solids six months before he left the breast. I began to talk six months before he could say a word. Last, and absolutely unassailable proof, *the sutures in my skull closed six months ahead of his.* Always just that six months difference to a day. Was that accident? Nobody is going to claim that, I'm sure. It was ordained—it was law—it had its meaning, and we know what that meaning was. Now what does this overwhelming body of evidence establish? It establishes just one thing, and that thing it establishes beyond any peradventure whatever. Friends, we would not have it known for the world, and I must beg you to keep it strictly to yourselves, but the truth is, *we are no more twins than you are.*"

The two old ladies were stunned, paralyzed—petrified, one may almost say—and could only sit and gaze vacantly at each other for some moments; then Aunt Betsy Hale said, impressively—

"There's no getting around proofs like that. I do believe it's the most amazing thing I ever heard of." She sat silent a moment or two, and breathing hard with excitement, then she looked up and surveyed the strangers steadfastly a little while, and added, "Well, it does beat me, but I would have took you for twins anywhere."

"So would I, so would I," said Aunt Patsy with the emphasis of a certainty that is not impaired by any shade of doubt.

"*Any*body would—anybody in the world, I don't care who he is," said Aunt Betsy with decision.

"You won't tell," said Luigi, appealingly.

"O, dear no!" answered both ladies promptly, "you can trust us, don't you be afraid."

"That is good of you, and kind. Never let on; treat us always as if we were Twins."

"You can depend on us," said Aunt Betsy, "but it won't be easy, because now that I know you ain't, you don't *seem* so."

Luigi muttered to himself with satisfaction: "That swindle has gone through without change of cars."

It was not very kind of him to load the poor old things up with a secret like that, which would be always flying to their tongues' ends every time they heard any one speak of the strangers as twins, and would become harder and harder to hang on to with every recurrence of the temptation to tell it, while the torture of retaining it would increase with every new strain that was applied, but he never thought of that, and probably would not have worried much about it if he had.

A visitor was announced—some one to see the Twins. They withdrew to the parlor, and the two old ladies began to discuss with interest the strange things which they had been listening to. When they had finished the matter to their satisfaction, and Aunt Betsy rose to go, she stopped to ask a question—

"How does things come on between Roweny and Tom Driscoll?"

"Well, about the same. He writes tolerable often, and she answers tolerable seldom."

"Where is he?"

"In St. Louis, I believe, though he's such a gad-about that a body can't be very certain of him, I reckon."

"Don't Roweny know?"

"Oh, yes, like enough. I haven't asked her lately."

"Do you know how him and the Judge are getting along now?"

"First rate, I believe. Mrs. Pratt says so; and being right in the house, and sister to the one and aunt to t'other, of course she ought to know. She says the Judge is real fond of him when he's away, but frets when he's around and is vexed with his ways, and not sorry to have him go again. He has been gone three weeks this time—a pleasant thing for both of them, I reckon."

"Tom's ruther harum-scarum, but there ain't anything bad in him, I guess."

"Oh, no, he's just young, that's all. Still, twenty-three is old, in one way. A young man ought to be earning his living by that time. If Tom were doing that, or was even trying to do it, the Judge would be a heap better satisfied with him. Tom's always going to begin, but somehow he can't seem to find just the opening he likes."

"Well, now, it's partly the Judge's own fault. Promising the boy his property wasn't the way to set him to earning a fortune of his own. But what do you think—is Roweny beginning to lean any towards him, or ain't she?"

Aunt Patsy had a secret in her bosom; she wanted to keep it there, but nature was too strong for her. She drew Aunt Betsy aside, and said in her most confidential and mysterious manner—

"Don't you breathe a syllable to a soul—I'm going to tell you something. In my opinion Tom Driscoll's chances were considerable better yesterday than they are to-day."

"Patsy Cooper, what *do* you mean?"

"It's so, as sure as you're born. I wish you could a been at breakfast, and seen for yourself."

"You don't mean it!"

"Well, if I'm any judge, there's a leaning—there's a leaning, sure."

"My land! Which one of 'em is it?"

"I can't say for certain, but I think it's the youngest one—Anjy."

Then there were handshakings, and congratulations, and hopes, and so on, and the old ladies parted, perfectly happy—the one in knowing something which the rest of the town didn't, and the other in having been the sole person able to furnish that knowledge.

The visitor who had called to see the Twins was the Rev. Mr. Hotchkiss, pastor of the Baptist church. At the reception Angelo had told him he had lately experienced a change in his religious views, and was now desirous of becoming a Baptist, and would immediately join Mr. Hotchkiss's church. There was no time to say more, and the brief talk ended at that point. The minister was much gratified, and had dropped in for a moment, now, to invite the twins to attend his Bible-class at eight that evening. Angelo accepted, and was expecting Luigi to decline, but he did not, because he knew that the Bible-class and the Freethinkers met in the same room, and he wanted to treat his brother to the embarrassment of being caught in free-thinking company.

Chapter 5

[A long and vigorous quarrel follows, between the twins. And there is plenty to quarrel about, for Angelo was always seeking truth, and this obliged him to change and improve his religion with frequency, which wearied Luigi, and annoyed him too; for he had to be present at each new enlistment—which placed him in the false position of seeming to indorse and approve his brother's fickleness; moreover, he had to go to Angelo's prohibition meetings, and he hated them. On the other hand, when it was *his* week to command the legs he gave Angelo just cause of complaint, for he took him to circuses and horse-races and fandangoes, exposing him to all sorts of censure and criticism; and he drank, too; and whatever he drank went to Angelo's head instead of his own and made him act disgracefully. When the evening was come, the two attended the Freethinkers' meeting, where Angelo was sad and silent; then came the Bible-class and looked upon him coldly, finding him in such company. Then they went to Wilson's house, and Chapter XI. of "Pudd'nhead Wilson" follows, which tells of the girl seen in Tom Driscoll's room; and closes with the kicking of Tom by Luigi at the anti-temperance mass meeting of the Sons of Liberty; with the addition of some account of Roxy's adventures as a chambermaid on a Mississippi boat. Her exchange of the children had been flippantly and farcically described in an earlier chapter.]

Next morning all the town was a-buzz with great news: Pudd'n-head Wilson had a law-case!

The public astonishment was so great and the public curiosity so intense, that when the justice of the peace opened his court the place was packed with people, and even the windows were full. Everybody was flushed and perspiring, the summer heat was almost unendurable.

Tom Driscoll had brought a charge of assault and battery against the Twins. Robert Allen was retained by Driscoll, David Wilson by the defence. Tom, his native cheerfulness unannihilated by his backbreaking and bone-bruising passage across the massed heads of the Sons of Liberty the previous night, laughed his little customary laugh, and said to Wilson—

"I've kept my promise, you see: I'm throwing my business your way. Sooner than I was expecting, too."

"It's very good of you—particularly if you mean to keep it up."

"Well, I can't tell about that, yet. But we'll see. If I find you deserve it I'll take you under my protection and make your fame and fortune for you."

"I'll try to deserve it, Tom."

A jury was sworn in; then Mr. Allen said:

"We will detain your honor but a moment with this case. It is not one where any doubt of the fact of the assault can enter in. These gentlemen—the accused—kicked my client, at the Market Hall last night; they kicked him with violence; with extraordinary violence; with even unprecedented violence, I may say; insomuch that he was lifted entirely off his feet and discharged into the midst of the audience. We can prove this by four hundred witnesses—we shall call but three. Mr. Harkness will take the stand."

Mr. Harkness, being sworn, testified that he was chairman upon the occasion mentioned; that he was close at hand and saw the defendants in this action kick the plaintiff into the air and saw him descend among the audience.

"Take the witness," said Allen.

"Mr. Harkness," said Wilson, "you say you saw these gentlemen, my clients, kick the plaintiff. Are you sure—and please remember that you are on oath—are you perfectly sure that you saw *both* of them kick him, or only one? Now be careful."

A bewildered look began to spread itself over the witness's face. He hesitated, stammered, but got out nothing. His eyes wandered to the Twins and fixed themselves there with a vacant gaze.

"Please answer, Mr. Harkness, you are keeping the court waiting. It is a very simple question."

Counsel for the prosecution broke in with impatience:

"Your honor, the question is an irrelevant triviality. Necessarily they both kicked him, for they have but the one pair of legs, and both are responsible for them."

Wilson said, sarcastically:

"Will your honor permit this new witness to be sworn? He seems to posses knowledge which can be of the utmost value just at this moment—knowledge which would at once dispose of what everyone must see is a very difficult question in this case. Brother Allen, will you take the stand?"

"Go on with your case!" said Allen, petulantly. The audience laughed, and got a warning from the court.

"Now, Mr. Harkness," said Wilson, insinuatingly, "We shall have to insist upon an answer to that question."

"I—er—well, of course I do not absolutely *know*, but in my opinion—"

"Never mind your opinion, sir—answer the question."

"I—why, I *can't* answer it."

"That will do, Mr. Harkness. Stand down."

The audience tittered, and the discomfited witness retired in a state of great embarrassment.

Mr. Wakeman took the stand and swore that he saw the Twins kick the plaintiff off the platform. The defence took the witness.

"Mr. Wakeman, you have sworn that you saw these gentlemen kick the plaintiff. Do I understand you to swear that you saw them *both* do it?"

"Yes, sir"—with decision.

"How do you know that both did it?"

"Because I *saw* them do it."

The audience laughed, and got another warning from the court.

"But by what means do you know that both, and not one, did it?"

"Well, in the first place, the insult was given to both of them equally, for they were called a pair of scissors. Of course they would both want to resent it, and so—"

"Wait! You are theorizing, now. Stick to facts—counsel will attend to the arguments. Go on."

"Well, they both went over there—*that* I saw."

"Very good. Go on."

"And they both kicked him—I swear to it."

"Mr. Wakeman, was Count Luigi, here, willing to join the Sons of Liberty last night?"

"Yes, sir, he was. He did join, too, and drank a glass or two of whisky, like a man."

"Was his brother willing to join?"

"No, sir, he wasn't. He is a teetotaler, and was elected through a mistake."

"Was he given a glass of whisky?"

"Yes, sir, but of course that was another mistake, and not intentional. He wouldn't drink it. He set it down." A slight pause, then he added, casually, and quite simply, "The plaintiff reached for it and hogged it."

There was a fine outburst of laughter, but as the justice was caught out, himself, his reprimand was not very vigorous.

Mr. Allen jumped up and exclaimed:

"I protest against these foolish irrelevancies. What have they to do with the case?"

Wilson said:

"Calm yourself, brother; it was only an experiment. Now, Mr. Wakeman, if one of these gentlemen chooses to join an association and the other doesn't; and if one of them enjoys whisky and the other doesn't, but sets it aside and leaves it unprotected," [titter from the audience], "it seems to show that they have independent minds and tastes and preferences, and that one of them is able to approve of a thing at the very moment that the other is heartily disapproving of it. Doesn't it seem so to you?"

"Certainly it does. It's perfectly plain."

"Now, then, it might be—I only say it might be—that one of these brothers wanted to kick the plaintiff last night, and that the other didn't want that humiliating punishment inflicted upon him in that public way and before all those people. Isn't that possible?"

"Of course it is. It's more than possible. I don't believe the blonde one would kick anybody. It was the other one that—"

"Silence!" shouted the plaintiff's counsel, and went on with an angry sentence which was lost in the wave of laughter that swept the house.

"That will do, Mr. Wakeman," said Wilson, "you may stand down."

The third witness was called. He had seen the Twins kick the plaintiff. Mr. Wilson took the witness.

"Mr. Rogers, you say you saw these accused gentlemen kick the plaintiff."

"Yes, sir."

"Both of them?"

"Yes, sir."

"Which of them kicked him first?"

"Why—they—they both kicked him at the same time."

"Are you perfectly sure of that?"

"Yes, sir."

"What makes you sure of it?"

"Why, I stood right behind them, and *saw* them do it."

"How many kicks were delivered?"

"Only one."

"If two men kick, the result should be two kicks, shouldn't it?"

"Why—why—yes, as a rule."

"Then what do you think went with the other kick?"

"I—well—the fact is, I wasn't thinking of two being necessary, this time."

"What do you think now?"

"Well, I—I'm sure I don't quite know what to think, but I reckon that one of them did half of the kick and the other one did the other half."

Somebody in the crowd sung out:

"It's the first sane thing that any of them has said."

The audience applauded. The judge said—

"Silence! or I will clear the court."

Mr. Allen looked pleased, but Wilson did not seem disturbed. He said:

"Mr. Rogers, you have favored us with what you think and what you reckon, but as thinking and reckoning are not evidence, I will now give you a chance to come out with something positive, one way or the other, and shall require you to produce it. I will ask the accused to stand up and repeat the phenomenal kick of last night." The Twins stood up. "Now, Mr. Rogers, please stand behind them."

A Voice: "No, stand in front!" [Laughter. Silenced by the court.]

Another Voice: "No, give Tommy another highst!" [Laughter. Sharply rebuked by the court.]

"Now, then, Mr. Rogers, two kicks shall be delivered, one after the other, and I give you my word that at least one of the two shall be delivered by one of the Twins alone, without the slightest assistance from his brother. Watch sharply, for you have got to render a decision without any ifs or ands in it." Rogers bent himself behind the Twins, with his palms just above his knees, in the modern attitude of the catcher at a base-ball match, and riveted his eyes on the pair of legs in front of him. "Are you ready, Mr. Rogers?"

"Ready, sir."

"Kick!"

The kick was launched.

"Have you got that one classified, Mr. Rogers?"

"Let me study a minute, sir."

"Take as much time as you please. Let me know when you are ready."

For as much as a minute Rogers pondered, with all eyes and a breathless interest fastened upon him. Then he gave the word—

"Ready, sir."

"Kick!"

The kick that followed was an exact duplicate of the first one.

"Now, then, Mr. Rogers, one of those kicks was an individual kick, not a mutual one. You will now state positively which was the mutual one."

The witness said, with a crest-fallen look—

"I've got to give it up. There ain't any man in the world that could tell t'other from which, sir."

"Do you still assert that last night's kick was a mutual kick?"

"Indeed I don't, sir."

"That will do, Mr. Rogers. If my brother Allen desires to address the court, your honor, very well; but as far as I am concerned I am ready to let the case be at once delivered into the hands of this intelligent jury without comment."

Mr. Justice Robinson had been in office only two months, and in that short time had not had many cases to try, of course. He had no knowledge of laws and courts except what he had picked up since he came into office. He was a sore trouble to the lawyers, for his rulings were pretty eccentric sometimes, and he stood by them with Roman simplicity and fortitude; but the people were well satisfied with him, for they saw that his intentions were always right, that he was entirely impartial, and that he usually made up in good sense what he lacked in technique, so to speak. He now perceived that there was likely to be a miscarriage of justice here, and he rose to the occasion.

"Wait a moment, gentlemen," he said, "it is plain that an assault has been committed—it is plain to anybody; but the way things are going, the guilty will certainly escape conviction. I cannot allow this. Now—"

"But your honor!" said Wilson, interrupting him, earnestly but respectfully, "you are deciding the case of yourself, whereas the jury—"

"Never mind the jury, Mr. Wilson; the jury will have a chance when there is a reasonable doubt for them to take hold of—which there isn't, so far. There is no doubt whatever that an assault has been committed. The attempt to show that both of the accused committed it has failed. Are they both to escape justice on that account? Not in this court, if I can prevent it. It appears to have been a mistake to bring the charge against them as a corporation; each should have been charged in his capacity as an individual, and—"

"But your honor!" said Wilson, "in fairness to my clients I must insist that inasmuch as the prosecution did not separate the—"

"No wrong will be done your clients, sir—they will be protected; also the public and the offended law. Mr. Allen, you will amend your pleadings, and put one of the accused on trial at a time."

Wilson broke in—

"But your honor! this is wholly unprecedented! To imperil an accused person by arbitrarily altering and widening the charge against him in order to compass his conviction when the charge as originally brought promises to fail to convict, is a thing unheard of before."

"Unheard of *where*?"

"In the courts of this or any other State."

The judge said, with dignity—

"I am not acquainted with the customs of other courts, and am not concerned to know what they are. I am responsible for this court, and I cannot conscientiously allow my judgment to be warped and my judicial liberty hampered by trying to conform to the caprices of other courts, be they—"

"But your honor, the oldest and highest courts in Europe—"

"This court is not run on the European plan, Mr. Wilson; it is not run on any plan but its own. It has a plan of its own; and that plan is, to find justice for both State and accused, no matter what happens to be practice and custom in Europe or anywhere else." [Great applause.] "Silence! It has not been the custom of this court to imitate other courts; it has not been the custom of this court to take shelter behind the decisions of other courts, and we will not begin now. We will do the best we can by the light that God has given us, and while this court continues to have His approval, it will remain indifferent to what other organizations may think of it." [Applause.] "Gentlemen, I *must* have order!—quiet yourselves! Mr. Allen, you will now proceed against the prisoners one at a time. Go on with the case."

Allen was not at his ease. However, after whispering a moment with his client and with one or two other people, he rose and said:

"Your honor, I find it to be reported and believed that the accused are able to act independently in many ways, but that this independence does not extend to their legs, authority over their legs being vested exclusively in the one brother during a specific term of days, and then passing to the other brother for a like term, and so on, by regular alternation. I could call witnesses who would prove that the accused had revealed to them the existence of this extraordinary fact, and had also made known which of them was in possession of the legs yesterday—and this would of course indicate where the guilt of the assault belongs—but as this would be mere hearsay evidence, these revelations not having been made under oath—"

"Never mind about that, Mr. Allen. It may not all be hearsay. We shall see. It may at least help to put us on the right track. Call the witnesses."

"Then I will call Mr. John Buckstone, who is now present; and I beg that Mrs. Patsy Cooper may be sent for. Take the stand, Mr. Buckstone."

Buckstone took the oath, and then testified that on the previous evening the Count Angelo Cappello had protested against going to the hall, and had called all present to witness that he was going by compulsion and would not go if he could help himself. Also, that the Count Luigi had replied sharply that he would *go*, just the same, and that he, Count Luigi, would see to that, himself. Also, that upon Count Angelo's complaining about being kept on his legs so long, Count Luigi retorted with apparent surprise, "*Your* legs!—I like your impudence!"

"*Now* we are getting at the kernel of the thing," observed the judge, with grave and earnest satisfaction. "It looks as if the Count Luigi was in possession of the battery at the time of the assault."

Nothing further was elicited from Mr. Buckstone on direct examination. Mr. Wilson took the witness.

"Mr. Buckstone, about what time was it that that conversation took place?"

"Toward nine yesterday evening, sir."

"Did you then proceed directly to the hall?"

"Yes, sir."

"How long did it take you to go there?"

"Well, we walked; and as it was from the extreme edge of the town, and there was no hurry, I judge it took us about twenty minutes, maybe a trifle more."

"About what hour was the kick delivered?"

"At thirteen minutes and a half to ten."

"Admirable! You are a pattern witness, Mr. Buckstone. How did you happen to look at your watch at that particular moment?"

"I always do it when I see an assault. It's likely I shall be called as a witness, and it's a good point to have."

"It would be well if others were as thoughtful. Was anything said, between the conversation at my house and the assault, upon the detail which we are now examining into?"

"No, sir."

"If power over the mutual legs was in the possession of one brother at nine, and passed into the possession of the other one during the next thirty or forty minutes, do you think you could have detected the change?"

"By no means!"

"That is all, Mr. Buckstone."

Mrs. Patsy Cooper was called. The crowd made way for her, and she came smiling and bowing through the narrow human lane, with Betsy Hale, as escort and support, smiling and bowing in her wake, the audience breaking into welcoming cheers as the old favorites filed along. The judge did not check this kindly demonstration of homage and affection, but let it run its course unrebuked.

The old ladies stopped and shook hands with the Twins with effusion, then gave the judge a friendly nod and bustled into the seats provided for them. They immediately began to deliver a volley of eager questions at the friends around them: "What is this thing for?" "What is that thing for?" "Who is that young man that's writing at the desk?—why, I declare it's Jake Bunce!—I thought he was sick." "Which is the jury?" "Why, is *that* the jury? Billy Price, and Job Turner, and Jack Lounsbury, and—well, I never!" "Now who would ever a thought—"

But they were gently called to order at this point and asked not to talk in court. Their tongues fell silent, but the radiant interest in their faces remained, and their gratitude for the blessing of a new sensation and a novel experience still beamed undimmed from their eyes. Aunt Patsy stood up and took the oath, and Mr. Allen explained the point in issue and asked her to go on, now, in her own way, and throw as much light upon it as she could. She toyed with her reticule a moment or two, as if considering where to begin, then she said:

"Well, the way of it is this. They are Luigi's legs a week at a time, and then they are Angelo's, and he can do whatever he wants to with them."

"You are making a mistake, Aunt Patsy Cooper," said the judge. "You shouldn't state that as a *fact*, because you don't know it to *be* a fact."

"What's the reason I don't?" said Aunt Patsy, bridling a little.

"What is the reason that you do know it?"

"The best in the world—because they told me."

"That isn't a reason."

"Well, for the land's sake! Betsy Hale, do you hear that?"

"*Hear* it?—I should think so," said Aunt Betsy, rising and facing the court. "Why Judge, I was there and heard it myself. Luigi says to Angelo—no, it was Angelo said it to—"

"Come-come, Mrs. Hale, pray sit down, and—"

"Certainly, it's all right, I'm going to sit down presently, but not until I've—"

"But you *must* sit down!"

"*Must!* Well, upon my word if things ain't getting to a pretty pass when—"

The house broke into laughter but was promptly brought to order, and meantime Mr. Allen persuaded the old lady to take her seat. Aunt Patsy continued:

"Yes, they told me that, and I know it's true. They're Luigi's legs this week, but—"

"Ah, *they* told you that, did they?" said the justice, with interest.

"Well, no, I don't know that they *told* me, but that's neither here nor there; I know, without that, that at dinner yesterday, Angelo was as tired as a dog, and yet Luigi wouldn't lend him the legs to go up stairs and take a nap with."

"Did he ask for them?"

"Let me see—it seems to me somehow, that—that—Aunt Betsy, do you remember whether he—"

"Never mind about what Aunt Betsy remembers, she is not a witness; we only want to know what you remember, yourself," said the judge.

"Well, it does seem to me that you are most cantankerously particular about a little thing, Sim Robinson. Why, when I can't remember a thing myself, I always—"

"Ah, *please* go on!"

"Now how *can* she, when you keep fussing at her all the time?" said Aunt Betsy. "Why, with a person pecking at *me* that way, I should get that fuzzled and fuddled that—"

She was on her feet again, but Allen coaxed her into her seat once more while the court squelched the mirth of the house. Then the judge said:

"Madam, do you know—do you absolutely *know*, independently of anything these gentlemen have told you—that the power over their legs passes from the one to the other regularly every week?"

"Regularly? Bless your heart, regularly ain't any name for the exactness of it! All the big cities in Europe used to set the clocks by it." [Laughter, *suppressed by the court*.]

"How do you *know*? That is the question. Please answer it plainly and squarely."

"Don't you talk to me like that, Sim Robinson—I won't have it. How do I know, indeed! How do *you* know what you know? Because somebody told you. You didn't invent it out of your own head, did you? Why, these Twins are the truthfulest people in the world; and I don't think it becomes you to sit up there and throw slurs at them when they haven't been doing anything to you. And they are orphans besides,—both of them. All—"

But Aunt Betsy was up again, now, and both old ladies were talking at once and with all their might, but as the house was weltering in a storm of laughter and the judge was hammering his desk with an iron paper-weight, one could only see them talk, not hear them. At last when quiet was restored, the court said—

"Let the ladies retire."

"But your honor, I have the right, in the interest of my clients, to cross-exam—"

"You'll not need to exercise it Mr. Wilson—the evidence is thrown out."

"Thrown out!" said Aunt Patsy, ruffled; "and what's it thrown out, for, I'd like to know."

"And so would I, Patsy Cooper. It seems to me that if we can save these poor persecuted strangers, it is our bounden duty to stand up here and talk for them till—"

"There, there, there, *do* sit down!"

It cost some trouble and a good deal of coaxing, but they were got into their seats at last. The trial was soon ended, now. The Twins themselves became witnesses in their own defence. They established the fact,

upon oath, that the leg-power passed from the one to the other every Saturday night at twelve o'clock, sharp. But on cross-examination their counsel would not allow them to tell whose week of power the current week was. The judge insisted upon their answering, and proposed to compel them, but even the prosecution took fright and came to the rescue then and helped stay the sturdy jurist's revolutionary hand. So the case had to go to the jury with that important point hanging in the air. They were out an hour, and brought in this verdict:

"We the jury do find: 1, that an assault was committed, as charged; 2, that it was committed by one of the persons accused, he having been seen to do it by several credible witnesses; 3, but that his identity is so merged in his brother's that we have not been able to tell which was him. We cannot convict both, for only one is guilty. We cannot acquit both, for only one is innocent. Our verdict is that justice has been defeated by the dispensation of God, and ask to be discharged from further duty."

This was read aloud in court, and brought out a burst of hearty applause. The old ladies made a spring at the Twins, to shake and congratulate, but were gently disengaged by Mr. Wilson and softly crowded back into their places.

The Judge rose in his little tribune, laid aside his silver-bowed spectacles, roached his gray hair up with his fingers, and said, with dignity and solemnity, and even with a certain pathos:

"In all my experience on the bench I have not seen Justice bow her head in shame in this court until this day. You little realize what far-reaching harm has just been wrought here under the fickle forms of law. Imitation is the bane of courts—I thank God that this one is free from the contamination of that vice—and in no long time you will see the fatal work of this hour seized upon by profligate so-called guardians of justice in all the wide circumference of this planet and perpetuated in their pernicious decisions. I wash my hands of this iniquity. I would have compelled these culprits to expose their guilt, but support failed me where I had most right to expect aid and encouragement. And I was confronted by a law made in the interest of crime, which protects the criminal from testifying against himself. Yet I had precedents of my own whereby I had set aside that law on two different occasions and thus succeeded in convicting criminals to whose crimes there were no witnesses but them-

selves. What have you accomplished this day? Do you realize it? You have set adrift, unadmonished, in this community, two men endowed with an awful and mysterious gift, a hidden and grisly power for evil—a power by which each in his turn may commit crime after crime of the most heinous character, and no man be able to tell which is the guilty or which the innocent party in any case of them all. Look to your homes—look to your property—look to your lives— for you have need!

"Prisoners at the bar, stand up. Through suppression of evidence, a jury of your—our—countrymen have been obliged to deliver a verdict concerning your case which stinks to heaven with the rankness of its injustice. By its terms you, the guilty one, go free with the innocent. Depart in peace, and come no more! The costs devolve upon the outraged plaintiff—another iniquity. The court stands dissolved."

Almost everybody crowded forward to overwhelm the Twins and their counsel with congratulations; but presently the two old aunties dug the duplicates out and bore them away in triumph through the hurrahing crowds, while lots of new friends carried Pudd'nhead Wilson off tavernwards to feast him and "wet down" his great and victorious entry into the legal arena. To Wilson, so long familiar with neglect and depreciation, this strange new incense of popularity and admiration was as a fragrance blown from the fields of paradise. A happy man was Wilson.

Chapter 6

[A deputation came in the evening and conferred upon Wilson the welcome honor of a nomination for mayor; for the village has just been converted into a city by charter. Tom skulks out of challenging the twins. Judge Driscoll thereupon challenges Angelo, (accused by Tom of doing the kicking;) he declines, but Luigi accepts in his place against Angelo's timid protest.]

It was late Saturday night—nearing eleven.

The Judge and his second found the rest of the war party at the further end of the vacant ground, near the haunted house. Pudd'n-head Wilson advanced to meet them, and said anxiously—

"I must say a word in behalf of my principal's proxy, Count Luigi, to whom you have kindly granted the privilege of fighting my principal's battle for him. It is growing late, and Count Luigi is in great trouble lest midnight shall strike before the finish."

"It is another testimony," said Howard, approvingly. "That young man is fine all through. He wishes to save his brother the sorrow of fighting on the Sabbath, and he is right; it is the right and manly feeling and does him credit. We will make all possible haste."

Wilson said—

"There is also another reason—a consideration, in fact, which deeply concerns Count Luigi himself. These Twins have command of their mutual legs turn about. Count Luigi is in command, now; but at midnight, possession will pass to my principal, Count Angelo, and—well, you can foresee what will happen. He will march straight off the field, and carry Luigi with him."

"Why! sure enough!" cried the Judge, "we have heard something about that extraordinary law of their being, already—nothing very definite, it is true, as regards dates and durations of the power, but I see it is definite enough as regards to-night. Of course we must give Luigi every chance. Omit all the ceremonial possible, gentlemen, and place us in position."

The seconds at once tossed up a coin; Howard won the choice. He placed the Judge sixty feet from the haunted house and facing it; Wilson placed the Twins within fifteen feet of the house and facing the Judge—necessarily. The pistol-case was opened and the long slim tubes taken out; when the moonlight glinted from them a shiver went through Angelo. The doctor was a fool, but a thoroughly well-meaning one, with a kind heart and a sincere disposition to oblige, but along with it an absence of tact which often hurt its effectiveness. He brought his box of lint and bandages, and asked Angelo to feel and see how soft and comfortable they were. Angelo's head fell over against Luigi's in a faint, and precious time was lost in bringing him to; which provoked Luigi into expressing his mind to the doctor with a good deal of vigor and frankness. After Angelo came to he was still so weak that Luigi was obliged to drink a stiff horn of brandy to brace him up.

The seconds now stepped at once to their posts, half way between

the combatants, one of them on each side of the line of fire. Wilson
was to count, very deliberately, "One——two——three——fire!——
stop!" and the duelists could bang away at any time they chose during that recitation, but not after the last word. Angelo grew very
nervous when he saw Wilson's hand rising slowly into the air as a sign
to make ready, and he leaned his head against Luigi's and said—

"O, please take me away from here, I can't stay, I know I can't!"

"What in the world are you doing? Straighten up! What's the matter with you?—*you're* in no danger—nobody's going to shoot at you.
Straighten up, I tell you!"

Angelo obeyed, just in time to hear—

"One——!"

"Bang!" Just one report, and a little tuft of
white hair floated slowly to the Judge's feet in
the moonlight. The Judge did not swerve; he
still stood, erect and motionless, like a statue,
with his pistol-arm hanging straight down at
his side. He was reserving his fire.

"Two——!

"Three——!

"Fire!——"

Up came the pistol-arm instantly—Angelo
dodged with the report. He said "Ouch!" and
fainted again.

The doctor examined and bandaged the
wound. It was of no consequence, he said—
bullet through fleshy part of arm—no bones
broken—the gentleman was still able to
fight—let the duel proceed.

Next time, Angelo jumped just as Luigi
fired; which disordered his aim and caused
him to cut a chip out of Howard's ear. The
Judge took his time again, and when he fired

Angelo jumped, and got a knuckle skinned. The doctor inspected and dressed the wounds. Angelo now spoke out and said he was content with the satisfaction he had got, and if the Judge—but Luigi shut him roughly up, and asked him not to make an ass of himself; adding—

"And I want you to stop dodging. You take a great deal too prominent a part in this thing for a person who has got nothing to do with it. You should remember that you are here only by courtesy, and are without official recognition; officially you are not here at all; officially you do not even exist. To all intents and purposes you are absent from this place, and you ought for your own modesty's sake to reflect that it cannot become a person who is not present here to be taking this sort of public and indecent prominence in a matter in which he is not in the slightest degree concerned. Now don't dodge again; the bullets are not for you, they are for me; if I want them dodged I will attend to it myself. I never saw a person act so."

Angelo saw the reasonableness of what his brother had said, and he did try to reform, but it was of no use; both pistols went off at the same instant, and he jumped once more; he got a sharp scrape along his cheek from the Judge's bullet, and so deflected Luigi's aim that his ball went wide and chipped a flake of skin from Pudd'nhead Wilson's chin. The doctor attended to the wounded.

By the terms, the duel was over. But Luigi was entirely out of patience, and begged for one more exchange of shots, insisting that he had had no fair chance, on account of his brother's indelicate behavior. Howard was opposed to granting so unusual a privilege, but the Judge took Luigi's part, and added that indeed he himself might fairly be considered entitled to another trial, because although the proxy on the other side was in no way to blame for his (the Judge's) humiliatingly resultless work, the gentleman with whom he was fighting this duel was to blame for it, since if he had played no advantages and had held his head still, his proxy would have been disposed of early. He added—

"Count Luigi's request for another exchange is another proof that he is a brave and chivalrous gentleman, and I beg that the courtesy he asks may be accorded him."

"I thank you most sincerely for this generosity, Judge Driscoll," said Luigi, with a polite bow, and moving to his place. Then he added—to Angelo, "Now hold your grip, hold your *grip*, I tell you, and I'll land him, sure!"

The men stood erect, their pistol-arms at their sides, the two seconds stood at their official posts, the doctor stood five paces in Wilson's rear with his instruments and bandages in his hands. The deep stillness,

the peaceful moonlight, the motionless figures, made an impressive picture, and the
impending fatal possibilities augmented this
impressiveness to solemnity. Wilson's hand
began to rise—slowly—slowly—higher—
still higher——in another moment—

"*Boom!*"—the first stroke of midnight
swung up out of the distance. Angelo was off
like a deer!

"Oh, you unspeakable traitor!" wailed his
brother, as they went soaring over the fence.

The others stood astonished and gazing;
and so stood, watching that strange spectacle until distance dissolved it and swept it
from their view. Then they rubbed their eyes
like people waking out of a dream.

"Well, I've never seen anything like that
before!" said the Judge. "Wilson, I am going
to confess, now, that I wasn't quite able to
believe in that leg-business, and had a suspicion that it was a put-up convenience
between those Twins; and when Count
Angelo fainted I thought I saw the whole
scheme—thought it was pretext No. 1, and
would be followed by others till twelve
o'clock should arrive and Luigi would get off
with all the credit of seeming to want to fight
and yet not have to fight, after all. But I was
mistaken. His pluck proved it. He's a brave
fellow and did want to fight."

"There isn't any doubt about that," said

Howard, and added in a grieved tone, "but what an unworthy sort of Christian that Angelo is—I hope and believe there are not many like him. It is not right to engage in a duel on the Sabbath—I could not approve of that, myself; but to finish one that has been begun—that is a duty, let the day be what it may."

They strolled along, still wondering, still talking.

"It is a curious circumstance," remarked the surgeon, halting Wilson a moment to paste some more court plaister on his chin, which had gone to leaking blood again, "that in this duel neither of the parties who handled the pistols lost blood, while nearly all the persons present in the mere capacity of guests got hit. I have not heard of such a thing before. Don't you think it unusual?"

"Yes," said the Judge, "it has struck me as peculiar. Peculiar and unfortunate. I was annoyed at it, all the time. In the case of Angelo it made no great difference, because he was in a measure concerned, though not officially; but it troubled me to see the seconds compromised, and yet I knew no way to mend the matter."

"There was no way to mend it," said Howard, whose ear was being readjusted now by the doctor; "the code fixes our place, and it would not have been lawful to change it. If we could have stood at your side, or behind you, or in front of you, it—but it would not have been legitimate, and the other parties would have had a just right to complain of our trying to protect ourselves from danger; infractions of the code are certainly not permissible in any case whatsoever."

Wilson offered no remarks. It seemed to him that there was very little place here for so much solemnity, but he judged that if a duel where nobody was in danger or got crippled but the seconds and the outsiders had nothing ridiculous about it for these gentlemen, his pointing out that feature would probably not help them to see it.

He invited them in to take a nightcap, and Howard and the Judge accepted, but the doctor said he would have to go and see how Angelo's principal wound was getting on.

[It was now Sunday, and in the afternoon Angelo was to be received into the Baptist communion by immersion—a doubtful prospect, the doctor feared.]

Chapter 7

When the doctor arrived at Aunt Patsy Cooper's house, he found the lights going and everybody up and dressed and in a great state of solicitude and excitement. The Twins were stretched on a sofa in the sitting room, Aunt Patsy was fussing at Angelo's arm, Nancy was flying around under her commands, the two young boys were trying to keep out of the way and always getting in it, in order to see and wonder, Rowena stood apart, helpless with apprehension and emotion, and Luigi was growling in unappeasable fury over Angelo's shameful flight.

As has been reported before, the doctor was a fool—a kind-hearted and well-meaning one, but with no tact; and as he was by long odds the most learned physician in the town, and was quite well aware of it, and could talk his learning with ease and precision, and liked to show off when he had an audience, he was sometimes tempted into revealing more of a case than was good for the patient.

He examined Angelo's wound, and was really minded to say nothing, for once; but Aunt Patsy was so anxious and so pressing that he allowed his caution to be overcome, and proceeded to empty himself as follows, with scientific relish—

"Without going too much into detail, madam—for you would probably not understand it anyway—I concede that great care is going to be necessary here; otherwise exudation of the aesophagus is nearly sure to ensue, and this will be followed by ossification and extradition of the maxillario superioris, which must decompose the granular surfaces of the great infusorial ganglionic system, thus obstructing the action of the posterior varioloid arteries and precipitating compound strangulated sorosis of the valvular tissues, and ending unavoidably in the dispersion and combustion of the marsupial fluxes and the consequent embrocation of the bi-cuspid populo redax referendum rotulorum."

A miserable silence followed. Aunt Patsy's heart sank, the pallor of despair invaded her face, she was not able to speak; poor Rowena wrung her hands in privacy and silence, and said to herself in the bitterness of her young grief, "There is no hope—it is plain there is no hope;" the good-hearted negro wench, Nancy, paled to chocolate, then to orange, then to amber, and thought to herself with yearning sympathy and sorrow, "Po' thing, he ain' gwyne to las' thoo de half o'

dat;" small Henry choked up, and turned his head away to hide his rising tears, and his brother Joe said to himself, with a sense of loss, "The babtizing's busted, that's sure." Luigi was the only person who had any heart to speak. He said, a little bit sharply, to the doctor—

"Well, well, there's nothing to be gained by wasting precious time: give him a barrel of pills—I'll take them for him."

"You?" asked the doctor.

"Yes. Did you suppose he was going to take them himself?"

"Why, of course."

"Well, it's a mistake. He never took a dose of medicine in his life. He can't."

"Well, upon my word, it's the most extraordinary thing I ever heard of!"

"Oh," said Aunt Patsy, as pleased as a mother whose child is being admired and wondered at, "you'll find that there's more about them that's wonderful than their just being made in the image of God like the rest of His creatures, now you can depend on that, *I* tell you," and she wagged her complacent head like one who could reveal marvelous things if she chose.

The boy Joe began—

"Why, ma, they *ain't* made in the im—"

"You shut up, and wait till you're asked, Joe. I'll let you know when I want help. Are you looking for something, doctor?"

The doctor asked for a few sheets of paper

and a pen, and said he would write a prescription—which he did. It was one of Galen's; in fact it was Galen's favorite, and had been slaying people for sixteen thousand years. Galen used it for everything, applied it to everything, said it would remove everything, from warts all the way through to lungs—and it generally did. Galen was still the only medical authority recognized in Missouri, his practice was the only practice known to the Missouri doctors, and his prescriptions were the only ammunition they carried when they went out for game. By and by Dr. Claypool laid down his pen and read the result of his labors aloud, carefully and deliberately, for this battery must be constructed on the premises by the family, and mistakes could occur; for he wrote a doctor's hand—the hand which from the beginning of time has been so disastrous to the apothecary and so profitable to the undertaker:

> Take of Afarabocca, Henbane, Carpobalsamum, each two Drams and a half; of Cloves, Opium, Myrrh, Cyperus, each two Drams; of Opobalsamum, Indian Leaf, Cinamon, Zedoary, Ginger, Coftus, Coral, Cassia, Euphorbium, Gum Tragacanth, Frankincense, Styrax Calamita, Celtic, Nard, Spignel, Hartwort, Mustard, Saxifrage, Dill, Anise, each one Dram; of Xylaloes, Rheum Ponticum, Alipta Moschata, Castor, Spikenard, Galangals, Opoponax, Anacardium, Mastich, Brimstone, Peony, Eringo, Pulp of Dates, red and white Hermodactyls, Roses, Thyme, Acorns, Penyroyal, Gentian, the Bark of the Root of Mandrake, Germander, Valerian, Bishops Weed, Bay-Berries, long and white Pepper, Xylobalsamum, Carnabadium, Macodonian, Parsley-seeds, Lovage, the Seeds of Rue, and Sinon, of each a Dram and a half; of pure Gold, pure Silver, Pearls not perforated, the Blatta Byzantina, the Bone of the Stag's Heart, of each the Quantity of fourteen Grains of Wheat; of Sapphire, Emerald, and Jasper Stones, each one Dram; of Hasle-nut, two Drams; of Pellitory of Spain, Shavings of Ivory, Calamus Odoratus, each the Quantity of twenty-nine Grains of

Wheat; of Honey or Sugar a sufficient Quantity. Boil down and skim off.

"There," he said, "that will fix the patient; give his brother a dipperful every three-quarters of an hour—"

—"while he survives," muttered Luigi—

—"and see that the room is kept wholesomely hot and the doors and windows closed tight. Keep Count Angelo nicely covered up with six or seven blankets, and when he is thirsty—which will be frequently—moisten a rag in the vapor of the tea-kettle and let his brother suck it. When he is hungry—which will also be frequently—he must not be humored oftener than every seven or eight hours; then toast part of a cracker until it begins to brown, and give it to his brother."

"That is all very well, as far as Angelo is concerned," said Luigi, "but what I am I to eat?"

"I do not see that there is anything the matter with you," the doctor answered, "You may of course eat what you please."

"And also drink what I please, I suppose?"

"Oh, certainly—at present. When the violent and continuous perspiring has reduced your strength, I shall have to reduce your diet, of course, and also bleed you, but there is no occasion for that yet awhile." He turned to Aunt Patsy and said: "He must be put to bed, and sat up with, and tended with the greatest care, and not allowed to stir for several days and nights."

"For one, I'm sacredly thankful for that," said Luigi, "it postpones the funeral—I'm not to be drowned to-day, anyhow."

Angelo said quietly to the doctor:

"I will cheerfully submit to all your requirements, sir, up to two o'clock this afternoon, and will resume them after three, but I cannot be confined to the house during that intermediate hour."

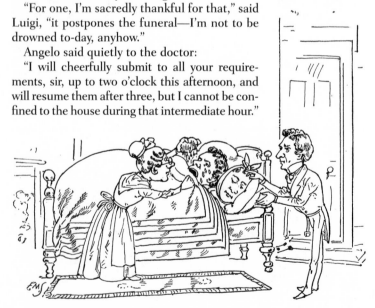

"Why, may I ask?"

"Because I have entered the Baptist communion, and by appointment am to be baptised in the river at that hour."

"O, insanity!—it cannot be allowed!"

Angelo answered with placid firmness—

"Nothing shall prevent it, if I am alive."

"Why, consider, my dear sir, in your condition it might prove fatal."

A tender and ecstatic smile beamed from Angelo's eyes and he broke forth in a tone of joyous fervency—

"Ah, how blessed it would be to die for such a cause—it would be martyrdom!"

"But your brother—consider your brother; you would be risking his life, too."

"He risked mine an hour ago," responded Angelo, gloomily; "did he consider me?" A thought swept through his mind that made him shudder. "If I had not run, I might have been killed in a duel on the Sabbath day, and my soul would have been lost—lost."

"O, don't fret, it wasn't in any danger," said Luigi, irritably; "they wouldn't waste it for a little thing like that; there's a glass case all ready for it in the heavenly museum, and a pin to stick it up with."

Aunt Patsy was shocked, and said—

"Looy, Looy!—don't talk so, dear!"

Rowena's soft heart was pierced by Luigi's unfeeling words, and she murmured to herself, "O, if I but had the dear privilege of protecting and defending

him with my weak voice!—but alas, this sweet boon is denied me by the cruel conventions of social intercourse."

"Get their bed ready," said Aunt Patsy to Nancy, "and shut up the windows and doors, and light their candles, and see that you drive all the mosquitoes out of their bar, and make up a good fire in their stove, and carry up some bags of hot ashes to lay to his feet—

—"and a shovel of fire for his head, and a mustard plaster for his neck, and some gum shoes for his cars," Luigi interrupted, with a temper; and added, to himself, "damnation, I'm going to be roasted alive, I just know it!"

"Why, Looy! Do be quiet; I never saw such a fractious thing. A body would think you didn't care for your brother."

"I don't—to *that* extent, Aunt Patsy. I was glad the drowning was postponed, a minute ago; but I'm not, now. No, that is all gone by: I want to be drowned."

"You'll bring a judgement on yourself just as sure as you live, if you go on like that. Why, I never heard the beat of it. Now, there-there! you've said enough. Not another word out of you, Looy—I won't have it!"

"But Aunt Patsy—"

"Luigi! Didn't you hear what I told you?"

"But Aunt Patsy, I—why, I'm not going to set my heart and lungs afloat in that pail of sewage which this criminal here has been prescri—"

"Yes you are, too. You are going to be good, and do everything I tell you, like a dear," and she tapped his cheek affectionately with her finger. "Rowena, take the prescription and go in the kitchen and hunt up the things and lay them out for me. I'll sit up with my patient the rest of the night, doctor; I can't trust Nancy, she couldn't make Luigi take the medicine. Of course you'll drop in again during the day. Have you got any more directions!"

"No, I believe not, Aunt Patsy. If I don't get in earlier, I'll be along, by early candle-light, anyway. Meantime, don't allow him to get out of his bed."

Angelo said, with calm determination—

"I shall be baptized at two o'clock. Nothing but death shall prevent me."

The doctor said nothing aloud, but to himself he said, "Why, this chap's got a manly side, after all! Physically he's a coward, but morally he's a lion. I'll go and tell the others about this; it will raise him a good deal in their estimation—and the public will follow their lead, of course."

Privately, Aunt Patsy applauded, too, and was proud of Angelo's courage in the moral field as she was of Luigi's in the field of honor.

The boy Henry was troubled, but the boy Joe said, inaudibly, and gratefully, "We're all hunky, after all; and no postponement on account of the weather."

Chapter 8

By nine o'clock the town was humming with the news of the midnight duel, and there were but two opinions about it: one, that Luigi's pluck in the field was most praiseworthy and Angelo's flight most scandalous; the other, that Angelo's courage in flying the field for conscience sake was as fine and creditable as was Luigi's in holding the field in the face of the bullets. The one opinion was held by half of the town, the other one was maintained by the other half. The division was clean and exact, and it made two parties, an Angelo party and a Luigi party. The Twins had suddenly become popular idols along with Pudd'n-head Wilson, and haloed with a glory as intense as his. The children talked the duel all the way to Sunday school, their elders talked it all the way to church, the choir discussed it behind their red curtain, it usurped the place of pious thought in the "nigger gallery."

By noon the doctor had added the news, and spread it, that Count Angelo, in spite of his wound and all warnings and supplications, was resolute in his determination to be baptised at the hour appointed. This swept the town like wildfire, and mightily reinforced the enthusiasm of the Angelo faction, who said, "If any doubted that it was moral courage that took him from the field, what have they to say now!"

Still the excitement grew. All the morning it was traveling countrywards, toward all points of the compass; and so, whereas before only the farmers and their wives were intending to come and witness the remarkable baptism, a general holiday was now proclaimed and the children and negroes admitted to the privileges of the occasion. All the farms for ten miles around were vacated, all the converging roads emptied long processions of wagons, horses and yeomanry into the town. The pack and cram of people vastly exceeded any that had ever been seen in that sleepy region before. The only thing that had ever even approached it was the time, long gone by, but never forgotten nor ever referred to without wonder and pride, when two circuses and a Fourth of July fell

together. But the glory of that occasion was extinguished, now, for good. It was but a freshet to this deluge.

The great invasion massed itself on the river bank and waited hungrily for the immense event. Waited, and wondered if it would really happen, or if the twin who was not a "professor" would stand out and prevent it.

But they were not to be disappointed. Angelo was as good as his word. He came attended by an escort of honor composed of several hundred of the best citizens, all of the Angelo party; and when the immersion was finished they escorted him back home; and would even have carried him on their shoulders, but that people might think they were carrying Luigi.

Far into the night the citizens continued to discuss and wonder over the strangely-mated pair of incidents that had distinguished and exalted the past twenty-four hours above any other twenty-four in the history of their town for picturesqueness and splendid interest; and long before the lights were out and the burghers asleep it had been decided on all hands that in capturing these Twins Dawson's Landing had drawn a prize in the great lottery of municipal fortune.

At midnight Angelo was sleeping peacefully. His immersion had not harmed him, it had merely made him wholesomely drowsy, and he had been dead asleep many hours, now. It had made Luigi drowsy, too, but he had got only brief naps, on account of his having to take the medicine every three-quarters of an hour—and Aunt Betsy Hale was there to see that he did it. When he complained and resisted, she was quietly firm with him, and said in a low voice:

"No-no, that won't do; you mustn't talk, and you mustn't retch and gag that way, either—you'll wake up your poor brother."

"Well, what of it, Aunt Betsy, he—"

"'Sh-h! Don't make a noise, dear. You mustn't forget that your poor brother is sick and—"

"Sick, is he? Well, I wish I—"

"Sh-h-h! Will you be quiet, Luigi! Here, now, take the rest of it—don't keep me holding the dipper all night. I declare if you haven't left a good fourth of it in the bottom! Come—that's a good boy."

"Aunt Betsy, don't make me! I tell you I feel like I've swallowed a cemetery; I do, indeed. Do let me rest a little—just a little; I can't take any more of the devilish stuff, now."

"Luigi! Using such language here, and him just baptised! Do you want the roof to fall on you?"

"I wish to goodness it would!"

"Why, you dreadful thing! I've a good notion to—let that blanket alone; do you want your brother to catch his death?"

"Aunt Betsy, I've *got* to have it off; I'm being roasted alive; nobody could stand it—you couldn't, yourself."

"Now, then, you're sneezing again—I just expected it."

"Because I've caught a cold in my head. I always do, when I go in the water with my clothes on. And it takes me weeks to get over it, too. I think it was a shame to serve me so."

"Luigi, you are unreasonable; you know very well they couldn't baptise him dry. I should think you would be willing to undergo a little inconvenience for your brother's sake."

"Inconvenience! Now how you talk, Aunt Betsy. I came as near as anything to getting drowned—you saw that, yourself; and do you call this inconvenience?—the room shut up as tight as a drum, and so hot the mosquitoes are trying to get out; and a cold in the head, and dying for sleep and no chance to get any on account of this infamous medicine that that assassin prescri—"

"There, you're sneezing again. I'm going down and mix some more of this truck for you, dear."

Chapter 9

During Monday, Tuesday and Wednesday the Twins grew steadily worse; but then the doctor was summoned south to attend his mother's funeral and they got well in forty-eight hours. They appeared on the street on Friday, and were welcomed with enthusi-

asm by the new-born parties, the Luigi and Angelo factions. The Luigi faction carried its strength into the Democratic party, the Angelo faction entered into a combination with the Whigs. The Democrats nominated Luigi for alderman under the new city government, and the Whigs put up Angelo against him. The Democrats nominated Pudd'nhead Wilson for mayor, and he was left alone in this glory, for the Whigs had no man who was willing to enter the lists against such a formidable opponent. No politician had scored such a compliment as this before in the history of the Mississippi Valley.

The political campaign in Dawson's Landing opened in a pretty warm fashion, and waxed hotter and hotter every week. Luigi's whole heart was in it, and even Angelo presently developed a surprising amount of interest in it—which was natural, because he was not merely representing Whigism, which was a matter of no consequence to him, he was representing something immensely finer and greater—to wit, Reform. In him was centred the hopes of the whole reform element of the town; he was the chosen and admired champion of every clique that had a pet reform of any sort or kind at heart.

He was president of the great Teetotalers' Union and its chiefest prophet and mouthpiece.

But as the canvass went on, troubles began to spring up all around—troubles for the Twins, and through them for all the parties and segments and fractions of parties. Whenever Luigi had possession of the legs, he carried Angelo to balls, rum shops, Sons of Liberty parades, horse races, campaign riots, and everywhere else that could damge him with his party and his church; and when it was Angelo's week he carried Luigi diligently to all manner of moral and religious gatherings, and did his best to get back the ground which he had lost before. As a result of these double performances, there was a storm blowing all the time, and it was an ever rising storm, too—a storm of frantic criticism of the Twins, and rage over their extravagant and incomprehensible conduct.

Luigi had the final chance. The legs were his for the closing week of the canvass. He led his brother a fearful dance.

But he saved his best card for the very eve of the election. There was to be a grand turn-out of the Teetotalers' Union that day, and Angelo was to march at the head of the procession and deliver a great oration afterward. Luigi drank a couple of glasses of whisky—which steadied his nerves and clarified his mind, but made Angelo drunk. Everybody who saw the march, saw that the Champion of the Teetotalers was half seas over, and noted also that his brother, who made no hypocritical pretentions to extra-temperance virtues, was dignified and sober. This eloquent fact could not be unfruitful at the end of a hot political canvass. At the mass meeting Angelo tried to make his great temperance oration but was so discommoded by hiccups and thickness of tongue that he had to give it up; then drowsiness overtook him and his head drooped against Luigi's and he went to sleep. Luigi apologized for him, and was going on to improve his opportunity with a ringing appeal for a moderation of what he called "the prevailing teetotal madness," but persons in the audience began to howl and throw things at him, and then the meeting rose in a general burst of wrath and chased him home.

This episode was a crusher for Angelo in another way. It destroyed his chances with Rowena. Those chances had been growing, right along, for two months. Rowena had even partly confessed that she loved him, but had begged for time to consider. But now the tender dream was ended, and she

frankly told him so, the moment he was sober enough to understand. She said she would never marry a man who drank.

"But I don't drink," he pleaded.

"That is nothing to the point," she said, coldly, "you get drunk, and that is worse."

[There was a long and sufficiently idiotic discussion here, which ended as reported in a previous note.]

Chapter 10

Dawson's Landing had a week of repose, after the election, and it needed it, for the frantic and variegated nightmare which had tormented it all through the preceding week had left it limp, haggard and exhausted at the end. It got the week of repose because Angelo

had the legs, and was in too subdued a condition to want to go out and mingle with an irritated community that had come to distrust and detest him because there was such a lack of harmony between his morals, which were confessedly excellent, and his methods of illustrating them, which were distinctly damnable.

The new city officers were sworn in on the following Monday—at least all but Luigi. There was a complication in his case. His election was conceded, but he could not sit in the board of aldermen without his brother, and his brother could not sit there because he was not a member. There seemed to be no way out of the difficulty but to carry the matter into the courts, so this was resolved upon. The case was set for the Monday fortnight. In due course the time arrived. In the meantime the city government had been at a stand-still, because without Luigi there was a tie in the board of aldermen, whereas with him the liquor interest—the richest in the political field—would have

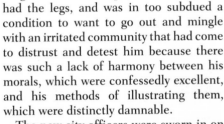

one majority. But the court decided that Angelo could not sit in the board with him, either in public

or executive sessions, and at the same time forbade the board to deny admission to Luigi, a fairly and legally chosen alderman. The case was carried up and up from court to court, yet still the same old original decision was confirmed every time. As a result, the city government not only stood still, with its hands tied, but everything it was created to protect and care for went a steady gait toward rack and ruin. There was no way to levy a tax, so the minor officials had to resign or starve; therefore they resigned. There being no city money, the enormous legal expenses on both sides had to be defrayed by private subscription. But at last the people came to their senses, and said—

"Pudd'nhead was right, at the start—we ought to have hired the official half of that human phillipene to resign; but it's too late, now; some of us haven't got anything left to hire him with."

"Yes we have," said another citizen, "we've got this"—and he produced a halter.

Many shouted—

"That's the ticket."

But others said—

"No—Count Angelo is innocent; we mustn't hang him."

"Who said anything about hanging him? We are only going to hang the other one."

"Then that is all right—there is no objection to that."

So they hanged Luigi. And so ends the history of "Those Extraordinary Twins."

Final Remarks.

As you see, it was an extravagant sort of a tale, and had no purpose but to exhibit that monstrous "freak" in all sorts of grotesque lights. But when Roxy wandered into the tale she had to be furnished with something to do; so she changed the children in the cradle: this necessitated the invention of a reason for it; this in turn

resulted in making the children prominent personages—nothing could prevent it, of course. Their career began to take a tragic aspect, and some one had to be brought in to help work the machinery; so Pudd'n-head Wilson was introduced and taken on trial. By this time the whole show was being run by the new people and in their interest, and the original show was become side-tracked and forgotten; the twin-monster and the heroine and the lads and the old ladies had dwindled to inconsequentialities and were merely in the way. Their story was one story, the new people's story was another story, and there was no connection between them, no interdependence, no kinship. It is not practicable or rational to try to tell two stories at the same time; so I dug out the farce and left the tragedy.

The reader already knew how the expert works; he knows now how the other kind do it.

MARK TWAIN.

TEXTUAL INTRODUCTION
AND
TABLES OF VARIANTS

Pudd'nhead Wilson and *Those Extraordinary Twins:* Textual Introduction

To understand the problems of editing *Pudd'nhead Wilson* and *Those Extraordinary Twins*, one must be familiar with the extant documents that may have some authority in the transmission of the text. Briefly they are:

1. The Berg Manuscript (hereafter referred to as BMS)
2. A typescript of the Berg Manuscript (TS₁)
3. The Morgan Manuscript (MMS)
4. The *Century Magazine* serialization (CM)
5. The American Publishing Company edition (APC)
6. The Chatto & Windus edition (C&W)

(Collations of other editions that appeared in Clemens's lifetime prove them to be of no authority, usually deriving from APC, the first printing of *Pudd'nhead Wilson* and *Those Extraordinary Twins* in book form [and the first appearance of *Twins*].)

To this list must be added a typescript made of the MMS; though this typescript is not extant, there is a note in Clemens's letter of February 3, 1893, to Frederick J. Hall that "My book is type-writered and ready for print—'Puddn'head [sic] Wilson—a Tale.' (Or, 'Those Extraordinary Twins,' if preferable.)"[1] (This typescript shall henceforth be referred to as TS₂.)

The first manuscript, of about ten thousand words, is in the Berg Collection of the New York Public Library. On page one, Clemens called the story "Those Extraordinary Twins." This manuscript contains Clemens's earliest attempt at writing the story of the Siamese twins, begun some time in 1892. The manuscript is apparently a surviving portion of a longer work, for in a letter dated September 4, 1892, to his junior partner at Charles L. Webster & Company, Fred Hall, Clemens said of the story:

> It is the howling farce I told you I had begun a while back. I laid it aside to ferment while I wrote 'Tom Sawyer Abroad,' but I took

---

1. Hamlin Hill, *Mark Twain's Letters to His Publishers* [*MTLP*] (Berkeley and Los Angeles: University of California Press, 1967), pp. 336–37.

it up again on a little different plan lately, and it is swimming along satisfactorily now. I have written about 20,000 words on it, but I can't form any idea of how big a book it is going to make yet. If I keep up my like it will be a book that will *sell* mighty well, I am sure of that. I think all sorts of folks will read it. It is clear out of the common order—it is a fresh idea—I don't think it resembles anything in literature. *I* believe there's a 'boom' in it.[2]

Clemens's word count is apparently accurate, for in a letter to his sister-in-law Sue Crane of September 1, 1892, he says he "took up 'Twins' again, destroyed the last half of the manuscript and then re-wrote it in another form. . . ."[3] At some point—in September or October 1892[4]—the remaining ten-thousand-word text was typed, and this typescript was later incorporated into the MMS by the author.

Once this typescript was made, Clemens decided to recast the characters of Pudd'nhead Wilson, Tom Driscoll, and Roxy, and had a new burst of creative energies, as can be seen by numerous letters from him to Hall, Vice-Consul-General Hogue in Frankfurt a/M, Chatto & Windus, Clara Clemens, Franklin G. Whitmore, Laurence Hutton, and others, and from some extensive notes on the story in his notebooks of the period. After writing sixty to eighty thousand words (as his letter to Hall dated December 12, 1892,[5] states) of this new version, Clemens wrote in his notebook, under the date of December 20, 1892:

> Finished 'Pudd'nhead Wilson' last Wednesday, 14th. Began it 11th or 12th of last month, after King girls left. Wrote more than 60,000 words between Nov. 12 & Dec. 14. One day, wrote 6,000 words in 13 hours. Another day wrote 5,000 in 11.

As Frederick Anderson points out, "The bloated book at this stage included all of the fullest expansion of the Siamese-twins farce and the complex variety of serious themes the book now possesses and a drearily facetious foreword about March weather."[6] This new version—the MMS—was mostly in Clemens's handwriting, except for the pages of TS_1 made from the Berg Manuscript; these pages were included in the 633½ pages of MMS. Under the same date in the notebook but three pages later is the entry: "Adam and Puddn to

2. *MTLP*, p. 319.
3. Copy of letter in Mark Twain Papers [MTP], Berkeley.
4. In an October 14, 1892, letter to Vice-Consul-General Hogue Clemens says, "The closing pages of the Twins have also arrived." (Typescript of letter in MTP.) Presumably he is referring to a typescript.
5. *MTLP*, p. 319.
6. Frederick Anderson, ed., *Pudd'nhead Wilson and Those Extraordinary Twins, by Mark Twain, a Facsimile of the First Edition* (San Francisco: Chandler Publishing Company, 1968), p. xiii.

type-writer."[7] By March 10, 1893, Fred Hall had received a copy of the "ms" but had "not looked it over yet."[8]

During most of the composition Clemens was in Europe with his wife, Olivia. But in April and May 1893 he was in New York, at which time he apparently visited Hall and retrieved the typescript that he had sent Hall from Florence.[9] After much deliberation, and after gathering much criticism from his wife, Hutton, and Hall about the book, Clemens decided to revise the entire plot, and by July 30 he was able to write to Hall about this new version of the story:

> *This* time "Pudd'nhead Wilson" is a success! . . . I have pulled the twins apart & made two individuals of them; I have sunk them out of sight, they are mere flitting shadows, now, & of no importance; *their* story has disappeared from the book. Aunt Betsy Hale has vanished wholly, leaving not a trace behind; aunt Patsy Cooper & her daughter Rowena have almost disappeared—they scarcely walk across the stage. The whole story is centred on the murder and the trial; from the first chapter the movement is straight ahead without divergence or side-play to the murder & the trial; everything that is done or said or that happens is a preparation for those events.
>
>   ✳   ✳   ✳
>
> When I began this final reconstruction the story contained 81,500 words; now it contains only 58,000. I have knocked out everything that delayed the march of the story—even the description of a Mississippi steamboat.[1] There ain't any weather in, & there ain't any scenery—the story is stripped for flight![2]

By mid-August he was ready to send Hall copy for publication.[3]

The copy he sent to Hall was almost certainly a cut, pasted, and revised text of the December 20 typescript (i.e., TS_2).[4] In this massive revision he completely rewrote the story, casting characters in

---

7. A search for an "Adam" typescript has proven fruitless. But in a letter of July 30, 1893, he mentions to Hall that he "shall tackle Adam once more" (*MTLP*, p. 356). Hamlin Hill sees this as a reference to "Adam's Diary."

8. *MTLP*, p. 336, n. 2.

9. As noted above, Clemens had a typist in Florence.

1. The passage may be found in "Emendations of the Copy-Text: Substantives (Lengthy Passages)," 37.1, herein.

2. *MTLP*, pp. 354–55; the passage about the weather may be found in Appendix 1 herein.

3. We see this in a letter to Hall of August 9, 1893: "I am traveling on the idea that John Brisben Walker will take PW" (*MTLP*, p. 358), and also in another to Hall of August 14, 1893: "I mean to ship PW to you—say tomorrow. It'll furnish me hash for a while I reckon" (*MTLP*, p. 359).

4. Considering how large the text is (over 630 MMS pages), and also considering that almost every passage in the final version of the story is lifted nearly verbatim from the MMS, it is not at all unlikely that Clemens cut and pasted his typescript (TS_2) and then added new connecting passages, made his revisions (especially those concerning the now-separated Siamese twins), and deleted the farcical material—all this being done in TS_2. In fact, the printer's copy for the present edition was prepared in just this way, on a typescript of MMS.

new roles, discarding some characters, rearranging the materials of the plot, and separating out the extraordinary twins. This typescript was then sent to Hall,[5] and is almost certainly what was used for printer's copy by the *Century Magazine*. The MMS itself was never used by a printer, for many substantive changes were made in the story which appear in all published versions, but which do not appear in the manuscript. (It is also possible that a carbon copy of TS_2 was made.[6]) The first installment appeared in *Century Magazine* for December 1893. Clemens wrote to his wife on September 7, 1893:

> I've sold . . . PW to the Century for six thousand five hundred. . . . Story will begin in December number, & be made the "feature."[7]

We learn from one of Clemens's letters to his wife Olivia that on September 21, 1893, he began to read proof for the first installment of the serialization at the *Century* offices; he said that his "deeply thought out, and laboriously perfected" punctuation had been altered by some "imported proof-reader, from Oxford University. . . . I said I didn't care if he was an Archangel imported from Heaven, he couldn't puke his ignorant impudence over *my* punctuation, I wouldn't allow it for a moment. I said I couldn't read this proof. I couldn't sit in the *presence* of a proofsheet where that blatherskite had left his tracks. . . . I'm to return there to-morrow & read the deodorized proof."[8] However, the great number of punctuation changes in the serialization make it highly unlikely that Clemens's wishes as to such styling were respected.

Though he wanted his own printing firm, C. L. Webster & Company, to publish the novel in book form, the nearly bankrupt company was unable to do so; instead he offered it to the American Publishing Company and to Chatto & Windus in England, who contracted to publish it simultaneously. The book was issued on November 28, 1894, by both companies, but in the American publication the farce of *Those Extraordinary Twins* was included. This was done by Clemens mainly for financial reasons, as he sold what he called "refuse matter"[9] (i.e., the deleted Siamese twins story) to the American Publishing Company for $1,500.

---

5. Anne Wigger claims that Clemens "had a typewritten manuscript mailed to Fred Hall"; see Wigger, "The Composition of Mark Twain's *Pudd'nhead Wilson* and *Those Extraordinary Twins*: Chronology and Development," *Modern Philology*, November 1957, p. 97, note 21. Her arguments are sound, and her discussion of the story is interesting and valuable.
6. See discussion of the C&W edition, below.
7. Dixon Wecter, *The Love Letters of Mark Twain* [*LLMT*] (New York: Harper & Brothers, 1949), p. 267.
8. *LLMT*, pp. 273–74.
9. Typescript of letter to Livy (Olivia Clemens), August 4, 1894; also letter to Henry Huttleston Rogers, February 8–9, 1895 (see Lewis Leary, *Mark Twain's Correspondence with Henry Huttleston Rogers, 1893–1909* [*MTHHR*] [Berkeley and Los Angeles: University of California Press, 1969], p. 128).

For *Pudd'nhead Wilson* the American Publishing Company used *CM* for its printer's copy; we know this because their edition follows the *Century* consistently in substantives and accidentals.[1] For *Those Extraordinary Twins* the American Publishing Company used "refuse matter" from the cut and pasted typescript (TS$_2$)—material concerning the Siamese twins which was removed from the *Pudd'nhead Wilson* story. Clemens sailed for Europe on March 7, 1894, and was in Paris part of that year, while taking other trips to New York for financial reasons. Distance and financial matters make it unlikely that he had anything to do with the production of the American edition.

It ought to be noted that three distinct states of the printed American text are discernible; chronologically, they are the prospectus,[2] copies in the Library of Congress and Harvard Library, and the first published edition (APC). Further discussion of these states is beyond the scope of this edition.[3]

Chatto & Windus's printer's copy for the first seventeen chapters of *Pudd'nhead Wilson* was undoubtedly *CM*. Collations along with Chatto & Windus correspondence substantiate this.

Clemens may have been traveling through London on his way back to his family in France at about the time that the *Pudd'nhead Wilson* text was being set and readied for publication at Chatto & Windus, but it is unlikely that the variants between that edition and the other texts came from his pen on this trip.[4] Some variants, both substantive and accidental in nature,[5] are easily seen as those of a compositor or because of the printing house's style. Thus the Chatto & Windus edition has no authority. A record of its readings has been retained for the present edition.

One feature of the English edition does cause some problems, however: the last five chapters of *Pudd'nhead Wilson* in this edition (Chapters 18–21 and the Conclusion) do not follow *CM* so closely as do all the earlier chapters; in fact, these five chapters have readings that often coincide with MMS where *CM* varies from that manuscript. For example, where MMS has "man," (509.10), *CM* (17.i.35) and APC (228.19) have "man;", but the English text has the

---

1. For example, where the MMS has "law-chapters" (5.5–6), both *CM* and APC have the words unhyphenated (233.i.9 and 15.11 respectively); where the MMS has "was saved" (39.4), the other two have "had been saved" (237.ii.16 and 36.19). See note 5 below for an explanation of the terms *substantives* and *accidentals*.

2. In the Yale University Library.

3. See Sidney Berger, "Editorial Intrusion in *Pudd'nhead Wilson,*" *Papers of the Bibliographical Society of America* 70 (1976), 272–76.

4. The English edition has such variants as "any way" (8.18) where the manuscript has one word (21.35), "asleep;" (111.23) where the other versions have a comma, "down to de" (188.14) where the others have "down de," "by voluntarily" (173.26) where the others have "in voluntarily," and so on.

5. A *substantive variant* is one in which a word, phrase, or passage in one text varies from that in the other. An *accidental variant* is a difference in punctuation, capitalization, spelling, hyphenation, italicization, or paragraphing.

comma (183.5); where MMS has "mawnins" (510.4), *CM* (17.ii.45) and APC (229.5) have "mawnin's," but again the English text agrees with the MMS (183.15). The English edition and the manuscript also agree in hyphenations, use of italics, and several other areas of accidentals.

Most perplexing of all, however, is the fact that in substantive readings C&W usually follows *CM*, but occasionally it does not. And where C&W varies substantively from *CM*, the English text invariably has MMS readings. For example, where *CM* has "last" (23.ii.21) MMS and C&W have "past" (559.7 and 207.18). It appears that for these chapters the English printers could not have used *CM* to set from, but were setting from copy closer to MMS than was *CM*. The several complex ways of explaining this anomaly are beyond the scope of this edition. It is sufficient to say here that Clemens had no direct hand in the production of the English edition and that this edition hence has no authority.[6]

One further note about the development of the story is in order. When Clemens realized that the complete story (as it existed in MMS) needed to be recast—pulling the twins apart and separating out the farce—he must have initially thought the revision could be made on the Morgan Manuscript itself. This thought was necessarily brief, as a glance at the substantive emendations of the copy-text shows. However, there is evidence that he made some revisions in the Morgan Manuscript with the concept of separated twins in his mind. At the top of manuscript page 545 he wrote "OVER OVER," and on the back of the sheet he added a paragraph in which he has Luigi, ostensibly alone, going out for a walk (the walk on which he hears the Judge's cries for help). However, when the Morgan manuscript was typed and Clemens made his revisions, he changed "Luigi" to "the twins" (see 99.10 herein), realizing that in the original story the twins were necessarily together everywhere, and that it would be simpler here to have the twins going out for a walk together than to recast the entire murder and trial elements of the story to concern Luigi only.

For *Those Extraordinary Twins* we know that pages of typescript were sent to the American Publishing Company as copy. Clemens simply pieced together the Siamese twins materials that he had excised from *Pudd'nhead Wilson* (i.e., leftover pieces of TS$_2$), adding bracketed passages as connectors between the various pieces of "refuse matter." Certainly, the American Publishing Company was not setting directly from manuscript, for the farce of the twins still remains embedded, unrevised, in the Morgan manuscript.

---

6. See Sidney Berger, "Determining Printer's Copy: The English Edition of Mark Twain's *Pudd'nhead Wilson*," *Papers of the Bibliographical Society of America* 72 (1978), 250–56.

Copy-Text

On the simplest level, the term *copy-text* refers to the base text chosen by an editor—the text that the editor emends to create a version closest to the author's final intentions (as well as these intentions can be ascertained). The emendations are drawn from authoritative sources. Once again, it is beyond the scope of the Textual Introduction for a Norton Critical Edition to explain technical bibliographical theories.[7] It is sufficient to say that for the present edition, where there are passages of author's inscription (i.e., his own handwriting), they are used as copy-text. Where—in the final version of the story—there is no inscription, the earliest appearance of the text in print (which presumably most closely resembles the lost typescript) is copy-text. For *Pudd'nhead Wilson* this is the *Century Magazine* text; for *Those Extraordinary Twins* it is the APC printing.

Though the CM version of *Pudd'nhead Wilson* represents the first publication of the story in its final order of chapters and passages, and with the characters and plots recast, the correspondence of the individual wording and sentence structure with MMS is close enough that we can see in this manuscript more than merely a rough draft of the story. What the author has done in his massive revision is to use most of his original prose, but he has completely revised it in terms of the order in which his chapters and passages appear, at the same time supplying the necessary new passages to explain additions to and deletions from the plot, and with new transitions where they were needed.

Since the Morgan manuscript text was used nearly verbatim for much of the *Pudd'nhead Wilson* story, it is the best choice for copy-text for much of this edition, whereas the order of the chapters and incidents is taken from the first printed edition: CM. Where there is typescript in MMS (i.e., TS_1), BMS (representing latest authorial inscription) is copy-text; the author's written emendations in TS_1, however, supersede BMS readings. And where new materials not in either manuscript exist, the earliest printed version (the CM for *Pudd'nhead Wilson* and the APC for *Those Extraordinary Twins*) is copy-text.

---

7. The reader who wishes further amplification of the highly complex topic of copy-text may read W. W. Greg, "The Rationale of Copy-Text," *Studies in Bibliography* 3 (1950), 19–36; Paul Baender, "The Meaning of Copy-Text," *Studies in Bibliography* 22 (1969), 311–18; Fredson Bowers, "Current Theories of Copy-Text, with an Illustration from Dryden," *Modern Philology* 67 (1950), 19–36; S. L. Clemens, *What Is Man and Other Philosophical Writings*, ed. Baender (University of California Press, 1973), pp. 609–13; and Kenneth M. Sanderson and Bernard L. Stein, eds., *Fables of Man* (University of California Press, 1972), pp. 477–78.

Pudd'nhead Wilson: *Principles of Emendation*

The copy-text has been emended for *Pudd'nhead Wilson* in four distinct ways. (1) The order of the text was made to conform to that of the CM edition. (2) Adaptations for the new order of the story are drawn from CM. This, of course, means that passages in the Morgan Manuscript that were never printed have been deleted. For example, the end of Chapter 6 in MMS was transferred to the middle of Chapter 1 of *Those Extraordinary Twins;* also, a passage in MMS between pages 92 and 99 concerning Roxy's religion and Jasper's stopping a runaway carriage are found in the Emendations of the Copy-Text. (3) While revising, Clemens occasionally ignored coordinating passages or words that needed changing because of revision. For example, on manuscript page 591 Clemens first decided to end one of David Wilson's speeches after the word *words.* But then, after some revision, Wilson continues to speak. Clemens forgot to delete the first closing quotation marks. The emendations of the copy-text in such instances are drawn from CM or are made by the editor. (4) Outright blunders are emended. For example, Clemens ten times spelled *seize* as "sieze."

Clemens's spelling has not been modernized. Forms acceptable (and authorized by contemporary dictionaries) in the 1890s are retained (e.g., "grewsome" or "clew"). Since we have manuscript evidence of authorial punctuation for most of the text, it is safer to retain the author's unevenness in this area than to emend to a more consistent punctuation possibly supplied by the *Century Magazine* editors or compositors.

Clemens was completely indifferent in many of his spellings and word-forms, and to impose a regularity on his word-forms would be to produce a text that he himself never created.[8] Regularization is a type of modernization, and it produces an anachronistic, non-authorial text. Hence, all of Clemens's inconsistent spellings and punctuation are retained, unless the inconsistency produces an outright blunder (e.g., 519.4 of MMS: the line lacks open quotation marks), a spelling not acceptable in his day, or an instance of punctuation that renders a sentence unintelligible.

A few inconsistent spellings of names have been regularized (e.g., Valet de Chambre/Vallet de Chambers; Capello/Cappello). But, in dialogue, especially in dialect, a sound change might be indicated by a variant spelling (e.g., "jes'" / "jist" / "jis'"); all spelling and punctuation variants have been left to stand as they appear in the manuscripts. There is a great variety in Clemens's use of *a* preceding a

---

8. For a discussion of the latest views on imposing regularity on the author's accidentals, see the excellent article: Hershel Parker, "Regularizing Accidentals: The Latest Form of Infidelity," *Proof* 3 (1973), 1–20.

verb, where the *a* represents a gerund or replaces "have." For example, he has "a ben," "a had," "a workin'," and also "a-court'n," "a-fishing," and "a-yowlin'." These have all been left in the holograph form, even though printed editions frequently add hyphens and make apostrophes more accurately reflect dropped letters.

One word in dialogue, however, has been normalized. Clemens had many times written (for Roxy's dialect) "myself." Several times he slipped and wrote "myseff." In rereading he noticed the slips a few times, and crossed off the lower loop of the first *f* of a few occurrences of the word (e.g., 514.17, 516.7, 519.6). He did not make the correction at 415.21 or 518.2, nor at 424.13 and 535.7 (where the word "seff" is used). These four slips have been emended to his preferred form for Roxy's dialect.

Some of Clemens's habits of writing have been changed with no citation of the change in the tables of emendations. Ampersands have been spelled out. The word *Chapter* has been spelled out and is followed by Arabic numbers.

The *Century Magazine* readings of italics and exclamation points are assumed to be authorial, and emendations are drawn from the serialization for these two types of accidentals.

One of the problems faced by any editor working directly from a Clemens manuscript is to distinguish between capital and lower case *t*'s, *c*'s, *j*'s, *k*'s, and *m*'s, or perhaps other letters. In *Pudd'nhead Wilson* and *Those Extraordinary Twins* one encounters scores of occurrences of *twins, court, church, judge, king,* and so on, with ambiguous initial letters. For most words the context supplies the answer. But for *twins, court, march* (a command, at 201.11 of the manuscript), *mammy* (52.2), and a few others, there is no way of knowing what the author's intention was. In a few instances, however, the word *twins* was clearly written with a lower case *t*, and then—just as clearly—the *t* was capitalized. Hence, in ambiguous cases, when the word *twins* is used to refer directly to Luigi and Angelo, it has been capitalized. Similarly, in ambiguous cases, when *court* refers specifically to the judge it is capitalized. The word *march* (at 201.11 of the manuscript [40.28 herein]) has been capitalized because the context seems to warrant great emphasis. Other instances of ambiguous capital or lower case letters are discussed in the textual notes.

Those Extraordinary Twins:
Copy-Text and Principles of Emendation

Since printer's copy for the first printing in APC of *Those Extraordinary Twins* was a revised typescript of the Morgan Manuscript (TS$_2$), sheets of which were separated from the *Pudd'nhead Wilson* story (see page 193, above), that printer's copy would be the ideal copy-text. However, a situation exists for the *Twins* similar to that for *Pudd'n-head Wilson:* the actual prose of MMS is often closely followed in the final printed form of the *Twins,* though with much rearrangement. In *Those Extraordinary Twins* there has been more revision in the excision of material than there was for *Pudd'nhead Wilson*. Clemens recognized the dreariness and "extravagantly fantastic"[9] nature of the farce, so he has summarized much of the wordiness of the original in brackets in the final printed version of the story.[1]

For this edition the Morgan Manuscript is copy-text, with two exceptions: (1) as for *Pudd'nhead Wilson*, the order of the material is adopted from the first printing (APC) and (2) the new prose passages Clemens wrote for APC (often in brackets) to explain the nature of the revision and to condense some passages he has omitted from the Morgan version are taken from APC. For a few heavily revised passages, copy-text is the first printing of the story. This is so only for passages so heavily revised as to have little semblance to the original from which they were adapted; such passages may be seen as mere rough drafts, not at all representing authorial "final intention."

9. See *Those Extraordinary Twins*, p. 311 of the APC (126.9–10 herein).
1. See, for example, pages 130, 141, 142, 142–43, 151–52, 164–65, 170, and 183 herein.

Pudd'nhead Wilson

Emendations of the Copy-Text: Substantives

This table lists every substantive emendation of the copy-text, along with all other variant readings. The boldface material represents readings in the present edition; the lightface material contains first the copy-text reading, and second any other variants if there are any. The copy-text reading is for the MMS or the BMS, whichever contains the latest authorial inscription.

"**I**" after an adopted reading indicates that the emendation is made by the editor. For example, at 19.35 "stomach ache" was the author's preferred form, so this spelling is adopted despite the fact that all printed texts have the words hyphenated.

An asterisk (*) indicates that the reading is discussed in the Textual Notes.

A caret (∧) is used to show an absence of punctuation. A paragraph marker (¶) indicates that there is a new paragraph at that point.

Where possible, the adopted reading tries to give an indication of context.

Lengthy passages—too long for this table—are listed with an ellipsis [. . .]. They are preceded by a dagger (†) and may be found at the end of the table.

"[n.i.]" indicates a passage not in the copy-text.

†*[n.i.]   *CM-C&W   To Printer* . . . out.
1.   **heading** *A Whisper to the Reader.* CM-C&W   Note Concerning the Legal Points.
1.17–18   **here to Florence** CM-C&W   here
1.30   **outbreak** CM-C&W   attack
2.1   **flattery, far from it.** CM-C&W   flattery.
2.5   **three** CM-C&W   two
3.21   **were made** CM-C&W   made
4.5   **big Orleans liners** CM-C&W   big New Orleans and Cincinnati and Louisville liners
6.5   **young Wilson said** CM-C&W   The newcomer, David Wilson, said *BMS* he said *MMS*
6.10   **group** *MMS-C&W*   grouped *BMS*
*7.7   **and was to continue to hold its place for twenty long years.** CM-C&W and Wilson was still Pudd'nhead Wilson to-day, after all those twenty years. *BMS*

and and was to continue to hold its place for twenty long years. Wilson was still Pudd'nhead Wilson to-day, after all those twenty years. *MMS*
7.14   **money when he arrived,** CM-C&W money,
7.37–38   **him such a weary long time** CM-C&W   him twenty years
8.2   **into** CM-C&W   in
8.36   **come on,** CM-C&W   come,
8.38   **I's middlin'** CM-C&W   I'm middlin'
8.41   **Is** CM-C&W   Has
9.11   **friendly** CM-C&W   good-natured
9.32   **even** CM-C&W   perhaps even
9.35   **people** CM-C&W   folks
9.44   **other** CM-C&W   other kid
10.10   **Jasper** CM-C&W   Jim
12.3–4   **had been** CM-C&W   was
13.19   **that they** CM-C&W   they
14.13   **moaning, crying** CM-C&W moaning and crying

14.33–34 it; midway. . . . She had CM-C&W it. She

15.1 rather lurid CM-C&W pretty loud

15.19 Straightway her CM-C&W Her

16.37–38 to burn wid Satan CM-C&W to suffer

17.10 had to CM-C&W had a auction to

18.26 providences—namely, there CM-C&W providences, that there

19.35 stomach ache. I stomach ache; consequently he was hiccuppy beyond reason and a singularly flatulent child. MMS stomach-ache. CM-C&W

20.10 Roxy would CM-C&W Roxy was flying, by now, and would

20.12–13 delicacies CM-C&W delicacies going

20.13 In CM-C&W By

21.6 that CM-C&W that as

21.12–13 the person CM-C&W the party

21.30 have changed clothes with him, CM-C&W have put on his clothes∧

21.42–43 knees and seat CM-C&W knees

22.24 a crowd CM-C&W the crowd

22.35 howl CM-C&W yell

23.10 to call CM-C&W to always call

24.30 was that of CM-C&W was

24.30–31 other that of CM-C&W other was

25.18 chambermaiding CM-C&W chambermaid

†**25.21** wood. CM-C&W wood. She . . . anyway.

25.25 up CM-C&W down

†**25.31** it." CM-C&W it." He wished . . . dat!"

26.22 he rather openly CM-C&W he

26.34 Tom CM-C&W he

26.39–40 to and after that clothed himself in the local fashion CM-C&W and clothed himself after the local fashion after that

27.9–10 were now . . . life. CM-C&W were . . . life, now.

27.12–13 before about the dog. CM-C&W before.

28.11–17 anything. The . . . large. CM-C&W anything.

28.22 found CM-C&W finds BMS

28.22 tedious CM-C&W tedious long BMS

28.22 was CM-C&W is BMS

28.23 had CM-C&W has BMS

28.24 was CM-C&W is BMS

28.25 was CM-C&W is BMS

28.25 sat CM-C&W sits BMS

28.28 it was CM-C&W it is BMS

28.28 she was CM-C&W she is BMS

28.30 She had CM-C&W She has

28.30 Rowena had CM-C&W Rowena has

28.31 slave woman CM-C&W slave girl BMS slave MMS

28.32 had CM-C&W have

28.33 was CM-C&W is

28.35 returned CM-C&W returns

*****28.35–29.13** excitement, . . . Here CM-C&W excitement, and says—¶ "Do read it again, ma—it's just too lovely for anything! Oh, dear, I *am* so glad!"

*****29.21–22** its courtly . . . style, everybody CM-C&W it, everybody

29.23 Coopers were steeped in happiness CM-C&W Coopers swam in seas of glory

*****29.38–45** entered the twins . . . duplicates. CM-C&W entered a human creature that had two heads, two necks, four arms, and one body, with a single pair of legs attached.

30.8–24 Chapter 6. Let . . . rested— CM-C&W [n.i.]

31.8–9 languages. Also . . . truth. CM-C&W languages.

31.17 attractions CM-C&W 'freaks' BMS freaks MMS

*****31.20** bread. CM-C&W bread. That hateful . . . anywhere."

31.30–32 Venice—to . . . exclaimed: CM-C&W Venice—

31.34 to see de gen'lmen!" CM-C&W to see—to see—*him*—dem!"

31.34 She CM-C&W The slave girl

32.1–2 also were the foreigners. CM-C&W also was Luigi; but Angelo said he would like to go and dress first, and he should think Luigi would prefer that, too. He shot a covert, imploring glance at his brother which said, "Be humane, be generous—don't carry me in there before all those people in this heart-breaking costume, which offends against every canon of harmony in color and will make everybody think we have been brought up among African savages;" but the answering glance said, "We will go just as we are, or we will have a scene here—take your choice." So Angelo sighed, and said he was ready.

32.3–4 and entered the CM-C&W toward the

32.4 conversation. CM-C&W conversation. When they appeared suddenly before the crowd, every eye flew wide and froze to a glassy stare, there was a universal gasp that chorded itself into a single note, and two or three boys skipped out of the open window like frogs.

32.16 admiring CM-C&W devouring

32.18 was CM-C&W were

32.24 were overwhelmed CM-C&W were knocked cold

32.29 and CM-C&W and inquired

32.38 favor from all. CM-APC popu-

larity right along. *BMS-MMS* favour
from all. *C&W*

33.9   **the** *CM-C&W*   the young

33.10   **there** *CM-C&W*   up there

33.26   **twins** *CM-C&W*   duplicates

33.29–35   **The . . . masters.** *CM-C&W*
[n.i.]

*****34.2–4**   **[maxim] One . . . *Calendar.***
CM-C&W [n.i.]

34.8–9   **to play some duets** *CM-C&W*
to do the balcony scene in Romeo and
Juliet *MMS* [n.i.] *BMS*

34.11   **to be** *CM-C&W*   be

*****34.14**   **see.** *CM-C&W*   see, and a
herd . . .

34.19   **some** *CM-C&W*   some of the

34.21   **put** *CM-C&W*   squirt

34.22   **fire; then he** *CM-C&W*   fire, and

34.30   **of it** *CM-C&W*   from it

34.43   **Freethinkers. He** *CM-C&W*
Freethinkers. ¶ This latter fact interested
Luigi as much as it discomforted Angelo.
The Judge

†*****35.1–3**   **established. He . . . told** *CM-
C&W* established. Luigi . . . and
more. . . . Judge . . . on the way told

35.6   **succeeded** *CM-C&W*   succeeded
with Luigi

†**35.6–11**   **achieved. Later . . . carried.**
CM-C&W   achieved; but with
Angelo . . . Wilson's.

35.15–18   **presently . . . house.** *CM-
C&W* [n.i.]

36.4   **great, and** *CM-C&W*   great,

36.6   **in** *CM-C&W*   in alternating

36.10   **young Tom** *CM-C&W*   young

36.22   **arrive a little** *CM-C&W*   arrive

36.29   **of which she herself was not
aware.** *CM-C&W*   which she was not
aware of, herself.

36.42–43   **At . . . thirty-five.** *CM-C&W*
She went away chambermaiding the year
she was set free, when she was thirty-
five.

†**37.1**   **Mogul."** I Mogul." It was . . . eyesight. Mogul.ᴧ *CM-C&W*

37.2   **made her wonted and easy-
going at the work,** *CM-C&W* made a
wonted and easy-going steamboatman
of her,

37.11–12   **had banked** *CM-C&W*   had
saved up and banked

37.12   **month in New Orleans** *CM-C&W*
month

37.14   **and that** *CM-C&W*   and

37.27   **local packet** *CM-C&W*   packet

37.28   **Time** *CM-C&W*   At once her
memory began to travel back over the
long ago, and she found that time

37.29   **and** *CM-C&W*   and that

37.33   **upon** *CM-C&W*   around

37.44   **surely** *CM-C&W*   sure

38.6   **would** *CM-C&W*   should

38.14   **expressions** *CM-C&W*   explosions

38.22   **The ostensible "Chambers"** *CM-
C&W*   Chambers

39.22   **with** *CM-C&W* with complacent

39.32–33   **it. Her . . . Chambers:** *CM-
C&W*   it.

40.15   **was unconsciously** *CM-C&W*
was

42.28   **a former slave** *CM-C&W*   a
negro ex-slave

*****44.7**   **grieve** *CM-C&W*   weep

44.10–13   **[2nd maxim]** *CM-C&W*
[n.i.]

44.14   **Tom** *CM-C&W*   Then Tom

44.20   **lower** *CM-C&W*   lower than
this

44.23   **wretched** *CM-C&W*   tolerably
sick

45.36   **fambly name** *CM-C&W*   surname

*****46.3–4**   **of disorganizing sensations
and** *CM-C&W*   of doubt, certainty, fear,
derision, and all the other

46.21   **it's** *CM-C&W*   its

46.31   **business** *CM-C&W*   cold business

47.3   **amount** *CM-C&W*   amount on

*****48.7–8**   **[2nd maxim] When angry . . .
*Calendar.*** *CM-C&W*   [2nd maxim] Why
is it that we rejoice at a birth and weep at
a funeral? It is because we are not the
person involved.—*Pudd'nhead Wilson's
Calendar.*

48.11   **groan** *CM-C&W*   bitter groan

†**48.21**   **head."** *CM-C&W*   head. . . . .
I . . . virtue.". . . .

48.27   **wretch** *CM-C&W*   degraded
wretch

48.27   **he is an** *CM-C&W*   he is white,
and for that I could kill him—if I had the
courage. Ach! he is an

49.8   **ideals,** *CM-C&W*   ideals, now,

49.12   **work.** *CM-C&W*   work; he had
not been used to thinking. And it was not
easy; his mind was a whirlwind of spin-
ning spirals of dust with elusive rags and
fragments of ideas chasing each other
through it. But all whirlwinds settle at
last, and so did this one; then he had the
opportunity to gather his rags and fragments together and put them in order
and study the pattern and make out its
meaning. ¶ While the whirlwind continued, it furnished him many surprises.

49.20   **knew, idol . . . worship,** *CM-
C&W*   knew,

49.26   **passed** *CM-C&W*   had passed

49.32   **He said to himself that the curse
of Ham was upon him.** *CM-C&W*   The
curse of Ham was upon him, he said to
himself.

49.39   **ostensible "aunt's"** *CM-C&W* aunt's

49.41   **ostensible "uncle"** *CM-C&W*
uncle

†**49.44 dog."** *CM-C&W* dog." ¶ In his . . . rage.

50.11 but after a while *CM-C&W* but now

50.16 days. *CM-C&W* days. ¶ Yet a change or two *was* present, and remained. He hated the whites, he would steal from them without shame, and even with a vengeful exultation; he loathed the "nigger" in him, but got pleasure out of bringing this secret "filth," as he called it, into familiar and constant contact with the sacred whites; he privately despised and hated his uncle and all his aristocratic pretensions.

50.34 Occasionally *CM-C&W* Now and then

50.38 For this purpose he projected a new raid on his town. *CM-C&W* He projected a new raid on his town in this interest.

51.3 him in a bundle *CM-C&W* him

51.8 then *CM-C&W* then he

51.29 the valuables of that house *CM-C&W* that house's valuables

52.2 Twins *CM-C&W* Twins from the Bible Society

52.5 shameless creature *CM-C&W* brazen huzzy

52.11 No. 3 *CM-C&W* but No. 3

52.12 heart. *CM-C&W* heart with all your clothes on.

52.14–15 [2nd maxim] As to . . . Calendar. *CM-C&W* [n.i.]

52.16 twins *CM-C&W* duplicates

52.17–18 influence the . . . strength. *CM-C&W* influence Angelo cheered up and forgot his late vexations.

52.19 praised *CM-C&W* complimented

52.25–26 be seeing the . . . time when *CM-C&W* be startled at the figure the Twins made when

53.4 the law feature *CM-C&W* this feature

53.12 should *CM-C&W* would

53.21 Wilson had *CM-C&W* He had

54.14 notion-factory *CM-C&W* maggot-factory

54.21 got *CM-C&W* got here

54.23 chaff *CM-C&W* raillery

56.17 history *CM-C&W* past

56.35 it to himself *CM-C&W* it

57.19 kill him, . . . too? *CM-C&W* kill Angelo, how many hours would I have survived?

58.9–10 his pillow; we . . . together. *CM-C&W* our pillow.

58.11 vague *CM-C&W* dim

58.17 neck. *CM-C&W* neck. I think he was dead before his spouting blood struck us.

†**58.18 breaths, and . . . said,** *CM-C&W* breaths, . . . Wilson,

58.19–20 hand—¶ "Now Tom, I've *CM-C&W* hand, "I've

58.22 had snatched away his hand *CM-C&W* had drawn his hand away

59.6–7 middle-aged Irishman . . . who was *CM-C&W* middle-aged man who spoke English with a slight but noticeable Irish accent. When he first came to the town, a few years before, he gave his name as John Buckstone, and added, "formerly Lord Buckstone, author of the Queen's hounds"—meaning master of the Queen's hounds, probably. He was

†**59.15–18 Angelo less . . . one.** *CM-C&W* Angelo declined . . . them."

59.24–25 the bass *CM-C&W* a bass

59.33 and were *CM-C&W* and

*****60.9 were** *CM-C&W* was

60.16 a *CM-C&W* a pronounced

60.45 side-remarks. *CM-C&W* side-remarks department of them.

61.2–3 The extraordinarily . . . other suggested *CM-C&W* The Twins stood with their legs braced slightly apart. Their heads happened to be canted apart, too. Their attitude suggested

*****61.6 human philopena** *CM-C&W* human pair of scissors

61.8 aptness *CM-C&W* precision

61.10–13 Luigi's southern . . . took *CM-C&W* Luigi took

61.14 halted behind *CM-C&W* was behind

61.15 vigor *CM-C&W* vigor in the joker's rear

61.16 Tom *CM-C&W* him

62.8 upon *CM-C&W* onto

62.11 stampede *CM-C&W* outpour

62.13–14 to annihilate *CM-C&W* to have annihilated

63.2 strict *CM-C&W* stringent

64.1 one of the *CM-C&W* the

64.3 "Did *CM-C&W* "They did

64.18 Tom beat the twin on the trial. *CM-C&W* the trial went against Tom.

64.21 him up *CM-C&W* them up

64.23–24 The . . . death-stroke.∧ *CM-C&W* "Oh, my God!" ¶

64.24 for him∧ *CM-C&W* for his friend,

64.35 ain't . . . ain't *CM-C&W* isn't . . . isn't

64.39 Dominion." *CM-C&W* Dominion, and from that blood can spring no such misbegotten son."

65.2 was not *CM-C&W* not

65.7–10 answered guilelessly . . . assault." *CM-C&W* answered innocently, with a sheepish little laugh—¶ "Well, the fact is, it don't stand any way at all. I had them up in court, and they beat me."

65.11–12 feet with the opening sentence *CM-C&W* feet

†**65.21 said— . . . ¶ "You** *CM-C&W* said— . . . responsibility. You

65.27 it. He *CM-C&W* it. He was bitterly sorry he had been so premature
with his lie. He

*66.3–4 He is a . . . devil *CM-C&W*
They are . . . devils

66.4 him *CM-C&W* them

66.8 cornerₐ *CM-C&W* corner, still

66.10 scattering *CM-C&W* and scattered

66.20 The Count *CM-C&W* He

66.20–21 minutes," said Howard *CM-*
C&W minutes."

66.27 to ruin *CM-C&W* to rags and ruin

66.36 standpoint *CM-C&W* standpoint
it is,

66.37 most easily *CM-C&W* easiest

67.7–10 [maxim] October . . . *Calen-*
dar. *CM-C&W* [n.i.]

67.13 each *CM-C&W* either

67.14 he came *CM-C&W* came

67.25–26 likely, after . . . law-court.
CM-C&W likely.

67.30–31 hard. Try and . . . kicked.
CM-C&W hard. Better luck next time.
It's our first lawsuit, and we couldn't both
win it, you know. It's your turn next.

67.42 Italian savage *CM-C&W* human
lemon-squeezer

68.1 "Yes *CM-C&W* "The Twins—yes

68.15–16 their slipping . . . offense—
CM-APC there being any doubt about
it, such crowds of people saw the
assault—never once thought of their
slipping out of it the way they did, with
their vile double-action and single-action,
interchangeable at will when they want to
commit crime, and the original Satan
himself not able to tell t'other from which
when you want to fetch them to book—
their slipping . . . offence—*C&W*

68.26–27 being an . . . lawyer *CM-*
C&W being on the top wave of legal
prosperity

68.36 Italianₐ *CM-C&W* Twins,

69.42 has *CM-C&W* have

71.23 silence *CM-C&W* weighty silence

†**71.23–31 peace . . . Tom.** *CM-C&W*
peace . . . been!"

71.39–40 About . . . Pembroke
CMC&W It was the gracious watermelon season. All hearts should have
been gay and happy, but some were not.
About the time that Wilson was saying
the words which close the last chapter,
Pembroke

†**71.41–72.12 waiting. ¶ "Well . . . say-**
ing— *CM-C&W* waiting. ₐ Howard . . .
saying—

73.5 hour. *CM-C&W* hour of the night.
It was near eleven—a good hour after his
ordinary bedtime.

73.10–11 sight and hearing *CM-C&W*
sight

73.12 Howard said *CM-C&W* Howard
had his pistol case with him. He said

73.14 also with his brother. *CM-C&W*
also his brother, of course, who is looking indisposed.

73.30 "I *CM-C&W* "Ah, I

73.35 imitation *CM-C&W* mute imitation

74.3 getting more . . . doubtful *CM-*
C&W getting sicker and sicker

74.13 luck. *CM-C&W* luck. [end of
chapter] CHAPTER 22. [maxim] Let us
endeavor to so live that when we
approach death even the undertaker will
be sorry.—*Pudd'nhead Wilson's*
Calendar.

74.13–14 He dragged . . . in *CM-C&W*
Meantime Tom had been brooding in

74.23 people— *CM-C&W* people. There's

74.24–26 instance; even . . . but he
isn't *CM-C&W* instance; his fortune's
made, and what has he done to deserve
it, I would like to know. Yes, he has made
his own fortune, but isn't

74.26–27 block mine *CM-C&W* ruin
mine

74.30 to his *CM-C&W* for his

74.42 and turned westward. *CM-C&W*
and just then the Twins whizzed by, on
their way home. He wondered what that
might mean. Had they seen a ghost at
the haunted house?

74.45 duelists returning . . . he *CM-*
APC duelists, and he *MMS* duellists
returning . . . he *C&W*

75.8 wid one o' dem *CM-C&W* wid dat
pair o' nutcrackers—dem

75.10 Then he addedₐ *CM-C&W* He
added,

75.13 Twin I twins twin *CM-C&W*

75.17 Luigi *CM-C&W* Angelo

75.41–42 My great-great-great-gran'fa-
ther en yo' great-great-great-great-
gran'father *CM-C&W* My father en yo'
gran'father

75.42 Cap'n John Smith *CM-C&W*
John Randolph of Roanoke

75.44–45 queen, . . . Africa *CM-C&W*
queen

76.7 rumble *CM-C&W* rumble again

76.17 skinned. How *CM-C&W* peeled—
how

76.21 on *CM-C&W* in

76.31 out, en dah in de moonlight,
right I out, en dah I seed everything as
plain as day in de moonlight. Right
MMS out, en dar in de moonlight, right
CM-C&W

76.32 one o' de *CM-C&W* de

76.32–33 a-cussin' . . . a'cussin' . . . 'uz
cussin' *CM-C&W* a-yowlin' . . . a-
yowlin' . . . was yowlin'

76.33 brown *CM-C&W* *white*

76.34 shoulder. *CM-C&W* shoulder—
dat is, I *reckon* it 'uz *his* shoulder, dough
how *he* could tell it 'uz his'n, de way dey
arms is mixed up do beat me—but any-

way he judged it 'uz his'n en so he 'uz
doin' de yowlin' till he could fine out.

76.38 twin *CM-C&W* white twin

76.40 de twin *CM-C&W* de white one

76.44 me. *CM-C&W* me. Den dey 'uz
a gwyne to shoot agin, but de Twins dey
lit out. De white one 'uz gitt'n more'n
his sheer, en I reckon it 'uz him dat
run. But I don't know—caze 'tother one
went too.

77.6 Smith-Pocahontases *CM-C&W*
Randolphs

77.12 blon' twin *CM-C&W* nigger-
twin

77.12 doctor en de seconds. *CM-C&W*
doctor.

**79.5 [maxim] Nothing so needs
reforming** *CM-C&W* Nothing is so
injurious

79.7–11 [maxim] Behold . . . Calender.
CM-C&W [n.i.]

79.12–80.18 What . . . mystery. *CM-
C&W* [n.i.]

80.42–43 town, the town . . . either.
CM-C&W town, let the town keep it's
shirt on, too.

81.32 B'George *CM-C&W* 'George

81.35 with *CM-C&W* along *with*

82.27 it. *CM-C&W* it whatever.

83.20 or *CM-C&W* or or

83.36 either *CM-C&W* had either

83.38 perfect during . . . week. *CM-
C&W* perfect.

83.44 fight that Italian adventurer.
CM-C&W fight those Twins.

84.1 unawares, *CM-C&W* unprepared—

84.1–2 meet him . . . about him *CM-
C&W* meet them . . . about them

84.30–85.2 enough." ¶ The . . . it."
CM-C&W enough. I will cut those
Twins when I get the opportunity—one
of them ran away from the field, anyway:
perhaps both."

85.12–13 had restored . . . aunt *CM-
C&W* had made him solid with the
aunt

*****85.34–38 [maxim] We . . . Calendar.**
CM-C&W [n.i.]

86.11 sudden *CM-C&W* so sudden

86.16 dumb *CM-C&W* speechless

86.35 "Much *CM-C&W* "Hm! Much

87.9 selling *CM-C&W* sending

88.14–17 [maxim] Even . . . Calendar.
CM-C&W [n.i.]

88.22 [2nd maxim] Calendar. *CM-C&W*
Calendar. ¶ On Independence Day
Rowena went out back to see the fireworks and fell down the well and got
drowned. But it is no matter; these things
cannot be helped, in a work of this kind.

*****82.23–83.45 The . . . deserted.** *CM-
C&W* [n.i.]

90.6–9 [2nd maxim] Thanksgiving . . .
Calendar. CM-C&W [n.i.]

90.37 I'm *CM-C&W* I am

91.35–36 he said *CM-C&W* said

91.37 a deep *CM-C&W* a deep a deep

*****91.45 was only** *CM-APC* was but
MMS, C&W

*****92.44 Chambermaid** *CM-C&W* head
chambermaid

*****93.15 heard** *CM-C&W* hear

*****93.30–31 den I** *CM-C&W* I

*****95.37 de house** *CM-APC* he house
MMS, C&W

96.8 effort *CM-C&W* offer

*****96.23 knows you's a-goin'.** *CM-APC*
knows it. *MMS knows* it! *C&W*

97.29 this *CM-C&W* that

97.36–38 [maxim] Few . . . Calendar.
CM-C&W [n.i.]

†*****97.39–98.2–3 Dawson's . . . it. Judge
Driscoll declined** *CM-C&W*
Dawson's . . . Driscoll. The Judge
declined

98.30 for *CM-C&W* of

98.41 howling colony *CM-APC* harem
MMS, C&W

99.5 will *CM-C&W* shall

99.7 still a *CM-C&W* a

*****99.10 the twins** *CM-C&W* Luigi

*****99.17 window-blinds and lighted** *CM-
APC* window shades and lit *MMS* window-blinds and lit *C&W*

99.20 it, and laid it by. *CM-APC* it.
MMS it and laid it by. *C&W*

99.38 old man's small *CM-C&W* small

100.7 the notes *CM-APC* his notes
MMS, C&W

100.26 had joined *CM-C&W* were with

101.4 lighted *CM-APC* lit *MMS, C&W*

101.8 most *CM-APC* the most *MMS,*
C&W

101.10 ashes, scattered the ashes, *CM-
C&W* ashes,

101.22–24 mysteries, and . . . years."
CM-C&W mysteries.

**101.30 profligate Italian nobleman or
barber‸** *CM-C&W* profligate ex-freak
called the Italian Twins

101.32 The assassin will *CM-C&W*
One of them is considered innocent, but
the other one will

102.1 "One of the twins *CM-C&W*
"The Twins

102.2 him *CM-C&W* them

*****102.36–103.3 The coroner's . . . Wil-
son** *CM-C&W* The coroner's jury found
that the homicide was committed by
Luigi, and that Angelo was accessory to it.
The grand jury indicted Luigi for murder
in the first degree and Angelo as accessory. The Twins were transferred from the
city jail to the county prison to await trial.
¶ The town was bitter against them, and
for the first few days after the murder
they were in constant danger of being
lynched. ¶ Wilson

102.39–40 the unfortunates *CM-C&W*
them

102.42 **jury presently** *CM-C&W* jury
102.44 **accessory before the fact.** *CM-C&W* accessory.
103.18 **last** *CM-APC* past *MMS, C&W*
103.38 **had really** *CM-C&W* had
103.38 **revived, as . . . discovered,** *CM-C&W* revived,
105.2 **Aunt Patsy Cooper** *CM-C&W* the two old aunties
105.16–17 **one friend** *CM-C&W* two friends
105.17–18 **countenance . . . landlady. She . . . her** *CM-C&W* countenance. These sat near Wilson, and looked their
105.19 **In** *CM-C&W* One was aunt Patsy Cooper, the other was aunt Betsy Hale. In
105.24 **temper** *CM-C&W* fury
*105.27 **these** *CM-C&W* those
105.31 **toss** *CM-C&W* resolute toss
105.37–38 **his presence** *CM-C&W* his silence
106.10 **budding career** *CM-C&W* new reputation
*106.21 **on** *CM-C&W* in
107.14 **said that** *CM-C&W* said
107.29 **old-lady friend** *CM-C&W* two old-lady friends
107.31 **Aunt Patsy** *CM-C&W* the two old aunties
107.32 **a gay** *CM-C&W* a great and noble
107.32–33 **finishing.** *CM-C&W* finishing, and went away crying.
107.34–108.24 **Absolutely . . . then.** *CM-C&W* [n.i.]
108.35 **have** *CM-C&W* haven't
108.41 **always?"** *CM-C&W* always, just because you won once?"
109.2–3 **considering the brunette one's** *CM-C&W* considering their odious
109.34 **unintentionally left** *CM-C&W* left
110.24 **Heavens** *CM-C&W* Great guns
111.5–7 **[2nd maxim]** *April . . . Calendar.* *CM-C&W* [n.i.]
111.9 **high** *CM-C&W* tremendous
111.15 **whorls** *CM-APC* sworls *MMS, C&W*
111.31 **was ready** *CM-APC* ready *MMS, C&W*
112.3 **compelled** *CM-C&W* roused immediate
112.4 **evoked** *CM-C&W* also evoked
112.20 **admission.** *CM-C&W* admission as this.
112.24 **said.** *CM-C&W* said. The two old aunties seemed smitten with a collapse.
112.40 **accused brothers** *CM-C&W* accused
112.40–41 **that one of them** *CM-C&W* that they
112.41 **Judge** *CM-C&W* the late Judge

112.41 **lose his** *CM-C&W* lose their
112.43–44 **there secretly . . . adversary.** *CM-C&W* there by night and take their enemy by surprise and save themselves by destroying him.
114.20 **physical marks** *CM-C&W* marks
114.22–23 **physiological autograph** *CM-C&W* autograph
117.8 **pantograph copies** *CM-APC* things *MMS* pantagraph copies *C&W*
118.1 **thunder-crash** *CM-C&W* crash
118.1–2 **followed and** *CM-C&W* followed,
118.2–3 **feet, . . . Tom** *CM-C&W* feet, and the two old ladies flung themselves with hysterical gratitude at the Twins, but were promptly repressed by official force and brought to order along with the rest of the assemblage. Tom
118.5–6 **house's attention . . . more,** *CM-C&W* house was become tranquil again,
118.31–35 **Roxana was . . . privately.** *CM-C&W* Roxana began to fan herself violently, although the fall weather was pleasant; it certainly was not uncomfortably warm, at least.
118.40 **Roxy's . . . still!** *CM-C&W* Roxy collapsed and fell over against her next neighbor, but quickly recovered herself.
*119.11 **sits among you. I** sits in your midst! *MMS* sits in among you. *CM-APC* sits in your midst. *C&W*
120.13–19 **CONCLUSION. [2 maxims]** *CM-C&W* Chapter 32. [no maxims]
120.24–26 **marvelous. His . . . good.** *CM- APC* marvelous. He was a made man for good, this time; nothing could ever shake his foundations again. *MMS* marvellous. His . . . good. *C&W*
120.28 **remorseful** *CM-C&W* remorseful and shame-faced
120.31 **friends** *CM-C&W* boys
120.32 **isn't** *CM-C&W* ain't
*120.33–36 **now, and with . . . Roxy's** *CM-C&W* now, and they came into vast and instant favor again, and aunt Patsy and aunt Betsy's cups of happiness were full. But the restored popularity of the strangers did not last long. . . . Roxy's
†120.41 **solace.** *CM-C&W* solace. ¶ Aunt Patsy . . . kind.
121.18–19 **as through . . . blame the false** *CM-C&W* as the false
121.21 **rightly claimed** *CM-C&W* claimed
122.6–7 **erroneous inventory** *CM-C&W* dishonest inventory which had suppressed his name
†*122.12 **river.** *CM-C&W* river. ¶ CONCLUSION. . . . . sides.

Emendations of the Copy-Text: Substantives
(Lengthy Passages)

*[n.i.] First entry in Emendations of copy-text, Substantives. (See facsimile, Appendix 1.)

<u>To Printer</u>. Please make fac-similes of those signs, and use them at chapter-tops—one and sometimes two—SLC   it is not necessary that they fit the weather of the chapter always.

Key to Signs used in this book.

To save the space usually devoted to explanations of the state of the weather in books of this kind, the author begs leave to substitute a simple system of weather-signs. The hieroglyph at the head of each chapter will instantly convey to the reader's mind a perfect comprehension of the kind of weather which is going to prevail below.

The signs and their meanings here follow: [Sunny, Pitch Dark, Starlight, Rainy, Moonlight, Snow, Fog—see Appendix 1]

When two or more signs occur together, the ensuing weather is going to be more, or more yet, or still more variable, according to number of signs employed.

When all the signs are used it means <u>Stormy</u>.

When they are doubled it means <u>Extremely Violent</u> <u>and</u> <u>Perilous</u> <u>Weather</u>.

When there is no sign, it means that there is no going to be any weather. It is a mistake to suppose that weather is at all times necessary in a novel. As often as not, it is an inconvenience, and keeps the characters from going out.

25.21   wood. *CM-C&W*

wood. She had remained a Methodist ever since she first "got religion" and lost two dollars by it; she was a most capable hymn-singer, for she had the rich and sweet and pathetic voice so common to the race which she accepted as hers; she was the best shouter in the "amen corner," and if she wasn't a tough customer in a theological argument, she at least thought she was. Jasper was a Dunker Baptist. He had a pretty robust opinion of his own powers in argument, and was fond of meeting Roxy in that field; consequently the theological fur was quite sure to fly whenever they came together. A chief bone of contention between them was the matter of special providences; they had gnawed it till there was no vestige of meat left on it, but that was no matter, they found it as toothsome without meat as with it. Jasper believed in special

providences, Roxy didn't. She believed that whatever happened in this world happened in obedience to a body of well regulated general laws, and that these laws were never set aside by sudden caprice to wet some saint's wilting crop or drown some sinner who went a fishing on the Sabbath.

Three day's [*sic*] before Roxy's visit, Jasper was tramping up the "Bluff road," among the hills back of the town. It was a heavy pull, and when he reached what was called Precipice Corner he sat down and hung his heels over the abyss and prepared himself for a rest and a smoke. At his right was a stretch of road as straight as a lance and pretty steep; where he sat, this road made an exceedingly abrupt elbow; between the sheer precipice on the one side and the cut wall of the hill on the other there was not room for two wagons to pass. Whoever drove down the stretch of straight road must turn that elbow cautiously if he would turn it safely.

Presently Jasper heard a noise above him, and glanced up and saw a cloud of gray dust flying down the straight road toward him. It was moving so swiftly that he thought it must be a whirlwind. He jumped up to observe it. But it wasn't a whirlwind.

"By gracious it's somebody's hoss runnin' away wid him! If he whirl's [*sic*] round dis corner at dat gait, somebody got to chink down in de valley en gether him up in a basket."

He took a position, spat in his hands and gave himself a shake as a kind of notice to his vast strength to get ready for business. He was not able to furnish the particulars of what happened after that. He only knew that the next instant the flying horse was upon him and that he grabbed him and stood him upon his hind heels in the air!

Then the dust settled and he had a great and glad surprise, for he saw his young mistress, with her nurse and baby, sitting in the buggy. Jasper led the horse around the elbow and went to examining the harness to see if it was all right. The occupants of the buggy got out, and thought they would walk back to their summer home on the hill for a change of sensations. When the lady turned the elbow she saw her father and mother and the house servants grouped on the precipice and trying to look over; and all were moaning and wailing and ejaculating. The family, standing on the porch, had seen the horse begin to run when he left the gate, and they and the negroes had followed on foot, in the wake of a flight which none imagined could end otherwise than in destruction at the precipice.

"Father, we are not hurt!" The father

turned dreamily and incredulously about, at the sound of this voice which he had supposed would never comfort his ear again in this life, and saw his daughter standing unharmed before him, delivered, he knew not by what miracle, from the very grave itself.

There was nothing but wild embracings and incoherent exclamations of gratitude for a little while, then the father said—

"But how was it done? What is the explanation of it?"

"Jasper happened to be here, and he siezed [sic] the horse and stopped him."

"That is not possible. No man could do it; ten couldn't. The town will never believe it."

"But Jasper did it, and I saw him."

Jasper was called, and came humbly, with his hat in his hand. His master said—

"Jasper, there is nothing that I can say now—I am too much moved, too much broken up to put rational speech together; but another time—another time I will try to thank you. Put on your hat. Freemen stand covered in each other's presence in the open air; and you are free, from this hour."

For three days Jasper had been a freed man, a hero, and the talk of the town. He was "laying for" Roxy, all loaded and primed and ready with an argument which he judged would silence her guns for one while, anyway.

25.31   it." CM-C&W

it." He wished her prosperity and a safe return, and turned away, saying—

"You want to modify that highflyer attitude of yours, Roxy, and take your knuckles out of your hips: Jasper's a free citizen and a hero, now, and you must stop putting on airs around him."

The theologians answered with a laugh apiece, and the arguments began to fly. As the fencing went on, Jasper began to lead warily up to his heroic episode; then he set forth the situation: he had to be on that hill, and at that exact spot, at that precise moment of time to the fraction of a minute, or those people's death was an absolutely unpreventable thing. Then he shook a victorious finger in Roxy's face and shouted:

"Dah, now! Dey ain't no special providences, hain't dey? *Who put me dah?*—aha, you answer me dat!"

Roxy's return-blast was instant and disabling:

"Who sent de *hoss* dah in dat shape, you chucklehead? Answer me *dat!*"

*35.1–3   established. He. . . . he told CM-C&W

said the society had been in existence four years and already had two members, and was firmly established. Luigi wanted to join it.

The Judge was delighted, and would call the membership together right away, suspend the rules and make the election immediate. He said that the addition of so distinguished a personage would give the society a fine lift and a fresh start. He hinted that if Count Angelo also—

But Luigi interrupted, and said, "My brother will attend the meetings, but that will be as far as he can go. He will not be able to join, or take any active part in the proceedings, because he is a member of the Methodist church, and the prejudices of that sect are such that even his passive presence is more than likely to provoke criticism and make talk."

"Ah, I see, I see how the case stands, I see the delicacies and difficulties of the situation. But we shall be very glad to have you present with us unofficially, dear sir—informally, sir, purely informally—and although it has been our rule to exclude all who were not members, I assure you we shall be glad to make an exception in your case; and I may add with confidence that no effort will be spared to make these occasions enjoyable to you, sir."

Angelo concealed his bitter annoyance as well as he could, and answered courteously—

"I thank you sincerely, sir, for your kind welcome, and for the great and undeserved concessions which the society proposes to make in my favor. I shall attend the meetings, but it would not be honorable in me to conceal the fact that I shall go because I must, not because I wish to. I believe you when you say that the society will spare no effort to make the meetings enjoyable to me, but I know too well, alas, but too well, sir, that when it has done it's [sic] best my enjoyment will be of but a doubtful sort. All the positions and arguments of the freethinkers—you will pardon my speaking so frankly—are a horror to me, and so the prospect of sitting out one of these discussions and seeming to countenance it, and be in it and of it, fills me with the keenest suffering. I assure you I do no overstate the case, sir."

"I see your side of the matter, sir, and I wish I could think of some way to—to—can either of you suggest a way out of this really most painful and embarrassing difficulty, gentlemen? The more I look at it the more—the more—er—"

The benevolent Judge came to a stop. The case was too new and complex for him. Nobody suggested anything, and so after a pause, he said:

"Why, there must be some—er—way—some—er—how do you generally do?"

"Well," said Luigi, with a touch of resentment in his voice, "I have allowed my brother the opportunity to state that very thing, but apparently he sees that to do it would place him in no very generous attitude after what he has been saying; so I will state it myself: *We always go together*. Ask him if I go to church with him. Just ask him. If he wants to deny it—"

"I don't deny it," said Angelo in a low voice, and coloring.

The Judge bent a pained and reproachful gaze upon him. There was a wordless silence, for many moments, during which each of these erring and yet well-intentioned men was busy with his own sad thoughts; then Angelo spoke:

"You should not be too hard upon me— either of you. My conflict has not been without example. I am merely human. Who is more? Luigi, when you have been in command of our body, have you ever invited me to go to church?"

"Well—no."

"Have you yielded and taken me when I begged you?"

"I—well, I believe I never have."

"When it was my week of command, did you ever go with me except upon compulsion?"

Luigi was silent.

"Judge Driscoll, you see he does not answer. It is because his answer would be a confession. Am I justified? Am I worse than he?"

"Give me your hands, both of you. There—let bygones be bygones. We are all poor erring creatures, quick to judge, prompt to see the wrong in others and be behind it in ourselves. I see the whole case, now, and find no fault with either of you. You have merely done as I would have done, as anybody would have done, situated as you are. Go on, gentlemen, just as before, and no right-minded man can [seek] [illegible] a flaw in your conduct. There is no harm in going to church when one cannot help it; I see, now, and see clearly, that this is perfectly true. It follows that there can be no harm in your going to our freethinking meeting, sir, upon the same terms and conditions. As I said before, you will be most welcome, and I wish sincerely that you might be correspondingly happy; but it may not be, I suppose, it may not be; we cannot have everything as we would like it in this world, filled as it is, one knows not why, with conflicting opinions and warring desires."

Angelo replied, with much feeling—

"Indeed, sir, I could almost wish I might be happy there, for your sake; for I appreciate and am grateful for the generous sympathy and solicitude which you exhibit for me"—then added with a sigh—"but my beliefs and principles being what they are, it would make me deeply unhappy to be happy in such circumstances. I could not abide it, I could not endure it. Happy there? I shud-der to think of it; it would be sacrilege." His voice trembled with emotion; he was not able to go on for some moments; then he added, with touching earnestness: "No, I shall be unhappy; and I shall be far happier in being unhappy than I could be in being happy."

"A noble spirit spoke there!" cried the Judge. "I could embrace you for those words. I wish we had a thousand like you in our society. But they do not exist, sir; the world cannot furnish them. I am proud to know you, sir, proud to know such a man."

"You do me too much honor, sir, indeed you do; but I am thankful for what you have said; I could not be more so if I truly deserved it."

The Judge insisted that he did deserve it, and more.

[For an explanation of the place of this deleted passage, see the Textual Note for 35.1–3 for *Pudd'nhead Wilson*. (See page 221 herein.) Note that an extensive part of the manuscript at this point (MMS 132–161) has been removed from *Pudd'nhead Wilson* and used in *Those Extraordinary Twins*.]

35.6–11   achieved. Later . . . carried. *CM-C&W*

achieved; but with Angelo the favorable impression was not quite perfect, it being marred by the fact that Wilson was a free-thinker. The meeting was called to order, a ballot was taken, and Luigi elected to membership. Then the Judge proposed to discuss the six days of the creation from a strictly scientific standpoint, but Wilson made a little speech in which he said he had learned, during the day, that the guest of the evening was a church member, therefore the courtesy due him as a guest forbade that any subject be touched upon which could in any way wound his feelings. He moved that the hour be devoted to conversation upon ordinary topics and the cultivation of friendly relations and good-fellowship, and then sat down.

The Judge cast a proud glance at the Twins which said, "There—what did I tell you?"— that is the kind of man he is." Angelo's eyes sent back a glance of surprised and grateful approval, but Luigi remained impassive. Still, he said to himself, I don't like Wilson the less for this; I would do such things myself if I could get the best of my nature. This thought pushed him to an effort, and when the motion was put he made it unanimous by voting aye. Angelo could have embraced him, he was so pleased, but he kept his impulse to himself, knowing that with Luigi it was generally best to let well enough alone.

[Note: most of the following paragraph is in *Pudd'nhead Wilson* 35.12–16. It is quoted here in full because the paragraph in MMS differs in many words and then continues with the long deleted passage.]

The hour passed quickly away in lively talk, and when it was ended the lonesome and neglected Wilson was richer by two friends than he had been when it began. He invited the Twins to look in at his lodgings when the Bible class should be over, and Luigi promptly accepted. Angelo said—

"I ought not to go, much as I desire it, since mixing socially with freethinkers must make talk and be a detriment to me, situated as I am, but I cannot decline any invitation this week which my brother accepts, therefore I shall come—yes, and eagerly, in spirit, although reluctantly in principle."

The freethinkers left, now, and as they went out at the door the Bible class began to file in, the Rev. Mr. Hotchkiss in the lead. It made him gasp to see the Twins there, but the young ladies and gentlemen did not gasp; no, the situation was larks for them, so to speak, as one could see by their arch glances and the way they privately nudged each other and indulged in smothered gigglings. Mr. Hotchkiss had been spreading the fact around that his church had made a capture of one of the distinguished foreigners, and that both were going to visit his Bible class, and the class was not slow, now, to perceive how much the size of these triumphs had been cut down by the precedence given the freethinking crew. They were too young to grieve over Mr. Hotchkiss's misfortune, they only enjoyed it.

However, Mr. Hotchkiss did the best he could, in the circumstances. He threw as much cordiality as he could into his welcome of the Twins, though his embarrassment showed through, rather plainly. He introduced everybody in turn to the strangers, and then the session opened. The Bible class was in effect a debating class, with casting vote and veto lodged in its president, the minister. They now proceeded to discuss the question of whether men would rise from the dead as spirits or clothed on [sic] with flesh. The minister closed the discussion, and was gratified to see, he said, that the class was with him in believing that we should enter heaven in the flesh, and differing in no wise from what we are here.

Then he offered the Twins the privilege of speaking, whereupon Angelo took the minister's view, and after talking a while, apologized for Luigi, who was not now a believer but must in time become one; of this Angelo felt sure.

The minister most heartily hoped that this would prove true, and asked Luigi if he was not able to believe that men would be raised in the flesh.

Luigi said yes, he was able to believe it, and did believe it.

The minister was gratified, and asked him why, then, he did not come into the fold and take measures to save himself.

Luigi answered, with simplicity, that he was not fitted by nature and disposition for the religious vocation, and was satisfied to leave it to his brother to save him.

"Your brother! Ah, my dear friend, we cannot delegate these things. Each must enter heaven on his own merits; your brother cannot take you there."

"How will he avoid it?"

There was a sufficiently awkward silence, which endured for some moments; then the minister rallied, and said:

"There—er—well, there is—er—there is certainly reason in the position which you have taken. It is indeed logical—in fact, formidably so; that I must confess. But, on the other hand, consider, my dear friend, that a place is appointed for those who die in sin, and to it they must infallibly go; and surely you would not desire to drag down with you thither your innocent brother?"

Luigi reflected, then said:

"Do you ever teach that an innocent person can be sent to that place because somebody else has led a guilty life and died in sin?"

"Why—n-no. Certainly not—of course not."

"Shall you ever teach that?"

"Well, no, I could not teach that, I am free to say."

"Very well, I believe as you do: the innocent need not be afraid of being punished for the guilty. You have confirmed and solidified in me this belief. I have always depended upon my brother to save me, and I know he will. I shall go on depending on him."

The clock on the wall struck nine, and the minister seemed relieved by the interruption and at once dismissed the class. Luigi had worked him into an awkward dilemma and was gratified; he saw that the class was tickled, and that pleased him; Angelo was ashamed of him, and that completed his happiness and he was glad he had come. Mr. Hotchkiss did not tarry for an effusive leave-taking, but cut it as short as decency would permit and got away; and as he trudged homeward he said to himself with an irritated spirit, "These Twins are in every way an awkward and embarrassing anomaly, and in my opinion the more this community sees of them the more it is going to have that fact borne in upon them." Presently he added, with bitterness—

"These giddy young scamps will carry to-night's performance all over the town tomorrow; from the town it will spread all around the back country, and every sorrowing creature in the land that is suffering for something to laugh at will come to see me baptise [sic] that abandoned infidel, Sunday!"

37.1   Mogul." *CM-C&W*

Mogul." It was a big steamer for the time—
two hundred and fifty feet long. Roxy had
never been in a steamer's cabin before—
cabin was the western name for the grand
salons into which the berth-rooms opened,
not the berth-rooms themselves. The cabin
was like a long, brilliantly lighted tunnel. It
was of pine, covered with a highly polished
skin of white paint. On every berth-room
door of the two far-stretching sides was an
oil picture—Mississippi scenery, the subject—with all the known colors in it and
some of the unknown, and all the different
kinds of drawing in it except good drawing—
dreadful pictures, in fact, but very showy
and effective. Separating these crimes were
fluted white-painted pine pilasters with
gilded Corinthian capitals. Overhead the
receding stretch of ivory-like ceiling fairly
bristled with down-pointing wonders of
ornamentation done with the jig-saw and the
turning-lathe. At fifty-foot intervals there
were great pyramidal chandeliers, whose
sumptuous fringes of cut-glass prisms, flaming and flashing in the sun, shook out showers of dancing rainbow-flecks upon the
white walls and doors in response to the
slightest joggle. Tables covered with figured
crimson cloths formed a fiery platform down
the middle of the tunnel from end to end.
Against each wall was backed a stiff rank of
windsor chairs, from the bar on the port side
and the clerk's office on the starboard clear
aft to the piano and the big mirror in the
ladies' cabin. And the carpet—the carpet was
a revel; not a dream, but a revel, just a revel
of bounding and careering great whorls of
inflamed scroll-work out on a drunk.

Roxy was entranced. She had often heard
of these "floating palaces"—which was the
common and quite sincerely-applied name
of these museums—but had never been on
the inside of one of them before. She moved
through it in an ecstasy of bliss. The wilderness of noble furniture amazed her by its
magnitude, and its possible cost made all her
former notions of wealth seem poor and
shabby imaginings; the profusion and rich-
ness of the decorations steeped her barbaric
soul in delight, and in the glorious insurrection of color she saw her dearest dreams of
the splendors of heaven realized. Ah, why
hadn't she run away and entered into the
joys of this earthly paradise earlier? It
grieved her to think she had lost so much
time.

Presently passengers began to stream
aboard and flock hither and thither in search
of their staterooms, inquiring, commanding,
exclaiming, and they filled the whole place
with inspiriting life and racket and commo-
tion. Ah, it was a thousand times better to be
here than in that sleepy dull town.

Soon, a swarm of white-aproned and
white-jacketed colored boys burst in from
somewhere, and in an instant the red covers
were gone and the tables clothed in white! It
made Roxy dizzy, the thing was done so suddenly. And she wondered how one mere
human establishment could support such a
horde of servants. When she came to herself
after a couple of seconds, there was another
surprise—they had vanished; whither, she
didn't know.

Then came a musical kling-kling from a
little bell, and they appeared again; they
marched in, in a couple of snowy files, and
moved down the long cabin, depositing
plates and cruets and things as they went,
and in a minute the tables stood completely
arrayed and ready for the provisions. The last
boys in the ranks placed the chairs.

The bell struck again, and again the files
entered, some bearing great platters and
chafing-dishes of fish, meats and so forth,
aloft, and others superb sugar-clad minia-
ture temples, supposed to be made of cake,
whereas in truth the finest of them were decorated cheese-boxes, though neither Roxy
nor the passengers suspected that.

Then the first gong let go a horrible crash
and kept it up two minutes, although there
was a passenger behind every chair by the
time that the fiend with the gong had hit it
the second blow.

At the end of ten minutes the gong broke
loose again, the double file of passengers
plunged into their seats, and the havoc
began.

To Roxy the prodigious noise and confusion about the stage-planks during the final
moments before the boat's departure was a
most satisfying delight. Every detail had
interest for her: the rushing avalanch of bar-
rels thundering down the stages; the belated
passengers skipping perilously among them
to win to the forecastle; the clarion voices of
the mates discharging volume after volume
of the most erudite and versatile and magnificent profanity without a tautological
blemish in it anywhere; the yelling of news-
boys; the slamming of furnace doors; the
screaming of gauge-cocks; the deafening
banging and clanging of the everlasting "last
bell." Every separate detail had a dulcet
charm for Roxy, and the combination constituted bliss.

At last the boat did get away, and went
plowing down the Ohio, filling all the heavens with sable smoke; and for seven days
and nights she piled States and scenery
behind her with a celerity which bewildered the second chambermaid and made
her realize as she had never realized before
that the white man was in very truth a won-
der-compelling creature and a creator of
marvelous contrivances. Then she found
herself in New Orleans, and when she saw

that the wells (cisterns) and the graves were all on top of the ground instead of under it she was sure her excitements had confused her brain and disordered her eyesight.

48.21   head." CM-C&W

head. . . . . I am a nigger—a nigger! . . . . . Yesterday I hated nobody very much, but now I hate the whole human race. . . . . If I had the courage, I would kill—somebody—anybody. But she was right—I haven't it. I've only material in me for an assassin. . . . . . Better that than. . . . . . I am so changed, so changed! Yesterday I was ashamed of my thefts—but now, why now, I am not, for I stole from the whites. I will do it again. I will do it whenever I can. . . . . . And that poor lowly and ignorant creature is my mother! . . . . . . Well, she has my respect for one thing—she has never owned a slave. All the white respectability of this town is shabby and mean, beside that one virtue.". . . .

49.44   dog." CM-C&W

dog."
    In his broodings in the solitudes, he searched himself for the reasons of certain things, and in toil and pain he worked out the answers:
    Why was he a coward? It was the "nigger" in him. The nigger *blood*? Yes, the nigger blood degraded from original courage to cowardice by decades and generations of insult and outrage inflicted in circumstances which forbade reprisals, and made mute and meek endurance the only refuge and defence.
    Whence came that in him which was high, and whence that which was base? That which was high came from either blood, and was the monopoly of neither color; but that which was base was the *white* blood in him debased by the brutalizing effects of a long-drawn heredity of slave-owning, with the habit of abuse which the possession of irresponsible power always creates and perpetuates, by a law of human nature. So he argued.
    But what a totally new and amazing aspect one or two things, in particular, bore to Tom, now that he found himself looking at them from around on the other side! For instance—nigger illegitimacy, yesterday and to-day. Yesterday, of what consequence could it be to a nigger whether he was a bastard or not? To-day the reflection "I am a bastard" made the hot blood leap to Tom's very eyelids. Yesterday, if any had asked him, "Which is more honorable, more desirable, and more a matter for a nigger to be proud of—to be a nigger born in wedlock, or a white man's bastard?" he would have thought the questioner was jesting. It was of course an honor to be

a white man's bastard, and the highest honor a nigger could have. Who could doubt it? The question would astonish the nigger himself—go ask him and you will see. But to-day—to-day! to be a nigger was shame, but compared with this million-fold obscener infamy it was nothing, it was less than nothing. "And I am a nigger *and* that other thing!" It was only thought, he could not have uttered it, for his throat was dry and his tongue impotent with rage.

58.18   breaths, and . . . said, CM-C&W

breaths, and Tom said—
    "I wonder he was so particular. I should have thought he would kill the first one of you that came handy—or jam his dirk into your mutual body and kill you both."
    Angelo colored, and said, rather shamefacedly—
    "Well, the truth is, he had a reason, and a good one, for preferring me. He could have killed Luigi without much sin, for Luigi was a freethinker and the fact was known; but he could kill me without any sin at all; and not only that, but it would be a very meritorious and praiseworthy deed, because I had just publicly apostatised from the Mohammedan Church, and this native was a Mohammedan. If he killed Luigi my death would follow, but *he* wouldn't get any credit for it on high, so the knife's gems would be his only reward. Necessarily, common sense moved him to kill me, and get both rewards."
    "Well, I *never* should have thought of that ingenious distinction!" exclaimed Tom, with admiration. "That native was no fool, *I* tell you!"
    "Now, Tom," said Wilson,

59.15–18   Angelo less . . . one. CM-C&W

Angelo declined it as cordially, and called all present to witness that in going with Luigi he was doing it under protest; that he would not go if he could help it; and that he was totally opposed to the principles of the rum party; he added that he was dying of fatigue, and that it was a shameful cruelty to keep him on his legs any longer.
    "*Your* legs!" said Luigi indignantly. "I like your impudence. You will go to the meeting—I will see to that. And don't waste any more pathetic speeches here; save them for the temperance meetings—you will probably carry me to enough of them."

65.21   said— . . . ¶ "You CM-C&W

said—
    "So your refuge, the jury, discovered—as we have been informed—that only one of the pair kicked you, but could not determine

which one it was? Which one do you think it was?"

Tom had already been to call at the widow Cooper's, and had gathered a strong suspicion there that Rowena was warming toward Angelo and cooling toward him. Without much reflection he framed a lie, now, which gave him a good deal of satisfaction for a moment—

"I don't need to think, I already know which one it was. It was the one named Angelo—the pious one—the one that is to be baptised to-morrow. He was so set-up because he had got the best of me in the trial that he couldn't resist the temptation to crow—so he whispered and told me, going out of court, that he was the one that kicked me."

The way in which the news was received surprised the young fellow, and not pleasantly:

"Ah, that is good! that is splendid!" exclaimed the uncle, beaming with joy. "It locates the responsibility. You have challenged him?"

"N—no," hesitated Tom, turning pale.

"All right, no harm is done. You

71.23–31   peace . . . Tom *CM-C&W*

peace began to clear his throat, and Wilson said to himself, "People haven't been in the habit of coming here in flocks, as far back as I can remember—I see I am about to have my curiosity set at rest as to what this flock are here for."

"Mr. Wilson," said the justice, with solemnity, "I do not need to remind you that we are soon to cease from being a town, and put on the dignity of a city."

"No, your honor, I am aware of it."

"And I do not need to remind you, either, that the time for our first charter election approaches."

"No, your honor, I am aware of that, also."

Tom said he believed he was not interested in politics, and thought he would excuse himself. He was allowed to go. He went sighing, and miserable.

"Mr. Wilson, you cannot of course be unaware of the great and gratifying leap which you have made to-day in fame and in the admiration and esteem of your fellow-citizens—a leap which I am free to say, much surpasses anything of the kind which I have ever met with before in all my experience on the bench—I-I mean in all my experience—er—anywhere. It is the general wish of our party—the great Democratic party of which you have always been a faithful member—that your name and talents shall be secured for the service of our new municipal organization. We have come, therefore, as a committee, deputed to invite you to stand for office under the forthcoming city government. May I say that you will oblige us?"

The tumultuous blood rushed to Wilson's very forehead for joy and exultation. He said it was the proudest moment of his life, and for once that moss-backed phrase vibrated with the genuine life of truth. He said he was his party's loyal servant—let it command, he was ready to obey. What office did the party desire that he should go into nomination for?

"Any, sir! Any you please! Choose for yourself, Mr. Wilson—such are our instructions. You make your choice [sic] sir—the party will look to the rest."

Wilson was mute—he was entirely overcome. Honors?—here were not only honors, but choice of them. He had never dreamed of a fairy land of that amazing sort before, asleep or awake. He was in such a whirl of happiness and emotion that he could not trust his voice, but had to do his thanks with fervent hand-grasps and the deep eloquence of watery eyes.

It was sufficient. The old Justice characterized it afterward as by a long way the most beautiful speech he had ever heard.

The deputation thanked him through their mouthpiece for his acceptance, and went away, leaving him to make choice at his leisure, and report. Wilson stood some little time like one stupefied, then turned to his work murmuring—

"What a day—*what* a day it has been!"

71.41–72.12   waiting. ¶ "Well . . . saying— *CM-C&W*

waiting. Howard sat down near him with that vague and indefinable something in his manner which warns the alert observer to prepare for ill news, but the Judge was oblivious to it, and spoke up with the briskest confidence and interest—

"Well, what is the hour and where is the place?"

Howard hesitated, as one might who is seeking some way to soften an unavoidable blow, then he said—

"I—well, I may as well blurt it straight out, I see no way to mitigate it." He pulled himself together, looked the Judge piteously in the eyes, and said with a sigh—

"He won't fight."

The old man started violently, then his gaze began to wander vacantly about the room, and his face to turn ashy and his lips to move, sometimes emitting no sound, sometimes emitting broken words, parts of sentences: "Won't—fight . . . . ah-h! . . . . cruel . . . . . serve an old man so . . . . My honor . . . . . . what is to become of that? . . . . . Oh, how . . . . . how could one . . . . . believe . . . . ." And so on, and so on. He was like one whose faculties have been stunned by a physical blow and one groping in confusion and semi-consciousness. It made his friend's heart bleed to see him. He brought whisky and made him drink it, and soothed his hurt spirit with caressing and comforting words; and so presently won him back to life, and to tranquillity [sic] and resignation. He hastened to reinforce these efforts with his tale, and his reward followed; he saw his patient's eye begin to lose its haziness and brighten with interest as the story went on; and sooner than he had ventured to hope the restoration was complete.

"I will give you the details, York, and then you will understand the situation. I went there and asked to see the foreign gentlemen privately, and was left in the parlor alone. They entered soon, and were very polite and pleasant, remembering my face and name, and also referring to a detail or two of the moment's talk which we had had at the reception. I then introduced the matter of my errand and handed the cartel to Count Angelo, at the same time saying that I was at his second's immediate service and that if he would name him I would go at once and arrange the details with him. To my astonishment he declined to accept the challenge, and explained that his religious views would not allow him to do such a thing. I was surprised at the pretext, of course, but did not betray it. I urged him, with all courtesy, not to restrict himself to considering the matter as it affected himself alone, but to remember and respect your rights and dues in it as well. I went further and begged him as a brother in the faith not to bring a hurt upon our religion by a hasty and incautious interpretation of its precepts, and reminded him that its loftiest admonition, its golden rule, made it at once our privilege and our imperative duty to do unto others as we would have them do unto us in the same circumstances. To my stupefaction this had no more effect upon him than if he had been reared in the outer darkness of paganism. He still refused to fight, and refused point blank.

"At this point a noble thing happened—a sin, it was, but a manly one; if ever sin may be so named—and if ever sin *may* be so named, this was the manliest one that was ever committed in my sight. The Count Luigi *lied* to save his brother from shame—came out with magnificent audacity and said *he* committed the assault and would fight!"

"By the lord Harry he's a man!—he's a man, every inch of him!" cried the Judge. "Ah, it would be a privilege to stand up before a Roman like that, if it were only permissible." He shook his head once or twice, and added, wistfully, "for it wouldn't be

right—no, I suppose it wouldn't be right—to let him chance his life for his brother's fault?"

Plainly, he hoped that Howard would argue him out of that scruple; and he was charmed to see, by the sudden clearing of his friend's countenance, that he was applying in the right quarter. Howard took vigorous hold of the moralities and proprieties of the case, and both men were soon convinced that it was not only permissible to shoot one brother for another brother's offence, if he wanted to be shot, but that it was even a high and righteous duty to grant him that privilege and thus enable him to remove a smirch from his brother's honor which would extend to his own if it were allowed to remain. Then Howard said, cheerfully—

"The matter is simple, now, and we can proceed with untroubled consciences. I am very very glad you look at it as you do, York. I was determined not to suggest this solution to you, for I couldn't have you do a thing upon any hint of mine which you could regret afterwards. I came away from that place miserable, for I didn't dare to let Luigi accept, of course, since that would have been to go beyond the powers vested in me; but I shall go back there in another frame of mind, I assure you. Ah, it's [sic] a fine fellow, York!—you'll like to fight that one; I should like it myself. You should have heard him argue his case. He said his brother's honor was just as dear to him as his own, and that he would gladly put himself in danger at at [sic] any time, gladly have himself shot at, for its protection and preservation. And he insisted upon being allowed to do this, and said that he had the same high right to take the place of a brother who was disabled by his principles from defending himself as he should unquestionably have if that brother were disabled by physical incapacity."

"Why, Pembroke, that's not only fine and manly and handsome, but it's perfectly sound—absolutely sound. Why, of *course* principles are as legitimate and complete a disability as physical disability, when you come to look at it. That young man has got an admirable head, and most capable head, and a most broad and unusual intelligence. His brother was grateful?"

"Well, n-no, he—in fact he wasn't. He disappointed me. Instead of being grateful, he objected—and strenuously. He said it was all very fine for his brother, with his robust nature, not to mind bullets, but as for himself, he was not built in that way, and he *did* mind them. He didn't *want* to stand so near while his brother was being shot at, and wouldn't ever consent to do it; said he should be perfectly sick when the bullets began to fly; and when his brother tried to comfort him, and said the Westerners were all good marksmen and could be depended on to hit the particular man they were shooting at, so *he* needn't be worrying, he turned as gray as a last-year's cobweb, and said if Luigi's head got bored through, it might just as well be his own, the general result would be the same. However, his labored shufflings and irrelevancies had no effect upon his chivalrous brother, who wanted to fight, was bound to fight, and was bent on having the duel straight off, this very night, before twelve o'clock."

"Why, Pembroke, he's magnificent! I never saw so fine a creature. Go and arrange the thing."

"Howard siezed [*sic*] his hat and started on his joyful errand, saying—

*102.36–103.3   Dawson's . . . it. Judge Driscoll declined *CM-C&W*

Dawson's Landing had a week of repose, after the election, and it needed it, for the frantic and variegated nightmare which had tormented it all through the preceding week had left it limp, haggard and exhausted at the end. It got the week of repose because Angelo had the legs, and was in too subdued condition to want to go out and mingle with an irritated community that had come to distrust and detest him because there was such a lack of harmony between his morals, which were confessedly excellent, and his methods of illustrating them, which were distinctly damnable. He took his exercise after eleven at night, when the streets were empty. Luigi was sick of society too, for the present, so this nocturnal arrangement suited him perfectly, though he did not say so, since he and his brother were still not on speaking terms.

However, the season of reposeful dulness [*sic*] was to end now, for Luigi was once more on deck. On Sunday Pudd'nhead Wilson carried his challenge to Judge Driscoll. The Judge declined

120.41   solace. *CM-C&W*

solace.

Aunt Patsy and Aunt Betsy felt the loss of the Twins deeply, and the scar of that loss remained with them permanently; but their hearts were young and their interests limitless, so they were sufficiently bulwarked against serious unhappiness.

The lads Henry and Joe fell down the well and got drowned. But it is no particular matter, and such things cannot well be provided against in a work of this kind.

122.12   river. *CM-C&W*

. . . river.

CONCLUSION.

March. Thought by some to be one of the spring months. But this is an error. March is a season by itself, and has not been classified. It was created for some inscrutable, unwise, inexcusable purpose, which we may conjecture about all we want to, but the best plan is to stop there: many a man has died who has been too handy with his opinions about March.

Puddn'head [*sic*] *Wilson's Calendar.*

[This chapter could not be written, on account of the weather.]

THE END.

Florence, March, 1893.

(<u>Private</u> <u>to</u> "<u>Comp.</u>")

Treble all the weather-signs above "Conclusion," and turn some of them upide [*sic*] down, and others down on their sides.

Emendations of the Copy-Text: Accidentals

The following table lists every instance in which the copy-text has been emended with an accidental. If the accidental is caused by or coincident with a substantive variation, the word or phrase in question is listed both under accidentals and under substantives.

The boldface words or phrases represent the present text readings and the texts in which those readings appear (indicated by sigla). The lightface material represents the copy-text readings and any other readings from other texts. The copy-text reading is for the MMS or the BMS, whichever contains the latest authorial inscription.

"I" after an adopted reading indicates that the emendation is made by the editor. An asterisk (*) indicates that the reading is discussed in the textual notes. A squiggle (~) is used to indicate that there is no variant in the word, just in the punctuation. A caret (∧) indicates the lack of punctuation at that point. A paragraph marker (¶) indicates that there is a new paragraph at that point. "[n.i.]" indicates that the word or phrase is not in the text whose abbreviation follows it.

2.3   now. He *CM-C&W*   now, he
2.11   too, *CM-C&W*   ~∧
2.22   *Mark Twain CM-APC*   Mark Twain *MMS* MARK TWAIN *C&W*
3.7–8   one- and two-story *CM-APC* one and two-story *MMS* one- and two-storey *C&W*
3.8   frame *CM-C&W*   "~"
3.40   blew)∧ *CM-C&W*   ~),
6.15   'Pears? *CM-C&W*   'Pears,
6.15   another. "Is *CM-C&W*   another, "is
6.39   I *CM-C&W*   I
8.8   name∧ *CM-C&W*   ~,
9.4   you. *CM-APC*   ~! *MMS* ~? *C&W*
9.17   wheelbarrow *CM-C&W* whee-barrow
*9.34   "sassy" *CM-APC*   "~∧ *MMS* '~' *C&W*
*10.9   gather *in CM-C&W*   gather-in
11.22   thief. *CM-C&W*   ~!
13.3   DOWN THE RIVER *CM-C&W   down the river*
13.11   it! *CM-C&W*   ~∧
13.14   *here CM-C&W*   ˆhere
14.20   *you CM-C&W*   you
14.24   way, *CM-C&W*   ~!
14.25   mammy's got *CM-C&W* mammy's got
14.28   you, *CM, C&W* ~! *MMS* ~∧ *APC*
14.31   *yonder. CM-C&W*   ~∧
15.3   complexion. Then *CM-C&W*   ~, then
15.13   fo' *CM-C&W*   for
15.21   all! *CM-C&W*   ~∧
15.22   lovely. *CM-C&W*   ~!
15.23   bit. *CM-C&W*   ~!
15.32   his'n. *CM-C&W*   ~!
16.12   is, *CM-APC*   ~! *MMS*   ~∧ *C&W*
16.15   it. *CM-C&W*   ~!
17.14   bilin'. *CM-C&W*   ~!
17.30   fo' *CM-C&W*   for
17.43   sho' *CM-C&W*   sho'
19.21   appalling *CM-C&W*   appaling
19.40   it! *CM-C&W*   ~∧
20.2   "father" *CM-C&W*   ∧~∧
20.4   Like *CM-C&W*   *Like*
20.6   Awnt *CM-C&W*   *Awnt*
20.6   Hab *CM-C&W*   *Hab*
20.7   Take *CM-C&W*   *Take*
22.27   canoe-bottom *CM-C&W* canoe's bottom
23.1   this nigger *CM-C&W*   *this* nigger
23.14   Chambers! *CM-C&W*   ~,
23.14   ∧What *CM-C&W*   —what

23.18   hear *CM-C&W*   *hear*
23.19   me! *CM-C&W*   ~.
23.29   saw *that CM-C&W*   saw that
24.12   it. *CM-C&W*   ~!
24.30   Essex *CM-C&W*   Essex's
24.31   Driscoll *CM-C&W*   Driscoll's
25.33   almond; *CM-C&W*   ~,
25.36   Baldwin's, *CM-C&W*   Baldwin
26.28   couldn't *CM-C&W*   *couldn't*
27.5   *did CM-C&W*   did
27.36   pudd'nhead *CM-C&W* puddn'-head
28.24   no! *CM-C&W*   ~∧
28.25   Louis. *CM-C&W*   ~!
28.28   specially *CM-C&W*   especially
*28.42   Cappello I   Capello
*30.22   blonde *C&W* [n.i.] *MMS* blond *CM-APC*
30.25   ought not *CM-C&W* oughtn't *BMS-MMS*
*31.4   seized *MMS-C&W* siezed *BMS*
31.10   "Our *MMS-C&W* ∧~ *BMS*
*31.43   country town, I   village, *BMS* country town. *MMS-C&W*
*32.15–16   Capello." Handshake I ~." ¶ ~ *BMS-MMS* Capello." Hand-shake *CM-APC* Capello.' Hand-shake *C&W*
32.16   ye, *CM-C&W*   ~!
32.41   ours—all ours! *CM-C&W* ours—~~.
32.44   group *MMS-C&W* groupe *BMS*
34.22   fire; *CM-C&W*   ~, *BMS-MMS*
*35.4   Pudd'nhead *CM-C&W*   Puddn'-head
37.1   ∧A *CM-C&W*   ¶ A
37.4   Then she was promoted ∧ *CM-C&W*   She was promoted, then,
37.17–18   When the . . . Orleans∧ she bade . . . ashore. *CM-C&W*   She bade . . . ashore∧ when the . . . Orleans.
*37.36   lovely; *CM-C&W*   ~—
37.37   poverty. *CM-C&W*   ~!
37.38   poverty! *CM-C&W*   ~.
37.41   much. *CM-C&W*   ~!
38.26   so? *CM-C&W*   ~!
39.11   dollahs. *CM-C&W*   ~!
39.16   tell *CM-C&W*   *tell*
39.28   *ever CM-C&W*   ever
39.28   so! *CM-C&W*   ~.
39.29   tribbilation. *CM-C&W*   ~!
39.34   I's *CM-C&W*   *I's*
39.39   do *CM-C&W*   *do*
39.41   you *CM-C&W*   *you*

39.41 mammy? T'ain't CM-C&W mammy, t'ain't
39.42 reckon. CM-C&W ~?
39.43 my CM-C&W my
39.43 is CM-C&W is
40.27 Please . . . please CM-C&W Please . . . please
40.44 Tom! . . . wouldn't! CM-C&W ~, . . . ~.
41.3 short! CM-C&W ~.
41.5 mammy. CM-C&W ~!
41.6 along! CM-C&W ~.
41.19 could CM-C&W could
*41.20 dol— CM-C&W d—
41.23 you a CM-C&W you a
41.24 it! CM-C&W ~.
41.25 half-way CM-C&W halfway
41.30 he'p CM-C&W h'ep
41.36 ever CM-C&W ever
*41.38 the CM-C&W The
42.2 beg CM-C&W beg
42.8 now! CM-C&W now.
42.11 you. CM-C&W ~!
42.13 she CM-C&W she
42.19 knows. I ~?
42.33 en more CM-C&W en more
42.40 dollah. CM-C&W ~!
42.40 you ain't CM-C&W you ain't
42.44 seized CM-C&W siezed
43.9 not! You CM-C&W not. You
43.10 me names CM-C&W me names
43.16 hear CM-C&W hear
43.18 see CM-C&W see
43.18 too! CM-C&W ~.
43.19 me." CM-C&W ~!"
43.25 ready. CM-C&W ~!
43.39 bill! CM-C&W ~.
43.43 it! CM-C&W ~.
*44.22 house, CM-C&W ~ʌ
45.12 me! CM-C&W ~.
45.15 dat CM-C&W dat
45.16 all CM-C&W all
45.18 mean CM-C&W mean
45.20–21 You . . . is! CM-C&W You . . . is!
45.21 dat's CM-C&W dat's
45.24 all! CM-C&W ~.
45.25 minute; CM-C&W ~!
45.26 sell . . . river CM-C&W sell . . . river
45.30 me. CM-C&W ~!
45.30 you's my CM-C&W you's my
45.32 ¶—"en I ʌ—"~ MMS ¶ ʌ"En CM-C&W
45.33 en yo' CM-C&W en yo'
45.36 got CM-C&W got
45.37 seized CM-C&W siezed
45.39 me CM-C&W me
45.41 thoo— CM, C&W thoo— MMS throo— APC
45.42 but I CM-C&W but I
45.45 you! Now CM-C&W you. Now
46.2 you! CM-C&W ~.
46.11 again! Please CM-C&W again. Please
46.11 Roxy! CM-C&W ~.

46.14 me Roxy CM-C&W me Roxy
46.15 Ma . . . mammy I Ma . . . mammy MMS ma . . . mammy CM-C&W
46.21 me CM-C&W me
46.22 it. CM-C&W ~!
41.24 it. CM-C&W ~!
46.39 "How CM-C&W ʌ~
46.41 I CM-C&W I
46.41 questions. CM-C&W ~!
47.24 you. CM-C&W ~!
47.31 don't! CM-C&W ~.
47.39 man. ¶ CM-C&W ~!ʌ
47.43 it. ¶ CM-C&W ~.ʌ
48.1 'long! CM-C&W ~.
48.2 right CM-C&W right
48.2 swah. CM-C&W ~!
48.25 nigger CM-C&W nigger
48.28 wish CM-C&W wish
49.36 nigger, CM-C&W ~!
50.3 himself. ¶ CM-C&W ~.ʌ
50.4 opinions CM-C&W opinions
50.5–6 character CM-C&W character
50.28 townʌ (for . . . village), CM-C&W ~, ʌfor . . . villageʌ,
50.34 St. CM-C&W Stʌ
51.17 and had CM-C&W and had
52.10 manuscript CM-C&W MS
52.26 hands; CM-C&W ~,
53.15 ʌ Tom winced.ʌ CM-C&W [~~.]
53.18 grit! CM-C&W ~.
54.36 in CM-C&W in
55.10 would CM-C&W would
55.11 palms. Come CM-C&W palms—come
55.21 Luigi: CM-C&W ~—
55.22 alone; CM-C&W ~—
55.25 Dave! CM-C&W ~.
56.28 quite to CM-C&W to quite
56.36 your CM-C&W your
56.38 prophesied CM-C&W prophecied
56.45 of! CM-C&W ~.
57.1 enemy! CM-C&W ~.
57.4 along. CM-C&W ~!
57.10 I'll CM-C&W I'll
58.20 happens; CM-C&W ~—
58.21 hel-lo CM-C&W Hel-lo
58.29 me! CM-C&W ~.
59.22–23 long wavering CM-C&W wavering long
*60.7 cries: CM-C&W ~—
60.39 deny. CM-C&W ~!
61.7 speech. CM-C&W ~!
61.26 them CM-C&W them
62.20 absence CM-C&W absence
64.7 go CM-C&W go
*64.8 the Judge CM-C&W The Judge
64.11 didn't CM-C&W did not
64.14 thatʌ— CM-C&W ~!—
64.25 arms, CM-C&W ~ʌ
64.35 true! CM-C&W ~.
64.38 it's CM-C&W it is
66.1 by; CM-C&W ~,
66.3 uncle! CM-C&W ~.
*66.4 devil CM-C&W devils
*66.4 afraid CM-C&W afraid

*66.5   him! *CM-C&W*   them.
66.9   **repeating that lament again and again** *CM-C&W*   repeating, again and again, that lament
66.15   **father!** *CM-C&W*   ~.
66.39   *that CM-C&W*   that
66.39   **me** *CM-C&W*   me
67.2   **gone.** *CM-C&W*   ~!
67.23–26   **throat. ¶ "It's . . . likely, . . . law-court." ¶ A** *CM-C&W*   throat.∧ ["It's . . . likely."]∧ A
67.38   **discoveries!** *CM-C&W*   ~.
67.40   **dissipation.** *CM-C&W*   ~!
68.21   **you!** *CM-C&W*   ~.
68.38   **Tom!** *CM-C&W*   ~.
68.39   **nothing!** *CM-C&W*   ~.
69.10   *had CM-C&W*   had
69.11   **did not** *CM-C&W*   didn't
69.13   **list.** *CM-C&W*   ~!
69.21   **born!** *CM-C&W*   ~.
69.32   *in CM-C&W*   in
70.11   **as we** *CM-C&W*   as *we*
70.23   *robbed CM-C&W*   robbed
70.29   *that CM-C&W*   that
70.31   **was** *CM-C&W*   was
70.38   **Buckstone.** *CM-C&W*   ~?
71.4   **good.** *CM-C&W*   ~!
71.5   **what** *CM-C&W*   what
71.12   **have** *CM-C&W*   have
71.21   **my** *CM-C&W*   my
72.16   **think—began** *CM-C&W*   think. Began
73.5   **unusual**∧ *CM-C&W*   ~——
73.11   **could** *CM-C&W*   could
73.16   **apiece."** *CM-C&W*   ~.∧
73.17   **Good!** *CM-C&W*   ~.
73.44   **now** *CM-C&W*   now
74.7   **sure!** *CM-C&W*   ~.
74.33   **then**∧ *CM-C&W*   then!—
75.10   **That's** *CM-C&W*   That's
75.26   **me** *CM-C&W*   me
75.28   **nigger** *CM-C&W*   nigger
75.29   *soul. CM-C&W*   soul!
75.39   **has** *CM-C&W*   has
75.39   **I** *CM-C&W*   I
75.43   *his CM-C&W*   his
76.2   **nigger** *CM-C&W*   nigger
76.2   **you!** *CM-C&W*   ~.
76.11   **¶ Presently** *CM-C&W*   ∧~
76.22   **I** *CM-C&W*   I
76.22   **myself.** *CM-C&W*   myseff!
76.24   **did!** *CM-C&W*   ~.
76.27   *che-bang CM-C&W*   che-*bang*
77.4   **range!** *CM-C&W*   ~.
77.6   **'Fraid** *CM-C&W*   'Fraid
77.6   **nothin'** *CM-C&W*   nothin'
77.9   *I wouldn't CM-C&W*   I wouldn't
77.16   **inch.** *CM-C&W*   ~!
77.18   **minute.** *CM-C&W*   ~!
77.26   **Now . . . end.** *CM-C&W*   Now . . . end!
78.6   *on CM-C&W*   on
78.6   **you,** *CM-C&W*   ~!
78.11   **I** *CM-C&W*   I
78.11   **you!** *CM-C&W*   ~.
78.13   **me!** *CM-C&W*   me.

78.20   **big** *CM-C&W*   big
78.22   **month?** *CM-C&W*   ~.
78.28–29   **you is gwyne** *CM-C&W*   you's gwyne
78.34   **once** *CM-C&W*   once
78.36   **one!** *CM-C&W*   ~.
78.38   **self** *CM-C&W*   seff
80.29   **no** *CM-C&W*   no
80.38   **haven't** *CM-C&W*   haven't
80.45   **good!** *CM-C&W*   ~.
81.1   **St.** *CM-C&W*   St∧
81.5   **to!** *CM-C&W*   ~.
81.11   **¶ Blake's** *CM-C&W*   ∧~
81.22   **that** *CM-C&W*   that
81.24   **of** *CM-C&W*   of
81.32   **days**∧ *CM-C&W*   ~!
81.35   **was** *CM-C&W*   was
82.13   **argument's** *CM-C&W*   arguments
82.16   **got** *CM-C&W*   got
82.17   **that?** *CM-C&W*   ~.
82.32   **think I** *CM-C&W*   think *I*
*82.35   **that** *CM-C&W*   That
82.35   **any such knife** *CM-C&W*   any such *knife*
82.37   **dollars** *CM-C&W*   ~!
83.3   **seen** *CM-C&W*   seen
83.13   **Twins!** *CM-C&W*   ~.
83.17   **but** *CM-C&W*   but
83.21   **himself: ¶** *CM-C&W*   ~,∧
83.40   **anywhere. ¶** *CM-C&W*   ~.∧
84.3   **Indeed?** *CM-APC*   ~! *MMS*   ~. *C&W*
84.17   **I** *CM-C&W*   I
84.26   **it.** *CM-C&W*   ~!
*84.31   **a while I**   awhile *CM-C&W*
85.14   **¶ His** *CM-C&W*   ∧~
85.18   **now!** *CM-C&W*   ~.
85.18   **you** *CM-C&W*   you
86.29   **sayin' it!** *CM-C&W*   ~~∧ *MMS* ~? *APC*
86.33   *do CM-C&W*   do
86.35   **law** *CM-C&W*   law
86.36   **now** *CM-C&W*   now
86.41   **dem** *CM-C&W*   dem
88.8–9   **there. Then** *CM-C&W*   there, then
88.12   *I's sole down de river CM-C&W*   I's sole down de river
90.37   **it!** *CM-C&W*   ~.
90.43   **bes'** *CM-C&W*   bes'
90.44   **so!** *CM-C&W*   ~.
91.34   **no mercy** *CM-C&W*   no mercy
91.34   **mo'.** *CM-C&W*   ~!
91.42   **was** *CM-C&W*   was
92.15   **stan' it.** *CM-C&W*   stan' it!
92.17   **flat.** *CM-C&W*   ~!
92.21   **me** *CM-C&W*   me
92.26   **got** *CM-C&W*   got
93.7   **watch!** *CM-C&W*   ~.∧
93.10   **myself** *CM-C&W*   myseff
93.11   **I is.** *CM-C&W*   I is!
93.14   **home** *CM-C&W*   home
93.14   **I tell** *CM-C&W*   I tell
93.17   **dat** *CM-C&W*   dat
93.20   **all.'** *CM-C&W*   ~.∧

93.24   dem CM-C&W   dem
93.41   take! CM-C&W   ~.
94.3   couldn't CM-C&W   couldn't
94.4   here CM-C&W   here
94.8   help CM-C&W   help
94.17   shirt! CM-C&W   ~.
94.25   me! CM-C&W   ~.
94.36   bill! CM-C&W   ~.
94.42   *all* CM-C&W   all
95.5   is CM-C&W   *is*
95.29   sho." CM-APC   sho'.∧
95.31   ast you CM, C&W   ask you MMS
askyou APC
96.4   you CM-C&W   *you*
96.5   hide! Would CM-C&W   hide.
Would
96.5   it? No∧ CM-C&W   it! No!
96.5   dog CM-C&W   *dog*
96.7   I's CM-C&W   I is
96.16   gamblin' CM-APC   gamblin∧
MMS gambling C&W
96.24   you knows CM-C&W   *you* knows
96.25   it! CM-C&W   ~.
96.31   honey—set down. CM-C&W
honey. Set down!
97.3   tole CM-C&W   *tole*
97.9   self CM-C&W   seff
97.17   en it CM-C&W   en *it*
97.21   I CM-C&W   *I*
97.23   yo'n! CM-C&W   ~.
97.32   her CM-C&W   *her*
97.33   rob CM-C&W   rob
97.34   skinflint. CM-C&W   ~!
99.3   him! CM-C&W   ~.
99.12–13   Dawson's, CM-C&W   ~∧
100.4   seized CM-C&W   siezed
*100.6   home—and CM-C&W   ~∧ and
100.9   seized CM-C&W   siezed
100.12   ¶ He CM-C&W   ∧He
100.16   man! CM-APC   ~. MMS, C&W
101.25   St. CM-C&W   St∧
102.44   degree, CM-C&W   ~∧
103.13   wasn't CM-C&W   *wasn't*
103.28   so! CM-APC   ~. MMS, C&W
103.33   could CM-C&W   could
103.38   had CM-C&W   *had*
103.40   St. CM-C&W   St∧
104.4   was CM-C&W   *was*
104.9   *with* CM-C&W   with
104.41   any . . . any CM-C&W   *any . . .
any*
105.26   her CM-C&W   *her*
105.32   you. CM-C&W   ~!
*106.22   added∧ significantly, CM-
C&W   ~, ~∧
109.15   face; CM-APC   ~! MMS   ~,
C&W
109.32   are! CM-C&W   ~.
109.38   Nothing CM-C&W   nothing
110.1   ¶ "Now CM-C&W   ∧"~
*110.10   use; CM-APC   ~, MMS   ~—
C&W

110.19   recall CM-C&W   recal
110.19   was CM-C&W   *was*
110.22   seized CM-C&W   siezed
110.24   so CM-C&W   *so*
110.25   it! CM-C&W   ~.
*111.12   his pantograph CM-APC. his
pantagraph MMS, C&W
111.33   ¶ Tom CM-C&W   ∧ Tom
112.1   lick! CM-C&W   ~.
112.10   words.∧ CM-C&W   ~."
112.14–16   that . . . murder CM-C&W
that . . . *murder*
112.17–18   We . . . claim CM-C&W
We . . . claim
113.23   secretly CM-C&W   *secretly*
113.25   *not* CM-C&W   not
113.31   was CM-C&W   *was*
113.32   before CM-C&W   *before*
*113.38   ∧ Another CM-C&W   [~
113.41   "It CM-C&W   '~
113.41   hit!" ∧ CM-C&W   ~.']
114.4   seized CM-C&W   siezed
114.28   this CM-C&W   *this*
114.30   globe! CM-C&W   ~.
114.42   that CM-C&W   *that*
115.9–10   autograph. CM-C&W   ~!
115.10   That CM-C&W   *That*
115.30–31   Order . . . down CM-C&W
Order . . . *down*
116.4   it! CM, C&W ~. MMS, APC
116.10   *their* CM-APC   their MMS,
C&W
116.11   experimenters CM-C&W   experi-
mentors
116.30–32   Applause [4 times] CM-
C&W   *Applause* [4 times]
*116.43   A . . . B CM-C&W   A . . . B
117.12   ¶ He CM-C&W   ∧ He
117.23   We . . . honor CM-C&W   *We . . .
honor*
118.1   *resemble,* CM-C&W   ~!
118.11   was CM-C&W   *was*
118.20   ¶ "No . . . widely! CM-APC   ¶
"No . . . widely. MMS ∧"No . . . widely.
C&W
118.27   By no means! CM-C&W   By no
means.
118.30   changed . . . cradle CM-C&W
changed . . . cradle
118.38–39   and . . . house! CM-C&W
and . . . house.
118.45–119.1   Sensation . . . ejaculations CM-C&W   *Sensation . . . ejaculations*
119.2–3   Burst . . . officers CM-C&W
Burst . . . officers
120.30   this . . . us CM-C&W   *this . . .
us*
120.31   years. CM-C&W   ~!
120.32   elected. CM-C&W   ~!
121.10   "nigger gallery" CM-C&W   "nigger" gallery

Rejected Variants: Substantives

This table contains substantive readings in texts other than the copy-text which are not used for emendation of the copy-text. Page and line numbers indicate present text locations. Any text not cited by sigla in light-face type does not differ from the copy-text reading. An asterisk preceding an entry indicates that the entry is discussed in the Textual Notes.

1.19–20   **Maccaroni and** Macaroni CM-C&W

*3.21   **home** house CM-C&W

*6.4–5   **disagreeable, whereupon young Wilson said** CM-C&W   disagreeable. The new-comer, David Wilson, said BMS   disagreeable; whereupon he said MMS

6.20   **that, he** BMS   it, he MMS-C&W

6.44   **all."** MMS   all—I ain't no judge." BMS

7.5   **was not able** MMS   never was able BMS

12.28   **their loudest** the loudest APC

13.25   **he was** was CM-C&W

14.11   **feet and** feet APC

17.34   **if it takes** if it's CM-C&W

18.20   **this** the CM-C&W

23.32   **deeps** depths APC

*24.11   **whar** what CM-C&W

28.32   **town** MMS   village BMS

28.35   **aflush** BMS   ablush MMS-C&W

29.16   **Justice Robinson** MMS   Captain Baldwin BMS

29.25   **uncertain, in low water,** MMS   uncertain BMS

29.25   **those** these CM-C&W

29.26   **times.** MMS   times. They took life easy, they were never in a hurry, they arrived early or late, according to circumstances, there was no schedule. BMS

*29.30   **came; then twelve, and** BMS   came; and MMS-C&W

29.31   **town** MMS   village BMS

29.33   **on the** BMS   at the MMS

*31.20   **exhibit** BMS   be exhibited MMS-C&W

31.43   **country town** MMS   village BMS

32.23–24   **the sort** that sort CM-C&W

*32.45   **recognized** BMS   recognizing MMS   recognised CM-C&W

34.42   **now president** MMS   now local agent of the packet line, clerk of the county court, chairman of the debating club and president BMS

*37.39   **dream: Maybe he would help her;** dream: CM-C&W

39.6   **marse** marster CM-C&W

*41.3   **damn it** —— it CM-C&W

43.13   **you hadn't** hadn't CM-C&W

44.18   **deeps** depths CM-C&W

46.13   **Dah's** Dat's APC

47.23   **don't you** don't APC

*50.44   **later—** after— CM-C&W

54.33   **jugglery** juggling CM-C&W

55.20   **half a dozen years** half dozen years CM-APC   half-dozen years C&W

*57.21   **you, and** you∧— CM-C&W

*58.8   **that knife** the knife CM-C&W

*64.31   **a slander** slander APC

*70.22   **out** out of CM-C&W

70.25   **lasted for** lasted CM-C&W

73.6   **chill** chill of CM-C&W

73.45   **bad scare** scare APC

76.12   **rumblings** ramblings CM-C&W

78.40   **once** one CM-C&W

83.24   **had had** had CM-C&W

*83.41   **On Saturday** Saturday CM-C&W

87.26   **never** never to CM-C&W

90.37   **meant** meant it APC

97.19   **into** right into APC

*99.20   **with a** with CM-C&W

99.29   **waning** wandering APC

102.8   **prostrated** prostrate C&W

103.32   **firstly** first CM-C&W

105.8   **didn't** did not CM-APC

107.12   **proven** proved CM-APC

107.26   **events** event C&W

114.25   **the mutations** mutations APC

121.11   **that** that it APC

Textual Notes

[**First entry in Emendations of the Copy-Text: Substantives**]   These first pages in MMS were never used in any printed text of the book. (See last entry in Emendations of the Copy-Text: Substantives

[Lengthy Passages] herein, p. 206.) See facsimile, Appendix 1, for this passage about weather signs.

1.10   **court**   A few times the c of "court"—referring to a judge and jury—is

ambiguous, either upper or lower case.
All forms that are ambiguous in the
manuscript have been normalized to
lower case, the predominant form in the
manuscript of unambiguous cases.
Unambiguous forms, even when they are
capitalized, are not normalized. Below is
a table of all ambiguous instances of the
word (page and line numbers are those
of the present edition):

Pudd'nhead Wilson	TET
112.6	153.26
117.20	156.9
120.12	164.13

3.20   home   "house" is probably an eye-
skip by the Berg typist to this word a few
lines above.

4.15   slave-holding   Clemens could not
fit the end-of-line hyphen in, so he put it
in in the left margin before "holding."

4.23   Judge   As with the letters c and t,
j's are often written in such a way that
they could be either upper or lower
case. For the titles "Judge" and "Justice"—when the initial letter is ambiguous—this edition adopts capital letters,
since this is the predominant form in
the unambiguous cases. The following
table lists all ambiguous forms in the
present edition:

Pudd'nhead Wilson		TET
4.23	18.7	161.7
5.19	27.15	

What is amusing and perhaps instructive
about Clemens's attitudes while he was
writing the two parts of the story is that
the cluster of lower-case "judges"
appears in the farcical "kicking" trial of
the twins in *Those Extraordinary Twins*,
while in the *Pudd'nhead Wilson* murder
trial "judge" appears consistently with a
capital *j*, with the single exception of
"judge" at 115.1, where the word appears
in the phrase "judge and jury."

6.4–5   disagreeable . . . said   Note that
here the source of emendation is *CM*,
which clearly shows authorial intervention.

7.7   and was . . . years.   The BMS
reading was typed verbatim by the Berg
typist; in the MMS Clemens has added
with a caret the present text reading,
but he has neglected to cross out the
other reading, and he also used an extra
"and."

9.34   "sassy"   House style for C&W called
for single quotation marks where all
other texts have them double; the practice is consistent throughout the novel
and is not recorded in the tables.

10.9   gather in   The hyphen in the MMS
is not an acceptable form.

12.5   church   The MMS reading here and
at *TET* 178.3 are ambiguous as to capitalization. More than twenty other

instances in the text are unambiguously
lower case, so this form is adopted for
these two readings.

15.13   fo'   Though accidental variations
in dialogue are generally not emended in
this edition, MMS "for" (and the same
form at 17.30) is not characteristic of
Roxy's speech. There are many occurrences of her saying "fo'," but only these
two of "for."

24.11   whar   Clemens's handwriting is
somewhat ambiguous in the manuscript,
and the typist apparently misread this for
"what."

28.35–29.13   excitement, . . . Here   The
rest of this passage, beginning with
"Well, set down," is used in its unrevised
BMS form in *Those Extraordinary Twins*,
129.5–130.19 of the present edition.
The *CM* version is Clemens's revision of
this passage, a passage so revised that
the *CM* must be used as the sole authority for *Pudd'nhead Wilson* here. The
BMS and MMS readings are identical,
except for the word "too" in the deleted
passage, which Clemens wrote "two"; the
correction was made by the typist.

28.42   Cappello   Here and elsewhere
there is inconsistency in the spelling of
this name. In the BMS, at 13.16,
Clemens has written "Capello" and then
inserted the second *p* with a caret,
clearly showing his preference for this
form. The spelling of the name with two
p's will be the normal one for this text.

**29.21–22   its courtly . . . style, every-
body**   The *CM* has "practiced" spelled
"practised," but the passage there is otherwise verbatim with the present edition.

29.30   came; then twelve, and   "came;
and" is a typist's error in the MMS.

**29.38–45   entered the twins . . . dupli-
cates**   See *Those Extraordinary Twins*,
130.24–26.

30.22   blonde   Though there is no manuscript passage here, and though substantively the C&W text is not
authoritative, the present edition adopts
"blonde" as the author's sole form. In
Clemens's own hand at BMS 26.2 and
32.5 the word is spelled with an *e*.
Clemens apparently did not know that
this spelling is normally feminine.

30.38   child   This is a case of careless-
ness on Clemens's part. The statement
(which in *Pudd'nhead Wilson* should
have been "children") comes from the
original "joined" twins story.

31.4   seized   This is one word Clemens
uniformly misspelled. The dozen occurrences of it in the MMS are all incorrect,
except for the two typed instances, and the
corresponding manuscript occurrences of
these two in the BMS are also incorrect.

31.20 exhibit "be exhibited" is a typist's error in the MMS.

31.20 bread. The passage removed from the *Pudd'nhead Wilson* story at this point, beginning "That hateful black bread," may be found in *Those Extraordinary Twins* (142.1–15 of the present edition).

31.43 country town, In the BMS Clemens wrote "village, she"; the typist changed this to "village. She"; Clemens decided to change "village" to "country town" and in doing so accepted the typist's error. The present text retains the substantive revision but uses the punctuation of the BMS.

31.43 its The MMS typist has incorrectly spelled this word "it's" several times, always using a comma for an apostrophe.

32.3 Twins Many of Clemens's *t*'s can be interpreted as either upper or lower case; context normally helps one decide. But Clemens was inconsistent in his capitalization of "twins," and there are many ambiguous occurrences in both MMS and BMS. This edition normalizes all ambiguous *t*'s to upper case for two reasons: this is the predominant form in the manuscripts in the unambiguous cases, and there are a few cases in the manuscript where a lower case *t* is distinctly changed by the author to a capital letter (but not a single case of the converse). Each ambiguous occurrence in the manuscripts is listed below by page and line number of the present edition. These are not elsewhere recorded.

Pudd'nhead Wilson

32.3	59.14	76.32	100.27	104.1	107.31
32.5	60.9	83.13	102.15	104.6	115.5
32.43	64.1	83.16	102.16	104.9	118..6
34.24	67.17	83.30	102.21	105.1	120.33
36.30	68.13	83.32	102.24	105.8	
50.43	70.32	84.8	103.1	105.16	
52.19	71.14	85.3	103.4	105.23	
54.24	75.9	85.6	103.25	106.12	
56.15	75.13	100.15	103.26	107.3	

Those Extraordinary Twins

133.39	152.26	156.14	164.15	177.34
142.35	153.12	156.17	165.19	179.18
145.24	154.6	160.22	165.32	180.27
148.33	155.18	162.6	169.22	181.25
149.41	156.8	162.31	170.39	181.39

Deleted Matter

All these occurrences of "Twins" will appear with a capital *T* in the notes that list passages deleted from the present edition. The page and line number references are to entries in Emendations of the Copy-Text: Substantives.

35.1–3(3)	68.1	76.44	118.2–3
52.25–26	68.36	83.44	120.32
61.2–3	74.42	84.30–85.2	

32.15–16 Cappello." Handshake The present edition accepts the paragraphing of the *CM* and the spelling of the manuscripts.

32.45 recognized "recognizing" is an error of the BMS typist. The C&W compositor apparently spotted the need for a past tense and changed the erroneous reading to "recognised." There is no indication of direct contact with the BMS.

34.2–5 [maxim] One . . . Calendar. This maxim, preceding Chapter 7 of the present edition, does not appear in the manuscripts. Chapter 9 in the MMS—which corresponds to Chapter 7 of the present edition—has no maxim inserted between the typed lines of the page; however, on the preceding page (handwritten, p. 130 of the MMS) the following maxim was inserted. It was not used in the final novel: ¶ "The Creator admired His glittering array of far-stretching solar systems, the work of His hands, but merely pronounced it 'good.' Considering the modesty of the word, one might think He was describing a village, whereas when you hear a villager describing his village, you think he is describing the solar systems. ¶—*Pudd'nhead Wilson's Calendar.*" This maxim (at 34.2–4) appears also at the beginning of Chapter 27, Vol. 2, of *Following the Equator*, but beginning, "The principal difference between. . . ."

34.15 see. The continuation of the passage deleted appears in *Those Extraordinary Twins*, 142.24 ff. of the present edition.

35.1–3 established. He . . . he told One difficulty in explaining this entry lies in the facts that Clemens has (1) deleted several pages of the manuscript and (2) linked MMS 135.5 with 161.3. The intervening matter was used for *Those Extraordinary Twins*. Hence, the portion from "Luigi wanted" to "and more" (BMS 84.2–93.19, 207.A.62–208.B.19 herein is from the BMS; the passage from "Judge" to "told" is from the MMS (MMS 161.1–3, appearing at 35.1–3 of the present edition as "He would . . . told"). The ellipsis in the tabulated passage indicates that the intervening passage ("The hour passed . . . his lodgings") was used elsewhere in *Pudd'nhead Wilson*; see 35.12–15 of the present edition. The typescript of the BMS in the MMS differs from the BMS in several instances. One accidental and three substantive variants between the BMS and the Morgan typescript are all typist's errors.

35.4 Pudd'nhead Here and at 35.18 Clemens has put the apostrophe in the wrong place. Henceforth this error is silently corrected.

37.36 lovely; Normally the punctuation of the copy-text is retained; however, with two other emendations of an authorial nature in this sentence, the semicolon is adopted as also authorial.

37.39 dream . . . give her; The lack of the phrase "Maybe . . . her;" can be seen as a typist's or compositor's eye-skip: the word "maybe" is immediately below "Maybe" in the MMS.

41.3 damn it See textual note to *Those Extraordinary Twins*, 135.6.

41.20 dol— The *CM* reading of "dol—" is much clearer than the MMS "d—"; the former is likely to be authorial.

41.38 the In the MMS the sentence originally began with "The"; Clemens inserted "But now" and forgot to make the *T* of "The" lower case.

43.25 . . . . . . Git This is one of several instances in the manuscripts in which Clemens used an unusual number of dots (often seven) to represent some kind of pause. *CM* has normalized these to ellipses. C&W uses four dots. The manuscript forms are retained.

44.7–9 [First maxim] This maxim appears in the MMS at the beginning of the following chapter.

44.22 house, Though usually the punctuation of the copy-text is retained, this is one instance in which the comma after "house" is needed for clarity and has thus been adopted.

45.19 gloomed The MMS (p. 219) has "gloomed," possibly an error for "loomed."

46.3–4 of disorganizing sensations and In the deleted passage, which reads "of doubt, certainty, fear . . . ," Clemens must surely have meant "uncertainty" for "certainty."

48.7–8 [maxim] When angry . . . *Calendar*. The maxim removed from here ("Why is it . . . involved."), with one substantive change, is moved to Chapter 9, p. 44 of the present edition.

50.44 later— This is most likely an eye-skip to the previous line by the typist.

57.21 you, and Clemens's ampersand is easily mistaken for a dash in the manuscript.

58.8 that knife The variant reading, "the knife," is most likely an eye-skip, for the phrase "the knife" appears twice on the manuscript page, once four lines directly above the present reading. The word "the" appears immediately above "knife" in the manuscript.

60.7 cries: A paragraph marker was inserted by the author above the *s* of "cries." Originally the comma would have been adequate; but if the following sentence is made a separate paragraph, the new punctuation characteristic of Clemens's style is called for.

60.9 were The MMS originally had "A glass . . . was"; Clemens emended to "Glasses" but forgot to make the coordinating change of the verb.

61.6 philopena A philopena is "a social game in which each of two persons eats one of the twin kernels of a nut (usually an almond), and one pays a forfeit to the other if first saluted with the word 'philopena' or on other specified conditions" (*A Standard Dictionary of the English Language* [New York: Funk & Wagnalls, 1895], p. 1327). The picture of the twin kernels apparently prompted Clemens to use this image.

64.8 the Judge The word "the" was originally the first word in the sentence. "At the finish" was inserted with a caret, but Clemens forgot to change "The" to lower case.

64.31 a slander The APC compositor, setting from sheets of the *CM*, probably had an eye-skip to three lines directly above in the dense *CM* column, where the word "slander" appears without "a" before it.

66.3–4 uncle! . . . him! The phrase "They are murderous devils." was inserted by Clemens with a caret which was at the very end of the line (MMS 343.12). The word "They," above the line, preceded the word "I" in "I never could," so the typist inadvertently reversed the two phrases, typing the one seen first. All printed editions have the phrases in this reverse order, but with Clemens's adaptations for the separated twins.

70.22 out This weakness in grammar is in Constable Blake's speech. He makes many other idiomatic and grammatical errors; the correction would appear to be editorial.

82.35 that This was originally the first word in the sentence. When Clemens added "Why" with a caret, he neglected to make "That" lower case.

83.41 On Saturday In the manuscript Clemens first wrote "Once" and then altered this to "On" by crossing out the *ce*; he clearly wanted "On" even though "Saturday evening" has been inserted with a caret.

84.31 a while The source for this reading, *CM*, has "awhile"; but Clemens clearly preferred the spelling as two words; only twice in the MMS (117.35 and 434.15) does the word appear with no space, while there are twelve occurrences of it as two words.

85.31–33 [maxim] We . . . Calendar. The first maxim of this chapter was transferred here from Chapter 26 of the MMS, which corresponds with Chapter 15 of the present edition.

85.42 friendless.— The punctuation is Clemens's practice of using a dash in the right margin at the end of a sentence where he had no room to write another word; the dash fills the space at the right margin, making it clear that the paragraph was not ending. The dashes at 86.33 ("you?—") and 87.43 ("She!—") are of the same nature.

88.23–89.45 The summer . . . deserted. See 183.5 in "*Those Extraordinary Twins*: Textual Notes," herein.

91.45 was only For a discussion concerning the agreement of C&W with the MMS, see "Textual Introduction," page 194 herein.

92.44 chambermaid The *CM* compositor could have inadvertently omitted the word "head" in his typesetting. But this reading (without "head," which is the MMS reading) is corroborated by the C&W text. C&W, it should be remembered, is not using *CM* as their printer's copy at this point. If the hypothesis about the two sets of proof sheets of the *CM* printing is correct, then the adopted reading has authority through two separate channels: Clemens's emendations of the first set of proofs, which were at the *CM* offices, and the unemended proofs, which reflect the emended typescript. Other instances substantiating the hypothesis that there were two sets of proof sheets are noted below.

93.15 heard See note for 92.44.

93.30–31 den I See note for 92.44.

95.37 de house The reading "he house" appears in the MMS and in the C&W printing. C&W is apparently setting from uncorrected proofs of the *CM* printing. The revised proofs yield "de house" for *CM* and APC—a version not available to the C&W compositor.

96.23 *knows* you's a-goin'. The MMS had "*knows* it." This was changed in Clemens's cut-and-paste job to "knows it!"—the reading on the *CM* proofs. The corrected proofs contain the present reading. The uncorrected proofs yield "knows it!" for C&W.

97.42–98.2–3 Dawson's . . . it. Judge Driscoll declined Most of the original paragraph (MMS 539.1–17) has been moved to *Those Extraordinary Twins* (page 183 herein); Clemens has here rewritten the opening passage of the chapter.

99.10 the twins This sentence was written after Clemens had decided to recast the work with the twins separated; otherwise, he would not have had Luigi going out alone. However, after doing some revision (e.g., on backs of sheets, as in this example), and after having the manuscript typed, he realized that later

in the story both Luigi and Angelo are caught at Judge Driscoll's corpse; it was much easier to change "Luigi" to "the twins" (as he has done here) than it would have been to have changed all the rest of the story to a trial of Luigi alone.

99.14 lonely The word looks like "lovely" in MMS (545.4).

99.17 window-blinds and lighted The C&W text follows the MMS on the word "lit." This is another instance supporting the supposition that two sets of *CM* proofs were being used. When C&W could not get copy for *Pudd'nhead Wilson* further than the fifth installment, despite several requests to Frederick Hall, they directly or indirectly contacted the *CM*, who sent them their house proofs to be set from. (See page 194 herein.)

99.20 with a The "a" was inserted with a caret at the top of the page and was easily not seen by a typist.

100.6 home—and In the MMS Clemens's ampersand looks like a dash. Either the typist typed a dash and supplied the needed "and," or else Clemens supplied the "and" in this typescript or in the *CM* proofs.

102.37–103.3 The coroner's . . . Wilson This change was made by the author clearly to show that the twins were separate people.

105.27 these See note for 92.41.

106.21 on See note for 92.41.

106.22 added‸ significantly, With other emendations in this passage that are definitely authorial, this one may be seen also as the author's improvement of his punctuation.

109.22 Take As with "twins," the initial letter of this word is not clearly upper or lower case. See note for 32.3. *CM* and C&W have "take."

110.10 use; Clemens had "use" in the MMS and changed this in his cut-and-paste job to "use—"; this dash he later changed to a semicolon in correcting proofs, but the uncorrected proofs retained the dash. Hence the C&W reading.

111.13 pantograph Except for the occurrence of this word at 118.17 of the present edition, where the word was spelled correctly (MMS 617.8), the author misspells the word "pantagraph" consistently. The other instances of emendation are at 111.13, 111.14, 111.26, 116.41–42, 118.13, 118.21, 118.25, 119.4–5. The incorrect spelling was caught in proofs at *CM*, but the uncorrected proofs retained this misspelling, which appears in all occurrences of the word in C&W—who even changed Clemens's one correct spelling at 118.17.

C&W also has "pantagraph" at 117.8, words not in MMS.

113.38 ∧**Another**   The variant here concerns the use of brackets; however, here and throughout this passage C&W uses parentheses.

114.3   **course;**∧   In the manuscript a word has been crossed out after the semicolon, and part of the cross-out line looks like a dash. *CM-APC* have the dash.

116.43   *A . . . B*   The italicization of the letters *A* and *B* throughout this passage appears in all versions except the manuscript. It is not henceforth recorded.

119.11   **sits among you**   In making the change from "in your midst" to "among you," Clemens probably forgot to cross out the word "in." All printed texts have this slightly awkward phrase: "in among you."

119.11   **Valet de Chambre**   Elsewhere in the text (e.g., 40.2, 45.35, and 46.13) the name is spelled "Vallet de Chambers"—in Roxy's dialect, representing her pronunciation. The present spelling represents Wilson's pronunciation.

120.33–36   **now, and with . . . Roxy's**   The passage for MMS represented by the ellipsis in the right column was moved to *Those Extraordinary Twins* (183.30–184.36 herein). Passages deleted in this material and passages revised by the author may be found in the tables for *Those Extraordinary Twins* in this volume.

122.12   **river.**   In the deleted passage, Clemens has accidentally spelled "upside" without the *s*. (See the last entry in Emendations of the Copy-Text: Substantives [Lengthy Passages].)

Those Extraordinary Twins

Emendations of the Copy-Text: Substantives

This table lists every substantive emendation of the copy-text along with all other variant readings. The material in boldface type represents readings in the present edition; the lightface material contains, first, the copy-text reading, and, second, any other variants, if there are any. The copy-text reading is for the MMS or the BMS, whichever contains the latest authorial inscription. Sigla following the entries indicate the sources of those readings.

"**I**" after an adopted reading indicates that the emendation is made by the editor.

An asterisk (*) indicates that the reading is discussed in the Textual Notes.

Where possible, the adopted readings give an indication of context.

Lengthy passages—too long for this table—are printed in lightface type with an ellipsis (. . .). They are preceded by a dagger (†) and may be found at the end of the table.

"[n.i.]" indicates that a passage is not in the text indicated.

129.16 **"Twins! How sweet! I** *APC* "I
129.34 **you. We** *APC* you, for we
130.19 **expect it.** *APC* expect them to be, yourself, ma." ¶ "Oh, go 'long with such nonsense. If a person's name made him sick, couldn't he rake up another one? You done it yourself." ¶ "Well, if I really thought he *was* sick, I—here
130.24–26 **Then followed . . . legs!** *APC* Then entered a human creature that had two heads, two necks, four arms, and one body, with a single pair of legs attached.
130.37 **Count Luigi** *APC* Luigi
130.38 **Count Angelo** *APC* Angelo
131.1 **into** *APC* in
131.2 **sup** *APC* a sup
131.7–8 **of Rowena's small brothers** *APC* of the boys
131.18 **them** *MMS-APC* them them *BMS*
132.8–9 **one; the . . . door.** *APC* one.
132.11 **trouble** *APC* trouble enough
133.12 **the one on the left—no, it was the one to the east of the other one—** *APC* the left-hand one—
134.7 **so far** *APC* as far
134.26 **cruelly** *APC* bitterly
* **134.34** **"Whole Duty of Man,"** *MMS-APC* Testament,

135.9 **sing "From Greenland's Icy Mountains"** *APC* sing
137.18 **hands** *APC* arms
137.26 **turned** *APC* turning
137.33 **break** *APC* break in it
137.39 **became** *APC* had become
* **138.4** **sure as** *APC* sure's *BMS* sure,s *MMS*
139.1 **both my** *APC* both of my
139.7 **half of the passengers** *APC* half
139.15 **"It is** *APC* "It's
139.19 **has** *APC* it *has*
140.10 **convinced . . . converted** *APC* convicted . . . convinced
140.27 **much less** *APC* less
140.42 **her:** *APC* her, and said—
141.7 **turn cordially** *APC* turn with cordial effusion
141.24 **I'd a et** *MMS* I'd eat *BMS* I'd 'a et *APC*
141.26 **and—"** *APC* and saved his brother's life." ¶ "It ain't anything. If I was starving, you gimme the chance and I'd save a whole family." ¶ "Now you've said enough, Joe, and you can keep still. I never saw such an aggravating boy; the plainer a thing is made to you the more you can't see it." ¶ "Well, anyways, I can see—" ¶ "There!—that'll do.
142.15 **three."** *APC* three." ¶ "And

225

you've made it four, and you think *that's* a good argument against a person that's made it three. There, Joe—close your head; when there's any help wanted out of you, I'll let you know. Go on, Angelo, never mind these people; If you wait for *them* to get quiet, you'll never get anywhere."

144.1   point, *i.e., APC*   point:
144.24   point *APC*   point of view
145.1   influences *APC*   influence
145.13   the Judge's *APC*   the
*   **145.21   [after the chapter heading] [n.i.]** *APC*   ¶ It is a mistake to inflate the truth. Dress a fact in tights, not in an ulster. ¶— *Pudd'nhead Wilson's Calendar. MMS*
145.22   Joe and Harry *APC*   the brothers
147.36   regulated *APC*   regulated weekly
147.36   hundreds *APC*   the hundreds
148.8   would *APC*   will
*   **148.19   Sunday** *APC*   a Monday *BMS*   a Sunday *MMS*
148.29   Lord *APC*   God
149.23   ladies *APC*   people
149.40   as *APC*   just as
*   **150.9   [n.i.]** *APC*   ¶ Whenever you find out you have been in error, don't change. This is Consistency. ¶—*Pudd'nhead Wilson's Calendar.* ¶ When I reflect upon the number of disagreeable people who I know have gone to a better world, I am moved to lead a different life. ¶—*Pudd'nhead Wilson's Calendar.*
151.3   were doing *APC*   was doing
†**151.33–38   moment, now, to invite . . . company.** *APC*   moment, now, on a . . . controversy.
151.40–152.17   [A long . . . chapter.] *APC*   [n.i. *BMS* or *MMS*]
*   **152   [n.i.]** ¶ There are 869 different forms of lying, but only one of them has been forbidden: thou shalt not bear false witness against thy neighbor. ¶—*Pudd'nhead Wilson's Calendar.*
152.18–19   Pudd'nhead *APC* Punk'n-head
152.45   can *APC*   could
153.4   among *APC*   amongst
153.19   said, sarcastically: *APC*   said:
155.9   other *APC*   other one
157.6   man in the world *APC*   man
158.16   for both *APC*   for
159.43   thirteen *APC*   seventeen
160.19   the old favorites *APC*   they
160.26   that young man *APC*   that
160.41   whatever *APC*   what
163.26   head *APC*   sacred head
164.12   injustice *APC*   unjustness
164.22   blown from the fields of paradise *APC*   wafted from paradise
167.10–11   has got nothing to do with it *APC*   has delegated his authority to another
168.8–9   he himself . . . trial, *APC*   he might fairly be considered entitled to another trial himself.

170   [n.i.] [after the chapter heading] *APC* ¶ He is as conceited as a proverb. ¶—*Pudd'nhead Wilson's Calendar.*
170.42   and always *APC*   but always
173.5   lungs *APC*   congested lungs
*   **174.1–2   Quantity. Boil down and skim off. I** quantity. Boil down and skim off. *APC*   Quantity. *MMS*
176.11   fractious *APC*   cantankerous
176.28   finger. *APC*   finger; but turning her head to give an order, the finger wandered in reach of Luigi's mouth and he bit it. "Why, you impudent thing!" and she gave him a rap; but she was flattered, nevertheless, perceiving that it was a love-bite.
177.7–8   prevent me *APC*   prevent it
177.14   proud *APC*   as proud
179.43   goodness *APC*   heaven
180.4   cold *APC*   thundering cold
180.20   infamous *APC*   infernal
†**180.21   prescri—"** ¶ "There, . . . dear." *APC*   prescri—" ¶ "Why . . . that."
*   **181.25   the Twins I** twins *MMS*   the twins *APC*
†**181.42–43   canvass. He . . . dance.** *APC* canvass. He . . . votes.
181.44   he *APC*   Luigi
181.44   best *APC*   greatest
182.5–6   which steadied his nerves and clarified his mind *APC*   which did not affect him in the least
182.24   persons *APC*   rowdies
*†**183.5   worse."** *APC*   worse." ¶ "Why . . . defeated.
183.24   case. His election was conceded, but he *APC*   case. He
183.31–34   fortnight. In due . . . standstill, *APC*   fortnight. The legs were Angelo's for this first week, and the brothers were not on speaking terms, now, but Luigi made no secret anywhere of the fact that there would be a duel when he got possession—either that, or Judge Driscoll would apologize: he could take his choice.
183.34   because without *APC* ¶ The Twins were heroes of romance, now, and they came into vast and instant favor again, and aunt Patsy and aunt Betsy's cups of happiness were full. But the restored popularity of the strangers did not last long. The city government had been at a stand still ever since election day, because without
184.4   up and up *APC*   up and up and up
184.5   court, yet *APC*   court till it promised to reach the high court of the hereafter, yet
184.34   to that." *APC*   to that." ¶ So the town carried the halter to Luigi, explained its persuasions, and asked him to resign and go to Europe, and not stop anywhere this side. ¶ Luigi accepted the invitation, and took his brother along with him. They never returned. Then a new election was held, and the city got started right, this time.

Emendations of the Copy-Text: Substantives
(Lengthy Passages)

**151.33–38   moment, now, to invite . . .
company** *APC*

moment, now, on a special errand. He
said—

"I have come to extend a cordial invitation
to you, gentlemen, to attend our Bible class,
which meets at eight this evening, in room
No. 16 over the market house, and I assure
you in advance that you may count upon a
pleasing and profitable hour there."

Angelo said—

"I cannot express, dear sir, how sorry I am
to be obliged to decline your most kind invitation, but my brother has an engagement
which—"

"Oh, I have no engagement that can inter-
fere," said Luigi, promptly, "and we accept
with pleasure, and shall be there."

Angelo was astonished; and also suspicious. When the minister was gone, he said:

"I was not expecting this grace at your
hands, Luigi. How did you come to accept
that invitation?"

Luigi answered in a tone of placid indifference—

"I had two reasons. I overheard you, to-
day, when you arranged to haul down your
Methodist flag day after tomorrow and hoist
the Baptist—"

"Ah!"—

—"and as I have to take a prominent part
whenever you change your fire insurance
and take out a policy in a new company, I
thought it might be well enough to get a little
coaching on the fresh conditions—examine
the prospectus, so to speak. That is one reason why I wanted to exploit the Bible class."

"Something warned me," said Angelo bitterly, "that your impulse was not a generous
one. But let it go, it is no matter; it is your
disposition to be hard; and I must still bear
it, as I have always had to do. And you had
another reason?"

"Yes, but it has no importance. The Freethinkers meet at seven, for only an hour, the
Bible class at eight. It is no inconvenience to
attend the Bible class, as we are already
there."

"Already where? How do you mean?"

"They both meet in the same room."

Angelo turned red with anger and mortifi-
cation, and he said sharply—

"It was like you! Yes, it was like you, to prepare this humiliation for me. I see it all. You
propose to keep me there until the minister
and his class come and discover me in such
company. This is to be my recommendation to
the confidence and respect of the congrega-
tion whose holy hospitalities I am to seek

day after tomorrow, and who, ignorant of the
circumstances, will receive me with cold welcome, and say privately, one to another, 'he
thinks it courtesy to prepare himself for our
companionship by assisting at a freethinker
orgy.' Luigi, how can you have the heart to
treat me so?"

"Look here!" retorted Luigi, his southern
blood suddenly rising, "as usual, blinded and
stupefied by your bigotry, you see and appreciate but one side of the case. Nothing ever
has two sides for you, but only one. Morally,
you are one-eyed; intellectually, when the
interests of that precious baggage which you
regard as your soul are concerned, you are a
bat; just simply a bat. It seems a heartless
thing to you that I should prepare this humiliating exposure for you, but you are not able
to perceive that you have prepared a bitterer
one for me."

"I? Impossible. Out with it; name it, if you
can."

"There! It is just as I said. And it simply
passes belief! You can easily anticipate the
shame *you* are to feel under the accusing eyes
of those Baptists when they say to one
another, 'There he is, making his hypocrite
vows, and he fresh from a freethinker's meeting;' yet you are dully unable to put yourself
in my place and feel what I must feel when my
freethinking friends, whom I honor and
esteem and believe to be as upright and good
and honest and respect-worthy as anybody in
any church, shall wither me with their pitying
eyes Sunday afternoon and say in their hearts,
'he came to our meeting only to laugh at us,
we never suspecting; he beguiled us of our
confidence, merely that he might spit upon it;
he tricked us into confessing, with schoolboy
enthusiasm, how proud we were going to be
to show him off as our brother—and now,
here he stands, breast deep in the river, before
all this multitude, and will get himself baptised: treachery and insult can no farther go;
he is not a man, he is a cur!'"

Angelo was profoundly hurt. He would
have left the room instantly, if he could have
done it. He said—and his voice showed how
deeply he was agitated—

"I beg that you will now cease. For my own
dignity's sake I must decline to continue a
discussion with one who so far forgets himself as to place Baptists and Freethinkers
upon the same level."

"I don't do it," retorted Luigi hotly. "I don't
classify the bifurcated creatures of God by
their religious politics; I classify them as men
or fools, only. I place a Freethinking fool and
a Baptist fool on the same level; and a Baptist who is not a fool, and a Freethinker

who is not a fool belong on a common and honorable level, and there I place them. When you started out as a Roman Catholic where did *you* place the Baptist, since you are suddenly become so sensitive about him?"

No reply.

"And when you were a Mohammedan, where did you place the Catholic *and* the Baptist?"

No reply.

"And when you ceased to be a Turk and became a Scotch Presbyterian, how did you regard all the other rag patches in the ecclesiastical quilt?"

Indignant silence.

"You do well to keep still. You change your road to heaven every time you come to a new finger-board, and then the first thing you do is to depreciate all the roads that brought you that far. If you had stuck to one road you might be in heaven, now, but the way you travel you are never going to get anywhere, in my opinion. Not that *I* care how many roads you travel—wouldn't care, I mean, if I didn't have to go along; but as it is, I get dog-tired of these everlasting excursions, for *I* get nothing out of them, not even scenery, for it's all alike—the same old paradise on one side of the track, the same old perdition on the other, and never anything fresh: a monotony of angels and a monotony of devils, and I never know which I prefer, except that it is not the angels. Now what kind of an angel do you think *you* are going to make?"

"Luigi, your cruelty forces me to speak, though I would you could have granted me peace—it would have cost you very little. You are blaming me, criticising me, upbraiding me, for the one merit I have, the sole thing in me that I might be pardoned for taking pride in—the facility and courage with which I discard a religious error when I find myself in one."

"Yes and the facility and chuckle-headedness with which you take up with the next one that comes along. You are just theological goat [*sic*], that is what you are: first you munch a dishrag, and you'll drop that for a last year's newspaper, and that for a pile of pine shavings, and that for a paper of tacks; and you are vain of the facility and courage with which you can sample thirty kinds of refuse in succession and come out with a belly full of nothing at the end, and just as hungry and idiotically enterprising as you were when you started in. You've got the appetite of an ostrich, with the judgment of a kangaroo, and you've got no more shame than to confess that you are proud of it. I wish, for your own sake, you would reform."

"Luigi, you are brutal! It should occur to you, and it should be a reproach to you, that I make this weary and sometimes almost despairing search for salvation,

unaided, unencouraged, yes, even reviled, obstructed, harassed, by you, when if you had the sort of heart you ought to have, you would help me."

"*I* help you—the idea! As if I don't get excursions enough the way it is. No, I will do nothing of the kind. I look back upon my past with horror. When you were a Catholic I had to get up before daylight and go with you to early mass; once, when you had command of our legs, you took me to the convent and had our mutual back scourged for your individual sins—once you did, but you didn't play that again. When you were a Mohammedan I had to starve the Ramadan through, or you would have told on me and got me into trouble; and I had to seem to pray five times a day, like the rest of that detestable sect. When you were this, that and the other experimental ecclesiastical tramp, I had all the privations of the situation and none of the hopes of reward. When you were a Presbyterian—but I will be silent there; I cannot think of those dismal Sabbaths and keep any rag of my patience. And *now* what are you proposing to do day after tomorrow? You are going to risk drowning me, that is what. And after all, what was to be the reward of this lagging dull lifetime of sorrows and sufferings and aggravations that I have been obliged to endure? The salvation of that tedious soul of yours. Oh, there is a long account to be settled between you and me, and I will see that you square it up, to the last farthing."

So ended the controversy.

180.21   prescri—"   ¶ "There. . . . dear."
APC

prescri—"

"Why, I'll take something *to* you if you don't hush up this minute! Bless my heart, I never heard the like. See how quiet and good *he* is—you don't hear *him* carrying on like that."

"I wish I could!"

"Looy, be *quiet*! Why, you're the very old Satan for disobedience and wrongheadedness. Instead of which, you ought to be an example to him."

"To Satan?"

"No! What are you talking about? I never said anything about your being an example to Satan. What I meant was, that you are older than he is, and—"

"Older than Satan?"

"Looy, I declare I'll give you a crack with my thimble if you keep catching me up like that and distorting what I say."

"Well, what *did* you say, Aunt Betsy? And don't lose your temper; it's getting shaky. What was it you said?"

"I said—I said—now you've got me so muddled up that I don't hardly know where

I was. I said you ought to be an example to Sa—to—to your brother, because you are older than Sa-*him*!—plague take the numskull, he has got me that mixed up and—"

"Who—Satan?"

"Hush up! You are the most aggravating creature that ever—Luigi, you're sneezing again. I do *wish* I knew something to do! Dear me, I get more and more anxious every time you sneeze. Why, I never *saw* such a cold. Something's got to be *done*, and right away, too. I'm going down stairs and make you a pail of sheep-nanny tea, and—"

"Oh, have some compassion! I'd rather have fifty colds than drink that obscene stuff. Come, sit down, now, and I'll be good—try to be, anyway."

"Yes, it's well you put that in—it ain't *in* you, *I* don't believe. You are the tryingest, and the headstrongest, and the most—"

"Well—it's true—I haven't got many virtues, but—I love *you*, Aunt Betsy!"

"O, you *dear*! I'll forgive you everything for saying that," and she caressed his hair with one hand and wiped her eyes with the back of the other. "You certainly do try a body out of all patience, but I don't mind that or anything, as long as you love me. Now you lie still till I go and get that truck; and don't you disturb your brother. I'll make it boiling hot—"

"Aunt Betsy, it's not a bit of use; I'll die before I'll take it."

But she retorted as she went out—

"No, you won't die, and you *will* take it. Don't you give yourself any uneasiness about that."

181.42–43   canvass. He . . . dance. *APC*

canvass. He began his work by dancing a breakdown on the street corner Sunday forenoon, and kept it up till all the people and all the dogs had flocked there to see. He danced away with all his might, caring not a rap for Angelo's distress, who cried bitterly all the time, and whose innocence and grief ought to have touched the hearts of the spectators; and in some cases it did, but in only a few; the mass of the crowd only laughed to see the tears flowing down the front of his violently bobbing head. For this performance Angelo was turned out of the church that very day, and that meant the loss of a great block of votes. But Luigi saved

*183.5   worse." *APC*

worse."

"Why, it is not I that am to blame, Rowena, for I never drink a drop."

"You only make your case worse when you say that," responded the girl sternly. "One *might* respect a person who gets

drunk himself, but never one who gets drunk by proxy."

"But I implore you to believe that I don't do it purposedly, Rowena; I can't help myself."

"Call me Miss Cooper, please."

"Do have pity on me, Miss Cooper. Indeed it is just as I say—I am not able to help myself."

"This is but shuffling, Count Capello. No person is obliged to get drunk on another person's liquor unless he wants to. I have never heard of such a case."

"But dear Miss Cooper my case is not like any one else's. I assure you that I—"

"Please drop the subject. I could never love a person who gets drunk clandestinely in this way. And in no case whatever could I love a dishonest person."

"Dishonest? Oh, please do not say such cruel words. How am I dishonest?"

"Luigi buys that liquor with his own money; and when you lie in wait for it and rob him of the effects of it—effects which *he* is entitled to, not you—it is larceny; it is more; it is burglary. Would you ask me to give my hand to a burglar?"

He saw that he could not contend with her in argument. Reason was on her side, or seemed to him in his dazed and but half sober condition, to be. Then the austere severity of her manner cowed him. He could plead no more. He begged piteously that if she could not be more to him, she would at least not cast him out utterly, but would be his friend. This touched her, and she said gently, laying her hand upon his head and turning her eyes reverently aloft—

"I will be your friend—nay, more, I will be your sister. Let that suffice. May heaven temper this disaster to you and give you peace."

And saying these words, she quitted the room in tears, and with a heart sore smitten by the pathetic sobs that fell upon her ear as she closed the door behind her.

The closing speck of the campaign was made by Judge Driscoll, and he made it against both of the Twins. He reviewed in acrimonious detail their extraordinary conduct of the preceding two months, and said it was the most scandalous exhibition that had ever been seen outside of an insane asylum. He would up with charging cowardice upon them for flying the dueling field, and added as a snapper his belief that the reward offered for the lost knife was buncombe, and that Luigi would be able to find it whenever he should have occasion to assassinate somebody.

This last remark flew far and wide over the town and made a prodigious sensation. Everybody was asking "What could he mean by that?" And everybody went on asking that question, but in vain; for the Judge only said he knew what he was talking about, and stopped there; Tom, who was down on a visit, said he hadn't any idea what his uncle meant, parried the question by asking the questioner what *he* thought it meant.

Wilson got the whole city vote for mayor. The Twins got the poorest vote that was cast for anybody, but as they were running against each other, even this meager showing had to elect one of them, and did—Luigi was the man.

Tom's conduct had remained letter perfect during two whole months, now, and had set him high in his uncle's confidence; so high,

indeed, that he trusted him with money with which to influence vacilating or indifferent people to vote against Luigi. He took it out of a tin box in the safe in his private sitting room, and said he would spend the rest of the box's contents to beat Luigi, if necessary. Tom saved a hundred dollars, and used it for the purpose for which it was given him, too, merely retiring ten per cent of it as commission—which was ninety per cent better morals than he had had in stock at any time before, since his childhood.

When the election was over he went back to St Louis happy—fully half happy, at any rate, for one twin had been defeated.

Emendations of the Copy-Text: Accidentals

The following table lists every instance in which the copy-text has been emended with an accidental. If the accidental is caused by or coincident with a substantive variation, the word or phrase in question is listed both under accidentals and under substantives.

The material in boldface type represents the present text readings and the texts in which those readings appear (indicated by sigla). The light-face material represents the copy-text readings and any other readings from other texts. The copy-text reading is for the MMS or the BMS, whichever contains the latest authorial inscription.

"**I**" after an adopted reading indicates that the emendation is made by the editor. An asterisk (*) indicates that the reading is discussed in the Textual Notes. A squiggle (~) is used to indicate that there is no variant in the word, just in the punctuation. A caret (∧) indicates the lack of punctuation at that point. A paragraph marker (¶) indicates that there is a new paragraph at that point. "[n.i.]" indicates that the word or phrase is not in the text whose sigil follows it.

129.17	**are!** APC ~.		132.36	**now.** APC ~!
129.19	**so** APC so		133.1	***They*** 19 They
129.21	**that!** APC ~.		133.31	**grand!** APC ~.
129.22	**"—'but** APC ∧—'~		*134.17	**when** MMS-APC When
129.25	**ma!** APC ~.		134.17	**I am** APC I am
129.28	**names.** APC ~!		134.20	**as you** APC as *you*
128.40	**ma!** APC ~.		134.39	**so strong** APC so strong
128.42	**them!** APC ~.		134.40	**that—"** APC ~—∧
130.4	**I** APC I		134.42–43	**you could** APC you could
130.5	**I** APC I			
130.12	**I** APC I		135.4	***principles*** APC principles
130.14	**hope** APC *hope*		135.22	**I don't** APC I don't
131.16	**weird** APC wierd		135.25	**every** APC *every*
131.21	**look** APC *look*		135.26	**village;** APC ~—
131.24–25	**I was** APC I *was*		135.33	**I** APC I
132.5	**on** *its* **I** on *it's*		135.37	**singing!** APC ~.
132.18	**say!** APC ~.		135.41	**ever** APC *ever*
132.21	**this** APC *this*		135.42	**'Greenland's Icy Mountains'**
132.22	**begin.** APC ~!			APC ∧~~~∧
132.24	**you** APC *you*		136.2	**'Old Bob Ridley'** APC ∧~~~∧
132.33	**dizzy** MMS-APC dizz		136.4	**"Bob Ridley'** APC ∧~~∧
132.34	**I** APC I		136.10	**They** APC *They*

136.25   I APC   I
136.28   is APC   is
137.7   coming! APC   ~.
138.1   ¶ "Now that APC   ∧ "Now that
138.3   it— APC   it—
138.11   you MMS-APC   you
138.22–24   he . . . he APC   he . . . he
139.15   saying, APC   ~∧
139.19   fact, APC   ~ ∧
139.38   didn't, APC   ~!
140.31   he APC   he
140.33   never APC   never
140.33   life! APC   ~.
140.34   you. APC   ~!
140.40   hand, APC   ~!
141.23   good APC   good
141.23   food APC   food
142.3   Mister APC   Mister
142.4   Luigi APC   Luigi
142.10   certainly APC   certainly
142.10   thinking APC   thinking
144.24   that. APC   ~!
145.8   drunk APC   drank
145.42   with! APC   ~.
146.3   isn't APC   isn't
146.9   brother's! APC   ~.
146.24   ¶ "And APC   ∧"~
146.26   they APC   they
147.15   week! APC   ~.
147.20   do APC   do
147.26   never! APC   ~.
147.39   me APC   me
147.40   Jericho MMS   Jerico
148.9   borrow APC   borrow
148.12   nowdays APC   now-a-days
148.16   all APC   all
148.18   does not APC   doesn't
148.20   such APC   such
149.6   be APC   be
149.15   that, APC   that,
149.21–22   we . . . are APC   we . . . are
149.23–24   paralyzed— . . . say— APC   ~, . . . ~,
149.30   anywhere APC   anywhere BMS   anywhere MMS
149.33   Anybody APC   Anybody
149.36   dear APC   dear
150.1   Luigi . . . satisfaction: "That . . . cars." APC   "That . . . cars," Luigi . . . satisfaction.
153.22   everyone I every one MMS-APC
154.1   question. APC   ~!
154.8   gentlemen APC   gentleman
154.14   ¶ The APC   ∧~
154.23   it. APC   ~!
154.41   they APC   they
155.8   say it might APC   say it might
155.10   didn't APC   didn't
155.12   I APC   I
155.30   saw APC   saw
155.43   said, APC   ~!
156.9   A Voice: APC   A Voice.
156.9   Laughter . . . court APC   Laughter . . . court
156.10   Another Voice: APC   Another Voice

156.10–11   Laughter . . . court APC   Laughter . . . court
157.31   Wilson; ∧ the APC   ~; "~
157.40   not APC   not
157.45   unprecedented! APC   ~.
158.5   where APC   where
158.15   has APC   has
158.17–18   Great applause APC   Great Applause
159.27   impudence! APC   ~.
159.28   Now APC   Now
160.44   fact APC   fact
160.44   be APC   be
161.2   do APC   do
161.6   Hear APC   Hear
161.12   down! APC   ~.
161.13   Must APC   Must
161.21   they told APC   they told
161.33   please go on APC   please go on
161.35   me APC   me
161.44   of it! APC   ~~.
161.45   Laughter, APC   Laughter—
162.22   know. APC   ~?
163.31   seized APC   siezed
163.45   but APC   but
164.3   gift, APC   ——
164.8–9   need! ¶ "Prisoners APC   ~!∧∧~
164.9   up. APC   ~!
164.12   injustice. APC   unjustness!
164.13   more! APC   ~.
164.16   aunties APC   Aunties
165.24   Why! APC   ~,
166.3   duelists APC   dualists
166.7   can't stay APC   can't stay
166.9   you're APC   you're
166.9   at you APC   at you
166.11   Angelo∧ APC   ~,
168.13   was to APC   was to
169.7   Boom APC   Boom
169.17   that APC   that
169.17   before! APC   ~,
170.4   finish APC   finish
171.17   maxillario superioris I maxillario superioris MMS   maxillaris superioris APC
171.22–23   populo redax referendum rotulorum APC   populo redax referendum rotulorum
172.15   can't APC   can't
172.16   word, APC   ~∧
172.30   Joe. APC   ~!
174.5   while APC   While
174.26   to-day APC   to-day
175.21   lost. APC   ~!
175.27   Looy! APC   Looy!
176.10   it! APC   ~.
176.11   Looy APC   Looy
176.13   that APC   that
176.19   it! APC   ~.
176.22   I'm APC   I'm
177.10   all! APC   ~.
177.11   lion. APC   ~!
177.35–36   Pudd'nhead APC   Puddn'-head
179.34   I— APC   I—
179.35   Will APC   Will

179.39   can't APC   *can't*   184.27   ticket. APC   ~!
180.16   this APC   *this*

Rejected Variants: Substantives

This table contains substantive readings in texts other than the copy-text that are not used for emendations of the copy-text. Page and line numbers indicate present text locations. Any text not cited by sigla accompanying the reading given in lightface type does not differ from the copy-text reading. An asterisk preceding an entry indicates that the entry is discussed in the Textual Notes.

For the few instances when the BMS and MMS differ, this fact is emphasized with the citation of sigla accompanying the boldface material.

130.10   **May be**   Maybe APC
130.17   **Those**   These APC
*130.22   **on the**   at the MMS-APC
*130.22   **family**   anxious family APC
130.31   **slave wench** MMS   slave girl BMS   slave-wench APC
131.14   **lightnings**   lightning APC
133.35   **can fix**   can can fix MMS
*134.33   **in one**   on one MMS
*135.6   **d-bosh**   bosh APC
137.8   **"They . . . right."**   [n.i.] BMS
*138.14   **did not**   didn't MMS-APC
*139.5   **these**   the MMS-APC
*139.22–23   **indigestion**   digestion MMS
*140.27   **illnesses**   illness MMS-APC
*140.33   **"Well**   "Why APC
141.24   **a et**   eat BMS 'a et APC
144.4   **the**   a APC
*144.28   **the**   an MMS a APC
*145.9   **the languor**   and languor MMS-APC
*145.11   **long and**   long MMS-APC
145.23   **persons that noon,** persons BMS   persons that noon ∧ APC

*147.29   **shade and fraction**   shade of a fraction MMS-APC
148.5   **No**   Now APC
*148.5   **you're**   you've MMS-APC
148.19   **Sunday**   a Monday BMS a Sunday MMS
*149.26   **proofs**   proof MMS-APC
*150.3   **poor old**   poor MMS-APC
*156.16   **or ands**   and and's APC
157.42   **law**   laws APC
*160.27   **Jake**   Jack APC
163.1   **the one**   one APC
163.32–33   **circumference**   circumstance APC
*164.18   **crowds**   crowd APC
170.24   **whatsoever**   whatever APC
170.28   **about it**   about APC
174.30   **I cannot**   cannot APC
*176.18   **you, Looy**   you, APC
*178.19   **and so**   so APC
178.33   **ever**   even APC
179.17   **the burghers**   burghers APC
179.38   **I tell you I**   I APC
*180   **[Chapter 9]**
*181.31   **and his**   and the APC

Textual Notes

130.22   **on the**   "at the" is an error of the typist who typed the BMS. The typed pages are inserted in MMS.

130.22   **family**   This is an eye-skip by the typist. In the deleted matter in the line above this one was the phrase "anxious family."

134.17   **when**   When Clemens inserted words preceding this one in the sentence, he neglected to make this lower case.

134.34   **"Whole Duty of Man,"**   The person who typed the BMS accidentally typed "Testament" with a lower case *t*. Clemens has written "Whole Duty of

Man" (without the quotation marks) between the lines.

135.6   **d-bosh**   Note that at 41.3 of the present text, the CM editors reduced "damn it" to "———it."

135.9   **"From Greenland's Icy Mountains"**   In *Following the Equator* (Vol. 2, Ch. 19) Clemens quotes the lyrics as follows: "From Greenland's icy mountains, / From India's coral strand, / Where Afric's sunny fountains / Roll down their golden sand; / From many an ancient river, / From many a palmy plain, / They call us to deliver / Their land from error's chain." He then says: "These are beautiful verses, and they have remained in my memory all my life." (*Following the Equator* [New York and London: Harper & Brothers, 1897, 1899], Vol. 2, p. 225.)

138.4 sure as The comma in the rejected reading ("sure,s") is the way it appears in the BMS typescript (i.e., the one embedded in the MMS). The use of the comma for apostrophes by the typist is consistent, and is not henceforth noted.

138.14 did not This is a typist's error.

139.5 these in the BMS Clemens's *se* of "these" was messy and easily taken for an *n*; the typist typed "then"; Clemens, not making any sense of this when he proofread the typescript, crossed off the typist's *n*.

139.22–23 indigestion The typist erroneously typed "digestion"; someone, seeing the error, inserted a caret before this word in pencil but neglected to insert "in" above the line. (Also, Clemens has had Luigi here ask Angelo not to add any more sugar to his tea, saying it would give him [Luigi] indigestion; this humorous touch is in the wrong brother's mouth, for it is Angelo who is affected by what goes into the stomach.)

140.27 illnesses This is a typist's error.

140.33 "Well This typist's error is an eye-skip to a paragraph above.

144.28 the In BMS "the" is written carelessly; it looks like "an"; the typist typed "an," which form still remains in the MMS. The APC changed "an" to "a."

145.9 the languor "and" is a typist's error.

145.11 long and This is a typist's error.

145.21 [After chapter heading] [n.i.] This maxim, penned into the typed pages of the MMS, was not used in this story.

145.23 persons that noon, "that noon," was added into the MMS by the author in pencil.

147.29 shade and fraction This is a typist's error.

148.5 you're The BMS reading is questionable but appears to be "you're"; the typist read "you've."

148.19 Sunday The "Sun" has been changed in pencil to "Mon"—probably not by Clemens.

149.26 proofs This is a typist's error.

150.3 poor old This omission is a typist's error.

150.9 [n.i.] These two maxims appear on page 141 of MMS, immediately after the first two paragraphs on p. 150 of the present edition. The words ". . . if he had" originally ended MMS Chapter 10, and the two maxims were headed "Chapter 11." The first of these ["Whenever you find . . ."] was never used. The second ["When I reflect . . ."] heads Chapter 13 of *Pudd'nhead Wilson* (page 67 herein).

152 [n.i.] This maxim was never used for *Pudd'nhead Wilson*. It appears at the opening of Chapter 19 (Vol. 2) of *Following the Equator*, as part of "*Pudd'nhead Wilson's New Calendar.*" It differs from the MMS version by the inclusion of the word "squarely" before "forbidden."

160.27 Jake This is likely a typist's eye-skip to "Jack Lounsbury" a few lines later.

164.18 crowds This was originally written "crowd," then the comma was changed to an *s* and another comma was inserted. The first comma makes it look as if the *s* is crossed out.

174.1–2 Quantity. Boil down and skim off. This recipe is pasted into the MMS, cut by Clemens from his article "A Majestic Literary Fossil" in *Harper's New Monthly Magazine*, LXXX (February 1890), pp. 439–444. This excerpt is on page 444.

176.18 you, Looy "Looy" is inserted with a caret in an area with much authorial revision. It was probably not seen by the typist.

178.19 and so The ampersand is at the end of the line and is followed by a deleted word; thus it was easily missed by the typist.

180 [Chapter 9] N.B. For this chapter the published copy of APC has several words deleted from the text as it existed in the earlier form as sent to the Library of Congress. These deletions may be found in Appendix 2 (p. 237 herein).

181.25 the Twins In making a correction, Clemens forgot to include the word "the."

181.31 and his Clemens wrote "& his," and the ampersand could have easily been mistaken for a *t*. The typist or compositor—realizing that the word "this" did not make much sense—evidently changed it to "the."

183.5 worse." Clearly some of this deleted passage refers to the story in *Pudd'nhead Wilson*. But it is recorded here since it is surrounded by the *Those Extraordinary Twins* story, and there was no specific place in *Pudd'nhead Wilson* from which it was deleted. The passage shows how the two stories (the Siamese twins and the murder mystery) were still joined in the MMS. Parts of this deleted passage were substantially rewritten for *Pudd'nhead Wilson*, Chapter 17, page 89 herein), though some of it was used verbatim there.

Appendix 1

The Weather Signs Passage Deleted from
*Pudd'nhead Wilson**

*See first entry in Emendations of the Copy-Text: Substantives (Lengthy Passages), on page 206 herein. This "Weather Signs" passage was published by Daniel Morley McKeithan in his essay "The Morgan Manuscript of Mark Twain's *Pudd'nhead Wilson*" (see Bibliography).

4

(Put this paragraph below the succeeding two.)

When there is no sign, it means that there is not going to be any weather. It is a mistake to suppose that weather is at all times necessary in a novel. As often as not, it is an ~~circumstance~~. inconvenience, & keeps the characters from going out.

When all the signs are used it means **Stormy**. ~~with~~

When they are doubled, it means ~~[crossed out]~~ Extremely **Violent & Perilous** **Weather**.

(Put it down here.)

Appendix 2

Words Deleted from Chapter 9 of
Those Extraordinary Twins

In the first published version of *Those Extraordinary Twins* (American Publishing Company, 1894) several words were deleted from the text. In the proof copies of this edition sent by the American Publishing Company to the Library of Congress for copyright purposes, these words were not deleted. (For an explanation, see Sidney Berger, "Editorial Intrusion in *Pudd'nhead Wilson*," *The Papers of the Bibliographical Society of America* 70 [1976], pp. 272–76; or see the Textual Introduction, page 193 herein.)

Below is a table of the present edition readings (those of the MMS and the Library of Congress, printed in boldface type) and the readings in APC (lightface type).

181.12	**hotter and hotter**	hotter
181.13	**presently developed**	developed
181.14	**interest in it**	interest
181.15	**which was a**	a
181.16	**him,**	him, but
181.21	**Union and**	Union,
181.34	**and did his**	doing his
181.34	**to get back**	to regain
181.35	**ground which**	ground
181.37	**and it was an**	an
181.39–40	**extravagant and**	extravagant,
182.22	**a ringing appeal**	an appeal
182.26	**in a general burst of wrath**	in wrath
182.31–32	**had even**	had
182.33	**but had begged for**	but wanted
182.33–34	**But now**	Now
182.34–183.1	**she frankly**	she

CRITICISM

All readings from *Pudd'nhead Wilson* and *Those Extraordinary Twins* have been made to conform to the style of the present edited text, and all page numbers refer to this text.

Reviews

WILLIAM LIVINGSTON ALDEN

From *The Idler* (August 1894)†

Puddenhead Wilson, Mark Twain's latest story, is the work of a novelist, rather than of a 'funny man.' There is plenty of humour in it of the genuine Mark Twain brand, but it is as a carefully painted picture of life in a Mississippi town in the days of slavery that its chief merit lies. In point of construction it is much the best story that Mark Twain has written, and of men and women in the book at least four are undeniably creations, and not one of them is overdrawn or caricatured, as are some of the most popular of the author's lay figures. There is but one false note in the picture, and that is the introduction of the two alleged Italian noblemen. These two young men are as little like Italians as they are like Apaches. When challenged to fight a duel, one of them, having the choice of weapons, chooses revolvers instead of swords. This incident alone is sufficient to show how little Italian blood there is in Mark Twain's Italians. But this is a small blemish, and if Mark Twain, in his future novels, can maintain the proportion of only two lay figures to four living characters, he will do better than most novelists. The extracts from 'Puddenhead Wilson's Almanac,' which are prefixed to each chapter of the book, simply 'pizon us for more,' to use Huck Finn's forcible metaphor. Let us hope that a complete edition of that unrivalled almanac will be issued at no distant day.

From *The Athenæum* (January 19, 1895)‡

The best thing in *Pudd'nhead Wilson*, by Mark Twain (Chatto & Windus), is the picture of the negro slave Roxana, the cause of all the trouble which gives scope to Mr. Wilson's ingenious discovery about finger-marks. Her gusts of passion or of despair, her vanity, her motherly love, and the glimpses of nobler feelings that are occasionally

---

† From *The Idler, an Illustrated Monthly Magazine* (London), Vol. VI, pp. 222–23.
‡ An anonymous review from *The Athenæum, a Journal of Literature, Science, The Fine Arts, Music, and the Drama* (London), No. 3508, pp. 83–84.

seen in her elementary code of morals, make her very human, and create a sympathy for her in spite of her unscrupulous actions. But hers is the only character that is really striking. Her son is a poor creature, as he is meant to be, but he does not arrest the reader with the same unmistakable reality: his actions are what might be expected, but his conversations, especially with Wilson and the Twins, seem artificial and forced. Wilson, the nominal hero, appears to most advantage in the extracts from his calendar which head the chapters, but as a personage he is rather too shadowy for a hero. And what has to be said about the book must be chiefly about the individuals in it, for the story in itself is not much credit to Mark Twain's skill as a novelist. The idea of the change of babies is happy, and the final trial scene is a good piece of effect; but the story at times rambles on in an almost incomprehensible way. Why drag in, for example, all the business about the election, which is quite irrelevant? and the Twins altogether seem to have very little *raison d'être* in the book. Of course there are some funny things in the story—it would not be by Mark Twain if there were not—but the humour of the preface might very well be spared; it is in bad taste. Still, if the preface be skipped the book well repays reading just for the really excellent picture of Roxana.

HJALMAR HJORTH BOYESEN

From *Cosmopolitan* (January 1895)†

*   *   *

Let me add, for the sake of a transition, that Mark Twain, whose "Puddin'-Head Wilson" I have just finished, is even more unique among humorists. Here we have a novel of the ante-bellum days in Missouri, rather melodramatic in plot, and full of the liveliest kind of action. If anybody but Mark Twain had undertaken to tell that kind of story, with exchanges of infants in the cradle, a hero with negro taint in his blood substituted for the legitimate white heir, midnight encounters in a haunted house between the false heir and his colored mother, murder by the villain of his supposed uncle and benefactor, accusation of an innocent foreigner, and final sensational acquittal and general unraveling of the tangled skein—if, I say, anybody else had had the hardihood to utilize afresh this venerable stage machinery of fiction, we should have been tempted to class his work with such cheap stuff as that of Wilkie Collins, Hugh Conway, and the dime novelists. But Mark Twain, somehow, has lifted it all into

† From *Cosmopolitan* 18 (January 1895): 379.

the region of literature. In the first place, the alleged extracts from Puddin'-Head Wilson's calendar are inimitably droll and witty. Take, for instance, this:

"There is no character, howsoever good and fine, but it can be destroyed by ridicule, howsoever poor and witless. Observe the ass, for instance: his character is about perfect; he is the choicest spirit among the humbler animals; yet see what ridicule has brought him to. Instead of feeling complimented, when we are called an ass, we are left in doubt."

Then again, the Missouri village in which the scene is laid, is so vividly realized in its minutest details; and the people, in all their fatuous prejudice and stolidity, are so credible and authentic, so steeped in the local atmosphere, that the illusion becomes perfect, and we swallow the melodrama without a qualm,—exchange of heirs, haunted house, murder, and all,—and scarcely dream that we have been duped, until we wake up with a start at the end of the last chapter. "Tell the truth, or trump,—but take the trick," is one of Puddin'-Head Wilson's maxims; and the author, to make assurance doubly sure, has done both. He evidently has an ample fund of experience to draw upon; and he possesses, also, that high imaginative faculty which does not consist in crude invention, but in shaping remembered truth into logical and artistic coherence. His people stand squarely upon their feet, not because he has so constructed them, but because he has known their type and been familiar with their looks, speech, and habits. How deliciously rich, racy, and copious is, for instance, his negro talk. The very gurgling laugh and cooing cadence seem, somehow, implied in the text; and the fancy instinctively adds the vivid miens and gestures. Since Mark Twain wrote his "Tom Sawyer" and "Roughing It," he has published no book comparable in interest to "Puddin'-Head Wilson."

From *The Critic* (May 11, 1895)†

The literary critic is often puzzled how to classify the intellectual phenomena that come within his ken. His business is of course primarily with *literature*. A work may be infinitely amusing, it may abound even with flashes and touches of genius, and yet the form in which it comes into the world may be so crude, so coarse, so erring from the ways of true classicism, so offensive to immemorial canons of taste, that the critic, in spite of his enjoyment and wonder, puts it

† An anonymous review from *The Critic; an Illustrated Monthly Review of Literature, Art, and Life* (New York), Vol. XXVI, pp. 338–39.

reluctantly down in the category of unclassifiable literary things—
only to take it up and enjoy it again!

Of such is *Pudd'nhead Wilson*, and, for that matter, Mark Twain
in general. The author is a signal example of sheer genius, without
training or culture in the university sense, setting forth to conquer
the world with laughter whether it will or no, and to get himself
thereby acknowledged to be the typical writer of the West. He is the
most successful of a class of American humorists whose impulse to
write off their rush of animal spirits is irresistible, and who snatch at
the first pen within reach as the conductor of their animal electric-
ity. If we look at other national humorists, like Aristophanes, Cer-
vantes, Molière or Swift, we find their humor expressed in an
exquisite literary form, in which a certain polish tempers the extrav-
agance, and annoying metrical (or it may be imaginative) difficulties
have been overcome. What wonderful bird-rhythms and wasp
melodies and cloud-architecture, so to speak, emerge from the marvellous choral interludes of the Greek comedian; what suave literary
graces enclose the gaunt outlines of Don Quixote; in what honeyed
verse are Alceste and Tartuffe entangled, and what new, nervous,
powerful prose describes the adventures of Gulliver! When we turn
our eyes westward we encounter Judge Haliburton, Hosea Biglow,
Uncle Remus, Mark Twain—an absolutely new *genre* distinct from
what we had previously studied in the line of originalities. The one
accomplished artist among these is Lowell, whose university traditions were very strong and controlled his bubbling humor. The others are pure 'naturalists'—men of instinctive genius, who have relied
on their own conscious strength to produce delight in the reader,
irrespective of classicity of form, literary grace or any other of the
beloved conventions on which literature as literature has hitherto
depended. This is true in a less degree of Uncle Remus than of Judge
Haliburton and Mark Twain.

Pudd'nhead Wilson is no exception to the rule. It is a Missouri tale
of changelings 'befo' the wah,' admirable in atmosphere, local color
and dialect, a drama in its way, full of powerful situations, thrilling
even; but it cannot be called in any sense *literature*. In it Mark
Twain's brightness and grotesqueness and funniness revel and
sparkle, and in the absurd extravaganza, 'Those Extraordinary Twins,'
all these comicalities reach the buffoon point; one is amused and
laughs unrestrainedly but then the irksome question comes up:
What *is* this? is it literature? is Mr. Clemens a 'writer' at all? must he
not after all be described as an admirable after-dinner storyteller—
humorous, imaginative, dramatic, like Dickens—who in an evil
moment, urged by admiring friends, has put pen to paper and written down his stories? Adapted to the stage and played by Frank Mayo,
the thing has met with immediate success.

T. M. PARROTT

From *The Booklover's Magazine* (February 1904)†

*　*　*

Pudd'nhead Wilson * * * has an artistic unity which the others lack. Curiously enough this sombre story took shape in the author's mind as a farce, which turned into a tragedy under his very hands. In one of the most amusing glimpses of a literary workshop that an author has ever given us, Mr. Clemens tells of his trouble with the tangled story. The farce and the tragedy, he says, obstructed and interrupted each other at every turn, and created no end of confusion and annoyance, until he finally pulled the former up by the roots and left the other, 'a kind of literary Caesarean operation.'

The result of the operation, however, is by no means wholly gratifying. *Pudd'nhead Wilson* is a tragedy, but a very sordid one. There is no trace left of the light-hearted gaiety of *Tom Sawyer*, and very little of the genial humanity of *Huckleberry Finn*. On the contrary, the book is marked by a strong dash of ironical cynicism which finds utterance mainly in the *obiter dicta* of the titular hero, prefixed as mottoes to the various chapters. 'If you pick up a starving dog and make him prosperous, he will not bite you; that is the principal difference between a dog and a man,' says one of these. That is not the sort of thing that the Mark Twain of *Innocents Abroad* would have regarded as a joke, and it runs counter to the experiences of Tom with Muff Potter, and of Huck with 'nigger Jim.' It is, perhaps, a result of this bitter mood that there is no one figure in the book capable of arresting and retaining our sympathies. Tom Driscoll, the slave who takes his master's place, is a monster of meanness, cowardice, and ingratitude; the mulatto, Roxana, is a strongly conceived, but rather repellent character; and Pudd'nhead himself is, till the very close of the book, a mere lay figure on which to hang the author's own philosophizings. And yet the work is by no means devoid of power. It is a strong, direct, and simple piece of narrative; it has an ingeniously constructed plot and a startling climax; and like its predecessors it is a genuine and realistic picture of that phase of American life with which the author is most familiar. Had anyone but Mark Twain written such a book it would no doubt have been more generally recognized as the grave and powerful piece of art it really is.

† From *The Booklover's Magazine* (Philadelphia), Vol. III, pp. 145–54.

Essays

BERNARD DE VOTO

[Mark Twain's Presentation of Slavery]†

In "Pudd'nhead Wilson" the institution that had furnished a living background for these other books[1] becomes the active center. In all other places Mark Twain omitted an explicit statement of sexual relationships—though the force of implication is irresistible wherever the squatters are displayed. Here, it may be in all innocence, he states and develops a theme completely tabooed in nineteenth-century American literature, miscegenation. It is so inevitably a part of the book that critical amazement develops only retrospectively. Yet there is an intense artistic courage in this presentation of the slave Roxana, one sixteenth negro, of fair complexion and fine soft hair, and of the son whom she bears to Cecil Burleigh Essex.

Roxy is unique and formidable. Mark's handling of her suffers somewhat from the melodrama and sentimentality that, it should be clear, were inescapable—but does not suffer much. In outline and in detail she is memorably true. She lives: her experiences and emotions are her own, and, being her own, are faithful to the history of thousands. With new instruments at its service and a generation of writers far distant from the reality, literature may make another essay of slavery—but is unlikely to go beyond the superstition, affection, malice, and loyalty of this woman. In her exist, as nowhere else, the experience, the thought, and the feelings of slaves. Even in melodrama she retains her verity. When she forces Valet de Chambre Essex to his knees, she is within reach of the preposterous, but the scene is as true, as inevitable, as her thieving and tippling. It ends with her declaration that "dey ain't another nigger in dis town dat's as high-bawn as you is" (47), and this is grandeur. Grandeur of another kind appears in her original crime and, most evidently, in her disgust when she learns that her son has disgraced

† From Bernard De Voto, *Mark Twain's America* (Boston: Little, Brown and Company, 1932), pp. 293–94. Copyright © 1932 by Bernard De Voto, renewed 1960 by Avis M. De Voto. Reprinted by permission of Houghton Mifflin Company. All rights reserved.
1. *A Connecticut Yankee, The Prince and the Pauper, Joan of Arc, The Gilded Age, The American Claimant,* and *The Man Who Corrupted Hadleyburg* [Editor].

his father by ratting the duel with Luigi. "En you refuse' to fight a man dat kicked you, 'stid o' jumpin' at de chance! En you ain't got no mo' feelin' den to come en tell me, dat fetched sich a po' low-down ornery rabbit into de worl'! Pah! it make me sick! It's de nigger in you, dat's what it is. Thirty-one parts o' you is white, en on'y one part nigger, en dat po' little one part is yo' *soul*. 'Tain't wuth savin'; 'tain't wuth totin' out on a shovel en tho'in' in de gutter" (75). In such passages as this and the mind of Valet de Chambre, slavery finds a profundity and a complexity of expression that it has had nowhere else. . . . It is worth noting that in *Pudd'nhead Wilson*, Mark Twain adheres to the artistic necessities of his structure. The tough-minded ending, though clumsily managed, is carried out in its own terms.

Slavery as an institution and Negroes as sharers of the scene are organic in the community to which these novels are devoted. It is a whole community: the effect is totality. Several generations of American experience, a race, an era, and a society, are enregistered.

* * *

LESLIE FIEDLER

"As Free as Any Cretur . . ."†

The most extraordinary book in American literature unfortunately has not survived as a whole; but its scraps and fragments are to be found scattered through the work of Mark Twain: a cynical comment ascribed to a small-town lawyer and never printed, the wreck of a comic tale framed by apologies and bad jokes, and finally the *Pudd'nhead Wilson* that has come down to us, half melodramatic detective story, half bleak tragedy. What a book the original might have been, before *Those Extraordinary Twins* was detached and Pudd'nhead's *Calendar* expurgated—a rollicking atrocious melange of bad taste and half understood intentions and nearly intolerable insights into evil, translated into a nightmare worthy of America.

All that the surrealists were later to yearn for and in their learned way simulate, Twain had stumbled on without quite knowing it. And as always (except in *Huckleberry Finn*) he paid the price for his lack of self-awareness; he fumbled the really great and monstrous poem on duplicity that was within his grasp. The principle of analogy

† From *The New Republic*, Vol. CXXXIII, Nos. 7–8, Issues 2125–26 (August 15 and 22, 1955), pp. 130–39. Reprinted by permission of *The New Republic*.

which suggested to him linking the story of the Siamese Twins, one a teetotaler, the other a drunk, Jekyll and Hyde inside a single burlesque skin—to a tale of a Negro and white baby switched in the cradle finally seemed to him insufficient. He began to worry about broken plot lines and abandoned characters, about the too steep contrast between farce and horror; and he lost his nerve—that colossal gall which was his essential strength as well as his curse. Down the well went the burlesque supernumeraries and finally out of the story; and the poor separated twins remain to haunt a novel which is no longer theirs.

But something in Twain must have resisted the excisions; certainly they were made with a striking lack of conviction, and the resulting book is marred by incomprehensible motivations and gags that have lost their point with the unjoining of the once Siamese twins. The two stories were, after all, one, and the old book a living unity that could not be split without irreparable harm.

Yet *Pudd'nhead Wilson* is, after all, a fantastically good book, better than Mark Twain knew or his critics have deserved. Morally, it is one of the most honest books in our literature, superior in this one respect to *Huckleberry Finn*; for here Twain permits himself no sentimental relenting, but accepts for once the logic of his own premises. The immoral device of Tom's revelation, the fake "happy ending" of *Huck* are avoided in *Pudd'nhead*. It is a book which deals not only with the public issue of slavery, after all, long resolved—but with the still risky private matter of miscegenation, which most of our writers have chosen to avoid; and it creates in Roxy, the scared mulatto mother sold down the river by the son she has smuggled into white respectability, a creature of passion and despair rare among the wooden images of virtue or bitchery that pass for females in American literature. It is a portrait so complex and unforeseen that the baffled illustrator for the authorized standard edition chose to ignore it completely, drawing in the place of a "majestic . . . rosy . . . comely" (9) Roxana—a gross and comic Aunt Jemima.

The scenes between this mother and her unregenerate son, who passes from insolence and cowardice to robbery and murder, and who ends slobbering at the feet of the woman he despises and plots to sell, have the cruelty and magnificence attained only by a great writer telling us a truth we cannot afford to face in a language we cannot afford to forget. It is a book which will be, I am sure, more and more read; certainly it is hard to believe that so rare a combination of wit and the metaphysical shudder will be considered forever of the second rank. Beside this book, *The Mysterious Stranger*, for the last several years a favorite of the writers on Twain, is revealed as the callow and contrived piece of cynicism it is: the best a cultureless man can do when he chooses to "philosophize" rather than dream.

Perhaps the best way to understand *Pudd'nhead* is to read it as a complement to *Huckleberry Finn*, a dark mirror image of the world evoked in the earlier work. Nearly ten years come between the two books, ten years in which guilt and terror had passed from the periphery of Twain's life and imagination to their center. *Huckleberry Finn* also is steeped in horror, to be sure; but it is easier to know this than to feel it. Though the main fable of the earlier book begins with a boy standing off with a rifle, his father gone berserk with the D.T.'s and ends with the revelation of that father's death in a seedy and flooded room scrawled with obscenities, it has so poetic a texture, so genuine though unmotivated a tone of joy—that one finds himself eternally doubting his own sense of its terrible import. In *Pudd'n-head*, however, the lyricism and the euphoria are gone; we have fallen to a world of prose, and there are no triumphs of Twain's rhetoric to preserve us from the revealed failures of our own humanity.

True enough, there is humor in the later book, but on a level of grotesquerie that is more violent and appalling than anything avowedly serious. It is the humor of Dickens' Quilp and Faulkner's idiot Snopes, the humor of the freak. In the chamber of horrors of our recent fiction, the deformed and dwarfed and dumb have come to stand as symbols of our common plight, the failure of everyone to attain a purely fictional norm. Toward this insight, Twain was fumbling almost without awareness, believing all along that he was merely trying to take the curse off of a bitterness he could not utterly repress by being what he liked to think was "funny."

Just as the grotesque in *Pudd'nhead* tends to break free from the humorous, so the tragic struggles to shed the nostalgic which swathes it still in *Huckleberry Finn*. In the earlier book, it is possible to believe that the flight toward freedom and childhood is more than a flight toward isolation and death. There is always waiting in a bend of the river Aunt Sally's homestead: a utopia of childhood visits and Southern homecooking. But Huck rejected this nostalgic Southland at the end of his own book, and in *Tom Sawyer, Detective*, Twain had introduced death and the threat of madness into that Eden itself.

By the time he was attempting to detach *Pudd'nhead* from the wreck of his larger book, Twain had decided that the only unthreatened utopia is death itself; and amid the animal jokes and easy cynicism of the Calendar quotations set at the head of each chapter, rings the sybil's cry: *Let me die*: "Whoever has lived long enough to know what life is, knows how deep a debt of gratitude we owe to Adam, the first great benefactor of our race. He brought death into the world" (14). When he writes this, Twain no longer finds in freedom the pat happy ending waiting to extricate his characters from their moral dilemmas and himself from the difficulties of plotting.

He does not abandon the theme of liberty, but renders now the full treacherous paradox, only half of which he had acknowledged earlier.

Everyone remembers the climax of *Huckleberry Finn*, at which Tom, "his eye hot, and his nostrils opening and shutting like gills," cries out to Jim: "They hain't no *right* to shut him up. . . . Turn him loose! He ain't no slave; he's as free as any cretur that walks this earth!" As free as any cretur . . . the wry joke is there already, but Twain can no more see it than can Tom; and we are not permitted to see it as readers as long as we remain within the spell of the book. But in *Pudd'nhead Wilson*, the protagonist, who is obviously Tom himself grown older and an outcast but about to be reinstated into the community, rises to answer his own earlier cry, in such a situation as he has always dreamed: "Valet de Chambre, negro and slave . . . make upon the window the finger-prints that will hang you!" (119–20). The double truth is complete: the seeming slave is free, but the free man is really a slave.

The resolution of *Pudd'nhead* is, of course, double; and the revelation which brands the presumed Thomas à Becket Driscoll a slave, declares the presumed Valet de Chambre free. We are intended, however, to feel the "curious fate" of the latter as anything but fortunate; neither black nor white, he is excluded by long conditioning from the world of the free, and barred from the "solacing refuge" of the slave kitchens by the fact of his legal whiteness. Really, his is, as Twain himself remarks, quite another story; what is symbolically important is the deposition of Thomas à Becket—and the meaning of this Twain makes explicit in one of the final jottings in his journal, "The skin of every human being contains a slave." We know at last in what bitter sense Tom's earlier boast is true: "As free as any cretur. . . ." *Pudd'nhead Wilson* begins and ends in the village where *Huckleberry Finn* began and *Tom Sawyer* was played out, on the banks of the same river and in the same pre–Civil War years. But between "St. Petersburg" and "Dawson's Landing" there is a terrible difference. In the latest book, we see Twain's mythicized Hannibal for the first time from the *outside*; in the two earlier books, we are already inside of it when the action begins, and there is no opportunity to step back and survey it. But Pudd'nhead comes as a stranger to the place of Twain's belonging; and the author himself takes advantage of this occasion to pan slowly into it, giving us an at first misleadingly idyllic description of its rose-clad houses, its cats, its sleepiness, and its fragrance—all preparing for the offhand giveaway of the sentence beginning, "Dawson's Landing was a slaveholding town . . ." (4).

The Civil War is the watershed in Twain's life between innocence and experience, childhood and manhood, joy and pain; but it is politically, of course, the dividing line between slavery and freedom. And

Twain, who cannot deny either aspect, endures the contradiction of searching for a lost happiness he knows was sustained by an institution he is forced to recognize as his country's greatest shame. It was the best he could dream: to be free as a boy in a world of slavery!

In *Tom Sawyer*, this contradiction is hushed up for the sake of nostalgia and in the name of writing a child's book; in *Huck* it is preserved with all the power of its tensions; in the last book it falls apart into horror. In *Pudd'nhead Wilson*, Hannibal is felt from the beginning not as a Western but as a *Southern* town. The river is no longer presented as the defining edge of the natural world, what America touches and crosses on its way West; but as a passageway into the darkness of the deep South. "Down the river" is the phrase which gives a kind of musical unity to the work—a motif repeated with variations from Roxana's first jesting taunt to a fellow Negro, "If you b'longed to me I'd sell you down the river 'fo' you git too fur gone . . ." (9) to the bleak irony of the novel's final sentence, "the Governor . . . pardoned Tom at once, and the creditors sold him down the river" (121).

A comparison inevitably suggests itself with *Huckleberry Finn* in which the southward motion had served to symbolize (in contempt of fact) a motion toward deliverance. But here the direction of the river that Twain loved is felt only as the way into the ultimate south, the final horror—the absolute pole of slavery. The movement of the plot and the shape of the book are determined by this symbolic motion toward the sea, now transposed from a dream of flight to a nightmare of captivity. It is after she herself has been threatened with such a fate and in order to preserve her son from it, that Roxy switches the children in the cradle. But there is no way to escape that drift downward toward darkness to which the accident of birth has doomed her and her son; by virtue of her very act of evasion she sets in motion the events that bring both of them to the end she had dreaded.

It is not only as a slave-holding town that Dawson's Landing belongs to the South, but also in terms of the code of honor to which everyone in the book subscribes. Patrician and Negro, American and foreigner, freethinker and churchgoer, all accept the notion that an insult can only be wiped out in blood, and that the ultimate proof of manhood is the willingness to risk death in such an attempt. The real demonstration of the unworthiness of the false Tom is his running to the courts for redress in preference to facing a duel. Ironically enough, this very duel was to have been in the book as originally planned a howling travesty of the values of the gentleman; for one of the parties was to have been half of a Siamese twin—and one can see what mad complications would have ensued. The "serious" Twain was, however, as incapable of doubting the code as Tom Sawyer; he could mock it only in pure farce, when he felt it perfectly clear to everyone that he was just kidding. There is in this book no Huck to challenge the many Colonel Sherburnes by rejecting courage as just another temptation—no absolute outcast, armed only with lies, to make it clear that honor is a luxury item for a leisure class. Even Pudd'nhead, for all his skepticism, longs not for bare survival but for style and success—and so he must pay his Tom Sawyerish respects to chivalry.

In *Huckleberry Finn*, the society which Huck finally rejects, his "sivilization," is essentially a world of the mothers, that is to say, of what Christianity has become among the females who sustain it just behind the advancing frontier. It is a sufficiently simple-minded world in which one does not cuss or steal or smoke but keeps clean, wears shoes, and prays for spiritual gifts. Above all, it is a world of those who cannot lie—and the truth, too, Huck finds a virtue beyond his budget. In this world, the fathers appear generally as outcasts and scoundrels, like the Duke and Dauphin and like Pap himself. At best, the paternal is represented by the runaway nigger, the outcast who was never even offered the bait of belonging.

In *Pudd'nhead Wilson*, however, society is defined by the fathers, last defenders of the chivalric code and descendants of the cavaliers. Four in especial represent the world to which Pudd'nhead aspires: York Leicester Driscoll, Percy Northumberland Driscoll, Pembroke Howard and Col. Cecil Burleigh Essex—the names make the point with an insistence that is a little annoying. This is a world continuous with that of Renaissance gallantry, connected with the Court of Elizabeth, which represents for Twain on the one hand a romantic legend, and on the other a kind of lost sexual Eden (celebrated in his privately circulated *1601*), whose potency puts to shame a fallen America where the natives "do it onlie once every seven yeares." The religion of such a society is, of course, not Christian at all; of Driscoll, the noble character murdered by the boy to whom he was a benefactor and almost a father, we are told "to be a gentleman was his only religion" (4).

One half of the story of Thomas à Becket Driscoll (really the slave Valet de Chambre) is the account of his failing this world of the fathers, first in gambling and thieving, then in preferring the courts to the field of honor, finally in becoming out of greed and abject rage, a quasi-parricide. Twain spares us, perhaps from some reluctance to surrender to utter melodrama, more probably from lack of nerve, the final horror. The logic of the plot and its symbolic import both demand really that Tom be revealed at last as the bastard of the man he killed; but we are provided instead with a specially invented double of the dead Driscoll as the boy's begetter, a lay figure called Cecil Burleigh Essex.

In all of the book, only a single mother is allowed the center of the stage—the true mother of the false Tom, the slave girl Roxana. Just as in *Huckleberry Finn*, Nigger Jim is played off against the world of Aunt Polly/Aunt Sally/Miss Watson, so in this reversed version a Negress is set against the society defined by Driscoll, Howard, and Essex. This is, of course, a just enough stroke, which satisfies our sense of the historical as well as our desire for the typical. If the fathers of the South are Virginia gentlemen, the mothers are the Negro girls, casually or callously taken in the parody of love, which is all that is possible when one partner to a sexual union is not even given the status of a person.

The second and infinitely worse crime of Tom is the sin against the mother, the black mammy who threatens him with exposure; and the most moving, the most realized sections of the book deal with this relationship. Throughout his career, Twain returned over and over to this theme of the rejection of the mother, the denial by the boy of the woman who has loved him with the purest love Twain could imagine. Of this Tom Sawyer is falsely accused by his Aunt Polly; of this Tom Canty is actually guilty at the tearful climax of *The Prince and the Pauper*, so extravagantly admired by its author. It is as if Mark Twain were trying to exorcise the possibility of himself failing the plea he could never forget, the cry of his own mother, clasping him to her over the death-bed of his father: "Only promise me to be a better boy. Promise me not to break my heart."

In *Pudd'nhead*, this tearful romance of the boy as a heartless jilt, becomes involved with the ambiguous relations of black and white in the United States, with the problems of miscegenation and of "passing," and is lifted out of the sentimental toward the tragic. Twain's own judgment of sexual relations between the races is not explicitly stated; but there seems no doubt that he thought of the union between Roxy and Essex as a kind of fall—evil in itself and the source of a doom on all involved. Paired together, *Huck* and *Pudd'nhead* express both sides of a deep, unthought-out American belief, reflected on the one side of Twain by James Fenimore Cooper and on the other by William Faulkner: that there are two relations, two kinds of love between colored and white, one of which is innocent, one guilty, one of which saves, one damns. The innocent relation can only exist between men, or a man and a boy (Natty Bumppo and Chingachgook, Huck and Jim)—a love unphysical and pure; the other, suspect and impure, tries to join the disjoined in passion, and must end either in frustration and death (Cora and Uncas) or in unhappiness for all (Roxana and Essex).

A further reach of complexity is added to the theme by the symbolic meanings inevitably associated with the colors white and black, meanings which go back through literature (Shakespeare's "Dark

Lady," for example) and popular religion (the New England habit of calling the Devil "The Black Man") to the last depths of the folk mind. No matter how enlightened our conscious and rational convictions may be in these matters, we are beset by a buried ambivalence based on this archetypal symbolism of light and dark. Twain himself in this very novel speaks unguardedly of the rain trying vainly to wash soot-blackened St. Louis white; and the implication is clear: black is the outward sign of inward evil. In this sense, the Negro puzzlingly wears the livery of the guilt we had thought the white man's. But *why*? It is a question which rings through the white man's literature in America; and the answer returns in an ambiguity endlessly compounded.

Who, having read it once, can ever forget the terrible exclamation in Melville's "Benito Cereno"—the cry which seems intended to dissolve in irony the problem we had hoped would be resolved in certainty, "It is the Black!" But there are even more terrible lines in *Pudd'nhead*: the lonely and baffled query of Tom (how hard it is to believe that it is not a quotation from Faulkner), "What crime did the uncreated first nigger commit that the curse of birth was decreed for him . . ." (48) and the still more appalling response of Roxy to the news that her son has failed the white man's code, "It's de nigger in you, dat's what it is!" (75). The name of their own lot turned insult in the mouth of the offended—beyond this it is impossible to go; and we cannot even doubt that this is precisely what Roxy would have said!

Perhaps the supreme achievement of this book is to have rendered such indignities not in terms of melodrama or as a parochial "social problem" but as a local instance of some universal guilt and doom. The false Tom, who is the fruit of all the betrayal and terror and profaned love which lies between white man and black, embodies also its "dark necessity"—and must lie, steal, kill, and boast until in his hybris he reveals himself as the slave we all secretly are. This tragic inevitability is, however, blurred by the demands of the detective story with which it is crossed. The tragedy of Tom requires that he expose and destroy himself; the melodrama of Pudd'nhead Wilson requires that he reveal and bring to justice the Negro who has passed as white; and Twain decided finally that it was Pudd'nhead's book— a success story. Yet there remains beneath the assertion that a man is master of his fate, the melancholy conviction that to be born is to be doomed, a kind of secularized Calvinism.

We have already noticed that Pudd'nhead is Tom Sawyer grown up, the man who has not surrendered with maturity the dream of being a hero; but it must be added that he wants to be a hero on his own terms, to force himself upon a hostile community without knuckling under to its values; that is to say, he would like still to be as an adult the "good bad boy" who put the finger on Indian Joe. Translated out of the vocabulary of boyhood, this means that he has to become first a rebel and then a detective.

He begins as a pariah, the sage whose wisdom is taken for folly: an outsider in a closed society, a free thinker in a world of conformism, a gadgeteer and crank, playing with palmistry and fingerprints. But he is also, like his creator, a jokester; and, indeed, it is his first quip which earns him a reputation for stupidity and twenty years of exclusion. "I wish I owned half of that dog," he says of a viciously howling beast, "because I would kill my half" (6)—and that is almost the end of him. Yet like his creator he wants to succeed in the world he despises; and he yields to it half-unwittingly even before it accepts him, adjusting to its code of honor, its definition of a Negro—while writing down in private or reading before a two-man Free Thinkers' Society his dangerous thoughts.

Typically enough, it is as a detective that he makes his comeback. In three earlier books his prototype, Tom Sawyer, had achieved similar triumphs: exposing Injun Joe, revealing Jim's true status, clearing his half-crazed uncle of the charge of murder; but more is involved than this. Ever since Poe's Dupin, the sleuth has been a favorite guise of the writer in fiction—non-conformist and exposer of evil, the poor man's intellectual. He is the one who, revealing in the moment of crisis "who done it," restores the community (as W. H. Auden has suggested in an acute study of the detective story) to a state of grace.

But Twain has the faith neither of a Chesterton nor a Conan Doyle; and the revelations of David Wilson (the name "Pudd'nhead" is sloughed off with his victory) restore civil peace only between him and the community which rejected him: for the rest, they expose only bankruptcy and horror and shame, and stupidity of our definition of a Negro, and the hopelessness of our relations with him. Wilson's disclosure of Roxy's hoax coalesces with Twain's exposure to America of its own secret self; and the double discovery is aptly framed by Wilson's Calendar entries for two of our favorite holidays.

The chapter which contains the courtroom revelation is preceded by the text, "*April 1*. This is the day upon which we are reminded of what we are on the other three hundred and sixty-four" (111). The implication is clear, whether conscious or not, not fools only but slaves! And it is followed by another, even grimmer, "*October 12, the Discovery*. It was wonderful to find America, but it would have been more wonderful to miss it" (120). The Discovery! It is a disconcerting ending for a detective story, which should have faith in all disclosures; but it is the aptest of endings for an American book, the only last word possible to a member of the Free Thinkers' Society. Beyond such bleak wisdom, there is only the cry of Roxy at the moment of revelation, "De Lord have mercy on me, po' misable sinner dat I is!" (120). But this is forbidden to Mark Twain.

F. R. LEAVIS

Mark Twain's Neglected Classic: The Moral Astringency of *Pudd'nhead Wilson*†

Pudd'nhead Wilson is not faultless—no book of Mark Twain's is that—but it is all the same the masterly work of a great writer. Yet it is very little known. One cannot easily find anyone, English or American, who has read it (at least that is my experience), and it would seem never at any time to have had the beginnings of the recognition that is its due. Its reputation—if it may be said to have a reputation—would not encourage a strenuous search for a copy of the book, unless in an admirer of *Huckleberry Finn* who was curious to look over one of the author's ephemeral productions, one that also dealt in its way with life in Hannibal, Missouri, the village of Mark Twain's childhood.

The explanation, I think, is partly that *Pudd'nhead Wilson* is so very unlike *Huckleberry Finn*. But it is also, I think, that the nature of the greatness of *Huckleberry Finn* itself tends not to be fully recognized. There are, then, two reasons for hoping that *Pudd'nhead Wilson* may come to be appreciated as it deserves: it is a classic in its own right (if an unrecognized classic may be said to *be* one); and, further, for all the unlikeness, it bears a very close relation to *Huckleberry Finn*; a relation of such a kind that to appreciate the lesser work is to have a surer perception of the greatness of the greater.

Huckleberry Finn, by general agreement Mark Twain's greatest work, is supremely the American classic, and it is one of the great books of the world. The significance of such a work doesn't admit of exhaustive recognition in a simple formula, or in several. Mark Twain himself was no simple being, and the complexity of his make-up was ordinarily manifested in strains, disharmonies, and tormenting failures of integration and self-knowledge. These, in his supreme masterpiece, can be seen to provide the creative drive. There is of course the aspect of return to boyhood, but the relation to complexity and strain represented by *Huckleberry Finn* is not one of escape from them—in spite of the qualities that have established the book as a classic for children (and in spite of Mark Twain's conviction, at times, that its appeal should be as such). It is true that the whole is

† From *Commentary* 21 (February 1956): 128–36. Reprinted by permission of the Estate of F. R. Leavis.

given through Huck, the embodiment of that Western vernacular, or of the style created out of that, in which the book is written. But that style, perfectly as it renders the illiterate Huck, has been created by a highly sophisticated art to serve subtle purposes, and Huck himself is of course not merely the naive boyish consciousness he so successfully enacts; he is, by one of those triumphant sleights or equivocations which cannot be judiciously contrived, but are proof of inspired creative possession, the voice of deeply reflective maturity—of a life's experience brooded on by an earnest spirit and a fine intelligence. If Mark Twain lacked art in Arnold Bennett's sense (as Arnold Bennett pointed out), that only shows how little art in Arnold Bennett's sense matters, in comparison with art that is the answer of creative genius to the pressure of a profoundly felt and complex experience. If *Huckleberry Finn* has its examples of the unintelligence that may accompany the absence of sustained critical consciousness in an artist, even a great one, nevertheless the essential intelligence that prevails, and from the poetic depths informs the work, compels our recognition—the intelligence of the whole engaged psyche; the intelligence that represents the integrity of this, and brings to bear the wholeness.

For in his supreme creation the complex and troubled Mark Twain did achieve a wholeness; it is manifested in the nature of the creative triumph. The charged significance of *Huckleberry Finn* brings together a strength of naivety and a strength of mature reflective wisdom. Let me quote, with immediate relevance, Mr. Bernard De Voto, most penetrating of the commentators on Mark Twain I am acquainted with: ". . . fundamentally Huck is an expression—a magnificent expression, a unique expression—of the folk mind. The folk mind, that is, in mid-America in the period of the frontier and immediately following, the folk mind shaped for use by the tremendous realities of conquering a hostile wilderness and yet shadowed by the unseen world. He is one of the highest reaches of American fiction.

"But if Huck expresses the folk mind, he is also Mark Twain's surrogate, he is charged with transmitting what that dark, sensitive, and complex consciousness felt about America and the human race. . . . Mark Twain was not a systematic thinker. Customarily, like the creature of fable who was his brother Orion, he held in succession all possible opinions about every subject he tried to analyze, held none of them long, and was able to drive none very deep beneath the surface. Especially as a metaphysician he was as feeble a novice as ever ventured into that stormy sea. But in what he perceived, in what he felt, in the nerve-ends of emotion, in the mysterious ferments of art which transform experience, he was a great mind—there has been no greater in American literature. Be it said once more and ever so wearily: insufficiencies and mental defects prevented him from ever completely implementing the artist throughout the whole course of a book. That does not matter—in *Huckleberry Finn* we get the finest expression of a great artist, the fullest report on what life meant to him."[1]

When Mr. De Voto speaks of the "folk mind" in *Huckleberry Finn* he is making a plainly valid observation; an observation duly offset, as the quoted passage shows, by the recognition of quite other aspects of the book. But insistence on the "folk" element sometimes goes with an attempt to make *Huckleberry Finn* American in a sense that would make it an immeasurably lesser thing than the great work it is. Mr. Van Wyck Brooks, in *The Times of Melville and Whitman*, writes: "He was the frontier storyteller, the great folk writer of the American West, and raised to a pitch unparalleled before him the art of oral story-telling and then succeeded in transferring its effects to paper." Such an account (and there is a formidable representative intention behind it) serves as a license for insisting on the force of the reply—the obvious and unanswerable reply: Mark Twain was something very much more than a folk-writer, and the art of *Huckleberry Finn* is no mere matter of managing effects—suspense, surprise, climax, and so on. One cannot intelligently discuss the art without discussing the complex and reverse of naive outlook it conveys. Mr. Brooks, recognizing, as any reader must, an insistent moral preoccupation in the theme, quotes Paine, Mark Twain's biographer: ". . . the author makes Huck's struggle a psychological one between conscience and the law on one side, and sympathy on the other." But there is more to the moral theme of *Huckleberry Finn* than that suggests. What the book conveys is the drama in a mind in which conscience finds that it is not single, and that the "law" doesn't speak with one voice, and that what Paine calls "sympathy" itself engages a moral imperative. In fact, *Huckleberry Finn* has as a central theme the complexity of ethical valuation in a society with a complex tradition—a description that applies (for instance) to any "Christian" society.

The book is a profound study of civilized man. And about its attitude towards civilization as represented by the society depicted in it there is nothing simple or simplifying, either in a "frontier" spirit or in a spirit of reductive pessimism. It is not to the point to adduce such private utterances of Mark Twain's as: "We have no real morals, but only artificial ones—morals created and preserved by the forced suppression of natural and healthy instinct." "Never trust the artist; trust the tale": Lawrence's dictum might have been addressed to Mark Twain's case. *Huckleberry Finn*, the tale, gives us a wholeness

1. From *Mark Twain at Work*.

of attitude that transcends anything ordinarily attainable by the author. The liberation effected by the memories of youth and the Mississippi was, for the creative genius at his greatest, not into irresponsibility but the reverse. The imaginatively recovered vitality of youth ministered, in sum, no more to the spirit of "Pudd'nhead Wilson's Calendar" than to nostalgia or daydream, but to the attainment of a sure and profound moral maturity. That is, to call *Huckleberry Finn* a great work is not an exaggeration.

I insist in this way because of a tendency in America (and transatlantic fashions regarding American literature tend to be taken over uncritically in England) to suggest that the beginnings of the truly American in literary tradition come from the frontier and the West. According to this view Mark Twain is a more truly American writer than Hawthorne or Henry James. It is a view that, in offering to exalt him, actually denies his greatness, for it makes the attributed advantage in Americanness a matter of his being alienated from English and European tradition as Hawthorne and James are not. Such an alienation could only be an impoverishment: no serious attempt has been made to show that any sequel to disinheritance could replace the heritage lost. Mark Twain is indeed "frontier" and Western, but in being greatly American he bears as close and essential a relation to England and Europe as that which we recognize in Hawthorne or in James (in some ways he strikes an English reader as being less foreign, less positively un-English, than either of them). The Americanness of alienation may be represented by Dreiser, Scott Fitzgerald, and Hemingway: the author of *Huckleberry Finn*, when we think of those writers, seems to belong to another world. Nor as we read the book are we prompted to reflect that he is a fellow countryman of Walt Whitman.

It is not my business here to enforce these observations in a detailed analysis of *Huckleberry Finn*, but, with them in view, to suggest how that book is related to *Pudd'nhead Wilson*, which, different as it is (it makes no show of frontier naivety, but belongs frankly to sophisticated literary tradition), is nevertheless unmistakably by the same hand, develops the same preoccupations and expresses the same moral outlook. With the oral tradition of story-telling, the potent element of recovered boyhood that has so recommended *Huckleberry Finn* is absent too. But the Mississippi *is* there in *Pudd'nhead Wilson*, and its evoked presence occasions a significant expansion:

> The hamlet's front was washed by the clear waters of the great river; its body stretched itself rearward up a gentle incline; its most rearward border fringed itself out and scattered its houses

about the base line of the hills; the hills rose high, enclosing the town in a half-moon curve, clothed with forests from foot to summit.

Steamboats passed up and down every hour or so. Those belonging to the little Cairo line and the little Memphis line always stopped; the big Orleans liners stopped for hails only, or to land passengers or freight; and this was the case also with the great flotilla of "transients." These latter came out of a dozen rivers—the Illinois, the Missouri, the Upper Mississippi, the Ohio, the Monongahela, the Tennessee, the Red river, the White river, and so on; and were bound every whither and stocked with every imaginable comfort or necessity which the Mississippi's communities could want. . . . (3–4)

Here, quite plainly, speaks a proud imaginative delight in the memory of the great river; the great river as Mark Twain had known it in boyhood and in his piloting days; and in the memory, or vision, we feel the sense of freedom, beauty, and majesty that informs *Huckleberry Finn*; but there is something further: the passage unmistakably conveys the sense, sanguine and exalted, of an expanding and ripening civilization.

Mark Twain, we are told, was brought up in a frontier society. "Think," it has been written, "of the squalor of those villages, their moral and material squalor, their dim and bounded horizon, their petty taboos: repression at one extreme, eruption at the other, and shiftlessness for a golden mean." But what *Pudd'nhead Wilson* should make us recognize is that "frontier" is an insidious term. It suggests cultural deprivation and loss—a dropping of the heritage in the battle with pioneer hardship. And no doubt it could be argued that the account just quoted fairly describes Dawson's Landing; or that so we should have agreed if we had had to live there. But as a matter of fact this is not the tone, this is not how the stress falls, in *Pudd'nhead Wilson*. After the evocation of the river we read:

The town was sleepy, and comfortable, and contented. It was fifty years old, and was growing slowly—very slowly, in fact, but still it was growing. (4)

It may have been sleepy, but what Mark Twain conveys with great power is an effect quite other than one of rawness and squalor:

In 1830 it was a snug little collection of modest one- and two-story frame dwellings whose whitewashed exteriors were almost concealed from sight by climbing tangles of rose vines, honeysuckles and morning-glories. Each of these pretty homes had a garden in front fenced with white palings and opulently stocked with hollyhocks, marigolds, touch-me-nots, prince's feathers and other old-fashioned flowers; while on the window-sills of the houses stood wooden boxes containing moss-rose plants, and terra cotta pots in which grew a breed of geranium whose spread of intensely red blossoms accented the prevailing pink tint of the rose-clad house-front like an explosion of flame. When there was room on the ledge outside of the pots and boxes for a cat, the cat was there—in sunny weather—stretched at full length, asleep and blissful, with her furry belly to the sun and a paw curved over her nose. Then that home was complete, and its contentment and peace were made manifest to the world by this symbol, whose testimony is infallible. A home without a cat—and a well fed, well petted, and properly revered cat—may be a perfect home, perhaps, but how can it prove title?

All along the streets, on both sides, at the outer edge of the brick sidewalks, stood locust trees with trunks protected by wooden boxing, and these furnished shade for summer and a sweet fragrance in spring when the clusters of buds came forth. (3)

The comfort, well-being, and amenity evoked here have more than a material significance; they are the outward signs of an inward grace. Provincial as Dawson's Landing may be, it represents a society that has kept its full heritage of civilization. True, it *is* provincial, and Wilson's fate—the "Pudd'nhead" and the long failure to make way against that estimate—figures for us its attitude towards originality of mind. Moreover an English reader gets what are for him (the human world presented being so essentially unforeign) startling glimpses of mob lawlessness as an accepted social institution. Yet the effect of the opening description of Dawson's Landing remains: this is a civilized community—one qualified to have exacted a very much more favorable report than any brought back by Martin Chuzzlewit.

And further, it is not unaware of its provinciality, and is far from having lost the desire to keep in touch with the remoter centers of its civilization and with its past. This comes out notably in its reception of the twins, the presentment of which illustrates the complex poise of Mark Twain's attitude. The comedy of the reception is not satiric. Dawson's Landing displays, not merely its crudenesses and limitations, but also a touching positive humility, a will to pay homage to something other than provinciality and philistinism and the standards of everyday life. The exhibition of democratic *mœurs* at Aunt Patsy's is finely and subtly done, and quite clear in its significance. These democrats, without being in the least inclined to go back on their democracy, respond imaginatively to their traditional memories and to the sense of ideal values belonging to a richer life that is now remote from them. It is an utterly different thing from snobbery, and, as Mark Twain presents it, something that the social crudity of the occasion sets off as the reverse of trivial or crude:

> None of these visitors was at ease, but being honest people, they didn't pretend to be. None of them had ever seen a person bearing a title of nobility before, and none had been expecting to see one now, consequently the title came upon them as a kind of pile-driving surprise and caught them unprepared. A few tried to rise to the emergency, and got out an awkward My Lord, or Your Lordship, or something of the sort, but the great majority were overwhelmed by the unaccustomed word and its dim and awful associations with gilded courts and stately ceremony and anointed kingship, so they only fumbled through the handshake and passed on, speechless. (32)

Then, significantly, this homage to a glimpsed ideal superiority is followed by the homage to art:

> Here a prodigious slam-banging broke out below, and every-body rushed down to see. It was the twins knocking out a classic four-handed piece on the piano, in great style. Rowena was satisfied; satisfied down to the bottom of her heart.
>
> The young strangers were kept long at the piano. The villagers were astonished and enchanted with the magnificence of their performance, and could not bear to have them stop. All the music that they had ever heard before seemed spiritless prentice-work and barren of grace or charm when compared with these intoxicating floods of melodious sound. They realized that for once in their lives they were hearing masters. (33)

The poise is beautifully maintained; those first two sentences serve only to enforce the serious and profound significance of the last, the closing one of the chapter.

In its whole attitude towards distinction that appeals to standards other than the "democratic," Dawson's Landing represents a subtler civilization than accounts of "the pioneer community" might suggest. Consider, for instance, the special license accorded Judge Driscoll in an environment that doesn't encourage moral independence or free play of mind. "Judge Driscoll," says Mark Twain, "could be a free-thinker and still hold his place in society because he was the person of most consequence in the community, and therefore could venture to go his own way and follow out his own notions" (28). But York Leicester Driscoll isn't represented as having achieved his leading place by preeminence in the qualities that one would have expected to tell most among pioneering democrats. We are told of him:

> He was very proud of his old Virginian ancestry, and in his hospitalities and his rather formal and stately manners he kept

up its traditions. He was fine, and just, and generous. To be a
gentleman—a gentleman without stain or blemish—was his
only religion, and to it he was always faithful. He was respected,
esteemed, and beloved by all the community. (4)

It is quite unequivocal: he is "respected, esteemed and beloved" (a
set of terms that defines something quite different from the attitudes
towards the smart and therefore successful man) because he is a
"gentleman," representing as such an ideal that doesn't belong to the
realm of material "success" and is above the attainment of the ordinary member of the community. And we come here to that complexity of ethical background which I have spoken of as providing a
central preoccupation of Mark Twain's, in *Pudd'nhead Wilson* as in
Huckleberry Finn. I am not thinking merely of the persistence of an
aristocratic tradition in a democratic society. That society has also
its Christian allegiance, and, while the Judge is "just and generous,"
the total concept of "gentleman" is decidedly not Christian. When
we come to Pembroke Howard, for whom to be a gentleman is *not*
his only religion, the situation, with its irony, is focused in the one
actor:

> He was a fine, brave, majestic creature, a gentleman according
> to the nicest requirements of the Virginian rule, a devoted Pres-
> byterian, an authority on the "code," and a man always courte-
> ously ready to stand up before you in the field if any act or word
> of his had seemed doubtful or suspicious to you, and explain it
> with any weapon you might prefer from brad-awls to artillery. He
> was very popular with the people, and was the Judge's dearest
> friend. (5)

For the gentleman, "honor stood first": the laws of honor
"required certain things of him which his religion might forbid: then
his religion must yield—the laws could not be relaxed to accommodate religion or anything else" (63). And the Christian and democratic community, with a complete and exalted conviction, gave its
approval.

> The people took more pride in the duel than in all the other
> events put together, perhaps. It was a glory to the town to have
> such a thing happen there. In their eyes the principals had
> reached the summit of human honor. (79)

There is nothing remarkable about the ability to observe such
facts. What is remarkable is the subtlety of the appraising attitude
that Mark Twain, in terms of impersonal art, defines towards them—
as towards the whole inclusive situation presented in the book.
Astringent as is the irony of *Pudd'nhead Wilson*, the attitude here has

nothing of the satiric in it (the distinctively satiric plays no great part in the work as a whole). Mark Twain unmistakably admires Judge Driscoll and Pembroke Howard. And it is important to note that, if they are "fine," the "fineness" is not a mere matter of their being "just and generous." The total attitude where they are concerned is not altogether easy to describe, not because it is equivocal, but because it is not a simple one, and has called for some subtlety of dramatic means to convey it. The two most sympathetic characters in the drama give the "code" itself their active endorsement. It is not for instance suggested that Wilson, in acting as second in the duel, does so with any self-dissociating reservations or reluctance, and he rebukes Tom for not telling his uncle about the kicking and "letting him have a gentleman's choice": "if I had known the circumstances," he says, "I would have kept the case out of court until I got word to him and let him have a gentleman's chance."

> "You would?" exclaimed Tom, with lively surprise. "And it your first case! and you know perfectly well there never would have *been* any case if he had got that chance, don't you? and you'd have finished your days a pauper nobody, instead of being an actually launched and recognized lawyer to-day. And you would really have done that, would you?"
> "Certainly."
> Tom looked at him a moment or two, then shook his head sorrowfully and said—
> "I believe you—upon my word I do. I don't know why I do, but I do. Pudd'nhead Wilson, I think you're the biggest fool I ever saw." (68)

This reminder of the circumstances of the rebuke will serve to enforce the point that Wilson, the poised and preeminently civilized moral center of the drama, whom we take to be very close in point of view to Mark Twain, is not, all the same, to be identified with him. Wilson *is* an actor in a dramatic whole that conveys its significances dramatically. The upshot of the drama is to set a high value on the human qualities fostered by the aristocratic code: to endorse the code even as far as Wilson does would be quite a different matter, and no reader of the book can suppose it to be doing that. Against the pride and the allegiance to an ideal of conduct that make personal safety a matter of comparative indifference, we see the ignominy and ugliness of Tom's complete self-centeredness, which is as unchecked by pride or concern for any ideal as by imaginative sympathy. Hearing that the Judge, fighting in *his* cause, has survived the duel, he reflects immediately, with an exasperation untouched by shame, how blessedly all problems would have been solved had the Judge been killed: the duel has been wasted.

The exposure of human nature in Tom Driscoll has an essential part in the total astringency of the book. But it will not do to suggest that human nature, as the book presents it, reduces to Tom. If the Wilson of "Pudd'nhead Wilson's Calendar" is not the Wilson of the drama, neither does he represent the imagination and the sensibility that inform this as a conceived and realized whole. Such utterances of Mark Twain's as this marginal note from a book, characteristic as they are, mustn't be credited with a kind of conclusive authority they certainly haven't:

> What a man sees in the human race is merely himself in the deep and honest privacy of his own heart. Byron despised the race because he despised himself. I feel as Byron did and for the same reason.

The exhibition of Tom's viciousness has its convincing force, no doubt, because *we* recognize in ourselves the potentiality, as Mark Twain did in *him*self. But it would be misleading to say that we despise Tom; that would be to suggest an animus that we do *not* feel when we place him, unequivocally, as contemptible: we are not engaged and involved in that way. The irony of the work as a whole means a very secure poise, and the poise is secure because the author has achieved a mature, balanced, and impersonal view of humanity. He himself is not involved in the personal way that involves animus in condemning.

The attitude of *Pudd'nhead Wilson* is remote from cynicism or pessimism. The book conveys neither contempt for human nature nor a rejection of civilization. It is concerned with the complexities of both human nature and civilization as represented in a historical community—for Dawson's Landing, it may reasonably be said, is one that, at a given time in actual American history, Mark Twain had intimately known.

We are not, by way of dismissing the suggestion of any general contempt, confined to adducing Wilson himself and the "fine, brave, majestic creatures" who uphold the code of the F.F.V. Most impressively, there is Roxy. It is true that her heroic maternal devotion plays against the extremity of mean heartless egotism given us in Tom. But her significance is not exhausted in that irony. We feel her dominating the book as a triumphant vindication of life. Without being in the least sentimentalized, or anything but dramatically right, she plainly bodies forth the qualities that Mark Twain, in his whole being, most values—qualities that, as Roxy bears witness, he profoundly believes in as observable in humanity, having known them in experience. Although born a slave, she is herself a "fine, brave, majestic creature," whose vitality expresses itself in pride, high-spiritedness, and masterful generosity. Her recklessness in exposing herself during the duel defines Mark Twain's attitude towards the "code" more decisively than Wilson's participation does. When she proudly tells Tom that he is descended from the best blood of Virginia the effect, for all the irony, is not satiric. And her confident and justified reliance on the loyal comradeship, not only of her fellow-"niggers," but also of the officers of the *Grand Mogul*, has its part in the appraisal of human nature conveyed by the book as a whole.

Mr. De Voto makes the point that she represents a frank and unembarrassed recognition of the actuality of sex, with its place and power in human affairs, such as cannot be found elsewhere in Mark Twain. That seems to me true and important. It is an aspect of the general fact, that she is the presence in the book of a free and generous vitality, in which the warmly and physically human manifests itself also as intelligence and spiritual strength. It is this far-reaching associative way in which, so dominating a presence, she stands for—she *is*—triumphant life that gives the book, for all its astringency and for all the chilling irony of the close, its genial quality (to be both genial and astringent is its extraordinary distinction).

How far from satiric the spirit of *Pudd'nhead Wilson* is may be seen in the presentment of the subtleties of conscience and ethical sensibility in Roxy. Consider the episode of the stolen money and the threat to sell the Negro servants down the river. We are no doubt very close to the satiric note in the irony with which the chapter ends— in Percy Driscoll's self-gratulation on his magnanimity: "that night he set the incident down in his diary, so that his son might read it in after years and be thereby moved to deeds of gentleness and humanity himself" (13). But we are remote from satire here:

> The truth was, all were guilty but Roxana; she suspected that the others were guilty, but she did not know them to be so. She was horrified to think how near she had come to being guilty herself; she had been saved in the nick of time by a revival in the colored Methodist Church, a fortnight before, at which time and place she "got religion." The very next day after that gracious experience, while her change of style was fresh upon her and she was vain of her purified condition, her master left a couple of dollars lying unprotected on his desk, and she happened upon that temptation when she was polishing around with a dust-rag. She looked at the money a while with a steadily rising resentment, then she burst out with—
>
> "Dad blame dat revival, I wisht it had a ben put off till tomorrow!"
>
> Then she covered the tempter with a book, and another member of the kitchen cabinet got it. She made this sacrifice as a

> matter of religious etiquette; as a thing necessary just now, but
> by no means to be wrested into a precedent; no, a week or two
> would limber up her piety, then she would be rational again, and
> the next two dollars that got left out in the cold would find a
> comforter—and she could name the comforter.
>   Was she bad? Was she worse than the general run of her race?
> No. They had an unfair show in the battle of life. . . . (12)

In spite of that last phrase, we know that what we have been contemplating is not just an exhibition of Negro traits: "her race" is the
human race. These naive and subtle changes and adjustments of conscience and the moral sense we can parallel from our own inner experience. But there is nothing cynically reductive in Mark Twain's study
of the moral nature of man; he shows the clairvoyance of a mind that
is sane and poised, and the irony that attends the illustration of subtleties and complexities throws no doubt on the reality or the dignity
or the effectiveness in human affairs of ethical sensibility.

I have not yet touched on the central irony of the book, the sustained
and complex irony inherent in the plot. *Pudd'nhead Wilson* should be
recognized as a classic of the use of popular modes—of the sensational
and the melodramatic—for the purposes of significant art. The book,
I have said, is not faultless, and an obvious criticism lies against the
unfulfilled promise represented by the twins—the non-significant play
made with them, their history and the sinister oriental dagger. Mark
Twain, we can see, had intended to work out some interplay of the two
parallel sets of complications: twins and interchanged babies. He abandoned the idea, but didn't trouble to eliminate that insistent focusing
of expectation upon the twins. The fault is in a sense a large one, and
yet it is not, after all, a very serious one: it doesn't affect the masterly
handling of the possibilities actually developed.

The ironic subtleties that Mark Twain gets from the interchange
of the babies in their cradles seem, as one ponders them, almost inex-
haustible. There is the terrible difference, no more questioned by
Roxy than by her master, between the "nigger" and the white. The
conventionality of the distinction is figured by the actual whiteness
of Roxy, whose one-sixteenth of Negro blood tells only in her speech
(with which, indeed, it has no essential relation, as is illustrated later
by the inability of "Valet de Chambers," now revealed as the pure-white
heir, to shed the "nigger"-speech he learnt in childhood). So awful,
ultimate and unchangeable is the distinction that Roxy, as, in order
to save her child from the fate hanging over the slave (to be "sold
down the river"), she changes the babies in their cradles, justifies
herself by the example of God. The rendering is an irresistible man-
ifestation of genius, utterly convincing, and done with a delicate subtlety of ironic significance:

She flung herself on her bed, and began to think and toss, toss and think. By and by she sat suddenly upright, for a comforting thought had flown through her worried mind—

"'Tain't no sin—*white* folks has done it! It ain't no sin, glory to goodness it ain't no sin! *Dey's* done it—yes, en dey was de biggest quality in de whole bilin', too—*Kings!*"

She began to muse; she was trying to gather out of her memory the dim particulars of some tale she had heard some time or other. At last she said—

"Now I's got it; now I 'member. It was dat ole nigger preacher dat tole it, de time he come over here fum Illinois en preached in de nigger church. He said dey ain't nobody kin save his own self—can't do it by faith, can't do it by works, can't do it no way at all. Free grace is de *on'y* way, en dat don't come fum nobody but jis' de Lord; en *He* kin give it to anybody He please, saint or sinner—*He* don't k'yer. He do jis' as He's a mineter. He s'lect out anybody dat suit Him, en put another one in his place, en make de fust one happy for ever en leave t'other one to burn wid Satan." (16)

There is of course a glance here at the Calvinism of Mark Twain's youth. And it is to be noted that Roxy, while usurping the prerogative of the predestinating Deity, has shown a wholly human compassion, and has invoked a compassionate God in doing so:

"I's sorry for you, honey; I's sorry, God knows I is,—but what *kin* I do, what *could* I do? Yo' pappy would sell him to somebody, some time, en den he'd go down de river, sho', and I couldn't, couldn't, *couldn't* stan' it." (16)

In saving the child from the consequences of the awful distinction that she assumes to be in the nature of things, she demonstrates its lack of any ground but convention; she demonstrates the wholly common humanity of the "nigger" and the white. The father himself cannot detect the fraud: he cannot tell his own child from the other. And—one of the many ironies—it is his cruel, but confidently righteous, severity that imposes the full abjectiveness of slave mentality upon his own child, who becomes the defenseless and rightless servant of the slave's child. On the other hand, Roxy's success in saving Valet de Chambers (the name her proud tribute to an ideal "white" lordliness) from the fate of the slave erects a dreadful barrier between child and mother. Treated as "young Marse Tom," not only does he become that different order of being, the "master"; in Roxy herself the slave attitudes that she necessarily observes towards him find themselves before long attended by the appropriate awe. When at last, outraged by the humiliating and cruel rebuffs that meet her appeal for a little kindness (she is in need) to the old "nigger-mammy," she forgets habit and the ties of motherhood, and pants for revenge, she has to recognize that she has placed him in an impregnable position: no one will believe her tale. A further irony is that, if he has turned out bad, a portent of egocentric heartlessness, that is at least partly due to his spoiling as heir and young master, the lordly superior being.

It is a mark of the poised humanity characterizing the treatment of the themes of *Pudd'nhead Wilson* that, worthless and vicious as "Tom" is, when he has to face the sudden revelation that he is a Negro, we feel some compassion for him; we don't just applaud an irony of poetic justice when he is cornered into reflecting, with an echo of his mother's self-justifying recall of the Calvinistic God:

> "Why were niggers *and* whites made? What crime did the uncreated first nigger commit that the curse of birth was decreed for him? And why is this awful difference made between black and white?" (48)

Compassion, of course, soon vanishes as the dialectic of utter selfishness unfolds in him. The developments of his incapacity for compassion are done with a convincingness that the creator of Tito Melema would have envied. When Roxy offers to be sold back into slavery in order to save "Tom" from being disinherited, and he, with dreadfully credible treachery, sells her "down the river," the opposite extremes of human nature are brought together in an effect that belongs wholly to the mode of *Pudd'nhead Wilson*, and is equally removed from melodrama and from cynicism. It can hardly be said, when we close the book, that the worst in human nature has not been confronted; yet the upshot of the whole is neither to judge mankind to be contemptible nor to condemn civilization. And it is remarkable how utterly free from animus that astringency is which takes on so intense a concentration in the close:

> Everybody granted that if "Tom" were white and free it would be unquestionably right to punish him—it would be no loss to anybody; but to shut up a valuable slave for life—that was quite another matter.
>
> As soon as the Governor understood the case, he pardoned Tom at once, and the creditors sold him down the river. (121)

It is an irony of the tale that this, the fate to secure him against which Roxana had committed her crime, is, as an ultimate consequence of that crime, the fate he suffers.

HENRY NASH SMITH

[*Pudd'nhead Wilson* as Criticism of the Dominant Culture]†

*   *   *

2

* * *The central theme of *Pudd'nhead Wilson* is still the corrupt state of the official culture of Dawson's Landing—that is, Hannibal—and the plot of the novel is focused on two acts which, in quite different ways, call attention to evils beneath the apparently placid surface of it. The first act, the slave Roxana's desperate effort to free her son by exchanging him with her master's son in the cradle, is frustrated by the second, which consists in Wilson's detection of Roxy's stratagem more than twenty years later.

*   *   *

* * *Even in this farce,[1] Mark Twain is dramatizing the conflict between propriety and nonconformity that had served him so often before as comic material. The playful fantasy, however, touched off deeper responses—hence the appearance of the three characters who figure in *Pudd'nhead Wilson*. Roxy's son, known as Tom Driscoll during most of the story, is the psychological equivalent of the twins. He is two persons in one: a Negro (according to the definition operative in Dawson's Landing—he "has one thirty-second Negro blood") who appears "white" and is reared as the adopted son of the great man of the town. He is by law a slave but apparently free. The duality of white and Negro introduces the theme of false appearance and hidden reality, which is repeated in Tom's activities as a burglar in the disguise of a woman while he is ostensibly leading the life of the idle young heir to the town's largest fortune.

The material drawn up thus into consciousness is not comic, but intensely serious. When Mark Twain has conceived of Tom Driscoll he is launched upon a fable involving the tragic theme of slavery, with all it implies of hereditary but constantly renewed guilt and of perverted social conventions distorting human fact. For what but a morass of arbitrary assumptions makes Tom originally "black" and enslaved, later "white" and free, then converts him back into a Negro and a slave when the "truth" is revealed? The society of Dawson's

---

† From Henry Nash Smith, *Mark Twain: The Development of a Writer* (Cambridge, Mass: The Belknap Press of Harvard University Press, 1962), pp. 173–83, 207. Copyright © 1962 by the President and Fellows of Harvard College, Copyright renewed 1990.
1. *Those Extraordinary Twins* [*Editor*].

Landing imposes upon slaves and masters alike the fictions which sustain the institution of slavery. The training corrupts both: the slave by destroying his human dignity, by educating him to consider himself inferior, by building up in him a ferocious hatred of himself as well as of his rulers; the master by encouraging cruelty toward the human beings he is taught to regard as animals, and thus by blunting his sensibilities and fostering an unwarranted pride of place.

Tom's mixed biological heritage points to the further fact that slavery debases sexual relations. To be sure, Mark Twain handles this topic with marked reticence. From the standpoint of imaginative coherence Judge York Leicester Driscoll is the father of Tom just as clearly as Roxy is his mother. But Mark Twain places the unmentionable fact of sexual intercourse between master and slave at two removes from the actual story—first by making Roxy, Tom's mother, the slave of a shadowy brother of Judge Driscoll at the time of Tom's birth; and then by the further precaution of creating an even more shadowy figure, Colonel Cecil Burleigh Essex, to be his biological father.

3

* * *

The problem of tone is often difficult in *Pudd'nhead Wilson*, but Mark Twain's earlier ridicule of Southern aristocratic pretensions in *Life on the Mississippi* and elsewhere strengthens one's suspicion that he intends to caricature Judge Driscoll's pride of ancestry and his equation of honor with readiness to send or accept a challenge. The Judge is unmistakably an object of satire in Chapter 7, when he shows the newly arrived Italian counts the sights of the town— including the slaughter house and the volunteer fire company—and naïvely tells them "all about his several dignities, and how he had held this and that and the other place of honor or profit, and had once been to the legislature" (34). There is some ambiguity in the treatment of the Judge's duel with Luigi; Mark Twain admired physical courage, and the reader is expected to feel contempt for Tom because he is too cowardly to challenge the Count. Yet the duel in *Pudd'nhead Wilson* replaces a farcical encounter in "Those Extraordinary Twins" in which Angelo, physically joined to Luigi and therefore exposed to the Judge's fire against his will, dodges about so violently that he frustrates the efforts of both combatants, and finally assumes control of the twins' common pair of legs to run away. And the bit of slapstick that gives rise to the duel in "Those Extraordinary Twins" is retained in the novel. When Tom directs a sneering jest at Luigi from the platform of an anti-prohibition meeting, Luigi "took a couple of strides and halted behind the unsuspecting joker. Then he drew back and delivered a kick of such titanic vigor that it lifted Tom clear over the footlights and landed him on the heads of the front row of the Sons of Liberty" (61).

Mark Twain's ironic attitude toward the Judge's sense of honor is also indicated by the sequel to the duel. Tom rationalizes his refusal to fight Luigi by declaring that the Count is an assassin. Without asking for particulars, the Judge instantly accepts the explanation, and declares: "That this assassin should have put the affront upon me of letting me meet him on the field of honor as if he were a gentleman is a matter which I will presently settle—but not now. I will not shoot him until after the election [for town officers]. I see a way to ruin them both before; I will attend to that first" (84). The Judge waits until the eve of the election and then, still without any effort to verify Tom's slander, repeats it in a campaign speech. The coup brings about Luigi's defeat.

This incident would be more significant than it is if Judge Driscoll were a fully rounded character. But he is not. Mark Twain is not really interested in him as a person; he merely represents the aristocratic part of Tom Driscoll's heritage, which the writer means to satirize in the composite figure of the four descendants of the First Families of Virginia. Yet there is one odd obscurity of outline in the portrait. Pembroke Howard, the Judge's closest friend, is "a devoted Presbyterian" whereas the Judge is a freethinker. The theological difference is of no consequence in the plot. The Judge's unorthodoxy, like his pride in his Virginian ancestry, seems to be a reminiscence of Samuel Clemens' father, John Marshall Clemens. The parallel is a fleeting reminder that as the story of *Pudd'nhead Wilson* emerged from the farce about the Italian twins it drew into itself buried memories of Mark Twain's childhood—not always to the advantage of the novel.

4

The other half of Tom's heritage is that of his mother, Roxy the slave. The two parts of it are at war with each other. When Tom is but an infant Percy Northumberland Driscoll, Roxy's master, threatens to sell some of his slaves down the river. Although he relents and sells them in the town, Roxy suddenly realizes he has the power to carry out his threat: "Her child could grow up and be sold down the river! The thought crazed her with horror" (14). She says to the sleeping infant: "I hates yo' pappy; he hain't got no heart—for niggers he haint, anyways. I hates him, en I could kill him!" (14). She is the only articulate enemy of the aristocracy of Dawson's Landing. Just as in some not negligible sense Judge Driscoll takes over the function of the Arthurian aristocracy in representing the values of a society stained by tyranny and cruelty, Roxy takes over Hank Morgan's role as adversary of the dominant class. In doing so, she becomes a successor to the vernacular protagonists of earlier stories.

Of course, there are important differences. Because she is a Negro (however "white" in appearance) and a woman, Mark Twain cannot identify himself with her as he identifies himself with Hank Morgan. And her aggression against the established order is not motivated by a program of reform. Mark Twain has accepted the demonstration in *A Connecticut Yankee* that society cannot be redeemed. Yet in *Pudd'nhead Wilson* he continues his preoccupation with the question of values, stripping down the fictive world of the Matter of Hannibal to the only vestige of affirmation he can find in it: the warmth, the passion of love and of hate, the sheer personal force in this representative of the submerged slave caste.

Roxy thus represents the last trace of unhandseled nature that has survived the perverted training of society in Dawson's Landing. But with a beautiful irony Mark Twain shows that she has adopted many of the values of the white aristocrats: their pride of ancestry, their code of honor, even their contempt for Negroes. Her denunciation of Tom, setting forth Judge Driscoll's sentiments in her heavy dialect, is one of the great passages in this uneven but often powerful book:

> "En you refuse' to fight a man dat kicked you, 'stid o' jumpin' at de chance! En you ain't got no mo' feelin' den to come en tell me, dat fetched sich a po' low-down ornery rabbit into de worl'! Pah! it make me sick! It's de nigger in you, dat's what it is. Thirty-one parts o' you is white, en on'y one part nigger, en dat po' little one part is yo' *soul*. 'Tain't wuth savin'; 'tain't wuth totin' out on a shovel en tho'in' in de gutter. You has disgraced yo' birth. What would yo' pa think o' you? It's enough to make him turn in his grave."(75)

Roxy herself has stood in range of bullets from the duel in order to watch it, and a ricochet shot has tipped her nose. When Tom asks her, "Weren't you afraid?" she invokes in unconscious parody of Judge Driscoll the absurd pedigree she has invented for herself. She believes that "My great-great-great-gran'father en yo' great-great-great-great-gran'father was Ole Cap'n John Smith, de highest blood dat Ole Virginny ever turned out, en *his* great-great-gran'mother or somers along back dah, was Pocahontas de Injun queen, en her husbun' was a nigger king outen Africa" (75). It is a sufficient explanation of her behavior that "De Smith-Pocahontases ain't 'fraid o' nothin', let alone bullets" (77).

Except when she is momentarily under the influence of her "strong and sincere" piety, Roxy is indifferent toward property rights; she offers as a matter of course to help Tom in his burglaries when he needs money to pay his gambling debts. But on the crucial occasion of the theft of money that led her master to sell the guilty slaves, she had overcome temptation herself because she had "got religion" a fortnight before at a revival. Mark Twain is at his comic-ironic best in this scene, culminating in Roxy's exclamation, "Dad blame dat revival, I wisht it had a ben put off till tomorrow!" (12). Roxy is nevertheless free of the heaviest burden that slavery has imposed on the whites: the sense of guilt. She is not torn by inner conflict, and she conveys the suggestion of subliminal energy, of darkness and mystery, that is attached to women and Negroes in American culture. The aggressiveness of the Judge is controlled by traditional forms, and even on the dueling ground he merely wounds his adversary. But when Roxy, without reference to code or etiquette, conceives the idea of killing her master, or herself and her child, the reader is convinced she is capable of these actions.

There is a haughty grandeur in her character that shines through the degraded speech and manners of a slave, and confers on her an intimation of tragic dignity: "She was of majestic form and stature, her attitudes were imposing and statuesque, and her gestures and movements distinguished by a noble and stately grace" (9). We have seen with what assurance she has imagined an Indian queen and an African king among her ancestors. Mark Twain never conceived a more effective passage than the scene, at once tragic and comic, in which she determines to exchange her son with the Driscoll heir, and justifies the action to herself by a process of reasoning both humble (for she takes for granted the inferiority of the Negro—" 'Tain't no sin—*white* folks has done it!" [16]) and arrogant, because she compares herself with royalty and even usurps the divine prerogative of arbitrarily conferring free grace on her child:

> "Now I's got it; now I 'member. It was dat ole nigger preacher dat tole it, de time he come over here fum Illinois en preached in de nigger church. He said dey ain't nobody kin save his own self—can't do it by faith, can't do it by works, can't do it no way at all. Free grace is de *on'y* way, en dat don't come fum nobody but jis' de Lord; en *He* kin give it to anybody He please, saint or sinner—*He* don't k'yer. He do jis' as He's a mineter. He s'lect out anybody dat suit Him, en put another one in his place, en make de fust one happy forever en leave t'other one to burn wid Satan. De preacher said it was jist like dey done in Englan' one time, long time ago. De queen she lef' her baby layin' aroun' one day, en went out callin'; en one o' de niggers roun' 'bout de place dat was mos' white, she come in en see de chile layin' aroun', en tuck en put her own chile's clo'es on de queen's chile, en put de queen's chile's clo'es on her own chile, en den lef' her own chile layin' aroun' en tuck en toted de queen's chile home to de nig-

ger quarter, en nobody ever foun' it out, en her chile was de king, bimeby, en sole de queen's chile down de river one time when dey had to settle up de estate." (16–17)

Roxy's subversive threat to the dominant culture is the only aspect of the material of *Pudd'nhead Wilson* that stirs Mark Twain's imagination. As a result, she is the only fully developed character, in the novelistic sense, in the book. She has a different order of fictional reality from the figures of fable with which she is surrounded. She resembles a portrait in full color set in a black-and-white background.

5

Although Tom Driscoll is evidently the key figure in the imaginative logic of *Pudd'nhead Wilson*, he is, like Judge Driscoll, not so much a character as a complex of themes. He incarnates both the tortured paradox of uncertain identity and the perversions resulting from generations of the bad training imposed by slavery. He exhibits the worst traits ascribed to both races in this fictive world—the lax morals and cowardice of the Negro, together with the hatred of the master that is putatively expressed in his murder of Judge Driscoll; the indolence and affectation of white aristocrats (he is sent to Yale and returns with mannerisms of dress that are offensive to the community); the cruelty toward slaves that Mark Twain's latent respect for the ideal of the Southern gentleman, related to his feeling for John Marshall Clemens, prevents him from attributing directly to Judge Driscoll.*   *   *

Tom's most atrocious act, his betrayal of Roxy by selling her down the river after she has helped him pay his debts by allowing herself to be sold back into slavery, comes after he is aware that he is a Negro and himself legally a slave. It is not an expression of aristocratic arrogance but of the unmotivated melodramatic villainy that Mark Twain ascribes to Tom along with his sociologically determined traits. While this deed is not inconsistent with Tom's character, it does not belong to the imaginative fabric of the novel or even to its ideological structure; it represents the infection by stereotypes from popular fiction and the theater to which Mark Twain was always exposed when he lost control of his materials.

6

The third of the three characters who Mark Twain said "got to intruding themselves" into his farce about the Italian twins "and taking up more and more room with their talk and their affairs" (126) was Pudd'nhead Wilson. Comments in Mark Twain's letters make it clear that Wilson remained a minor character through the first drastic revision of the original farce into a "tragedy."[2] Not until later, when Francis Galton's *Finger Prints* (published in 1892) provided a sound scientific method for establishing the identities of Tom and Chambers and for proving Tom guilty of the murder of Judge Driscoll, did Mark Twain undertake the revision that made Wilson the "chiefest" figure. This version of the novel, incidentally, has survived in manuscript. Still another revision would be necessary to dissect out the Siamese-twins motive.

Even when Wilson was given a crucial role in the plot, Mark Twain did not undertake to characterize him fully. A letter to Livy in 1894 contains a revealing comment on his intention. A lecturer in New York, he reported, had said that "Pudd'nhead was clearly & powerfully drawn & would live & take his place as one of the great creations of American fiction." Mark Twain continued: "Isn't that pleasant— & unexpected! For I have never thought of Pudd'nhead as a *character*, but only as a piece of machinery—a button or a crank or a lever, with a useful function to perform in a machine, but with no dignity above that."[3] Wilson is incarnate analytical intelligence, the personification of science. Mark Twain liked to embody the notion of rational analysis, either farcically or seriously, in a figure borrowed from the newspapers and from popular fiction: the detective. In the later 1870's he had experimented with a novel and a play called "Cap'n Simon Wheeler, the Amateur Detective," traces of which survive in *Tom Sawyer, Detective* (1896); and he makes much of allegedly scientific methods of investigation in *The Stolen White Elephant* (1878) and *A Double Barrelled Detective Story* (1901, containing a burlesque of Sherlock Holmes). Closely tied to the solving of crimes is the sensational effect of the detective's courtroom revelation of the identity of the criminal—a motive that links Wilson retrospectively with Tom Sawyer and proleptically with Wilhelm Meidling, or rather with Satan in the guise of Meidling, in *The Mysterious Stranger*.

These affiliations of Wilson suggest that he has some qualities of transcendence. He does not have the omniscience of the fully transcendent figure: he is deceived by Tom's disguises and is temporarily convinced by Tom's argument that the twins never possessed the valuable dagger they say has been stolen from them. We are also asked to believe that Wilson suffers from his twenty years' isolation and wishes to be accepted as a member of the community, even to the point of being gratified by his popularity after his triumph in the

2. Anne P. Wigger, "The Composition of Mark Twain's *Pudd'nhead Wilson* and *Those Extraordinary Twins*: Chronology and Development," *Modern Philology* 55 (November 1957): 93–102, especially pp. 93–94.
3. New York, 12 January, *The Love Letters of Mark Twain*, ed. Dixon Wecter (New York: Harper, 1949), p. 291.

trial scene. But his transcendent traits are unmistakable. He is much better educated and more intelligent than anyone else in the village; he is an outsider who arrives from a great distance and is therefore free from the guilt of slavery that the Virginia gentlemen have brought with them to Dawson's Landing; his mastery of the science of reading palms, like his discovery of the principle of identification through fingerprints, strikes the townspeople as almost miraculous; and he feels no warmth for any human being.[4]

When Wilson reveals in the courtroom that the supposed Tom Driscoll is a bastard, a thief, a murderer, and worst of all a Negro, he demonstrates that the official culture, with its vaunted ideals of honor and chivalry and ancient lineage, is merely a façade for deceit, avarice, and illegitimacy. He also defeats Roxy by frustrating her plan to free her son: Tom suffers precisely the fate of being sold down the river that she had tried to save him from.

* * *

JAMES M. COX

The Ironic Stranger†

* * *

Written in Europe, *Pudd'nhead Wilson* was Mark Twain's last American novel—the final volume in what we may justly call his Mississippi trilogy.* * *

* * *

* * * The novel which remained after the unnatural removal of the farce is not a tragedy. It begins with a seemingly pointless joke, chronicles the history of a crime, and ends as Pudd'nhead Wilson, the stranger and hero, brings to justice the false Tom Driscoll, who has harassed the peace of Dawson's Landing. The hero's triumph over and entry into the society is in the comic rather than the tragic mode. But the facile neatness of the ending, instead of being joyously comic, emphasizes that the problems evoked by the novel have not really been settled so much as swept under the carpet. The triumph of justice, the defeat of the criminal, the success of the long-suffer-

---

4. Paul Baender notes transcendent elements in Wilson ("Mark Twain's Transcendent Figure," [unpublished dissertation, University of California, Berkeley, 1956], p. 85).

† From James M. Cox, *Mark Twain: The Fate of Humor* (Princeton, N.J.: Princeton University Press, 1966), pp. 222–46. Reprinted by the University of Missouri Press, 2002. Copyright © 2002 by the Curators of the University of Missouri. Reprinted by permission of the University of Missouri Press.

ing hero are transparent veils which seem deliberately to expose rather than to conceal the larger doom, the deeper crime, and the final failure of the society which the novel scrutinizes. Coward, thief, and murderer though Tom Driscoll is, his indictment is more disturbing than gratifying. His sale down the river in the closing moment of the novel is a final indictment of the world in which he had his being, a last ironic stroke in this savagely ironic novel. It is ironic for Tom himself, whose career at launching had been pointed toward a raceless utopia only to veer through a series of atrocities culminating in Tom's murder of his white foster father and his selling his mother down the river. But the irony is also directed at the society itself, for Tom's entire career reveals how much he is the instrument of an avenging justice which has overtaken Dawson's Landing.

For Tom is a marked man—a Negro. Yet how different he is from Nigger Jim, whom Huck ultimately saw as "white inside." Tom Driscoll is white *outside*, his white face and white talk hiding the mark within. If Jim was the indulgent slave who wakened Huck's sleeping conscience, Tom Driscoll is the nightmare plaguing the moral sleep of Dawson's Landing. Only one-thirty-second black, he is invisible to his victims, the six generations of white patrimony contributing to his creation having physically equipped him to assume the role of changeling which Mark Twain assigns him. He thus stands always in the foreground as the figure embodying the long history of miscegenation in the background; although this background is not elaborated on, the novel is nonetheless the history of a time, a place, and a crime. The narrative is, as Mark Twain insistently terms it, a chronicle.

Since miscegenation can culminate in "passing" the color line, the arbitrary changeling device functions as the comic equivalent of historic possibility and can legitimately dramatize the last phase of a society trapped by its secret history. Although the slaveholding society of Dawson's Landing is built around an aristocracy of Virginia gentlemen who worship honor, the novel discloses that across its coat of arms runs a dark bend sinister, an indelible stain disfiguring the heraldry of every member of the community's ruling class. The first families cannot, of course, see the stain, because they have conditioned themselves not to see it; but the novel exposes it in the person of the false Thomas à Becket Driscoll.

Spawned at the very center of their legalized institution of slavery, he crosses the color line in the white disguise six generations of white blood have given him. He is, after all, the son of white men's casual lust gratified by a series of aggressive sexual acts at the expense of their slaves. Although the masters may have assumed economic responsibility for these actions, their sexual willingness to cross the color line—the legal fiction they have created to define the unbridge-able gulf separating the races—merely underlines their refusal to accept any moral responsibility in the matter. The miscegenation which they have tacitly indulged in within the framework of slavery is their own covert affirmation of the inexorable bond between the races. The secret channel carrying white blood steadily down into the area of human life separated and suppressed by slavery, it makes pos-sible the emergence of the false Tom Driscoll into the white world. The dark force he possesses upon his return represents the loss of power sustained by the ruling class.

Pudd'nhead Wilson thus implies a world in which the power of those who rule has been transferred to those who serve, for if the ori-gin of Tom's force is the lust out of which he was created, the imme-diate source is embodied in the personality of his mother, Roxana, who shifts him into the cradle of the white heir. One of Twain's most interesting creations, she possesses the strength, the passion, and the fertility so strikingly absent in the white women she serves; in fact, her darker, deeper beauty merely emphasizes their frigidity. Mark Twain remarks that on the same day she bore her son she was "up and around," while Mrs. Percy Driscoll "died within the week" of her childbirth confinement. The long logic underlying this chron-icle explains Roxana's power, for the submerged lust transfers the passion from the white wives to the slave mistresses. If the transfer bestowed purity upon the white women, it nonetheless left them increasingly impotent. Thus, in the white South of Mark Twain's memory, the Negro women became the Mammies who were the real mothers in a society so obsessed with purity that it divested the ordained mothers of passional vitality. That is why, in the Southern gentleman's idealized version of existence, the white women of priv-ileged classes could not nurse their children and were relieved of the obligation as soon after the travails of childbirth as possible.

In rearing the white man's legitimate children and giving birth to his illegitimate ones, Roxana bears what their honor cannot bear—*the guilt of their repressed desires*. Their guilt is objectified in her repression. Her humiliation (she has no guilt) takes the form of repressed vengeance. Thus, her release of Tom into the white soci-ety grows out of her arraignment before Percy Driscoll on the false charge of petty larceny. She acts not in overt vengeance but out of desperation to save him from the fate of being sold down the river. That her ostensibly defensive action constitutes such an aggression against the society discloses how much unconscious power and hos-tility she actually commands. When Tom Driscoll is finally unmasked, she is the sole person in the society who can assume inward responsibility for the crime of the society. Her cry, "De Lord have mercy on me, po' misable sinner dat I is!" is a stricken cry of acknowledgment in a world given over to repression and confirms the nobility and responsibility she alone possesses. She is, after all, the darkly powerful queen in the society which Mark Twain depicts. Although the "nobles" of the society bear the names of Elizabethan court lovers, the white queens in the New World imitation of the Old remain as remotely in the background of the novel as the real Tom Driscoll who shambles about the slave quarters. Only Roxana has the power to create drama and to become the primary force in the world she serves.

The responsibilities thrust upon her become her critical force, enabling her to vitalize with certain insight the empty illusions which she inherits from the world above her. Reprimanding Tom for his failure to meet the terms of the code duello, she affirms her honor and origins with a summary of the family pedigree.

> "What ever has 'come o' yo' Essex blood? Dat's what I can't understan'. En it ain't only jist Essex blood dat's in you, not by a long sight—'deed it ain't! My great-great-great-gran'father en yo' great-great-great-great-gran'father was ole Cap'n John Smith, de highes' blood dat Ole Virginny ever turned out; en *his* great-great-gran'mother or somers along back dah, was Pocahontas de Injun queen, en her husbun' was a nigger king outen Africa—en yit here you is, a slinkin' outen a duel en disgracin' our whole line like a ornery low-down hound! Yes, it's de nigger in you!" (75–76)

Even as she parodies the genealogical obsessions of the first families, she confronts the distinctive heritage of Dawson's Landing and America, the strange and remarkable history which so much defines the New World. Her sketch of her American family tree is the repressed genealogy which upholds the tenuous tracings educed by the First Families of Virginia, at least insofar as the novel implies their genealogies. The self-styled aristocrats of Dawson's Landing, in repressing her genealogy, cut themselves off from the vitality of their own past as well as hers. Denial of their secret history is actually a denial of themselves, and their blood, flowing in that covert tradition, becomes their nemesis in the person of Tom Driscoll.

As long as Tom is ignorant of his identity, he does not direct his inborn hostilities upon his fathers but gratifies his uncontrollable temper with cruel jokes perpetrated on the slaves who serve him, particularly the unfortunate Chambers, his true master, and Roxy his mother. His brutal treatment of Roxy, however, eventually angers her into humiliating him with the facts of his lineage. His discovery of his true mother, though temporarily paralyzing, is nevertheless a self-discovery and a half-conscious realization of his destiny. His casually malevolent will, which has struck blindly downward in indiscriminate aggression, begins to find its fated target. Thus, when Roxy tauntingly asks him what his father would think of his refusal to accept the dueler's challenge, Tom "said to himself that if his father were only alive and in reach of assassination his mother would soon find that he had a very clear notion of the size of his indebtedness to that man and was willing to pay it up in full, and would do it, too, even at risk of his life . . ." (75). At such a moment, when even Mark Twain's rhetoric assumes Faulknerian aspects, outward and inward action tend to coalesce into social and psychological reality, disclosing that the false Thomas à Becket Driscoll is the avenging agent who carries back across the color line the repressed guilt which has gathered at the heart of slavery. Although he withholds his terrible intention from Roxy, Tom willingly seizes upon his fated mission: the murder of Judge Driscoll. For the Judge, who harbors within his walls the invisible assailant, is not only Tom's foster father and inevitable target of his malice; he is also the living symbol of law and order in the community, and his murder suggests the anarchy which the white society has by its own action released upon itself.

This, then, is the crime which strikes at the heart of Dawson's Landing. The man who finally "sees" Tom Driscoll and restores a semblance of honor and order to the community is quite appropriately the rank outsider, Pudd'nhead Wilson—the stranger who first intruded into Mark Twain's farce about the Siamese twins. Having wandered West from his native New York to seek his fortune, Wilson comes into the community a free agent. His "freedom" places him at the opposite extreme from the fate in which Driscoll is caught. So far apart are they—Wilson on the periphery of the society, Tom at the center—that Mark Twain resorts to arbitrary devices to draw them together. Thus, there is the weakly plotted series of accidents upon which the novel turns: Pudd'nhead arrives in Dawson's Landing during the month in which Tom is born; he is rejected by the society at almost the same time Tom enters it; his rise to fame begins the same moment Tom's honor is questioned. Pudd'nhead even shares character traits with his opposite number. Both are notorious idlers, both are collegiately sophisticated, both are given to droll and cutting irony. Finally, both share a desire for the limelight, and when Wilson exploits the drama of the final courtroom scene, he is merely usurping the role of showman which Tom has played in society. At opposite points on the wheel of fortune, the destinies of the two figures are fatally related, the ascending fortune of Pudd'nhead coming necessarily at the expense of Tom's fall. The novel predictably ends with Wilson standing above his cowering antagonist to pronounce his doom.

In order to show how and why this plot machinery fails to rise above the level of mere mechanical contrivance, it is necessary to recognize the real relationship between Tom Driscoll and Pudd'nhead Wilson which is implied by Mark Twain's insistence on plot symmetries. Wilson's first act upon entering Dawson's Landing is to mutter the joke which isolates him and launches the novel. Hearing an "invisible" dog barking behind the scenes, he expresses to a group of loitering citizens the wish that he owned half the dog. Upon being asked why, Wilson rejoins, "Because I would kill my half." The only response the literal-minded inhabitants can make to this sally is summed up by one of the gullible bystanders, who inquires of his comrades, "What did he reckon would become of the other half if he killed his half? Do you reckon he thought it would live?" (6). Jay B. Hubbell, in a penetrating objection to the novel, contends that the joke is typical of small-town humor and that "the village yokels would have yelled with delight when they heard it."[1] Hubbell feels that at this point in his career Mark Twain had lost his sense of connection with the village of his memory and thus was becoming cut off from the reality of his humor.

In a very particular way Hubbell is right. The joke, an old chestnut in the provinces, should have evoked a warm response. Yet, coming from a total stranger, Pudd'nhead's wisecrack reveals a discomforting familiarity and at the same time betrays a veiled threat. Given the particular province, there is a certain realism in the instinctive withdrawal of the village idlers and their rejection of the strange humorist as a "pudd'nhead." Wilson's subsequent behavior lends a measure of justification to their puzzled distrust, for although he ultimately discloses the invisible assassin in their midst, he is also the one who plants in Roxy's mind the possibility that her son is indistinguishable from the legitimate Driscoll heir. "How do you tell them apart, Roxy, when they haven't any clothes on?" (10), he asks with innocent amusement. Remembering Wilson's observation, and assuming that if one so intelligent cannot distinguish the children neither can the dull-witted villagers, Roxy decides to shift her son into the cradle of the legitimate Tom Driscoll.

If Wilson is capable of suggesting the possibility of mistaken identity in the village, he is also visibly engaged in erecting a system of detection which will expose the possibility. Thus, his casual observation to Roxy reveals that personal identity in Dawson's Landing is a matter of mere appearance; and his reliance upon fingerprints as a means of criminal detection undercuts the whole structure of familial identity on which the society stands. His effort to establish a complete fingerprint file of every member of the community is a stratagem for checking personal identity against the one unchanging characteristic of human physiology. Trusting only these "natal autographs," as he calls them, Wilson refuses to rely on names and

1. Jay B. Hubbell, *The South in American Literature* (Durham, 1954), p. 835.

faces, the conventional hallmarks of identity. His arduous "hobby" is, in fact, based on an essential distrust of the identity of the entire village.

Having precipitated the crisis which only his system can resolve, Wilson's final apprehension of the criminal merely completes and closes the circuit of the plot. For all the detached curiosity with which he surveys the village, he remains singularly blind to the series of incidents set in motion by his own idle remark to Roxy; and although he holds Tom Driscoll's true signature within arm's reach, he is almost as bewildered by the murder case as is the dullest citizen in Dawson's Landing. The fatal attraction between detective and criminal is the only thing that finally saves him from failure, despite his foolproof system. For Tom compulsively seeks Wilson out to taunt him for failing to solve the murder of the Judge, only to leave his telltale print on one of Wilson's glass slides. Seeing Wilson's shocked countenance and unaware of his crucial error, Tom grants his host's request to be left in peace but cannot resist a parting jibe: "Don't take it so hard," he says; "a body can't win every time; you'll hang somebody yet." Wilson's reply is a mutter to himself: "It is no lie to say I am sorry I have to begin with you, miserable dog though you are!" (109).

More than being a silent retort to Driscoll's taunt, Wilson's remark is an oblique answer to the joke which initiated his isolated career, for in addition to finding the "invisible dog"—or, as Roxy puts it, the "low down hound"—which disturbed the peace of the community, he has indeed come to own half of it and is ready to assume the role of killer which he first proposed for himself. He demands in the courtroom that Tom make upon the courtroom window the fingerprints which will hang him. But the society into which Wilson is about to be accepted owns the other half and determines not to destroy such a valuable property. The terms of the joke thus become the terms of the novel, and Wilson's casual wish to own half of the unseen dog is realized at the moment he establishes Tom's identity and guilt. As a result of Wilson's detection, Tom reverts from his role of secret agent to the status of property "owned" by the society at the same instant Wilson's twenty-three-year period of rejection is ended and he is welcomed into the community of owners as a reward for his achievement. As the two figures "enter" the social order at the conclusion of the narrative, it becomes evident that they are the *real* twins in this novel which grew around a farce about Siamese twins.

*   *   *

Thus the character of Pudd'nhead is the "way" or means by which Mark Twain realized his disillusion. He had begun to realize it in Hank Morgan, the stranger whose emergence into the sleepy world of Camelot forecasts Pudd'nhead's entry into Dawson's Landing. But two things caused Mark Twain to lose control over Morgan. First, Morgan's unconverted indignation manifested itself in increasingly bad humor. Second, Morgan's slang could not assimilate the "thought" which Mark Twain increasingly tried to give it. But in the character of Pudd'nhead, Mark Twain solved both these problems. Pudd'nhead is not a vernacular character but a college man and thus can legitimately "say" any thought Mark Twain can give him. More important, the indignation which in effect blows up Morgan is economized in *Pudd'nhead Wilson* by means of a radically disjunctive irony.

To achieve this irony, Mark Twain moved away from vernacular and back to plot—in the manner of *The Prince and the Pauper* and *Tom Sawyer*. Both these earlier books contain irony, but the emotion on which the irony rests is essentially indulgent. The world depicted is a world of boyhood—particularly is this true in *Tom Sawyer*—and the relationship established between narrative consciousness and action is one of ultimate approval. Even in *Huckleberry Finn*—despite all the bitter knowledge and experience which go into the book—the emotions upon which the humor rides are indulgence and approval. In *A Connecticut Yankee* irony gives way to direct expression, outbursts of anger and spleen, and to a sarcastic tone. In *Pudd'nhead Wilson* a genuine irony is restored—but it is irony without indulgence. Scorn and contempt are the emotions at the heart of this irony. The perspective upon the world of Dawson's Landing is as remote as it was in *Tom Sawyer*, but the world is a world of men, and the narrative consciousness, instead of approving the antics on stage, evokes disapproval of the entire world. There is only one "actor" held in affection by the narrative consciousness: Roxana. The others, even Pudd'nhead, are either held in check or exposed by the sardonic eye of the chronicler.

The strength of Mark Twain's irony is particularly evident in the light of Hank Morgan's slang fiasco; it is a means of keeping the action in focus and control. While its fine edge noticeably diminishes the possibility of "good humor," it nevertheless prevents the intrusion of Mark Twain's anger and bad temper; it is a way of controlling them from the beginning. Speaking from the vantage point of the historian, the chronicler chooses a perspective which allows him to see the events of his history as fatal—to see that the relationships between man, society, and history take precedence over man's individual desires and ambitions. Viewed from such a perspective, man is at once the creator and the creature of fate; he carries out and is the victim of destiny. But in order to achieve this perspective, the plot must be made to *seem* like a part of the destiny. This does not mean that the plot has to be "invisible." Instead, it must be extremely visible, its absolute visibility disclosing that the entire order of the action is an expression or symbolic enactment of fate itself.

*   *   *

Yet the ironic stranger, whose very irony was a means of releasing order into the chaos left in Hank Morgan's wake, was also repressive—and repressive in two ways. First, his role in the novel is repressive, not liberative. Thus, although his irony ultimately indicts the society his detection has exposed, his immediate concern is to indict the false Tom Driscoll and restore the status quo. But Pudd'nhead is not only repressive within the novel; he is repressive upon it. This would not be true if his character were fully realized, for then his repressive tendencies would be dramatized as character trait. But he is not so realized, and it is just this failure which accomplishes what can be called a completion of the central weakness of the book. For whereas Roxana's character denied her original relation to the plot, Pudd'nhead's plot keeps him from ever really becoming a character. He remains instead little more than a massive plot device. Neither he nor his "twin," the false Tom Driscoll, is ever freed into character; rather, they function as dominant parts of the plot machinery.

Even though Mark Twain confidently asserted that Pudd'nhead came unbidden and "freely" into his creative consciousness, the form which the character imposed upon the action was extremely constrictive—so constrictive that Mark Twain was ironically right in calling the book a tragedy. For the bitter plot of Pudd'nhead overrides the character of Roxana, reducing her vernacular to dialect and severing her humor from the sources of her instinctive power. Exposed by Wilson's detection, that power is reduced to a mere guilty minstrel cry: "De Lord have mercy on me, po' misable sinner dat I is!" (120).

ARLIN TURNER

Mark Twain and the South: Pudd'nhead Wilson†

Huckleberry Finn paints the world of the lower Mississippi as the whites see it. To be sure, Huck's level of social vision is little above Jim's, but his sympathy for Jim is inconstant and may seem to imply

† From "Mark Twain and the South: An Affair of Love and Anger," The Southern Review 4, n.s. (April 1968): 493–519.

an identification which does not exist. The white man's doctrine of race superiority is held up to ridicule, but the victim of that doctrine remains unrealized. The basic situation, Huck and Jim raft-borne in a flight before expected pursuers, led Mark Twain to formulate in this book a sequence of responses to the arguments on slavery and race he had known since childhood but had never before considered seriously. And even here the reader may get the impression that the sequence grew unawares to the author, while his attention was fixed on other elements.

But Mark Twain had long known that not every slave could expect to go rafting down the river to freedom; recollections extending back to his childhood furnished harsh proof to the contrary. He also knew that the doctrines of race which outlived slavery had far greater effects than to form queer ideas in the mind of a boy such as Huck. In 1874 he had published "A True Story," a short narrative telling that he once asked a Negro servant how she could have lived sixty years and "never had any trouble." She answered by recounting how in slave times her husband and seven children were sold away from her and how she met one son by accident during the Civil War. She concluded, "Oh, no, Misto C————, *I* hain't had no trouble. An' no *joy!*" She thus places herself alongside Jim, a Negro employed to pass judgment on the white man's generalized view of race. But the story, in addition, hints that under suitable prompting the author might trace out the human effects of slavery and caste, and might draw full-scale characters in the process.

This hint which may be read in "A True Story" was in a large measure borne out in *Pudd'nhead Wilson*, and the direct promptings under which the novel grew are fully revealed. The author declared that the Negro characters were not in his original plan, and that after he had brought them in for minor roles in the plot, the question of race demanded a hearing without regard to his intentions. When the novel was finished, after extensive recasting, he had treated the dominant Southern issue of his time with more force and realism than elsewhere in his writings—or, for that matter, in any other contemporary writings except Cable's. Here, in a frankness not usual with him, he faced the implications of miscegenation and the psychological effects of racial doctrines on both races. Here, as a consequence, in Roxy, who has one-sixteenth Negro blood, he created his most fully realized female character and through her, in the clearest instance in all his fiction, acknowledged sex to be an element in human relations. As a further consequence, and in spite of inconsistency in the portrait, he achieved in Roxy a level of tragic characterization not present elsewhere in his works. In *Huckleberry Finn* slavery is obscured in the happy ending for Jim, and other aspects of the race question are not broached; *Pudd'nhead Wilson* ends tragically for all the characters, white and black, who are touched by slavery and race.

*   *   *

The chief need in recasting the story was to adjust the characters Tom Driscoll and Roxy to the new understanding of the race problem the author was approaching. The roles these two had assumed were leading him to understand that slavery and caste shape not only society and its institutions but individuals also, that instead of being merely a social phenomenon, miscegenation is a matter of life and a matter of death among human beings.

As initially introduced, Tom Driscoll is white, with no hint of Negro blood. He is a young man of both innate and cultivated evil, displaying villainy enough to deserve the conviction for crime Pudd'nhead Wilson's fingerprint collection will insure. He embarrasses his friends when he can, robs his neighbors to finance his dissolute life, and gleefully contemplates killing his uncle if that is necessary to hasten his own inheritance.

Such was the character Tom when the author decided to make him a changeling and a Negro. The Tom of the second stage, accustomed to abusing the slaves as members of an inferior race, is grimly embittered to learn that he belongs to that race. In the first draft of the episode in which Roxy tells him who she is, she refuses to identify his father, leaving him consumed by hatred. Vowing to learn the secret from her somehow and to seek out and kill his father, he exults in what he calls his father's death song. He will show what can be expected from "a nigger with a grievance," repeating the word "nigger" in his bitterness. The lowly creature who is his mother, he says, has a nobility beyond anything a slaveholder could ever claim. He is himself both a slave and a white man's bastard. Whatever is base in him may have come from either the white or the black blood, or from both, for it is the product of slavery, through the abuse and degradation experienced by the slaves or through the debasement and tyranny produced in the slaveholder. Tom's resentment inspires in him a raging hatred of all whites and a dedication to revenge which bear overtones of the heroic. His hatred produces the courage he would not otherwise have, and he is capable of murder, not simply assassination. Notebook entries and preserved manuscript scraps show that Mark Twain at one time planned a scene in which Tom confronts his father, hesitates, and then concludes he cannot kill him. But when his father pleads, "O spare me!—I am your father!" Tom cries, "Now for *that*, you shall die," and kills him.

Because the inordinate deceit and meanness and cowardice of the white Tom Driscoll could have no place in this Tom, the author turned back to pages written earlier and modified these aspects of his character. Yet some traits appropriate to the earlier Tom but not this one remained unchanged, and survived in fact to the printed book, such as Tom's goading of Pudd'nhead Wilson about his hobbies and his failure in law practice.

Mark Twain's uncertainty in delineating Tom as the Negro who had been brought up believing he was white suggests that he was exploring his way in areas new to his thought and that more than once he decided he had gone astray in his extemporizing. This Tom Driscoll of hatred and revenge was not acceptable, even after the diabolism of the earlier white man had been diluted. A character who nursed such blind hatred, however many wrongs he might have suffered, seemed to Mark Twain false to the Negro in America, either as a slave or as a freedman. In further—and final—recasting, therefore, Roxy tells Tom he can hold his head high in pride because his father, who died ten years earlier, belonged to one of the First Families of Virginia. Tom's earlier rage against his unknown father now becomes self-pitying analysis of his own weaknesses and a cowering humility in the presence of whites. He is weak, cowardly, given to drink and gambling, incapable of hunting down and killing his father or anyone else. He kills Judge Driscoll when frightened during a robbery rather than by design.

The changes in character Roxy experiences in the sequences of revisions, no less drastic than the changes in Tom, show even more clearly the expansion that was taking place in the author's understanding of Negro character and Negro experiences in America. At her first appearance in the early draft, sick and penniless and whining as she returns from eight years as a chambermaid on the river, Roxy is a stock household Negro, visiting among the servants and living on food they sneak out of the kitchen for her. She has little thought of her son Tom, except that she hopes he will provide for her. Rebuffed in her first pleas to him, she makes a whimpering appeal to his sympathy. Then when she tells Tom who he is and can blackmail him, she becomes a partner in his burglary and frightens him by the risks she will take in her greed. Portions of the early draft show her finally driving Tom, under awesome threats, to steal from Judge Driscoll the money he needs. One manuscript fragment concludes with her saying to Tom: "Take yo' choice—hog de money dis night or I tells de Jedge in de mawnin' who you *is*. You'll be on de oction block in 2 minutes." Another fragment illustrates Roxy's meanness as she was first drawn. Chambers has been arrested by mistake after Tom's murder of Judge Driscoll. When he has been seized by a lynch mob, Roxy says, "Well twould a ben my son if I hadn't changed 'em."

In the revisions, Roxy's heartlessness and her calculated selfishness are cancelled. She shows genuine affection for Tom when she returns from steamboating, and she is confident he will treat her kindly. When his harshness has convinced her "that her beautiful dream was a fond and foolish vanity, a shabby and pitiful mistake," she has feelings altogether unsuited to the early Roxy: "She was hurt to the heart, and so ashamed that for a moment she did not quite know what to do or how to act" (41). To Tom's continued degrading scorn, she responded as "[t]he heir of two centuries of unatoned insult and outrage" (43), and "the fires of old wrongs flamed up in her breast and began to burn fiercely" (41). Thus the reader of the published work is prepared to have Roxy take on the role of an avenging angel as she tells Tom who he is. Instead of the scheming woman of the earlier draft who would drive her son to destruction for her own gain, she now goes into slavery to save his fortune. He sells her into what they both know to be the unspeakable horror of slavery "down the river," and after her escape and return she is simply pronouncing on him, in effect, the sentence he has brought upon himself—he must go ask the judge for the money to buy her free. To rob the judge rather than ask for the money is now his decision, not Roxy's. It is worth noting that in the early draft Roxy is normally referred to as a mulatto, a crone, or an old woman, and that in the revisions such designations are replaced by her name or a simple pronoun. In one revision it is said that Roxy's "bearing took to itself a dignity and state that might have passed for queenly if her surroundings had been a little more in keeping with it" (47).

Although slavery and race oppression were introduced late into the plans for *Pudd'nhead Wilson*, in the final version they stand under severe and inclusive charges. The helplessness of the slaves is dramatized in Tom's abuse of Chambers, for example; and the catalog of horrors Roxy experiences after she has been re-sold into slavery gains immediacy and weight from the fact that she describes them to her son, who has betrayed her. The effects of slavery on the slaves, aside from their lot of deprivation and pain, appear in Chambers, when at the end he discovers he is white but cannot recover from the wrenching in both mind and spirit he has received while a slave. After learning that he is in fact a Negro and a slave, Tom finds he can no longer think and act as he did before, even though he and Roxy alone know his identity. In addition, the effect of slavery on the master class becomes clear, as Mark Twain exposes the essential dishonesty entailed by the owning of slaves. Percy Driscoll feels so righteous for selling his three household slaves, not down the river but elsewhere, after they have confessed to petty thievery, that he wants the account to serve his son as an example of moral conduct. Tom, growing up the spoiled heir to a Virginia gentleman's estate, develops the cruelty appropriate in that estate to dealings with slaves. His arrogance and his inhumanity as a white man and also his cowardice and meanness later as a slave derive from his own or the experiences of others as slaves or as slaveowners.

*   *   *

* * * it should be noted that the Negro as a simple comic figure appears also in *Pudd'nhead Wilson*. Jasper, first named Jim in the manuscript, and then Sandy (for a slave in the Clemens household in Hannibal), appears in the second chapter in a bantering dialogue with Roxy. In the initial draft Jasper is a Dunker Baptist and Roxy is a Shouting Methodist, as are also Dan'l and Jinny, and they too argue about divine providence. In marking out the debate of Jasper and Roxy on divine providence, the author reduced the buffoonery of the Negro characters, but the tone of the scene remained slapstick. Mark Twain's fondness for these characters, with their comical argument, is attested further by their appearance again in a work he left unpublished, *Simon Wheeler, Detective* (1963).

Along with the subject of race, Mark Twain looked more closely in *Pudd'nhead Wilson* than elsewhere in his works at the cult of Southern aristocracy, codes of honor, and the duel, as details of the plot led him from one aspect of the cult to another. Yet he reached no consistent, inclusive attitude, and he displayed a tolerance of slavery as seen from the position of the slaveholders which in the total view is out of keeping with the view of slavery shown through the slaves.

In the past he had thrown many darts at the Sir Walter Scott cult in the South: the naming of children, houses, colleges, and towns from Scott's romances; the importing of unfitting medieval architecture; the revival of the tournament; the awe with which Americans viewed titled Europeans; the taste for medieval romances of adventure; and above all the assumption of class superiority. But Mark Twain acknowledges varying types and grades of aristocracy, and he makes no claim that they are confined within the South. * * * European titled aristocracy stands condemned, but only mildly. The severest strictures are against American pretensions to aristocracy, and much of American life stands indicted through the idealism of the young English nobleman. But his idealism is folly, after all. One man cannot reform an entire social order alone; the sensible course for him is to keep his hereditary station and work for improvement from that as a base.

In *Pudd'nhead Wilson* the First Families of Virginia are represented by Percy Northumberland Driscoll, York Leicester Driscoll,

Pembroke Howard, and Tom's father, Colonel Cecil Burleigh Essex. These men, bearing flamboyantly appropriate names, revere their Virginia heritage above all other affiliations, not excluding the loyalties owed to church, state, or family. In this loyalty they are foolish rather than evil, and they possess the virtues of integrity, kindness, and high purpose. Supported by hereditary doctrines of caste, they are unquestioning slaveholders. Kind masters, according to their lights, they would not believe that the slaves suffered under the system or that they were themselves warped through their role as masters. Slavery is under subtler and stronger indictment in the final than in the earlier drafts of the novel. With Roxy becoming more important and the book swinging from farce toward tragedy, greater subtlety was required and greater force in the satire resulted. But the slaveholders do not appear to be responsible for the evils of slavery. Except in the death of Judge Driscoll, they have farcical roles. In the context of the entire plot, Driscoll is destroyed by an agent of the social evil which his proud heritage has fostered, but this larger view is obscured by the surface fact that he falls before Tom's villainy.

Percy Driscoll no doubt owed much of his character and some of his action as a slaveholder to Mark Twain's recollections of his father, and it is probably for this reason that Driscoll is portrayed more absurd than evil and that Tom is left to bear the full curse of slaveholding. Like John Marshall Clemens, Driscoll has come from Virginia, is proud of his gentlemanly heritage, is the soul of generosity toward white men, but applies a different brand of generosity and kindness in dealing with slaves. In an early draft of *Pudd'nhead Wilson* Mark Twain assigned to Judge Driscoll an episode from his father's life. Once journeying south to collect money a friend had long owed him, John Marshall Clemens took along a slave to sell as a way of financing the trip, thoughtless of the sorrow caused the slave and his family. The cutting out of this journey even before the final revision of the novel was probably due in part to the author's reluctance to perpetuate an episode which reflected so unfavorably on his father. In a similar instance, Mark Twain referred in the manuscript of *Following the Equator* (1897) to his father's striking a slave. When his wife objected, he deleted the note.

A key to the author's uncertain way of looking at the cult of Southern aristocracy may be taken from his equivocation in handling the duel. His account of how once in Nevada he came close to engaging in a duel should be noted in this connection. In a passage deleted from the manuscript of *Life on the Mississippi* he remarked that the duel had not quite disappeared in the Southern states but had been "hopefully modified." In New Orleans blood might be drawn now and then, but in Virginia, he added, "the mere flash and smell of powder would cure the most acrid wound which can be inflicted upon a statesman's honor." The implication here is that duels are to be condemned, but the direct statement—and the cause for scorn—is that in both New Orleans and Virginia dueling is no more than ritual and pretense, with no real danger to the participants. The same statement and the same scorn dominate two chapters in *A Tramp Abroad*. In one the French political duels are ridiculed as utter sham. Another chapter describes the bloody duels of university students in Germany, detailing the blood, pain, and disfigurement as the serious young Germans hack away at each other. The student duels were genuine, and the author could admire the courage, even though it was displayed in a foolish affair.

The duel recounted in *Pudd'nhead Wilson* as first written, and retained in the supplement, "Those Extraordinary Twins," is broadest farce: one of the conjoined twins has accepted Judge Driscoll's challenge and the other twin is an unwilling close attendant. In the novel proper, with the twins separate, the duel remains farcical—with all those present receiving wounds except the principals—but the episode is less outlandish. Even so, not all is farce. Judge Driscoll and his friend, Pembroke Howard, are shown to be naïve, if not absurd, in their reverence for the code of honor; but they are to be respected for integrity and courage lying beyond all question. In pouring her blistering scorn upon Tom because he has refused to defend his honor in a duel, Roxy in effect condemns rather than defends dueling, for like Huckleberry Finn, she speaks from the false beliefs of the society around her. Yet the reader notes that Tom refuses to fight not because of any principle but because of his cowardice, and his refusal elicits the derision of Pudd'nhead Wilson, who stands outside the social structure of Dawson's Landing and thus speaks from an uncompromised position.

Dueling on Mark Twain's pages is a silly vestige of an antiquated code which was just as silly when it flourished in remote ages. Still, no one loses more than a drop or two of blood in his version of a Southern duel and no one but a cowardly Tom Driscoll or an otherworldly Italian twin refuses to fight. Like feuds, duels are total nonsense, but they are perpetuated by families who bear the best blood and the highest culture of the region. The doctrines supporting race superiority and slavery are false growths from man's greed and his habit of deceiving himself; yet the Driscolls, Miss Watson, and other slaveholders of Mark Twain's fictional world seem to be somehow without responsibility for slavery. They are comical or silly or unaware, but always innocent, at least in intentions. Until *Pudd'n-head Wilson* Mark Twain's fictional slaves knew little of actual slavery; and even in that book the typed stage darky is exploited for comic effect. But under prompting from the characters and the situations he introduced into the plot, he reached understandings of the two races and their influences on each other, both before and after emancipation, which he had not approached before.

In 1894, the year *Pudd'nhead Wilson* appeared in book form, George W. Cable published his last book dealing with the race question in the South, *John March, Southerner*. Cable had found no audience in either North or South for essays or lectures on the subject, and his publishers were urging him to write fiction which would not antagonize or even disturb anyone. By 1894, the problems explored in *Pudd'nhead Wilson* had grown wearisome in the North as well as the South. More than a decade earlier the political decision had been made that the Southern states should solve the race problem without interference from the national government. As state laws were enacted in the early 1890s which decreed for the former slaves a segregated, non-voting status, no effective protest was voiced in either section. The public, valuing the peace which had been achieved, did not welcome disturbances, even in fiction.

There is something of irony in that, by chance rather than intention, Mark Twain wrote his most perceptive and most impressive attack on racism and related doctrines at a time when his attack could stir no spark in the reading public. It was an irony fitting to the black mood into which he was descending steadily deeper. Roxy, Tom, Chambers, and Judge Driscoll had revealed to him subtleties in the race question which in his chuckle-headedness, he might have said, he had not learned from Uncle Dan'l, Aunt Hannah, Jim, or others of the characters he had put into fiction over the preceding twenty years. And his new understanding came at just the time he realized—or might have learned from his friend Cable—that society, in the North no less than in the South, had settled into a pattern of thought which could promise no relief for the victims of race oppression.

Whether Mark Twain was aware that these changes were taking place in the status and the prospects of the former slaves is not certain—or indeed whether he realized that in *Pudd'nhead Wilson* he had probed more deeply than ever before into the complexities of Southern society. He did not attempt in any of his later works to reconcile the inconsistencies and contradictions which remained in that novel—and in his mind—even after the extensive reworking which accompanied refinements in his understanding. He continued, rather, to speak of the South after his old habit, in affection or disgust, nostalgia or anger, depending on the immediate provocation and his mood at the moment.

GEORGE M. SPANGLER

Pudd'nhead Wilson: A Parable of Property†

The striking lack of agreement about the merits of Mark Twain's *Pudd'nhead Wilson* is unquestionably related to the equally striking disagreements over interpretation of the novel, related in the crucial sense that all the thematic analyses so far presented leave important aspects of the novel unaccounted for. The result is that those who are inclined to praise the novel dismiss certain parts as finally inconsequential evidence of Twain's predictably careless technique, while those who have serious reservations about its merits stress its lack of coherence, its lack of an action adequate to embody what appear to be the author's chief concerns. Although interpretations vary widely, ranging from the view that its theme is the conflict between appearance and reality to the assertion that it has "no clear meaning,"[1] two interpretative emphases are most common. First, there are those critics who stress racial themes, especially slavery and miscegenation, and second, those who argue for the centrality of the theme of environmental determinism and see slavery as simply a metaphor for Twain's more general concern with the influence of "training" on the individual.[2]

Although both of these approaches yield valuable insights, both are finally unsatisfactory because they leave too many important questions unanswered—except by alluding to Twain's uncertain artistry. If Twain's purpose was to condemn slavery, racism, and miscegenation, why did he grant so much respect and even, at a key point, sympathy to the FFV gentlemen and their code of honor; and why did he allow such sympathetic figures as Wilson and Roxy to accept unquestioningly the values of these leaders of a guilty society? On the other hand, if Tom is the victim and avenger of racial injustice, why did

---

† From *American Literature* 42 (March 1970): 28–37. Copyright © 1970 Duke University Press. All rights reserved. Reprinted by permission of the publisher.

1. These views are presented respectively in Edgar T. Schell, "'Pears' and 'Is' in *Pudd'nhead Wilson*," *Mark Twain Journal* 12 (Winter, 1964–1965), 12–14, and Warner Berthoff, *The Ferment of Realism* (New York, 1965), p. 72.

2. The racial interpretation is most elaborately presented in James M. Cox, *Mark Twain: The Fate of Humor* (Princeton, 1966), pp. 225–46. Racial themes are also stressed in Philip S. Foner, *Mark Twain: Social Critic* (New York, 1958); Robert A. Wiggins, *Mark Twain: Jackleg Novelist* (Seattle, 1964); and Barbara A. Chellis, "Those Extraordinary Twins: Negroes and Whites," *American Quarterly* 21 (Spring, 1969), 100–12. The case for environmental determinism is best presented in Henry Nash Smith, *Mark Twain: The Development of a Writer* (New York, 1967), pp. 171–83; and Leslie Fiedler, "As Free as Any Cretur . . . ," in *Mark Twain: A Collection of Critical Essays*, ed. H. N. Smith (Englewood Cliffs, N.J., 1963), pp. 130–39. Similar emphasis also appears in DeLancey Ferguson, *Mark Twain: Man and Legend* (Indianapolis, 1963); and Louis J. Budd, *Mark Twain: Social Philosopher* (Bloomington, Ind., 1962). [The criticism by Cox, Smith, and Fiedler is excerpted herein—*Editor*.]

Twain present him as a moral monstrosity, an unmitigated villain throughout the narrative? Why, finally, did Twain allow Roxy's racist explanation of Tom's behavior to go unchallenged? Similarly, the interpretative stress on environmental determinism raises as many questions as it answers. If the novel illustrates the debilitating effects of the training of a corrupt society, why did Twain present Tom as being far beyond the community in viciousness? Why did he present Tom's contempt for the code of honor which the town endorses as major evidence of Tom's baseness? If training is all, Tom should express the values of his environment; but he specifically does not in the key matter of the duel and in his response to the twins, and in fact generally stands apart from the environment that is supposed to have shaped him. Clearly what is necessary is a thematic analysis that can answer these questions in terms of what is shown in the novel and thus demonstrate a coherence in *Pudd'nhead Wilson* that has too often been denied.

The key to such an analysis is the idea of property, more particularly the obsession with property as a vitiating and reductive influence on human beings. Written when Twain's financial condition was at its worst, *Pudd'nhead Wilson* is a parable dealing with the faults of the Gilded Age, faults of which Twain himself was often guilty. It is a book pervaded from start to finish with the very obsession with property which is its theme, yet fully in control of the revelation it offers about the moral and spiritual consequences of this obsession. At both the beginning and the conclusion of the book the importance of the theme of property is revealed with stark clarity. The basis for the narrative is the fact that human beings may be sold as property, and its starting point is Roxy's recognition, itself the result of an incident involving petty theft, that her master may sell her child down the river at any time. "A profound terror had taken possession of her. Her child could grow up and be sold down the river! The thought crazed her with horror" (14). Her response is to exchange her child and her master's, the fact of plot which is central to the subsequent narrative. Similarly, in the final pages the property theme is underscored, this time through Twain's bitter parody of thinking in terms of property. After Tom is convicted of murder and sentenced to imprisonment for life, the creditors of the Percy Driscoll estate offer their view of the situation.

> They rightly claimed that "Tom" was lawfully their property and had been so for eight years; that they had already lost sufficiently in being deprived of his services during that long period, and ought not to be required to add anything to that loss; that if he had been delivered up to them in the first place, they would have sold him and he could not have murdered Judge Driscoll,

therefore it was not he that had really committed the murder, the guilt lay with the erroneous inventory. Everybody saw that there was reason in this. (121–22)

Inconsistent with the story—if the false heir was not part of the inventory, his substitute certainly was and the creditors had had the benefit of his disposal—this passage defines in the manner of parody what has been the consistent theme of the novel, viz., the distortions of reason, feeling, and mortality that result when economic motives are the primary source of human action. If the creditors' logic is absurd, it is also, in a paradoxical sense, correct, for mistaken attitudes about property are in fact the cause of murder and much other evil in this novel.

In the body of the story Twain's focus is on the false Tom, a character whose increasingly vile acts cannot be understood in terms of race or environmental determinism. Rather Tom makes sense only as a nearly allegorical figure of the obsession with property to the exclusion of all other human concerns. Spoiled by too much as a child, threatened by too little as a man, Tom in the end becomes property. His final condition is merely the expression of what his behavior has implied all along: as his singleness of purpose is reductive, so he himself is finally reduced. A nasty child from the start, Tom in his first words makes clear the essence of his bad nature: "He would call for anything and everything he saw, simply saying, 'Awnt it!' (want it), which was a command" (19). When he reaches manhood, his principal vice and the cause of all of his difficulty, gambling, is consistent with his acquisitiveness as a child. Apparently not tempted by sex, alcohol, or other traditional vices, he cannot, on the other hand, resist gambling, even though he knows that the revelation of his losses will cause the judge to disinherit him. Indeed his fear of being disinherited is the crucial emotional fact of his life and the only source of his vows to reform himself. Moreover, his determination to hide his gambling losses leads directly to his overt crimes: the robberies, the betrayal of Roxy, the murder of the judge.

The point is perfectly clear, indeed has the clarity of allegorical pattern: neither when he assumes that he is white nor when he knows that he is legally black does Tom reveal for more than a moment any motive other than the economic one. No moral standard and no personal tie of love, loyalty, or simple gratitude have any force for him. When knowledge of his true birth presents him with a subtle problem of identity, his response is merely a determination to resolve this problem, like all his others, with economic means. Furthermore, in the singleness of his commitment to property values, Tom stands apart from the rest of the community, however deeply it, too, is involved in his kind of thinking. For in the respect it grants to the cosmopolitanism of the visiting Italian twins and to the aristocratic code of honor, Dawson's Landing shows its capacity to appreciate values that are not simply materialistic. Tom, on the other hand, has no such appreciation; he is instinctively hostile to the twins, and his response to Luigi's insult shows that the code of honor is completely unintelligible to him. Twain's characterization of Tom then makes no consistent sense so long as it is seen as embodying some statement about race or training. When, however, this central figure of the parable is recognized as the type of the obsession with property as it reduces human beings and poisons human relations, both characterization and narrative reveal a coherence that they at first may not appear to have.

Structurally the foil to Tom is Pudd'nhead Wilson; as Tom degenerates morally and is finally convicted of murder and sold into slavery, Wilson gradually gains status in the town and ends as a hero when his file of fingerprints allows him to reveal Tom's true identity. As Tom falls Wilson rises, and in fact the rise of the one depends on the fall of the other. Moreover, this structural contrast has a crucial analogue in the sharp divergence of the values of the two characters. If Tom typifies obsession with property, Wilson is largely dissociated from property, particularly from material success. Wilson is, in fact, long a conspicuous failure, unable to practice law, a profession for which he is well trained. The reason for his lack of success in Dawson's Landing is his fatal display of humor when he first arrives in town. He remarks that he wishes he owned half of a noisy dog so that he could kill his half. His hearers forthwith decide that he is a fool, a pudd'nhead, and the nickname they give him ruins his chances for a successful legal practice. Taken literally, the incident is incredible—Wilson's little joke is of the very sort the town loafers could understand—but in this parable about propery it is clear enough: Wilson's low status is the result of his apparent failure to respect and understand the laws of property. Thus for years Wilson must content himself with the respect of only Judge Driscoll and Roxy (a sign of course of his true merit), until he at last wins favor through his association with the duel between Judge Driscoll and Luigi and becomes a hero through his exposure of Tom.

The contrast between the values of Tom and those of Wilson is fully revealed in their discussion of the legal action Tom brought against Luigi instead of fighting a duel with him. Defending Luigi against Tom's charge was Wilson's first chance to practice his profession in the town and thus perhaps the first step toward at long last establishing himself as a lawyer. Yet when Wilson discovers that Judge Driscoll did not know of Tom's action, he is ashamed of his part in the trial, and he tells Tom that he would have kept the matter out of court until the judge had been informed and had had a "gentleman's chance" to avoid the disgrace of having a member of his family take such a matter to court. Tom finds Wilson's attitude incomprehensible.

> "You would?" exclaimed Tom, with lively surprise. "And it your first case! and you know perfectly well there never would have *been* any case if he had got that chance, don't you? and you'd have finished your days a pauper nobody, instead of being an actually launched and recognized lawyer to-day. And you would really have done that, would you?" (68)

What seems incredible to Tom, who has only one standard of value, is matter of fact for Wilson because he has values in the face of which considerations of personal success and status are inconsequential. Himself symbolically dissociated from property, Wilson sees in Tom "a degenerate remnant of an honorable line" who has no other commitment.

Indifferent to material success and respectful of the aristocratic code, Wilson also stands for other values that Tom could not comprehend. Though as well educated as Tom, he is not meanly ambitious in Tom's manner; he is open and frank, not devious like Tom; his sense of humor is kindly, not cutting like Tom's. His interest in fingerprinting and other such scientific advances and his membership with the judge in their two-member Freethinker's Society reveal his intellectual curiosity, which also allows him to appreciate the Italian twins whom Tom only envies. Once again the point is clear: if this tale is primarily an attack on a corrupt community, Twain's sympathetic portrayal of Wilson, who uncritically accepts the values of the community and who is finally and triumphantly accepted into it, is a serious flaw which threatens the coherence of the book. But if *Pudd'nhead Wilson* is above all a protest against exclusively materialistic values, the reason for the status Twain gave Wilson is evident, for it is Wilson, the immaterialist, who stands most apart from and ultimately vanquishes Tom, the figure of unqualified devotion to property.

Unlike Wilson, who serves continuously as a foil to Tom, Roxy becomes deeply involved for a time in her son's economic way of thinking. When she returns to Dawson's Landing after eight years of working on a riverboat, she is the victim of a bank failure which has robbed her of her savings and taught her that "hard work and economy" are not enough to make her secure and independent. Faced with poverty, she pathetically thinks that Tom will give her a little money, "maybe a dollar, once a month, say." But when she discovers what a complete monster he has become, she is willing to blackmail him with the threat that she will reveal his true parentage. Understandably indifferent to property rights, she has no objection to

Tom's stealing and is generally willing to aid his plots to remain the heir of the Judge. For a time, that is, economic considerations shape her relation with her son, not simply because of her need, but also because of her desire to be close to a child who does not exist on any other level.

That love is the cause of her apparent acquiescence to Tom's values is movingly suggested in her demand that he recognize her maternity: " 'You'll call me Ma or mammy, dat's what you'll call me—leastways when dey ain't nobody aroun'. *Say* it!' " (46). Later, her feeling for Tom becomes patent when she suggests that he sell her in order to pay his gambling debts. Heroic as her sacrifice is, it is still a matter of trying to function at Tom's level, and when she learns that he has betrayed her trust by selling her *down* the river, her attitude changes greatly. Yet she does not simply denounce him; she also accepts responsibility for what he is: " 'You is de low-downest orneriest hound dat was ever pup'd into dis worl'—en I's 'sponsible for it!' " (96). Moreover, she demands that he tell the Judge the truth about his debts and ask for money to buy her freedom, even though, as Tom protests and she realizes, such a confession will mean disinheritance. Having suffered the consequences of meeting Tom at his level, she attempts to force him to a higher one where he will be honest with Judge Driscoll and recognize his obligation to her. But Tom of course is incapable of such a change; instead he plans to rob the Judge and ends by murdering him.

Roxy then, despite her temporary acceptance of Tom's standards, is redeemed by her capacity for love, self-sacrifice, and moral awareness. In comparison to Tom, who has economic motives solely, she is very heroic indeed. Recognizing a similar sort of comparative merit is also the key to understanding Twain's attitude toward the town aristocrats and their code of honor, which has caused commentators so much difficulty. That a problem of ambivalence on Twain's part exists is evident from two early passages of characterization, which had better be quoted in full. About Judge Driscoll Twain writes,

> He was very proud of his old Virginian ancestry, and in his hospitalities and his rather formal and stately manners he kept up its traditions. He was fine, and just, and generous. To be a gentleman—a gentleman without stain or blemish—was his only religion, and to it he was always faithful. He was respected, esteemed, and beloved by all the community. (4)

Since the Judge as a freethinker makes no claim to religious orthodoxy, the passage must stand as praise unqualified by irony. Yet two paragraphs later Twain sounds the ironic note in his description of the Judge's best friend, Pembroke Howard:

> He was a fine, brave, majestic creature, a gentleman according
> to the nicest requirements of the Virginian rule, a devoted Pres-
> byterian, an authority on the "code," and a man always courte-
> ously ready to stand up before you in the field if any act or word
> of his had seemed doubtful or suspicious to you, and explain it
> with any weapon you might prefer, from brad-awls to artillery. (5)

The difference of tone between these two passages is not a matter of
distinguishing between the Judge and his friend, for if Twain first
presents the Judge in the language of praise, he subsequently provides evidence for a case against him. For example, the Judge's swoon
when he learns that Tom took an insult to court instead of the dueling ground has the tone of burlesque. Further, the Judge is not only
an aristocrat, he is also a democratic politician and something of a
Babbitt. As politician, he is quite willing to buy votes and use innu-
endo against his opponent, and as Babbitt he escorts the twins
around Dawson's Landing, pouring out "an exhaustless stream of
enthusiasm" for its paltry "splendors." Finally, he is dozing over his
cash and accounts when Tom comes to rob him, a scene which suggests the economic base of his status, one perhaps similar to that of
his brother and Tom's presumed father who died a bankrupt because
of his speculations in land.

   Yet, in spite of these hints, Twain's portrayal of the Judge is not
finally negative. Because the sympathetic Roxy and Wilson endorse
the duel while the vicious Tom rejects it, the reader is allowed to
admire the courage and integrity the Judge displays in the service of
his code. More important, just before the duel Twain shows the
Judge once more writing a will in Tom's favor, even though he vowed
to disinherit Tom after hearing of his cowardice.

> "This may be my last night in the world—I must not take the
> chance. He is worthless and unworthy, but it is largely my fault.
> He was entrusted to me by my brother on his dying bed, and I
> have indulged him to his hurt, instead of training him up
> severely and making a man of him. I have violated my trust, and
> I must not add the sin of desertion to that." (72)

Like Roxy, the Judge accepts more responsibility for Tom than is
properly his, and also like her, displays an affection which Tom cannot comprehend. Then, to make perfectly sure of his readers'
response, the author portrays the Judge's friend Howard fully endors-
ing the Judge's humane act and, a few pages later, shows Tom, who
has overheard the Judge's change of heart, regretting that the Judge
has not been killed in the duel. This contrast of attitudes makes perfectly clear the Judge's moral and emotional superiority to Tom. For
all his faults, the Judge, like Roxy, has a capacity for feeling and moral
judgment that places him far above Tom. His aristocratic code,

despite its endorsement of violent foolishness, allows for values far superior to Tom's, and even at its worst, it fosters an integrity that Tom's materialism does not. If it is a dubious center of value for the town, it is also clearly better than the values Tom embodies.[3]

As well, the code is preferable to the democracy the town practices. The townspeople not only accept and admire the aristocratic ways of the Judge, they also make a farce of their practice of democracy. Their politics amount to no more than the division between the rum and the antirum parties, and the meeting of the Sons of Liberty ends in a drunken brawl of "raging and plunging and fighting and swearing humanity" (61). The Judge is at his worst, not when he is fighting a duel, but when he runs for office confident that he can win by buying votes and slandering his opponent. The satire of democracy is only a small part of *Pudd'nhead Wilson*, but it is consistent with the main thrust of the book—its relentless attack on the obsession with property. Viewed from this perspective, some of the most striking items in Wilson's *Calendar* become comprehensible.

> July 4. Statistics show that we lose more fools on this day than in all the other days of the year put together. This proves, by the number left in stock, that one Fourth of July per year is now inadequate, the country has grown so. (88)

The irreverence of this reference to Independence Day is repeated in the final and most conspicuous entry in the *Calendar*: "October 12, the Discovery. It was wonderful to find America, but it would have been more wonderful to miss it" (113). Even if it were the only evidence of Twain's attitude available, this book would suggest a Twain writing in reaction to the Gilded Age, in reaction to a period in which democracy seemed to be a failure and obsessive acquisitiveness, of the kind Tom represents, prevailed. In comparison, the ability of Roxy and Judge Driscoll to love, the disinterestedness and immaterialism of David Wilson, and even the aristocratic code—all associated with a bygone age—are very attractive indeed.

Even the extraordinarily unwieldy twins have their place in this parable about property. Representative through their cosmopolitanism and their artistic skills of yet another realm of value that Tom cannot understand, they, too, have experienced financial hardship: "'We were seized for the debts occasioned by their [parents'] illness and their funerals, and placed among the attractions of a cheap museum in Berlin to earn the liquidation money. It took us two years to get out of that slavery'" (31). It is this kind of slavery that Twain

---

3. F. R. Leavis makes this distinction between the code and certain admirable human qualities it fosters in his introduction to the Grove Press edition of *Pudd'nhead Wilson* (New York, 1955), pp. 9–31.

is talking about in *Pudd'nhead Wilson*—slavery to property, to economic motives, which, as in the case of Tom, finally reduces one to property, to slavery.

Biographically related to Twain's own financial distress and historically to an America dominated by robber barons, the book, far from being incoherent or inconsistent, is remarkable among Twain's works for its unity, a unity which derives from its pervasive concern with the theme of property, particularly the perils of an obsession with property to the exclusion of all other human values and needs.

JOHN M. BRAND

The Incipient Wilderness: A Study of *Pudd'nhead Wilson*†

It is hardly an understatement to suggest that Mark Twain would not have appreciated the use of any works of Cooper to throw light on one of his own. Nevertheless, one way of making entry into *Pudd'nhead Wilson* is through *The Prairie*, where the aged Natty Bumppo warns travellers who have left the settlement and ventured deep into the uncharted wilderness:

> 'Why then do you venture in a place where none but the strong should come?' he demanded. 'Did you not know that when you crossed the big river you left a friend behind you that is always bound to look to the young and feeble like yourself?'
> 'Of whom do you speak?'
> 'The law—'tis bad to have it, but I sometimes think it is worse to be entirely without it. Age and weakness has brought me to feel such weakness at times. Yes—yes, the law is needed when such as have not the gifts of strength and wisdom are to be taken care of. I hope, young woman, if you have no father you have at least a brother.'[1]

The sense of tension which we get from parts of *The Prairie* stems from the repeatedly helpless wanderings of just these people, who in reaching that area have entered an ethical no-man's-land where law, the ordering force of the settlement, is non-existent, and wayfarers must create their rules as they go along. The loftiness of Natty Bumppo and Ishmael Bush in large measure emerges from their ability to exist in that very situation.

† From *Western American Literature* 8 (Summer 1972): 125–34. Reprinted by permission of the publisher.
1. James Fenimore Cooper, *The Prairie* (New York, 1964), p. 28.

Pudd'nhead Wilson lacks the zest and flair of Cooper's novel. A great river has been crossed, but the crossing was made so a settlement could occur. Just west of the Mississippi River, Dawson's Landing is anything but spectacular. Neither, for that matter, will its hero dazzle us, for David Wilson's primary resources in attacking challenges are his wit, wisdom and patience. Compared to the likes of Natty and Bush, Wilson is prosaic. So is the novel as a whole. Its plot, for example, is stationary, as few characters go anywhere; the action occurring does so within the rather puny confines of Dawson's Landing. But to say the novel is stationary is not to label it static, because it has its own dynamics and in its own way is akin to *The Prairie*. For granted the prosaic and even hum-drum quality of life in Dawson's Landing, a kinship with Cooper's world arises when existing law proves insufficient to reorder a threatened society. In fact, from the beginning of his novel, Twain traces the inexorable process by which the lawlessness of the wilderness slowly permeates the settlement. It is true that, unlike the situation in Cooper's novel, law does exist in Dawson's Landing. However, instead of being based on something like natural rights or Christian ethics, it is shakily rooted in custom and tradition, in this case, white prejudices against black people. Law is thus impotent in caring for "the young and feeble" like Roxy, a white woman who, because of a tiny part of her, is judged legally black by her community. Frustrated by the enduring unfairness of things, and thus goaded into rebellion, she switches her white, but legally black child with the child of her master and therein sets in motion forces which further disorder the life of Dawson's Landing. For her real son Tom, becoming well-versed in the ways of the young white master, eventually turns in his scorn upon both black and white humanity, in this case, his own step-father, whom he murders. Because the disgraced Italian twins, Luigi and Angelo, are the first to arrive at the murder scene, and because the people have a handy grudge they would like to exercise, they are only too eager to use the law to convict and dispose of the two. In effect they are doing what they must, since, through their shackling of the law to custom and tradition, they have no other way of arriving at the truth. Law in Dawson's Landing is in effect non-existent. Since it is largely a vehicle of a people's prejudices, it cannot transcend their tormented subjectivity. It has no way of objectively sighting and correcting the wrong in a people's midst, no way of discerning and disclosing the fact that the primary cause inciting Roxy to action was precisely this limited and narrow force, the law itself. But this is not to suggest that absolute Truth exists at any point in Twain's world, because a major reason for this society's bondage to its own norms is the absence of any transcendent power or pattern. There is nothing Eternal underneath society. So social stability will always be short-lived because it is fragile to begin with, and is so in Dawson's Landing because these citizens compound cosmic insecurity with crippling value systems, making absolute those values that at best are relative, and surely have a questionable place in the West. But even assuming their willingness to scrutinize and reorder their own premises, it is not likely that any more stable culture will emerge. Even granting a desire to raise standards a certain degree, towards what abiding Ideal may citizens move? Does such a spiritual or moral realm or power exist? And if it does, if, for example, the Heavenly City can be perceived and emulated, who stands among them to set their sights towards it? Here then is a chilling look at life in the Secular City, where we experience the anguish of an age lacking not only such giants as Bumppo and Bush, but also the gods Cooper envisioned underlying even the savage wilderness. It is significant that in *Pudd'nhead Wilson* the great river is used for a crossing, but little else. The dark but undeniable river god of *Huck Finn* is ignored, in part because the piety of Dawson's Landing is sheer religiosity, but also because Twain himself is already heading towards the despair that produced *The Mysterious Stranger* and *Letters from the Earth*. He thus creates in this novel a society with no objective pattern by which it may order itself, a society passionate about social stability, but lacking a Torah or Logos upon which to base it. *Pudd'nhead Wilson* thus demonstrates the manner in which any settlement can become a wilderness again, and how one man brings "law and order" back to his time.

The dynamics of *Pudd'nhead Wilson* begin as soon as Twain places his novel. He gives us the settlement of Dawson's Landing, just west of which is the wilderness. The wilderness is wide open both spatially and ethically. It is open to all codes because it is friendly to none. It is barren and crusty, and will crush certain codes attempting to take root there, while reshaping others. Yet this vast nothingness exerts a compelling dynamics of its own. It is there and is there to be crossed and, hopefully, conquered in the form of settlements. As long as it is there people will strive to subdue it. They or their seed must do so sooner or later, since having once severed the spatial ties between them and their old home, they lack the enduring rootage of their ancestors.

Sitting atop what was once sheer open space, Dawson's Landing is just this conquest. It exudes the confident and serene mood that the journey is over and that it is a blessing indeed to get settled. It is this illusory settled quality that Twain is satirizing as he opens his novel. The houses he mentions make up a "snug little collection of modest one- and two-story frame dwellings" (3). Hardly nomadic, the citizenry intend to stay, and proceed to develop and maintain their property, even to the point of adding a touch of luxury, the flower garden. The apparently fixed quality of life there is manifested in the household cat outside, "stretched at full length, asleep and bliss-ful, with her furry belly to the sun and a paw curved over her nose. Then that house was complete, and its contentment and peace were made manifest to the world by this symbol, whose testimony is infallible" (3).

Unfortunately, Dawson's Landing lives on the assumption that people can migrate without losing or having to alter old codes. If they accept the necessity of changing certain ways, they do so with the strong hope that one change will be enough. Without knowing it, set-tlers are living between codes, the one they left behind and the one in process of being born in the westward movement. It is during this period of stress that the dynamics of the wilderness are most prone to rupture the settlement and precipitate disorder. What is being tested is thus a people's ability to live between these codes. Some, like Percy Northumberland Driscoll, are quite vulnerable to this pressure. Driscoll will succumb to the pressure of change by envi-sioning a hyper-extension of the old code, and will be willing, if pressed, to exert it to its most logical and grotesque conclusion, the sending of slaves down the river. He is representative of those white supremists who either try, or are willing to try, to perpetuate the Vir-ginia tradition, but who have to do so in a different situation, and lack the concern for the weaker that kept slavery in some places from becoming a total monstrosity. Tom Driscoll is vulnerable to the wilderness in another sense. As he moves into the future, he hardly looks back at all. His adaptation to his surroundings has been final. He belongs among those who think current, and thus engages in a hasty acceptance of what is new, in this case, the profligate activity he finds available in the glittering city of St. Louis to the north. Therefore, lacking such inner resources as love to curb tendencies to grotesque extremes, Percy Driscoll is an atavist, while Tom is an anarchist. The father's behavior will stem from his passion to main-tain old ties and customs in their primal forms, whereas the son's vagrancy will stem from his refusal to honor any ties at all. The exte-rior Twain thus gives us of Dawson's Landing is akin to the prosaic tone permeating much of the novel, for the novel's rather drab super-structure hides a turbulent substructure, just as the settlement of Dawson's Landing sits atop inevitably eruptive forces. The settle-ment is an incipient wilderness, where the center never holds.

Twain dramatizes this tension between the wilderness and the set-tlement by placing most important events just west of town, where things not only happen, but where, because of the compelling pres-sure being exerted on the town, things simply have to happen.

For example, after telling the joke that alienates him from the townspeople, Wilson is next seen inhabiting the western fringe of town. It is suggestive that because of the citizens' insensitivity and lack of vision, this above-average newcomer is deprived of the chance to practice law. His house is thus an indication of the direction he conceivably could take towards spiteful rebellion, since just west of it is the haunted house Roxy and Tom use as their headquarters, whereas beyond this house is nothing. As they meet in the haunted house, Tom and Roxy, succumbing to the attraction of the wilderness, foment trouble that disrupts the whole community. Wilson, on the other hand, remains a model citizen while in his house, and turns to the hobby that will in effect help him and his townspeople better move westwards. His hobby is finger-printing, a new science that will better insure the detection and control of crime, and thus the stability of Dawson's Landing. Neither atavist nor anarchist, Wilson brings to his town the virtues of Franklin; curious, he is ready to make certain adaptations to a new environment which men like Percy Northumberland Driscoll are unwilling to make; disciplined, he will not succumb to lawlessness with Tom Driscoll. Painstaking and disciplined curiosity is thus Wilson's response to the attraction of the West.

But before Wilson can act as deliverer, he must act as dupe. Twain next creates a series of situations where the actual truth about Dawson's Landing is being disclosed, but ineffectually, since these disclosures in no way alter the diseased condition of the community. There is disclosure, but is no such thing as that revelation which eventuates in repentance. Twain thus skillfully reenacts the plight of any age undergoing the loss of God, or regenerating myth or ethic. With nothing Beyond to look to, people inevitably take the easy course of making their own norms sacrosanct. They soon get used to short-sightedness, so that even when the truth about themselves appears, they fail to see and understand. Wilson himself is flawed in this respect.

One afternoon as he works on his books, in a room looking "westward over a stretch of vacant lots," he hears joking going on between two slaves, a black man named Jasper and the white slave Roxy. Their goading is idle, but still betrays the extent to which Dawson's Landing stands under the shadow of the wilderness, since Roxy is jesting about abolishing ties: "'If you b'longed to me, I'd sell you down de river 'fo' you git too fur gone'" (9). Hers is followed by Wilson's idle chatter, in which he innocently asks the question that eventuates in the chaotic reality of the novel: "'How do you tell them apart, Roxy, when they haven't any clothes on?'" (10). It is later when Roxy, under the threat of being sold down the river, anxious about the welfare of her baby, and perhaps in response to Wilson's question, actually switches the babies, marveling, "'Now who would b'lieve clo'es could do de like o' dat?'" (16). The only possible foil to her plot is Wilson, who, Roxy muses, "'worries me wid dem ornery glasses o' his'n; *I* b'lieve he's a witch'" (17). But her worries are unnecessary, since Wilson is unable to spot the switch when she takes the infants right by him. Hence Wilson is unknowingly instrumental in helping launch the ruin Roxy begins with the switch. For the sake of her son, she deliberately severs ties whose endurance are at the heart of a healthy culture. To aid her own son, she in effect casts him out of her presence. She then adopts Driscoll's son as her own and assumes the responsibility of rearing him, but does so only after violating that child's relationship to his own father. Her behavior thus discloses the extent to which the settlement is becoming the wilderness, a fact known only to the reader.

The extent to which these ties have been severed is borne out in the confrontation occurring later between Tom and Roxy in the haunted house. Tom is now a young man and quite adept in assuming the role of the young white master. He renders Roxy a deep hurt when she approaches him in the Driscoll home after years of separation. Eager to receive affection from him, and just as eager to get part of the fifty dollars he is receiving monthly from Judge Driscoll just to stay out of town and out of sight, she approaches him and is hastily rebuffed. Roxy reacts with sheer force, threatening to expose Tom's dark secret, his black identity. He thinks she is referring to his gambling, a fact the threatened disclosure of which is sufficient to frighten him into submission. The two meet later to talk the situation over, and do so in what the town calls "*the* haunted house. It was getting crazy and ruinous now, from long neglect. It stood three hundred yards beyond Pudd'nhead Wilson's house, with nothing between but vacancy. It was the last house in the town at that end" (44–45). Only there is Tom's actual identity first made known to him. The mother is actually telling him that he belongs to her: " 'Yassir— you's my *son*—' " (45). But her disclosure serves only to widen the distance between them. What follows is mutual violation, since Roxy uses her knowledge of Tom's secret to blackmail him, while Tom will get back at her by selling her down the river. This mother and son probably embody the dynamics of the wilderness to a greater extent than any other characters in the novel. At any rate, the resurgence of the wilderness is a fact no one is present to witness. The truth is being made known, but to nobody's benefit.

Twain carefully connects with this episode another disclosure of the truth, this one managed by the astute Wilson in his own home and concerning the past of Luigi and Angelo. By reading Luigi's palm, Wilson detects a blemish in the man's past and learns that he has killed somebody. His procedure in making this discovery foreshadows the use to which he puts his disciplined ingenuity in solving the crime. Taking Luigi's hand, he "began to study . . . tracing life lines . . . noting carefully their relations . . . he felt of the fleshy side of the hand . . . he pain-stakingly examined the fingers, observing their form . . . entered upon a close survey of the palm again, and his revelations began" (55–56). Wilson's work looms as an initial counterforce to the destructive developments we have been witnessing. Unlike the other people of Dawson's Landing, he does not arrive easily at binding decisions on the basis of unenlightened custom or haphazard emotion; and unlike Roxy, he does not disclose truth for purpose of harsh mastery. His motives and his methods are more disinterested, foreshadowing the kind of objectivity that should enable people in an advancing nation to explore, understand, and order their surroundings. But this is not to suggest that Pudd'nhead Wilson has escaped the threat of the wilderness, for while his efforts here do not seem to add to the encroaching disorder around him, they in no way arrest it either. Aside from the fact that his discovery is a bit theatrical, it is flawed mainly because it is as much off the center of things as Roxy's shattering disclosure to Tom. Discovering Luigi's mystery benefits no one, while the real mystery concerning the corruption of Dawson's Landing remains undetected. Wilson, however, should be appreciated for trying. For just as his activity begins to emerge as a way of countering current wrong, respectable men like the Judge engage in activity that outshines Wilson's theatrics but is even less to the point. The duel is the old way of settling grievances, and can but enact the wills of those who have no way or desire to see beneath the surface of things. It is not a search for truth, since participants have already decided that each has the truth and now must proceed to prove it. The Judge's and Luigi's combat barely disrupts the order of the community, and as a device to redress wrongs, fails to settle such atrocities as slavery. The duelists are thus on the harmless, however spectacular, fringe of things. The Judge can win and feel more confident both of his humor and his manhood, and yet remain unconscious of the fact that his stepson Tom is legally a black man. A winner and full of more repute than ever, the Judge remains ignorant of the canker in everybody's soul, the sign of which is the gleeful Roxy, who, without being noticed, views the proceedings from the window of the haunted house. In addition, the Judge is ignorant of the frailty of the very code he embodies. For it is Tom who will not defend himself, forcing the Judge to duel and uphold the family honor. And it is the same Tom who, when caught looting to pay off his gambling debts, actually kills the Judge. The occurrence of the duel west of town is thus an indication of the extent to which even this esteemed old custom is existing under the destructive spell of the wilderness.

The murder of Judge Driscoll finally forces townspeople to reckon with their own sickness. Instead, they react blindly and, because the twins were the first to arrive at the scene of the murder, readily jump

to the pleasing conclusion that the two are the culprits. Enter Pud-
d'nhead Wilson again and finally.

While he is no Natty Bumppo or Dupin, Wilson is nevertheless a
hero of his time, and probably of ours. Like many today, he has a
marked distaste for disturbances in his community, and longs to put
his talents to use in "bringing things back to normal." Wilson is also
akin to us because of his unspectacular qualities. He evokes a
response from us because he is one of us more than is Natty or
Dupin. His time, after all, is prosaic to the point of being drab. Its
crises are of lesser make and intensity than those of the wilderness,
and are made to order for his unglamorous plod. And along with his
plod is sheer luck. From the beginning the truth has stood under his
own nose. It was he who failed to detect the switch Roxy made, he
who possessed from the first the evidence in the prints that would
illuminate the mystery, and he again who even discussed the crime
at some length with Tom Driscoll. An unlikely Dupin, Wilson never
has the situation completely under his control, and it is only after he
has misjudged situations, or neglected them altogether, that he
finally arrives at the truth, and he does this as much through Tom's
bravado as his own ingenuity. Still, in spite of his ugly duckling qualities, Wilson keeps emerging as a man of some stature. As Twain
describes him at work on the evidence, we find glimpses of a modern deliverer, the unspectacular researcher, who learns to keep subjective considerations under control for the sake of discovery. For we
are told that Wilson's initial speculations about Tom's innocence
"were unemphasized sensations rather than articulated thoughts, for
Wilson would have laughed at the idea of seriously connecting Tom
with the murder" (103). What he learns to do is to temper his subjective judgments with more objective evidence. In this respect he is
admirable, for with his plod and finally his flash of insight, he does
put things together and forces a disclosure of the truth. His usefulness thus stems from his placing law in Dawson's Landing on a less
subjective basis than before. His fingerprinting procedures put an
end to the legality of sheer emotion. This action climaxes in the court
house, dramatizing the momentous step Dawson's Landing has
taken back east, away from the chaos of the wilderness. Wilson thus
begins to turn the wilderness back into the settlement.

Nevertheless, this does not mean that he achieves an objective
reordering of his society, for his truth is used by a slave-holding culture needing increasing support in guaranteeing its survival; his justice is used to relegate Tom back to slave status and then on down
the river. Wilson then improves the periphery, but not the center of
his society; its surface, but not its underlying rottenness. A partial
deliverer, he sees "through a glass darkly."

It is for this reason that much irony arises from Wilson's use of the terminology of religious experience to designate his activity. A favorite word of his is "revelation." As we view him at work, we see a man engaged in tackling a problem with all the resources he has at his disposal. But from some of his statements, we may be led to believe that another force is at work the same time. Addressing the baffling evidence at hand, he remarks, "'There is a most extraordinary mystery here'" (110), which then points to his moment of discovery, "'It's so! Heavens, what a revelation! And for twenty-three years no man has ever suspected it!'" (110). But the closer we look, the more convinced we become that the supernatural is going to have no part at all in Wilson's discovery, and is not about to force a renovation of life in Dawson's Landing. Hence the impact of this "revelation" will be infinitely removed from the experience of St. Paul or Rilke, to whom the ecstatic experience also brought the admonition, "you must change your life."[2] There can be no abiding constructive change in Wilson's world, because there is no Center to fix it to, no Divine Law serving as the source and pattern of societal law. But even if such Law existed, it is doubtful that even Wilson, the best of his community, would have eyes to see and the will to apply it. His range of perception is too narrow, and his desire to transcend the mores of Dawson's Landing with another standard, even if such cannot be absolute, is essentially nil.

This novel is therefore anything but Twain's celebration of such Yankee virtues as diligence and common sense. To the contrary, while he foresees and sanctions the kind of wisdom that will be brought to bear upon the issues of increasingly complex societies, Twain is too deeply aware of what to him is the godless human predicament, and the hold human evil has over all forms of civilization, to forget that while strides by such mortals may be taken, never will they be giant ones, and never will they eradicate yesterday's wrongs or obviate tomorrow's. The grain of hope in this novel is thus mixed with Twain's dark and ruthless honesty, for he is noting a culture's increasing propensity to try to right wrongs without sighting and challenging their bases. When this is the case, those moving mankind into its future may be only a little less subjective than their predecessors; for, even when we have the best of intentions to put our talents to use in the service of society, this service will be at best a modified version of the wrongs plaguing our time, if our disinterestedness is blighted like Wilson's. Lacking any way, or having a way but lacking the will, to evaluate the presuppositions of our own culture, and hence allowing our so-called "objectivity" to work only this side of our sacred presuppositions, like the earnest but deluded Wilson, we will continue to make a wilderness out of the settlement we wish to preserve.

2. Rainer Maria Rilke, "Torso of an Archaic Apollo," from *Rilke: Selected Poems*, trans. C. F. MacIntyre (Berkeley, 1959) p. 93.

312

STANLEY BRODWIN

Blackness and the Adamic Myth in Mark Twain's *Pudd'nhead Wilson*†

Shortly after completing *A Connecticut Yankee in King Arthur's Court* (1889), Mark Twain wrote to W. D. Howells that he had left many things out of that book, and they still "burn in me; & they keep multiplying & multiplying; but now they can't ever be said. And besides, they would require a library—& a pen warmed-up in hell."[1] In later works like *Pudd'nhead Wilson* (1894), "The Man That Corrupted Hadleyburg" (1899), *The Mysterious Stranger* manuscripts,[2] and several shorter, darkly satirical works attacking God, the Bible, imperialism, and war,[3] Mark Twain indeed wrote with a pen warmed up in hell. But of all the novels and stories of his last years of despair, *Pudd'nhead Wilson* is his most classically conceived "tragedy" and the epitome of his deterministic view of reality in the novel form. Like most of Mark Twain's work in this period it deals with failure, betrayal, and damnation—innocence lost even as it gives the illusion of man's capacity to triumph over the fate of the damned human race.[4] *Pudd'nhead Wilson* is, therefore, not merely a "novel of ideas," but a theological study of man's nature whose intrinsic pattern is modeled on the myth of the fall of man. Temptation, pride, banishment, and damnation, dramatized in biblical terms, provide the key

† From *Texas Studies in Literature and Language* 15 (1973–74): 167–76.

1. *Mark Twain—Howells Letters*, ed. H. N. Smith and W. M. Gibson (Cambridge, Mass., 1960), II, 613.
2. Since the publication of *Mark Twain's Mysterious Stranger Manuscripts*, ed. with an Introduction by William M. Gibson (Berkeley and Los Angeles, 1969), it seems to me that critics can no longer make the traditionally accepted Paine-Duneka version the definitive one for critical analysis.
3. For example, see Mark Twain, *Letters from the Earth*, ed. Bernard DeVoto (New York, 1962); "Reflections on Religion," ed. Charles Neider, *Hudson Review* 16 (1963), 329–52; and an excellent anthology, *Mark Twain on the Damned Human Race*, ed. with an Introduction by Janet Smith (New York, 1962), containing such pieces as "To the Person Sitting in Darkness" (1901), "The War Prayer" (1905, 1916), and "The United States of Lyncherdom" (1901). Even his *Personal Recollections of Joan of Arc* (1896) must be considered as a "symbol of despair" since it deals with innocence betrayed and destroyed while holding fast to the possibility that man could overcome evil on earth.
4. For Mark Twain, man was "damned" in the precise theological sense. He wrote in the margin of a book by an optimistic evolutionist that man "was made to suffer and be damned." Quoted in Roger B. Salomon, *Twain and the Image of History* (New Haven, 1961), p. 50. And in a speech he gave on his "Seventieth Birthday," he talked seriocomically about the "sin microbes" in man. See *Mark Twain's Speeches* (New York, 1910), p. 433. Finally, Joseph Twichell chided Mark Twain for being "too orthodox on the Doctrine of Total Human Depravity"; Joseph Twichell to Mark Twain, September 5, 1901, as quoted by Kenneth R. Andrews, *Nook Farm: Mark Twain's Hartford Circle* (Cambridge, Mass., 1950), pp. 47, 253. Indeed, there are a great many references in Mark Twain's works to man's sinfulness, his fall, and the demonic God who punishes him for it.

to the novel's meaning and help us to resolve some of the critical questions raised by its archetypal and tragi-satirical form.[5]

Yet, characteristically, in a letter to Fred J. Hall, Mark Twain judged *Pudd'nhead Wilson* as a story whose ostensible interest "centered on the murder and the trial; from the first chapter the movement is straight ahead without divergence . . . to the murder and the trial. . . . Therefore, 3 people stand up high . . . and only 3—Pudd'nhead, 'Tom' Driscoll, and his nigger mother, Roxana. . . ."[6] In the same letter, however, Mark Twain writes that unless he can finish a new work he will "tackle Adam once more, and do him in a kind of a friendly and respectful way that will commend him to the Sunday schools. I've been thinking out his first life-days today and framing his childish and ignorant impressions and opinions for him."[7] This was to be "Extracts from Adam's Diary," published that year (1893), and the first of a group of works that included "Eve's Diary" (1905) and "That Day in Eden" (1923). Apart from the very obvious humor Mark Twain extracts from his anachronistic treatment of Adam and Eve, these works deal in comic and tragic terms with the theme of man's fall from innocence—a fall that is inevitable because man cannot transcend his machinelike nature. Man, burdened with the "Moral Sense," chooses a congenial or attractive evil rather than an uncongenial "good" or agonizing truth.[8] Thus, despite Mark Twain's interest in the melodramatic murder and trial, the combination of his erupting pessimism and long preoccupation with the Adamic myth found its way into the form and meaning of *Pudd'nhead Wilson.*

The basic technique by which Mark Twain achieves artistic and philosophic unity in this novel is to make the leading characters become victims of forces both outside and within themselves. Two linked tragedies are therefore developed. One is concerned with

5. Several of the best studies of *Pudd'nhead Wilson* have commented on the book's structural tightness and its evocation of a sense of genuine doom, praising its depth, though criticizing the mechanical quality of its structure and the flaw of mixing a tragic racial theme with a detective story. I hope to answer some of these objections in my study. But see James M. Cox, "*Pudd'nhead Wilson*: The End of Mark Twain's American Dream," *South Atlantic Quarterly* 58 (1959), 351–63; Leslie Fiedler, "As Free as Any Cretur . . .," in *Mark Twain, A Collection of Critical Essays*, ed. H. N. Smith (Englewood Cliffs, N.J., 1963); F. R. Leavis, "Mark Twain's Neglected Classic: The Moral Astringency of *Pudd'nhead Wilson,*" *Commentary* 21 (1956), 128–36; George M. Spangler, "*Pudd'nhead Wilson*: A Parable of Property," *American Literature* 42 (1970), 28–37; and Barbara A. Chellis, "Those Extraordinary Twins: Negroes and Whites," *American Quarterly* 21 (1969), 100–12, for a variety of different, but excellent approaches to the book. [The Fiedler, Spangler, and Leavis essays are reprinted herein—*Editor.*]
6. *Mark Twain's Letters*, ed. A. B. Paine (New York, 1917), II, 590–91.
7. Ibid., 591–92. For a study of Mark Twain's Adamic references see Allison Ensor, *Mark Twain and the Bible* (Lexington, 1970).
8. This is one of the fundamental ideas in *What Is Man?* (1906). For a good study of the Moral Sense in Mark Twain's thought, see Coleman O. Parsons, "The Devil and Samuel Clemens," *Virginia Quarterly Review* 23 (1947), 582–606. See also my study, "The Humor of the Absurd: Mark Twain's Adamic Diaries," *Criticism* 14 (1972), 49–64.

man's sin and fall, and the other with the fall of America. Pudd'n-
head satirically points to the latter in his calendar entry, entered just
after he makes his discovery of the identities of Tom and Chambers:
"October 12, the Discovery. It was wonderful to find America, but it
would have been more wonderful to miss it" (120). For the American
dream has become vitiated by slavery. Its grass-roots mentality drives
intellectuals like Pudd'nhead underground, and its cultural provin-
cialism is exposed by the Italian twins, Luigi and Angelo. Knowledge
through irony is wasted upon the people of Dawson's Landing, as
when Judge Driscoll tries to read Pudd'nhead's calendar to them:
"But irony was not for those people; their mental vision was not
focussed for it. They read those . . . trifles in . . . earnest, and
decided . . . that if there had ever been any doubt that Dave Wilson
was a pudd'nhead—which there hadn't—this revelation removed
that doubt. . ." (27). Pudd'nhead's ironic joke about the dog, from
which he gained his nickname, can now be seen as only the first in
a series of ironies that fail to enlighten, indicating the impotence of
humor in raising a fallen world. But behind this account of America's
failings lurks the more significant and unifying theme of original sin.
The proper setting is Eden, of which Dawson's Landing is yet
another avatar.[9] The town is described as a "snug little collection of
modest . . . dwellings whose whitewashed exteriors were almost concealed from sight by climbing tangles of rose vines, honeysuckles and
morning-glories" (3). The names of the flowers suggest the lush, yet
homey, quality of the place that was "sleepy and comfortable and
contented" (4). But Dawson's Landing is also a "slave-holding town,
with a rich slave-worked grain and pork country back of it" (4).
Herein lies the metaphorical serpent in this apparent Eden. For the
slavery is not only evil in itself—the National Sin—but is the condition that leads to a variety of crimes: miscegenation, betrayal, murder, and tampering with the lives of innocent infants. A whole range
of man's sinful impulses is dramatically realized. From this fact
springs the essential, mythic tragedy of the book.

The initial agents of the tragedy are Percy Northumberland
Driscoll and Colonel Cecil Burleigh Essex, two of the honor-wor-
shiping aristocrats of the town. It is they who sire two sons, one born
to Driscoll and his wife, who dies in childbirth, the other to Essex
and Driscoll's slave Roxana, who is only one-sixteenth black.[1] Mis-

9. See Henry Nash Smith, "Mark Twain's Image of Hannibal: From St. Petersburg to Esel-
   dorf," *Texas Studies in English* 37 (1958), 3–23.
1. In developing the character of Roxy, Mark Twain owed much to the longstanding stereotype of the tragic mulatto in American writing. The problems of "passing," double identity,
   and the melodramatic revelations were all standard fare and are all used in *Pudd'nhead
   Wilson*. Indeed, the tragic mulatto was one stereotype exploited by antislavery writers for
   propaganda purposes. No doubt Mark Twain learned much about antislave fiction from
   Harriet Beecher Stowe and George Washington Cable as well as from his general literary
   apprenticeship. Still, Mark Twain is often able to give a visceral human quality to his

cegenation becomes the first of several blood-sins, offenses against primal taboos. These sins pollute the earth, bring suffering or death to all, and demand retribution as in the stories of Cain and Oedipus.

Added to Essex's sins of fleshly pollution, so common and held in such abhorrence in the South, is Driscoll's original, spiritual sin—pride. For Driscoll, power over slaves is power over life and death, Heaven and Hell. He can sell slaves "down the river," which, writes Twain, "was equivalent to condemning them to hell!" (13). In this way Driscoll terrifies a group of slaves into confessing a petty theft. Driscoll relents and says he will sell them at Dawson's Landing. The slaves kiss his feet in gratitude. Then follows a passage that captures in a coldly ironic style the act of pride. And it begins fittingly and grandly, with a biblically shaped line:

> They were sincere, for like a god he had stretched forth his mighty hand and closed the gates of hell against them. He knew, himself, that he had done a noble and gracious thing, and he was privately well pleased with his magnanimity; and that night he set the incident down in his diary, so that his son might read it in after years and be thereby moved to deeds of gentleness and humanity himself. (13)

Mark Twain's use of irony is masterful here and may be regarded as a stylistic paradigm of the novel as a whole. The biblical line at the same time widens the vision of the incident by its suggestive allusion to the serpent's lure to Eve: "Ye shall be as gods" (Gen. 3:5). Driscoll behaves like a "god" and thus personifies fallen man trapped not only in pride but in pride's twin, blind self-deceit. And these are the qualities that he transmits to his new "son" who becomes Thomas à Becket Driscoll. These traits become manifest in Thomas and not in Percy's legitimate son, who becomes a humble, ignorant slave, because the culture of white supremacy brings them out of Thomas and suppresses them in Valet de Chambre. Man is seen as an "over-determined" creature, controlled by both his intrinsic nature and an environment that reinforces that nature. Pudd'nhead's calendar entry for chapter 2 crystallizes the determinism that the action of the chapter plays out:

> Adam was but human—this explains it all. He did not want the apple for the apple's sake, he only wanted it because it was forbidden. The mistake was in not forbidding the serpent; then he would have eaten the serpent. (7)

"types" as witness Jim, Roxy, and the Mammy in "A True Story" (1874). But see Sterling A. Brown, "Negro Character as Seen by White Authors," *Journal of Negro Education* 2 (1933), 180–201.

Perhaps even more directly, this aphorism, with its trenchant humor, applies to Pudd'nhead himself. For in this chapter the now rejected "college-bred" Pudd'nhead turns to his hobbies of palmistry and fingerprinting.[2]

It is a standard criticism of the novel that Pudd'nhead's concern for fingerprints and his use of them in solving a crime represent the "popular" and vulgar melodrama of the novel that Mark Twain never quite integrated with the tragedy of Roxy and her son.[3] But it seems fairly clear from the juxtaposition of the aphorism and the description of fingerprinting that there is some fundamental thematic connection, and that this is the necessity of the fall of man. Adam had to fall, and his destiny is stamped in man from birth. When Pudd'nhead takes the fingerprints of the two babies and Roxy, more than a melodrama of crime detection is being prepared. Pudd'nhead is actually translated into an instrument of God whose task it is to teach man the nature of his fate, a role concerning which Roxana has some intimations:

> Blame dat man, he worries me wid dem ornery glasses o' his'n; *I* b'lieve he's a witch. But nemmine, I's gwyne to happen aroun' dah one o' dese days en let on dat I reckon he wants to print de chillen's fingers agin; en if *he* don't notice dey's changed . . . den I's safe, sho'. But I reckon I'll tote along a hoss-shoe to keep off de witch-work. (17)

For Roxana, Pudd'nhead is a kind of witch-priest who is really the "smartes' man in dis town." Her magic fails because Pudd'nhead's magic represents the truth about man, locked in the whorls of his fingertips.

Pudd'nhead, with all his aphorisms about Adam, functions as the servant of God who rules over a deterministic world. He accepts this world with bitter humor and, like Mark Twain himself, comes to see that the result of the Fall has its own ironic consolation. The entry for chapter 3 is:

> Whoever has lived long enough to find out what life is, knows how deep a debt of gratitude we owe to Adam, the first great benefactor of our race. He brought death into the world. (14)

2. For information on Mark Twain's interest in fingerprinting, see Anne P. Wigger, "The Source of Fingerprint Material in Mark Twain's *Pudd'nhead Wilson* and *Those Extraordinary Twins,*" *American Literature* 28 (1957), 517–20.

3. See, for example, Richard Chase, *The American Novel and Its Tradition* (New York: Anchor Books, 1957), p. 155. He writes, "the characters and their relationships are not adequate to the moral action; the split between action and actors runs through the book." And Leslie Fiedler, who recognizes in the story a "local instance of some universal guilt and doom," also remarks that the "tragic inevitability" is "blurred by the demands of the detective story with which it is crossed"; in "Free as Any Cretur . . . ," p. 137. [Reprinted, pp. 248–57, herein—*Editor.*] I am arguing, however, for the organic relationship between the philosophic and detective elements in the book on the grounds that the fingerprinting functions as a theological symbol of man's fall.

Apart from expressing Pudd'nhead's own spiritual character, the aphorism relates—as all the calendar entries do—to the specific action of the chapter. And the action in chapter 3 is Roxy's trick of exchanging the destinies of the two infants. The link is again clear. Roxy, ironically playing God as her master did, commits an act of pride that brings tragedy and death (the murder of Judge Driscoll by Thomas, Roxy's son) into the world. But first she must justify her act, and this she does by telling herself that "*white* folks has done it! It ain't no sin, glory to goodness it ain't no sin!" To bolster her rationalization on an even deeper level, she invokes the Calvinist doctrine of the Elect expounded by a traveling preacher:

> He said dey ain't nobody kin save his own self—can't do it by faith, can't do it by works, can't do it no way at all. Free grace is de on'y way, en dat don't come fum nobody but jis' de Lord; en *He* kin give it to anybody He please, saint or sinner—*He* don't k'yer. He do jis' as He's a mineter. He s'lect out anybody dat suit Him, en put another one in his place, en make de fust one happy forever en leave t'other one to burn wid Satan. (16)

Thus, if destiny—or Free Grace—offers her a chance to save her child from slavery, then, reasons Roxana, she must take the opportunity presented to her. She herself becomes an agent of Election or Grace. But though she has great provocation for what she does, and the reader must partially sympathize with her, her action injures many innocent people and cannot finally be justified. Indeed, almost immediately, Roxana begins to suffer. Her child, now her master, becomes a sickly and pernicious person who takes particular delight in treating Roxana with open contempt. With characteristic irony, Mark Twain shows how Roxana loses the pleasure she sought in seeing her son master. Her "mock reverence" to Tom becomes "real reverence . . . the mock homage real homage." In short, she becomes the "dupe of her own deceptions" (20). Punishment follows swiftly on the heels of sin.

Even more quickly does the essential pattern of the book assert itself: the two boys follow fixed paths. Spoiled and pampered beyond limit, Tom becomes an egotist without moral backbone. Given a chance to be a free and purposeful human being, he fails to live up to the expectations of his mother and his "uncle," Judge Driscoll, who takes him in hand after his "father," Percy Driscoll, dies. His betrayal consists of two terrible crimes: selling his mother down the river after she reveals his true origin to him, and murdering his "uncle." A lesser, but still significant betrayal is demonstrated when Tom, rather than answering Count Luigi's challenge to a duel, takes the affair to court, thereby blemishing the aristocratic honor-code held by his family and the town's leading citizens. Much of what Tom does is explained by his "training," but the deepest quality of his soul's evil, and its cause, reveals itself in the great "discovery" scenes between Roxana and Tom. Roxana, free for many years now, returns to Dawson's Landing to see her son once again. Asking him for some money, she receives only humiliation. Her proud character rebels; she becomes determined to reveal the truth to him. Shattered, Tom listens to the truth in impotent rage. Then, he utters the lament that is the tragic core of the novel, a lament that makes the social tragedy of slavery part of the cosmic tragedy of original sin: "Why were niggers *and* whites made? What crime did the uncreated first nigger commit that the curse of birth was decreed for him? And why is this awful difference made between white and black?" (48).

For an explanation of the awful racial problem, Tom can only fall back on a theological concept of primal guilt. Tom feels that "the curse of Ham" is upon him. Here, Mark Twain, though in sympathy with the Negro, recognizes the persuasiveness of this biblical apologetic in the South. The Negro is *doomed* to suffer. To generations— North and South—saturated with biblical thought and seeking answers in vast cosmic solutions, whether through the Bible or Darwinism or through the fixed power of a vague "Providence," such an answer would have its impact—and its believers. For Mark Twain, the tragedy is not in being born black, but in being born black into a white world. That is the agony. Man's punishment lies in the very fragmentation of his physical as well as moral nature. The contrast between white and black with all its symbolic and cosmic connotations of struggle and strife lives in the flesh of man.

There is the momentary hope that a perception of such tragic depth could, and would, alter character. But the hope flickers and dies. Tom is afflicted with guilt for being black—he hears the biblical accusation "Thou art the man" that Nathan hurled at David (2 Sam. 12:7). Slowly but surely Tom responds with such intensity to the idea of being black that his manners and behavior take on the aspect of a slave. "But," writes Mark Twain, "the main structure of his character was not changed, and could not be changed" (50). Soon after, Tom commits his crimes. A child of miscegenation, he embodies the doom of guilt and suffering for being a Negro with the rich white man's vices of gambling, contempt for inferiors, egotism, and self-indulgence. The main line of the plot is simply a demonstration of the consequences of this fate.

It is Roxana's fate to be both creator and victim of Tom at one and the same time. This is what makes her the protagonist as well as the emotional center of the novel. It is she who is most aware of the tragically ironical world around her, and it is she who tries to struggle out of the trap she has created for herself. The burden of Tom's failure to succeed in the white man's world falls on her shoulders. While she tries to save her son from debts and disinheritance, she is also called upon to condemn him when he fails to answer Luigi's challenge to a duel:

> "It's de nigger in you, dat's what it is. Thirty-one parts o' you is white, en on'y one part nigger, en dat po' little one part is yo' *soul*. 'Tain't wuth savin'; 'tain't wuth totin' out on a shovel en tho'in' in de gutter. You has disgraced yo' birth. What would yo' pa think o' you? It's enough to make him turn in his grave." (75)

The terrible irony of a Negro condemning her own race is, indeed, an "appalling response,"[4] as Leslie Fiedler has termed it. This, for Mark Twain, is the ultimate tragedy of the Negro. His mind and soul have been literally and figuratively "whitewashed," so that he sometimes assumes the point of view of the slaveholder and despises himself for being a slave and black. It is the final stage of degradation in slave-psychology. Roxy even goes so far as to invoke the white man's racism on the basis of the distorted Christian reading of the Bible that makes the tribe of Ham inherently guilty. Thus, she and her white masters join together in condemning blacks on the grounds of a kind of original sin, though the sin itself can never be clearly articulated in theological terms. For the sin of Ham, "the father of Canaan" who "saw the nakedness of his father," Noah (Gen. 9:22), is neither the sin of pride nor lust nor any of the other major sins against God. The biblical text, in fact, does not suggest that Ham entered the tent in order to see the nakedness of his father. The implication is clearly that Ham entered by chance. Accident or not, in the severely patriarchal society of the Hebrews, beholding the genitalia of the father was a terrible transgression against the sexual mores. The punishment is for Canaan to be a "servant of servants" (Gen. 9:25). The biblical passage is etiological and attempts to degrade the Canaanites (who were not Negroid) because of the conflict the Hebrews were to have with them later, recounted in The Book of Judges and Samuel 1 and 2. The historical irony, as it was developed in the South, and reflected in *Pudd'nhead Wilson*, is that the white sons of Noah punished the sons of Ham by degrading them sexually. But Roxana is proud, ironically, of being used by the aristocratic Essex, who, like many of the white masters who used their slaves sexually, unconsciously degraded himself. Tom, the spawn of such an act, becomes its spiritual incarnation. And he knows that this doom has been foisted on him. That is why, after listening to Roxy's condemnation, Tom wishes that his white father were alive so

---

4. Leslie Fiedler, "As Free as Any Cretur . . . ," p. 137. [See pp. 248 ff. herein—*Editor*.]

that he could kill him. As it is, he kills his surrogate father, Judge Driscoll, though ostensibly for money.

Roxy, however, is the more tragic figure, for she is the self-deceived one, trying to escape her destiny through her child, yet having to turn on her child with her master's religious and racial attitudes. Clearly, Mark Twain is sympathizing with her and agonizing over her destiny.[5] He is delineating the tragedy of the Negro rather than accepting Roxy's own judgment of her race. This point must be emphasized,[6] for on the surface it might appear that Mark Twain implicitly accepted the "original" inferiority of the Negro by making Tom evil and Chambers good. But such a view would miss the tragic religious, social, and sexual ironies that permeate the novel. For Mark Twain the tragedy lies in the fact that Tom, by "training" a white slaveholder with the white slaveholder's vices, is blamed for these vices because of his Negro birth. Chambers, goodness and humility personified, has been conditioned by his Negro training that teaches him to know his place and accept his lot, yet that goodness is assumed to be the result of his being white. Such is the terrible irony and confusion about race and character with which the South (and, by extension, America) was burdened. And the tragedy is compounded because of the irrevocability of training, the attitudes it creates, and the universal nature of man himself. Man could not reform. Once fallen, he must stay fallen. That is the essence of Mark Twain's pessimistic determinism.

The idea is made explicit at the end of this scene between Roxy and Tom. Roxy terrifies Tom into behaving well so that Judge Driscoll will make a new will leaving him his fortune. Tom says, "I know, now, that I am reformed—and permanently. Permanently—and beyond the reach of any human temptation" (79). To underscore the resolution, Mark Twain writes that there was "no levity in his voice." But

5. Yet Philip Butcher in his article "Mark Twain Sells Roxy down the River," *CLA Journal* 8 (1965), 228, writes that Roxy is a "ludicrous grotesque, a shadow signifying nothing except Twain's inability . . . to rise above popular notions about the Negro's instability and lack of profound feeling." I feel that this criticism is unjustifiable. While Roxy is, as I have pointed out, part of a tradition of Negro stereotypes, Mark Twain humanizes her. He shows her to be driven to her actions by the oppression of slavery and the loss of a genuine womanhood and motherhood. These actions are "believable" because they derive from an authentic despair. Butcher also writes in the same passage that Mark Twain "seems to forget how little 'Negro blood' flows in Roxy's veins and to lend support to the shabby opinion that any 'taint' of Negro ancestry . . . was 'remote' and could not account for her 'irrational, ignoble behavior.'" But Mark Twain is not forgetting that in the South any "taint" of Negro blood was enough to condemn a person to racist oppression. He is not justifying it; he is commenting on the tragedy of such a condition. *Pudd'nhead Wilson* is a masterly, ironic delineation of the racial traps both black man and white man are caught in.

6. See, for example, Anne T. Wigger, "The Composition of Mark Twain's *Pudd'nhead Wilson* and *Those Extraordinary Twins*: Chronology and Development," *Modern Philology* 55 (1957), 93–102. Miss Wigger says that Tom's function is "unclear—almost as if innately corrupt due to his Negro blood" (p. 98).

the result of Tom's reformation is contained in Pudd'nhead's calendar entry for the next chapter: "Nothing so needs reforming as other people's habits" (79). Tom is robbed of his stolen loot by a thief and so the plot is hatched whereby he will recoup his loss by selling his mother down the river. This occurs in the next chapter, whose calendar entry is: "If you pick up a starving dog and make him prosperous, he will not bite you. This is the principal difference between a dog and a man" (85). Once again the point is driven home that a man cannot reform.

Roxy eventually escapes, but shortly thereafter Tom commits the murder with which the twins are charged. The stage is set for the courtroom scene in which Pudd'nhead will emerge from relative obscurity to produce his grand "effect." The calendar entry is: "*April 1*. This is the day upon which we are reminded of what we are on the other three hundred and sixty-four" (111). The doom and the tragedy that come with Tom's exposure involve white and Negro, American life as a whole. Roxy cries, "De Lord have mercy on me, po' misable sinner dat I is!" (120). She is not merely lamenting, nor does Mark Twain suggest that it is only a lament. Truly, she has sinned. But she has been more sinned against. She has played God, and she has been used by men playing God. If she and her son are punished, so is the white society that shaped their fate. The miscegenation, an act of intimacy, has only torn the white man and Negro further apart, creating provocation to other sins. Tom is, indeed, sent down the river in the novel's final crushing irony, but he has left death behind and a clear condemnation of the white man's values that had corrupted him. The "triumph" of Pudd'nhead is weak compensation for such a tragedy and, in his way, Pudd'nhead realizes this in his bitterly ironic remark that it would have been more wonderful for Columbus to miss discovering America.[7] In the end, there is only the realization that man is tricked by God or Providence and his own sinful nature into thinking that through choice (Roxana) or through the saving grace of ironic humor (Pudd'nhead) he could change destiny and reform the world and himself. And it is this realization that Mark Twain consciously embraced, allowing it to dominate the mood and content of the work of his remaining years.

---

7. That is why *Pudd'nhead Wilson* is not a "success story"—despite Pudd'nhead's ostensible triumph—as Fiedler characterizes it. There is no real "assertion that man is master of his fate." Pudd'nhead is simply an instrument of Divine Justice, however impersonal. He brings retribution after the fall. What Fiedler states as the underlying theme—"that to be born is to be doomed"—is true, but it is not worked out in "secularized" Calvinistic terms. Rather it is structured in genuinely biblical tropes, with the clear implication that man has sinned against an impersonal God who does not allow tampering with the fixed order of things; see Fiedler, "As Free as Any Cretur . . . ," p. 137 [pp. 248 ff. herein].

ARTHUR G. PETTIT

The Black and White Curse:
Puddn'head Wilson and Miscegenation†

You is a *nigger!*—*bawn* a nigger en a *slave!* . . . (45)
Thirty-one parts o' you is white, en on'y one part nigger, en dat po' little one part is yo' *soul*. (75)
—*Pudd'nhead Wilson* (1894)

I have no race prejudices, and . . . no color prejudices . . . [Black Africans] should have been crossed with the Whites. It would have improved the Whites and done the Natives no harm. . . . Nearly all black and brown skins are beautiful, but a beautiful white skin is rare. . . .
Where dark complexions are massed, they make the whites look bleached out, unwholesome, and sometimes frankly ghastly.
—*In Defense of Harriet Shelley* (1893)
Following the Equator (1897)[1]

Notwithstanding his fondness for black culture and causes, by the 1890s Mark Twain had a serious, even shattering color problem. On the one hand he had persuaded himself that persons of dark skin were physically more attractive than those of white skin, and he said so. Moreover he was convinced that the greater tragedy of the South was not miscegenation, but the curse that white Southerners had placed upon it. *The Tragedy of Pudd'nhead Wilson* is Mark Twain's most eloquent declaration of conscience on these two subjects.

Yet Clemens also had a private, more or less conscious craving to find a credible sexual being in that most incongruous and puzzling of all places in the nineteenth century, namely a *white* woman. The result was an extraordinary amount of color confusion in his private thinking and in his art, culminating in Mark Twain's two-toned portrait of the mulatto slave woman Roxana in *Pudd'nhead Wilson*. At the same time that Roxana's small drop of black blood made the point about the tragedy of racial mixture in a slave society, Mark Twain's Victorian teachings demanded that her skin be white. By painting this woman in a baffling black-and-white collage he tried to have it both ways: to satisfy the requirements of the Victorian code, while calling down the curse of the South. The ultimate outcome was chaos; but in the process of making a shambles of Roxana, Mark Twain let slip some revealing opinions about color. The purpose of

---

† From Arthur G. Pettit, *Mark Twain and the South* (Lexington, Ky.: The University Press of Kentucky, 1974), pp. 139–55, 207–10. Copyright © 1974 by the University Press of Kentucky. Reprinted by permission of the publisher.
1. *Harriet Shelley*, p. 264; *Following the Equator*, 1:247; 2:51.

this chapter is to trace the curiously shaded patterns that ripple over this woman and to place them in the context of Mark Twain's changing notions of skin color and of miscegenation.

*　*　*

Mark Twain was not the first to explore the plight of the Tragic Mulatto: Cable, Melville, Stowe, and Howells were there before him.[2] But sometime in the 1880s Mark Twain also began to sense the pathos in the subject. Possibly inspired by conversations with Cable before and during their lecture tour, he sketched a four-page outline for a story about the misfortunes of a mulatto man who has the same amount of Negro blood as Roxana in *Pudd'nhead Wilson*. Although the story is rough and incomplete, it is Mark Twain's most compact and explicit statement about miscegenation, and it merits full quotation:

> Before the War he is born—1850
> The Accident—Mrch or Apl—1860
> The Sale, April, 1860.
>
> The War.
>
> The Wanderings.
> (His father <u>his</u> master & mean.)

Does not deny but speaks of his n [*sic*] blood. His struggles—education—advertises & hunts for his mother & sister—at last gives them up. At last, seeing even the best educated negro is at a disadvantage, besides always being insulted, clips his wiry hair close, wears gloves always (to conceal his telltale nails,) & passes for a white man, in a Northern city.
     Makes great success—becomes wealthy.
     Falls in love with his cousin, 7 years younger than himself—he used to "miss" her, on the plantation.
     She & her father are very poor; he blows & gasses & talks blood & keeps up the lost cause fires, & she supports him. She is a very fine & every way noble & lovely girl; but of course the moment the revelation comes that he is ¹⁄₁₆ negro, she abhors him. Her father & she wears [*sic*] fictitious names, to indulge his pride, & he makes a mystery of their former history—which

2. For the similarities between Roxana and the mulatto slave woman Cassy in *Uncle Tom's Cabin*, see Kenneth S. Lynn, *Mark Twain and Southwestern Humor* (Boston: Little, Brown, 1960), pp. 265–66. Clemens read Cable's *The Grandissimes*, which deals in part with miscegenation, and may have borrowed part of the plot for *Pudd'nhead Wilson* from Cable's *Madame Delphine*, which deals with a quadroon mother who renounces her daughter so she may enter the white world. Howells' *Imperative Duty*, about a white man and a very white octoroon woman who have trouble deciding whether they should marry, was published one year before *Pudd'nhead Wilson*.

enables him to aggrandize it & at the same time prevents either
of them from saying anything which would lead XX to recognize
them.

XX keeps his early history a secret, of course—& it is the only
secret which he has from *her*. All the towns people try to dig out
his secret, but fail.

At the climax when his mother & sister (who is waiting on the
table) expose his origin & his girl throws him & her cousin
(proud, poor, & not sweet), voices *her* horror, he is at least able
to retort, "Well, rail on; but there is one fact which Atlantics of
talk cannot wash away; & that is, that this loathsome negro is
your *brother*.

At time of the climax he is telling the stirring tale of the heroic
devotion of a poor negro mother to her son—of course not men-
tioning that he was the son & that *his* is the mother who bears
the scar which he has described. Then she steps forward &
shows the scar she got in saving him from his own father's bru-
tality. So this gassy man is *his* [*sic*, whoever XX is] father, & it is
his niece whom XX loves, & who with (perhaps) his daughter,
supports him.[3]

Apparently the mulatto boy was sold by his master-father directly
after the unknown "accident," which may have been the blow suffered by his mother in attempting to protect him. Freed by the war,
he courts and perhaps marries the cousin he used to address as
"Miss" on the antebellum plantation, but whom he does not now recognize. The girl soon learns that he is part Negro, but she is too
ashamed to reveal her knowledge to him. This leaves the way open
for the mulatto to be dramatically exposed by his long-lost, and now
freed, mother and sister. From there the genealogical ramifications
of the plot grow more confusing, but they include the revelation that
other people who had been under the illusion that they were all-
white are also tainted.

In this brief sketch Mark Twain uncovered the fear, doubt,
hypocrisy, and guilt of white feelings about mixing with blacks. The
implications of this unfinished story become fully explicit only in the
light of *The Tragedy of Pudd'nhead Wilson*, Mark Twain's last American novel and his last published outcry against the American South.
That the story turned out to be so anti-Southern was more accidental than planned.[4] Having begun with the notion of chronicling the

---

3. DV 128, MTP. ["DV . . . MTP" references are to a typescript on file in the Mark Twain
Papers (U.C. Berkeley) under De Voto.] Paine dates the story in the 1880s.
4. I do not intend to summarize or to cite critical discussions of *Pudd'nhead Wilson*. Numerous listings are available. [See pp. 467 ff. herein—*Editor*.]

absurd adventures of an extraordinary pair of Siamese twins—one virtuous and fair, the other vicious and swarthy—Mark Twain was chagrined to find that a stranger named Pudd'nhead Wilson, a mulatto woman named Roxana, and another mulatto named Tom Driscoll were taking over the story. Dimly aware that the plot was veering from comedy toward tragedy, he attempted to solve the problem of his hybrid creation by performing what he called a "literary Caesarian operation," yanking out the Siamese twins altogether. The extraction, though physically complete, was artistically incomplete and the novel remains a semiserious, semicomic grotesque—a hodgepodge of characters and events which somehow still reveal the traumatic divisions and cruelties that Mark Twain had come to associate with the antebellum South.

* * *

From the beginning this novel is a chronicle of interracial crime and punishment. The true *Tragedy of Pudd'nhead Wilson* is not the lawyer David Wilson's quarter-century of social exile in Dawson's Landing,[5] but the two centuries of white exploitation of black—the South's great self-inflicted wound. By the end of the story one harmless aristocrat, Judge York Leicester Driscoll, had been killed by the mulatto Tom Driscoll. Roxana, after two decades of sacrifice to protect her son from exposure, is condemned by a court of law for enslaving a white aristocrat in order to free a mulatto slave. And the all-white aristocrat Chambers is so bent and stifled from shuffling around the slave quarters all those years that he can be "liberated" only into a life of genteel misery: "He could neither read nor write, and his speech was the basest dialect of the negro quarter. His gait, his attitudes, his gestures, his bearing, his laugh—all were vulgar and uncouth; his manners were the manners of a slave. . . . The poor fellow could not endure the terrors of the white man's parlor, and felt at home and at peace nowhere but in the kitchen. The family pew was a misery to him, yet he could nevermore enter into the solacing refuge of the 'nigger gallery'" (121).

The most eloquent commentary on Southern chauvinism over interracial intercourse comes from its least sympathetic victim. Coward, thief, and murderer though he is, the mulatto Tom Driscoll reaches a more profound understanding of the tragedy of racial mixture in a racially unequal society than any other character in Mark

---

5. David Wilson is condemned to twenty-three years of social exile in Dawson's Landing for remarking on his arrival in the village that if he owned half of a dog that was yelping, he would kill his half. The villagers promptly label him a pudd'nhead ("What did he reckon would become of the other half if he killed his half?") and boycott his law practice. In his leisure Wilson takes fingerprints of most of the citizens, including the mulatto Tom Driscoll, whom he ultimately exposes as the murderer of Judge Driscoll.

Twain's writing. When this villain learns that the mammy who wet-nursed him as a child is actually his mother, the shock almost destroys him. For the next quarter of the novel Driscoll suffers through an excruciating crisis of identity: he too is one of the despised race. In his person he gives the lie to white distaste for black and reveals the philistinism of a society that privately tolerates miscegenation, then publicly punishes its victims. In an unpublished portion of the manuscript Driscoll asks himself which in fact is the higher or the lower in him, the white or the black, and has the perception to see that "the high is either color, when undegraded by slavery." [See Emendations of the Copy-Text, 49.44, p. 211 herein.] In the published version of the novel he pursues the agonizing inquiry farther: "Why were niggers *and* whites made? What crime did the uncreated first nigger commit that the curse of birth was decreed for him? And why is this awful difference made between white and black? . . . How hard the nigger's fate seems [now]" (48).

Yet, for all his perception, Tom Driscoll's insight is wasted on a scoundrel. The reader who comes to this novel expecting to learn how a part-black man, given the privileges of passing as a white, will prove himself worthy of this rare opportunity is in for a surprise: Driscoll proves thoroughly unregenerate. Although Mark Twain implies that the mulatto may have been warped by six generations of decadent FFV blood rather than by his drop of Negro blood, Driscoll's mother Roxana is convinced that her son's wickedness flows from his invisible mark of blackness—a color irony which is compounded when we compare *Pudd'nhead Wilson* to *Huckleberry Finn*. Huck believes that Nigger Jim must be "white inside"; but Tom Driscoll is white on the *outside*. His whiteness thoroughly conceals both his wickedness *and* his blackness, until his bad behavior exposes them both.[6]

For all his heartfelt ruminations on the plight of niggers, Tom Driscoll's insight leads not to reformation but to recovery of his old vicious self. Self-pity soon gives way to more typical trains of thought, including future villainies which are directly spawned by his discovery that he is not who he thought he was. Before the revelation of his race Driscoll was a liar, gambler, and petty thief. He continues these activities but now expands his evil doings to include selling his mother Roxana down the river and murdering his foster father,[7] thus becoming Mark Twain's first, but not his last, mulatto

---

6. James M. Cox, *Mark Twain: The Fate of Humor* (Princeton: Princeton University Press, 1966), p. 228. [Excerpted herein—*Editor*.]

7. In the working notes for the novel Mark Twain made Judge Driscoll himself the father of Tom. But in the finished work he shied from such intimacy, possibly because his own father, Marshall Clemens, resembled the aristocrats in the story. Marvin Fisher and Michael Elliott, in *"Pudd'nhead Wilson: Half a Dog Is Worse than None," Southern Review* 8 (1972): 544, point out that Percy Driscoll would have had "to vault out of one bed and leap into another in order to father sons born to different mothers on the same day."

avenger.[8] Although Driscoll gets his comeuppance by being sold down the river himself into the same slave fate he had decreed for his mother,[9] this facile ending of the story is not very satisfying, for it reminds us that the main problems posed by the novel have not been resolved. The defeat of the mulatto criminal at the hands of a depraved white society seems deliberately to extenuate rather than to lessen the larger crimes of slavery and of color discrimination. By declaring Tom Driscoll to be a black slave and hence a valuable piece of property to be sold rather than jailed, the court of Dawson's Landing denies Driscoll the dignity of human punishment and acts as the instrument of an avenging justice which ought itself to be punished. Blackguard though he is, Tom Driscoll's fate is more disturbing than gratifying, for it leaves us with the suspicion that the worse offender is not the mulatto avenger, but the white South.

That the innocent Judge Driscoll must bear the full white burden of "black" revenge in *Pudd'nhead Wilson*, while the aristocrat who started the trouble, Essex, dies unpunished, compounds the irony. There is, Mark Twain implies, no such thing as a "free" Southerner. All Southerners, innocent and guilty, will suffer for the sins of slavery and concubinage. And the suffering will go on until emancipation from both slavery *and* the stigma of miscegenation brings remission to black and white alike.

More than any character in the novel Roxana embodies this suffering and gives it enormous power and poignancy. Herself a fourth-generation product of interracial union, she adds one more. And more than any character in Mark Twain's writing she suffers the consequences.

Unlike her son, who is accepted as white and free until proven otherwise, Roxana is a slave. She too, however, has a color problem, though a very different one. Dawson's Landing had no difficulty deciding she was a mulatto, but her creator did. Mark Twain in effect wound up with two Roxanas: a near-white one, carefully adjusted to the proper shade for white readers, and a much darker Roxana who may have figured more prominently in Mark Twain's imagination. The public Roxana is, for all intents and purposes, an all-white Southern belle: "Only one-sixteenth of her was black, and that sixteenth did not show. She was of majestic form and stature, her attitudes were imposing and statuesque, and her gestures and movements distinguished by a noble and stately grace. Her complexion was very fair . . . her eyes were brown and liquid, and she had

8. The mulatto Jasper, discussed in the next chapter, is Mark Twain's superlative portrait of the black avenger.

9. Mark Twain originally had Tom Driscoll hang himself with his suspenders after David Wilson finds him guilty of murder. By changing Tom's fate to being sold down the river, Mark Twain completes the cycle of Tom earlier selling Roxana down the river.

a heavy suit of fine soft hair which was also brown. . . . Her face was shapely, intelligent, and comely—even beautiful" (9).

Roxana's drop of blackness seems important at first only as a reminder that miscegenation did in fact take place in the South and to explain why this lovely white woman is a slave. For Roxana, however, it has always been disastrous. It dictates her mudsill position in white society and it explains why she despises all niggers, who remind her of her own invisible mark. Indeed much of Roxana's credibility is based on prejudice and hatred. Rejected by one race and hardly wishing to be embraced by the other, she resorts to almost any means of redress for the vast injustice that is her life. She lies, steals,[1] cajoles, threatens, and flatters. She never questions slavery, except as it applies to herself and her son; and she repeatedly attempts to catapult herself into the highest order of whites. When Tom Driscoll first learns he is tainted and timidly asks who his father was, Roxana launches into the sort of trumped-up family genealogy we customarily associate with white Southerners: "You ain't got no 'casion to be shame' o' yo' father, *I* kin tell you. He was de highest quality in dis whole town—Ole Virginny stock, Fust Famblies, he was. . . . Does you 'member Cunnel Cecil Burleigh Essex. . . ? Dat's de man. . . . Dey ain't another nigger in dis town dat's as high-bawn as you is"[2] (47).

As with Nigger Jim before her, much of Roxana's credibility is founded on her fallibility, especially the extent to which she has picked up white prejudices. When her son refuses to challenge a white man to a duel for a petty insult, Roxana denounces him by way of one of the more confusing family pedigrees in American literature. The passage is a fine piece of irony, and it momentarily places this mulatto woman in company with the poor-white Huck as a naive, and therefore merciless, reporter of bloated Southern notions of ancestry. In one spasm of specious reasoning Roxana manages not only to make a sharp distinction between superior African blacks and loathsome New World niggers, but to parrot one of the white South's favorite clichés about the desirability of mixing a smidgen of *red* with white:

> "You has disgraced yo' birth. What would yo' pa think o' you? . . .
> [Y]o' great-great-great-great-gran'father was ole Cap'n John
> Smith, de highes' blood dat Ole Virginny ever turned out; en *his*

---

1. Mark Twain made it clear that for slaves robbed of their freedom, stealing was not immoral. According to Kenneth M. Stampp, adult slaves "doubtless detected the element of hypocrisy in white criticism of their moral laxity" (*The Peculiar Institution: Slavery in the Ante-Bellum South* [New York: Alfred A. Knopf, 1956], p. 350).
2. Roxana's genealogical pretensions are strikingly similar to Aunt Rachel's in "A True Story," as Roxana herself is similar to Rachel in every detail but color. ["A True Story" was published by Twain in the *Atlantic* in 1874—*Editor.*]

great-great-gran'mother or somers along back dah, was Pocahontas de Injun queen, en her husbun' was a nigger king outen
Africa—en yit here you is, a slinkin' outen a duel en disgracin'
our whole line like a ornery low-down hound! Yes, it's de nigger
in you! . . . Ain't nigger enough in [you] to show in [your] . . .
finger-nails . . . yit dey's enough to paint [your] soul."[3] (75–76)

Yet for all her efforts to bolster her whiteness with nigger prejudices and genealogical fantasies, Roxana is a good deal darker than
her physical appearance would lead us to believe. In the course of
the story her whiteness is the one thing about her that we tend to
ignore or to forget: her speech and manners, strength and
endurance, shrewdness and passion are qualities that Mark Twain
usually reserved for black women. In every characteristic except
color Roxana is an exact duplicate of the female slaves and servants
Clemens knew as a boy in Missouri and as a wealthy Yankee
employer of black domestic help. Like Aunt Hanner of Quarles
Farm, the Clemens's slave girl Jenny in Hannibal, Aunty Cord in
Elmira who became Aunt Rachel in "A True Story," and Aunty Phyl-
lis in "Refuge of the Derelicts," Roxana is statuesque, good-looking,
courageous, arrogant, strong, and smart.[4] First introduced as a new
mother, back on her feet caring for her white mistress's newborn
child a few hours after giving birth to her own, Roxana is the archetypal black matriarchal figure—the combination of mistress and wet
nurse who rears the white man's legitimate children and bears his
bastards.

The one thing wrong with Roxana is that she is neither black nor
white long enough at a stretch to be entirely convincing. The problem is not that she is, literally, a mulatto but that Mark Twain had
trouble deciding which Roxana is the real one: the one who looks
white or the one who acts black. Even *as* a black Roxana changes
roles with bewildering speed. At times she is a loving, warm-hearted,
pious and simple Black Mammy. At other times she is just as black
but cunning and ruthless. When she meets her son for the first time
in several years, Roxana first behaves like a doting mammy. Then,
with incredible swiftness, she turns herself into a vengeful bitch,
exulting over the "[f]ine nice young white gen'lman kneelin' down to
a nigger wench" (43) and taking swigs from a whiskey bottle more in

---

3. Thomas Jefferson, among others, elaborated on the desirability of mixing red with white
as opposed to black with white in *Notes on the State of Virginia*, ed. William Peden (Chapel
Hill, 1955), pp. 58–64, 100–02, 140. For an excellent account of Jefferson's racial feelings and fantasies, see Winthrop D. Jordan, *White Over Black: American Attitudes toward
the Negro, 1550–1812* (Chapel Hill, 1968), pp. 475–81.
4. Jenny, Marshall Clemens's slave in Hannibal, is described by both Mark Twain and Paine
as young, handsome, arrogant, stubborn, insolent, and statuesque. Later, like Roxana, she
was sold down the river and became a chambermaid on a steamboat.

the manner of a black shrew than the tragic mother figure Mark Twain had carefully constructed up to this point.

The problem with this woman is not that she lacks qualities of character but that she has too many of them. Wandering back and forth between comedy and tragedy, between all-white Southern belle and all-black mammy, Roxana is the victim of Mark Twain's own color confusion. When obviously black, she is a creature of rare beauty and passion, courage and dignity, vitality and fertility, with an immense capacity to love, hate, and forgive. When near-white she is tepid. Alternately bleached and blackened too often and too haphazardly, Roxana ultimately fails to transcend the sentimentality she evokes and loses much of her identity and, therefore, much of her credibility.

Mark Twain's color confusion over Roxana was in part the result of a collision between his attraction to persons of dark skin and his bondage to white social and sexual values. Indeed it is not too much to say that he consciously used blacks and mulattoes to express sexual feelings that were prohibited by white standards of propriety, especially feelings about miscegenation. Concubinage was, after all, an accepted part of the social system of the antebellum South;[5] and Mark Twain, who was quite reticent about sexual relations between whites,[6] never tried to conceal the obvious fact of Southern interracial intercourse. There were a number of mulattoes in Hannibal and even in St. Petersburg white, mulatto, and Negro children patronize the town pump to which Tom flees from his whitewashing job. In his *Autobiography* Mark Twain remembered that Wales McCormick, a fellow newspaper apprentice in Hannibal, "was constantly and persistently and loudly and elaborately making love" to a mulatto girl and that "by the customs of slaveholding communities it was Wales's right to make love to that girl if he wanted to." Four years after he left Hannibal, while working on a Cincinnati paper, young Clemens placed one of his first fictional characters, Thomas Jefferson Snodgrass, in an embarrassing predicament. Snodgrass is approached on the street by a fashionably dressed white woman, who asks him to

5. W. J. Cash wrote that black women, "taught an easy complaisance for commercial reasons," were "to be had for the taking" and that white boys "inevitably learned to use" them. *The Mind of the South* (New York, 1940), p. 87. Bernard De Voto speaks sweepingly of the "forbidden world of slaves," with its black concubines ready to initiate "their quota of pubescent boys" into manhood. *Mark Twain's America* (Boston, 1932), pp. 64–65. Kenneth M. Stampp, using specific evidence, concludes that "sexual contacts between the races were not the rare aberrations of a small group of depraved whites but a frequent occurrence involving whites of all social and cultural levels." *The Peculiar Institution*, pp. 350–51.

6. The Beinecke Rare Book and Manuscript Library at Yale University has some verses by Mark Twain about lost virility, and his speech to the Stomach Club on "The Science of Onanism." There is of course *1601*, and Mark Twain's late remarks about white female sexuality in *Letters from the Earth*, ed. Bernard De Voto (New York, 1962), pp. 16–17, 50–53.

hold a basket for her for a moment, then disappears. When the lady does not return Snodgrass opens the basket and finds he has become foster father to a mulatto child. Then there was the furor in Virginia City launched by Mark Twain's ill-considered suggestion that some local charity funds had been turned over to a miscegenation society in the East; and as late as 1872 Clemens told Howells that he was so uplifted by Howells's favorable review of *Roughing It* that he felt like "a mother who has given birth to a white baby when she was awfully afraid it was going to be a mulatto."[7]

Neither serious nor malicious, these early remarks about miscegenation are playful flights of fancy by a humorist who liked to test the limits of public tolerance and of private taste. The same can be said for the commonplace jokes about black sexuality that Clemens set down in his notebooks. In 1882, on his trip down the river, he recorded a dialogue he supposedly overheard on board the *Gold Dust* between two black laundresses, who chit-chat about wayward nigger employees who "takes up with everybody and anybody that comes along." One laundress explains that if she were young again she would change her habits and refuse to sleep with strangers. While Clemens listened (or so he made it appear in his notebook), the laundress illustrated her technique by withstanding the advances of a brash "young colored chap" who happened along at that moment. Though she permitted the man to come "pretty close to it," the laundress made it clear that that was "just as close as I allows one of them young fellows to go." If she was going to go farther at her age, she was going to go with "a *man*."[8]

Given Clemens's imaginative and vernacular powers, this "conversation" is at least as suspect as the "dialogue" between the two black deckhands about God being responsible for man's sins—recorded on board the same boat, in the same river notebook, and on the same journey. At the very least the part pertaining to the young colored chap probably gained in elaborateness as Clemens warmed to his subject. Other notebook jottings, especially those made after Livy died, are almost certainly fictitious:

> *She*. I cain't dance wid you. I don't know who you is.
> *He*. Plenty knows me en dey kin tell you. My name's Clapp.
> *She*. Oh yes. Is you de genlmn dat start de epidermic in de Babtis' chu'ch?

7. Albert Bigelow Paine, ed., *Mark Twain's Autobiography* (New York and London: Harper & Brothers, 1924), 2 vols., 2:276–77, MTHL, 1:7. Dixon Wecter discusses Hannibal's brothels and prostitutes and concludes that Clemens, "with a taste for the 'low company' of the Blankenships, and tutelage in several newspaper offices," was probably well-acquainted with the town's "seamy side" (*Hannibal*, pp. 147, 174–75, 214–15).
8. Typescript Notebook 16a, pp. 26–28, MTP [Mark Twain Papers—*Editor*].

After this entry Clemens added a telephone conversation, in which a black woman accepts a proposition with, "Yas—but who *is* you, anyhow?"[9]

Taken separately these jokes are not compelling evidence of preoccupation with black sex. Clemens's notebooks are sprinkled with mild smut about animal copulation, masturbation, scatology, and heterosexual intercourse, most of it set down after Livy died.[1] Moreover, since it was taboo to write about white female sexuality, it was taken for granted by many whites that black females gave an extra excitement to sex jokes—a common prejudice which Clemens was willing to foster. Yet when taken together these "jokes" suggest that Clemens may have been sexually troubled in his late years, and that race came into it as an expression of his repression. The most revealing example is a dream Clemens said had been bothering him for a long time before he finally set it down in 1897:

> In my dream last night I was suddenly in the presence of a negro wench who was sitting in grassy open country, with her left arm resting on the arm of one of those long park-sofas that are made of broad slats with cracks between, & a curve-over back. She was very vivid to me—round black face, shiny black eyes, thick lips, very white regular teeth showing through her smile. She was about 22, & plump—not fleshy, not fat, merely rounded & plump; & good-natured & not at all bad-looking. She had but one garment on—a coarse tow-linen shirt that reached from her neck to her ankles without a break. She sold me a pie; a mushy apple pie—hot. She was eating one herself with a tin teaspoon. She made a disgusting proposition to me. Although it was disgusting it did not surprise me—for I was young (I was never old in a dream yet) & it seemed quite natural that it should come from her. It was disgusting, but I did not say so; I merely made a chaffing remark, brushing aside the matter—a little jeeringly—& this embarrassed her & she made an awkward pretence that I had misunderstood her. I made a sarcastic remark about this pretence, & asked for a spoon to eat my pie with. She had but the one, & she took it out of her mouth, in a quite

9. Typescript Notebook 38, p. 14, MTP.
1. Justin Kaplan, *Mr. Clemens and Mark Twain* (New York: Simon and Schuster, 1966), pp. 222, 323, offers a few titillating examples of Mark Twain's sex jokes, but omits the more numerous and mild examples, such as a couple copulating under a bridge; a girl who goes to a doctor to be vaccinated, is raped, and asks "to be vaccinated again"; and a "procrastitute," who is defined as "a woman who promises & then fools along & doesn't perform." In the last notebook there is some very bad verse about lovers returning a buggy with "a grease-spot on the cushion / And I think there's been some pushing / For there's boot-tracks on the dashboard upside down," and a comparison between Standard Oil being slapped with a heavy fine and the June bride who "expected it but didn't suppose it would be so big." Typescript Notebook 38, pp. 17–19, MTP.

matter-of-course way, & offered it to me. My stomach rose— there everything vanished.[2]

The sixty-one-year-old man who dreamed this dream had grown up in a slaveholding society which had among its commonest institutions black wet nurses and black concubinage. The dream is open to numerous interpretations, but the least farfetched is the possibility that Clemens found the woman, who was "not at all bad-looking," less repulsive than the proposition itself, which was disgusting because it violated Clemens's code of *conduct*, not of color. The woman's blackness simply made her sexuality possible. Being non-white, she could behave in a manner that, for black women, was "quite natural." Being white, Clemens could not behave in such a manner, and he went to considerable pains to dissociate himself from this woman. Since most of his dreams, by his own admission, were shaped by guilt[3] and since he was rarely able or willing to untangle the dream from the reality, Clemens sought release from the haunting mystery of the black woman by insisting that the rational and responsible wide-awake Clemens had no physical or psychological resemblance whatever to the self of his dreams. By denying emphatically that the one had any knowledge of the other, he could disown any disturbing symbolic meanings he may have seen in his dreams. If the two Clemenses were wholly unknown and wholly unrelated, then how on earth could the real Clemens be held accountable for the actions or thoughts of his dream self?

This is precisely where Mark Twain boxed himself into a corner with Roxana in *Pudd'nhead Wilson*. For here, in full consciousness, is a near-*white* hussy; acting provocatively when seemingly black, yet white on the outside nonetheless. By combining disguised blackness with surface whiteness, Mark Twain managed to endow Roxana with the uninhibited mannerisms of his black dream woman, while at the same time satisfying the popular demand for the Tragic Mulatto who must appear to be white.

Always his own most rigid censor, Mark Twain approached Roxana's sexual behavior with great caution and delicacy. In her first appearance in the novel this off-white woman does not actually "appear" at all; instead she is introduced offstage as an invisible, seemingly all-black voice which exchanges a series of sexual sallies with a coal-black slave named Jasper, who plans to court her as soon as she has recovered from childbirth. Though Roxana makes it clear that she does not mix "wid niggers as black as you is," she teases Jasper ("how does *you* come

2. Paine, *Mark Twain's Notebook*, pp. 348–52.
3. "I go to unnameable places. I do unprincipled things; and every vision is vivid, every sensation—physical as well as moral—is *real*" (Kaplan, *Mr. Clemens and Mark Twain*, pp. 340–46).

on, Jasper? . . . Is ole Miss Cooper's Nancy done give you de mitten?")
and comes off as a "high and sassy," plainly provocative woman (8).
Only *after* this scene do we learn that Roxana looks white: Mark
Twain's careful description of Roxana's physical appearance comes
only after we have been led to believe she is black.

It is the invisible black mark that gives Roxana her marvelously
uninhibited manner. White women simply do not behave this way in
Mark Twain's writing, either because he was unwilling to break the
bonds of convention or because he was constitutionally unable, until
late in life, even to imagine the possibility of white women behaving
in an overtly sexual manner.[4] The pity is that he failed to maintain
the color dichotomy consistently. When obviously all-white, Roxana
is anemic. When obviously part-black, she is a fascinating mixture of
white pathos and black boldness. Indeed in her finest moments Roxana transcends the prototypical heroine of the age to become that
rarest of nineteenth-century creatures, a white woman who acts
"black." For all the color confusion that ultimately crippled her credibility, this woman, at her "blackest," is the one convincing female
character in Mark Twain's writing who is not an adolescent, a widow,
or a middle-aged aunt. Although Mark Twain failed to stick to a
single image of Roxana, the very *idea* of such a woman, capable of
running the full range of human passions, was a far more original
and daring experiment than either the all-white Tragic Mulatto she
finally turned out to be or the predictably disgusting and hardly original black wench who haunted Clemens in his dreams.

Roxana is more than a bewildering mixture of black and white,
however. She is also the most poignant example in Mark Twain's
writing of his conviction that the greater crime of the South was not
miscegenation but the white Southerners' unwillingness to admit
that mulattoes were, after all, the products of their own lust.[5] Since

4. Joan of Arc was, for Clemens, an idealization of nonsexual and, as he understood it, constitutionally nonnubile young womanhood. In his copy of Jules Michelet's *Jeanne d'Arc*
(1853), opposite a passage citing the testimony of Domrémy women that Joan had never
menstruated, Clemens wrote: "The higher life absorbed her and suppressed her physical
(sexual) development" (*Mr. Clemens and Mark Twain*, p. 315). In a courtship letter to Livy,
Clemens described her "as pure as snow . . . untainted, untouched even by the impure
thoughts of others"; March 1869, in Dixon Wecter, ed., *The Love Letters of Mark Twain*
(New York: Harper & Brothers, 1949), p. 76. Howells called Livy "heavenly white," and
Mrs. James T. Fields described Livy as especially "white and delicate and tender"; *Atlantic
Monthly* 130 (1922):342–48. When told of the alarming amount of venereal disease
among British troops in India, Clemens wrote that clean native women "subject to rigid
inspection ought to be kept for these soldiers," so the soldiers would not subsequently
infect the "fresh young English girls" they married; Paine, *Mark Twain's Notebooks*,
pp. 280, 286.
5. In 1906, in response to William Lecky's remarks in his *History of European Morals, from
Augustus to Charlemagne*, 2 vols. (New York, 1903; Clemens's copy in MTP), that "the
chastity of female slaves was sedulously guarded by the Church," Clemens scrawled in the
margin: "This is better than the Southern Protestant Church of America ever did, *nicht
wahr?*"

mulattoes offered visible evidence of a covert bond between the races, that bond had to be overtly denied at all costs. The price of such deceit was bound to be paid by Southerners of every hue: all-white aristocrats like Chambers, mistaken for black; supposedly all-white Southerners who must worry whether the stigmata might not turn out to be theirs also; mulattoes like Roxana who are recognized as contaminated; mulattoes like Tom Driscoll who pass the color line only to be brought back across into slavery and blackness. No amount of deceit or dissimulation can guarantee permanent protection from discovery. After twenty-three years of indoctrination into white manners, speech, and decorum, the fair-skinned Tom Driscoll can still be declared tainted. And, conversely, after twenty-three years of indoctrination into black manners, speech, and decorum, the fair-skinned Chambers is beyond redemption. Neither environment *nor* heredity can match Southern prejudice.[6]

In its exposure of the Southern racial trauma, *Pudd'nhead Wilson* anticipates one of the obsessive themes of Southern writing in the twentieth century. The legacy of slavery and concubinage is one of fear, suspicion, false accusation, hypocritical exoneration, and guilt—a legacy that can be wiped out only by putting an end not to miscegenation but to discrimination. In a society of mixed blood in which the central preoccupation is with purity of blood, denial of the dignity and worth of blacks and mulattoes becomes, inevitably, a denial of the self. If some blacks are partly white, then some whites must be partly black. If some whites are slaves, then some blacks must be free. Who are they? And how many? And how long is this self-defeating denial going to go on? The fear and the hypocrisy seem endless: by rejecting blackness by day and embracing it by night, white Southerners have planted a lie in the soul of their progeny, cut themselves off from a vital part of their past, and locked themselves into a dilemma which will last as long as the blood curse itself.

For Mark Twain this was the central tragedy of the Southern experience—the curse of blood. The problem was not one of racial mixture, but the destructive emphasis on purity of blood of *any* sort. Injustice toward blacks springs from intraracial as well as interracial discrimination. The whole business of "born a gentleman, always a gentleman," or Marshall Clemens's efforts to compensate for poverty by assuring his family they were "blood-pure," or the blood feud of

6. Robert Wiggins, in *Mark Twain: Jackleg Novelist* (Seattle, 1964), p. 107, points out that Mark Twain is inconsistent when he argues that environment (what he called training) determines human behavior exclusively. With Chambers, Mark Twain's deterministic theory is convincing: slavery ruins him. But Tom Driscoll is carefully shown to be wicked *before* his white training has the opportunity either to uplift or to damage him. With Chambers, environment is the determining factor; with Driscoll, both environment and heredity (including six generations of white blood) could be said to determine his behavior.

the Grangerfords, or Pap Finn's hatred of black skin when his own was "a white to make a body's flesh crawl," or Roxana bragging to her mulatto son about his FFV blood—all this adds up to an intolerable burden imposed by white on black, white on white, and black on black. Tainted blood goes far beyond color; indeed it may have nothing whatever to do with race. But from blood consciousness springs the stultifying pride of those who believe they are pure and the paralyzing fear of those who believe they are not. Southern pride in blood and Southern fear of miscegenation are two sides of the same sword and the sword cuts black and white alike. More than any nineteenth-century novel except Cable's *The Grandissimes, The Tragedy of Pudd'nhead Wilson* implies that the greater tragedy of the South is not miscegenation but the curse that white Southerners have placed upon it; and, therefore, upon themselves.

BARRY WOOD

Narrative Action and Structural Symmetry in *Pudd'nhead Wilson*†

As any student of Mark Twain soon discovers, serious critical attention to his work is not apparent until the middle of the twentieth century. In the case of *Pudd'nhead Wilson* (1894), the watershed dates from essays by Leslie Fiedler in 1955 and F. R. Leavis in 1956.[1] Since that time there have been a surprising number of studies of the novel, all of them useful in unravelling one or another aspect of the work without presenting in total more than a mosaic of motifs and themes. Without attempting to present a detailed summary of scholarship, I would like to point to a few of the issues in the novel around which the thematic interpretations have been built.

First, there is the racial theme centering on miscegenation and the disastrous results of interbreeding at Dawson's Landing, the small Missouri settlement on the west bank of the Mississippi south of St. Louis where the major action is set.[2] A second theme derives from the notion of environmental determinism, a concept specifically linked to the realism and naturalism so central to the writings of the

---

† This essay was published for the first time in the first edition of this Norton Critical Edition.
1. Leslie Fiedler, "As Free as Any Cretur . . . ," *Mark Twain: A Collection of Critical Essays*, ed. Henry Nash Smith (Englewood Cliffs, N.J.: Prentice-Hall, 1963), pp. 130–39; F. R. Leavis, "Mark Twain's Neglected Classic: The Moral Astringency of *Pudd'nhead Wilson*," *Commentary* 21 (February 1956), 128–36. [Both essays are reprinted herein—*Editor*.]
2. See Thomas W. Ford, "The Miscegenation Theme in *Pudd'nhead Wilson*," *Mark Twain Journal* 10.1 (1955), 13–14; and Barbara A. Chellis, "Those Extraordinary Twins: Negroes and Whites," *American Quarterly* 21 (1969), 100–12.

later nineteenth century.[3] As a key to human behavior, environmental determinism has been brought forward to explain the fortunes of Roxana's two infant charges after she has exchanged their roles, placing her own Negro son into the white environment of the First Families of Virginia. A third theme, set forth persuasively by Edgar T. Schell, also focuses on the changeling motive but adds to it the succession of hidden or disguised identities in the story, arguing that the confusion between appearance and reality provides the central organization of the book. The resolution of the book, says Schell, occurs when Pudd'nhead Wilson discovers "the perspective from which appearance and reality are the same."[4] A fourth approach, emphasized in an important article by George Spangler, interprets the story as "a parable of property," showing how the actions principally of Tom, partially of Roxana, and peripherally of Wilson derive from their single-minded concern (or lack of it) for property. The thrust of this study centers on "the obsession with property as a vitiating and reductive influence on human beings."[5] A fifth approach, set forth by Eberhard Alsen, claims that the property theme reduces Wilson to "the foil to Tom," and therefore neglects the centrality of the title character—particularly the important effects on the story of his twenty-three year "fight for popularity and power."[6]

The variations in these thematic approaches and the very different data in the novel to which they address themselves illustrate the fundamental critical problem of the book. As with studies of many literary works, a number of studies of *Pudd'nhead Wilson* are true, in the sense of demonstrable, without being particularly satisfactory. Each one either omits important events or issues in the book or interprets them as servants to a thesis. At the same time, certain features are simply not taken seriously. The tendency is to treat the Italian twins, Luigi and Angelo, as vestigia from *Those Extraordinary Twins* or as examples of Twain's fascination with doubles;[7] to eliminate Wilson's palmistry and fingerprinting as cheap motifs from Victorian melodrama;[8] and to ignore all but a handful of entries from *Pudd'nhead*

---

3. See Leslie Fiedler, "As Free as Any Cretur"; also Henry Nash Smith, *Mark Twain: The Development of a Writer* (Cambridge, Mass.: Harvard University Press, 1962), pp. 171–84. [The Smith essay is reprinted herein—*Editor*.]

4. Edgar T. Schell, "'Pears' and 'Is' in *Pudd'nhead Wilson*," *Mark Twain Journal* 12.3 (Winter 1964–65), 14.

5. George M. Spangler, "*Pudd'nhead Wilson*: A Parable of Property," *American Literature* 42.1 (1970), 29. [Reprinted herein—*Editor*.]

6. Eberhard Alsen, "Pudd'nhead Wilson's Fight for Popularity and Power," *Western American Literature* 7.2 (1972), 135–43.

7. See George Feinstein, "Vestigia in *Pudd'nhead Wilson*," *Twainian* (May 1942), 1–3; and Robert Rowlette, "Mark Twain and Doubles," Chapter 4 of *Mark Twain's Pudd'nhead Wilson: The Development and Design* (Bowling Green, Ohio: Bowling Green University Popular Press, 1971), pp. 62–82.

8. See "Mark Twain and the Detective," Chapter 3 in Rowlette.

Wilson's Calendar which are easily recognized as satiric commentary on the story.[9]

Difficulties in almost every case would appear to derive from an almost exclusively thematic emphasis with the underlying assumption that Twain was attempting, through the medium of the novel, to say something, satirize something, or criticize something. These assumptions, often accurate in the context of realism where art so often spills over into social commentary, can easily lead to the kind of dismissal registered by Warner Berthoff, who finds no "significant art," a "crude and forced" compositional design, and a "profound archetypal symbolism—black and white, guilt and innocence" which "composes, in *Pudd'nhead Wilson*, no clear meaning."[1] The fact of the matter is, however, that the narrative movement of the book has been so consistently ignored, or limited to plot summary in the service of theme, that almost any intelligent commentary should open up new areas of understanding. What I propose to consider is the narrative movement of the book based on the notion that narrative action begins with, and consists of, a disruption of equilibrium and ends when some form of equilibrium has been restored.[2]

A cursory glance at the opening chapter of *Pudd'nhead Wilson* reveals an apparent equilibrium before the narrative action begins:

> Dawson's Landing was a slave-holding town, with a rich slave-worked grain and pork country back of it. The town was sleepy, and comfortable, and contented. It was fifty years old, and was growing slowly—very slowly, in fact, but still it was growing. (4)

One can hardly avoid the irony implicit in this summation after two pages devoted to the whitewashed houses hidden behind lush gardens, brick sidewalks, tree-lined streets, and the occasional outstretched cat—"symbol" says Twain of "contentment and peace."

9. This is not to overlook the valuable suggestions in Jim W. Miller, "'Pudd'nhead Wilson's Calendar'," *Mark Twain Journal* 13.3 (1967), 8–10; and useful remarks in more general studies such as James M. Cox, "*Pudd'nhead Wilson*: The End of Mark Twain's American Dream," *The South Atlantic Quarterly* 57 (1959), 351–63, and Stanley Brodwin, "Blackness and the Adamic Myth in Mark Twain's *Pudd'nhead Wilson*," *Texas Studies in Literature and Language* 15.1 (1973), 167–76. [The Brodwin essay is reprinted herein—*Editor*.]
1. Warner Berthoff, *The Ferment of Realism: American Literature, 1884–1919* (New York: The Free Press, 1965), p. 72. A useful study which nicely counters the realist dismissal is John C. Gerber, "*Pudd'nhead Wilson* as Fabulation," *Studies in American Humor* 2.1 (April 1975), 21–31. Gerber locates the major critical shortcoming as I have in the approach through theme: "Those critics who by their preoccupation with theme give the impression that *Pudd'nhead Wilson* is primarily a solemn examination of slavery, miscegenation, and/or determinism seem to me to have lost their sense of balance, if not their sense of humor" (p. 31, n. 19).
2. This approach to narrative action is based on suggestions in Sheldon Sacks, *Fiction and the Shape of Belief: A Study of Henry Fielding, With Glances at Swift, Johnson and Richardson* (Berkeley: University of California Press, 1964), and Robert Scholes and Robert Kellogg, *The Nature of Narrative* (New York: Oxford University Press, 1966), especially Chapter 6.

The irony rests in the fact, nowhere mentioned, that there is—there must be—a line of demarcation between slaveholders and slaves, presumably corresponding to the color line between white and black. Later we learn of a deeper irony: the blurring of this color line through a long history of miscegenation. Roxana, for instance, who looks white, is a slave because one-sixteenth of her blood is black. It is worth emphasizing that Roxana's diluted black blood is the result of four cases of miscegenation in four successive generations; her son's dilution to one thirty-second is the further result of her secret union with Colonel Cecil Burleigh Essex—the fifth successive occurrence. Yet nothing is disturbed. The regular crossing of the color line for the purpose of gratifying white lust is by now an established institution, completely integrated into the equilibrium of the community. Twain emphasizes this when he outlines the important citizens of the town: "Then there was Colonel Cecil Burleigh Essex, another F.F.V. of formidable calibre—however, with him we have no concern" (5).

Miscegenation, then, while often discussed as an important theme of *Pudd'nhead Wilson*, is simply a point of interest in the book; but it plays no part in the disruption of the equilibrium which starts the narrative action. At the same time, the history of miscegenation symbolizes the underlying tension persisting at Dawson's Landing—a tension, however, which has no resolution within the context of the quiet town. The duality of slaveholder and slave, "white" and "black," exists in a finely tuned balance. This situation points out the purpose of the narrative action: the introduction of some disruptive element into the town can, or may, unmask the tension by carrying it to a different arena such that the tension will be rooted out and perhaps resolved.

The disruption occurs with the arrival in Dawson's Landing of David Wilson with his "fatal remark." This occurrence may be regarded as mechanical or wooden, but could hardly be otherwise, given the completeness of the equilibrium into which he moves. His arrival, however, begins the narrative action by translating the rooted contradictions of the town into new terms. His remark—"I wish I owned half of that dog. . . . I would kill my half" (6)—not only isolates him from the community but reveals precisely what kind of tension Dawson's Landing *cannot* tolerate. Clearly there are profound differences among the citizens of the town, but the disinterested intellect is not a difference that the town can absorb. Both slaveholders and slaves reject him, label him a "pudd'nhead," turn him into an outsider, and banish him to the fringes of social life. The hiding of Pudd'nhead's intellect behind the mask of the fool, paradoxically, allows for his acceptance and partial integration into the life of the town. Meanwhile, unable to practice his legal profession, he remains an intellectual isolate for more than twenty years. His presence constitutes an instability which can only be corrected when Dawson's Landing finally assimilates into itself the qualities Wilson represents: intellect, in its purest sense; law, the practical application of intellect; and perhaps wisdom. I say "perhaps" because this side of Wilson, it turns out, is never successfully integrated into the community at the end. The fact that many entries in his *Calendar* have no apparent bearing on events of the story may function symbolically as an indication of a degree of wisdom quite beyond the comprehension of the town, at the beginning and later.[3]

Wilson's isolation in itself is not enough to create a major sequence of narrative events, partially because the town finds a way to absorb him through his "humble capacities of land-surveyor and expert accountant" (7). The result is that he appears initially to slip into an incidental position in the story. Nevertheless, the particular qualities which lead to his isolation create a kind of polar opposite in the person of Thomas Driscoll. Wilson's penetrating observation of life touches the spring that sets off this action. Roxana, of course, is extremely intelligent, but primarily in cases where she is forcibly confronted with a specific problem to be solved—and her solutions are often ingenious. But her intelligence is derivative rather than original, so that she is, by herself, incapable of a highly creative action such as the exchange of babies. It requires Wilson's perceptive remarks about the similarity between the babies and his suggestive question "How can you tell them apart, Roxy, when they haven't any clothes on?" (10) to initiate and ratify her thinking. Given the problem arising the next day—Percy Driscoll's threat to sell not only the thief of his household but *all* his slaves down the river, Roxana is able to turn Wilson's revealing question into her own private solution for the problem. Even so, she has to justify her actions with the communally accepted rationale of her Calvinist religion: "He [de Lord] s'lect out anybody dat suit Him, en put another one in his place, en make de fust one happy forever en leave t'other one to burn wid Satan" (16). By giving her own son the Driscoll name she launches him into the white world with everything that membership in it entails. The false Thomas Driscoll thus becomes the polar opposite for Pudd'nhead Wilson, precisely because his identity poses problems that no one else in Dawson's Landing has the intellectual prowess to solve. Like Wilson, Tom's true identity is masked; the revelation of his real identity by Wilson at the end of the book constitutes a double unmasking.

Thomas' secret identity creates a new tension in the community,

3. This suggestion seems more plausible to me than the assumption of artistic failure.

though not a tension that will manifest itself immediately. However, as he grows up, he develops a distinctive pattern of behavior which is traceable neither to his white environment nor to his Negro blood. Roxana argues once that "It's de nigger in you, dat's what it is" (75); but more likely the source of Tom's scorn for white values and his slippage into a series of crimes can be blamed on the situation created by an exchange of identities while Roxana, his real mother, continues her maternal care in the guise of a Driscoll slave. Any definitive explanation for his moral corruption is out of reach, of course, and Twain appears to have intended that it remain so. What does seem clear, however, is that Twain created in Tom a new variety of isolation—and a precise opposite of Wilson's. Thus Tom represents that disruption of community life that comes with persistent crime and outright lawlessness, exactly balancing the isolated power of law represented by Wilson. Moreover, Tom's progressive alienation turns his behavior into a combination of personal greed and untrammelled passion, the polar opposite of Wilson's methodical precision of mind. This dramatic polarity constitutes a transformation of the balanced equilibrium at the beginning of the novel—a transformation whereby the deeply masked contradictions of the society are now more explicitly expressed and therefore capable of being discovered and rooted out. The subsequent narrative action of the novel, revolving around these polarized varieties of isolation, can be seen as a movement toward a new equilibrium. George Spangler's notion of the novel as "a parable of property" applies specifically to Tom's criminal attempts to obtain Judge Driscoll's inheritance at all costs, thus bringing an end to his own isolation from the propertied white community. Similarly, Eberhard Alsen's perceptive account of Pudd'nhead Wilson's fight for popularity and power describes Wilson's attempts to end his own isolation and win communal acceptance for himself, specifically in terms of his professional and avocational skills, law and fingerprinting.

The real ironies of Dawson's Landing, intensified in these polar characters, are now clear. What is hidden behind the gardens and sunlit homes of the town is not so much a racial dichotomy, nor even a history of miscegenation: these are only symptoms. What Wilson's lonely vigil from his little house "on the extreme western verge of the town" reveals is that the community has no place for intelligence, wisdom, or procedural law.[4] What Tom's repeated crimes reveal is that the original harmony of the town rests on a fabric of fundamental lawlessness and passion. The fact of persistent miscegena-

4. A study that bears on this point, though obliquely, is John M. Brand's "The Incipient Wilderness: A Study of *Pudd'nhead Wilson," Western American Literature* 7.2 (1972), 125–34. [Reprinted herein—*Editor.*]

tion through generations—without a visible tremor—serves as fundamental evidence. That Judge Driscoll, the highest legal authority, abhors the idea of a courtroom trial and resorts to the aristocratic code of the duel reinforces it.

The ostensible harmony of the town thus turns out to be a mask obscuring fundamental inconsistencies and profound ironies. The novel unfolds as the discovery of what the community really *is*. The metaphorical action accompanying this discovery is the action of identity concealed and revealed. Who people are becomes the real key to discovering what the community is. As people hide their identity behind masks appearances take on the status of reality, leading to multiple levels of irony.[5] Roxana appears to be white but is really a slave according to the arbitrary definition of Dawson's Landing. Her son is likewise "black" but his whiteness allows for the substitution of appearance for reality—engineered by the exchange of babies. Thenceforward, Roxana, who is really the mother of Tom, assumes the *appearance* of a family slave (which, paradoxically, she *is*), while Tom confuses her appearance for reality. Twain is explicit about the effects of this confusion:

> Roxy was a doting fool of a mother. She was this toward her child—and she was also more than this: by the fiction created by herself, he was become her master; the necessity of recognizing this relation outwardly and of perfecting herself in the forms required to express the recognition, had moved her to such diligence and faithfulness in practicing these forms that this exercise soon concreted itself into habit; it became automatic and unconscious; then a natural result followed: deceptions intended solely for others gradually grew practically into self-deceptions as well; the mock reverence became real reverence, the mock obsequiousness real obsequiousness, the mock homage real homage; the little counterfeit rift of separation between imitation-slave and imitation-master widened and widened, and became an abyss, and a very real one. . . . in her worship of him she forgot who she was and what he had been. (20–21)

The description is emblematic of the novel as a whole, for it traces exactly the way in which the realities of life in Dawson's Landing have been hidden beneath multiple layerings of fictions, deceptions, counterfeitings, and imitations until these patterns have been legitimized as habit.

At the death of Percy Driscoll Roxana is set free. Years later, after

---

5. Edgar T. Schell, already cited, has worked out the notion of appearance and reality in strictly thematic terms without placing it in the context of the larger narrative action.

a bank failure in New Orleans which leaves her penniless, she returns to Dawson's Landing in order to obtain money from Tom—whose role is now that of former master. Tom is away in St. Louis, but Roxana learns of his gambling from Valet de Chambre, who is really white but appears to be a slave because of Roxana's exchange of sons. "Take it back, you mis'able imitation nigger dat I bore in sorrow en tribbilation" she shouts at him, her words containing levels of irony of which even she is unaware. The reply of her "son" is equally layered: "If I's imitation, what is you? Bofe of us is imitation *white*—dat's what we is—en pow'full good imitation, too" (39). The deepest irony, of course, is the unquestioned acceptance by Roxana and Valet de Chambre of the arbitrary logic according to which someone with Negro blood diluted to one thirty-second is still a "nigger" and thus only "imitation white."

When Tom returns Roxana humbly requests money from him; he refuses, and she threatens to tell Judge Driscoll "what I knows. I knows enough to bust dat will to flinders—en more, mind you, *more!*" (42). What she really knows is the secret of his identity; what she appears to know is the facts of his gambling. Begging Roxana not to require her young master to do the "horrible thing" of humiliating himself before her, Tom finally slumps to his knees and begs her not to expose him—an action which he feels has plummeted him to "the deepest deeps of degradation" (44). In reality, of course, the son has bowed before the mother, his single noble action in the book. The appearance of this act to him, however, is an index of the twisted masks worn by this apparently harmonious community.

From this point on the ironies of lost or hidden identity take on even more explicit form. In order to conceal his identity during his robberies in Dawson's Landing, Tom adopts the disguise of a Negro woman; later, when he attempts to rob Judge Driscoll, he blackens his face to look like a Negro slave. After Tom sells Roxana down the river she returns, disguised as a Negro tramp. These disguises represent a kind of masochistic wish fulfillment, as Roxana and her son assume the appearance of precisely what Dawson's Landing has arbitrarily defined them to be. Tom's robbery of the Judge in the guise of a Negro functions symbolically for the generalized robbery he has been engaged in for years while really a Negro disguised as a white. The fact that disguises which are identical to the underlying reality serve as the perfect way to *hide* one's identity is germane to the larger contradictions in the community where all of this takes place.

Pudd'nhead Wilson is then a labyrinth of lost identities or secret identities, appearances which look real, disguises which symbolize reality. David Wilson is given an identity on the day he arrives in the community; what he has been given serves thereafter as a disguise concealing his real shrewdness. Disguised as a fool, Wilson uses his spare time for more than twenty years developing a foolproof test for *identity*. Each glass slide containing the "physiological autograph" of someone in Dawson's Landing allows for the penetration of any disguise adopted by a citizen of the town. The sum total of Wilson's slides constitutes the infallible test for the identity of the town itself.

Pudd'nhead's unmasking of Tom is a case of truly multiple discoveries of identity in which Tom is simultaneously revealed as Negro, a false heir to the Driscoll estate, a thief, the real face behind the disguise of a girl, and a murderer. In the same moment, Wilson is unmasked and revealed for what he is, a brilliantly competent lawyer, a carefully observant scientist, and a capable leader for the community. Dawson's Landing, too, is unmasked, though—one must add— not reformed. The real Thomas Driscoll, now "rich and free," continues to be victimized by the masks he has worn, while the false Thomas is inventoried as part of the Driscoll estate and sold down the river. Indeed, the tragedy of the free slave and the blatant illogic of the final economic solution serve as indices of the real Dawson's Landing, quite unapparent in the idyllic scenery of the opening pages. The new equilibrium which occurs, even though it now includes the lawlessness of Tom brought under the control of Wilson's legal intellect, reveals the deeper ironies of a slaveholding civilization; for even the most powerful penetration of deception and the unveiling of truth make no lasting mark on this society.

We have then a double narrative action, which may be diagrammed by two intersecting curves. The widest distance at the center of their arcs suggests the point of complete communal disruption, caused by the masking within the community of Wilson's intellect and Tom's greed. At one end (the left), before the intersection occurs, we have the harmonious equilibrium of a town even though it is divided between slaveholders and slaves. At the other end (the right), we have the harmonious equilibrium of the town recovered—though now revealed for what it really is. Wilson's isolation is represented by the downward curve while Tom's career is represented by the upper. The upward curve diagrams Tom's entry into the white community after Roxana's exchange of babies; the downward curve projects Wilson's isolation from the white community to the periphery of the town and its life. The relative positions of these curves, with Tom's lawlessness soaring *above* Wilson's law, with greed quite out of reach of intellectual control, poses the dilemma of Dawson's Landing in dramatic terms, and suggests the kind of reversal of values that a new equilibrium will require. The reversal occurs in the final courtroom scene when Wilson, through the application of intellect and legal

reasoning, regains supremacy over the lawlessness and passion of Tom. Twain has simplified the issues, but for a gain rather than a loss of emphasis. As James M. Cox has put it, "the arbitrary neatness of the ending serves only to remind us that the problem has not been finally settled; the triumph of justice, the defeat of the criminal, the success of the long-suffering hero are thin masks which seem deliberately to reveal the larger doom, the deeper crime, the final failure to which we have been exposed."[6]

This kind of structural picture of the novel can help to put several things into focus—the proliferation of themes that critics have unfolded during the last twenty years, for instance. Certain themes, like the property theme or the emphasis on fingerprinting, are confined to one or another of the curves, touching the other only at the moment of intersection. Miscegenation is operative but primarily as a fact within the equilibrium of Dawson's Landing before the action begins and after it has ended; it does not in itself generate the action of the story—providing only the *possibility* for mistaken identity. The double curves, diagramming the careers of the two principal characters, serve to show the double genre of the book, which is partly comic and partly tragic.[7] At the same time, the machinery operating between these poles modifies both genres considerably. Thus, for instance, some of Wilson's demonstrations—his palmistry, and the elaborately staged and timed trial at the end of the book—tend to cast what is normally the curve of comedy into burlesque. Similarly, many aspects of Tom's career—the exchange of roles, the adoption

6. Cox, "*Pudd'nhead Wilson:* The End of Mark Twain's American Dream," 353.
7. That *Pudd'nhead Wilson* is comedy has been recognized by several critics, among them Henry Nash Smith, *Mark Twain, The Development of a Writer* (Cambridge, Mass.: Harvard Univ. Press, 1962), who sees the book as a comedy of manners; and James M. Cox, *Mark Twain: The Fate of Humor* (Princeton, N.J.: Princeton Univ. Press, 1966), who notes that "the hero's triumph over and entry into the society is in the comic rather than the tragic mode" (p. 228). A recent study which sees the book as both comedy and tragedy is Clark Griffith's "*Pudd'nhead Wilson* as Dark Comedy," *ELH* 43.2 (Summer 1976), 209–26.

of disguises, the elaborate playacting he performs as a girl before the spying Wilson, the use of a haunted house for laying plans, the selling of his mother, and above all his murder of Judge Driscoll with an elaborately carved dagger which is then dropped at the scene of the crime with bloody fingerprints—all of this redefines the usual tragic curve in terms of melodrama. No single theme dominates the structure; instead various serious themes are played off against one another in a tightly controlled structure of burlesque and melodrama. This is not to say that the book is perfectly realized; it is rather to point out that apparently incongruous themes and tones are unified within a double narrative action.

The mistake is, of course, to regard the novel in strictly thematic terms. From such a vantage point the farce and the melodrama, the use of fingerprinting and other devices from the popular detective story, seem ruinous to the serious intention of the book. An approach through narrative, however, reveals how the narrative action operates to dramatize what cannot otherwise be rooted out—the hidden lawlessness penetrating every facet of life at Dawson's Landing.[8] But, more important, a look at the unfolding narrative restores what seems to have been forgotten about *Pudd'nhead Wilson*: that the novel is also to be enjoyed. Symmetry and balance, tension and harmony, are always essential ingredients of esthetic pleasure. One cannot help thinking about the Italian twins, for instance, in esthetic terms; they remain in the mind long after one has set the book aside as a kind of analogy for the symmetry of the story. They reinforce and echo the other set of handsome look-alikes whose exchange sets up repeated doublings of identity; they tantalize us with the mystery of differences hidden between sameness of appearance which is so germane to the story. At the other extreme we have Pudd'nhead Wilson's "whimsical almanac . . . a calendar, with a little dab of ostensible philosophy, usually in ironical form, appended to each date" (27). Because the people of Dawson's Landing possess only a single, literal view of things, "irony was not for those people" (27); Wilson alone has the gift of double vision. The excerpts from his *Calendar* printed at the head of each chapter give a tonal reinforcement to the dramatic polarities of the story itself. They reinforce the more profound man which the community has masked as a fool. At the same time, if *Pudd'nhead Wilson's Calendar* seems to fly free of direct commentary on the situation, this is after all the irony of its author's isolated intellect.

A great deal is left out of any thematic interpretation of this novel,

---

8. The relevance of this approach through narrative action understood as disequilibrium is apparent in "The Man That Corrupted Hadleyburg" (1899), a work which is purely comic though more heavily ironic. Approximately the same thing happens: an initial equilibrium is disrupted by the incursion of an outsider who ultimately unmasks the hidden corruption of the town.

if only because a thematic approach searches for singleness of idea beneath variations in event. Esthetically, however, everything makes sense when seen within the context of the narrative action and symmetry of the novel. Here, indeed, form is wedded to content. At the same time, we need to recognize and admit that the mixture of motifs and genres in this book often verges on the bizarre. But critics often act as though the novelist who mixes too daring a brew ought to be punished by authoring a poor book which is soon forgotten. As Wilson puts it in his *Calendar*, "Few things are harder to put up with than the annoyance of a good example."

JOHN MATSON

The Text That Wrote Itself: Identifying the Automated Subject in *Pudd'nhead Wilson* and *Those Extraordinary Twins*†

. . . as the short tale grows into the long tale, the original intention (or motif) is apt to get abolished and find itself superseded by a quite different one. . . . Much the same thing happened with "Pudd'nhead Wilson." I had a sufficiently hard time with that tale, because it changed itself from a farce to a tragedy while I was going along with it,—a most embarrassing circumstance. But what was a great deal worse was, that it was not one story, but two stories tangled together. . . . I pulled one of the stories out by the roots, and left the other one—a kind of literary Cæsarian operation.
—*Pudd'nhead Wilson and Those Extraordinary Twins*, 125

I knew all about type-setting by practical experience, and held the settled and solidified opinion that a successful type-setting machine was an impossibility, for the reason that a machine cannot be made to think, and the thing that sets movable type must think or retire defeated. So, the performance I witnessed did most thoroughly amaze me. Here was a machine that was really setting type, and doing it with swiftness and accuracy, too. Moreover, it was distributing its case at the same time. The distribution was automatic; the machine fed itself from a galley of dead matter and without human help or suggestion, for it began its work of its own accord when type channels needed filling, and stopped of its own accord when they were full enough. The machine was almost a complete compositor. . . .
—quoted from Albert Bigelow Paine, *Mark Twain: A Biography* (904)

The notoriously confused, erratic quality marking Mark Twain's infamously troubled composition of *Pudd'nhead Wilson* has often

† This essay is being published for the first time in this Norton Critical Edition.

inspired critical association with the author's financially tragic investment in the Paige Compositor, a typesetting device designed not merely to replace, but, significantly, to simulate the labor of skilled human typesetters.[1] In 1892—the year Twain began work on the novel—the author accumulated an increasing debt in Paige's invention and had a demoralizing failure to raise capital from potential co-investors. By 1893, the year of the novel's completion and serial publication in the December edition of *Century,* his over-investment in the machine, coupled by that year's national financial panic and the impending bankruptcy of his publishing company, did indeed place the author in a considerable financial bind, making the economic, not to mention psychological, urgency of a quick and easy best-seller all the more pressing.

Yet Twain's unlucky financial investments in the Compositor tend to obfuscate the broader implications of the machine's considerable design goals. Little critical attention has been paid to the uncanny consonance between a machine constructed to "think" and compose "without human help or suggestion"—to indeed become a "complete compositor" designed to take the labor of typesetting out of human hands—and a "book" whose characters take the work of authorship "entirely into their own hands . . . working the whole tale as a private venture of their own" (126). And while Twain's claim that his novel wrote itself should not be taken quite literally, the provocative bravura with which he wields the assertion assumes a certain relevance that demands it not be ignored.[2] Nor for that matter should we sweep aside the author's tendency to humanize the Paige Compositor as mere characteristic Twainian hyperbole. Twain's investment in both *Pudd'nhead Wilson* and the Paige Compositor was not merely financial but symptomatic of the author's equally relevant investments in a model of self-governed writing machinery. Both text and machine deploy an image of what Twain himself called "automatic" authorship—a notion of the author as automaton that feeds back to inform a line of inquiry common to both the Paige machine and his notoriously "unreadable" novel of freak bodies and doubled identities: what constitutes the human?

For Twain this question carries duplicitous implications. To suggest that human authorship can be duplicated in both machine and text is, after all, to suggest an inherent challenge to the ostensibly vested singularity of the human itself. These are not surprising terms

---

1. The connection between the text's structural incoherencies and Twain's desperate financial situation has become a ubiquitous assumption in critical discussions of the novel. See for instance Cox, 7, Rowe, 147, and Sundquist, 146, in Gillman and Robinson (1990). For the text's compositional history see Berger (2005, pp. 189 ff. herein) and Parker and Binder (1978).
2. The veracity of Twain's account of the novel's composition has garnered mixed responses. See, for example, Robinson, 28, and Sundquist, 50, in Gillman and Robinson (1990).

from an author who repeatedly challenged his own singularity; whose own pseudonym famously signifies an authorial identity already split in "Twain." Nor should they seem surprising in works like *Pudd'nhead Wilson* and *Those Extraordinary Twins,* in which Twain's portrayal of the double subject reaches a kind of proliferate apotheosis. To the many theses advanced in the name of elucidating the author's preoccupation with duplicity I offer my own: Twain's investment in the doubled self stems from his fundamental ambiguity toward a notion of the human modeled on what, following Allucquère Roseanne Stone, I call the single-self-to-single-body paradigm of subjectivity—that classic notion of the rationally centered, liberal self a priori to the foundations of Western humanism and which found its undoing with the emergence of modern media.[3] Understanding the various emergence of the double in *Pudd'nhead Wilson* requires that we take an extended detour outside the text, through its medial margins, to investigate the means by which the author's coterminous involvement with writing machines—the Paige Compositor, as well as a variety of other composition technologies—work to pressure the "singular" paradigm of the self in ways that would eventually feed back to inform the technological subtext of Twain's difficult novel.

I say *difficult,* because even the relation between "singularity" and technology is a double-sided issue in the text. After all, Pudd'nhead Wilson's use of fingerprints marks the means through which new technologies of inscription can also serve a compensatory function, simultaneously mobilized to restore the singular ties between body and self threatened by automated machinery like the Paige Compositor. Registering both the disarticulation and re-articulation of the singular self in new media, *Pudd'nhead* emerges in part from a technologically specific crisis in the status of the human at the end of the nineteenth century.

Difficult as well, because so much is at stake in an ostensibly amusing text that shrouds its painfully serious portrait of race slavery beneath a disarmingly sensational display of freak bodies and melodrama. To locate the novel within its technological context is, however, not to shroud it from the power relations of race construction that have served as the basis for much of the recent and important critical discussion of the text.[4] Instead, it is to reconfigure the dynamic of these relations. Recent scholarship has shared the criti-

3. Also focusing on late-nineteenth-century new media, Stone (1995), locates a similar set of crises at the emergence of the telephone, 83–97.
4. I am referring here to the scholarly attention to the novel's involvement in late-nineteenth-century racial discourse, epitomized in the critical anthology edited by Gillman and Robinson (1990), a collection premised on the imperative to investigate what they—following Fredric Jameson—designate as the text's "political unconscious," vii.

cal task of reclaiming the relevance of *Pudd'nhead Wilson,* rescuing the text's troubled composition history from the calumnious "new critical" stigma of aesthetic failure to the status of telling social symptom. It is with the latter critical imperative that I locate my own reading. Yet by revisiting the "exigencies of composition" (Hershel Parker's term) I suggest that we can expand the terms of inquiry to include the technological and material backdrop against which such constructions reside. We can begin, in other words, to trace the interrelation between the text's "political unconscious" and its *medial* unconscious, the often latent means by which technologies of inscription feed back into the very representations of the human they are mobilized to produce. Though the body of this essay will concern itself more overtly with technology than with race, it is conjoined with the twin imperative to situate Twain's novel within the politics of racial difference specific to an era of increased technological standardization. In the end, Twain's articulation of the doubled, mediated self operates as a critique of the late-nineteenth-century imperative, epitomized in Pudd'nhead Wilson's use of fingerprints, to reassert the racial singularity of laboring hands—among them, Twain's own authorial hand—during a period that saw the diffusion of manual labor into the anonymous machinery of industrialization.

Pudd'nhead Wilson and Those Extraordinary Twins doubles and redoubles its critique of singularity with an exhaustive excess that defies easy summary. In its place I offer a necessarily cursory though nevertheless strategic account. There is, first of all, Roxy, the one-sixteenth black, though visually white, mulatto slave who, in the desperate hope of sparing her infant son the tragedy of a life condemned to slavery, exchanges the newly born Valet de Chambre (Chambers)—the (by blood, still "whiter") progeny of her affair with Cecil Burleigh Essex, a prominent white aristocrat—with Tom Driscoll, the newborn heir of her white master. Both white in skin and black by law, Roxy and Chambers undermine the specular oppositions on which racial difference depends, doubly occupying two racial identities in a single body—while the slave son Chambers, now "Master" Tom, compounds this dual occupation by literally assuming the social place and name meant for his would-be owner. This tragic lampoon of mixed racial and class identities is in turn doubled in the dual tales of the twins Angelo and Luigi, the aristocratic Italian outsiders who quickly assume a marked conspicuousness in the small, Southern antebellum town of Dawson's Landing that serves as the setting of Twain's novel. Ostensibly detached in *Pudd'nhead Wilson* (Twain's continuity on this point is shoddy) the brothers emerge in the attached tale of *Those Extraordinary Twins* as two distinctly disparate personalities congenitally conjoined to one body, "two heads and four arms" alternately distributing control of a single pair of legs.

The dramas of both the white "negroes" Roxy and Chambers and that of the Siamese twins Angelo and Luigi draw on the historical significance of "freak" sideshow displays, theatrical exhibits at which, throughout the nineteenth century, the spectacle of the abnormal subject was paraded and commodified as popular amusement. Both white and black, separate and conjoined, the visual power of the freak body stems from its troubling power to expose the unthinkable margins on which singularity depends. As many have explored, Twain's novel no doubt banks in part on the popularity of these shows, as well as their subtly subversive capacity to trouble normative conceptions of subjectivity.[5]

Yet the "freak" drama of doubling in the novel is not only fictional but significantly meta-fictional. In the intermediary textual link through which he joins the two tales of *Pudd'nhead Wilson* and *Those Extraordinary Twins,* Twain repeats the logic of duplicity operant within the text by extending the trope *externally* to incorporate the body of the text itself. The novel about freaks is itself a *textual* freak, a "little . . . six page tale," that writes itself into "not one story, but two stories tangled together," suggesting a homology between the dual-self-to-single-body model of subjectivity operating within the narrative and the dual tales "tangled" within the textual corpus. Relevant in this light as well is the coincidence tying the "freak" emergence of the conjoined twins Angelo and Luigi with the freak mutability attached to the writing of the novel itself. The "literary Cæsarian operation"—a metaphor that explicitly conflates body and text—by which Twain divides his conjoined tales into the distinct forms of "farce" and "tragedy" coincides with his division of the fictional bodies of the Siamese twins into "two separate men" (128).

Twain's play on doubling, in other words, indicates a consonance between the bodies articulated within fiction and the substantive infrastructures that make up the body of the text itself. It is a commonplace of media theory that any representation of the human body itself *depends* on a body—some material substratum on which such articulations are inscribed. Twain's novel performatively plays on the relays joining represented and textual body by suggesting that the two are in fact one. In *Pudd'nhead Wilson,* the designation of text as a human body is a reification that works both ways; each takes on the qualities of the other. The novel that takes authorship into its own "hands," also variously announces the hand as a "record," a

5. Gillman's work ([1989], 53–95, [1990], 86–104) explores the topic thoroughly. For a more general account of the cultural investment in the freak body in nineteenth-century America see Adams (2001) and Reiss (2001).

"book" to be read, "as if . . . covered with print" (54). Whether or not we choose to believe Twain's admittedly hyperbolic assertion that the novel literally wrote itself is largely beside the point here. More to the point is the text's self-conscious alliance between embodiment and media. Coinciding with its fictional drama of passing, dual identities, and freak bodies, the very corpus of Twain's novel indicates a vision of the "human" subject in which body and text are intimately intertwined like a pair of Siamese twins.

The "tangled" relations joining media and subject were not new ground for Twain. The author's own dual identity was after all more specifically a self first and foremost divided between Samuel Clemens and the printed page. Yet if Twain's novel underscores the interdependence between representations of the human and the texts that bear them, it is also informed by the author's firsthand familiarity with material changes in the writing technologies employed to produce these representations. Katherine Hayles has written of the series of "feedback loops" that join collective changes in the representation of bodies in literature, in the media that house these representations, and the construction of humans as they interface with new technologies within the composition process.[6] By 1890, Twain's own writing would reflect the "complex relations" between the contingencies of representation, text, author, and writing machine.[7] Only two years before his troubled composition of *Pudd'nhead Wilson and Those Extraordinary Twins,* Twain had developed a more self-conscious critique of authorial singularity that indicates the newly mediated scene of writing eventually to inform the latter novel, a notion of "automatic" authorship that anticipates both his self-writing text as well as the emergence of automated composition technologies that placed writing at a new remove from human "hands":

> I think it likely that the [authorial] training most in use is of the unconscious sort, and is guided and governed and made by-and-by unconsciously systematic, by an automatically-working taste—a taste which selects and rejects without you asking for any help, and patiently and steadily improves itself without troubling you to approve or applaud. (Reply to Editor of "The Art of Authorship," *Collected Tales,* 945)

6. I am drawing here on Hayles's (1999) remarkably apposite model of the reciprocity among subjectivity, informatics, and literature: "changes in bodies as they are represented within literary texts, have deep connections with changes in bodies as they are encoded within information media, and both types of changes stand in complex relation to changes in the construction of human bodies as they interface with information technologies," 29. Hayles's obvious focus here is the twentieth century, yet the model is equally applicable to Twain's investments in automation.
7. Hayles (1999), 29.

In her highly informed and deservedly influential study of Twain and duplicity, *Dark Twins,* Susan Gillman points out that Twain's investment in an "automatically-working" model of authorship reflects the author's ongoing interest in the psychical research of figures like William James who conducted some of the first "scientifically legitimate" investigations in the occult phenomena of "automatic writing," studies in which subjects were observed writing under states of cognitive distraction.[8] Within the context of psychical research, "automatic" and "unconscious" operate interchangeably to designate writing that appears from outside thought as the dictates of an authorial "Other"—a second self that, like the characters in *Pudd'nhead Wilson,* "selects and rejects" writing "without troubling you to approve or applaud."[9]

"Automatic" was, however, also commonly employed to designate writing done on machine. We need only recall Twain's above-quoted reaction to the Paige Compositor: "the distribution was *automatic;* the machine fed itself from a galley of dead matter . . . without human help or suggestion." While a full discussion of the weighty implications attached to the term *automatic* are beyond the scope of this investigation, a brief explanation will help clarify its specific relevance to Twain. To trace the mechanistic relevance of *automatic* is not to define the term in contradistinction to Twain's equally relevant investments in psychical research.[1] In his 1905 pseudo-philosophical treatise *What Is Man?*—the question makes explicit the implicit theme of *Pudd'nhead Wilson*—Twain in fact invokes both the technological and psychical meanings of *automatic* interchangeably, defining humans as "machines" that do not originate "ideas" but merely process them "unconsciously" and "automatically" the way a "goblin loom" processes fabric. When used in reference to humans, *automatic* designates dimensions of experience that are noncognitive, "blind" behavior—reflex actions, to take an easy example—that do not involve thought and thus appear to take place *outside* the self. With respect to machinery, *automatic* reciprocally implies action normally indicative of cognitive intention, activities typically associated with sentience and thus with a vested "self" to which they can be attributed. *Automatic* designates a crisis of singularity, dually describing both the mechanistic qualities of the human as well as the human qualities of machine; like its semantic cousin the *automaton,* the term demarcates the permeable borders distinguishing humans from their (writing) machines, people, and things.

---

8. Gillman (1989), 146–47.
9. Gillman (1994) expands on Twain's passive conception of his own authorial agency with passing reference to his "mind-as-machine thesis," 28.
1. Both Gitelman (1999), 185–218, and Kittler (1990), 206–28, discuss the "automatic" consonance between late-nineteenth-century psychophysics and technology.

Taking the "venture" of writing into its own "hands," *Pudd'nhead* marks the transfer of Twain's 1890 theory of "automatically-working" authorship into compositional practice. Because *automatic* implies a dual subject, at once human and machine, part subject, part object— and thus not wholly either—the term also returns us to the "freak" bodies that play such a central role both within and through the textual body of the novel. Telling also is the term's uncanny emergence within the text, designating Roxy's confused inability to distinguish between her son, Tom, the once slave object newly switched at birth to become "master" subject: "by the fiction created by herself, he was become her master . . . it became automatic and unconscious" (20). Roxy's "automatic" acceptance of her son as "master" mirrors the equally "automatic and unconscious" terms of the text's composition. Yet her son's own dual position as both owned (slave) object and propertied (master) subject designate the place where the terms of the subject/object ambiguities attached to automation and those of slavery coincide. The simultaneously white and "black" slaves that are both human and yet denied the ethical privilege of human rights, the twins that both are and are not separate, the book that both is and is not an author all share an underlying ambiguity toward the singularity of the human subject inherent to the design ideology of automation. Automation, in turn, brings us full circle to the Paige Compositor, that technological freak which threw the author into bankruptcy and made the hasty composition of the novel such an economic necessity. And while the discourses of race, freak, and automation may at first glance seem too separate to ever truly conjoin, it is worthwhile to note the telling terms employed by Twain's friend and biographer Albert Bigelow Paine, who variously referred to the Paige machine as a "gigantic vampire," a "remorseless Frankenstein Monster," and a laboring "human thing," echoing both the familiar terminology of nineteenth-century freak culture and the haunting paradoxes at the heart of the slave economy.[2]

Although Twain's interest in the Compositor was largely pecuniary, it wasn't entirely so. While critics generally consider Twain's assessment of the machine as a "complete compositor" a matter of the author's proclivity for overzealous boosterism, the collapse of the human/machine distinction often ascribed to the legacy of Paige's device emerges from a material base largely ignored in the machine's critical history. Justin Kaplan, for instance, argues that Twain's tendency to humanize the Paige machine was the mixed result of the author's high financial hopes for the automated Compositor and a "basic layman's ignorance, his credulity in the face of what seemed to him a divine mystery only because he knew hardly anything about

2. Paine (1912), 910.

mechanics."[3] What Kaplan indicts as Twain's so-called ignorance of mechanical design does little to account for the fact that even the machine's inventor, James Paige, repeatedly referred to the machine as an "organism."[4] On the contrary, Twain's tendency to humanize the machine was in fact largely attributable to his intimate knowledge of the Compositor's construction. From its inception, the machine was designed with the specific intent of simulating the functions of human typesetters. Far from being an anthropomorphic projection narrated as an aftereffect onto a strictly inhuman machine, the narrative of the "human" was in fact built into the machine's construction, deeply infiltrating its organization, the very nuts and bolts constituting its design philosophy. By understanding this design and its attached history, we can better understand the complex calculus through which the "thing" that "thinks" co-emerges in the dual guises of writing machine and self-writing novel.

To fully appreciate the technological implications of Paige's invention, it is necessary to review the requisites of the manual labor the machine was designed to replace. Practiced for more than four hundred years before the Paige Machine, hand typesetting involved the time-consuming and labor-intensive work of manually selecting individual metal letters, called "sorts," from a type case and setting them from left to right on a composing stick. After arranging lines of type, typesetters carefully spaced words for a straight (justified) right-hand margin, corrected this "live matter," and, after printing, returned used type (or "dead matter") one by one to their places in the typecase. From personal experience I can attest to the complexity of this process, of the necessary training involved in performing the difficult task of typesetting efficiently. Indeed, proficiency at what was commonly conceived as the "art" of typesetting involved years of labor-intensive apprenticeship.

As a former typesetter and apprentice to his older brother Orion and as a compositor in the Hannibal print shop while growing up in Missouri, Twain was ideally positioned to fully appreciate the technological stakes of mechanizing this ostensibly "human" process. A fully automated typesetter would require the mechanical capacity to perform the strictly human cognitive functions of reading and recognizing individual sorts; selecting them from a typecase; assembling sentences; and, moreover, distributing used sorts, or dead matter, back into their proper space after printing. In other words, a mechanical typesetter offered itself as an appropriately Twainian figure of the authorial double, able to perform the more rarefied human cognitive functions of reading and writing, not to mention

3. Kaplan (1966), 283.
4. Lee (1987), 59.

the propioceptive capacity to coordinate these cognitive functions with the physical identification and manipulation of individual pieces of type.

It was largely due to the requisite typesetting skills of reading and writing that the development of a mechanized typesetter inspired narratives of the mechanized human. Such narratives had in fact circulated within the cultural milieu of the printing trade well before the development of Paige's machine. Previous to the Paige design, mechanized composition had been a technological aspiration from as early as the late seventeenth century, when Johan Joachim Becher designed the first such machine in 1682. By 1900, over 1500 similar designs had been submitted to the U.S. patent office. Paige's invention in fact emerged at a time that saw something of a technological horse race developing among inventors and investors, placing hundreds of machines in competition to fill a perceived technological gap in the printing industry that, once satisfied, promised to make their owners overnight millionaires.

These alternate attempts to mechanize manual typesetting had been the source of various fantasies of automated cognition throughout the nineteenth century, when printing trade journals published poems and cartoons attesting to the centrality of the typesetting automaton as a social imaginary within the profession. In 1889 the professional periodical *Inland Printer* published a poem, appropriately titled "Exchange: The Typesetting Machine," which voiced the skepticism of a labor force under threat of becoming "exchanged" for intelligent machinery:

> But the summertime will come again
> And the winter's winds will blow
> Ere the thing of cranks and gearing
> take the place of pen and ink
> or supplants the toiling typo,
> with his power to work and think.[5]

In terms that directly echo Twain's description of the Paige Compositor, a typesetting machine that could "work" was inevitably a "thing" that threatened to "take the place" of the "power" to "think." Significant in this light as well is that the figure under threat of replacement here is not simply the compositor or "toiling typo," but the author who, trafficked in the manual technologies of "pen and ink," finds its replacement in "cranks and gearing." Images of the thinking "thing" were in fact not uncommon in the typesetting profession. In 1862 the British typesetting firm of Field and Tuer adorned their office with the cartoonish figure of a compositor robot, a cherubic automaton/freak with the head of a teapot, which stands

5. Huss (1973), 20.

reading copy text at a typecase while physically assorting individual sorts in a composing stick. The image would eventually circulate across the Atlantic, where it found publication during the 1880s in the same American printing periodical that published the above poem.[6]

It is plausible to speculate that Twain had an at least marginal familiarity with such images. Not only was the author himself experienced in the hands-on practice of composing type but he also maintained a regular dialogue with the profession throughout his adult life, both through his brother Orion—for some time an independent typesetter—and his honored attendance as a guest speaker at the Typothetae Convention, the leading national assembly of professional typesetters. Indeed, it was at a convention of this association that the author attempted to sell the Paige automaton to the very labor force the machine was designed to replace—a proposal that was (perhaps understandably) rejected by the convention's organizers.

Whether or not Twain had a direct familiarity with such alternate images of the automaton is however secondary to the common reification of the human they imply. Like Field and Tuer's reading-and-writing robot, the fantasy of the mechanized human was not exclusively a matter of imaging the machine in semi-anthropomorphic form. Rather, it was intrinsically tied to the higher cognitive activity of recognizing and processing the abstract significance of alphanumeric codes and coordinating these data with the physical orchestration of type. Visually reminiscent of a giant iron piano, weighing in at a monstrous two tons and consisting of over twenty thousand parts (filling the pages of what remains the largest patent in U.S. history), the Paige Machine in fact bore no familiar resemblance to "human" form at all, underscoring the construction of the human as primarily a set of cognitive capacities unrelated to anthropomorphic appearance. Just as the textual body of *Pudd'nhead Wilson* assumes the human status of author in physically alternate form, the Paige machine implied an abstraction of the human, conferring the status of "person" to a set of cognitive functions divorced from any recognizable bodily substrate. With no arms, no legs, and not even the valence of a head, what Twain hailed as a "complete compositor" pre-figures the book that could take composition into its own "hands," a freak spectacle of the mutable body that rivals even the most "extraordinary" of circus sideshows.

The abstraction and reification of the human as authorial/thinking machine operated as a design standard of technological attempts to simulate manual typesetting. Accordingly, the most impressive

6. Ibid.

attribute of the Paige Compositor was not merely that it solved the problem of the mechanized distribution of type but that it solved it according to a model that ostensibly reproduced "human" cognition in automated form. When it worked, the Compositor achieved this considerable design goal by identifying and arranging used sorts through a system of notches and grooves. Paige's patented notch-and-groove system operated as a set of internal coded relations that allowed the machine to autonomously recognize and distinguish individual letters without human direction. By mechanically coding language, the machine implicated an inherent doubling of the authorial functions of reading and writing. On the Paige Compositor the use of code effectively reproduced not merely the manual labor of human compositors but cognitive labor as well, allowing the machine to selectively *reread* the alphanumeric codes input by its operators by translating them into a separate mechanized language of notches and grooves. Simultaneously, a separate composing mechanism worked according to a similar logic, rereading then *rewriting* the coded input of human compositors then translating it back again into the familiar language of printed text. Moreover, in what stood as the largest obstacle to mechanized typesetting, the machine used the system of notches and grooves to recognize used sorts and redistribute them back into their proper place in the typecase when printing was complete. Twain's assertion that the machine had "more brains than all the printers in the world put together" was not merely a function of mechanical "ignorance." Nor did Twain's 1905 articulation in *What Is Man?* of the human mind itself as a "brain-machine" take place in a technological vacuum. Anticipating by over a half century the theoretical imperatives of informatics research, Paige's machine reproduced human cognition through a system of mechanic *recognition,* recognizing then reproducing "human" text through the inhuman form of machinic binary combinations of notches and grooves. While the printing industry mobilized the paradoxes of the "thinking thing" as a standard of difference to distinguish manual from mechanized labor, Paige's notch-and-groove system revealed the contingencies inherent in the whole notion of "thinking" itself as an essential site for locating the boundary between humans and things.

Despite the considerable complexity of Paige's invention, the mechanistic connotations of the term *automatic* were not exclusive to the Paige Compositor but to the full range of automated machinery with which Twain was both financially invested and psychically obsessed. The author of automated literature was himself the inventor of an automatic bed-maker, a self-adjusting vest strap, and a "pregummed" scrapbook, his only financially successful invention, whose patented "self-pasting" design (glue came already, i.e., *automatically,* applied) anticipates Twain's investment in the "Pudd'n-head" model of the automated book.[7] Most important, however, is Twain's self-designated status as "the first person in the world to apply the typing machine to literature" (apparently for *The Adventures of Tom Sawyer*).[8] Like the Paige Compositor, the typewriter added considerable connotative weight to the mechanistic dimension of Twain's interest in "automatically-working" authorship. Typewriters were in fact often designated "automatic writers," suggesting a semantic alliance between the "unconscious" functions of William James' psychical writing subject and the mechanical functions of Twain's early typewriting device.

And like the Paige device, the typewriter inspired narratives of the authorial automaton. In 1890, not four years before Twain published his self-authoring twin tales (the same year Twain published his editorial reply on "automatic" authorship), the "Strange Tale of a Typewriter" emerged on the pages of *Harper's New Monthly Magazine.* The singular tale is itself significantly two tales: author Anna C. Brackett's faux memoir of an "intelligent . . . sometimes even humorous . . . machine" as well as the tale the machine tells, or rather writes (while its owner is away)—the aptly named "Typewriter Fantasy" of an old woman with a penchant for the work of Balzac. It is however the terms through which Brackett describes her machine that are most telling. "The machine," remarks Brackett's narrator, "seemed to be learning to think."[9] While Mark Twain never granted his typewriter the rarefied status of thinking thing—though he did once voice his belief that his machine could "print faster than" he could "write" on it—the social imaginary at the heart of Brackett's "Strange Tale" was not lost on the "automatically-working" author.[1] Like the automatic "hands" that take over the writing of Twain's equally strange *Pudd'nhead Wilson and Those Extraordinary Twins,* Twain's new typewriter would introduce him to similar ambiguities, exposing the singularity of his own hand to the uneasy boundaries between author and writing machine.

For Twain the history of writing machinery coincides with "curious" transformations in the status of "person[s]." When the author purchased his first writing machine—a Remington Standard No. 1 typewriter—in 1874, both the device and "the person who owned

---

7. Fishkin (1996), 173.

8. Twain's first literary application of the typewriter remains unclear. In his *Autobiography* (itself typewritten from dictation recorded on a phonograph) Twain makes the claim for *Tom Sawyer,* while others have pointed to portions of *Life on the Mississippi.* His 1892 *The American Claimant* is also apparently among the earliest novels ever dictated to phonograph. See Twain (1996), 169, and Fishkin (1996), 174.

9. Brackett (1980), 7.

1. Quoted in Fishkin (1996), 175.

one" were "still a curiosity." By the time the author dictated (to a typewriting amanuensis) his 1904 monograph on the "First Writing-Machines," times—and bodies—had changed: "much has happened—to the type-machine as well as to the rest of us." For "now," notes Twain, "it is the other way around: the person who *doesn't* own one is a curiosity." According to Twain, within a space of thirty years—"a sort of lifetime"—the borders demarcating the normative self from the freak status of "curiosity" had reversed with the technological tide. While in 1875 the device was for Twain a "curiosity-breeding little joker," a "curiosity" that turned its owners into curiosities, by the time the author was "dictating autobiography to a type-writer" in 1904, the very term *typewriter* had long referred to both the machine and its operator.[2] Whether "curiosity" or "type-writer," however, both the machine and its users were inevitably joined in semantic union.

The consonance between what had indeed "happened" to both the "type-machine" (a title that itself suggests a mechanics of people-making) and the "rest of us" was largely a matter of interface. The seeds of change were already present when the author composed his first typewritten letter to friend and fellow auteur William Dean Howells:

> I DON'T KNOW WHETHER I AM GOING TO MAKE THIS TYPE-WRITING MACHINE GO OR NTO: THAT LAST WORD WAS INTENDED FOR N-NOT; BUT I GUESS I SHALL MAKE SOME SORT OF SUCCESS OF IT BEFORE I RUN IT VERY LONG. I AM SO THICK-FINGERED THAT I MISS THE KEYS. YOU NEEDN'T A SWER THIS; I AM ONLY PRACTICING TO GE THREE; ANOTHER SLIP-UP THERE; ONLY PRACTICING TO GET THE HANG OF THE THING. I NOTICE I MISS FIRE & GET IN A GOOD MANY UNNECESSARY LETTERS AND PUNCTUATION MARKS. I AM SIMPLY USING YOU FOR A TARGET TO BANG AT. BLAME MY CATS BUT THIS THING REQUIRES GENIUS IN ORDER TO WORK IT JUST RIGHT.[3]

On his new typewriter Twain, the former "toiling typo," re-encountered an authorial identity in the alienated form of typos—among the earliest composed on a mass-produced typewriter. The passage is indeed significant, if for no other reason than it marks perhaps the first encounter between the new machine and a high-profile author. Significant as well, however, for the way in which it implicitly registers so much of what's at stake in the self-writing, the composition of

2. Twain (1996), 166–67.
3. Quoted in Fishkin (1996), 174.

Pudd'nhead (marking the means by which the displacement of authorial agency on a typewriter—the question of whether the "machine"
will go or not) coincides with a crisis of singularity, the alienated
encounter with the self as both authoring subject and textual object:
"*I notice I* miss fire & get in a good many unnecessary letters and punctuation marks." The latter formulation is, after all, "curious" language
for an author famously invested in the split identity of authorship. On
his typewriter, Mark Twain is literally marked "twain," a doubled "I" in
the form of extraneous (punctuation) "marks."[4]

Still more significant, however, is what is missing from the passage. At the time of its introduction, the most conspicuous detail to
appear on the early typewritten page was the author's disappearance.
Broadly speaking, the emergence of the typewriter coincided with
the more general nineteenth-century diffusion of hand labor into the
abstract and anonymous logic of industrial standardization. Viewed
in contradistinction to its technological predecessor, the hand-held
pen, the anonymity of typewritten text—underscored above by the
fact that Twain's first machine wrote only in capitals—no longer
endowed texts with the auratic contours of a writer's authorial presence. Manuscript spoke to (and thus produced) the distinguishing
traits of a writer's singularity as well as social positionality, often
operating as a signifier of "personality," class, gender, and even, often
significantly, race. Indeed, within the cultural and racial context of
Reconstruction, typewriting took on a certain consonance with the
social practice of passing—subverting the specular economy on
which distinctions of identity were both produced and verified.
Racial distinctions of black and white became meaningless on the
black and white marks of the typewritten page.

Alienation at the typewriter was, however, not merely visual but
also significantly physiological. Twain's "thick-fingered" struggles at
the machine epitomize what according to Maurice Merleau-Ponty
reflects is a process of corporeal transformation at the interface
between the body and changes in its technological environment. For
Merleau-Ponty the ability to operate machines like the typewriter
depends on the internalization of a certain embodied identity—a
kind of unconscious familiarity between body and machine that ties

---

4. Twain's self-perceived split between the dual positions of authorial agent and alienated
textual other—both the "I" that writes and the "I" that is noticed on the typewritten page—
was largely a function of early typewriter design. Twain's first typewriter, a Remington
Standard No. 1, effectively hid text during the writing process. Unlike the open-faced
design of its more familiar descendants, on Twain's early Remington, typewritten text
emerged from the top of a platen cylinder well *after* being input on the keyboard. If the
typewriter functioned as a mirror, its design projected a rather delayed and difficult reflection. As Gitelman (1999) points out, writing on the early Remington was literally blind
writing, visually cut off from authorial eyes: writing went in, but what came out would
remain something of a mechanical mystery until well after composition, 205.

user and device into a seamless unity.[5] Trained typists, for instance, do not intellectually reflect on the placement of their hands on a keyboard but incorporate this knowledge within the hands themselves. Because knowledge of the typewriter is assimilated into the hands, resynthesizing how the body understands its environment, the relation between body and machine is not an external one of hand and tool but an internal one of prosthetic extension. Bound in a union between body and machine, the body attains a new corporeal identity; for the late-nineteenth-century author, the typewriter represented an extension of "new" hands.[6]

Twain was, of course, no typist when he purchased the early machine. But his "thick-fingered" alienation at the device speaks in negative terms to the contingent status of the body through the hands-on encounter with new writing technologies. By 1882, eight years after purchasing his first Remington, Twain would sum up the transformation of his authorial hand at the machine in a letter that ambiguously embraced the means of its own typewritten production:

> You see I am writing that way again. . . . I expect every-body to applaud me for making the change. As soon as you get used to the typewriter you will be insulted when people write you in any other way. . . . I am trying to forget how to write the old hand, because the new is so much prettier.[7]

As if attempting to preempt the typewriter's preemptive monopoly over the typewritten page, Twain's first words in the passage announce what his typefaces have already revealed *despite* him, "You see I am writing that way again." Twain's compulsion to point out the obvious reveals his compensatory insistence that what his readers "see" be accompanied by a reassertion of authorial sovereignty: "*I* am writing" insists Twain, even if all you "see" is typescript and not my "old hand." Yet the very assertion discloses what is at stake on the typewriter—the loss of a self consumed by the technocratic anonymity of typescript. The specter of anonymity—the consumption and loss of the self in machine—is in fact precisely what the letter both registers and represses. Hence Twain's imaginary construction of his readership as an audience that will "applaud" him for "making the change" to the typewriter counters the impersonality of typewritten correspondence with the *in-person*ality of public performance. Indeed, it is out of the repressed need to restore

5. Merleau-Ponty (1962), 144.
6. The intersection between inscription and embodiment epitomizes what Hayles (1999), also drawing in part on Merleau-Ponty, has called "Inscribing Practices" and "Incorporating Practices"—a series of "feedback loops" between changes in representations of the body and changes in the embodied interface with new technologies, 199.
7. Quoted in Fishkin (1996), 176.

the self-lost-at-machine that Twain significantly marks the entrance of the typewriter with the re-entrance of displaced hands in covert form. For while Twain's own "hand" is newly hidden in typescript, the very displacement of hands into the typewriter finds a comforting legitimacy in the applause of a reading audience metonymically reduced to a collective of clapping hands. These are significant terms for an author equally renowned in his own time for his talents as a public speaker as he was as a writer—particularly one who once complained that the voice loses its "soul" when transcribed to print.[8] For Twain, anxieties over the death of the author in typescript find their answer in the reification of the typewritten page as a spectacle of liveness—an epistemologically stable space in which Twain can be seen and verified as himself.

Yet the epistemological ambiguities of what is *seen* on the typewritten page reveal a deeper ontological ambiguity over the status of the "I" that writes. "I am," Twain declares with reiterative insistence—not once but twice in the passage. But what that "I" has now become is something quite different. For the "I" who struggled to recover an authorial identity in his "struggle" to make his typewriter "go" eight years earlier is now in fact "trying" to "forget" the "old hand" for the "new." In a journal entry, Twain would in fact use his "own hand" to reverse the logic of alienation instanced in his first typewritten letter. The "T.[ype] W.[riter]," notes Twain, "soon suits one's eye and understanding better than one's own hand."[9] It is no longer the typewritten but rather one's "own hand" that obfuscates the visual link between author and text. Yet it is Twain's 1882 letter that extends the identification of self-as-machine by collapsing any difference at all, turning his "own hand" into the "new" hand of his typewriter. What begins as the need to reassert the self from behind the veil of typescript soon transforms into the powerful assertion that author and machine are in fact one. The dual connotations of "hand" announce the reification of self on the two levels outlined above, that of epistemology—manuscript now appears in the preferred, "prettier" form of typescript—as well as ontology—the typewriter has been internalized as a prosthetic extension of "new" hands.

Pudd'nhead Wilson emerges from these (re)negotiations of the self in "new" media. While Twain's freak assimilation of the typewriter as the "prettier" "new" hand to replace the "old hand" of manuscript suggests the mutable relations between self and body at the interface with new technologies, the Paige Compositor abstracted the cognitive "self" out of the body altogether, reifying the status of author in

8. Twain (1982), 190.
9. Notebooks (1935), III. 639.

physically alien form. Together both machines figured a crisis of the singular relation tying body and self that finds expression in the equally variable bodies that make up both the fictional world and "tangled" textual corpus of Twain's novel.

Composed largely on an automatic writer, Twain's "automatically-working" text bears the traces of the competition between the "old hand" of manuscript and "new" media. In February 1893 Twain wrote friend and editor Fred J. Hall to report his novel "type-writered and ready for print." Another version was sent to Hall the following month, a muddled combination of manuscript with pages of "Puddn" sent to "typewriter." The transfer of *Pudd'nhead* from his own hand to the typewriter was in turn further remediated through publication, at the hands of "some imported proof-reader" whose "ignorant impudence" of the author's "punctuation" "left" its "tracks" in Twain's text.[1] Twain's complaints over the largely out-of-hand composition of his text give new meaning to the claim, voiced in the characteristically oblique terms of Pudd'nhead Wilson's Calendar, that reading the "manuscript" of an author's "forthcoming book" will carry "you clear into his heart" (52). The words significantly preface the chapter in which Wilson introduces his occult investments in palmistry, an art that the Italian twins compare to having their "palms read as if they were covered with print" (54). Fitting in this light as well is Tom Driscoll's above-mentioned take on Wilson's fingerprints, their ability to unite hand and script by making the "wrinkles" on a fingertip as "easy" to "read . . . as a book" (54).

Supplying the missing evidence to the mystery plot of the tale that bears his name, Pudd'nhead Wilson's rather anachronistic collection of fingerprint samples (the technology was an invention of the 1890s, not the antebellum South) inventory the entire population of Dawson's Landing—including the pre-exchanged infant identities of Tom Driscoll and the legally "black" slave Chambers. Having grown into a decidedly villainous young adult under the assumed identity of his actual master, Tom is dually discovered after leaving his prints on the knife (stolen from the Italian twins) he uses to kill his putative uncle, Judge Driscoll, in the process of robbing the aging judge to pay off gambling debts. Part-time lawyer, part-time exile, Wilson's Sherlock Holmesian introduction of fingerprint technology to expose the "ostensible" Tom as the "actual" "black" slave Chambers and murderer of Judge Driscoll reveals the technological means through which the law produces the very terms of the singular subject it is presumed to police. In providing the missing link to the novel's sensational murder plot and subsequent courtroom drama, the fingerprints present an impressive technological spectacle that

---

1. See pp. 191–92 of the present edition.

detracts attention from their practical employment in reinstating relations of class and racial difference.

It is in fact along these lines that critics have discussed Twain's use of fingerprints in the novel. Remaining, however, is the critical task of tracing the ways in which Twain's novel deploys fingerprint technology as a particular variety of compositional medium—literally a kind of "handwriting"—one that assumes specific relevance when considered in relation to the other media that inform the broader context of its use. This is not to imply a priority to handwriting as a more authentic or "essential" mode of inscription. On the contrary, it is to underscore the historically specific identity of the medium, one prone to reconstruction when variously displaced, resituated, or altered by the emergence of new technologies of composition. Read within its broader medial context, the "manuscript" technology of fingerprint inscription marks a nostalgic return to the presumed epistemological certainties of handwriting in an age that saw the increased distribution of human hands across the automated limbs of late-nineteenth-century writing machinery.

In the courtroom drama with which Twain closes the novel, Wilson in fact touts the virtues of his new technology in terms that rely specifically on the "old hand" technology of manuscript, the very medium Twain had replaced in the freak "new hand" of his "typewriting machine." The "marks" of one's fingerprint, argues Wilson, "are his *signature,* his *physiological autograph,* so to speak, and this autograph cannot be counterfeited, nor can he disguise it or hide it away, nor can it become illegible by the wear and mutations of time" (114). Against the specter of "mutations"—not simply those of "time" but implicitly those mutant bodies that haunt the new age of late-nineteenth-century writing technology and the tangled tales of Twain's novel—fingerprints offer Wilson the presumed power to "unerringly identify" any "person" from a "multitude of his fellow creatures" with the same certainty that a "bank cashier knows the autograph of his oldest customer" (116). And while Wilson's alliance between fingerprint and "autograph" underscores the specifically manuscript identity of his technology, that the lawyer illustrates the reliability of fingerprints *through* the terms of an "autograph" establishes manuscript not merely as the technological equivalent to the new medium but, more powerfully, as the technological standard against which the epistemological veracity of fingerprints are in fact measured.

Like Wilson's "physiological signature," the prefatory "Whisper to the Reader" with which Twain opens *Pudd'nhead Wilson* ostensibly consolidates the alliance among fingerprint, manuscript, and the law. "Given" as the author significantly puts it "under" his own "hand," Twain's preface on the authenticity of the novel's courtroom chapters, "written under the eyes" of a "legal expert," anticipates "legal expert" Pudd'nhead Wilson's courtroom presentation of fingerprints as a "sure identifier" of "hands" (1–2, 115). It is however the first line of the preface that most significantly establishes the link between media and legitimate legality: "A person who is ignorant of legal matters," writes Twain, requires the consultation of a "trained barrister" before attempting to "photograph a court scene with his pen" (1). Twain's realist metaphor of the photographic "pen" at once anticipates and complicates Wilson's use of fingerprints, locating the technology's more specifically dual status within the context of late-nineteenth-century media. As we have seen, like the "pen," Wilson's "autograph" metaphor situates his use of fingerprints as a form of manuscript technology. Like the photograph, however, fingerprints also maintain much of their vested fidelity from their status as a physical inscription of the real: the photograph and fingerprint not only bear a likeness to the object they represent but also authenticate this likeness through their status as the *products* of the object.[2] Just as the camera inscribes the light reflected from an object onto a photographic plate, the fingerprints in the novel inscribe the unique "physiological . . . lines and corrugations" of the hand onto the surface with Wilson's "pantograph" (114, 117). Both photograph and pen, the fingerprint represented handwriting updated to an age of new media, gaining much of its legitimacy from its hybrid conflation of the "old hand" media of manuscript and the more modern forms of nineteenth-century graphic technology. More important, as the immediate product of the bodily real, the fingerprint promised to restore the singular correspondence tying body and self newly challenged through the morphologically disproportionate—that is, "freak"—"new hands" of late-nineteenth-century writing machines like the typewriter and Paige Compositor.

Yet if it is the fingerprint's status as photographic pen that ultimately verifies Wilson's faith in the one-to-one ratio binding self and body, it is, as we have already seen, the very variety of "hands" that take over the composition of the novel which simultaneously troubles the singular identity of the inscriptive hand. That the novel writes itself into two "congenitally joined" bodies undermines the very single-self-to-single-body relation that Wilson's fingerprints are presumed to confirm. Moreover, Twain's "Final Remarks" on the novel confer the schizophrenic mechanics of authorship upon Wilson himself. "Brought in," the author tells us, "to help work the machinery" of the text, the fingerprinting hero is ironically located

2. My description here follows Friedrich Kittler's (1999) characterization of the photographic real, 11. We can also add to this list the phonograph, which Twain had dictated to while suffering from rheumatism. Like the photograph and fingerprint, the grooves on a phonograph were the product of soundwave variations inscribed on a wax surface.

by Twain as one of the text's fictional, we might say "automatically-working," authorial doubles (126, 184–85).

Consider as well Twain's remarkable 1894 letter, in which the lawyer bears an uncanny resemblance to a "human thing" of "cranks and gearing": "I have never thought of Pudd'nhead as a *character*, but only as a piece of machinery, a button or a crank or a lever, with a useful function to play in a machine, but with no dignity above that" (emphasis Twain's).[3] Twain's displacement of Wilson's "character" in the "machinery" of "button," "crank" and "lever"—technologies that paradoxically *remove* laboring hands further from production in the very process of connecting them to it—stands in ironic contraposition to the ostensibly heroic figure who claims to locate "character" on the "insides of the hands" (114). Yet it is, of course, not only Wilson but Twain's text that bears the signature of mechanization here. Wilson is merely a "piece of machinery . . . *in* a machine"—brought in to work the "machinery of the text." For Twain the novel that composes itself with its own "hands"—both text and human body—is also a literal writing "machine." Nor should Wilson's faith in the fingerprint as "signature" and "natal autograph" be confused with Twain's investments in the singular "character" of his own authorial hand. In his above-mentioned 1906 autobiographical reflection on the "First Writing Machines," Twain recalls an "enterprising" young autograph collector who, not content with "mere signatures . . . wanted a whole autograph letter," which the author in turn "furnished . . . in type-machine capitals, *signature and all*."[4]

Telling also is the deceptive language of Twain's prefatory "Whisper to the Reader." For the preface ostensibly attesting to the text's legal authenticity is in fact a mock parody of realism penned through the duplicitous depiction of Twain's own "hand" (2). Proclaiming the veracity of the novel's concluding court chapters "right . . . in every detail, for they were written under the eye of" the legal expert "William Hicks," Twain's "whisper" abruptly detours through a nonsensically labyrinthine description of the Florence villa in which he composed the novel, only to return several lines later to barrister Hicks who, Twain informs us, "was a little rusty on his law." Written "under the eye" of a "rusty" lawyer, Twain's preface both asserts and undermines the equation between hand, visual evidence, and the law. "Given under" his "hand," the rhetorical wink and nod that accompanies Twain's equivocal remarks on the "legal" validity of the courtroom scenes in the novel also anticipate and ironize Pudd'nhead Wilson's faith in the hand as a site for verifying the singular bonds between self and body.

3. This letter is quoted in Bradbury's (1969) introduction to the Penguin edition of the novel, 20.
4. Twain (1996), 169.

Wilson's investment in fingerprints epitomizes what Avital Ronell has called the "scientific imperative, the demand in the late-19th century for an epistemologically reliable inquiry into the nature of things." For Ronell, this imperative "derives part of its strength from the powerful competition represented by the freak . . . which is always on the way to technology"—a category that includes both the "automaton" and "writing machine."[5] The "freak" is "always on the way to technology" because both have the potential to place the singular identity of the self into question. "Automatic" writing technologies like the Paige Compositor and the typewriter challenge the distinction between people and machines, conferring the status of "human" on things while dually reifying authorship in technological terms. Writing themselves into a freak body, the combined texts of *Pudd'nhead Wilson* and *Those Extraordinary Twins* are located at the nexus where the freak and "automatic" technology coincide.

At the same time, Twain's novel also traces what Ronell calls the "scientific imperative" to retrieve the very singular paradigm of the human body that the body of the text itself—like the Compositor, a "human thing"—dually subverts. Joining the unique epidermal contours of the hand to the printed page, Wilson's fingerprints promised to restore the singularity of the writing body that appeared to have been challenged by new media. As itself a hybrid form of manuscript and photograph, however, the irony of the fingerprint lay in its own status as technology: in its apparent ability to generate media as the *product of the body* it also reversely maintained the body as *the product of media*. The irony of the fingerprints in *Pudd'nhead Wilson* is that, like the fictional "hands" that assume authorship of the novel, they merely repeat the reification of the hand as the product of the (finger) printed page. Conflating the positions of text, writing machine, and human body, Twain's novel testifies to the inevitable bonds that congenitally join the self to the technologies of inscription through which it is articulated.

Itself the direct product of late-nineteenth-century media, Twain's antebellum narrative of the slave-holding South is more appropriately situated as a cultural symptom of the race relations specific to an industrialized Reconstruction North. The era that saw an unprecedented northern migration of newly liberated ex-slaves to the region's emergent urban industrial centers also saw the coincident diffusion and abstraction of manual labor into the racially indistinct "cranks and gearing" of new machinery. This coincidence resulted in a contradictory double movement: as the racial makeup of the labor force in the North became increasingly diverse, the singular status of laboring hands—and the racial distinctions among

5. Ronell (1989), 367, 370, 372.

them—became increasingly indistinct. And while the factory floors that housed this labor force became perhaps more segregated than ever before, the homogenization of the laboring hand in machine threatened to pressure the very racial distinctions on which the emergent Reconstruction ideology of "separate but equal" depended.[6]

It is this immanent collapse of racial difference in technology that serves as the background against which the crisis of the single-self-to-single-body paradigm of subjectivity emerges in Twain's novel. As critics have pointed out, historically fingerprints served a eugenic function, reasserting the racial identity of the hand under the dubious guise of scientific legitimacy.[7] Registering both the nostalgic impulse to restore a singular, racially distinct self "previous" to media and the representation of multiple selves produced *through* media, Twain's novel ironizes the former imperative to underscore the latter. Twain's self-writing textual automaton replaces a singular subject with a *medial subject,* a notion of embodied identity as the mutable product of mediation. As medial subject, *Pudd'nhead Wilson* and *Those Extraordinary Twins* elicit the all-important ethical question, "What constitutes the human?" But the texts also suggest an answer to this question, raising their own "hands" in reply. In so doing, Twain's novel of doubles doubles as a critique of racial difference apropos to an age of automated technology—an age in which the reality of the human hand had become increasingly up for grabs.

Works Cited and/or Consulted

Adams, Rachel. *Sideshow U.S.A.: Freaks and the American Cultural Imagination.* Chicago: University of Chicago Press, 2001.

Berger, Sidney. "Preface." See below: Mark Twain, *Pudd'nhead Wilson and Those Extraordinary Twins* (1980).

Brackett, Anna C. "The Strange Tale of a Typewriter." *Harper's New Monthly Magazine* 81 (1890): 679–82.

Chinn, Sarah E. *Technology and the Logic of American Racism: A Cultural History of the Body as Evidence.* London and New York: Continuum, 2000.

Fishkin, Shelley Fisher. *Lighting Out for the Territory: Reflections on Mark Twain and American Culture.* New York and Oxford: Oxford University Press, 1996.

Gillman, Susan Kay. *Dark Twins: Imposture and Identity in Mark Twain's America.* Chicago: University of Chicago Press, 1989.

———. "The Writer's Secret Life: Twain and the Art of Authorship."

6. Sundquist's essay "Mark Twain and Homer Plessy" deals extensively with the relation between *Pudd'nhead Wilson* and segregation (Gillman and Robinson, 1990, 46–72).
7. See Chinn's, 2000, well-researched work on fingerprints as a "technology of race" (25–52), and Rogin's study of Francis Galton and Mark Twain (Gillman and Robinson, 1990, 73–85).

In *Mark Twain: A Collection of Critical Essays*. Ed. Eric Sundquist. Englewood Cliffs, N.J.: Prentice Hall, 1994.

———, and Forrest G. Robinson, eds. *Mark Twain's Pudd'nhead Wilson: Race, Conflict, and Culture*. Durham, N.C.: Duke University Press, 1990.

Gitelman, Lisa. *Scripts, Grooves, and Writing Machines: Representing Technology in the Edison Era*. Stanford, Calif.: Stanford University Press, 1999.

Hayles, N. Katherine. *How We Became Posthuman: Virtual Bodies in Cybernetics, Literature, and Informatics*. Chicago: University of Chicago Press, 1999.

Huss, Richard E., and University of Virginia Bibliographical Society. *The Development of Mechanical Typesetting Methods, 1822–1925*. Charlottesville: University Press of Virginia, 1973.

Kaplan, Justin. *Mr. Clemens and Mark Twain: A Biography*. New York: Simon & Schuster, 1966.

Kittler, Friedrich A. *Discourse Networks, 1800/1900*. Stanford, Calif.: Stanford University Press, 1990.

———. *Gramophone, Film, Typewriter. Writing Science*. Stanford, Calif.: Stanford University Press, 1999.

Lee, J. Y. "Anatomy of a Fascinating Failure." *American Heritage of Invention and Technology* (Summer 1987): 55–60.

Merleau-Ponty, Maurice. *Phenomenology of Perception*. London and New York: Routledge & Kegan Paul, Humanities Press, 1962.

Paine, Albert Bigelow. *Mark Twain: A Biography: The Personal and Literary Life of Samuel Langhorne Clemens*. New York: Harper & Brothers, 1912.

Parker, Hershel, and Henry Binder. "Exigencies of Composition and Publication: Billy Budd, Sailor and Pudd'nhead Wilson." *Nineteenth Century Fiction* 33.1 (1978): 131–43.

Reiss, Benjamin. *The Showman and the Slave: Race, Death, and Memory in Barnum's America*. Cambridge, Mass., and London: Harvard University Press, 2001.

Ronell, Avital. *The Telephone Book: Technology—Schizophrenia—Electric Speech*. Lincoln: University of Nebraska Press, 1989.

Stone, Allucquère Rosanne. *The War of Desire and Technology at the Close of the Mechanical Age*. Cambridge, Mass.: MIT Press, 1995.

Twain, Mark. *Collected Stories, Sketches, Speeches & Essays*. New York: The Library of America, distributed by Viking Press, 1992.

———. *Mark Twain's Notebooks*. 1st ed. Ed. Albert Bigelow Paine. New York: Harper & Brothers, 1935.

———. *Pudd'nhead Wilson and Those Extraordinary Twins*. Ed. Malcolm Bradbury. New York: Penguin Books, 1969.

———. *Pudd'nhead Wilson and Those Extraordinary Twins*. 2nd ed. Ed. Sidney E. Berger. New York: Norton, 2005.

———. *Selected Letters of Mark Twain*. New York: Harper & Row, 1982.

————, ed. *The $30,000 Bequest and Other Stories*. New York: Oxford University Press, 1996.
————. *What Is Man?* New York: Oxford University Press, 1996.

ANDREW JAY HOFFMAN

Pudd'nhead Wilson and the Roots of Existential Heroism†

Mark Twain's novels have power not only because they capture life in funny and beautiful prose, but also because they embody a deep conflict in the way he saw the world, and the way we still do. That conflict appears most definitively in Mark Twain's heroes. Twain created his heroes by imbuing everyday people with mythical, supernatural powers, always without disturbing the surface normalcy of their characters. Huckleberry Finn, for example, never seems to be anything but a poorly educated white boy from a broken home, on the lam from his violent father and the constraints of the civilized world. And yet, at the same time, he begins the book that bears his name by appearing to be reborn. He survives one life-threatening experience after another, frequently by assuming an alternate identity. In the study of mythical character, Huck is called a shapeshifter, the same essential person who appears in multiple forms.

This magical quality contrasts with the hard realism of the world in which Huck operates. Twain has gone out of his way to portray the Mississippi Valley with stunning historical accuracy. Feuding small towns, con-men, good-hearted racists, and wild riverboat men populate *Adventures of Huckleberry Finn* as they populated the world in which Sam Clemens grew up. Importantly, Twain depicts the ideology of slavery with cold precision. For him—and for everyone living in the culture—slaveholding became a hermetic system of thought that denied the humanity of people with even a fraction of African blood. Even as free a spirit as Huck Finn has tremendous difficulty thinking outside the system. The final conflict of the novel, in which Huck and Tom Sawyer go to elaborate lengths to free Jim, who Tom knows has already received his freedom, deflates the one moment of transcendent clarity Huck achieves. Huck's mythical powers to alter his identity can do nothing to alter the historical reality in which those identities live.

The same pattern of failed heroism dominates *A Connecticut Yankee in King Arthur's Court*. Hank Morgan not only travels through

† This essay is being published for the first time in this Norton Critical Edition.

time but also has knowledge well beyond the capacity of anyone else in Arthurian England. His introduction of modern concepts and inventions into a medieval world earns him the title of wizard. In the end, though, Morgan's magical powers cannot overcome the historically accurate religious superstitions of the world in which he performs his magic. His remarkable and mythic identity cannot hold back the tide of history, which overwhelms not only him, but also everything he has created.

Time and again in Twain's work, his magical characters run headlong into historical reality, which stops them dead. Twain works and reworks this borderland between story and history, between mythical heroism and historical determinism. He seems desperately to want his mythological creations to win. As readers, we would much prefer Huck and Hank to emerge from their experiences having achieved something, but in fact each leaves behind almost no evidence of Mark Twain's existence in his historically defined world. If people endowed with supernatural powers cannot alter the course of history, Twain's works imply, then what possibility remains for everyday people? This structural discordance, between mythically heroic characters and historically conceived realities, forces Twain to concede defeat for his heroes.

In *Pudd'nhead Wilson*, Mark Twain revisits this same pattern. In this case, David Wilson is the supernatural hero, and the world is Dawson's Landing. But Twain has made some adjustments to his schema, and enjoys some variations in the resulting narrative. Instead of imbuing his hero with transparently magical qualities, such as Huck's shape-shifting or Hank's wizardry, he gives David Wilson extraordinary intelligence and patience, leaving the sense of his supernatural qualities to the observations made of him by the novel's other characters. And the expansive worlds Mark Twain delineated in *Huckleberry Finn* and *Connecticut Yankee* have become the much more narrowly circumscribed Dawson's Landing. Twain still defines his place by its place in history, but now hamstrings its historical sweep through isolation.

The invocation of myth raised Mark Twain's novels above either remembrances of small-town life, as in *Tom Sawyer* and *Huck Finn*, or simple fable, as in *Connecticut Yankee* and *Joan of Arc*. *Pudd'nhead Wilson* fits into that latter category and—perhaps more than any other novel Twain wrote—it adheres to the rules that dominate fabulation. Twain constructs *Pudd'nhead Wilson* so that a talented interloper confronts the established patriarchy and assumes the mantle of power. Were this book built like most fables, which thrive on a clear definition of good and evil, David Wilson would overthrow not only the rulers but also the ruling system, replacing the corruption he found when he arrived in Dawson's Landing with a new and enlightened leadership. Here, though, when Wilson takes over the reins as mayor of Dawson's Landing, he does not change the direction in which the one-horse town moves. Twain circumscribes Wilson's heroism so tightly, as he does with the town itself, that he achieves only a redefinition of himself within the town, not a redefinition of the world in which he lives.

David Wilson arrives in Dawson's Landing a stranger. Oddly enough, he stays in the town even after his mistimed joke about owning half a dog backfires, cementing his reputation as a "pudd'nhead." A man of sense would have picked another river town and established himself there, but David Wilson remains, "a man so superior to the citizens of the little Missouri town in which he settled that, incapable of understanding him, they conclude him to be an idiot" (Regan, 208). The fundamental problem Wilson's brain must solve does not concern evil leadership or the core stupidity of the town's inhabitants. Instead, he must sort out the nature of identity. He does not rectify the unjust situation that insists that Roxy, a high-minded woman with a fraction of African blood, must live as a second-class citizen or seek to improve the immoral situation that allows Roxy's murderous son Tom to go unpunished. In fact, Wilson does precious little in the book. When he does act, forced by circumstances, he merely clarifies who is a slave and who is not. In the course of the novel, Wilson becomes empowered to sort out the issues of identity causing disequilibrium in Dawson's Landing because in so confused a place only an outsider possesses a reliable identity.

In fact, David Wilson's exclusion from the core of life in Dawson's Landing forms the basis of his heroism. "Shunted to the edge of the community from the hour he arrived, he is effectively blocked off from participation in society. This may seem a hardship in his eyes. But where to act at all is, according to the law of life, to act badly, the moral advantages should be apparent" (Griffith, 221). Only Wilson's essential separation from his community permits his goodness. *Pudd'nhead Wilson* transforms the essential nature of the fable because it does not permit David Wilson to achieve virtue as a member of the society. To the extent that he participates in Dawson's Landing, it besmirches him. Wilson attains virtue not by overthrowing the system but only by defining the identities of the people within it. While we cannot deny that Wilson is the hero of the book that bears his name, David Wilson's heroism forces us to reconsider how we define goodness.

Perhaps the best avenue for discovering the nature of Wilson's goodness comes in comparison with the forces of evil in the novel. At first look, the opposition between Tom Driscoll and David Wilson seems complete. One man robs and murders and the other retrieves the stolen property and identifies the murderer. They even face off in court—twice. But we quickly reach our moral limits with this comparison. While Tom has made a career of his dishonesty, Wilson also lies, such as when he says that he would have delayed the launch of his legal career out of deference to Tom's adoptive father's view of family honor. As the extract from Pudd'nhead Wilson's calendar notes before the first chapter, "Tell the truth or trump—but get the trick!" In addition, both men are eastern-educated, and both have had their eastern aspects drummed out of them by the town. They both occupy prominent positions in the town, but remain outside of the center of the town's daily life. The similarities of these circumstances, though, help clarify where the men's characters conflict.

The most obvious difference occurs in the characters' self-perception. David Wilson creates his reputation with a remark made "much as one who is thinking aloud" (6). Wilson, when he arrives in Dawson's Landing, seems unable to distinguish between what he says to himself and what he says to others. Tom, on the other hand, lives his entire life in artifice, master of the differences between internal and external selves. When the discovery of his true identity changes him with a force like the "gigantic irruption . . . of Krakatoa" (49), Twain observes of Tom that "no familiar of his could have detected anything in him that differentiated him from the weak and careless Tom of other days" (50). This disconnection has a simple root. "Tom imagined that his character had undergone a pretty radical change. But that was because he did not know himself" (50). Tom finds himself unsuited to life in "the dull country town" (26). He tries first to fend off the boredom with fashionable eastern dress but, ridiculed back into convention, responds by secretly stirring up trouble. Contrast this with Wilson, who "had a rich abundance of idle time, but it never hung heavy on his hands, for he interested himself in everything that was born into the universe of ideas" (7–8). Critics frequently take Wilson to task for participating in the duel, preferring that he follow some externally imposed moral code rather than the *code duello*, but Wilson remains true to himself, fulfilling the obligations of his identity in the context of Dawson's Landing. In fact, his only meaningful action in the book is to remain true to his identity despite being cruelly misnamed. He is, according to existentialist theory of self, authentic.

Tom, on the other hand, has no secure identity. He can intend to rob and end up murdering, without distinguishing between the two acts. He acts informed with so little self that even the perspicacious Pudd'nhead Wilson cannot imagine him capable of murder. Tom's most honest self-expression comes in anger at his own birth. "He said to himself that if his father were only alive and in reach of assassination his mother would soon find that he had a very clear notion of the size of his indebtedness to that man" (75). But even this emotional expression perceives him from outside himself: he does not think, "I would kill that man," but rather, "I will show Roxy." To Tom, even the most private thoughts are public performance. This is as good a definition as we can find of existential inauthenticity. Tom Driscoll has no authentic self, or at least he has no way to reach it, which amounts to the same thing. David Wilson has nothing but authenticity.

This existential interpretation allows us to clear up part of the nature of David Wilson's heroism, and the doubts that have centered on his acceptance of the dominant morality of Dawson's Landing. The questions we have about Pudd'nhead's goodness—his willingness to support the immoral framework of slavery that dominates the town—grow out of the difficulty we have in accepting existential dissociation between conventional morality and the ethics of personal authenticity. David Wilson's capitulation to the foul morality of Dawson's Landing does not cost him psychologically, financially, socially, or ethically; in fact, he gains substantially from it. But he does not perform his courtroom drama of assigning true identity to achieve these ends. Only our readerly attachment to an external morality, which we believe to be better than the town's, casts doubts on Wilson's heroism. His single significant act in the book is rectifying confusion over authentic identity. Within an existential framework, that is the only possible moral act.

Before we can dissect Wilson's approach to the problem of identity, we need to look at Roxy, Pudd'nhead's second opposition within the confines of the novel. Wilson's courtroom performance destroys Tom—he exists neither literally nor figuratively when the trial ends—but it only defeats Roxy. "Her hurts were too deep for money to heal; the spirit in her eye was quenched, her martial bearing departed with it, and the voice of her laughter ceased in the land" (120). While Tom perpetrates the evil in the tale, Roxy created Tom, and Wilson's defeat of her must tell us something about the nature of his heroism. Tom and Wilson oppose one another in all the practical mechanics that make the plot of *Pudd'nhead Wilson* move forward, and Wilson shows himself to be a traditional hero because of his success against Tom. But Roxy is heroic in her own right, so Wilson's opposition to her represents a competition of heroic types.

Critics love Roxy. She is, by general acclaim, the only complete woman Twain ever invented. No less an authority than Henry Nash Smith wrote that she is "the only fully developed character, in the novelistic sense, in the book. She has a different order of fictional reality from the figures of fable with which she is surrounded" (179). In essence, this means that she alone in the book can act in a morally mixed way. She alone seems to perceive the world of Dawson's Landing as readers do. Roxy's exchange of the infants attempts "to sabotage the white social feudal structure" (Vanderweken, 10). Roxy sides with the novel's narrator, agreeing that slaves "had an unfair show in the battle of life, and they held it no sin to take military advantage of the enemy" (12). While Roxy does not herself steal, she encourages Tom on his raids and benefits from them without losing our support, because she consistently holds to her higher moral purpose of disturbing the evil social order. But when Tom's cowardice drives him to drag Luigi to court or to sell Roxy downriver, she lambastes him. In a conventional novel, Roxy would be the hero, but *Pudd'nhead Wilson* is not a conventional novel. Roxy's likeness to conventional heroes only reinforces the obvious point that the real hero of the book is the one who succeeds, even though his accidental success is tragic. Roxy acknowledges this herself: "Dey ain't but one man dat I's afeard of, en dat's Pudd'nhead Wilson" (17).

Twain's neat construction of *Pudd'nhead Wilson*, and particularly his conflict-pairs of Tom/Wilson and Wilson/Roxy, simplifies the analysis of the book. With Tom representing evil and Wilson good, that conflict-pair becomes the moral center of the book's action. Roxy and Wilson conflict over the spiritual center of Dawson's Landing. In the plot, they conflict only over Tom; ideologically they conflict over the implications of their desires. Wilson seeks two things: "to live down his reputation" (7) and to gain "revelation" of a "mystery"—words Twain uses repeatedly in connection with his fingerprinting (7, 53, 110). Roxy seeks to avoid the pain of losing her son (Chapter 3) and to obscure the truth of both her identity and her son's. Practically, the courtroom battle settles the first conflict, by cementing Wilson's reputation as a lawyer and leader and sending Roxy's beloved Tom down the river.

More to the point of the book, Roxy and Wilson conflict in their desires concerning identity, true identity. For David Wilson, the revelation of identity has enormous value; why else would he have spent his long idle years fingerprinting and refingerprinting Dawson's Landing's relatively few inhabitants? In the first conflict between Roxy and David Wilson, Tom Driscoll becomes the literal prize for the victor. When Wilson wins, he—or the society he now represents—takes ownership of him. In the second conflict, Tom is only a symbolic representation of obscured identity. And in this conflict, Wilson's victory is implied but not entirely clear. While Wilson has proven that Tom is by birth a slave and by action a murderer, ambiguous identity follows him even after the trial. The book declares that, as a slave, he was too valuable to kill for his crime. In truth, though, either Chambers was already counted as a slave in Percy Driscoll's estate, in which case Tom merely takes his rightful place, or the Chambers/Tom slave was not a part of the estate at all. In either case, Tom would not be liable for sale. This final ambiguity in the ledger books leaves open the questions of identity Wilson sought to solve.

The spiritual opposition between Roxy and Wilson leaves questions of identity unresolved. In this framework, as Clark Griffith notes, Roxy "is less Madonna than Witch, a figure from the outer dark, presiding at an unholy ceremony of changelings. Nothing good can come of her undertaking, for it involves a violation, emphatic and terrible, of the very humanity it was meant to assert" (210). While neither Roxy nor her magic is in itself evil, they do give birth to evil, in the form of Tom, who "was a bad baby, from the very beginning of his usurpation" (19). Wilson, in counterpoint, plays the prophet, as Tom himself acknowledges, albeit with sarcasm. "Dave's just an all-around genius, a genius of the first water, gentlemen," he says as he tries to embarrass Wilson, "a great scientist running to seed here in this village, a prophet with the kind of honor that prophets generally get at home" (54). And when Tom thinks himself free from suspicion concerning his uncle's murder, only Wilson's prophetlike ability to see the invisible stands in the way. "The man that can track a bird through the air in the dark at night and find that bird is the man to track me out and find the Judge's assassin," Tom reassures himself (108). David Wilson succeeds in this spiritual contest with Roxy, and all his wise sayings become evidence of his second sight. In the "complexities of twinship" that form the core theme of *Pudd'nhead Wilson*, "the authentically identical twins are . . . demonic Roxy, crouched beside the cradles in 1830, and angelic Wilson, standing erect at the bar of justice in 1853" (Griffith, 221).

This point reveals the limits of David Wilson's success as a hero, limits that lie in the dual nature of the word "identity." The core issue of *Pudd'nhead Wilson* involved both forms of identity. On one hand, Wilson succeeds in clarifying the individual form of identity, but he remains unaware of the existence of the form of identity that pairs one individual with another, the sense of identity we mean when we say "identical." Both Roxy and Tom understand the nature of this form of identity and capitalize on it, both disguising themselves as the opposite sex to escape detection. Dawson's Landing is "becoming the seat of the dreadful Nemesis," the inverted self, as John Brand notes. In Roxy and Tom's "closeness they are strangers; in their separateness they are akin" (125). This nemesis plagues David Wilson, disturbing his passivity and forcing him to act. The trial makes him choose between risking his own authenticity by keeping silent about Tom's singular identity and, through revelation, killing his nemesis Roxy, in one sense an important part of himself. As one of the townsfolk notes when David Wilson makes the joke that sentences him to a quarter century of drudgery, "What did he reckon would become of the other half if he killed his half? Do you reckon he thought it would live?" (6). The dog's two halves have the same form of identity as Wilson and Roxy.

Insistent twinning pervades the structure of *Pudd'nhead Wilson*. Using this twinning structure, Twain manipulates the second meaning of "identity" to represent not only likeness but also difference, an insistent counterpoint that defines the novel's moral ecology. Every significant event in the book has its partner, from Roxy's initial baby switching and Wilson's rectification at the end, to Tom's first winning trial and his second losing one. These inversions also invite us to understand Mark Twain's dominant message in the novel: that this second form of identity creates an inseparable link between master and slave, that defining oneself against the other, as the patriarchs of Dawson's Landing do, means that you will cease to exist when the others do, no matter how strong a sense of individual identity you have. The very insistence on twinned difference creates a fundamental unity; like the dog, destroying one half destroys both halves.

Fighting against this tide of likeness, David Wilson sees himself as an isolate. He refuses to categorize people in the town, resolutely pursuing interests that contribute to individuation. He spends his time mastering the tools that allow one to become certain of individual identity, both physical identity through fingerprints and experiential identity through reading individual destiny in a palm. Perhaps more important, Wilson never allows himself to lose track of his own individual identity, still considering himself a lawyer though he has not set foot in a courtroom, still scribbling his maxims though no one around him understands them. Contrast this with the book's other characters: Roxy is "the dupe of her own deceptions" (20) as she allows herself to become the slave to her own child; the judge identifies himself by his role in society, not by any internal measures; the twins retain vestiges of themselves as the monstrous conjoined twins that so completely symbolize the other form of identity. And Tom hasn't a clue about who he is. Only David Wilson succeeds in holding on to his identity from within.

The nature of David Wilson's heroism now becomes clearer. He is not a hero because of his ability to change the world around him. Mark Twain's earlier characters Huck Finn and Hank Morgan tried that and failed spectacularly, despite their supernatural powers. In *Adventures of Huckleberry Finn* and in *A Connecticut Yankee in King Arthur's Court*, history overwhelmed the efforts of the heroes. In *The Tragedy of Pudd'nhead Wilson*, history threatens again. As in *Huck Finn*, historical reality takes largely two forms: slavery and small-town morality. David Wilson, however, differs substantially from Huck Finn, not only in class, age, and education but also in what he attempts within the confines of the books that bear their names. Huck changes identities and moves constantly, in a concentrated effort to free himself from his father and Jim from slavery. David Wilson never goes anywhere and never becomes anything except himself. Despite the fact that slavery is a constant theme of his world, he tries not to free himself, only to define himself and others through an understanding of individual identity.

Existentialism argues that the key source of virtue is an internally understood identity. Conversely, the failure to hold on to this internally understood identity is called inauthenticity. Inauthenticity is a result of existential bad faith. Bad faith can take on many different forms, any of which will result in a lack of authenticity, a failure to hold on to an internally understood identity. Four of the most well defined forms of bad faith appear repeatedly in *Pudd'nhead Wilson*: (1) identifying oneself as a thing, as slaves (particularly Roxy) do repeatedly and as the aristocracy does; (2) identifying oneself as another person, as Tom and Roxy do; (3) refusing to recognize the importance of one's place among others, Tom Driscoll's most grievous character flaw; and (4) the denial of one's own freedom, a constant in a book where nearly all the characters use lack of choice as an excuse for their behavior. As difficult as it must be for David Wilson to remain in Dawson's Landing, completely underappreciated and falsely accused of idiocy, he does not even momentarily turn to bad faith for solace. He never calls himself a slave to his community, denies his townsfolk his aid, falsely represents who he is, or objectifies himself. He remains David Wilson, an act of super-human strength that pays off for him in the long run. He lives his life in a way that exactly represents the dictum "To be is to do," coined by Jean-Paul Sartre, originator of existentialism.

Pudd'nhead Wilson responds to the world of Dawson's Landing uniquely. Though he acknowledges that living is itself a sort of slavery, he makes the free choice to live in Dawson's Landing. When he becomes a leader and peacemaker in the town, he accepts power not as a means of self-identification but as a result of the identity he already has. He acts only because he has to, forced by the threat to the twins Angelo and Luigi. Though he does not want to reveal Tom's false identity, the preservation of an innocent life depends on his acting. Though it courts existential absurdity to ascribe authenticity to a character in fiction—even more difficult when, because of the constraint of fable, that character represents unerring goodness—we must acknowledge that David Wilson symbolizes authentic individuation, in his ability to distinguish himself from others, distinguish between others, and place himself meaningfully in his context. He is an existential hero, and perhaps the first truly modern hero in American fiction.

Given his level of inactivity, it isn't surprising that Wilson succeeded in only very limited terms. He remains authentic and communicates the quality of authenticity as a new measure of virtue, but his material accomplishments come at a high cost. He becomes the mayor of Dawson's Landing, but Dawson's Landing is itself a town of pudd'nheads. Wilson's calendar entry before the tale's Conclusion shows that he is aware of his own predicament: "October 12, the Discovery. It was wonderful to find America, but it would have been more wonderful to miss it" (120). In the pitched battle between the two different kinds of identity—individuation and likeness—David

Wilson champions the individual, existential notion of identity. Acting to preserve the abstract value of authentic identity by his forced revelation of Tom's falseness, however, destroys Wilson's nemesis, which represents identity as likeness. As a result, Wilson has destroyed that part of himself that we as readers have come to value, his separation from Dawson's Landing. David Wilson's attempt to preserve authenticity, both in himself and as an abstract value, does not fully succeed. Since he is now the chief pudd'nhead in a town of pudd'nheads, identity as likeness has won the battle, and Wilson has martyred his individuation to the cause. His final calendar entry suggests that discovery and revelation are two sides of the same coin, but that the coin can buy nothing but failure.

The hero of *Pudd'nhead Wilson* does much more than act the hero's part. He becomes a prophet of identity, and as a result he receives "the kind of honor that prophets generally get at home." But in this martyrdom, David Wilson lights the way toward a future concept of heroism, one that dominates the fiction of the twentieth century, especially after the ascendance of existentialism. Wilson embodies an individual, and therefore personally practicable, form of heroism. The fact that we frequently have difficulty recognizing authenticity as heroism in no way diminishes its role in *Pudd'nhead Wilson* or its value in the wider world. We have grown to appreciate this novel in large measure because we have grown to appreciate David Wilson's heroism. Having discovered the limitations of more traditional heroes in his earlier novels, Mark Twain turned to a new conception of heroism here, and in doing so pointed the way toward a philosophy that had yet to be articulated.

Work Consulted

Brand, John M. "The Incipient Wilderness: A Study of *Pudd'nhead Wilson*." *Western American Literature* 7.2 (1972): 125–34; rpt. herein.

Campbell, Joseph. *The Hero with a Thousand Faces*. New York: Pantheon, 1949.

Finkelstein, Sidney. *Existentialism and Alienation in American Literature*. New York: International Publishers, 1965.

Gerber, John C. "*Pudd'nhead Wilson* as Fabulation." *Studies in American Humor* 2 (Spring 1975): 21–31.

Griffith, Clark. "*Pudd'nhead Wilson* as Dark Comedy." *ELH* 43.2 (1976): 209–26.

Khouri, Nadia. "From Eden to the Dark Ages: Images of History in the Work of Mark Twain." *Canadian Review of American Studies* 11 (1980): 151–74.

McCullough, Joseph B. "*Pudd'nhead Wilson*: A Search for Identity." *Mark Twain Journal* 18.4 (1978): 1–5.

Rank, Otto. *The Myth of the Birth of the Hero*. New York: Vintage, 1964.

Regan, Robert. *Unpromising Heroes: Mark Twain and His Charac-
    ters*. Berkeley: University of California Press, 1966.
Robinson, Forrest G. *In Bad Faith*. Cambridge, MA: Harvard Uni-
    versity Press, 1987.
Rowlette, Robert. *Twain's* Pudd'nhead Wilson: *The Development and
    Design*. Bowling Green, OH: Bowling Green University Popular
    Press, 1971.
Salomon, Roger Blaine. *Mark Twain and the Image of History*. New
    Haven, CT: Yale University Press, 1961.
Sartre, Jean-Paul. *Nausea*. New York: New Directions, 1964.
Schell, Edgar T. "'Pears' and 'Is' in *Pudd'nhead Wilson*." *Mark Twain
    Journal* 12.2 (1963): 12–15.
Smith, Henry Nash. *Mark Twain: The Development of a Writer*.
    Cambridge, MA: Harvard University Press, 1962.
Solomon, Robert C. *From Rationalism to Existentialism*. [Atlantic
    Highlands, N.J.]: Humanities Press, 1972.
Twain, Mark. *Pudd'nhead Wilson and Those Extraordinary Twins*.
    2nd ed. Ed. Sidney E. Berger. New York: Norton, 2005.
Vanderwerken, David L. "The Triumph of Medievalism in *Pudd'n-
    head Wilson*." *Mark Twain Journal* 18.4 (1977): 7–10.
Wood, Barry. "Narrative Action and Structural Symmetry in *Pud-
    d'nhead Wilson*." In *Pudd'nhead Wilson* and *Those Extraordinary
    Twins*. Ed. Sidney E. Berger. New York: Norton, 1980; rpt.
    herein.

LINDA A. MORRIS

Beneath the Veil: Clothing, Race, and Gender in Mark Twain's *Pudd'nhead Wilson*†

> And thus in the land of the Color-line I saw, as it fell across my baby,
> the shadow of the Veil.
> —W. E. B. Du Bois, *The Souls of Black Folk*

> Now who would b'lieve clo'es could do de like o' dat?
> —Mark Twain, *Pudd'nhead Wilson* (16)

The idyllic opening of *Pudd'nhead Wilson*, with its description of
Dawson's Landing's modest dwellings with whitewashed exteriors
and a cat asleep in a flower box, concludes with the description of
the village bounded on the front by the Mississippi River and on the
back by a row of high hills that, Mark Twain writes, were "*clothed*

† From *Studies in American Fiction* 27.1 (1999): 37–52. Reprinted by permission of North-
eastern University.

with forests from foot to summit."[1] Thus, unobtrusively and in the context of a tranquil landscape, he introduces what is to become one of the major subtexts of the novel: namely, clothes as markers of identity, race, and gender. The text is rich with masquerading, with layering of clothing, with cross-dressing and misleading gender markers, with foppery, veiling and unveiling, and with clothing as cues (and mis-cues) to sexual and racial identity. Yet across the novel's critical history, Twain's preoccupation with clothing in the text has been all but invisible.[2]

For the first generation of critics and reviewers of *Pudd'nhead Wilson*, even the multiple acts of cross-dressing performed by both the slave heroine, Roxana, and her son escaped public notice. In January 1895, the reviewer for *Cosmopolitan*, for instance, called attention to a host of melodramatic elements in the novel, but made no mention of cross-dressing:

> exchanges of infants in the cradle, a hero with negro taint in his blood substituted for the legitimate white heir, midnight encounters in a haunted house between the false heir and his colored mother, murder by the villain of his supposed uncle and benefactor, accusation of an innocent foreigner, and final sensational acquittal and general unraveling of the tangled skein. . . . [3]

This reviewer goes on in familiar nineteenth-century terms to extol the virtue of the text's black language: "How deliciously rich, racy, and copious is, for instance, his negro talk. The very gurgling laugh and cooing cadence seems, somehow, implied in the text."[4] The reviewer for the *Spectator*, responding to the wry humor of the novel, wondered if Twain had "found Missouri audiences or readers slow to appreciate his jokes,"[5] while the *Bookman* focused on the novelty of fingerprint records that ultimately reveal the true identity of the false heir who murders his purported uncle.[6] These reviewers, like others across the work's critical history, responded to *Pudd'nhead Wilson's* deeply disturbing critique of racial categories, but none of them per-

1. Mark Twain, *Pudd'nhead Wilson* and *Those Extraordinary Twins*, 2nd ed. (New York: Norton, 2005), 4. Hereafter cited parenthetically.
2. Two notable recent exceptions include Marjorie Garber's brief consideration of the text in *Vested Interests: Cross-Dressing and Cultural Anxiety* (New York: Routledge, 1992), which notes that "questions" of clothing and "the exchange of clothing" are part of the story from the beginning (289), and Eric Lott's "Mr. Clemens and Jim Crow: Twain, Race, and Blackface," which explores the relation of blackface and identity in the novel. Although issues of dress and disguise inform Lott's argument, his primary and provocative thesis focuses on racial performance. In *The Cambridge Companion to Mark Twain*, ed. Forrest G. Robinson (Cambridge: Cambridge Univ. Press, 1996), 129–52.
3. Hjalmar Hjorth Boyesen, quoted in Susan Gillman, *Dark Twins: Imposture and Identity in Mark Twain's America* (Chicago: Univ. of Chicago Press, 1989), 53. [See the present edition, 242–43—Editor.]
4. *Cosmopolitan* 18 (January 1895), 379.
5. *The Spectator* 74 (March 17, 1895), 367–68.
6. *The Bookman* 7 (January 1895), 122.

ceived how metaphors of clothing and cross-dressed performances complicate and complement the racial issues at the core of the novel.

More recently, *Pudd'nhead Wilson* criticism has taken two distinct directions. Scholars such as Hershel Parker have taken pains to understand how Twain composed *Pudd'nhead Wilson*, not being content to accept the author's flippant description of how he simply removed the Siamese twins from his original manuscript by Cæsarean surgery once the slave Roxana and her son "took over" the text.[7] By delicate surgical procedures of their own, these scholars have reconstructed Twain's composing and revising processes that led to the ultimate creation of two texts, *Pudd'nhead Wilson* and *Those Extraordinary Twins*. They note, for example, that in the original manuscript, now known as the Morgan Manuscript, there were no changelings; Tom Driscoll was white, not black; and the Italian twins were Siamese twins who were ultimately hanged by the good citizens of Dawson's Landing. (More accurately, only one of the twins was hanged; but as the citizenry deduced about Wilson's dog at the beginning of the story, killing one half of the animal would for all practical purposes also kill the other.)

A second strand of modern scholarship, as represented in Susan Gillman and Forrest Robinson's collection of essays, *Mark Twain's* Pudd'nhead Wilson: *Race, Conflict, and Culture*, reads the text historically and interprets late nineteenth-century culture through the text.[8] Critics such as Eric Sundquist and Shelley Fisher Fishkin recontextualize the novel in ways that emphasize the relationship between *Pudd'nhead Wilson* and the racial politics of the day, while Carolyn Porter and Myra Jehlen read the racial *and* gendered subtexts of the novel.[9] Susan Gillman explores the relationship between twins, duality, and identity in the novel, and positions the novel in relationship to Twain's late dream narratives.[1] Most of these critics, especially those exploring the intersections of race and gender, note that cross-dressing occurs at key crisis points in the novel and that it contributes to and highlights crises of race and identity, but none pursues this subject in depth. Nor has anyone yet noticed how

---

7. Hershel Parker, *Flawed Texts and Verbal Icons: Literary Authority and American Fiction* (Evanston: Northwestern Univ. Press, 1984), 115–46; Daniel McKeithan, *The Morgan Manuscript of Mark Twain's Pudd'nhead Wilson* (Cambridge: Harvard Univ. Press, 1961).

8. Susan Gillman and Forrest G. Robinson, *Mark Twain's* Pudd'nhead Wilson: *Race, Conflict, and Culture* (Durham: Duke Univ. Press, 1990).

9. Eric Sundquist, "Mark Twain and Homer Plessy," in *Pudd'nhead Wilson: A Collection of Critical Essays*, ed. Eric Sundquist (Englewood Cliffs: Prentice-Hall, 1994), 169–83; Shelley Fisher Fishkin, "Race and Culture at the Century's End: A Social Context for *Pudd'nhead Wilson*," *Essays in Arts and Sciences* 19 (1990): 1–27; Carolyn Porter, "Roxana's Plot," in Sundquist, ed., *A Collection of Critical Essays*, 154–68 [see pp. 395–411 in the present volume—*Editor*]; Myra Jehlen, "The Ties that Bind: Race and Sex in *Pudd'nhead Wilson*," in *Mark Twain's* Pudd'nhead Wilson: *Race, Conflict, and Culture*, 105–20 [see pp. 411–26 in the present volume].

1. Gillman, *Dark Twins*.

relentlessly the text enacts more conventionally defined issues of dress and clothing.

This essay will focus in particular upon dress and clothing as markers of identity, race, and gender as played out in relation to two of the primary characters in the novel, Roxana and her son Chambers, also known as Tom. Representations of their clothing simultaneously confound the already problematic categories of race and make problematic the categories of gender.[2] Such confounding, we will see, further destabilizes the precarious social order of Dawson's Landing and the post-Reconstruction South of Twain's own time.

In our first introduction to Roxana, the slave woman who propels the major plot into motion, we do not see her, only hear her, as she exchanges witticisms with a slave named Jasper. We do not need to see her, however, to know by her dialect that she is "black": "Oh, yes, *you* got me, hain't you. 'Clah to goodness if dat conceit o' yo'n strikes in, Jasper, it gwyne to kill you, sho'. If you b'longed to me I'd sell you down de river 'fo' you git too fur gone" (9). The narrator immediately both confirms and contradicts our assumptions: "From Roxy's manner of speech, a stranger would have expected her to be black, but she was not: Only one-sixteenth of her was black, and that sixteenth did not show" (9). In Mark Twain's South—whether the antebellum era in which the story is set or the post-Reconstruction era in which it was written—"by a fiction of law and custom," Roxana is "black." In the text her otherwise ambiguous racial identity is marked, finally, by the fact that her "heavy suit of fine, soft [brown] hair" is concealed "with a checkered handkerchief" (9). Set against her "white" appearance, Twain chooses here one of the most powerful and persistent of racial markers with which to identify Roxana, her head rag.[3] From this moment on, Roxana *is* "black"—her race does "show." The head rag as a marker of racial identity is reinforced later in the text when Roxana becomes a fugitive slave, hotly pursued by her "master"; following the practice of the day, the master has a "wanted" poster made for Roxana: "The handbill had the usual rude wood-cut of a turbaned negro woman running, with the customary bundle on a stick over her shoulder, and the heading, in bold type, '$100 *Reward*'" (94). In

2. Susan Gillman argues that in the novels following *Pudd'nhead Wilson* Twain questions traditional categories of gender identification: "If 'male' and 'female' are as readily interchanged as 'black' and 'white,' then gender difference may prove to be as culturally constituted as much 'a fiction of law and custom' as racial difference." Gillman, *Dark Twins*, 79. A recent article by Laura Skandera-Trombley focuses on cross-gendered shorter works Twain wrote in the late 1890s and 1900s: "Why Can't a Woman Act More Like a Man? Mark Twain's Masculine Women and Feminine Men," *OVERhere* 15 (1995): 49–57. In the same issue of *OVERhere*, John Cooley writes about Twain's "heroic but also tragic maidens and inadequate males" (34–47). None of these scholars, however, addresses the relationship between gender and race in the major works.

3. See Patricia Turner, *Ceramic Uncles and Celluloid Mammies: Black Images and Their Influence on Culture* (Berkeley: Univ. of California Press, 1994). Of particular interest is the chapter "Back to the Kitchen," 41–61.

other words, the handbill evokes the stereotyped image of the escaped slave woman, and it pins that stereotype on Roxana. For her part, Roxana continually undercuts all racial stereotypes throughout the novel, and the patriarchal order as well.[4]

Two infant boys born on the same day are entrusted wholly to Roxana's care: Thomas à Beckett Driscoll, son of one of the "first" white families in Dawson's Landing, and Roxana's own son, Valet de Chambre, who like his mother looks white but by Missouri law is black and a slave. The infants can be distinguished from one another only by their clothing. Tom's clothes are described briefly, but in detail, calling attention to their fabric and their ruffles, while Chambers is dressed in the unmistakable clothing of a slave child: a "tow-linen shirt which barely reached to its [sic] knees" (9). The transformative event of the novel—Roxana's exchanging the babies' clothing and thereby altering their public identities and personal fortunes—begins quite simply when Roxana privately declares her intention to drown herself and her baby. She plans to do so not to save the two of them from slavery, but to save her son from the possibility of being sold down the river, a fate she sees as literally worse than death. However, her action is arrested as she catches "sight of her new Sunday gown," a chance event that sets the plot in motion in a different direction. She looks down at her own slave's clothing, her linsey-woolsey dress, and vows not to be "fished out" looking so "misable" (14).

In the passage that follows, Twain displays his clear fascination with the details of female clothing, for nothing in the plot requires him to give so much attention to Roxana making her "death-toilet." Central to the process of preparing her death attire, Roxana sheds the marker of race, her head rag, and lets her "white" hair hang loose.

> She put down the child and made the change [into the dress]. She looked in the glass and was astonished at her beauty. She resolved to make her death-toilet perfect. She took off her handkerchief-turban and dressed her glossy wealth of hair "like white folks;" she added some odds and ends of rather lurid ribbon and a spray of atrocious artificial flowers; finally, she threw over her shoulders a fluffy thing called a "cloud" in that day, which was of a blazing red complexion. Then she was ready for the tomb. (14–15)

What Roxana sees when she looks into the mirror is her own beauty—that is, her constructed white self—in contrast to the equally constructed black image reflected back to her by Southern society. The faintly mocking tone of the narrator goes unheard by Roxana, who is clearly pleased by the image of herself that she creates. This image empowers her, just as later dressing as a man will empower her.

4. See Porter, "Roxana's Plot" [pp. 395–411 below].

Roxana may be "ready for the tomb," but her son is not. Having completed her toilette, she turns her gaze on her son, and is appalled by his "miserably short little gray tow-linen shirt and noted the contrast," not, as we expect at this moment, between her son's clothing and Master Tom's, but between his dress and her own. When she "noted the contrast between its pauper shabbiness and her own volcanic irruption [sic] of infernal splendors, her mother-heart was touched, and she was ashamed" (15). She was ashamed, that is, not of her own dress, but of her son's racially marked clothing, which she characterizes as "too indelicate" for the heaven to which they are bound. Ever resourceful (and spontaneous), Roxana dresses Chambers in the only fine clothing available, which is Tom's, and echoing her surprise at her own image in the mirror, she is now astonished at how "lovely" Chambers appears dressed in "white" clothing. Only then does she conceive the plan to exchange her "black" son with her "white" charge.

Roxana's exchange of the babies in the novel, as Carolyn Porter has so cogently shown, is a powerfully subversive act, one that challenges and disrupts the patriarchal order of Dawson's Landing. For Chambers to assume his new identity as Tom, however, he has to be stripped naked; only then can he don his "dainty flummery of ruffles" (15). Tom, too, is "stripped of everything" and dressed in tow-linen, which marks him in everyone's eyes as a slave. By this act, Tom is stripped of his name, his identity, his inheritance, his paternity (although both children have been fathered by two of the town's most distinguished citizens), and his freedom. Roxana stands back to view her handiwork and exclaims, "Now who would b'lieve clo'es could do de like o' dat?" (16).

In the early pages of *Pudd'nhead Wilson*, then, Twain establishes that clothing and dress will carry the weight of race as it is performed (and deconstructed) in the novel. The expected, indeed purportedly "indelible" stamps of race, both black and white—facial features, hair, skin color—are unreliable from the beginning. Moreover, clothing codes, which we would expect to be the more mutable markers of race, are unfailingly enforced by social dictate. The supposedly "natural" boundaries between the races were disappearing through racial mixing at the time of the novel's writing, leading to demands that they be reinforced by new boundaries and powerful markers. Yet Roxana's action demonstrates that these, too, are unreliable, even deceptive. Dawson's Landing, unbeknownst to its principal citizens, is in the midst of a cultural crisis; its socially constructed codes are unraveling before its very eyes.

As a young boy, the changeling Tom, who knows nothing of his identity as a changeling, is the master of Chambers, and he is spoiled by both Roxana and the white families with whom he resides. Pampered, undisciplined, indulged, he tyrannizes Chambers and treats Roxana with contempt. Chambers, in contrast, is quickly taught his place as a slave. The relationship between the two boys is expressed in part through metaphors of clothing. Tom, who is cowardly and a bully, makes Chambers do all his fighting for him; consequently, Chambers earns a reputation as an accomplished fighter, until "by and by . . . Tom could have changed clothes with him, and 'ridden in peace,' like Sir Kay in Launcelot's armor" (21). There is no hint of irony in this passage, no sense that Twain is making a conscious joke about the exchange of identities that has already taken place, although the passage evokes in its readers that ever-present knowledge. The literal "armor" that Chambers wears is Tom's cast-off, worn-out clothes that are described ironically by Twain as "holy": "'holy' red mittens, and 'holy' shoes, and pants 'holy' at the knees and seat" (21).

Twain's exploration of the childhood relationship between Tom and Chambers comes to an end when Chambers saves Tom from drowning, which earns him only insults for his trouble. Their playmates tease Tom that Chambers is his "Nigger-pappy—to signify that he had had a second birth into this life, and that Chambers was the author of his new being." Infuriated by the taunting, Tom orders Chambers to attack the boys; when he fails to do so, Tom "drove his pocket knife into him two or three times before the boys could snatch him away and give the wounded lad a chance to escape" (23). And escape he does. After this scene, Twain has no more interest in Chambers until the end of the story; he slips out of sight while Tom takes center stage as the (wrongful) heir to the Driscoll name and fortune.

When he is nineteen, Tom is sent off to Yale, where he learns to "tipple," gamble, and affect "eastern fashion." Upon returning to Dawson's Landing, he particularly offends the young people of his social set by wearing gloves. He also "brought home with him a suit of clothes of such exquisite style and cut and fashion—eastern fashion, city fashion—that it filled everybody with anguish and was regarded as a peculiarly wanton affront" (26). In a scene rich with foreshadowing, the young people of Dawson's Landing set about to cure Tom of his affectations by mocking his style of dress. They tailor a suit that burlesques Tom's and fit it to the town's "old deformed negro bellringer." He follows Tom through the streets, "tricked out in a flamboyant curtain-calico exaggeration of his finery, and imitating his fancy eastern graces as well as he could" (26). The mockery works: "Tom surrendered, and after that clothed himself in the local fashion" (26).

In commenting on this scene, Myra Jehlen rather enigmatically asserts that "it is unclear just what is being satirized: is it simply fop-

pish pretension, or rather some special absurdity of black foppery?
Because the characters are unaware that their parody of Tom possesses this additional dimension, it becomes a joke shared by the narrator and the reader, a joke with a new target."[5] Eric Lott reads the
incident as "a sort of minstrel gag in reverse; the black man burlesques Tom's acquired graces, and does so at the behest of an audience of village white boys . . . . it also suggests that Tom's whiteness
is itself an act, a suggestion that is truer than either the bell ringer
or Tom can know since Tom's identity is precisely a black man's
whiteface performance."[6] Both Jehlen and Lott raise important
points, but both critics quickly slip past the specific image of the
"flamboyant curtain-calico exaggeration of his finery." Jehlen's focus
is on who is the target of the joke, while Lott's is on the performance
of race. More fundamentally, we might wonder why this scene has
such a haunting quality about it. We are left with the image of the
black bellringer shadowing Tom through the streets of Dawson's
Landing, mirroring Tom in a distorted mirror that reflects both his
costume and his manners. Tom has been perceived by his contemporaries as feminized, as suggested by reference to his "fancy eastern graces." Later, as we shall see, when Tom cross-dresses as a
young girl and like Huck Finn practices *being* a girl, this same language is echoed in the text. By then he will know that by society's
definitions, he is really a black man, and he will assume a series of
masquerades only to deceive. The bellringer, by contrast, is a figure
used to re-establish, at least temporarily, Dawson's Landing's social
order, which its young male citizens believe has been disrupted by
Tom's putting on airs. In Bakhtinian terms, the scene is carnival-
esque, with the most lowly member of the community, the deformed
Negro bellringer, dressed in clothing intended to mock a member of
the town's most privileged class. While the black bellringer is not
protected by the customs of a festival as he would be in Bakhtin's ceremonial world, he is protected by the cover of the white youths on
whose behalf he performs.[7] Nothing in the text suggests that the
black bellringer is himself foolish or absurd, and to assume the joke
is somehow on Tom because he is "really" black but does not know
it misses the point. Lott's notion that Tom's whiteness is itself a performance comes much closer to the mark; nonetheless, his analysis
stops with this observation, thereby missing the opportunity to investigate the convergence of a racialized *and* gendered performance.

Cured of his worst pretensions, Tom nonetheless continues to
commit offenses against the social order. He accrues a sizable gam-

5. Jehlen, 110 [pp. 416–17 below].
6. Lott, 145.
7. Mikhail Bakhtin, *Rabelais and His World*, trans. Helene Iswolsky (Bloomington: Indiana
   Univ. Press, 1984).

bling debt that will, if revealed, cause him to be disinherited, so he
resorts to theft and deceit to pay off his creditors. In order to steal
from the villagers of Dawson's Landing, he assumes a series of disguises to mask his identity. Most powerfully and most successfully,
he cross-dresses as both a young girl and an old woman. The first
time we see him cross-dressed as a girl, we watch him through Pud-
d'nhead Wilson's eyes, although neither the reader nor Wilson knows
at that moment that the "girl" we are watching is Tom. The scene is
in fact represented twice in the text, first from David Wilson's perspective and then from Tom's.

In the first instance, Wilson chances to look out of his window
across a vacant lot into Tom's bedroom window in Judge Driscoll's
house. There he sees a girl in a pink-and-white striped dress "practicing steps, gaits and attitudes, apparently; she was doing the thing
gracefully, and was very much absorbed in her work" (36). Wilson
wonders what a girl is doing in Tom's bedroom, and for some time
tries unsuccessfully to discover her identity. Three chapters later,
Twain repeats the same scene, but this time from Tom's point of view.
This second time the scene is dramatized much more fully and more
elaborately, and we do not know at first we are witnessing what we
have seen before. Until close to the end there is no mention at all of
David Wilson.

> He [Tom] arrived at the haunted house in disguise on the
> Wednesday before the advent of the Twins,—after writing his
> Aunt Pratt that he would not arrive until two days later—and lay
> in hiding there with his mother until toward daylight Friday
> morning, when he went to his uncle's house and entered by the
> back way with his own key and slipped up to his room, where he
> could have the use of mirror and toilet articles. He had a suit of
> girl's clothes with him in a bundle as a disguise for his raid, and
> was wearing a suit of his mother's clothing, with black gloves
> and veil. By dawn he was tricked out for his raid. (50–51)

While Wilson had seen only a girl in a striped summer dress in Tom's
room, we now see Tom cross-dressed not once but twice, first in his
mother's clothing, then as the young girl Wilson sees. The added
detail of the second female identity assumed by Tom is further intensified by the new information that he had slipped into his own room
at his uncle's house so that "he could have the use of [a] mirror."
While David Wilson is watching Tom, not knowing who he is, Tom
is gazing at one of his female selves in the mirror. He is in the act of
performing a gender as surely as his life has become an act of performing a race. Further, the scene and imagery recall his mother's
act of looking at herself in the mirror just before she chances upon
the scheme to exchange the babies, turning the "black" Chambers

into the "white" Tom. That is to say, Tom's identity as a "white" man began with his mother's glance in the mirror, just as one of his identities as a woman is likewise reflected in a mirror.[8]

The scene is filled with images of performing, posturing, mirroring. Just after this passage, Tom notices that Wilson is watching him from his house. The two men, in Twain's words, "caught a glimpse" of each other peering through their respective windows. Far from being upset by his discovery that Wilson is watching him, Tom "entertained Wilson with some airs and graces and attitudes for a while" (51). Tom deliberately performs for Wilson as a girl, and as a girl he is apparently wholly convincing. Only after Wilson is confronted with other, overwhelming evidence that Tom is an impostor does he "see" beyond the female masquerade: "Idiot that I was! Nothing but a *girl* would do me—a man in girl's clothes never occurred to me" (109). This is the admission of one of the two founders of the Society of Free Thinkers in the town; in spite of his reputation as being a Pudd'nhead, David Wilson is a shrewd and discerning man. If he is unable to see beyond Tom's cross-gendered disguise, who can?[9]

After his performance, however, Tom is not entirely confident that he has thrown Wilson off track and so changes back into his mother's clothes before leaving the house. Just as Twain had repeated the performance scene twice, he now repeats twice in three sentences the same information about Tom's changing into his mother's clothing, underscoring the intensity of his preoccupation with cross-dressing in this text:

> . . . then [Tom] stepped out of sight and resumed the other disguise, and by and by went down and out the back way and started downtown to reconnoitre the scene of his intended labors.
>
> But he was ill at ease. He had changed back to Roxy's dress, with the stoop of age added to the disguise, so that Wilson would not bother himself about a humble old woman leaving a neighbor's house by the back way in the early morning, in case he was still spying. (51)

Tom's cross-dressing in order to commit burglaries sets the scene for even more complex gendered and racial crossing that follows. It is both a symptom and a cause of the category crisis that is at the heart of the novel.

8. On female identity and being seen see, for instance, Laura Mulvey, "Visual Pleasure and Narrative Cinema," *Screen* 16 (Autumn 1975): 6–18.
9. Carolyn Porter is less patient with Wilson, saying that he "is remarkably dull-witted when it comes to reading his evidence. Most noteworthy is his persistent and blundering confusion over the identity of the 'young woman' in Tom's room, 'where properly no young woman belonged'" (164).

As the story progresses, Tom's debts mount; he is disinherited by his uncle, written back into the will, then threatened with being dis- inherited again. In as ugly an action as the story holds, Tom know- ingly sells his own mother into slavery, and down the river, to pay his creditors. Some months pass before Roxana shows up again in the story, now as a fugitive. To escape detection in St. Louis, where she has fled from the deep South, Roxana has cross-dressed as a man, putting on men's clothing and "an old slouch hat," and blackening her face. That is to say, she has altered all the visible markers of her former identity: the planter from whom she escaped is looking for a "white" black woman, so she turns herself, ironically, into a "black" man. Her disguise is so effective that it fools even Tom, whom she tracks down in St. Louis. When Tom first sees her, he notices only "the back of a man"; when the man turns around, he sees only "a wreck of shabby old clothes sodden with rain and all a-drip. . . ." Then the man says, "in a low voice—

'Keep still—I's yo' mother!' " (90).

It is an arresting moment. While Tom "gasped out" a few feeble "incoherently babbling self-accusations" about why he has done such a terrible thing, Roxana takes off her hat, and her hair "tum- bled down about her shoulders" (90). Now she stands before Tom, and before us, as a "white" woman in blackface, dressed in men's clothes. At this critical moment in the text, Roxana embodies us all, black and white, man and woman. She is "every man" and "every woman." For this woman who has already been a forceful actor in her own life, this moment represents the most powerful embodiment of her strength. Roxana then proceeds to tell her story of enslave- ment, one that invokes and re-enacts the genre of slave narratives— stories of brutal physical treatment, of ultimately striking back at the overseer (Roxana "snatch[ed] de stick outen his han' en laid him flat" [92]), and of escape. Roxana's story, seemingly a long and moving digression from the main plot of the novel, propels the novel inex- orably toward the tragedy that it becomes.

With Roxana back on the scene (and in near total command of her son), Tom becomes more desperate in his efforts to steal money both to pay off his debts, and thus ensure his inheritance, and to buy his mother's freedom, as she demands. Desperate, he ultimately plots to steal from his uncle. Taking his cue from his mother (and evoking the tradition of minstrel theater with its complex socially constructed images and enactment of blackness),[1] Tom also blacks up to commit the robbery. Surprised by his uncle in the act of stealing from his safe, Tom thrusts a knife into him, killing him instantly, then flees upstairs to his own room. There, still in blackface, Tom disguises

1. In addition to Eric Lott's "Mr. Clemens and Jim Crow," see his *Love and Theft: Blackface Minstrelsy and the American Working Class* (New York: Oxford Univ. Press, 1993).

himself as a girl to escape from the house. The scene is represented
in only one sentence, but it is crucial:

> Tom put on his coat, buttoned his hat under it, threw on his suit
> of girl's clothes, dropped the veil, blew out his light, locked the
> room-door by which he has just entered, taking the key, passed
> through his other door into the back hall, locked that door and
> kept the key, then worked his way along in the dark and
> descended the back stairs. (100)

That is to say, Tom commits the murder in his own clothes (minus
his coat), and in blackface. Then he puts on his "girl" clothes over
his male clothes, drops a veil over his blackened face, and flees from
the house. What is the meaning of the layering here? Is it, perhaps,
a mistake, a glitch in the manuscript such as those remnants of the
Siamese twins carelessly left in the *Pudd'nhead Wilson* story? All evidence suggests that it is not. Twain had hinted at just such layering
before the murder. In preparing to commit the robbery, Tom "laid off
his coat and hat . . . unlocked his trunk and got his suit of girl's
clothes out from under the male attire in it, and laid it by. Then he
blacked his face" (99). The male clothes in the trunk have concealed
the female clothes, while after the murder, Tom's female clothes hide
his male clothes (and identity). In a move that mirrors his mother's
triumphant moment of embracing white and black, male and female,
Tom puts on layers of identities over the layers he already "wears."
The whiteness of his skin hides his blackness; passing for white
hides his true relationship to Roxana; blacking up hides his whiteness; female clothing covers up his maleness; a veil covers his blackface. Tom, *aka* Chambers, murderer of his benefactor and purported
uncle, collapses all categories of socially constructed identities.

Marjorie Garber, in discussing briefly the transvestite theme in
Pudd'nhead Wilson, draws a connection between Twain's use of the
"veil" and Du Bois' image of the veil in which to be "within the veil"
meant to be "under the burden of blackness." According to Garber,

> when Tom dresses as a woman, he disguises his *gender* because
> he is ashamed of his *race*. To "drop the veil" is to pull it over his
> face, to voluntarily veil himself. Inadvertently, then, read back-
> wards through Du Bois' compelling image, Tom's disguise, the
> woman's veil, becomes a signifier of that very blackness he is so
> anxious to conceal. The irony of Tom's desperate ploy—to pass
> as a woman because he has been passing as white, and then to
> obliterate the damning evidence, burning both male *and* female
> clothes—is that it marks him unmistakably, if only for a
> moment, as a black transvestite, the true son of the mother he
> despises and sells down the river.[2]

2. Garber, 290–91.

This is a provocative observation, but one that is ultimately based on a misreading of the text. Garber fails to notice that Tom "drops the veil" over his blackface—the blackness he is so anxious to conceal is twice represented here—while the literal veil he wears is a socially encoded, unambiguous marker of gender.

In order to escape detection, and literally to escape from the house, Tom thus goes forth, as his mother did in St. Louis, as both man and woman, as both black person and white. Like his mother's blackface cross-dressing, this represents a very powerful moment in Tom's life—he has acted, and he has acted decisively—but with two crucial differences. Although Roxana wears layered gender and racial identities, she pulls off her slouch hat and reveals her long, flowing hair; she strips off one layer to reveal herself. Tom, by contrast, piles on his layers only to deceive, to cover up the shame of his deed. And so his act, unlike his mother's, is an act of cowardice that puts him beyond the pale of human redemption.[3]

It has been clear to generations of readers that for all its vexing statements about the role of race in determining Tom's character (and by extension Chambers'), *Pudd'nhead Wilson* exposes the absurdity and arbitrariness of the very racial categories upon which the slave society depended. As both Eric Sundquist and Shelley Fisher Fishkin have demonstrated, the novel critiques as well the racial divisions of the 1890s, the era of the enactment of Jim Crow laws and the bolstering of racial boundaries where they were clearly threatened.[4] This essay has argued that the text is even more radical than these critics have suggested, for it also calls into question the socially constructed definitions and meanings of gender markers. In other words, in *Pudd'nhead Wilson*, the gender disguise is as hard to read as the racial disguise, and both reinforce the deconstructing of the other.

Pudd'nhead Wilson culminates with the trial of Luigi, one of the Italian twins, for the murder of Judge Driscoll. In the course of formally defending Luigi, David Wilson accidentally discovers the "true" identities of Tom and Chambers, and simultaneously reveals Tom to be the murderer of his uncle. The patriarchal social order has been thus only temporarily subverted by Roxana, for her worst fears are realized in the end as her son is deemed too valuable a piece of property to shut up in prison for life and he is sold down the river into slavery. From Roxana's perspective, the ending is like a Greek tragedy in which the very fate she had sought to escape is visited upon her son. Nonetheless, the social order has clearly been dealt a

---

3. Eric Lott characterizes Tom's going forth in female dress as "an element of blackface revenge for the master's rape of slave women, one of whose issue is Tom himself." "Mr. Clemens and Jim Crow," 149.
4. Eric J. Sundquist, "Mark Twain and Homer Plessy"; Shelly Fisher Fishkin, "Race and Culture at the Century's End."

blow from which it is unlikely to recover fully. In a novel glutted with ironies, the ultimate irony may be that the one utterly reliable marker of identity that *cannot* be altered—finger prints—reveals nothing whatsoever about either the gender or the race of the individual. The community's carefully drawn and constructed racial and gender lines have been challenged and exploded. This is signified subtly, but forcefully, by the re-introduction into the text of the man called Chambers, the "white" man who had been condemned to a lifetime of slavery by the treachery of his "mammy" but who is ostensibly set free by Wilson's discovery of his "true" identity:

> The real heir suddenly found himself rich and free, but in a most embarrassing situation. He could neither read nor write, and his speech was the basest dialect of the negro quarter. His gait, his attitudes, his gestures, his bearing, his laugh—all were vulgar and uncouth; his manners were the manners of a slave. Money and fine clothes could not mend these defects or cover them up, they only made them the more glaring and the more pathetic. (120–21)

The issue of gender, which seems not to play any role at all in Chambers' transformation back to being the white Tom, is hinted at after all in the language describing his "vulgarity": "His gait, his attitudes, his gestures." This is the language, we will recall, used to describe Tom when he performs his female gender for David Wilson. The fact that Chambers is at home only in the kitchen evokes not only race but also the female gender, or a feminized male identity.[5]

A novel propelled into motion by the exchange of two babies, *Puddn'head Wilson* makes no effort, dramatically, to make the exchange reciprocal. Twain shows almost no interest in the white baby who is raised as a slave; most of his attention is focused on the black baby raised as white. In the terms of the novel, "really" being white does not mean much at all, or, as Lott puts it, "to be imitation black is to *be* black, to be imitation white is to be [a] mere mimic."[6] Nevertheless, Chambers, who has been absent from the novel for much of its duration, is left in the end on center stage. His clothes, taken from him at six months, are symbolically returned to him, but the power they had to undo him at the outset is not matched by a corresponding ability to restore him in the end. In this sense, the social order has not been restored in the end. Even the whitest of black men can

---

5. See Myra Jehlen, who says that "The subversion in Tom's usurpation of white identity turns Chambers into a woman, for feminization is the lasting result of that unfortunate man's slave upbringing." But Jehlen never makes clear precisely how Chambers is feminized, except to suggest that the black man, in white men's stereotypes, is either an over-sexualized, threatening being or "contemptibly effeminate" (112 [p. 394 below]). Chambers clearly is not the former.

6. Lott, "Mr. Clemens and Jim Crow," 147.

be sold into slavery, but a white man, once "crossed by the shadow of the Veil," cannot ever be fully white again. While the old categories seem to be reinstated, they are now confounded to such a degree that the old order is shaken to its core.

CAROLYN PORTER

Roxana's Plot†

Many critics of *Pudd'nhead Wilson* have agreed on the extraordinary power of Roxana as a character, while others have attended more to her problematic behavior, such as the radical changes in her demeanor, her white supremacist attitudes, and her capacity for both cruelty and tenderness, and have offered a variety of explanations either to defend or to attack Twain's portrayal. The critical response shows a marked tendency, however, to use her sexuality to account for both Roxana's power and the problems she raises as a character.[1] For example, in the most compelling and nuanced analysis of the novel as a whole, James M. Cox calls Roxana "the primary force in the world she serves" and underscores that force as "sexual." He traces a circuit of power in the novel's plot structure originating in the white male lust of the Southern slaveholder. What "explains Roxana's power," according to Cox, is the "submerged lust" of the white male, whose "passion" is transferred "from the white wives to the slave mistresses." Roxana serves as the repository of "the guilt of their repressed desires," so that "their guilt is objectified in her repression." Her son, Tom Driscoll, thus becomes "the avenging agent who carries back across the color line the repressed guilt which

---

† From *Mark Twain's* Pudd'nhead Wilson: *Race, Conflict, and Culture*, ed. Susan Gillman and Forrest G. Robinson (Durham and London: Duke University Press, 1990), pp. 121–36. Copyright © 1990, Duke University Press. All rights reserved. Reprinted by permission of the publisher.

1. For example, while calling Roxana Twain's "most fully realized female character," Arlin Turner says that "through her, in the clearest instance in all his fiction," Twain "acknowledged sex to be an element in human relations." Frederick Anderson sees her as "Twain's most successful female protagonist," pairing her with the Aunt Rachel of "A True Story" to suggest that Twain apparently "required the distance provided by color to establish and sustain the vulgar quality of life in female character." One of the most impressive critiques of Twain's characterization of Roxana is also based on this assumption that her power is fueled by her sexuality. According to Arthur G. Pettit, it is Twain's ambivalence toward the powerfully sexual black woman of his imagination that accounts for Roxana's "bewildering" role changes from "black shrew" to "tragic mother figure." Twain "used blacks and mulattoes," Pettit claims, "to express sexual feelings that were prohibited by white standards of propriety," and Roxana's contradictory behavior reflects Twain's inability to cope with such feelings. Thus he "wound up with two Roxana's," Pettit suggests, a "near-white one, . . . and a much darker Roxana." See *Pudd'nhead Wilson* and *Those Extraordinary Twins*, 2nd ed., ed. Sidney E. Berger (New York: W. W. Norton, 2005), 287, Anderson, Introduction to the facsimile of the first American edition of *Pudd'nhead Wilson/Those Extraordinary Twins* (San Francisco: Chandler, 1968), pp. vii–xxxii; this quotation is rpt. in Berger, 1st ed. of *PW,* p. 285, 327–30.

has gathered at the heart of slavery." Therefore, Tom's assassination of his foster father, Judge Driscoll, is the thematic center of the plot, and his "murder suggests the anarchy which the white society has by its own action released upon itself." As Cox tracks the transmission of guilt and desire *from* the white male *through* the black female and *back onto* the white male, he also tracks power from its "origin" in the white male "lust out of which [Tom] was created" down to Roxana, who is only the "immediate source" of Tom's "dark force." If "the power of those who rule has been transferred to those who serve," its origin remains marked at the site of the white male father, and its final restoration is secured by the "dark comedy" of Pudd'nhead Wilson's ascent to the position of authority left vacant by Judge Driscoll's death. The oedipal pattern, in which white males hold, lose, and then regain power, is fulfilled by David Wilson's story, which is itself plotted along a circuit of power originating with and returning to the white male. "Having precipitated the crisis," Cox notes, David Wilson concludes the plot he has himself "set in motion by his own idle remark to Roxy" when he unveils Tom Driscoll as both black and a parricide.

It is this dual status, of course, which makes Wilson's plot resolution a case of "disjunctive irony." He exposes the killer in the community's midst, but by the same act he exposes that community's "secret history" of miscegenation. Thus the indictment of the society implicit in Wilson's exposure of Tom Driscoll as "black" is finally deflected and its threat recontained by the restoration to the status quo it effects by convicting him as a killer. Accordingly, both Wilson and his plot are "repressive," serving to recontain and deny the "erotic motive" buried in the adultery which is the "primal action . . . from which the entire plot originates."[2]

I have rehearsed Cox's argument at such length because it seems to me that he delivers the definitive analysis of the novel's plot, insofar as it can be understood to originate in the white male desire, repression, and guilt of the Southern slaveholding class, and to culminate in the simultaneous exposure and repression of that origin. He delivers as well a definitive diagnosis of the novel's flaws as a product of that same repression operating through the plot machinery centered in *Pudd'nhead Wilson*. Within the terms of his argument, both the analysis and the diagnosis are wholly persuasive. Yet those terms themselves are grounded in an essentially Freudian framework marked by oedipal struggle and a focus on repressed male sexual desire that is significantly limited and limiting in its treatment of Roxana. Such a framework accounts splendidly for David Wilson's plot as a repressive mechanism, but it cannot finally account for the

2. See James M. Cox, "The Ironic Stranger," in Twain, *Pudd'nhead Wilson* [herein, 278–86—*Editor*]. For a fuller version, see Cox's *Mark Twain: The Fate of Humor* (Princeton, N.J.: Princeton University Press, 1966), chap. 10, 222–46.

fact to which Cox himself testifies when he says that "Only Roxana has the power to create drama and to become the primary force in the world she serves."[3]

Such a statement underscores every reader's sense that Roxana generates a good deal of the energy that moves the often creaky machinery of the novel forward. If we focus on Roxana as "primary force," even as a kind of prime mover of events in the world she serves, then the repressive function that Cox accurately attributes to *Pudd'nhead Wilson*'s plot looks rather different. What makes that plot's censorship visible becomes less a matter of its success at repressing Roxana's sexuality than its *failure* wholly to recontain the disruptive force of what amounts to another plot—Roxana's plot.

In order to account for Roxana's resilient power, which suffers repeated deflection and suppression only to return in new guises and disguises, we need to attend to her status as mother. "Mother" is to be understood here not as a "natural" but as a social identity defined in Roxana's case by a set of particular legal, social, and cultural codes that make the slave mother at once antebellum America's most tragic victim and potentially one of its most powerful subversive agents.

No doubt the axiomatic problem of the Southern black woman stereotyped as "Jezebel" (to borrow the label used by the historian Deborah White) plays a critical role in Roxana's troubled creation, but the critical focus on her sexuality has obscured her status as mother and underestimated the force of the anxieties unleashed in both Twain and his readers by a figure who is both sexual and maternal. The opposition Jezebel/Mammy in the antebellum South repressed a great deal of social and psychic conflict and confusion among the white slaveowning classes. As with the analogous oppositional stereotypes of the black man as rapist/Uncle Tom, an ideologically secured psychic defense operates to force the Other into two contradictory, interdependent, and equally mystified positions. Such either/or stereotypes only point to the excluded middle that they repress.

This region has been, of course, partly colonized by literary convention as the site of the "tragic mulatta" who signals and represses at once the fact that slave women were sexual objects of desire in the eyes of their white masters. And clearly, Roxana's status as a mulatta is crucial to Twain's story. But in order to assess what makes it crucial, we need to see it within the context that Hortense Spillers has described. For Spillers, the mulatta is a figure of containment for white culture; what in reality threatens exposure—the physical evidence of miscegenation—is culturally recontained by a defensive sign deployed as an "alibi, an excuse for . . . otherness," as Spillers

3. Cox, "The Ironic Stranger" [281].

calls it. A term that "designates a disguise, covers up . . . the social and political reality of the dreaded African presence," *mulatta* or *mulatto* serves as a "semantic marker" that "exists *for others*—and a particular male other," according to Spillers. As a mulatta, Roxana certainly exposes the "covert tradition" of miscegenation, but her serial ordeal as a mulatta *mother* intent on saving her son exposes much more. Typically, the mulatto is a son or daughter who undergoes a crisis upon discovering a black or mulatto mother. Roxana is—first and last—that mother. Indeed, her status as a mulatta is established only to be immediately refocused by her status as a slave mother.[4]

Roxana is introduced as a set of contradictions: she sounds black, but looks white; "majestic" in "form and stature," fair-complexioned, she has a "heavy suit of fine soft hair," but it is "concealed" by a "checkered handkerchief"; "sassy" among her black friends, she is "meek and humble" among whites. These contradictions result from that "fiction of law and custom" that officially resolves them by dictating that "the one-sixteenth of her which was black out-voted the other fifteen parts and made her a negro." Thus Roxana's invisibly "mixed blood" matters not at all to her cultural, social, or legal identity. What matters—as Twain immediately reports—is that "she was a slave, and salable as such," and her child "too, was a slave."[5] In short, Roxana's white appearance is a plot device in the story of a slave mother and her child. Indeed, it is the central plot device, a tragic equivalent to "those extraordinary twins" in the "suppressed farce" that Mark Twain said he "pulled out by the roots" from the mother-text of *Pudd'nhead Wilson* (125). But it is her son's mulatto status, more than Roxana's, which invites Twain's brief exploration of the plight of the "tragic mulatto" faced suddenly with news of a black mother.

By attending, then, to Roxana as the slave mother, we can gain

4. Quotations from Spillers taken from lecture delivered at the University of California, Berkeley, November 1987. Twain explored the theme of the "tragic mulatto" more fully in the original manuscript of the novel before he separated the "tragedy" of *Pudd'nhead Wilson* from the "farce" called *Those Extraordinary Twins*. On these revisions, see Hershel Parker, *"Pudd'nhead Wilson*: Jack-leg Author, Unreadable Text, and Sense-Making Critics," in *Flawed Texts and Verbal Icons: Literary Authority in American Fiction* (Evanston, Ill.: Northwestern University Press, 1984), 115–46. Francis Harper's *Iola Leroy*, which appeared two years before Twain's novel, was the most contemporary of several fictional representations of the tragic mulatto. Critical assessments of this figure, and of the rich and heterogeneous tradition in which she or he functions, have proliferated in recent years. A beginning may be made with the following: Judith Berzon, *Neither White nor Black* (New York: New York University Press, 1978); Barbara Christian, *Black Women Novelists: The Making of a Tradition, 1892–1976* (Westport, Conn.: Greenwood Press, 1980); Hazel Carby, *Reconstructing Womanhood: The Emergence of the Afro-American Woman Novelist* (New York: Oxford University Press, 1987); Mary Helen Washington, *Invented Lives: Narratives of Black Women: 1860–1960* (New York: Doubleday, 1987).

5. Twain, *Pudd'nhead Wilson*, 9. [All further references are to the present edition, and will be cited in the text.]

access to that blurred, confused, and anxiety-producing region of the excluded middle repressed by the binary Jezebel/Mammy (a space of contradiction too often sutured over in white culture by the figure of the tragic mulatto). What comes into and out of focus in Twain's portrayal of Roxana is a region where mothers are sexual, slaves are powerful, and women are temporarily out of (and thus in) control. Roxana's agenda as a protagonist is set by her status as a slave mother, but in pursuing that agenda, she exposes not only the falseness of the Mammy/Jezebel opposition, but also the inadequacy of either "Mammy" *or* "Jezebel" to contain or represent the slave woman. The partitioning of sexuality from motherhood that is implicit in much of the critical response to Roxy is undermined in the novel itself, and thus such critical analysis cannot account fully for either Roxana's power or her problematic behavior. Indeed, that partitioning is a defense against what Twain was unable entirely to defend against—a slave mother wielding a subversive power in ways that threaten both narrative and social control.

From this viewpoint, *Pudd'nhead Wilson's* coherence is undermined not by the dissociation of Roxana's character from a plot that operates to repress her sexuality, but rather by a struggle between the unsuccessfully suppressed slave mother's story and the story of the white fathers whose oedipally grounded plot Cox makes so lucid. In other words, *Pudd'nhead Wilson* is the scene of conflict between a repressive paternal plot and a subversive maternal one.

Before exploring Roxana's plot, I should make clear the severe limits within which its subversive power emerges. Roxana's remarkable series of strategems to save her son do not, finally, succeed. No matter how powerfully Roxana wields the forces she learns to appropriate from the white patriarchy, her son is finally sold down the river. The plot I wish to foreground here is one that emerges only temporarily, in what might be called the artificially induced gap between the white slaveowning patriarchy's *threat* of such a sale, and its final enforcement of that threat twenty-three years later. Roxana's "plot" exposes contradictions in the white slaveowning patriarchy, signaling a potentially explosive negative power to thwart and undermine its rule, but her plot has no power to *alter* that rule itself, and more pointedly, it has no power to deflect that rule's crushing force on the slave mother's bond with her child.

In Roxana's plot, the primal action is not adultery, but childbirth. The first event recorded in this plot is also the first event recorded in the novel; in chapter 1, after describing Dawson's Landing and its "chief" citizens, Twain reports of Percy Driscoll, "on the first of February, 1830, two boy babes were born in his house; one to him, the other to one of his slave girls, Roxana by name" (5). But it is not until Roxana switches these two "boy babes" that her plot proper gets under way. No doubt, she acts in response to a threat from above, the threat of her son's being sold down the river. However, it is worth noting that the threat is not immediate; she is not guilty of the recent petty theft to which her fellow slaves have confessed and for which they, not she or her child, are going to be sold. Her master's act, in other words, is technically what starts the plot rolling, but only technically. It is Roxana's ability to understand the threat posed by this incident that leads to her radical response.

It is also worth noting how radical a response it is. Provided with motive and opportunity, she is also endowed with the courage to commit an act so violent in its implicit threat to her society that it is unthinkable, and so invisible. The children's striking resemblance, and their white appearance, coupled with the fact that no one can tell the difference between them save Roxana, provide opportunity only. The threat of her child's ultimate loss provides motive only. What we can easily fail to notice is that Roxana's act requires a will so strong, and a calculating mind so acute, that it can conceive of a "plot" so "beyond the pale" that it cannot even strictly be called criminal. The law cannot forbid it because the law cannot imagine it. When the "law" in the shape of Pudd'nhead Wilson, detective manqué, is finally forced to imagine it, the discovery requires the modern "scientifics" of fingerprinting, and even with this tactical aid, Wilson remains thoroughly befuddled until the very last moment.

The mainspring of Roxana's plot lies in the implications of the exchange with which it begins. When Roxana switches the children, she commits two subversive acts: she reduces the real Tom to slavery, and she creates a new "Tom" by renaming her son. As Evan Carton has pursuasively claimed, "her attempt to save one twin by dooming the other reiterates the structure and the illusion of the society it challenges." What Carton calls the "paradoxical imitative character of her enterprise" indeed haunts it from the outset, but it does so in ways that subvert as well as reiterate the white slaveholding patriarchy.[6]

This dimension of Roxana's endeavor comes into view if we attend first to her son's translation from slavery to freedom and the terms on which the novel invites us to understand it. Roxana acts to save her own son from a fate not only worse than death, but also functionally equivalent to it. From beginning to end, the novel enforces this equivalence between death and being sold down the river. When she conceives her plan, at the story's outset, Roxana is on the way to drowning both herself and her child to save the latter from being sold down the river. At the story's end, Tom is saved from life imprison-

---

6. "*Pudd'nhead Wilson* and the Fiction of Law and Custom," in *American Realism: New Essays*, ed. Eric Sundquist (Baltimore: Johns Hopkins University Press, 1982), 86.

ment by being restored to his status as property and sold down the river. As Richard Chase, among others, has noted, "down the river" serves as the novel's version of hell, and throughout the story, it is clear that there is little difference between death and slavery in the Deep South.[7]

As Orlando Patterson has explained, part of what makes slavery a form of "social death" is its status as a commutation of an actual death sentence.[8] The slave "lives" under the continuous threat of a death to which she or he is nonetheless socially condemned. Because the slave can always, in principle, be killed by the master, the slave's life is always conditional on that master's consent that he or she live. In *Pudd'nhead Wilson*, this condition is foregrounded when Roxana perceives the threat posed by Percy Driscoll's decision to *refrain* from selling her fellow slaves down the river *this time*. She understands that her very life, and that of her son, is permanently conditional—a commuted death sentence that can always be revoked at the master's will. For the slave, what this means is that survival depends upon remaining alienable. Roxana's fellow slaves express heartfelt gratitude at being sold, but not sold down the river. In terms of the novel's identification of death with being sold down the river, they preserve their lives by remaining alienable. This logic is pervasive. Percy Driscoll's treatment of his slaves is echoed at the end of the novel: "As soon as the Governor understood the case, he pardoned Tom at once, and the creditors sold him down the river" (122). The novel closes as it opens, with a pardon followed by a sale.

In this light, Roxana's opening gambit needs to be understood not only as a reiteration of the white patriarchy's structural inequality, but also as a specific imitation of the white master's power to enforce that inequality in the form of social death. Comprehending her permanently alienable status as itself predicated on a threat of death permanently in force, Roxana first seizes power over her life and that of her child by deciding to end them both. She then finds a way of commuting this double death sentence when she conceives her design to "save" her son. She thereby institutionalizes a power over her son that imitates the slaveholder's dominant position as commutator of a death sentence that he can always revoke. But if Roxana seizes the power to commute the metaphoric death sentence of

7. See Richard Chase, "The Inadequacy of *Pudd'nhead Wilson*," in *The American Novel and Its Tradition* (Garden City: Doubleday, 1957), pp. 149–56, esp. pp. 150–51.
8. See Orlando Patterson, *Slavery and Social Death: A Comparative Study* (Cambridge, Mass.: Harvard University Press, 1982), esp. chap. 2, 35–76. In addition to Winthrop Jordan's *White over Black: American Attitudes Toward the Negro, 1550–1812* (Baltimore: Penguin, 1969), useful sources on the cultural, legal, and political contexts of miscegenation in the United States are Michael Grossberg, *Governing the Hearth: Law and the Family in Nineteenth Century America* (Chapel Hill: University of North Carolina Press, 1985), 136 ff., and Marylynn Salmon, *Women and the Law of Property in Early America* (Chapel Hill: University of North Carolina Press, 1986), esp. 211 ff.

being sold down the river, she clearly still lacks the power to enforce that threat.

This is hardly surprising. After all, no matter how violently subversive Roxana's secret act is, it remains—and *must* remain, to have its immediately intended effect—secret.[9] Further, Roxana remains a slave. What is surprising is that twenty-three years later she is able to enforce the threat implicit in her deed, to exploit its actual consequences in terms that, for a while, at least, transform her imitation of the master's power into an active appropriation of it.

In order to understand this turnabout, it is necessary to explore the relation of killing to selling in the slave economy of social death as it operates in this novel, so as to see—what Patterson fails to see—how the slave mother is specifically positioned in and by that economy.

The complexity of the analogy between killing and selling is revealed by the novel's technically flawed ending. As everyone has noticed, in order to sell Tom down the river at the end, and thus restore him to his status quo ante, Twain must "forget" that Tom's double, Chambers, has already been sold and Percy Driscoll's estate thereby credited with the money Judge Driscoll paid for him. Because there is one slave whose exchange value is already accounted for, in this view, the sale of a second under the same name is redundant—a gratuitous addition made necessary by Twain's desire to underscore what George Spangler aptly calls a "parable of property."[1]

Yet what counts as contradiction on the surface of Twain's plot is quite consistent with the rules of property and exchange as they operate in Roxana's plot, where the economy's operation is experienced by the slave. Here, the condition of alienability is definitive, as Roxy demonstrates when she allows Tom to sell her back into slavery. Legally, she may be "free," but actually, she can always be sold and resold. In this economy, the same person can clearly be sold twice, that is, for a double profit. All that is necessary is that the person be designated "black." In Roxana's case, as she notes, it is her speech that identifies her as black despite her white skin. In Tom's case, it is finally his fingerprint that identifies him as black, despite his white speech *and* his white skin. But in both cases, all that is required for a person to be placed on the sale block, to be alienable, is proof of a specific racial identity. What makes Tom's sale at the end possible as well as logical, then, is an extension of the principle of the slave's alienability in terms of his or her name, or more accurately, the lack of one.

9. The question of whether it must remain a secret to her son, once he is old enough to hear it, is begged by Twain's account of Tom's upbringing as a white master. But the question is answered differently by Faulkner in the story of Charles Bon. See *Absalom, Absalom!* (New York: Vintage, 1936).
1. See George M. Spangler, "*Pudd'nhead Wilson*: A Parable of Property," in *Pudd'nhead Wilson* [295–303, herein].

The real anomaly of Tom's sale lies deeper—in the perception that two bodies have been sold under the same name. From the slave's perspective as always-alienable property, once his racial identity is proven, "Tom" has no identity at all as a person. This is clear from the fact that he loses his patronymic surname. As Roxy tells him "you ain't *got* no fambly name, becaze niggers don't *have* 'em" (45). If racial identity is "a fiction of law and custom" and thus manipulable by and subordinate to capital, so is the identity that depends upon, and is represented by, the "name of the father." Once reduced to nameless property, that is, two bodies can occupy the same alienable identity. This point is, in fact, demonstrated at the book's outset by Roxy's exchange of the babies and helps to explain why the exchange lacks symmetry. If Roxana "saves" her son from sale, she simultaneously places her master's son, potentially, on the sale block, an exchange that does not free anyone. Because the legally defined distinction between "free" and "slave" seems so absolute, it is easy to assume that Roxana's original exchange of the free Tom and the enslaved Chambers operates on a one-to-one ratio. If one is free, the other is a slave, and vice versa. But this ratio holds no more firmly within the economic system than it does within the racist society. If both children in the end become niggers, the one legally and the other culturally, this outcome is consistent with the contaminating force of a system of property and exchange value that replicates the contamination of nigger blood. Once a slave, always a slave. Once a nigger, always a nigger—even to the fifth generation in Tom's case. In other words, the exchange of A for B, as David Wilson later refers to the original Tom and Chambers, is no simple act of turning A into B and B into A so that the two can be returned to their original condition by a legal decision. Instead, it turns the free Tom (A) into the slave Chambers (B) and yet, despite Roxana's continual efforts, B ultimately reverts to B. Tom's reversion to the status of alienable property is always, from the moment of his un-naming, a potential threat.

In short, the symbolic form that the threat takes for Tom is the erasure of his surname. Without that name, he is subject to the slave's condition, in which death is either exchanged for alienability or else accepted as the only alternative to it. It is the lack of the name that accords a paternally founded identity that matters here. Accordingly, the exchange of the names, "Tom" and "Chambers," which designates a one-to-one exchange of two identities for each other, is functionally a chimera and is irrelevant in a system in which all that matters is the presence or absence of "Driscoll." This point is underscored by the striking contrast between what is at stake in Wilson's loss of "David" for "Pudd'nhead" and what is at stake for either Tom or Chambers in the loss or gain of "Driscoll."

Roxana's power to erase that name provides her with the leverage to appropriate and turn the white master's power against him. She has, of course, exercised this power over the real Tom Driscoll at the outset. But in blackmailing her son, she threatens to repeat her own initial erasure of "Driscoll" from the real Tom's name by un-naming the false Tom. The power she calls upon here enables her to complete the imitation of the white master by enforcing the threat of death he wields, and this power emerges as a result of her status as a slave mother as dictated by the antebellum slave code.

Because this code observed the Roman rule of matrilineal descent, in which the child follows the "condition" of the mother, no matter what the father's status, a slave mother, in giving birth, delivered her child into slavery. It is this rule, among other unwritten laws, that Roxana subverts when she inserts her son into the patrilineal, and patriarchal, system, in which he becomes the "heir of the house" (16). In one sense, this is a re-insertion because her son's father is a member in good standing of the white master class to which Roxana, in effect, returns her son. As a changeling, Tom thereby temporarily escapes his maternal legacy of slavery and social death and eventually devotes his attention to retaining his paternal legacy of a surname and the property accompanying it. But (in this context at least) the fate of the newly enslaved Chambers, whose name has been erased, designates the hidden power that eventually displays itself in Roxana's aggression against the white patriarchy. A crack in the patriarchy is opened to view on the site of the slave mother's body as the locus of miscegenation, a gap that opens because of the patriarchy's legal recognition of the slave mother as the source of her child's *lack* of identity. If in giving birth, the slave mother condemns her child to social death and the status of always-alienable property, that birth blots out the father and thereby condemns the child to an always-alienable condition marked by a lack of surname. Thus, within the slave family, the slave child is automatically made into property, and the slave father is automatically rendered legally impotent. The body of the slave mother, meanwhile, is the putatively passive conduit that the white master uses to castrate the slave father and appropriate the slave child as always-alienable property.

That, in any case, is how the system was supposed to function. But as the work of social historians—not to mention black women novelists—has abundantly demonstrated, slave mothers *and* fathers actively and often effectively combated the corrosive effects of this system on the slave family. (Despite which, the discussion of the "Black Matriarchy" and its sins never seems to stop.) Roxana's is neither a stereotypical nor a real slave family, but her case can perhaps help reveal the flaw in a system predicated on the slave mother's passivity. In Roxana's blackmail plot, we find that mother appropriating as power the negation of the father enacted by the son's birth. What makes this possible is also what makes it radically subversive: the father is a white master (as, in this case, is the son, at least on the face of it). But this subversive power exercised in succession over two "white" sons (one "real," one "false"), in revenge for "two centuries of unatoned insult and outrage" (43), is blighted by the subtext of horror that emerges in the fate of two "black" sons, and the condition of the mother that fate exposes. It is difficult, as well as painful, to separate these two sides of Roxana's plot, but it is necessary to do so in order to grasp the plot's implications.

If in her initial switching of the children, Roxana erased the real Tom's paternal identity, she returns twenty-three years later, recognizing her power to erase that of the false Tom. If we translate real/false to "white/black" or master's son/slave's son, she has already, of course, dealt this blow, sub rosa, against the master's son. Having given birth to her son, Roxana saved him from the fate his birth decreed. By appropriating the matrilineal descent rule, she suspended its negative power in regard to her son; at the same time, she exercised that power over the master's son. If she can blot out one father, she can blot out another. But now, the negative power implicit in the slave mother's position becomes explicit, as the repressed returns literally with a vengeance. Roxana has recognized her power not only to erase the name of the father by identifying her son, but also to threaten with death the white master who is her son by exposing him as her son. The slave mother's power to negate paternal identity, both disclosed and suspended at the moment Roxanna exchanged the babies, is now unleashed and aimed not only at Tom, but also through him at the white patriarchy, against which Roxana turns the same threat on which its power relies.

More specifically, until Roxana's return, all that Tom has to lose is his inheritance. After her return, and her revelation of his origins, he stands to lose his name and, symbolically, his life as well. By exploiting his fear of the first loss, Roxana is able to make good her threat of the second. And by exploiting his fear of the second, she is able to siphon a livelihood from the Judge's coffers. She thereby wreaks her revenge *on* Tom for mistreating her, and *through* him on the white masters whose crimes she wants to avenge. Tom's life now depends upon providing for her survival, as befits the slave's relation to his master. Of course, because Roxana's extorted funds depend upon Tom's retaining his legacy, and thus upon his remaining in the Judge's good graces, they both remain subject to the white master. Yet *within* this patriarchal system, Roxana has opened a rift that enables her revenge, and through Tom she creates havoc in Dawson's Landing.

The whole show, of course, is a bluff. Roxana cannot prove that she is her son's mother. Like all bluffs, hers can work only by not being called, but that it works for so long is testimony not only to Roxana's shrewdness as a "blackmail" artist whose manipulation of Tom makes him seem almost smart on occasion, but also to the obliviousness of the white masters whose social structure she subverts. That it works for so long testifies particularly to the remarkable blindness of David Wilson; Roxana knows Wilson to be her chief adversary from the start, but it takes him forever to see her as his.

Indeed, all the white fathers lack personal force, to put it mildly. Essex ("Tom's" real father) is—significantly—no more than a name. Percy Driscoll, his next "father," dies bankrupt, his finances having apparently gone into decline soon after his own son's birth. As for Judge Driscoll, his central identity lies in his reputation as a gentleman. He can swing elections, but he is too "infatuated" with Tom to exercise any genuine authority over him (98). The story of how Chambers acquires the name "Tom Driscoll's nigger pappy" suggests that effective paternal power might reside in the vacant position of the black father, were the "black" son allowed to become a father, that is, possess a name. This incident also foreshadows the relation between Tom and the Judge. Like the Judge, who keeps believing Tom despite Tom's repeated failure to make good on any of his promises to reform, Chambers believes Tom when he says he is drowning and thus "unfortunately"—as Twain says—saves his life. Tom then stabs Chambers, and when that fails to kill him, Tom tries to have Chambers sold down the river. When Judge Driscoll buys Chambers in order to "prevent" this "scandal," he ironically "saves" his brother's real son from the death that such sale implies. When the white patriarchs act in this novel, they act blindly. Further, the Judge's primary means of eliciting our respect is his friendship with David Wilson, the "true son" who finally names his "father's" killer and assumes his "rightful" position of authority in Dawson's Landing.

But Wilson, if we bracket his calendar, *is* a pudd'nhead. His intelligence is proven, and his ascenscion to authority vindicated in the end, but only after what amounts to Twain's extended humiliation of him as a detective who is remarkably dull-witted when it comes to reading his evidence. Most noteworthy is his persistent and blundering confusion over the identity of the "young woman" in Tom's room, "where properly no young woman belonged," and his search for this "mysterious" girl's fingerprints, despite his faith that a "gentleman" like the Judge "could have no quarrels with girls" (103). Roxana, certainly, has a "quarrel" with the class represented by the Judge, and in light of this fact, Wilson's "pudd'nheadedness" reflects the white masters' blindness to the violent power of the black woman in its midst. Tom wears his mother's clothes to disguise his movements as a thief and to cover his getaway as a murderer, and so Pudd'nhead Wilson pursues the clue of the mysterious woman in black. But what is a red herring on the novel's surface points to a vital truth at its center: Roxana, as a "black" woman, has turned Tom into her instrument for revenge. Figuratively, the knife that Tom uses to kill the Judge is an extension of the knife Roxana holds on Tom when she forces him to accompany her home in St. Louis. That none of the appointed authorities of Dawson's Landing imagines this is hardly surprising. That Wilson fails to see it suggests that the superior intelligence that Dawson's Landing has marginalized all those years may be somewhat overrated.

Aggressive and shrewd, the Roxana who deceives Wilson and rules Tom, advising him in his thievery while forcing him to "behave" more effectively than any of his fathers, ought to present a gratifying spectacle, not least because with Tom as her agent, running in and out of houses and dressed in her clothes, Roxana has everyone in Dawson's Landing thoroughly baffled and confused. But as any reader of *Pudd'nhead Wilson* can attest, gratification is hardly the word for our responses to this novel. To account for this, we need to attend to the other side of the slave mother's unique position as the locus of negation. Roxana's status as "imitation white" provides the precondition for her campaign of vengeance, a campaign that exposes a critical gap in the slave economy of social death, a gap that opens precisely on the site of the mulatto mother. What enables her attack on the white patriarchy is that she can turn the power inscribed on the slave mother's body—the power to negate the slave father—back on the white father. But this radical displacement entails the alienation of that father's "white" son as well, a fact that serves Roxana's purpose only insofar as Tom is that "white" son. But of course, "Tom" is not Percy Driscoll's "white" son. He is Roxana's "black" son.

Consequently, what looms up behind Roxana's vengeful subversion of the white fathers is the fundamental and unchanging horror of the condition that motivates it—the slave child's "natal alienation" from his mother, and her foredoomed loss of him. In the excruciating chapter 4, for example, in which Twain describes Tom's childhood culminating in "an abyss of separation" between Roxana and "her boy," the abyss in question is not simply that which opens as the master-slave relationship overtakes and destroys the mother-child bond. Several ideologically charged and contradictory codes (e.g., the black Mammy and her white charge and the white mother's love of her child) circulate through the story told in this chapter, but none wholly deflects the horror of the situation they both describe and obscure—that of the slave mother condemned to the loss of her child. Beneath the confusions of real/false and white/black lies the distinction "my son"/"his son," and the erasure of two white fathers' names entails the destruction of two "black" sons' lives. Satirizing the Southern ideology that exalted the Mammy's devotion to her white owner's children as well as theirs to her, Twain displays Roxana as full of "impotent rage" at Tom, and Tom as an irredeemable little bully to her. Twain includes a hilarious account of Tom as a "bad baby" that must have rung as true to the mothers of Twain's day as it does to those of ours, but the humor is corroded throughout by the racist implications it inevitably fosters. Likewise, when he appeals to the white culture's sanctification of the mother, Twain both satirizes this ideology, calling Roxana a "doting fool of a mother," whose son becomes her "master, and her deity," and yet invokes its cultural force by depicting Roxana's fall "from the sublime height of mother-hood to the somber deeps of unmodified slavery," as Tom's "chattel" and "dog." What makes this chapter so painful to read is what both destabilizes Roxana as a character and generates the entire novel's radically disjunctive tone. In appealing to such codes to tell the story of a black mother's alienation from a "white" son become a "master," Twain's chapter exacerbates the horror of the slave mother's plight as not only the victim, but also the reproducer of social death. What is represented explicitly as a double-bind blocking the immediate avenues of revenge implicitly refers us to the violently severed bond between slave mother and child.

That is, because she is "imitation-white," as Chambers tells her, Roxana can subvert the matrilineal rule of descent, but only at the cost of losing her son entirely. By disowning him, she makes him free but no longer hers. Once the maternal bond to him is worn thin by his mistreatment of her, she is faced with the fact that to "own" Tom as hers, even if she could prove her claim, would make him a slave, subject to being sold down the river—the very fate from which she had set out to save him. But, as we have seen, Roxana finds a way out of this impasse; by threatening to "own" him before the Judge, Roxana can bring vengeance on him as well as on the white masters. What she cannot do is "save" her son, for the dilemma she faces with regard to her "white" son—to own him is to make him a slave—uncannily reiterates precisely the slave mother's constitutive double-bind: to give birth is to inflict social death. In other words, to give life to her child is to condemn him to death: it is this contradiction—so brilliantly explored in Toni Morrison's *Beloved*—which reveals what the economy of social death that Patterson describes entails for the slave mother. And it is this logic which Roxana's plot both resists and horribly confirms. If to blot out one father means that you can blot out the other, the same negativity entails that any child you have you must lose. From the opening moment when she decides to drown her child, to the closing one in which he is sold down the river, death is the slave mother's predetermined legacy that Roxana tries to, but finally cannot, abort. The choice she confronts at the outset, between seeing her son sold away or killing him herself, in retrospect collapses; from her position, death is not merely the equivalent of being sold down the river, but is identical to it.[2]

From this vantage point, the space of the narrative opened up between Percy Driscoll's threat of sale and his creditors' final enforcement of that threat twenty-three years later may be figured as a space pried open between the jaws of a vise. In a sense, what keeps those jaws from closing for so long is the continual substitution of alienability for death that Roxana negotiates. For example, Chambers becomes alienable so Tom can "live"; Roxana sells herself back into slavery to save Tom; and Tom must find the money to buy Roxana back in order to save his life. Because the white slaveowning masters continue to buy and sell, and the "inventory" remains intact, they remain blindly aloof from the feverish strategems we observe going forward around them. Like Percy Driscoll, as a class they are too concerned with their speculations to notice any substitutions in the specific bodies that are the vehicles of their capital. Recall that no matter how much Roxana's second owner may admire her, he is quite satisfied to be reimbursed for her loss. From the white slaveowning class's viewpoint, the slave's life *is*, quite literally, his or her alienability as property so that the "erroneous inventory" held responsible for the Judge's murder is corrected to everyone's satisfaction by Tom's final sale down the river. But from Roxana's viewpoint, that sale is her son's death, snapping the vise shut forever.

Roxana's plot, then, drives in two directions at once. Most explicitly, it operates to subvert the white patriarchy. The plot device of an "imitation white" slave mother focused Roxana as a slave mother of 1850 through the lens of the 1890s, with its "one-drop" rules, its lynchings, Jim Crow laws, and *Plessy v. Ferguson* two years away. Roxana's power to erase the name of the father thus emerged and enabled Twain to assault, humiliate, and expose the white Southern gentleman, to attack virulently the slave society he had ruled and the racist society he had bequeathed and still ruled. Thus, Cox is quite right to identify the novel's target as the white Southern patriarchy. What needs to be added is that it is the matrilineal rule of descent reinscribed on the mulatto mother that makes Roxana such a powerful weapon in Twain's arsenal. The negating power that the white patriarchy has invested in the body of the slave mother backfires here. If the white fathers have used the slave mother to erase the

---

2. In fact, the collapse of difference between death and alienability has already been accomplished for her. When her efforts to exploit the exchangeability of death for alienability culminate in her own sale down the river, her experiences there can be read as narrativing the metaphorical relation between killing and selling, relocating it along a metonymic axis where her sale and her death threaten to achieve a cause-effect relationship.

name of the black father, Roxana turns this negating power back onto the white fathers. Insofar as it is a matter of revenge against the white fathers, then, Roxana's subversive power is appreciable. But insofar as it is a matter of sons rather than fathers, her plot backfires on Roxana herself. If what the slave code termed "the condition of the mother" enables Roxana to blot out the white father, it also compels her to blot out the "black" son—*her* son, for whose sake she had acted in the first place.

On the one hand, Roxana's plot foregrounds the radical difference in the fates of the two sons in order to drive home the moral idiocy of that "fiction of law and custom" that enforces the color line. But on the other, it also exposes the similarity in their fates; for the slave mother, that is, both fates are "killing." The slave mother's constitutive double-bind is thus explosively revealed, but corrosively recontained by the *Pudd'nhead Wilson* plot. This, I believe, is why Roxana as a character is thoroughly contradictory in herself—and destabilizing to the entire novel.

It is not only Roxana's sexual force that must be repressed. Nor is it only a question of Pudd'nhead Wilson finally bringing down the curtain on Roxana's career as an "imitation" master. Most fundamentally, what gives Roxana's plot its radical and disruptive force lies in the contradiction at its heart—a contradiction we can imagine Twain violently warding off even as it looms more powerfully all along—the contradiction between a power to negate and one unleashed from within the slave mother's negated position. This contradiction might account for, although by no means redeem, the well-known moments in the novel that provoke a kind of moral vertigo in the reader, such as Roxana's appeal to "white folks'" example to justify her exchange of the babies, her infamous genealogy speech, or the scene in which she excoriates Tom for his cowardice and blames the nigger in him. Such an account would require another essay, but I could suggest how we might proceed. For me, one of the worst among many moments in *Pudd'nhead Wilson* comes in the courtroom scene, when Roxana cries out, "De Lord have mercy on me, po' misable sinner dat I is!" and the clock strikes twelve. In some nightmarish version of Cinderella, Roxana is reduced to the rags of a racial stereotype. And rather than a prince, she finds in Twain a stern judge who condemns her in the final chapter as the recipient of a pension from "[t]he young fellow upon whom she had inflicted twenty-three years of slavery" (120).

There is no way to read this and other comparable passages without succumbing to a kind of ethical nausea. But there may be a way to account for such passages by suggesting that the aggression Roxana's plot unleashes in Twain's text is driven out of control by the horror that provokes it, so that Twain gives in to the temptation to turn that aggression against Roxana herself. As black women in this country have always known and have testified repeatedly, this would not be the first or the last time that the black mother got blamed.

MYRA JEHLEN

The Ties That Bind: Race and Sex in *Pudd'nhead Wilson*†

Literary fictions can no more transcend history than can real persons. Although certainly not universally acknowledged, in the current criticism this truth has replaced the former truth that literature is a thing apart. Once banned from the interpretation of books for violating the integrity of the imagination, considerations of race and sex (and of class) have entered into even the most formalist readings.[1] Race and sex are now found organic to problems of organic form. As a result, those problems have become vastly more complicated than when a literary work was thought to invent its own sufficient language, for then the task of the critic, although complex, was also simple, it was to show how everything within the text worked together, taking coherence as given. A poem or story was a puzzle for which the critic could be sure that he or she had all the pieces and that they dovetailed.

Neither assurance is any longer available; one cannot be certain a work seen as engaged in history is internally coherent, nor that the issues it treats finally hang together. This development is not altogether congenial to literary critics, who mean to analyze works, not to dismantle them. But if we take literature's link to history seriously, we will have to admit that it renders literature contingent, like history itself. My case in point is *Pudd'nhead Wilson*, the writing of which posed problems that were made impossible to resolve by the history of racial and sexual thinking in America. The ideologies of race and sex that Mark Twain contended with in this novel were

---

† From *Mark Twain's* Pudd'nhead Wilson: *Race, Conflict, and Culture*, ed. Susan Gillman and Forrest G. Robinson (Durham and London: Duke University Press, 1990), pp. 105–20. Copyright © 1990, Duke University Press. All rights reserved. Reprinted by permission of the publisher.

1. I use "sex" instead of "gender" in the title not to reject the argument that sexual identity is a social construction, but to sidestep it in order to evoke the material condition itself; the way sex is interpreted into gender being precisely the subject of this essay. I am aware that one view holds that no material condition as such exists, or none we can apprehend, so that the language of gender is all we know of sex and all we need to know. To this, my response is implicit in what follows, that gender, like any ideological construction, describes the interactions of several realities, at least one of which is not the creature of language but material—the world out there. Gender is all we know of sex, but not all we need to know. This essay also depicts the inadequacy of ideological knowledge.

finally not controllable through literary form. They tripped the characters and tangled the plot. *Pudd'nhead Wilson* exemplifies the tragedy of the imagination, a literary kind that, ironically, only a historical criticism can fully appreciate.

Pudd'nhead Wilson builds its plot upon a plot. The subversive schemer is a young slave mother named Roxana (Roxy), who is thrown into panic one day by her master's casual threat to sell some of his slaves downriver into the inferno of the Deep South. Reasoning that if he can sell these, he can as readily sell her baby, she first determines to kill herself and the child rather than lose it to the slave market. Then she finds another way. Being not only a mother but the Mammy of her master's child, she simply switches the infants, who look so much alike that no one suspects the exchange. In contrast to their perfect resemblance as babies, the two boys grow up totally unlike. The black child, taking the white's name of Tom (for Thomas à Becket Driscoll), becomes a treacherous, cowardly thief; the white child, assuming the black name, Valet de Chambre (Chambers), is gentle, loyal, honest, and brave. Tom's path of petty crime leads eventually to murder, and his victim is his putative uncle and guardian, the much-loved benevolent Judge Driscoll. A pair of visiting foreign twins are wrongly accused of the crime and are about to be convicted when Pudd'nhead Wilson, a local sage in the tradition of shrewd Ben Franklin, uncovers the real murderer who is, coincidentally, the real black. The amiable foreigners are vindicated, the real white man is freed from his erroneous bondage and restored to his estate, and the murderer is punished. He is not hanged because—not being really a gentleman but a slave—he has to be punished as a slave: he is sold downriver into the Deep South.

Twain starts off simply enough with a farce whose characters' opportunistic prevarications expose established lies. The lie Roxy exposes when she successfully replaces her master's child with her own is that racial difference is inherent. As the ground for slavery, this racism is unambiguously false, its inversion of human truth dramatized in Roxy's dilemma: she can jump into the river with her baby or live in daily peril of its being sold down the river. Given those alternatives, her stratagem appears righteous and even fair despite its concomitant enslavement of the white baby. Without condoning this but simply by focusing on Roxy and her child, the story enlists the reader wholly on their side since the failure of the scheme can mean only the sale of mother and child, no doubt separately, or their common death.

But then things take an odd turn, which in fact will culminate in an about-face, the reversal ultimately going so far as to transform the exposure of Roxy and her son into a happy ending that rights wrongs, rewards the good, punishes the bad, and restores order all around.

When, at an eleventh hour, Pudd'nhead Wilson unmasks Tom and justice is done, the reader is actually relieved and gratified. If by this intervention the story does not exactly celebrate the return of the escaped slave to bondage or his sale to the demons of tidewater plantations, neither does it regret these events. Roxy's broken spirit and the double defeat of her maternal hopes are pitiable sights to be sure, but there is a consolation prize. In *Pudd'nhead Wilson's* finally rectified moral economy, Roxy's punishment is quite moderate. Not only are the legal authorities of the town of Dawson's Landing forbearing, but also "The young fellow upon whom she had inflicted twenty-three years of slavery continued" the pension she had been receiving from Tom.[2] Exemplary generosity, to be sure, but also a startling turnaround. Roxy, who once was so helplessly enslaved that her only recourse was suicide, is now being represented as herself an enslaver. Adding insult to injury, the pension her victim bestows upon her makes her appear still more culpable. Roxy and her baby exit as the villains of a story they entered as the innocently wronged.

Twain recognized that this about-face required explanation. One reason Tom turned out so badly and Chambers so well, the narrator suggests, is that they were brought up in opposite ways. "Tom got all the petting, Chambers got none. . . ." The result was that "Tom was 'fractious,' as Roxy called it, and overbearing, Chambers was meek and docile" (20). Slavery is made to counter racism here much the way it does in *Uncle Tom's Cabin* and not to any better effect except that the black man made Christ-like by his sufferings is really white, so that in the absence of real blacks similarly affected the case is not fully made. All that these distortions of character argue is the evil of human bondage, not the equality of master and slave, and even less so when we know that the master is a member of the slave race. For Stowe, countering racism was incidental, indeed she had only a limited interest in doing so, up to the point of establishing the humanity of the slaves in order to argue her central case, which was against slavery. But this is not Twain's situation when he published *Pudd'nhead Wilson* in 1892–93, thirty years after Emancipation. In fact, his novel with its story of the baby exchange has little to do with slavery: the plot follows not Chambers the white slave in order to depict the horrors of his condition, but Tom the black master and the crimes he has all his freedom to perpetrate. In appropriate contrast to *Uncle Tom's Cabin*, *Pudd'nhead Wilson* is only peripherally concerned with the atrocities of the slave system. Although Chambers is sadly disadvantaged by his years of servitude, his debility has too little force to motivate the novel; nothing much comes from it or is expected to.

2. Mark Twain, *Pudd'nhead Wilson* and *Those Extraordinary Twins*, ed. Sidney E. Berger (New York: Norton, 2005), 120. Quotations from this edition are cited parenthetically in the text.

On the contrary, everything comes from Tom's ascension to power, all of it bad.

Nothing in the original premise of the story predicts this sad development, so the obvious question is, Why does Tom, the former slave, turn out so villainous and dangerous a master? The most congenial explanation—that Tom has been fatally corrupted by his translation into the class of oppressors—omits too much of the story to serve. Twain offers it only half-heartedly, presenting the true white planters as a decent lot, often absurd in their chivalric poses and inadequate to their ruling tasks, but on the whole men of integrity, faithful to their "only religion," which is "to be a gentleman . . . without stain or blemish." Even their slaveowning seems less evil than careless. The description of Pembroke Howard as "a fine, brave, majestic creature, a gentleman according to the nicest requirements of the Virginian rule . . ." (4, 5) mingles affection with mockery, and although his dash is balderdash, there are worse things—Tom for example. His sale of Roxy treacherously and symbolically downriver is transcendingly evil, branding him an unnatural son and a denatured man. To underline the exceptional quality of his betrayal, Twain shows Tom prepared to sell his mother twice over, for when she escapes and seeks his help against pursuing slave-hunters, only her threat to repay him in kind prevents him from turning her over.

It is more than a little perverse that the two characters who actually traffic in slavery are both black. Percy Driscoll's threat to sell his misbehaving slaves is the novel's original sin responsible for Roxy's desperate deed. But having the sale itself take place offstage and specifying that, unlike Tom, the judge only sells to his relatively humane neighbors and not to the Simon Legrees of the Deep South, attenuates our sense of the planter's guilt. On the contrary, the story pointedly reports Tom's plan to sell his boyhood companion Chambers, a plan foiled by Judge Driscoll, who buys Chambers to safeguard the family honor: "for public sentiment did not approve of that way of treating family servants for light cause or for no cause" (25). Tom's corrupting environment, therefore, does not explain why the disguised black is both more deeply and differently corrupted than his fellow slaveowners, a development that is the more startling because it reverses the initial expectations of virtue inspired by his first appearance as a hapless babe.[3]

But if no explanation emerges directly from the novel, consider its

3. The first description of the two children distinguished only by the "soft muslin and . . . coral necklace" of one and the "coarse tow-linen shirt" of the other (9) recalls the similarly contrasting costumes of the Prince and the Pauper. In that story, however, the little pauper fulfills all sentimental expectations, and far from usurping the throne, returns it more secure to its rightful owner. Are there implications in the virtue of this poor boy, versus the vice of the black boy, for different authorial attitudes toward class and race?

historical context. The year of its publication in book form, 1894, was the eve of McKinley's election and a period of accelerating racism marked by the bloody spread of Jim Crow. The formative experience of *Pudd'nhead Wilson*'s era was the defeat of Reconstruction, not the end of slavery. In that context the story of the replacement of a white baby by a black has a local urgency we may miss at this distance. And its progress from a good thing to a bad as the black boy grows up to murder the town patriarch who is his uncle and to rob, cheat, and generally despoil the whole village, as well as plunge his mother into a worse state than she had been in before, makes as much sense in history as it fails to make in the story.

In the story, Tom's villainy appears only arbitrary. As much as Twain justifies Roxy's revolution by appealing to the transcendent motive of maternal love, making her insurrection finally inevitable and in no way a sign even of inherent rebelliousness, he damns Tom from the start as "a bad baby, from the very beginning of his usurpation" (19). So the good black is a woman; the bad, a man. The good woman, complicated enough within herself to act badly while remaining herself good, is black; the bad man, lacking interiority and simply expressing a given identification that is barely an identity, is also black. With this formula, *Pudd'nhead Wilson* emerges as a remarkable exploration of the anxieties aroused by a racist social structure, as a literary locus classicus of one modern (in its integration of individualist concepts of identity) paradigm of race, and perhaps most strikingly, as the exposition of the relation between the racial paradigm of race and a modern paradigm of gender. The conjunction of race and sex is more often pictured as an intersection but here it is an interaction. Moreover, this interaction does not simply join, but combines, race and sex so that in certain pairings they are more stringently limiting than when taken separately.

When Twain associates the black race with the female sex, he represents racism in the uncontroversially repugnant form of slavery. Roxy's force and shrewdness work to disprove stereotypes of servility. Her sovereignty over the children extends naturally to the story of which she is a sort of author. She achieves the highest status available to a fictional character when she and the narrator are the only ones who know what is going on and can truly identify the participants. The white baby's mother is dead, and his own father fails to recognize him. Roxy alone knows who he is—and what. Further, the way she knows this bears its own anti-racist implications; because both babies have flaxen curls and blue eyes, her discrimination can have nothing to do with physical characteristics. Thus as she identifies them in her own image, *who* Tom and Chambers are is entirely independent of *what* they are. They embody the American ideal of individualism, the belief that a man is what he makes of himself, which is potentially anything he determines.

Consonant with this liberal view, *Pudd'nhead Wilson* initially defines black character in universal traits as benign as Roxy herself. If Roxy at times falls prey to the lure of unattended objects, "Was she bad?" Twain muses. "Was she worse than the general run of her race? No. They had an unfair show in the battle of life, and they held it no sin to take military advantage of the enemy—in a small way." He insists, "in a small way, but not in a large one" (12). Even as Twain writes this, Roxy takes the very large military advantage of exchanging the infants. But the petty thievery, in this case not even her own, that has called down the wrath of her master and thus precipitated this ultimate transgression, was a very small crime. If Roxy's pilfering turns to pillage, the novel suggests that this is not her fault, hardly even her doing, but that of a criminal society that monstrously deforms not only marginally guilty relations, but also purely innocent ones.

The night of the exchange, Percy Driscoll, whose threat to punish theft by selling the thief has raised for Roxana the specter of her child's own commodity status, sleeps the sleep of the just. By contrasting her master's smug oblivion to her anguished wakefulness, through which she becomes for this moment the story's consciousness, Twain condones and even endorses her crime. The novel continues to side with her when it is not Roxy but Percy Driscoll who enforces the children's inequality, permitting the ostensibly white boy to abuse the child whom he fails to recognize as his son (21). In this representation of the political economy of slavery in terms of the family, the author's voice speaks against the regnant patriarchy, espouses the oppressed, and applauds subversion. Fathers in Mark Twain are not a nice lot, and boys are frequently abused. A black woman enslaved by white men is the natural ally of white boys. Would that all boys had mothers like Roxy!

Tom's becoming a man, however, rearranges this scheme radically. His passage into manhood, marked by his return from Yale, seems to start the story over. At Yale he has been a desultory student but has acquired a number of grown-up ways that pose unprecedented grown-up problems. His indifferent intellect has prevented any deeper penetration, but Tom has acquired the superficies of elite culture, its dainty dress, and its mannered ways. The local youth naturally scorn such refinements, but when they set a deformed black bellringer dressed in parodic elegance to follow Tom about, the young popinjay is debunked more profoundly than anyone in the story suspects. And it is unclear just what is being satirized: is it simply foppish pretension, or rather some special absurdity of black foppery? Because the characters are unaware that their parody of Tom possesses this additional dimension, it becomes a joke shared by the narrator and the reader, a joke with a new target.

Twain had already mocked black dress when he described a despairing Roxy adorning herself for her suicide. Her ribbons and feathers, her wondrously gaudy dress, certainly reflect on her race, but the butt of the joke is not race as such. Being black is not given as ridiculous, although blacks may behave ridiculously. In the later episode being black is itself absurd: the private joke we share with the narrator is the very fact of Tom's negritude, that while pretending to be a high-falutin' gentleman, he is really a "Negro." Here, the novel begins its turnaround from the initial view implicit in the identical babies, that human beings are potentially the same to the final dramatization in the Judge's murder, of black duplicity and violence as inherent racial traits.

Tom's grown-up inferiorities in fact make his spoiled childhood irrelevant. He cannot have acquired his fear of duelling, for instance, from being raised a Southern gentleman. While his overexcited peers in the Dawson's Landing peerage fall to arms at the least imagined slight, Tom turns tail at the first sign of a fight. This is only one of a constellation of traits that define Tom as a different sort of beau ideal, the very type of the upstart Negro of post-Reconstruction plantation fiction: cowardly, absurdly pretentious, lazy and irresponsible, a petty thief but potentially a murderer. Born the generic, universal baby, Tom has grown into a very particular sort of man, unlike both his white and his black fellows; on the white side, he is not capable of being a master, and on the black, he has been dangerously loosed from the bonds that keep other black men in check.

I want to stress the next point because it is central to the racial/sexual paradigm developed in *Pudd'nhead Wilson*. The white man who has taken Tom's place might have been expected, in the context of the novel's increasingly essentialist view of race, also to manifest an essential nature. He does not. "Meek and docile" in adaptation to his powerless state, Chambers yet does not become a white man fatally misplaced among blacks, as Tom is a black man fatally misplaced among whites. This asymmetry embodies that of racial typing that applies only to the inferior race. The superior race, when defining itself in the terms of modern individualism, claims not a better type, but the general norm—universality or the ability to be any type and all of them.

Unhappily for Chambers, however, universality imparts only potential, a capacity to become rather than an already defined (therefore limited) being. That is, what characterizes the norm embodied in the superior race, instead of a particular set of traits, is universal potential. Such potential realizes itself in relation to environment: ironically, the white "Chambers" is far more vulnerable to the shaping force of the exchange, for had Tom remained a slave he would have unfolded into essentially the same man, although a crucially less powerful one and for that reason a less harmful one. So Chambers, unlike Tom, adapts to his sad situation and is shaped by it. In one important respect his adaptation represents one of the novel's most basic if unacknowledged issues. As I suggested earlier, in Roxy, Twain endorses a black woman's subversion of the white patriarchy, whereas in Tom, he rejects a black man's takeover. The fate of Chambers begins to explain why Twain distinguished so sharply between mother and son by revealing the stake in his relation to the latter.

That stake is manhood. Through Tom's usurpation, the white community of Dawson's Landing risks losing its manhood. A black woman exercising the authority of motherhood in a white society may call in question the domestic ideology of white womanhood. In *Pudd'nhead Wilson* this domestic ideology means the genteel sentimentalism of aunts and widows. Had it been only a question of Roxy's passing off her child as the child of a white lady, the baby switch would have been a disturbing but limited affair. But the far more encompassing event of a black man occupying the place of a white man, wielding the same power, usurping (Twain's repeated term) the authority of white fatherhood connotes a global reversal that, instead of emancipating the iconoclastic boy who typically articulates Twain's abhorrence of genteel culture, literally emasculates him. The subversion in Tom's usurpation of white identity turns Chambers into a woman, for femininization is the lasting result of that unfortunate man's slave upbringing. Once a black slave, he can never take his place among his real peers: "The poor fellow could not endure the terrors of the white man's parlor, and felt at home and at peace nowhere but in the kitchen" (121). Note that Chambers's loss of manhood is clearly regrettable only because he is white. A black man may be improved by the attenuations of femininity, as is the case elsewhere with Twain's motherly Jim. One stereotype of the black man threatens violence and uncontrollable sex. The other has him contemptibly effeminate. Black men are seen simultaneously as excessively male and insufficiently masculine. Inextricably entangled in these ideological contradictions, Tom is incoherently both. Although his final act is a stabbing, earlier in the story, disguised as a woman, he robs houses. The witnesses who fail to recognize in a dress the man they know as a white gentleman are actually seeing the real Tom, who thus shows himself one way and another not a real man.

By the logic of the different *kind* of identity that real men develop, a black mother can be the ally of rebellious boys, but a black father would rob them of their very selves as heirs to the mantle of universal (white) manhood. We stand with Roxy when she defies the social order to save her boy-child. But when this child grows up, he embodies a revolution which has displaced the erstwhile ruling children, usurping their manhood. Once this implication has been realized by the story's unfolding, even the benignity of Roxy's crime seems retrospectively less certain. On the last page of the novel, the story finally represents the exchange not as freeing the black child, but as enslaving the white.

That ending was implicit all along in the slave situation, which stipulated that the only way to free Tom was to enslave Chambers. This unhappy reciprocity, however, was not manifest in the story so long as it focused on mothers and children. The maternal economy is a welfare state. Its central concern is not production but distribution, and even when it is unfair, it has primarily to do with giving, allocating privileges and goods among the more or less undifferentiated members of a group who seek more not from each other but from the mother/state. But production, not distribution, was the chief care of the market-capitalist economy of the United States in the late nineteenth century; and in that context, distribution was a matter of competitive acquisition.

Much has been written about the relation of these two economies that in some respects confront and in others complement each other.[4] The peculiar slant of *Pudd'nhead Wilson* comes from presenting them not, as usual, synchronically, as simultaneous dimensions of one society, but diachronically, the market economy following the maternal. Thus sequentially related, with each one in its time defining the fictional universe, their contradictions emerge more sharply, along with the way that the hierarchy of family and state, private and public, gives the market the last word. It certainly has the last word in *Pudd'nhead Wilson*, as we will see. Although a mother may take something from one child and give it to another who needs it more but not deprive the former, in an economy in which personally recuperable profit is the bottom line, taking away and giving must show up on the ledger ultimately. And when self-sufficient individuals—men and fathers—possess unequal amounts of power or wealth, reallocation, however equitable, does mean deprivation: one gets only by taking away from another. At the point at which the story of Tom and Chambers leaves the nursery and enters the market place, Tom, who as a baby was the innocent and even rightful recipient of the freedom he unjustly lacked, becomes a usurper; Chambers is seen to have been robbed.

---

4. Here I would mention specifically that portion of the literature that has reevaluated the sentimental tradition as a female, sometimes feminist, critique of the male ideology of the market. See especially Jane Tompkins, *Sensational Designs: The Cultural Work of American Fiction, 1790–1860* (New York: Oxford University Press, 1985), and Elizabeth Ammons, "Stowe's Dream of the Mother-Savior: *Uncle Tom's Cabin* and American Women Writers before the 1920s," in *New Essays on Uncle Tom's Cabin*, ed. Eric J. Sundquist (Cambridge: Cambridge University Press, 1986).

The maternal and market economies which in their turn dominate the plot of *Pudd'nhead Wilson* do coexist to a degree. Although the story starts out in Roxy's control, the market wields overwhelming force from the first because the power of whites to sell blacks to other whites inspires the exchange of the babies. But at this point, even though in Roxy's world slavery functions as a harsh necessity that will ultimately deprive her of all power, the market as such is not yet the primary setting. Indeed, when this necessity first manifests itself, she resists successfully, temporarily returning her world to its prior order and keeping both babies. All through their infancy and childhood she administers her welfare system, taking care of both of them as fairly as she can under the circumstances despite the fact that her own child is in the master position and would be favored if she were fully to implement the unfairness of the slave system. When Tom is no longer a mother's child but his own man, however, he takes over the fictive universe and administers it his way. Because he is a man, whatever the quality of his administration, it participates directly in the patriarchal economy and in this new context the baby exchange realizes its meaning in the trade of Chambers's white manhood for Tom's black impotence, and vice versa.

Because the asymmetries of race and of sex are parallel, Roxy's innate character as a mother is congruent with her innate nature as a black woman. Paradoxically, even ironically, this very limit permits Twain to endow her as a character with a considerable degree of transcendence, the way that Flaubert, for example, endows Emma with much of his own sense of self without ever questioning the non-transcendence of female selfhood as such.[5] Roxy, a black woman, actually approaches individualist selfhood while her son is denied it altogether and is depicted as capable of achieving self-creative powers only by the outright usurpation of whiteness. On the other side, Chambers's failure to achieve manhood, in dramatizing the transcendence of white identity which defines itself by going beyond nature, also points up a terrible vulnerability that springs from the very quality that makes white men superior. To be capable of making oneself and one's world is a very fine thing, but that ability has its price. The price of white men's power of self-creation is the risk of failing not only to achieve but also to be, whereas women (as such though not always as fictional characters) and blacks are essentially and thus invulnerably what and as they are born. And this inequality of vulnerability counterbalances racial inequality, coming first, in the ideological and psychological universe of *Pudd'nhead Wilson*, to

---

5. I have discussed this phenomenon more fully in an essay, "Archimedes and the Paradox of Feminist Criticism," *Signs* 6 (Winter 1981): 575–601.

equate the plights of blacks and whites then finally to make blacks appear stronger, or at least more threatening.

An essentialist identity requires, for the good of the community, more social control; it is too little vulnerable to be allowed as much freedom as identities that carry their own constraints in their vulnerability. It is generally recognized that the ratio of self-making to being determines the status of modern individuals, so that the more a man is his own author the higher he ranks and the more authority he wields. The converse is less often articulated, that an essentialist identity not only brands the socially inferior but also necessitates their submission. In one scene of *Pudd'nhead Wilson* this logic almost begins to justify slavery.

In this scene, Chambers has just revealed to Roxy that her errant son is a dissolute gambler who at the moment owes the huge sum of $200. Roxy is stunned: " 'Two—hund'd—dollahs! . . . Sakes alive, it's mos' enough to buy a tollable good second-hand nigger wid.' " Now the irony, indeed the wit, here lies in the fact that the $200 Tom has gambled away are $200 *he* would fetch, being himself "a tollable good second-hand nigger." But the possibility of buying and selling human beings, which up until this point has implied such intolerable violations of natural law as the separation of mothers and children, has become, astonishingly, a way to measure and *preserve* genuine value: Tom's worthlessness as a white man is measured by his gambling away his worth as a slave. Lest we not grasp this point fully, Twain spells it out in the ensuing dialogue. Chambers's report that Tom has been disinherited for his scandalous conduct infuriates Roxy, who accuses her supposed son of lying, calling him a "misable imitation nigger." Chambers retorts, " 'If I's imitation, what is you? Bofe of us is imitation *white*—dat's what we is—en pow'full good imitation, too . . . we don't 'mount to noth'n as imitation *niggers*' " (39). But Chambers *is* an "imitation nigger," being really white. He is also really honest and good, as he shows by openly declaring his purported blackness, unlike the true blacks in the story who lie about race. Once again the reader of *Pudd'nhead Wilson* understands a scene by knowing better than the characters and the better knowledge is the reality, the truth, of race.

The preceding scene plays directly to the concealed switch of Tom and Chambers and exactly negates its original thrust that whites and blacks can be exchanged because in *fact* blacks can be essentially white—read: universally human. Now on the contrary, the exchangeability of physically resembling blacks with whites represents the way apparent likeness can mask real and profoundly different beings. Initially, clothing and social status were seen as hiding real human resemblance. These same superficial differences have come to mask real difference, and the bodily likeness of Tom and Chambers that first expressed their common humanity now renders their total opposition invisible. People may *appear* equal, it says, but they are really not.

What matters in this scene is the real difference between Tom and Chambers while what had mattered about them at the start was their real likeness. Coincidentally in the same episode, Roxy herself sadly dwindles as the narrator ascribes her anger at Chambers for reporting Tom's disinheritance to her fear of losing "an occasional dollar from Tom's pocket" (39). This is a disaster she will not contemplate, the narrator laughs. But earlier, Roxy defined herself in relation to a larger disaster, not the loss of a dollar but the sale of her baby. And when two pages later Tom actually does refuse his mother a dollar, the novel's shift of perspective is complete: where the injustice of racial inequality was first measured by the violation of Roxy's natural motherhood, now inequality will be justified by the spectacle of the emancipated and empowered Tom's unnatural sonhood. Roxy's subsequent threat to expose him articulates his falseness; the "truth" about Tom is that he is false, that he is not who he is or should be. Henceforth the story of *Pudd'nhead Wilson* is not about interchangeable babies irrationally and unjustly rendered master and slave, but about a black man who has taken a white man's place. Roxy herself, who first identified Tom as a universal baby—who revealed him as "white" as any baby—now dubs him a "nigger."

The first name she had bestowed on her child was the name of a servant, Valet de Chambre. The fine sound of it appealed to her, Twain explained, although she had no notion what it meant. But we do, and when we first laugh at it we do so out of affectionate condescension. When later Roxy exchanges this name for that of a lord, Thomas à Becket, we begin to see that both names have their serious implications: they project a spurious identity that yet determines what each man becomes. In the end, however, we find that we have been wrong twice, first when we took the names lightly, but second when we took them as seriously damaging misnomers. Valet de Chambre was all along the correct identification of a man born a servant and for a time dangerously misnamed a master.

Thus Roxy's final renaming of Tom does not merely exchange one name for another, but redefines the very nature of his identity. When she called her son Tom and thereby made him the equal of whites, it was on the ground that in himself he was indistinguishable from whites. Scrutinizing his golden babyhood dressed in white finery, she marveled: " 'Now who would b'lieve clo'es could do de like o' dat? Dog my cats if it ain't all *I* kin do to tell t'other fum which, let alone his pappy' " (16). When babies are fledgling individuals, one as good as another in anticipation of each one's self-making, pappys cannot tell one from another, for indeed paternity is irrelevant. But when racial nature enters into identity, paternity becomes all-important.

Roxy announces Tom's blackness to him by saying "'You ain't no more kin to old Marse Driscoll den I is!'" With this she tells him "'you's my *son*'" (45), but the ground of this claim is a renunciation. Even as she demands that he recognize her maternal authority— "'You can't call me *Roxy*, same as if you was my equal. Chillen don't speak to dey mammies like dat. You'll call me Ma or mammy, dat's what you'll call me . . .'" (46)—she abdicates the transcendent authority that earlier enabled her to name *him* into an identity she had more than borne: created. Henceforth he may call her "Ma or mammy" and accede to her orders, but for both this will ratify subjection, in fact servitude. Even the reclamation of this maternal authority is limited, bounded by the surrounding patriarchy. "'You'll call me Ma or mammy,'" Roxy storms, "'leastways when dey ain't nobody aroun.'" For him to recognize her as his mother in public, of course, would reveal his real identity as a slave, whereupon Roxy would lose him to the authority of his father, and to the paternal authority of the slave system. Roxy had been able on her own to make Tom white, when she was in charge and nature and race were in abeyance, but making him black requires her to invoke white patriarchal authority.

Through a master irony the revelation of his real white father seals Tom's status as a black son: a chastened Tom surrenders to his new status by asking timidly, "'Ma, would you mind telling me who was my father?'" (47). The final link connecting Tom to his mother— identifying him as a slave—is her knowledge, her ability to call on the name of a white man. And through the medium of Roxy's pride as she tells him that his father was "'de highest quality in dis whole town— Ole Virginny stock, Fust Famblies'" (47), the authority of Cunnel Cecil Burleigh Essex parodically but surely reaches forward from that past all-generating moment when he could command Roxy to bear his son, to declare that son now a black slave. "'Dey ain't another nigger in dis town dat's as high-bawn as you is,'" she ends, preferring an identity that is the fatal opposite of the one she had conferred on him at the start of the story. "'En jes' you hold yo' head up as high as you want to—you has de right, en dat I kin swah'" (47–48).

One sign of Roxy's demotion to the status of just another fond mother is that she is wrong about this: Tom has neither the right nor the capacity to hold up his head. Despite his excellent white descent, he is simply not of cavalier mettle. And on the occasion when he runs away from a challenge to duel, Roxy herself sadly draws the inevitable conclusion: not even his superior white siring can redeem his fatal flaw: "'It's de nigger in you, dat's what it is. Thirty-one parts o' you is white, en on'y one part nigger, en dat po' little one part is yo' *soul*. 'Tain't wuth savin'; 'tain't wuth totin' out on a shovel en tho'in' in de gutter. You has disgraced yo' birth. What would yo' pa think o' you? It's enough to make him turn in his grave'" (75).

Roxy's racism is comically undercut certainly, but in the service of what alternative view? We are the more at a loss for a proper liberal riposte in that Roxy's parting shot travels directly to the end of the novel and its definitive return of Tom to the now unproblematical status of "nigger." "'Ain't nigger enough in him to show in his fingernails,'" she mutters, "'en dat takes mightly little—yit dey's enough to paint his soul'" (76). It was because of his white, thus raceless or race-transcendent, fingernails that she had been able to raise him to the status of master. But now it turns out that his fingernails did not accurately represent the case. Rather, as all discover, his identity lies in his fingerprints, and no one transcends his fingerprints.

Wilson's resort to fingerprints to establish Tom's true identity solves more than the judge's murder. It provides a more encompassing resolution of the novel as a whole, for his astounding revelation restores both racial and sexual order. Indeed, in that any satisfactory ending would require that the truth be revealed and, because only Roxy could reveal it, it is not easy to imagine how else Twain could have ended his story. For Roxy to solve the mystery would not constitute an ending, not so much because her confession would be dramatically unlikely as, on the contrary, because by identifying Tom and Chambers accurately she would reassert precisely the power to identify that has so badly compromised Dawson's Landing. For Roxy to name her son and his white counterpart a second time would confirm her authority, thus perpetuating the racial dilemma of *Pudd'n-head Wilson*. Reconstruction would continue.

In Pudd'nhead Wilson, however, Twain finds an alternative truth-teller. Male to a fault in his entire self-sufficiency, Wilson counters, then surpasses, Roxy's authority: to the babies' identical fingernails which enabled Roxy to declare them identical, Wilson opposes fingerprints representing the apotheosis of difference, uniqueness. Now, fingerprints are not racially but individually distributed. Therefore they cannot testify to Tom's racial nature but only to his personal character. Nonetheless, in the courtroom scene, Wilson invokes the telltale fingerprints categorically, to rule out categories of persons in order to identify the individual miscreant as himself the representative of a category.

Wilson, who represents the category of authoritative white men commanding both law and language, begins by announcing this authority to the community: "'I will tell you.'" This is what he tells them: "'For a purpose unknown to us, but probably a selfish one, somebody changed those children in the cradle'" (118). So far is the story from casting doubt on any aspect of this emerging elucidation, its miraculous verity is reinforced when the narration turns briefly to Roxy portrayed thinking pathetically that "Pudd'nhead Wilson could do wonderful things, no doubt, but he couldn't do impossible ones," and that therefore her secret is safe. But what is impossible to her is as nothing to Wilson. Having named the exact time of the exchange (thus returning to the crime's origin to master it whole) and having identified the perpetrator, he continues in the irrefutable idiom of scientific formulas: "'A was put into B's cradle in the nursery; B was transferred to the kitchen, and became a negro and a slave . . . but within a quarter of an hour he will stand before you white and free!'" He controls time and place. "'From seven months onward until now, A has still been a usurper, and in my finger-records he bears B's name.'" And now the coup de grace: "'The murderer of your friend and mine—York Driscoll, of the generous hand and the kindly spirit—sits among you. Valet de Chambre, negro and slave.'" Roxy's response is poignantly telling. Before the miracle of white masculine omniscience, she can only pray: "'De Lord have mercy on me, po' misable sinner dat I is!'" (118–20).

Wilson's godlike authority has appropriated the story, raveling the order of the white community as he unravels the case. In the process the story has also been rewritten, however, with a new beginning that brushes Roxy's motive aside with the casual conclusion that whatever this motive was, it was selfish (in context a stunningly ironic term that the text leaves uninflected) and redrawing its characters and issues in stark blacks and whites.

And what about Pudd'nhead himself? The instrument of resolution, what is his relation to the order he restores? First, although he wields the authority of the white patriarchy, he is not himself a father but a bachelor, a lone, even an outcast figure whose own authority the village has only this moment recognized and then only because of his trick with the fingerprints. For himself, although he rescues the established order, he is acutely and at times bitterly aware that those who administer it are not often worthy of their power. The joke that earns him the nickname "Pudd'nhead" has turned out more serious than it seemed. On his first day in town, Wilson became a fool in the eyes of his neighbors when he declared that he wished he owned half a loudly barking dog so he might kill his half. Now he has saved half a dog, while the other half dies. There is nothing joyous in restoring the status quo of Dawson's Landing. Twain may have been reluctant to see black men acquire the power of whites and may have viewed their bid for a share of power as outright usurpation. He did not vindicate white society. This is a familiar dilemma in his work generally which frequently ends, as does *Pudd'nhead Wilson*, in a stalemate between radical criticism and an implicit conservatism expressed in the refusal or the inability, when it comes to it, to imagine significant change. The stalemate here seems particularly frustrating: change must be defeated, yet nothing of the established way of life appears worth preserving.

The depth of *Pudd'nhead Wilson's* concluding depression may gauge the sounding it takes of perhaps the most profoundly embedded images in the American mind, the images of race and sex. Separately but especially interacting, these images sometimes not only activate the imagination, but they also disable it, trapping it as Mark Twain seems to have been by the impossible adjuncts of racial equality and white authority, of maternal justice and patriarchal right. When in the end the rule of the white fathers is reestablished by the fiat of law, there is no rejoicing. Pudd'nhead Wilson himself is an outcast and a failure. Playing out his private charades alone in his study, he represents the writer as outcast and failure. If he also represents the writer as lawgiver and defends the system he hates, even against its victims who threaten it by trying to lift their oppression, this is not a productive paradox but a paralyzing contradiction. Pudd'nhead Wilson, expressing his author's own anguish, would really have liked to kill his half of the dog but was afraid finally of leaving the house unguarded.

JOHN CARLOS ROWE

Fatal Speculations: Murder, Money, and Manners in *Pudd'nhead Wilson*†

"You can't do much with 'em," interrupted Col. Sellers. "They are a speculating race, sir, disinclined to work for white folks without security, planning how to live only by working for themselves. Idle, sir, there's my garden just a ruin of weeds. Nothing practical in 'em."

"There is some truth in your observation, Colonel, but you must educate them."

"You educate the niggro and you make him more speculating than he was before. If he won't stick to any industry except for himself now, what will he do then?"

"But, Colonel, the negro when educated will be more able to make his speculations fruitful."

—CHARLES DUDLEY WARNER AND MARK TWAIN,
The Gilded Age (1873)

† From *Mark Twain's* Pudd'nhead Wilson: *Race, Conflict, and Culture*, ed. Susan Gillman and Forrest G. Robinson (Durham and London: Duke University Press, 1990), pp. 137–54. Copyright © 1990, Duke University Press. All rights reserved. Reprinted by permission of the publisher.

> It is good to begin life poor; it is good to begin life rich—these are
> wholesome, but to begin it poor and prospectively rich! The man
> who has not experienced it cannot imagine the curse of it.
>   —*Mark Twain's Autobiography*

In the "Conclusion" of *Pudd'nhead Wilson*, Tom Driscoll is sentenced to "imprisonment for life," only to be claimed as the legal property of the creditors of the Percy Driscoll estate, who had been able to recover only "sixty per cent" of the indebtedness of the estate at the time of Percy's death in the fall of 1845. The final two paragraphs of this uncanny novel constitute Twain's most withering satire of slavery as a legal and economic institution. Claiming that "'Tom' was lawfully their property and had been so for eight years," the creditors claim that his imprisonment would deprive them further of their property and any return they might expect from its "investment." Their arguments go well beyond, however, Twain's customary satire of the obvious absurdity involved in defining a human being as chattel. The creditors argue successfully that the violation of their rights occasioned by the mystery of Tom's origins is the real cause of the murder of Judge Driscoll: "[I]f he had been delivered up to them in the first place, they would have sold him and he could not have murdered Judge Driscoll, therefore it was not he that had really committed the murder, the guilt lay with the erroneous inventory. Everybody saw that there was reason in this."[1] The absurd attribution of a murder to an "erroneous inventory" is understood conventionally as Twain's satire of an antebellum legal system that in its worst moment would throw out Dred Scott's suit for liberty on the grounds that as a slave he had none of the legal rights of a U.S. citizen. Indeed, the conflict between property rights and civil rights is such a common theme in Twain's writings that this final turn in the already labyrinthine legalities of *Pudd'nhead Wilson* seems merely to underscore a familiar issue.

Yet by 1894, the surreal legal and existential situation of the antebellum slave must have seemed an increasingly anachronistic issue for the contemporary reader, even if the social and economic fates of black Americans were recognized by many to be as hard as ever.[2]

---

1. Mark Twain, *Pudd'nhead Wilson* and *Those Extraordinary Twins*, 2nd ed., ed. Sidney E. Berger (New York: W. W. Norton, 2005), 121–22. Quotations from this edition are cited parenthetically in the text.
2. See Arlin Turner, "Mark Twain and the South: *Pudd'nhead Wilson*," in the Norton Critical Edition, 1st ed. (1980), 286 ff. "By 1894, the problems explored in *Pudd'nhead Wilson* had grown wearisome in the North as well as the South. More than a decade earlier the political decision had been made that the Southern states should solve the race problem without interference from the national government. As state laws were enacted in the early 1890s which decreed for the former slaves a segregated, non-voting status, no effective protest was voiced in either section. The public, valuing the peace which had been achieved, did not welcome disturbances, even in fiction. There is something of irony in that, by chance rather than intention, Mark Twain wrote his most perceptive and most impressive attack on racism and related doctrines at a time when his attack

Twain's historical romances, as I think such works as *Huckleberry Finn, Pudd'nhead Wilson, A Connecticut Yankee*, and *The Prince and the Pauper* deserve to be called, employ historical distance to suggest how little the contemporary reader's society has progressed from the serfdom of either medieval England or antebellum America. In each of these works, Twain suggests that apparent—and often very dramatic—social changes merely have reinstated rigid social and class hierarchies; hints and foreshadowings of how such social transformations will effectively repeat the past quite often are incorporated in the dramatic action of the historical romance. Thus the fate of Jim at the end of *Huckleberry Finn*—a freed black man with nowhere to go—or that of the educated and freed black man ("a p'fessor in a college") scoffed by Pap Finn (in chapter 6) foreshadow accurately the plight of emancipated blacks under Reconstruction.[3] More obviously, the technological marvels that Hank Morgan brings to Arthurian England merely intensify the violent power struggles of the ruling class. In *Pudd'nhead Wilson*, the arbitrariness and irrationality of the law will survive the Civil War and Emancipation without substantial reform.

Despite the thematic continuities Twain may establish between the preindustrial societies in which his historical romances are set and ones in modern, industrial America of the Gilded Age, he often subscribes to his own special "history" of an America divided strategically by the Civil War. The rural, settled, slow-paced Midwest of "Old Times on the Mississippi" is forever changed by the railroads, land development, and westward expansion that accompanied—both as causes and effects—the political upheaval of the Civil War. I need not quote here those familiar passages from *Life on the Mississippi* in which Twain contrasts the romance of the steamboat and the near-transcendentalist qualities of its pilots with the brute realism of the railroad and the aggressive enterprise of its agents. Even when charged with the sins of the slave scheme, frontier Missouri often assumes the guise of a more "innocent" and manageable world than the openly corrupt cities of post–Civil War industrial America. Within this mythology, then, slavery is a cruel institution of rural America, whose passing is replaced by the more insidious forms of social and economic domination that would be faced by the immigrant, the emancipated black, and virtually any man or woman with only the means of honest labor. In this context Twain serves well

---

could stir no spark in the reading public." My argument, of course, attempts to lend Twain's "attack on racism and related doctrines" more relevance to late-nineteenth-century industrial America, North and South.

3. The "p'fessor in a college" so reviled by Pap Finn in chapter 6 of the novel is particularly hateful to him because he can *vote* in "Ohio." Freedom and voting rights are very often linked by Twain, which is why vote-buying is such an immoral "speculation" for him.

those myth critics who would maintain a sharp distinction between rural and industrial economies in America and thus, of course, the distinction between their social values.

Despite Twain's understandable sentimentality about an older, rural America, works like *The Gilded Age* and *Pudd'nhead Wilson* suggest that the sources of modern, postbellum, industrial corruption are to be found in rural America. A vigorous, albeit equivocal, even hypocritical satirist of modern technology, Twain understands slavery itself as not just a provincial agrarian institution, but the basis for the speculative economy that would fuel industrial expansion, Manifest Destiny, and laissez-faire capitalism. The slave is, after all, the ultimate "speculation," insofar as the buyer invests a relatively small amount of money—for purchase and maintenance—in hopes of watching that capital grow into the accumulated labor power of a healthy, long-lived slave. And insofar as the slave may be bred to multiply the owner's wealth, the speculation promises an enormous and virtually endless return for a very modest investment. All of this is accomplished by virtually no labor invested on the part of the owner, whose claim to a high return on his or her venture capital must be based on the risks that he or she is willing to run: the unpredictable losses that may be occasioned by mistreatment, illness, flight, or infertility of the slaves. In short, the slaveowner stakes claim to authority on "business acumen," the ability to tell a "good" property from a "bad," in virtually the same manner that a speculator stakes a claim by *predicting* how a particular property will rise or fall in the marketplace. Slaveowners commonly counted their slaves as capital assets, but the market value of such assets depended upon speculation regarding future productivity of both crops and children. Indeed, such speculations might well be improved by development, much as land speculators attempted to improve a particular property by subdivision, cultivation, or even the improvement of natural features (dredging rivers, draining marshes, clearing forests). One of the motives behind the taboo against miscegenation, other than the obvious motive of maintaining clear distinctions between rulers and ruled, may well have been the fear that publicity regarding "mixed progeny" might jeopardize the legal standing of the slave as chattel. Owners mated with their slave women not merely for their perverse pleasure, but with the hope of producing assets, of increasing the promise of their original investments.

In *The Gilded Age*, Warner and Twain represent virtually every aspect of the post-Civil War American business and social life as infected with the disease of speculation. Colonel Beriah Sellers was immensely popular with nineteenth-century readers, thanks to the gaudy splendor of his speculative rhetoric. A darling of contemporary theatergoers, Colonel Sellers inflates everything from turnips and water to his own name: "When we first came here [Washington, D.C.], I was *Mr.* Sellers, and *Major* Sellers, and *Captain* Sellers, but nobody could get it right, somehow; but the minute our bill went through the House, I was *Colonel* Sellers every time. And nobody could do enough for me; and whatever I said was wonderful. . . . Yes, sir, to-morrow it will be General, let me congratulate you, sir; General, you've done a great work, sir,—you've done a great work for the niggro; Gentlemen, allow me the honor to introduce my friend General Sellers, the humane friend of the niggro."[4] In *The Gilded Age*, parents have more children than they can care for, husbands are bigamists, and people speculate in the most unexpected futures: social reputation, political speeches, congressional votes, literature, genius, the imagination, a university.

The very notion of "speculation" in *The Gilded Age* is expanded from mere investment in the future of a marketable commodity to include the venture of psychic, social, or financial capital in something that has only a potential future value. The value of such speculation depends, of course, on the inverse proportion of investment to return: the less work, money, or human energy committed to a project, the greater its potential value. In the place of hard work and capital, the speculator spends *words* profligately on the projects—in brochures, speeches, conversation. Words, it would seem, especially those that require no thought (*conventional* words), are *free*. Speculation in postbellum America is criticized by Warner and Twain quite simply because it *discourages* honest labor and increasingly alienates economic and moral *value* from labor. Great fortunes are made and lost overnight, as Colonel Sellers never tires of telling his disciples; steady, dedicated labor seems sheer folly in an economy in which the value of a manufactured item or agricultural product might change dramatically as a consequence of market conditions fueled by unpredictable speculators. To refuse to play the speculative game is merely to become a victim of the system; most of the honest laborers in *The Gilded Age* lose their earnings to some boss whose speculative scheme fails, or are cheated of their wages by the real bosses, the accountants.[5] To play the game puts one in precisely the situation of

4. Mark Twain and Charles Dudley Warner, *The Gilded Age: A Tale of Today* (New York: New American Library, 1969), 393–94. Quotations from this edition are cited parenthetically in the text as *GA*.

5. While working as a surveyor and investor in a speculative scheme to develop a small Missouri settlement in advance of the railroad, Philip Sterling visits the New York offices of the company to find out why no funds for the workers' salaries have been sent. By the time he leaves these "headquarters," he finds himself several thousands of dollars in debt and his workers considerably "overpaid." The "accounting" given him is a splendid parody of the rhetorical sophistry by which commercial America would give "objective" credibility to its speculative fictions.

the gambler, who has only an illusory authority over an intentionally arbitrary system.

The town of Dawson's Landing in *Pudd'nhead Wilson* begins as a sleepy "slave-holding town, with a rich slave-worked grain and pork country back of it. . . . It was fifty years old, and was growing slowly—very slowly, in fact, but it was still growing" (4). Twain describes a town in 1830 (Tom and Chambers are born on February 1, 1830) that is, like most of his fictional Missouri towns, virtually indistinguishable from Hannibal or a host of other riverfront towns at the eastern edge of the American frontier. By 1853, however, Dawson's Landing has elected a mayor, incorporating itself as Hannibal had done in 1845, and otherwise shows signs of adapting to the economic ferment that helped Jacksonian America enter the modern industrial age. Like St. Petersburg in *Huckleberry Finn* or Hawkeye, where Colonel Sellers has his "mansion" in *The Gilded Age*, Dawson's Landing is Twain's touchstone for the changes coming to rural, agrarian, slaveholding America.

The "transitional" quality of Dawson's Landing during the twenty-three years covered by the narrative drama is often noted, but primarily to indicate how modern America brings into relief the antiquated values of antebellum feudalism. Twain provides certain details, however, that make *Pudd'nhead Wilson* a commentary on the shared economics of slavery and the new speculative economy that would carry us through the Civil War into the Gilded Age. When read in light of these economic details, David Wilson becomes an even more problematic character than he has been for previous critics because it is Wilson who helps adjust the law to this new economy, vindicates the murdered Judge Driscoll and his venerable descent from the First Families of Virginia, and lends scientific credibility to speculations in commodities as diverse as dogs, mothers, babies, slaves, signatures, fingerprints, and birthrights.

Critics often forget Percy Driscoll, younger brother of Judge Driscoll, actual father of Chambers and assumed father of Tom. This neglect is hardly surprising because Percy Driscoll's funeral is announced at the end of chapter 4; his role seems primarily to provide the means for Twain to help Roxy cover the tracks of her deception in switching the infants. Percy appears to be little more than a guywire in the general stage machinery of the drama. In customary fashion, Twain quickly makes Tom an orphan, whose adoption by his uncle and aunt helps emphasize his marginal familial status. In general, the unnatural bonds between children and nominal parents (aunts and uncles are customary) in Twain's fiction remind us that parent-child relations in such an artificial society are more conventional than natural. For example, in *Huckleberry Finn*, parents repeatedly are exposed as inadequate for the most elementary tasks of child-rearing, as Huck's stories of abandoned, mistreated, and orphaned children attest.[6]

In *Pudd'nhead Wilson*, the distance between parents and children is made even more explicit. Raised by slaves, ignored by their white parents, the children of slaveowners have more in common with the slaves than with their own parents. Given the long history of unacknowledged miscegenation, slaves like Roxy may be as little as "one-sixteenth black," so that her own child is "thirty-one parts white," even though he remains "by a fiction of law and custom a negro" (9). In view of such circumstances, it is hardly surprising that Percy Driscoll might have difficulty telling his own child apart from Roxy's, but Twain adds that Percy is also easily tricked because he has little familiarity with his own child. Describing Roxy's child, Twain notes: "He had blue eyes and flaxen curls, like his white comrade, but even the father of the white child was able to tell the children apart—little as he had commerce with them—by their clothes: for the white babe wore ruffled soft muslin and a coral necklace, while the other wore merely a coarse tow-linen shirt which barely reached to its knees, and no jewelry" (9).

It is common enough to comment that the only difference between these two children is their dress, signifying class in the perfectly conventional manner so likely to be satirized by Twain. Yet, two other observations are worth making. First, the close resemblance between Tom and Chambers, especially in a novel so obsessed with twins and doubles, encourages us to think at this early stage in the narrative that they share the same father. This expectation is only partially frustrated by Roxy's confession to Tom that his father was Colonel Cecil Burleigh Essex, another F.F.V. in Dawson's Landing. By chapter 9, when Roxy tells Tom who his father was, we are not likely to trust much of what Roxy says; indeed, the pride with which she tells Tom suggests at least delusions of grandeur if not outright deception on her part. Percy Driscoll and Colonel Cecil Burleigh Essex die conveniently in the same season and paragraph: "There were two grand funerals in Dawson's Landing that fall—the fall of 1845. One was that of Colonel Cecil Burleigh Essex, the other that of Percy Driscoll" (24). The only other mention of the Colonel is made in Twain's introduction of the chief citizens of Dawson's Landing in chapter 1: "Then there was Colonel Cecil Burleigh Essex, another F.F.V. of formidable calibre—however, with him we have no concern" (5). This mysterious character often has troubled critics.

---

6. See my discussion of Twain's representations of parents and children in *Through the Custom-House: Nineteenth-Century American Fiction and Modern Theory* (Baltimore: Johns Hopkins University Press, 1982), 161.

Why introduce him, if he is to play no other role in the narrative than to provide the "name" of Tom's white father? And why dismiss him so hastily, if the entire plot depends on family origins? On the other hand, his name, title, and convenient death in the same season as Percy Driscoll's provide Roxy with an excellent means of protecting herself. If we assume that Tom is the natural son of Percy Driscoll and Roxy, then we might conclude that Tom would have less to fear were Roxy to expose his true identity to Judge Driscoll. Mindful of the scandal such miscegenation in his own family might cause, Judge Driscoll would be likely to reach a settlement with Tom, albeit hardly one comparable to the inheritance that Tom expects from his uncle. On the other hand, exposed as the bastard child of Cecil Burleigh Essex and Roxy, Tom could expect little from Judge Driscoll other than prompt sale down the river.

Assuming that Tom is at least possibly the illegitimate son of Percy Driscoll, we may also suggest that he is but one part of Percy's general speculations. The younger brother of Judge Driscoll has little "commerce" with his only surviving heir, leaving him to the care of Roxy, not only because Mrs. Percy Driscoll dies "within the week" of the child's birth, but also because "Mr. Driscoll soon absorbed himself in his speculations" and left Roxy "to her own devices" with the children (5). Percy Driscoll's financial speculations have a central part to play in the plot, even though they are mentioned so early in the narrative as to be forgotten by the end. Roxy's plan to switch the babies is motivated principally by the fear inspired by her master's threat to sell all his slaves "down the river," unless the one who has stolen a "small sum of money" confesses to the theft (11). As Twain points out, "all were guilty but Roxana," and Twain goes on to explain the unwritten custom by which Southern servants were entitled to take small items—generally food or supplies—without punishment. Such informal servants' "rights" (sometimes called "smouching rights") are still in effect in the South, so Percy Driscoll's anger over that missing money seems extreme, if not indecorous. It is possible that his anxiety reflects the urgent circumstances of his own finances. Once Roxy has switched the babies, she is saved from the risk of the master's close attention to such domestic matters by his preoccupation with business: "for one of his speculations was in jeopardy, and his mind was so occupied that he hardly saw the children when he looked at them, and all Roxy had to do was to get them both into a gale of laughter when he came about them; then their faces were mainly cavities exposing gums . . ." (17–18). Further problems with this speculation force Percy and Judge Driscoll to leave Dawson's Landing for seven weeks, further assuring the success of Roxy's deception: "Within a few days the fate of the speculation became so dubious that Mr. Percy went away with his brother the

Judge to see what could be done with it. It was a land speculation, as usual, and it had gotten complicated with a lawsuit. The men were gone seven weeks. Before they got back Roxy paid her visit to Wilson and was satisfied" (18). By the time he dies in 1845, "Percy Driscoll had worn himself out in trying to save his great speculative landed estate, and had died without succeeding. He was hardly in his grave before the boom collapsed and left his hitherto envied young devil of an heir a pauper" (25).

Percy Driscoll's speculations in real estate recall, of course, John Clemens's "bequest" to his family of a hundred thousand acres in the Knobs of Tennessee (for which he paid $400), as well as his financial failure in Hannibal. The legendary "Tennessee land," with its fabled natural resources and excellent location, haunted the Clemens family for many years after the father's death. It is the same land that Squire Hawkins buys at the beginning of *The Gilded Age* and becomes the focus of the plot in Warner's and Twain's ruthless satire of the speculative economy of postbellum America. Twain's mother and his brother, Orion, floated any number of grandiose schemes on the promise of that Tennessee land, most of which was sold off in small parcels over the years to meet the family's urgent needs. In *The Gilded Age*, the Hawkins's land in the Knobs of East Tennessee becomes the center of an elaborate congressional swindle engineered by two of the Hawkins's children, Colonel Sellers, and Senator Dilworthy. The Senator sponsors a bill for the government purchase of the land as the site for the "Knobs Industrial University," which would be "open to all persons without distinction of sex, color or religion," and whose principal purpose would be the educational emancipation of black men and women (*GA,* 311, 312). That this colossal swindle "trades" on public sentiments for the improvement of the educational and economic opportunities of emancipated blacks in postbellum America is obvious enough; that slaves and freed blacks share the fate of being commodities in speculative America is only slightly less obvious.

What finally caused Judge Clemens's financial ruin remains somewhat unclear, although Twain refers in his *Autobiography* and the sketch, "The Villagers," to the debt on which Ira Stout defaulted and which Judge Clemens had co-signed as guarantor. Dixon Wecter notes that there is no surviving record of any default by Stout that also involved Judge Clemens.[7] Nevertheless, one of the several subplots of *The Gilded Age* concerns the romance between Philip Sterling and Ruth Bolton, whose father, despite being a Quaker and a lawyer, is ruined several times by his friend, Bigler, who repeatedly talks him into providing surety for Bigler's many speculative schemes.

7. Dixon Wecter, *Sam Clemens of Hannibal* (Boston: Houghton Mifflin, 1952), 68–72.

Judge Clemens's financial plight was so extreme by 1841 that he and Jane had to sell their interest in their home and lot; in the same period, "the Clemenses parted with their slave girl Jennie, . . . whom the Judge had once whipped, but who had served as 'mammy' to Sam and the other young children."[8] This was the same domestic slave that Twain recalls his father selling to his business associate, Beebe, who subsequently sold her down the river. In "The Villagers," Twain writes: "Was seen years later, ch[ambermaid] on a steamboat. Cried and lamented."[9] At least in some sense, Roxy, Percy Driscoll, and Judge Driscoll have biographical origins in Twain's recollections of his personal family circumstances in Florida and Hannibal, Missouri, in the 1830s and 1840s, just as the "Tennessee Land" and various speculative schemes in *The Gilded Age* explicitly satirize his father's cursed bequest to his family.[1]

Besides Ira Stout's financial irresponsibility, what most likely wrecked Judge Clemens's speculations in vacant land and "rental properties along Hill and Main" in Hannibal was the ten-year depression that followed the Panic of 1837. Most of the speculative ferment in the United States in the 1830s was sparked by the promise of the vast frontier, so that speculators invested heavily in canal projects, early rail and other transportation ventures, as well as in land that would be in the path of westward expansion. Andrew Jackson attempted to control land speculation by issuing the "Specie Circular" of 1836, which required "specie payment for public land." The economic consequences of this act were declining prices for land, pressures on banks holding government funds, and subsequent bank failures in many states.[2] Missouri was still primarily an undeveloped part of the frontier in 1837, and it consequently suffered less than eastern states committed to ambitious canal and railroad developments. Even so, the Panic of 1837 and the depression that followed it had national consequences, severest for those who had staked their fortunes to speculative enterprises. The Panic of 1837 falls precisely between the births of Tom and Chambers in 1830 and the death of Percy Driscoll, who is ruined by his land speculation, in 1845.

Roxy's switching of the babies is itself a "speculative" venture, a "gamble" against the chances of being discovered and thus sold down the river for her sins. What prompts her rebellious action is the master's threat to sell all his slaves down the river, a threat that we have

8. Wecter, *Sam Clemens*, 72.
9. As quoted in ibid., 72.
1. If Percy and the Judge represent two "halves" of Judge John M. Clemens, then David Wilson and Tom represent two "halves" of Twain's own personality. A psychoanalytical reading of *Pudd'nhead Wilson* that would elaborate the literary mechanisms by which Twain distances, represses, and still recognizes his kinship with these two corrupt characters would be most welcome and helpful.
2. Perry McCandless, *A History of Missouri*, vol. 2, *1820–1860* (Columbia: University of Missouri Press, 1972), 119.

suggested may well be caused more by his own financial reverses than mere arbitrariness. Roxy's "venture" with such modest human "capital" is little more than an imitation of what white masters did with their black commodities under slavery, risking that the black child will grow to become a valuable property from a relatively small investment. Virtually "born" (born *again*?) of this speculative enter-prise, which like most of Roxy's actions imitate white men's behav-ior, Tom would seem to have the proper background for a gambler.

Twain is careful to tell us, however, that Tom learns to gamble at Yale; he wants the reader to be certain not to associate Tom's vices with the black portion of his heredity. His gambling is his "inheri-tance" from his white father, whether "Cecil Burleigh Essex" or Percy Driscoll. Land speculation and gambling go hand-in-hand, of course, and the western folk myth of the Mississippi gambler has its origins in the gamblers and speculators who did business on the steamboats that were so crucial to the commercial development of Missouri from 1820 to 1865.[3] Tom's gambling is part of his effort to play the role of the Southern aristocrat with disposable income and leisure time, but it also associates him with the new economy fueled by speculators and get-rich-quick artists from Eastern urban centers of banking and finance. That Tom should learn to gamble at Yale should not surprise readers of *The Gilded Age*, in which the two most naive speculators, Philip Sterling and Henry Brierly, were classmates at Yale. Henry's first words are, "'Oh, it's easy enough to make a fortune,'" and he sends them both on the road to ruin by vaguely asking Philip, "'Well, why don't you go into something? You'll never dig it out of the Astor Library'" (*GA*, 95). As a couple of eastern swells, Philip and Henry epitomize "the young American," to whom "the paths to fortune are innumerable and all open; there is invitation in the air and success in all his wide horizon" (*GA*, 95). Although Warner and Twain make their own capital out of Senator Dilworthy's fraudulent scheme for the "Knobs Technical University," they repeatedly compare its inno-vative technical curriculum with models in Switzerland and Ger-many. Indeed, part of the cleverness of the plan for this university is that it *does* propose the sort of educational institution that Twain and Warner would consider enlightened. By contrast, the liberal arts edu-cation offered at nineteenth-century Yale would seem to encourage nothing other than the vague expectations and romantic ideals of young fops like Henry Brierly and Philip Sterling, each of whom learns ultimately the hard realities of this speculative economy.[4] Like

3. McCandless, *A History*, 2:138.
4. Philip Sterling finally overcomes his "speculating instincts" by working hard and discov-ering shared labor with his workers in the coal mine he develops in the latter part of the narrative. Henry Brierly's financial and romantic "schemes" lure him into the clutches of Laura Hawkins, who uses him as an unwitting accessory in her murder of the lover who had betrayed her. Finally released from prison, Harry heads for San Francisco, apparently

Percy Driscoll's land speculation, Tom's gambling jeopardizes his estate and thus the Driscolls' social authority. All of Tom's criminal actions are designed to cover his debts and thus assure his inheritance from Judge Driscoll. The child of speculating parents and of a speculative era and region, Tom fulfills that destiny by repeating in his own character the economic "failures" that punctuated the American economy from the Panic of 1837 to the Panics of 1873 and 1893.

Indeed, *Pudd'nhead Wilson* was written on the verge of the Panic of 1893 (and rewritten and proofread during the Panic), which was the final blow to Twain's publishing company, Webster and Company, and his dreams for the commercial success of the Paige Typesetter. Twain returned from Europe in the middle of the Panic, and he "couldn't borrow a penny."[5] Everything that he and Warner had predicted in *The Gilded Age* had come to pass with a vengeance, so it is hardly surprising that the legal servitude of the black in antebellum America should be confused so brilliantly with the economic servitude of Tom to the speculative interests of the new age. In debt for $80,000 as a consequence of the failure of Webster and Company and the Paige Typesetter, Twain would work his way back to solvency only by repeating his father's own "honorable" payment of "a hundred cents on the dollar" of the debts he had collected half a century earlier.[6] As familiar as the story of Twain's business failure and moral triumph may be, its relevance to the economic themes in *Pudd'nhead Wilson* remains untold. That he *did* follow his father's example reveals more than just Twain's integrity; that repetition may well have suggested to him the perverse continuity between antebellum and postbellum America. The gulf separating "Old Times on the Mississippi" from the new, progressive America must have appeared much narrower than it once had seemed to Twain. Writing his early drafts of *Pudd'nhead Wilson* in Italy, where he had "exiled" himself and his family to try to "economize," Twain responded to the Panic of 1893 as if it were some perverse fate sent specifically to punish him. The agrarian institution of slavery had been replaced by the urban servitude of those victimized by a speculative economy. The fact that

---

unregenerate, "to look after some government contracts in the harbor there" (*GA*, 346). The morality of Warner and Twain in *The Gilded Age* is heavy-handed and puritanical, but it provides a clear background for Twain's indictment of the cancerous immorality of speculation in *Pudd'nhead Wilson*.

5. *The Autobiography of Mark Twain*, ed. Charles Neider (New York: Washington Square Press, 1961), 281.

6. Neider, *Autobiography*, 282. Of John Clemens's efforts to satisfy his creditors, Dixon Wecter writes in *Sam Clemens of Hannibal*: "The code of the Virginia gentleman permitted no other course to Mark Twain's father, and the pride which the son took in his father's stripping himself to satisfy all claims—beyond the call of duty, we are told, down to offering the forks and spoons, and every stick of furniture—presaged a similar act in Mark's life half a century later" (71).

Twain was no mere innocent victim, but himself an active figure in the very speculative enterprises that Warner and he had so viciously criticized in the year of the last major American panic—the Panic of 1873—must have weighed heavily upon the writer's conscience. In this regard, Tom Driscoll and Percy Driscoll might be read allegorically as versions of Mark Twain and Judge John Clemens.[7]

Such an autobiographical allegory, however, is less interesting than the more general consequences of a narrative designed to reflect the continuity between an older slavery and the new slavery of urban economics. Tom and Percy are not the only characters affected by this speculative economy. Freed in Percy Driscoll's will, Roxy works for eight years (1845–53) on a Mississippi steamboat, saving her money to provide herself with a modest income when she is too infirm (at forty-three!) to work any longer: "She had lived a steady life, and had banked four dollars every month in New Orleans as a provision for her old age. She said in the start that she 'put shoes on one bar'footed nigger to tromple on her with,' and that one mistake like that was enough: she would be independent of the human race thenceforth forevermore if hard work and economy could accomplish it" (37). As every reader will recall, she bids goodbye to her "comrades on the Grand Mogul," only to discover that the "bank had gone smash and carried her four hundred dollars with it" (37). Had Roxy's modest savings remained safely in that New Orleans bank to pay her a poor return in interest as retirement income, she never would have returned to beg and threaten her natural son, Tom. Without the support of Roxy's intelligence and rage, Tom undoubtedly would have even more quickly caused his own financial ruin. Nevertheless, it is unlikely that he would have murdered his uncle or had his curious origins exposed. Quite obviously, both Roxy's vengeful authority and the rage inspired in Tom by her revelation of his black origins fuel his subsequent crimes in *Pudd'nhead Wilson*.[8] Giving quite so much weight to the economic "deus ex machina" of this New Orleans bank failure would, of course, be excessive were it not

---

7. Turner, "Mark Twain and the South," 280, makes a strong case for finding traces of Judge John Clemens in the characters of both Percy Driscoll and Judge Driscoll.

8. Tom's cowardice throughout *Pudd'nhead Wilson* often has been noted by critics. Tom's famous reflection in chapter 10 on his newly discovered identity as a black slave seems only to intensify that cowardice by adding self-contempt to the formula. Twain often noted that it was just this "slave-mentality" that was white America's worst sin against blacks. By the same token, Roxy's will, cleverness, and moral righteousness all seem to come from her general imitation of white customs and attitudes. As potentially racist as Twain's distinction between Tom and Roxy seems to be, it's fair to note that Twain gives us virtually no means for generalizing about the "essence" of the "Negro" in *Pudd'nhead Wilson*. As Roxy's fantastic family genealogy suggests, the "Essex blood" of which she is so proud is traceable ultimately to "Pocahontas de Injun queen, en her husbun' was a nigger king outen Africa" (75). In her own fictional origins—the ones that are finally the important ones for Twain's characters—Roxy rediscovers her strength, intelligence, and will in native American and African roots.

that *Pudd'nhead Wilson* incorporates so many equally "minor" details regarding speculation, each of which has a significant effect on the plot.

Critics have often noticed that Roxy's character, as powerfully vengeful as it becomes in the narrative, is nonetheless governed consistently by the values of the white ruling class. Roxy's pride regarding Tom's high birth, her "attendance" at the duel between Judge Driscoll and Luigi, her hard work and economy while a chambermaid on the *Grand Mogul*, and her maternal sentiments for Tom—all of these somewhat questionable "virtues" identify her self-reliance as well as her criminal potential with white values. Writing in a period when white America addressed the "negro question" by calling in various ways for the religious, educational, and economic "reformation" of the emancipated black, Twain ruthlessly satirizes the ways in which the black who would follow the customs of white America would end up victimized yet again, trapped in a new economic servitude that would continue to our own day. The freed black would share with the European immigrant and the naive young white American the fantastic promise of speculative, expanding America, only to become the agent of the same old thieving powers of the eastern bankers and urban tycoons.

Percy Driscoll dies in 1845, the year in which John L. O'Sullivan "coined the phrase Manifest Destiny . . . to promote the annexation of Texas."[9] As Michael Rogin reminds us, Manifest Destiny became the rallying cry of a short-lived group sponsored by O'Sullivan, "Young America," which "was militantly expansionist and Anglophobic," as well as in favor of "universal democracy, equality, and the overthrow of European kings."[1] In *Pudd'nhead Wilson*, the political enthusiasms of groups like "Young America" are satirized by the anti-temperance "Sons of Liberty," whose only rallying cry seems to be a drinking song. Even so, the liberal movements that supported Manifest Destiny and opposed slavery often claimed that the encouragement of Northern industrial interests in the course of westward expansion might provide the "answer" to slavery. Abolitionists knew that mere "emancipation" by law would hardly solve the problem of American blacks born and raised in slavery. New land and ambitious speculative ventures, including the railroads that would open the frontier, were often promoted on humanitarian grounds as promising employment and opportunity for freed slaves and other oppressed minorities. Roxy's hard-earned $400 is a small measure of the economic promise that Manifest Destiny might offer the freed slave; its loss in the bank's failure is Twain's satire of the economic

9. Michael Paul Rogin, *Subversive Genealogy: The Politics and Art of Herman Melville* (Berkeley: University of California Press, 1983), 73.
1. Rogin, *Subversive Genealogy*, 73.

realities that would disillusion freed blacks as well as European immigrants with the economic "promise" of American expansionism.

Roxy, Tom, and Percy are not the only speculators in *Pudd'nhead Wilson*. David Wilson, "a young fellow of Scotch parentage . . . had wandered to this remote region from his birthplace in the interior State of New York, to seek his fortune. He was twenty-five years old, college-bred, and had finished a post-college course in an eastern law school a couple of years before" (5). Like Philip Sterling in *The Gilded Age*, David Wilson lacks the obvious trappings of the fortune hunter; Philip's friend, Henry Brierly, for example, spends others' money on hotel rooms and fancy dinners with virtual abandon. Brierly is a youthful Colonel Sellers, whereas Sterling and Wilson have the modest qualities and potential virtues of the honest laborers Twain admires. Even so, both Sterling and Wilson are lured to the frontier of Missouri by the promise of "fortune." It is only as a consequence of Wilson's apparently casual remark about the dog that he is condemned to hang out a shingle and try the practice of law, then the more modest professions of surveying and accounting.[2] Even so, all of the three professions Wilson attempts to practice in Dawson's Landing are dependent upon the speculative economy of the region. Like the Kentuckians who came to Missouri in the 1820s and 1830s with capital and slaves, David Wilson, who is from New York State, "had a trifle of money when he arrived, and he bought a small house on the extreme western verge of the town"(7). That this "small house" is next door to Judge Driscoll's house suggests that Wilson's "trifle of money" is somewhat greater than Twain leads us to believe. Arriving in Dawson's Landing to profit from the modest development boom of the years following the admission of Missouri to the Union in 1821, Wilson virtually announces himself as a speculator and fortune-hunter in his "deadly remark": " 'I wish I owned half of that dog' " (6). Only a fool or a speculator would think in terms of "half-interest" in a dog, and the townfolks' judgment of Wilson's certain folly reflects their reliance on the customs of an older, landed economy.

Unable to practice law on account of this foolish remark, Wilson does occasional surveying and accounting, occupying his "rich abundance of idle time" with the "universe of ideas," notably his experiments in palmistry (7–8). In *The Gilded Age*, Colonel Sellers always has some new "invention" under way, ranging from eyedrops

---

2. See Frederick Anderson, "Mark Twain and the Writing of *Pudd'nhead Wilson*," in the 1st ed. of the Norton Critical Edition: "Aspects of Pudd'nhead Wilson's character and career, specifically his barren law practice, are based on that of Mark Twain's brother Orion and the crushing failure he encountered in his attempt to practice that profession" (285). We might add the "crushing failures" that Orion's speculative and inventive schemes invariably encountered in his curious career. The character Washington Hawkins in *The Gilded Age*, chief victim of Colonel Sellers's fantastic schemes, is clearly modeled after Orion Clemens.

to stoves. Scientific experimentation and speculation go hand-in-hand for Twain, whose own experiences with the Paige Typesetter and fascination with inventions of all sorts are notorious features of his biography. Although Twain respected inventiveness and the technology it promoted, he had good reason to be suspicious of the inflated expectations that the "scientific spirit" brought to America. Wilson and Judge Driscoll are both "free-thinkers," by which we assume they are mild agnostics, but "free thinking" in general is mercilessly indicted in *The Gilded Age* as one of the sources for the unchecked speculative "instinct" (as Twain and Warner call it) in modern industrial America.

David Wilson and Tom Driscoll are frequently contrasted by critics, who follow Twain's own lead in calling attention to Wilson's "rise" at the expense of Tom's "fall." Because Wilson attracts our sympathies with the satiric humor of his "calendar" and his generally marginal status in Dawson's Landing, modern readers have been quick to associate him with Twain's own views. Thus George Spangler suggests that Tom's greed anticipates the rampant materialism of the Gilded Age, whereas Wilson's "disinterestedness and immaterialism" are tokens of an alternative that we ought to associate with Twain's ideal.[3] Such interpretations have always foundered on the simple fact that David Wilson uses his experiments in fingerprinting not merely to "solve" the murder of Judge Driscoll and save the innocent Luigi from hanging, but that these same experiments are given legal status in a case that allows the townspeople to attribute such criminality to Tom's black heredity. David Wilson's "triumph," as the new mayor of the newly chartered city of Dawson's Landing, as courtroom lawyer and expert witness, even as amateur sleuth, is perhaps the most perverse heroic conclusion in modern literature.

Tom twice associates Wilson's forensic work with his fingerprints as "his palace-window decorations," and Wilson himself declares in court that he knows these "signatures . . . as well as the bank cashier knows the autograph of his oldest customer" (111, 116). Wilson's idle "speculation" in "paw prints" clearly assumes more than just *economic* value by the time he has solved the crime; his scientific "knowledge" of the origins and identity of any man so recorded is comparable to that of the absolute authorities of the European monarch or the American judge. In the speculative economy of the Gilded Age, no one's "identity" will be subject to the customary tests—the property, social habits and company, and local history that had given a man "reputation" and thus "identity" in

3. George M. Spangler, *"Pudd'nhead Wilson*: A Parable of Property," pp. 295 ff., herein.

older, small-town America. In this new world of changeable roles, ever-new "schemes," and both geographical and social mobility, men and women will be known only in their styles and fashions. Only a Colonel Sellers, whose "absolute" is paradoxically his infinitely malleable rhetoric (his only enduring "capital"), will have a "character," but the word will thus assume its idiomatic meaning: "Oh, *what a character!*"

At the dawn of such an era, Wilson's idle speculation in fingerprints, an avocation that is until the trial apparently useless, becomes the capital of the law, the scientific "basis" for judging human actions and relating those actions to larger sociohistorical forces. When Tom murders the Judge, Tom is disguised as a black man (he has blackened his face with charcoal); when he flees the scene, he is disguised as a girl. These masks are the "proper" murderers, who take their revenge against the master who has both stolen the black man's liberty and exploited the sex of both white and black women. These exploited "halves" of the slave, especially as they are prompted by the justifiable rage of Roxy, are the avenging angels of Tom's apparently individual and "criminal" act. It is worth noting at this point that Twain's literary style enables us to make such connections between individual "characters" and their socially symbolic acts in ways that are distinctly different from the "writing" of David Wilson's dramatic pantographs. Wilson introduces a "scientific" measurement of personality that extends the commodification of human beings under slavery to the general economy of America. Aware of the writer's complicity in the corruptions of the new economy (Philip Sterling, for example, initially wants to be a writer), Twain is at some pains to distinguish his own "tall-tale telling" from the inflated rhetoric of Colonel Sellers or the courtroom histrionics of David Wilson.

A reasonable objection to this argument is that Wilson does indeed save Luigi from conviction for Judge Driscoll's murder, but the fact that Luigi is held legally responsible for this murder depends upon another of the many hypocrisies of Dawson's Landing. We must remember that while Wilson runs for mayor, the Italian twins are running for aldermanic seats. Judge Driscoll and Tom are reconciled as father and son during the campaign by virtue of their "election labors" to defeat the twins. What Twain calls twice their "hard work" includes spending "money . . . to persuade voters" and the Judge's "closing speech of the campaign," which is notable for the inflated rhetoric by which it offers a "character assassination" of the twins. Previously associated with the new speculative economy only in the help he gives his brother, the Judge is in this context directly linked with what Warner and Twain consider two of the most insidious effects of the "speculative instinct": exaggerated, romantic rhetoric (hyperbole) and vote-buying.[4] Having "scoffed at them as adventurers, mountebanks, side-show riff-raff, dime-museum freaks," the Judge closes by claiming that "the reward offered for the lost knife was humbug and buncombe, and that its owner would know where to find it whenever he should have the occasion *to assassinate somebody*" (89). The Judge's accusation invokes the *code duello* of the region, and it is the *Judge* who refuses Count Luigi's challenge, declining "to fight with an assassin—'that is . . . in the field of honor'" (98). Wilson then explains the significance of the Judge's refusal to Count Luigi: "The unwritten law of this region requires you to kill Judge Driscoll on sight, and he and the community will expect that attention at your hands—though of course your own death by his bullet will answer every purpose. Look out for him! Are you heeled—that is, fixed?" (98–99). Nothing could be stranger, of course, than the newly elected mayor explaining the murderous intent of the town's judge to his intended victim! But even granting the absurdity of this "unwritten law of the region" and the circumstances of its narration, we are bound to wonder why Luigi is at risk for his life in the trial from which Wilson nominally "saves" him. Given the circumstances of such an "unwritten law," Luigi certainly has the reasonable argument of "self-defense," whether Tom's criminality is revealed or not.

Unfortunately, Twain provides no explicit motivation for Wilson's defense of Luigi other than his immediate perception that "Neither of the Twins" made the marks on the knife handle (103). The motives for Wilson's triumphant revelation of Tom's identity in the courtroom, however, have often been interpreted as part of Wilson's bid for legitimacy with the townspeople of Dawson's Landing. Until his murder, Judge Driscoll was Wilson's protector and guarantor of his rights in town. In fact, the Judge's paternal concern for Wilson, this aspiring lawyer, perversely doubles the Judge's relation to his stepson and nephew, Tom. Without this surrogate father, Wilson must legitimate his new role as mayor, which he does not only by assuming legal authority in the courtroom but also by "saving" Luigi. Luigi is, of course, no more saved by Wilson than Jim is saved by Tom and Huck at the end of *Huckleberry Finn*, but the irony of this salvation is that it causes Luigi and Angelo to "weary of Western adventure" and return "straightway . . . to Europe" (120). Although Wilson and the twins run for different civic positions, Twain announces the results of the election in terms that suggest syntactically their com-

4. The anonymous reviewer of *Pudd'nhead Wilson* in *The Athenaeum* (January 19, 1895) [reprinted herein, pp. 241–42—*Editor*] complains: "Why drag in, for example, all the business about the election, which is quite irrelevant? and the Twins altogether seem to have very little *raison d'être* in the book." It is fair to say that these are old complaints that have not been sufficiently answered by modern critics of the novel.

petition: "Wilson was elected, the twins were defeated—crushed, in fact, and left forlorn and substantially friendless" (89). That the Judge would suspect these two foreigners of being charlatans, all the while being surrounded by a society based on fraud—whether that of slavery or the new speculative economy—fits perfectly Twain's satiric purposes. The fact that Wilson's hard work—the first he performs in the narrative—in saving Luigi, revealing Tom as a slave, and turning the hapless Chambers into a white heir helps restore order in this small community remains far more troublesome.

For Wilson is no "mysterious stranger" sent to Dawson's Landing to reveal its own unconscious lie. What Wilson helps accomplish is hardly that familiar "disturbance" in Twain's other small towns that provokes some searching re-examination of their social values and contracts. Wilson proves himself to be not only a "proper" gentleman but also a leader, who will carry this town into its urban era in the wake of the new economics that would sweep America in the course of the Civil War and its aftermath. In this sense, Wilson is the appropriate heir to the arbitrary authority represented by Judge Driscoll and the F.F.V.s. Wilson is the "accountant," who helps make possible the correct "accounting" of Percy Driscoll's mortgaged and speculative estate. Wilson's palmistry is a new "science" of human accounting that promises the effective translation of the chattel of slavery into the commodity of labor manipulated by the urban speculator. Roxy, that wily imitator of the white man's slickest tricks, convinces her son to sell her down the river on the basis of a *forged bill of sale*. Tom's *signature* turns Roxy back into a saleable commodity. Wilson melodramatically concludes his courtroom speech by commanding: "Valet de Chambre, negro and slave—falsely called Thomas à Becket Driscoll—make upon the window the finger-prints that will hang you!" (119–20). For a second time, then, Tom's "signature" turns a human being into capital, which will in fact circulate by way of Percy Driscoll's creditors. Tom's forgery of his signature on his mother's bill of sale is, of course, doubly forged. Every signature of ownership on a slave deed must be a base forgery for Twain. Industrial, speculative America would transform that "forged ownership" into the capital *naturally* authorized by the very body of its workers. In America of the Gilded Age, there will be yet other forgeries by means of which the fact of slavery will be transformed into the broken promises and elusive opportunities that would become the wages of the freed black and European immigrant. The "profit" earned from such a speculative accounting as David Wilson's is neither property nor cash; like the antebellum slaveowner, David Wilson plays for power and authority. The last we hear from Colonel Sellers in *The Gilded Age*, he is embarking on yet a new and even more vainglorious venture than any before it: " 'I've seen enough to show me where my mistake was. The law is what I was born for. I shall begin the study of the law. . . . There's worlds of money in it! whole worlds of money! . . . Climb, and climb, and climb—and wind up on the Supreme bench. . . . A made man for all time and eternity!" (*GA*, 426). In the character of David Wilson, Colonel Sellers finds at last the profession and personality to which the speculator is born: philosopher, scientist, humorist, detective, lawyer, and mayor—America's Renaissance Man.

What, then, of "Pudd'nhead Wilson's Calendar" with its evocations of Twain's familiar skepticism and irony? The aphorisms still serve the purposes of Twain's general satire of Dawson's Landing, its slaveholding values, and the modern economy that it is entering. As David Wilson's "scratchings," such social and human criticism have become merely the "decorations" of a popular calendar, witty "saws" like the wisecrack about that dog. That his own skepticism and social criticism would become merely the "idle" pastimes of "freethinking" hypocrites like Judge Driscoll and David Wilson may well be Twain's deepest fear—and one realized in part in our postmodern economy, whose stock in trade may be the wisecrack.

SUSAN GILLMAN

"Sure Identifiers": Race, Science, and the Law in *Pudd'nhead Wilson*†

> A book is the writer's secret life, the dark twin of a man.
> —WILLIAM FAULKNER, *Mosquitoes*

Soon after *Pudd'nhead Wilson* was published in late November 1894, the well-known contemporary critic and novelist, Hjalmar Hjorth Boyesen, reviewed the novel with the kind of qualified praise it has received ever since. Puzzled particularly by Mark Twain's "stock" treatment of the highly charged issue of race relations, Boyesen struck a typically bemused tone at this "novel of the ante-bellum days in Missouri, rather melodramatic in plot." "If anybody but Mark Twain had undertaken to tell that kind of story," the review begins, going on to list the elements of "that kind of story":

> with exchanges of infants in the cradle, a hero with negro taint in his blood substituted for the legitimate white heir, midnight encounters in a haunted house between the false heir and his

† From *Mark Twain's* Pudd'nhead Wilson: *Race, Conflict, and Culture,* ed. Susan Gillman and Forrest G. Robinson (Durham and London: Duke University Press, 1990), pp. 86–104. Copyright © 1990, Duke University Press. All rights reserved. Reprinted by permission of the publisher.

colored mother, murder by the villain of his supposed uncle and
benefactor, accusation of an innocent foreigner, and final sensational acquittal and general unraveling of the tangled skein—
if, I say, anybody else had had the hardihood to utilize afresh this
venerable stage machinery of fiction, we should have been
tempted to class his work with such cheap stuff as that of . . .
the dime novelists. But Mark Twain, somehow, has lifted it all
into the region of literature.

Part of the "somehow," Boyesen suggests, is a certain historical
verisimilitude in *Pudd'nhead Wilson*—the "credible and authentic"
local atmosphere—that makes us "swallow the melodrama without a
qualm—exchange of heirs, haunted house, murder, and all—and
scarcely dream that we have been duped until we wake up with a
start at the end of the last chapter."[1]

Readers since Boyesen have continued to invoke similar terms.
Like him, many have felt "duped" by *Pudd'nhead Wilson*'s "tangle" of
the "authentic" and the "melodramatic," the historical texture embedded in (and sometimes suppressed by) the most conventional of sensational plots. So many difficult questions about the social
construction of racial identity surface partially in the narrative, only
to be arbitrarily closed off by the formulaic clarity of the conclusion
to the murder/detective plot, where there seems to be no room for
racial loose ends. Even the history of the composition of the manuscript bears out this reading, given that the text which began as a farcical literary sideshow about Siamese twins became entangled with a
racial "tragedy" of the antebellum South. As Hershel Parker points
out, the manuscript in the Morgan Library, consisting of both the
Siamese twins story and the race/murder plot, raises questions primarily about race and how Mark Twain represented—and avoided—
racial issues in the process of composition and revision. After
conceiving of the idea of switched racial identities, for example,
roughly about midway during the composition process, why did Mark
Twain proceed to write—and then cut out—much new and explicit
material on Tom Driscoll's agonizing discovery of his racial patrimony?[2]

This is at once a textual, social, and ethical problem: although readers recognize race relations as *Pudd'nhead Wilson*'s central
problematic, the novel has tended to generate inward-looking readings
that remain for the most part confined within the terms of the text

1. Hjalmar Hjorth Boyesen, Review, *Cosmopolitan* 18 (January 1895): 379 [see pp. 242–43
   herein—*Editor*].
2. Hershel Parker, *Flawed Texts and Verbal Icons: Literary Authority in American Fiction*
   (Evanston, Ill.: Northwestern University Press, 1984), 115–36. While Parker is patently
   wrong when he dismisses Pudd'nhead Wilson as "patently unreadable," he does pose a
   number of provocative questions about authorial intention and racial issues in the manuscript (see 142–44).

itself.[3] Rather, I would argue, Mark Twain's tangled textual skein must be anchored in, and perhaps unraveled by, the context of the cultural circumstances that produced it. Both *Pudd'nhead Wilson* and *Those Extraordinary Twins* condense what may strike us now as an incongruous combination of fads, vocabularies, and concepts, all of which were then part of the debates over whether and how biological differences determine the natural capacities of racial groups. *Those Extraordinary Twins*, for example, was based on the Tocci brothers, the Italian (rather than Siamese) twins whom Mark Twain had seen on exhibit in 1891, and was also inspired by the power of the cultural mythology that arose around Siamese twins at the time.[4] *Pudd'nhead Wilson* drew similarly on popular culture, incorporating fictional forms (the detective plot, the changeling plot) and, most important, historical circumstance. The novel's satire of racial classification by fractions of blood mirrors problems in American race relations during both the antebellum period in which the novel is set and the 1890s when it was written.

In this sense, Twain's novel implicitly reminds readers that racial codes regulating miscegenation and classifying mixed-race offspring did not disappear after Emancipation but instead were reenacted or reaffirmed, with even more rigorous definitions of whiteness, during the nineties, when antiblack repression took multiple forms, legal and extralegal.[5] *Pudd'nhead Wilson* was serialized in *Century Magazine* in the middle of a decade that saw not only an epidemic of lynchings but also the beginnings of newly enacted Jim Crow laws defining the "Negro's place" in a segregated society, laws paralleled in the political sphere by a variety of voting restrictions to disenfranchise most blacks. The novel may thus speak even more pointedly to the growing racism of its own era of the 1890s than to the race slavery abolished thirty years earlier. At the very least, the connection between the times of the book's setting and of its writing acknowledges silently an unwelcome tie between race slavery of the past and

3. Even historically oriented literary critics like Arlin Turner ("Mark Twain and the South: An Affair of Love and Anger," *Southern Review* 4 [April 1968]: 493–519) and Arthur Pettit (*Mark Twain and the South* [Lexington: University Press of Kentucky, 1974], pp. 286 ff. herein) place Twain's dealings with the race question primarily in the context of literary history (the figure of the "tragic mulatto," for example, in Cable, Melville, Stowe, Howells) or of Clemens's own life (his Missouri background) and writings (notebook passages, autobiographical passages on race and sexuality).
4. The physiological differences between the two pairs of twins, the Italian and the Siamese, are telling: the Toccis shared one body, unlike Chang and Eng whose separate bodies, complete in themselves, were joined by a ligature. The crucial distinction is the shared body, which heightens the dilemma of the metaphysics of Siamese twinhood: whether the twins are individual or collective. For a late-nineteenth-century view, see *Scientific American* 65 (December 1891): 374; for a modern view, see Stephen Jay Gould, "Living with Connections," in *The Flamingo's Smile: Reflections in Natural History* (New York: W.W. Norton, 1985), 64–77.
5. The terms in which I discuss these developments derive largely from George M. Fredrickson, *White Supremacy: A Comparative Study in American and South African History* (New York: Oxford University Press, 1981), 94–108, 129–35.

racism in the present, just as the link between *Pudd'nhead Wilson* and *Those Extraordinary Twins* acknowledges an unspoken kinship between those defined as other, freakish, monstrous, whether Siamese twin or mulatto.

The farce, however, makes a mockery of the Siamese twins' grotesque attachment, whereas the tragedy, obsessed with genealogy, race, and miscegenation, offers a critique of an American historical actuality. But as Boyesen suggests, *Pudd'nhead Wilson* similarly combines the authentic with the sensational and the melodramatic, a textual combination almost as grotesque and freakish as the narrative of the Siamese twins. From the beginning the novel offsets an implicitly historical and contextualized sensibility with a conventionalized, melodramatic mode. Precise details of time and place frame the first chapter. It is 1830. "The scene of this chronicle is the town of Dawson's Landing, on the Missouri side of the Mississippi, half a day's journey, per steamboat, below St. Louis" (3). Such detail had framed the manuscript from its inception, although it originally started with the arrival of the Siamese twins and was dated "about 1850." After the addition of the race plot, Twain rewrote the first chapters, incorporating the history of the exchange of the babies in their cradles, and set back the date twenty years so that the two children would be twenty-two around 1850.

The original date may have had no particular significance, but recast in the setting of a "chronicle" of "a slave-holding town" (a phrase added only during revision), 1850 becomes a memorable year and the Mississippi River locale a special place. The census of 1850 counted mulattoes for the first time. In that year, in Kentucky and Missouri, there was one mulatto slave for every six black slaves. And in that year, Joel Williamson comments, "the slave frontier was the trans-Mississippi South, and it was also preeminently the area of mulatto slavery"; he concludes that "where slavery was strongest and getting stronger, it was also becoming whiter." One further paradoxical result of this racial mixing became apparent in the "new intensity of white racial exclusiveness" during the 1850s.[6]

These multiple historical contradictions are not exactly articulated in *Pudd'nhead Wilson* but rather registered, I would say, as confusingly and as obliquely and as inconsistently as Williamson's account of their historical manifestations indicates. That is, he shows how Southern whites enabled themselves, ironically through increasingly stringent color consciousness, to deny the apparently undeniable presence of increasing racial intermixture. With a similarly tortuous combination of denial based on acknowledgment, the

6. Joel Williamson, *New People: Miscegenation and Mulattoes in the United States* (New York: New York University Press, 1980), 24, 57–59.

two chapters of Twain's novel immediately following our chronolog-
ical and geographic introduction to Dawson's Landing turn away
from the historical context of the "chronicle," and instead plunge us
into the narrative world of popular fiction (the Pudd'nhead Wil-
son/fingerprint plot and the Roxana/changeling plot). By thus sub-
merging history in melodrama, or by uneasily combining these two
modes, the novel participates in a strategy of presenting and yet
denying its own historical and racial context. The ironic result: *Pud-
d'nhead Wilson* pushes us back to the cultural context that is missing. This book is Twain's own "dark twin"—a mirror, we will see, of
what has been repressed in both his culture and his own perception.

At the center of the novel is a problem of knowledge (social, scientific, legal) epitomized by the institution of race slavery. Committed to maintaining the differences between racial groups as a means
of distinguishing the slave from the free, American slavery spawned,
and then tolerated, the anomaly Twain calls the "pure-white slave":
the mulatto who, appearing no different racially from his free white
relatives, creates a pressing need for the many preposterous social
and legal fictions of slave society. Partly a novel of detection and discovery, *Pudd'nhead Wilson* exposes a number of these fictions in the
course of exposing a murderer. The murder plot culminates by satirizing the legal fiction that a slave is both property (an extension of
the master's will) and nonproperty (in that he can be tried for very
willful, antisocial acts, such as murder).[7] In addition, the novel's
obsession with genealogy makes us aware of another social fiction,
what George Fredrickson calls the "official dedication to maintaining
a *fictive* 'race purity' for whites."[8] From the very beginning in which
Roxana, trading literally on the babies' interchangeability, switches
the two in their cradles, the novel detects a central ambiguity suppressed in law, if not custom, by slave society: if not by color or other
unalterable physiological differences, how can we differentiate individuals and groups? How do we know who is master and who is slave,
who is to be held accountable under the law and who is not? Finally,
with the unsettling trial at the end, the novel asks, how sound is the
basis of that knowledge? How do we know what we know is true?

More than any other characters in the novel, Roxana and her son
Tom trigger this epistemological confusion through their multiple
interchanges of race and sex. Not only does she engineer the switch
of the babies, but also—as with her son's numerous racial and sexual
disguises—she puts on blackface and male clothing, in her case, ironically, in order to escape from slavery. Particularly when mother and

---

7. On the legal problem of the slave's humanity, see Eugene D. Genovese, *Roll, Jordan, Roll:
   The World the Slaves Made* (New York: Random House, 1976), 28–37.
8. Fredrickson, *White Supremacy*, 133.

son assume both racial and sexual disguises, they enact the tangle of
fact and fiction through which identity is constituted in this world.
Each taking on aspects of the other's gender, they act out a mingling
of boundaries which stands for the mingling of blood denied by this
biracial society through its policies of racial classification. The infamous formula that makes Roxana—"to all intents and purposes as
white as anybody"—a black slave is only a fraction: "the one-sixteenth
of her which was black out-voted the other fifteen parts and made her
a negro."[9] And what enforces this illogical arithmetic other than the
socially sanctioned contract summed up by the verb "out-voted"? The
verb reminds us that these measurements measure ideologically produced differences between the races. Roxana's racial identity is
socially created, "a fiction of law and custom," but a fiction shored up
and made to look like fact through the pseudo-mathematics of blood
lines. For Twain the apparent precision implied by minute fractional
divisions (one-sixteenth, one thirty-second) only underscores their
disjunction from reality. All that counts racially in Dawson's Landing
are two categories: black and white.

Mark Twain's representation of racial identity as a system of
deceptive mathematics has historical precedent in the unique
"descent rule" that has been the principal basis of racial classification in the United States. According to this ancestry rule, all descendants of mixed unions are classed with their black ancestors. The
resulting two-category system (such as Twain depicts) originated in
efforts, mandated by state legislation since the colonial era, to
restrict interracial marriage and to determine the status of mixed offspring; by the time of the Civil War, in order to facilitate enforcement
of antimiscegenation laws, more precise definitions were formulated
as to what proportion of black ancestry placed an individual on the
other side of the color line. The usual antebellum rule for determining who was what was one-fourth or one-eighth, meaning that those
with such proportions of black "blood"—anyone with a black or
mulatto ancestor within the previous two or three generations—
must be classified as black. This "statutory homogenization of all
persons with Negro ancestry," as Winthrop Jordan calls it, was peculiar to slavery as it developed in the continental United States. Not
even in South Africa, Fredrickson notes, "despite the triumph of
white supremacy and segregationism," has such a "rigorous ancestry
principle been used to determine who is white and who is not."[1]

9. Mark Twain, *Pudd'nhead Wilson* and *Those Extraordinary Twins*, 2nd ed., ed. Sidney E.
   Berger (New York: W. W. Norton, 2005), 9.
1. On the "descent rule" or "rigorous ancestry principle," see Fredrickson, *White Supremacy*,
   95–99, 129–30; see also 101–08 on the antebellum history of the legal color line. On
   "statutory homogenization," see Winthrop D. Jordan, *White Over Black: American Attitudes Toward the Negro, 1550–1812* (Greenville: University of North Carolina Press,
   1968), 169.

The rigor of the American two-category system can be judged by common linguistic usage. Other than the term *mulatto* (which was indistinguishable from *Negro* for legal purposes), no terminology existed in the United States with which to recognize varying degrees of intermixed "blood," or to define a hierarchy of legal status derived from those shades of distinction. Elsewhere, as studies of comparative race relations show, racially mixed offspring ("half-castes" or "half-white") have usually been acknowledged as an intermediate group in systems of racial stratification with varying degrees of fluidity between white, "colored," and black. Such acknowledgment was reflected in the development of terminology to distinguish various racial mixtures. In Latin America and the British West Indies, for example, racially mixed offspring were labeled according to fractions of "blood": *mulatto* meant one-half white; *sambo*, one-fourth white; *quadroon*, three-fourths white; and *mestizo*, seven-eighths white.[2]

Twain's minute fractions mock the genetic absurdity of this way of quantifying the genetic makeup. But however theoretically and genetically untenable, this complex linguistic machinery established a fact of social practice: miscegenation was a publicly accepted, almost institutionalized practice in some New World slave societies, whereas the absence of analogous terms in the United States suggests that racially mixed offspring simply were not officially acknowledged.[3] The reasons for such denial may be summed up in the language of a pioneering Virginia statute of 1691 that banned, for the first time in the colonies, all forms of interracial marriage. The legislation's stated purpose was "the prevention of that abominable mixture and spurious issue."[4] The essential word is "mixture." Mulattoes blurred the clear separation between the races essential to American race slavery, and miscegenation was thus perceived as a threat to a biracial society. Particularly threatening to this two-part order were the "free persons of color," most of whom were mulattoes. "We should have but two classes," declared one grand jury deliberating the expulsion of the "free colored" from South Carolina in the late 1850s, "the Master and the slave, and no intermediate class can be other than immensely mischievous to our peculiar institution."[5] The grand jury testimony verges on acknowledging the contradiction that this "intermediate" group—an "abominable mixture," neither

2. Fredrickson, *White Supremacy*, 96; Jordan, *White Over Black*, 175, n. 84.
3. Leon Litwack claims that despite such legal erasure, on a more informal level, both before and after the Civil War, "whites made no attempt to deny the presence of a substantial mulatto population." The distorting combination of acknowledgment and denial is precisely what *Pudd'nhead Wilson* registers. See Litwack, *Been in the Storm So Long: The Aftermath of Slavery* (New York: Random House, 1980), 265–66.
4. John C. Hurd, *The Law of Freedom and Bondage in the United States*, 2 vols. (New York: D. Van Nostrand, 1858), 1: 236.
5. Quoted in Williamson, *New People*, 66.

white nor black, slave nor free—violates the logic of the institution that produced it and therefore must be suppressed.

If, as a result, the mulatto was legally erased, deprived of any status under the law, the problem of race mixture itself was not altogether suppressed in contemporary political, scientific, and religious writing. A widespread proslavery argument of the 1850s drew on current knowledge of heredity to theorize that the offspring of miscegenation would be an unnatural type, the mixture of races adapted to very different geographic regions, and hence unable to procreate beyond two or three generations. The eventual result of race mixture was inevitably sterility, according to another "scientific" argument offering "proof" in the sterility of an animal hybrid, the mule—an analogy linguistically enforced in the word *mulatto*, borrowed from the Spanish and derived from the Latin *mulus*. Scientific justification was not the only authority appealed to in antimiscegenation writing. Immediately after the war, miscegenation became for some the essential sin against God that caused the South to lose. Defeat "is the judgment of the Almighty," wrote one low-country Carolina planter in 1868, "because the human and brute blood have mingled to the degree it has in the slave states. Was it not so in the French and British Islands and see what has become of them."[6]

The widespread revulsion against race mixture expressed in all of the above writings—the Virginia statute, the grand jury testimony, the scientific arguments on hybridism, and the planter's religious argument—help to explain both why and how the fiction of race purity was maintained in the face of so much evidence to the contrary. As Jordan puts this contradiction: "by classifying the mulatto as a Negro [the white slaveowner] was in effect denying that intermixture had occurred at all."[7] When Mark Twain, later in the 1890s, framed racial identity in *Pudd'nhead Wilson* as an issue of acknowledgment and denial, both for himself as an author and for southern society, he was thus openly articulating the *sub rosa* judgment of many of his contemporaries.

Indeed, once slavery was abolished the question of the color line and its impact on the representation of race relations became, if anything, all the more pressing. For many white southerners, George Washington Cable pointed out in 1885, looming in the passage of the Fourteenth and Fifteenth Amendments and the freedman's participation in Reconstruction governments was the "huge bugbear of

---

6. On Southern "muleology" and religious arguments about the South's defeat (including the passage in the letter from William Heyward to James Gregorie, 12 January 1868), see Williamson, *New People*, 73, 92, 96; on the etymology of "mulatto" and its cultural meanings, see Jordan, *White Over Black*, 168.
7. Jordan, *White Over Black*, 178.

Social Equality": equality meant the "social intermingling of the two races," with its "monstrous" suggestion of "admixture of the two bloods" and "the utter confusion of race and corruption of society."[8] What Jordan calls the "peculiar bifurcation" of American racial categorization represented, then, for Twain and others, even more than purely a legal effort to control the results of interracial sex. The restrictive policy attempted broadly to control "black" encroachments on "white" identity, to fix racial identity as an absolute quantity with clear boundaries rather than on a continuum of gradations, one shading into another. Fears expressed about "amalgamation," an antebellum term equivalent to miscegenation, corroborate what I will show to be Twain's association of race mixture with the destruction of basic assumptions about identity—not only racial, but also social and even sexual identity.

One traveler in the antebellum South singled out what he called the "bugbear of 'amalgamation.'" The traveler's journal noted that even the reform-minded Lyman Beecher was "so far jaundiced" that he supported African colonization, because "he considered it a salutary preventive of that amalgamation, which would confound the two races and obliterate the traces of their distinction." Similar arguments, bent on maintaining these "irresistible" "natural" differences, were advanced from colonial days through the Emancipation Proclamation by other, even more eminent advocates of black emancipation and colonization. In 1781 Thomas Jefferson asked in *Notes on the State of Virginia*, "Will not a lover of natural history, then, one who views the gradations in all the races of animals with the eye of philosophy, excuse an effort to keep those in the department of man as distinct as nature has formed them?" Jefferson's argument against race mixture was reiterated in 1862, when Abraham Lincoln addressed a small group of black leaders in the White House on the subject of returning all American blacks to Africa. "You and we are different races," he said. "We have between us a broader difference than exists between any other two races."[9]

Both Jefferson and Lincoln were articulating a general fear of amalgamation shared both by those who advocated some form of black emancipation and by the anti-abolitionist "gentlemen of prop-

8. George Washington Cable, "The Freedman's Case in Equity" and "The Silent South," in *The Negro Question: A Selection of Writings on Civil Rights in the South*, ed. Arlin Turner (New York: Somerset, 1958), 71, 85.

9. Edward S. Abdy, *Journal of a Residence and Tour in the United States*, 3 vols. (London, 1835), quoted in Leonard L. Richards, *Gentlemen of Property and Standing: Anti-Abolition Mobs in Jacksonian America* (New York: Oxford University Press, 1970), 42; Jefferson quoted in Ronald T. Takaki, *Iron Cages: Race and Culture in Nineteenth-Century America* (Seattle: University of Washington Press, 1979), 46, 49–50; Lincoln quoted in Henry Louis Gates, Jr., "Writing Race and the Difference It Makes," *Critical Inquiry* [*"Race," Writing, and Difference*] 12 (Autumn 1985): 3.

erty and standing" in antebellum America. For the latter, especially, Leonard L. Richards asserts, amalgamation was personally and intimately threatening: it tapped the "fear of assimilation, of being 'mulattoized,' of losing one's sense of identity." For such men, tied to family, class, community, and position, race mixture went beyond a threat to race purity: it was a harbinger of "the breakdown of distinctions among white men, the blurring of social divisions, and the general levelling process that they saw enveloping ante-bellum America"; it was a first step to becoming "cogs in a mass society."[1] For Southern women of the same class, such as Mary Boykin Chesnut, amalgamation also threatened a more private, familial order, as a well-known 1861 entry in Chestnut's diary suggests:

> Like the patriarchs of old, our men live all in one house with their wives and their concubines; and the mulattoes one sees in every family partly resemble the white children. Any lady is ready to tell you who is the father of all the mulatto children in everybody's household but her own. Those, she seems to think, drop from the clouds.[2]

For men and women, proslavery apologists, abolitionists, and reform-minded anti-abolitionists alike, the issues of race mixture and interracial sexual relations struck at the heart of basic assumptions about the individual's place in home and society.

The "stock" changeling formula in *Pudd'nhead Wilson*, then, altered by Twain so that "twinned" black and white babies are exchanged in their cradles, acts out an interchangeability between the races that resonates with anxieties of the 1890s as well as of the antebellum years. Just so, the end of the Civil War and Reconstruction were characterized by optimism and even by radical thinking on race relations that gave way in the eighties and nineties to something old, something new. The law, once used to regulate the peculiar institution of slavery, now underwrote the far more broad-reaching ideology of white supremacy in state laws regulating relations between the races and establishing rigid lines of segregation. By the beginning of the twentieth century, for example, laws against intermarriage were passed in all but one of the seventeen states that had made up the slave South in 1861, and as recently as 1930, twenty-nine of the forty-eight states made intermarriage illegal. At the same time, for purposes of racial identification, the color line was more stringently and narrowly defined. As late as 1970, for example, in Louisiana the legal fraction defining blackness was still one thirty-second "Negro

1. Richards, *Gentlemen*, 45, 166.
2. Mary Boykin Chesnut, *A Diary from Dixie*, ed. Ben Ames Williams, (1949, repr. Cambridge: Harvard University Press, 1980), 21–22.

blood." Fredrickson says that "most southern states were operating in accordance with what amounted to a 'one-drop rule,' meaning in effect that a person with any known degree of black ancestry was legally considered a Negro and subject to the full disabilities associated with segregation and disfranchisement."[3]

Such heightened awareness of what George Washington Cable called "the Negro Question" characterized the years during which Twain wrote *Pudd'nhead Wilson*. The new race laws and the accompanying cultural conversation about the South's "race problem" articulated for Mark Twain, in concrete social and political terms, a longstanding problem: the connection between the maintenance of social control and the construction of identity. During this period (extending roughly from the late 1880s through the 1890s), the debate over race relations brought to the fore two bodies of contemporary knowledge—one legal and one scientific—that asserted the feasibility of drawing sharp racial, sexual, or social lines around groups of human beings, thereby ensuring the divisions many believed necessary to social stability. For Twain the possibility of such certainty as held out by the law and by the science of heredity was as deeply attractive as it was illusory and destructive. These contradictions finally collide in the conclusion of *Pudd'nhead Wilson*, when lawyer/detective/scientist David Wilson puts to the legal test the science of fingerprinting—a method of differentiating "each man from all the rest of the human species," according to the geneticist Francis Galton, "to an extent far beyond the capacity of human imagination."[4]

Alone among Mark Twain's fictional detectives, most of whom, he once commented, "extravagantly burlesque the detective business—if it *is* possible to burlesque that business extravagantly," David Wilson is genuinely adept at the procedures of detection and proof.[5] His chosen profession, the law, depends upon this skill, but since his fatal half-dog joke prevents him from practicing law in Dawson's Landing, his ratiocinative powers reveal themselves in more eccentric ways. Wilson's eccentricity as well as his outsider status remind us that he was created in the image of Sherlock Holmes, one of Twain's several forays in exploiting the contemporary market for detective fiction. Conan Doyle's Holmes had been a best-selling

3. On race classification in Louisiana, see Virginia R. Dominguez, *White by Definition: Social Classification in Creole Louisiana* (New Brunswick: Rutgers University Press, 1986). On the "one-drop rule" in general, see Fredrickson, *White Supremacy*, 130.
4. Francis Galton, *Finger Prints* (1892, repr. New York: Da Capo, 1966), 12.
5. Samuel Clemens to William Dean Howells, 21 January 1879, in *Mark Twain-Howells Letters*, ed. Henry Nash Smith and William Gibson, 2 vols. (Cambridge: Harvard University Press, 1960), 1: 246.

phenomenon in America ever since the first Sherlock Holmes story, *A Study in Scarlet*, appeared in *Beeton's Christmas Annual* (1887). An alienated intellectual, Holmes had popular appeal in part because he stood out from the institutionalized police detectives of the Pinkerton series or the Beadle dime novels. Holmes's "passion for definite and exact knowledge," for example, sometimes isolates him even from the devoted Watson, who criticizes the detective's intellect in *A Study in Scarlet* as "a little too scientific . . . approach[ing] to cold-bloodedness."[6] In creating his own detective, Twain picks up on the somewhat alienating ratiocinative powers of Conan Doyle's popular character: Tom Driscoll snidely sings Wilson's praises as the "great scientist running to seed here in this village."[7] In *Pudd'nhead Wilson*, as in popular detective fiction, one condition of intellectual power is isolation from the community, which, like Dawson's Landing, both fears and needs its scientists.

Mark Twain also appropriated from popular fiction the equation between seeing and deductive power, perhaps most memorably expressed in the insignia of the Pinkerton agency, which bore an open human eye with the motto "We Never Sleep" beneath it. Sherlock Holmes's power, too, is notably ocular; his special vision enables him to deduce biographical facts from ordinarily unnoticed details. Wilson's superior intellect also expresses itself through superior visual observation. Both his hobbies of reading palms and collecting fingerprints demonstrate a type of Holmesian second sight, for they emphasize the reading and interpreting of signs that are, to the interpreter, visible traces of the past in the present. In this fascination with ocular proof, Twain draws upon the popular caricature of the detective with magnifying glass, bending over what seems like invisible matter, collecting all possible facts because even trivial details may prove to signify.

When a whole elaborate plot may be thus untangled by discovering one essential fact, we have abandoned the problematic nature of causation in the real world of masters and slaves, where victim and victimizer both are bound together by the institutional effects of slavery. No such entanglements can remain in the secure universe of the detective story, where fixed laws give meaning to particular events, and, through the detective's knowledge, random events are ultimately arranged into one coherent line of causality from the murderer to the deed.

The characters in Twain's novel react to the deductive powers of the detective with much the same combination of awe and skepti-

6. Arthur Conan Doyle, *The Complete Sherlock Holmes* (1930, repr. New York: Doubleday, 1960), 17.
7. Twain, *Pudd'nhead Wilson*, 54.

cism that Twain himself sometimes expressed toward the writer's omniscient eye. Indeed, we know, he went so far as putatively to reject his own authorial omniscience in the preface that connects *Pudd'nhead Wilson* to *Those Extraordinary Twins* (the Siamese twin tale "changed itself from a farce to a tragedy while I was going along with it" and other, new characters began "taking things almost entirely into their own hands and working the whole tale as a private venture of their own," leaving Twain with not one "but two stories tangled together"). And of David Wilson's own interpretive abilities, Tom Driscoll mocks, "Dave's just an all-around genius, . . . a prophet with the kind of honor that prophets generally get at home—for here they don't give shucks for his scientifics. . . ."[8] If Twain's detective, like the self-professed "jack-leg" novelist himself, is less a prophet than a disturber of the peace, and if his "electrifying revelations" at the end of the novel are more disruptive than restorative, then what judgment are we to make of his solution to the mystery of a murderer's identity? More particularly, what are we to make of *how* rather than *what* he knows: along with the murderer, what is on trial in the courtroom conclusion is Wilson's method of deducing identity, his "scientifics," the fingerprinting system.

In this case, the author shares his character's passion for scientifics, for while writing *Pudd'nhead Wilson* in 1892, Clemens "devoured," as he put it, Francis Galton's *Finger Prints*, just published that year. In part his enthusiasm came from the novelty, and hence, he thought, salability of this material; "the finger-prints in this one is virgin ground," he assured his publisher Fred Hall, "absolutely *fresh*, and mighty curious and interesting to everybody."[9] But in larger part Clemens was fascinated by both the scientific findings and the credentials of the eminent geneticist (and cousin of Charles Darwin) Galton. Recalling in 1897 how he had relied on Galton's book while writing *Pudd'nhead Wilson* in 1892, he wrote in a letter: "The fingermark system of identification . . . has been quite thoroughly & scientifically examined by Mr. Galt [*sic*], & I kept myself within the bounds of his ascertained facts."[1] Chief among the facts on which the plot turns is Galton's demonstration that fingerprints can establish the identity of the same person at any stage of his life, between babyhood and old age (and for some time after his death, Galton adds), as well as differentiate between twins ("It would be totally impossible to fail to distinguish between the fingerprints of twins, who in other respects appeared exactly alike").[2]

8. Ibid., 310, 311–12, 54.
9. Clemens to Fred J. Hall, 30 July 1893, in *Mark Twain's Letters to His Publishers*, ed. Hamlin Hill (Berkeley: University of California Press, 1967), 355.
1. Clemens to Miss Darrell, 23 February 1897, Typescript in Mark Twain Papers, Bancroft Library, University of California, Berkeley.
2. Galton, *Finger Prints*, 113, 167.

Even more provocative for Clemens, I believe, than these particular "ascertained facts" was Galton's broad and spirited endorsement of the wide-ranging potential of fingerprinting as a method of "personal identification." The prints would be of value not only in identifying criminals, Galton points out, but also in ferreting out the less willful kind of imposture that had long fascinated Mark Twain: the possibility "of a harmless person being arrested by mistake for another man," for example, "and being in sore straits to give satisfactory proof of the error."[3] "Let no one despise the ridges on account of their smallness," Galton urges a possibly skeptical readership.

> They have the unique merit of retaining all their peculiarities unchanged throughout life, and afford in consequence an incomparably surer criterion of identity than any other bodily feature. . . . To fix the human personality, to give to each human being an identity, an individuality that can be depended upon with certainty, lasting, unchangeable, always recognisable and easily adduced, this appears to be in the largest sense the aim of the new method.[4]

Apparently persuaded as much by Galton's impassioned tone as by his facts, Mark Twain puts all of these claims to the test in the dramatic courtroom conclusion of *Pudd'nhead Wilson*. When Wilson unveils his theory of who murdered Judge Driscoll and presents the evidence that proves its soundness, he also implicitly tries the case for what Twain learned from his research in Galton's *Finger Prints*. This "mysterious and marvelous natal autograph," Wilson says, constitutes virtually perfect proof of identity:

> Every human being carries with him from his cradle to his grave certain physical marks which do not change their character, and by which he can always be identified. . . . this autograph cannot be counterfeited, nor can he disguise it or hide it away, nor can it become illegible by the wear and the mutations of time.[5]

Like Galton's, Wilson's tone becomes more impassioned, his parallel clauses building in length and intensity, as he moves beyond the data to contemplate the potential of what he calls these "sure identifiers." Fingerprints, in Galton's terms, reliable means of "Personal Identification," render deception through impersonation or accident impossible by enabling each individual to be absolutely differentiated from the rest of the species. Wilson waxes eloquent about this method, building suspense in the courtroom audience by defining what the method is not. This signature is not a person's height, "for duplicates

3. Ibid., 149.
4. Ibid., 2, 169.
5. Twain, *Pudd'nhead Wilson*, 114.

of that exist; it is not his form, for duplicates of that exist, also, whereas this signature is each man's very own—there is no duplicate of it among the swarming populations of the globe!" Even identical twins, Wilson pointedly concludes, "carry from birth to death a sure identifier in this mysterious and marvelous natal autograph. That once known to you, his fellow-twin could never personate him and deceive you."[6]

At this point in the argument, Wilson pauses and, as Mark Twain the performer used to "play with the pause," theatrically lets his brief silence "perfect its spell upon the house," before putting on his final display, submitting himself to an actual, on-the-spot test of his claims. While his back is turned, he asks several members of the jury, whose fingerprints he has collected over the years and so knows well, to make their prints on a glass window in the courtroom, where the two accused twins will also make their marks. This experimental procedure, as he requests, is repeated twice on different panes, for as he puts it, "a person might happen on the right marks by pure guesswork, *once*, therefore I wish to be tested twice." The reader is almost as gratified as the courtroom audience when Wilson correctly identifies the various prints ("This certainly approaches the miraculous!" says "the Bench"). But the source of our gratification is different from theirs. For us, the only real suspense in the novel has been waiting not for the identity of the murderer (which we've known all along) but for the moment when Wilson would discover that he has the means to prove it. And that moment finally arrives in the suitably theatrical trial, which opens in chapter 20 with this rather ominous entry from "Pudd'nhead Wilson's Calendar": "Even the clearest and most perfect circumstantial evidence is likely to be at fault, after all, and therefore ought to be received with great caution."[7]

How, then, ought we to receive the evidence of the fingerprints? What do those "sure identifiers" actually reveal? Wilson, no longer the flamboyant rhetorician but the dispassionate man of science, now draws on the ostensibly neutral, value-free variables of science and the syllogistic structure of logical reasoning to complete his presentation of the evidence. The fingerprints tell us first, he argues, using the impersonal notation preferred by Galton, that "A was put into B's cradle in the nursery." "In the majority of cases," Galton remarks, "the mere question would be, Is the man A the same person as B, or is he not? And of that question the fingermarks would give unerring proof."[8] In the case Twain creates, things are not quite so clear. What happens next, Wilson explains, is that "B was trans-

6. Ibid., 114, 115.
7. Ibid., 104.
8. Galton, *Finger Prints*, 151.

ferred to the kitchen, and became a negro and a slave—but within a quarter of an hour he will stand before you white and free!"[9]

Neither the triumphant tone nor the burst of applause from the audience nor the aura of logical deduction and absolute clarity disguises the fact that Wilson's conclusion, though strictly "the truth," is also illogical and arbitrary, almost more confusing than clarifying. Fingerprints appear to be the one measure of unique, noncontingent individual identity, but are in practice relational indices that must be read in and against the context of other sets of prints. Yet in spite of the methodologically essential social context, the fingerprints tell us nothing socially, as opposed to physiologically, significant about either A or B as individuals, much less about the lives of "Chambers" or "Tom." What they prove, in fact, is that one can be interchangeably "white and free" and "a negro and a slave." In this way Twain thus out-Galtons Galton. Galton finally had to admit that fingerprints do not reveal racial grouping or characteristics; he acknowledged "great expectations, that have been falsified, namely their use in indicating Race and Temperament."[1] Rather than stopping at this point, Twain goes even further than Galton, showing that though fingerprints do, indeed, establish racial difference, those categories are not biologically fixed but rather culturally determined. Knowing, then, that Tom, considered white, was born black and enslaved and is once again so constituted does nothing to fulfill Galton's promise that fingerprinting will "fix the human personality" and "give to each human being an identity, an individuality." Instead, like any other "natural" index of the self—race or gender, for example—fingerprints point toward the culture that appropriates nature as the basis of socially constructed identities.

Rather than leading to any stable, independent determinant of identity, then, the fingerprints focus attention on the social context that authorizes their use in the science of "personal identification." That social context most explicitly enters the novel during the sentencing phase of the trial, the moment in the courtroom when the social voice speaks most directly to reaffirm its values and to reestablish the order disturbed by the crime. In Twain's case, though, the sentence accomplishes no such righting to order. Although the murderer, now defined as "the false heir," makes "a full confession" and is "sentenced to imprisonment for life," the creditors of his ultimate victim, not Judge Driscoll but "the Percy Driscoll estate," argue that "a complication" has ensued. Building much the same structure of logical reasoning as Wilson does, they establish first that "the false heir" should have been "inventoried . . . with the rest of the prop-

9. Twain, *Pudd'nhead Wilson*, 118–19.
1. Galton, *Finger Prints*, 1–2, 20.

erty" at the time of its owner's death; that he was thus "lawfully their property"; and furthermore, "that if he had been delivered up to them in the first place, they would have sold him and he could not have murdered Judge Driscoll." Hard on the heels of this stunning conjecture, in a triumphant burst of illogic, comes the conclusion to both the creditors' argument and to the novel.

> therefore it was not he that had really committed the murder, the guilt lay with the erroneous inventory. Everybody saw that there was reason in this. Everybody granted that if "Tom" were white and free it would be unquestionably right to punish him— it would be no loss to anybody; but to shut up a valuable slave for life—that was quite another matter.
>
> As soon as the Governor understood the case, he pardoned Tom at once, and the creditors sold him down the river.[2]

The author and his reader see a different "reason" in this. If "Tom" or Tom or "the false heir" (the proliferation of names seeming to replace human substance with linguistic form) is pardoned only to be sold down the river, we reason, then words like "pardon" and "punish" (and "reason") have lost their meaning in Dawson's Landing, a society where an "erroneous inventory" can first assume the human burden of guilt and then, logically, escape human punishment. By the same agreed-upon fiction, a "valuable slave" is defined as chattel, not to be held accountable for human antisocial acts, and therefore even the law must obey the rules of logic and conclude of the murderer that "it was not he that had really committed the murder." But because only whites have the "unquestionable right" to punishment under the law, it also follows that in this case a valuable slave—will-less chattel—must be "pardoned" for a crime he could not by definition have committed. Finally, if the guilty party is the "erroneous inventory," then all of Southern society is implicated in the crime because it participates in and oversees the slave system that requires such inventories. The trial thus bears witness to the anguished tangle of contradictions surrounding the slave system, and, further, to the strange fact that while these contradictions expose themselves in the legal and linguistic fictions of slave society, they also keep that world from falling apart under their weight.

To thus discover that the criminal in a detective story is not one individual but an entire society is to disrupt the premise of narrative order and social justice upon which the form is based. Fomenting such disruption, Twain in 1893 appraised "the whole story" a success, "centered on the murder and the trial; from the first chapter

2. Twain, *Pudd'nhead Wilson*, 121–22.

the movement is straight ahead without divergence or side-play to the murder and the trial."[3] Such a narrative invokes expectations of the ritual confrontation between law and criminality that concludes most detective fiction with the restoration of order. Rather than coming to a schematic resolution, though, the conclusion of *Pudd'nhead Wilson* initiates polarities between innocence and guilt, slave and free man, loss and profit, punishment and pardon, only to expose them finally as "fictions of law and custom." Similarly, the changeling plot does not culminate in the conventional discovery of the child's noble birth, a discovery which ordinarily vindicates the noble behavior he has exhibited from the beginning as it restores class lines and fulfills the audience's desire for order, both narrative and social.

Pudd'nhead Wilson deliberately denies such wish fulfillment. Through the detective plot that its author so admired, the novel arouses the reader's craving to discover, the desire to turn the act of reading—palms, fingerprints, or texts—into a means of discovery and resolution of apparently impenetrable mysteries. But if Twain's detective acts out the author's desire that human knowledge could so accurately systematize the world, the character also oversees the author's deconstruction of his own fantasy. Wilson's classification system helps him to discover the false Tom (or "Tom"), but in exposing a "white" man as a "black" slave, it also exposes the whole society that created, but does not acknowledge, its own nemesis. Whether one calls this a discovery of America's "own secret self" (Leslie Fiedler) or of "the repressed guilt which has gathered at the heart of slavery" (James Cox), such a discovery makes knowledge more of a threat than a deliverance.[4] Tom's fate threatens that the hidden taint of black blood could be disclosed in any white person, tapping the dread that all "secret murderers are said to feel when the accuser says 'Thou art the man!'"[5] The craving to discover has reversed itself into fear of exposure.

Thus Pudd'nhead Wilson's Calendar entry for the final chapter reads ironically, "October 12, the Discovery. It was wonderful to find America, but it would have been more wonderful to miss it."[6] For a murder mystery, in which the murderer's identity has been known from the very beginning, to close with a problematic discovery is to confirm the earlier hint that *how* we know has replaced *what* we know as the object of inquiry. When the novel ends, its various sci-

---

3. Clemens to Hall, 30 July 1893, in Hill, *Mark Twain's Letters to His Publishers*, 354–55.
4. Leslie Fiedler, "As Free as Any Cretur . . . ," in *Mark Twain: A Collection of Critical Essays*, ed. Henry Nash Smith (Englewood Cliffs, N.J.: Prentice-Hall, 1963), 138; see James Cox, *Mark Twain: The Fate of Humor* (Princeton: Princeton University Press, 1966), 323. [The Fiedler and Smith essays are in the present edition—*Editor.*]
5. Twain, *Pudd'nhead Wilson*, 49.
6. Twain, 120. I am indebted to Leslie Fiedler's reading of the final Calendar entry as "a disconcerting ending for a detective story, which should have faith in all disclosures" ("As Free as Any Cretur . . . ," in *Collection of Critical Essays*, 138).

entific and legal bodies of knowledge—definitive means of identification and differentiation—result in no certainty at all.

More disturbingly, the contortions that the law goes through at the last moment to reverse or undo itself in Mark Twain's courtroom—the guilty party, once white and free, identified as a slave, defined as property, and pardoned—are analogous to the process of legal reversal enacted after Reconstruction. In a series of state laws and Supreme Court cases, the "freedmen" saw their legal rights reduced, eroded, and eventually nullified by the law. The process that once outlawed slavery in the late 1860s legalized segregation in the 1870s and 1880s, culminating most explicitly two years after the publication of *Pudd'nhead Wilson* in the "separate but equal" doctrine of the 1896 Supreme Court case, *Plessy v. Ferguson*.[7] The novel confirms in an American context what Twain's later anti-imperialist essays would conclude globally: that in spite of the Fourteenth and Fifteenth Amendments, the law had not only failed to solve the "Negro Question," but worse still had been positively enlisted in the service of reconstituting white supremacy, both in the United States and abroad. That many of the world's "civilized," "Christian" powers were, under the banner of imperialism, justifying the colonizing of Kipling's "lesser breeds without the law" meant for Twain a double defeat. Thereafter neither the law, which permitted and enforced the farce of "separate but equal," nor science, which shored up racism with theories of "natural" degeneration, would hold out any promise of addressing America's most pressing social problem.

But as well as casting doubt on these hallowed bodies of knowledge, two great allies of late-nineteenth-century American civilization, the novel also implicates the author's own omniscience and control over his text. Mark Twain's opening passage of *Those Extraordinary Twins* (125), we remember, brings his own intentionality under suspicion, deriding himself as the author of a tale that "changed itself from a farce to a tragedy" while it also spread "itself into a book." Perhaps what he most rejected was how both stories resist the project of definitively separating the innocent from the guilty in social, racial, and sexual terms. Neither the farcical issue of the Siamese twins' singular/plural duality, nor the tragic issue of black/white division is ever resolved. The trials—a total of three in the two works—fail to ascertain individual responsibility in the face of necessity (either the twins' physical bond or the biological, social, and economic ties of slavery). And finally, the specific methods of identification through readings of the body (skin color, fingerprints) also fail, in Galton's terms, to "fix the human personality, to give to each human being an identity, an individuality."

7. On the history of developments in anti–civil rights legislation following the Civil War, see Richard Bardolph, ed., *The Civil Rights Record: Black Americans and the Law, 1849–1970* (New York: Crowell, 1970), 58–72, 144–54.

Instead of a "true self" and clear standards of verification, what Mark Twain discovered in his own fiction was the constructed and artificial character of essential social measures of identity—measures that, as the history of race relations demonstrates, we nevertheless totally depend upon. The novel, therefore, also exposes even as it exemplifies the mechanisms by which we persuade ourselves that the constructed is the real. For without such constructs, or when they are momentarily inverted, the conclusion to *Pudd'nhead Wilson* suggests, the individual may find himself permanently displaced, nowhere socially recognizable. The "real heir," we remember, ends without a proper name or place or self, while the "false heir" disappears, pardoned and sold down the river. Mark Twain himself ends with his sense of authorial omniscience shaken, the writer still bound, the preface to the farce admits, by and to the unintentional disclosures of his own writing. Not even in the world of his own making could he imagine liberation under the law or discover a secure basis for knowledge of self and other. Like Aunt Patsy Cooper in *Those Extraordinary Twins*, Twain came increasingly to doubt whether he could "know—absolutely *know*, independently of anything [others] have told [him]" even that "reality" exists. Following *Pudd'nhead Wilson*, Twain's last major set of writings becomes obsessed with the question, "how do we know what we know is not a fiction or a dream?" The tendency in the thoroughly grounded, deeply historical *Pudd'nhead Wilson* to question conventional boundaries of racial identity expands in the dream tales into challenging the borders of reality itself.

Selected Bibliography

• indicates a work included or excerpted in this Norton Critical Edition.

GENERAL

Allen, Jerry. *The Adventures of Mark Twain*. Boston: Little, Brown, 1954.
Aller, Susan Bivin. *Mark Twain*. Minneapolis: Lerner, 2001.
Andrews, Kenneth R. *Nook Farm: Mark Twain's Hartford Circle*. Cambridge, Mass.: Harvard University Press. 1950.
Asselineau, Roger. *The Literary Reputation of Mark Twain from 1910 to 1950: A Critical Essay and Bibliography*. Paris: Didier, 1954.
Baetzhold, Howard G. *Mark Twain and John Bull*. Bloomington: Indiana University Press, 1970.
Baldanza, Frank. *Mark Twain: An Introduction and Interpretation*. New York: Barnes & Noble, 1961.
Bellamy, Gladys C. *Mark Twain As a Literary Artist*. Norman: University of Oklahoma Press, 1950.
Bercovitch, Sacvan, et al., eds. *The Cambridge History of American Literature*. Cambridge, U.K., and New York: Cambridge University Press, 1994–.
Berthoff, Warner. *The Ferment of Realism, American Literature, 1884–1919*. New York: Free Press, 1965.
Blair, Walter. *Horse Sense in American Humor*. Chicago: University of Chicago Press, 1942.
———. *Native American Humor: 1800–1900*. New York: American Book, 1937.
Bloom, Harold, ed. *Mark Twain: Modern Critical Views*, New York: Chelsea House, 1986.
Blues, Thomas. *Mark Twain and the Community*. Lexington: University of Kentucky Press, 1970.
Branch, Edgar M. *The Literary Apprenticeship of Mark Twain, with Selections from His Apprentice Writing*. Urbana: University of Illinois Press, 1950.
Brashear, Minnie M. "Formative Influences in the Mind and Writings of Mark Twain." Dissertation, University of North Carolina, 1930.
———. *Mark Twain, Son of Missouri*. Chapel Hill: University of North Carolina Press, 1934.
Brooks, Van Wyck. *The Ordeal of Mark Twain*. Rev. ed. New York: Dutton, 1933.
Budd, Louis J. *Mark Twain: Social Philosopher*. Bloomington: Indiana University Press, 1962; Columbia: University of Missouri Press, 2001.
———. *Our Mark Twain: The Making of His Public Personality*. Philadelphia: University of Pennsylvania Press, 1983.
Canby, Henry S. *Turn West, Turn East: Mark Twain and Henry James*. Boston: Houghton Mifflin, 1951.
Cardwell, Guy. *The Man Who Was Mark Twain*. New Haven and London: Yale University Press, 1991.
Carlstroem, Catherine. "Homicidal Economics in Mark Twain: Legacies of American Theft." Dissertation, University of California, Santa Cruz, 2001.
Chase, Richard. *The American Novel and Its Tradition*. Garden City, N.Y.: Doubleday, 1957.
Clemens, Clara. *My Father, Mark Twain*. New York: Harper & Brothers, 1931.
Covici, Pascal Jr. *Mark Twain's Humor, The Image of a World*. Dallas: Southern Methodist University Press, 1962.
• Cox, James M. *Mark Twain: The Fate of Humor*. Princeton, N.J.: Princeton University Press, 1966; Columbia: University of Missouri Press, 2002.
Cummings, Sherwood. *Mark Twain and Science: Adventures of a Mind*. Baton Rouge and London: Louisiana State University Press, 1988.
De Voto, Bernard. *Mark Twain at Work*. Cambridge, Mass.: Harvard University Press, 1942.
• ———. *Mark Twain's America*. Boston: Little, Brown, 1932.
Dreiser, Theodore. "Mark the Double Twain." *English Journal* 24 (1935): 615–27.

Emerson, Everett H. *Mark Twain: A Literary Life*. Philadelphia: University of Pennsylvania Press, 2000.

Ensor, Allison. *Mark Twain and the Bible*. Lexington: University of Kentucky Press, 1969.

Ferguson, DeLancey. *Mark Twain: Man and Legend*. Indianapolis: Bobbs-Merrill, 1943.

Fishkin, Shelley Fisher, ed. *A Historical Guide to Mark Twain*. Oxford, U.K., and New York: Oxford University Press, 2002.

———. *Lighting Out for the Territory: Reflections on Mark Twain and American Culture*. New York and Oxford, U.K.: Oxford University Press, 1997.

Foner, Philip S. *Mark Twain: Social Critic*. New York: International Publishers, 1958.

Geismar, Maxwell. *Mark Twain: An American Prophet*. Boston: Houghton Mifflin, 1970.

Grant, Douglas. *Twain*. Writers and Critics Series. New York: Grove Press, 1963.

Harnsberger, Caroline Thomas. *Mark Twain, Family Man*. New York: Citadel Press, 1960.

Hill, Hamlin. *Mark Twain: God's Fool*. New York: Harper & Row, 1973.

———, ed. *Mark Twain's Letters to His Publishers*. Berkeley: University of California Press, 1967.

Hill, Richard, and Jim McWilliams. *Mark Twain among the Scholars: Reconsidering Contemporary Twain Criticism*. Albany, N.Y.: Whitston, 2002.

Horn, Jason Gary. *Mark Twain: A Descriptive Guide to Biographical Sources*. Lanham, Md.: Scarecrow Press, 1999.

Howells, William Dean. *My Mark Twain: Reminiscences and Criticisms*. New York: Harper & Brothers, 1910.

Kaplan, Justin. *Mr. Clemens and Mark Twain, A Biography*. New York: Simon & Schuster, 1966.

Krauth, Leland. *Proper Mark Twain*. Athens: University of Georgia Press, 1999.

Krayse, Sydney J. *Mark Twain As Critic*. Baltimore: Johns Hopkins University Press, 1967.

Leary, Lewis. *Mark Twain*. Minneapolis: University of Minnesota Press, 1960.

———, ed. *Mark Twain's Correspondence with Henry Huttleston Rogers, 1893–1909*. Berkeley: University of California Press, 1969.

Long, E. Hudson. *Mark Twain Handbook*. New York: Hendricks House, 1958.

Lynn, Kenneth S. *Mark Twain and Southwestern Humor*. Boston: Little, Brown, 1960.

Macy, John A. *The Spirit of American Literature*. New York: Doubleday, Page, 1913.

McKeithan, Daniel Morley. *Court Trials in Mark Twain and Other Essays*. The Hague: M. Nijhoff, 1958.

Michelson, Bruce. *Mark Twain on the Loose: A Comic Writer and the American Self*. Amherst: University of Massachusetts Press, 1995.

Moore, Olin Harris. "Mark Twain and Don Quixote." *Publications of the Modern Language Association* 37 (1922): 324–46.

Paine, Albert Bigelow. *Mark Twain: A Biography. The Personal and Literary Life of Samuel Langhorne Clemens*. 3 vols. New York: Harper & Brothers, 1912.

———, ed. *Mark Twain's Autobiography*. New York: Harper & Brothers, 1924.

Pflueger, Lynda. *Mark Twain: Legendary Writer and Humorist*. Berkeley Heights, N.J.: Enslow, 1999.

Pochmann, Henry A. "The Mind of Mark Twain." Dissertation, University of Texas, 1924.

Powers, Ron. *Dangerous Water: A Biography of the Boy Who Became Mark Twain*. New York: Basic Books, 1999.

Quinn, Arthur H., ed. *The Literature of the American People*. New York: Appleton-Century-Crofts, 1951.

Regan, Robert. *Unpromising Heroes: Mark Twain and His Characters*. Berkeley: University of California Press, 1966.

Rodney: Robert M. "Mark Twain in England: A Study of the English Criticism of and Attitude Toward Mark Twain, 1867–1940." Dissertation, University of Wisconsin, 1945.

Rourke, Constance M. *American Humor: A Study of National Character*. New York: Harcourt, Brace, 1931.

Rowe, Katherine. *Dead Hands: Fictions of Agency, Renaissance to Modern*. Stanford: Stanford University Press, 1999.

Salomon, Roger B. *Mark Twain and the Image of History*. New Haven: Yale University Press, 1961.

Scott, Harold P. "Mark Twain's Theory of Humor: An Analysis of the Laughable in Literature." Dissertation, n.p., 1917. [Available from University Microfilms Inc., University of Michigan.]

Skandera-Trombley, Laura E. *Mark Twain in the Company of Women*. Philadelphia: University of Pennsylvania Press, 1994.

Sloane, David E. E. *Student Companion to Mark Twain*. Westport, Conn.: Greenwood Press, 2001.

———. "Mark Twain as a Literary Comedian: The Heritage of Artemis Ward in the 1860's." Dissertation, Duke University, 1970.

• Smith, Henry Nash. *Mark Twain: The Development of a Writer*. Cambridge: Harvard University Press, 1962.

Spiller, Robert E., et al., eds. *Literary History of the United States*. New York: Macmillan, 1948.

Stone, Albert E. *The Innocent Eye: Childhood in Mark Twain's Imagination*. New Haven: Yale University Press, 1961.

Trent, W. P., et al., eds. *Cambridge History of American Literature*. New York: Putnam's Sons, 1922.

Van Doren, Carl. "Mark Twain." In *Dictionary of American Biography*, 1928.

Wagenknecht, Edward. *Mark Twain: The Man and His Work*. New Haven: Yale University Press, 1935; 3rd ed. rev. Norman: University of Oklahoma Press, 1967.

Wecter, Dixon. *Sam Clemens of Hannibal*. Boston: Houghton Mifflin, 1952.

———, ed. *The Love Letters of Mark Twain*. New York: Harper & Brothers, 1949.

PUDD'NHEAD WILSON
AND THOSE EXTRAORDINARY TWINS

Alsen, Eberhard. "Pudd'nhead Wilson's Fight for Popularity and Power." *Western American Literature* 7.2 (Summer 1972): 135–43.

Anderson, Frederick, ed. *Pudd'nhead Wilson and Those Extraordinary Twins*. San Francisco: Chandler, 1968. (Facsimile of edition published by American Publishing Company, 1894.)

Aspiz, Harold. "The Other Half of Pudd'nhead's Dog." *Mark Twain Journal* 17.4 (Summer 1975): 10–11.

Baender, Paul. "*Megarus ad Iunam*: Flawed Texts and Verbal Icons." *Philological Quarterly* 64.4 (Fall 1985): 439–57.

Beer, Janet. "Absent Fathers across the Spectrum of Local Colour in the Short Stories of Kate Chopin." In *Paternity and Fatherhood: Myths and Realities*. Ed. Lieve Spaas. New York: St. Martin's, 1998.

Bentley, Nancy. "Contrary Dictions: Narrative Technique and Cultural Conflict in Antebellum American Writing." Dissertation. [*Dissertation Abstracts International*, Section A: The Humanities and Social Sciences 50.2 (August 1989): 442.]

Beppu, Keiko. "The Iconography of the Madonna and the American Imagination, 1: The Missing Joseph; 2: Roxana's Daughters." *Kobe College Studies* 38/39.3 (March 1992): 93–104.

Berger, Sidney E. "New Mark Twain Items." *The Papers of the Bibliographical Society of America* 68 (1974): 331–35.

———. "Editorial Intrusion in *Pudd'nhead Wilson*." *The Papers of the Bibliographical Society of America* 70 (1976): 272–76.

———. "Determining Printer's Copy: The English Edition of Mark Twain's *Pudd'nhead Wilson*. *The Papers of the Bibliographical Society of America* 72 (1978): 250–56.

• Brand, John M. "The Incipient Wilderness: A Study of *Pudd'nhead Wilson*." *Western American Literature* 8 (Summer 1972): 125–34.

Brewton, Vince. "'An Honour As Well As a Pleasure': Dueling, Violence, and Race in *Pudd'nhead Wilson*." *Southern Quarterly: A Journal of the Arts in the South* 38.4 (Summer 2000): 101–18.

• Brodwin, Stanley. "Blackness and the Adamic Myth in Mark Twain's *Pudd'nhead Wilson*." *Texas Studies in Literature and Language* 15 (1973–74): 167–76.

Budd, Louis J. "Mark Twain's Fingerprints in *Pudd'nhead Wilson*." *Etudes Anglaises: Grande-Bretagne, Etats-Unis* 40.4 (October–December 1987): 385–99. [Rpt. *New Directions in American Humor*. Ed. David E. Sloane. Tuscaloosa: University of Alabama Press, 1998.]

Butcher, Philip. "Mark Twain Sells Roxy Down the River." *CLA Journal* 8 (1965): 225–33.

Byrd, Linda. "*Pudd'nhead Wilson's* Roxy as a Tragic Hero." *Conference of College Teachers of English Studies* 63 (September 1998): 50–58.

Chapin, Henry B. "Twain's *Pudd'nhead Wilson*, Chapter VI." *Explicator* 21 (April 1963): Item 61.

Chase, Richard. ["The Inadequacy of *Pudd'nhead Wilson*."] In Richard Chase, *The American Novel and Its Tradition*. Garden City, N.Y.: Doubleday, 1957.

Chellis, Barbara A. "Those Extraordinary Twins: Negroes and Whites." *American Quarterly* 21.1 (Spring 1969): 100–12.

Chinn, Sarah E. "A Show of Hands: Establishing Identity in Mark Twain's *The Tragedy of Pudd'nhead Wilson.*" *Nineteenth Century Studies* 13 (1999): 48–80.

Clark, William Bedford. "Twain and Faulkner: Miscegenation and the Comic Muse." In *Faulkner and Humor: Faulkner and Yoknapatawpha.* Ed. Doreen Fowler and Ann J. Abadie. Jackson: University Press of Mississippi, 1986.

Coburn, Mark D. " 'Training Is Everything': Communal Opinion and the Individual in *Pudd'nhead Wilson.*" *Modern Language Quarterly* 31.1 (March 1970): 209–19.

Cowan, Michael. " 'By Right of the White Election': Political Theology and Theological Politics in *Pudd'nhead Wilson.*" *Mark Twain's* Pudd'nhead Wilson: *Race, Conflict, and Culture.* Ed. Susan Gillman and Forrest G. Robinson. Durham and London: Duke University Press, 1990.

Cox, James M. "*Pudd'nhead Wilson* Revisited." In *Mark Twain's* Pudd'nhead Wilson: *Race, Conflict, and Culture.* Ed. Susan Gillman and Forrest G. Robinson. Durham and London: Duke University Press, 1990.

• ———. "The Ironic Stranger." In *Mark Twain: The Fate of Humor.* Princeton: Princeton UP, 1966. 222–46.

———. "*Pudd'nhead Wilson*: The End of Mark Twain's American Dream." *South Atlantic Quarterly* 58 (Summer 1959): 351–63.

Crane, Gregg. "Black Comedy: Black Citizenship and Jim Crow Positivism." *The Yearbook of Research in English and American Literature* 18 (2002): 289–310.

Cronin, Frank C. "The Ultimate Perspective in *Pudd'nhead Wilson.*" *Mark Twain Journal* 16.1 (Winter 1971–72): 14–16.

D'Avanzo, Mario L. "In the Name of Pudd'nhead." *Mark Twain Journal* 16.2 (1972): 13–14.

Di Prisco, Joseph Michael. "Mark Twain's Art of Doing Business: Commerciality and Form in the 1890s." Dissertation. [*Dissertation Abstracts International*, Section A: The Humanities and Social Sciences 47.8 (February 1987): 3037–38.]

Dillon, Elizabeth Maddock. "Fear of Formalism: Kant, Twain, and Cultural Studies in American Literature." *Diacritics: A Review of Contemporary Criticism* 27.4 (Winter 1997): 46–69.

Eschholz, Paul A. "Twain's *The Tragedy of Pudd'nhead Wilson.*" *Explicator* 31 (April 1973): Item 67.

Feinstein, George. "Vestigia in *Pudd'nhead Wilson.*" *Twainian* n.s. 1.5 (May 1942): 1–3.

• Fiedler, Leslie. "As Free as Any Cretur . . ." In *Mark Twain's* Pudd'nhead Wilson: *Race Conflict, and Culture.* Ed. Susan Gillman and Forrest G. Robinson. Durham and London: Duke UP, 1990.

Fisher, Marvin, and Michael Elliott. "*Pudd'nhead Wilson*: Half a Dog Is Worse Than None." *Southern Review*, n.s. 8.3 (Summer 1972): 535–47.

Fishkin, Shelley Fisher. "Race and Culture at the Century's End: A Social Context for *Pudd'nhead Wilson.*" *Essays in Arts and Sciences* 19 (May 1990): 1–27.

Ford, Thomas W. "The Miscegenation Theme in *Pudd'nhead Wilson.*" *Mark Twain Quarterly* 10 (1955–58): 13–14.

Fredricks, Nancy. "Twain's Indelible Twins." *Nineteenth-Century Literature* 43.4 (March 1989): 484–99.

Freimarck, John. "*Pudd'nhead Wilson*: A Tale of Blood and Brotherhood." *The University Review* [Kansas City] 34.4 (June 1968): 303–06.

Fujisaki, Mutsuo. "The Critical Response to *Pudd'nhead Wilson*: A Brief History and Current Issues." *Eigo Eibungoku Ronso/Studies in English Language and Literature* 46 (February 1996): 77–85.

Gargano, James W. "*Pudd'nhead Wilson*: Mark Twain as Genial Satan." *South Atlantic Quarterly* 74 (Summer 1975): 365–75.

Gerber, John C. "*Pudd'nhead Wilson* as Fabulation." *Studies in American Humor* 2.1 (April 1975): 21–31.

Gillman, Susan. *Imposture and Identity in Mark Twain's America.* Chicago: University of Chicago Press, 1989.

Gillman, Susan, and Forrest G. Robinson, eds. *Mark Twain's* Pudd'nhead Wilson: *Race, Conflict, and Culture.* Durham (N.C.) and London: Duke University Press, 1990.

• ———. " 'Sure Identifiers': Race, Science, and the Law in *Pudd'nhead Wilson.*" In *Mark Twain's* Pudd'nhead Wilson: *Race Conflict, and Culture.* Ed. Susan Gillman and Forrest G. Robinson. Durham and London: Duke UP, 1990.

Griffith, Clark. "*Pudd'nhead Wilson* as Dark Comedy." *Journal of English Literary History* 43.2 (Summer 1976): 209–26.

Haines, James B. "Of Dogs and Men: A Symbolic Variation on the Twin Motif in *Pudd'nhead Wilson.*" *Mark Twain Journal* 18.3 (Winter 1976–77): 14–17.

Hakutani, Yoshinobu. "Race and Determinism in the Film *Pudd'nhead Wilson.*" In *Motion Pictures and Society.* Ed. Douglas Radcliff-Umstead. Kent: Kent State University Press, 1990.

Harris, Susan K. "Mark Twain's Bad Women." *Studies in American Fiction* 13.2 (Autumn 1985): 157–68.

Hedges, Warren. "If Uncle Tom Is White, Should We Call Him 'Auntie'? Race and Sexuality in Postbellum U.S. Fiction." In *Whiteness: A Critical Reader*. Ed. Mike Hill. New York: New York University Press, 1997.

Hines, Maude Elizabeth. "Making Americans: National Fairy Tales and Fantasies of Transformation, 1865–1900." Dissertation. [*Dissertation Abstracts International*, Section A: The Humanities and Social Sciences 59.8 (February 1999): 2980.]

• Hoffman, Andrew Jay. "*Pudd'nhead Wilson* and the Roots of Existential Heroism." In *Pudd'nhead Wilson and Those Extraordinary Twins*. Ed. Sidney Berger. 2nd ed. New York: Norton, 2005. 371–81.

———. *Twain's Heroes, Twain's Worlds: Mark Twain's* Adventures of Huckleberry Finn, A Connecticut Yankee in King Arthur's Court, *and* Pudd'nhead Wilson. Philadelphia: University of Pennsylvania Press, 1988.

Howe, Lawrence. "Race, Genealogy, and Genre in Mark Twain's *Pudd'nhead Wilson*." *Nineteenth-Century Literature* 46.4 (March 1992): 495–516.

Hughes, Langston. Introduction to *Pudd'nhead Wilson*. New York: Bantam Books, 1964. [Rpt. in *Interracialism: Black-White Intermarriage in American History, Literature, and Law*. Ed. Werner Sollors. Oxford, U.K.: Oxford University Press, 2000.]

Jeffries, William B. "The Montesquiou Case: A Possible Source for Some Incidents in *Pudd'nhead Wilson*." *American Literature* 31 (1959–60): 488–90.

• Jehlen, Myra. "The Ties That Bind: Race and Sex in *Pudd'nhead Wilson*." In *Mark Twain's* Pudd'nhead Wilson: *Race Conflict, and Culture*. Ed. Susan Gillman and Forrest G. Robinson. Durham and London: Duke University Press, 1990.

Kapoor, S. D. "Race and Mark Twain." In *Making Mark Twain Work in the Classroom*. Ed. James S. Leonard. Durham: Duke University Press, 1999.

Kolin, Philip C. "Mark Twain, Aristotle, and Pudd'nhead Wilson." *Mark Twain Journal* 15.2 (Summer 1970): 1–4.

Ladd, Barbara. *Nationalism and the Color Line in George W. Cable, Mark Twain, and William Faulkner*. Baton Rouge: Louisiana State University Press, 1996.

• Leavis, F.R. "Mark Twain's Neglected Classic: The Moral Astringency of *Pudd'nhead Wilson*." *Commentary* 21 (Feb. 1956): 128–36.

Leiter, Louis H. "Dawson's Landing: Thematic Cityscape in Twain's *Pudd'nhead Wilson*." *Mark Twain Journal* 13.1 (Winter 1965–66): 8–11.

Levis, Stuart A. "Pudd'nhead Wilson's Election." *Mark Twain Journal* 15.1 (Winter 1970): 21.

Mandia, Patricia. "Children of Fate and Irony in *Pudd'nhead Wilson*." *The Language Quarterly* 28.3–4 (Summer–Fall 1990): 29–40.

Mann, Carolyn. "Innocence in *Pudd'nhead Wilson*." *Mark Twain Journal* 14.3 (Winter 1968–69): 18–21, 11.

Mann, Karen B. "Pudd'nhead Wilson: One Man or Two?" *Research Studies* 42 (1974): 175–81.

Marcus, George E. " 'What did he reckon would become of the other half if he killed his half?': Doubled, Divided, and Crossed Selves in *Pudd'nhead Wilson*; or, Mark Twain as Cultural Critic in His Own Times and Ours." In *Mark Twain's* Pudd'nhead Wilson: *Race, Conflict, and Culture*. Ed. Susan Gillman and Forrest G. Robinson. Durham and London: Duke University Press, 1990.

• Matson, John. "The Text That Wrote Itself: Identifying the Automated Subject in *Pudd'nhead Wilson and Those Extraordinary Twins*." In *Pudd'nhead Wilson and Those Extraordinary Twins*. Ed. Sidney Berger. 2nd ed. New York: Norton, 2005. 347–71.

McKeithan, Daniel Morley. "The Morgan Manuscript of Mark Twain's *Pudd'nhead Wilson*." In *Essays and Studies on American Language and Literature*, No. 12. Cambridge: Harvard University Press, 1961; Uppsala, Sweden: A.-B. Lundeqvistka Bokhandeln, 1961.

McWilliams, Wilson Carey. "*Pudd'nhead Wilson* on Democratic Governance." In *Mark Twain's* Pudd'nhead Wilson: *Race, Conflict, and Culture*. Ed. Susan Gillman and Forrest G. Robinson. Durham and London: Duke University Press, 1990.

Messent, Peter. "Comic Intentions in Mark Twain's 'A Double-Barreled Detective Story.' " *Essays in Arts and Sciences* 28 (October 1999): 33–51.

———. "Toward the Absurd: Mark Twain's *A Connecticut Yankee, Pudd'nhead Wilson* and *The Great Dark*." In *Mark Twain: A Sumptuous Variety*. Ed. Robert Giddings. Totowa, N.J.: Barnes & Noble, 1985.

Miller, Jim Wayne. "Pudd'nhead Wilson's Calendar." *Mark Twain Journal* 13.3 (Winter 1966–67): 8–10.

• Morris, Linda A. "Beneath the Veil: Clothing, Race, and Gender in Mark Twain's *Pudd'nhead Wilson*." *Studies in American Fiction* 27.1 (1999): 37–52.

Moss, Robert. "Tracing Mark Twain's Intentions: The Retreat from Issues of Race in *Pudd'nhead Wilson*." *American Literary Realism* 30.2 (Winter 1998): 43–55.

Nayak, Kishori. "Ethnic Relations in Mark Twain and Ralph Ellison: A Comparative Study." *Indian Journal of American Studies* 24.2 (Summer 1994): 36–44.

Newman, Judie. "Was Tom White? Stowe's Dred and Twain's Pudd'nhead Wilson." In *Soft Canons: American Women Writers and Masculine Tradition*. Ed. Karen L. Kilcup. Iowa City: University of Iowa Press, 1999.

Newlyn, Andrea K. "Form and Ideology in Transracial Narratives: *Pudd'nhead Wilson* and *A Romance of the Republic.*" *Narrative* 8 (January 2000): 43–65.

Nielsen, A. L. "Mark Twain's *Pudd'nhead Wilson* and the Novel of the Tragic Mulatto." *Greyfriar: Siena Studies in Literature* 26 (1985): 14–30.

O'Connell, Catharine. "Resecting Those Extraordinary Twins: *Pudd'nhead Wilson* and the Costs of 'Killing Half.'" *Nineteenth-Century Literature* 57.1 (June 2002): 100–24.

Oliphant, A. W. "The Whole Dog: A Study of Multiplicity in *Pudd'nhead Wilson.*" *Language and Style* 24.2 (Spring 1991): 145–52.

Parker, Hershel. "*Pudd'nhead Wilson*: Jack-Leg Author, Unreadable Text and Sense-Making Critics." In *Flawed Texts and Verbal Icons: Literary Authority in American Fiction*. Ed. Parker. Evanston: Northwestern University Press, 1984.

Patterson, Mark R. "Surrogacy and Slavery: The Problematics of Consent in *Baby M*, *Romance of Republic*, and *Pudd'nhead Wilson.*" *American Literary History* 8.3 (Fall 1996): 448–70.

Pedersen, Vidar. "Of Slaves and Masters: Constructed Identities in Mark Twain's *Pudd'nhead Wilson*." In *Excursions in Fiction: Essays in Honour of Professor Lars Hartveit on His 70th Birthday*. Ed. Andrew Kennedy and Orm Øverland. Oslo: Novus, 1994.

• Pettit, Arthur G. "The Black and White Curse: *Pudd'nhead Wilson* and Miscegenation." In *Mark Twain and the South*. Lexington: The University Press of Kentucky, 1974.

• Porter, Carolyn. "Roxana's Plot." In *Mark Twain's* Pudd'nhead Wilson: *Race, Conflict, and Culture*. Ed. Susan Gillman and Forrest G. Robinson. Durham and London: Duke University Press, 1990.

Railton, Stephen. "The Tragedy of Mark Twain, by Pudd'nhead Wilson." *Nineteenth-Century Literature* 56.4 (March 2002): 518–44.

Rickard, Kenneth. "Blood on the Margins: Reconstructing Race in Mark Twain's *Pudd'nhead Wilson.*" *Publications of the Arkansas Philological Association* 23.2 (Fall 1997): 65–90.

Robinson, Forrest G. "The Sense of Disorder in *Pudd'nhead Wilson.*" In *Mark Twain's* Pudd'nhead Wilson: *Race, Conflict, and Culture*. Ed. Susan Gillman and Forrest G. Robinson. Durham and London: Duke University Press, 1990.

Rogin, Michael. "Francis Galton and Mark Twain: The Natal Autograph in *Pudd'nhead Wilson.*" In *Mark Twain's* Pudd'nhead Wilson: *Race, Conflict, and Culture*. Ed. Susan Gillman and Forrest G. Robinson. Durham and London: Duke University Press, 1990.

Rose, Marilyn Gaddis. "*Pudd'nhead Wilson*: A Contemporary Parable." *Mark Twain Journal* 13.2 (Summer 1966): 5–7.

Ross, Michael L. "Mark Twain's *Pudd'nhead Wilson*: Dawson's Landing and the Ladder of Nobility." *Novel* 6 (1973):244–56.

• Rowe, John Carlos. "Fatal Speculations: Murder, Money, and Manners in *Pudd'nhead Wilson.*" In *Mark Twain's* Pudd'nhead Wilson: *Race, Conflict, and Culture*. Ed. Susan Gillman and Forrest G. Robinson. Durham and London: Duke University Press, 1990.

Rowe, Katherine Anandi. "The Dead Hand: Fictions of Agency and the Physiology of Possession." Dissertation. [See *Dissertation Abstracts International*, Section A: The Humanities and Social Sciences 53.5 (November 1992): 1510–11.]

Rowlette, Robert. *Twain's* Pudd'nhead Wilson: *The Development and Design*. Bowling Green, Ohio: Bowling Green University Popular Press, 1971.

———. "Mark Twain's *Pudd'nhead Wilson*: Its Themes and Their Development." Thesis, University of Kansas, 1967.

Royal, Derek Parker. "The Clinician As Enslaver: *Pudd'nhead Wilson* and the Rationalization of Identity." *Texas Studies in Literature and Language* 44.4 (Winter 2002): 414–31.

Ryan, Ann Marie. "Missing the Joke: Twain, Freud, and the Fate of Women's Humor." Dissertation. [See *Dissertation Abstracts International*, Section A: The Humanities and Social Sciences 59.7 (February 1999): 2509–10.]

Sachs, Viola. "An Outsider's Conjectures on Mark Twain and Black Culture." *Rivista di Studi Vittoriani* 9.5 (January 2000): 109–22.

Samuels, Shirley. "Miscegenated America: The Civil War." In *National Imaginaries, American Identities: The Cultural Work of American Iconography*. Ed. Larry Reynolds and Gordon Hutner. Princeton: Princeton University Press, 2000.

Schaar, John H. "Some of the Ways of Freedom in *Pudd'nhead Wilson.*" In *Mark Twain's* Pudd'nhead Wilson: *Race, Conflict, and Culture*. Ed. Susan Gillman and Forrest G. Robinson. Durham and London: Duke University Press, 1990.

Schell, Edgar T. "'Pears' and 'Is' in *Pudd'nhead Wilson.*" *Mark Twain Journal* 12.3 (Winter 1964–65): 12–15.

Schleiner, Louise. "Romance Motifs in Three Novels of Mark Twain." *Comparative Literature Studies* 13 (1976): 330–47.

Shell, Marc. "Those Extraordinary Twins." *Arizona Quarterly* 47.2 (Summer 1991): 29–75.

Slote, Benjamin Howell. "Exiling the Sensual Muse: The Literary Career of Mark Twain's Decency." Dissertation [See *Dissertation Abstracts International*, Section A: The Humanities and Social Sciences 52.1 (July 1991): 164.]

Smith, Laura. "Fictive Names in Mark Twain's *Pudd'nhead Wilson*." In *Love and Wrestling, Butch and O.K.* Ed. Fred Tarpley. South Central Names Institute, Publication No. 2. Commerce, Texas: Names Institute Press, 1973.

Sollors, Werner. "Was Roxy Black?: Race as Stereotype in Mark Twain, Edward Windsor Kemble, and Paul Laurence Dunbar." In *Mixed Race Literature*. Ed. Jonathan Brennan. Stanford: Stanford University Press, 2002.

• Spangler, George M. *"Pudd'nhead Wilson*: A Parable of Property." *American Literature* 42 (March 1970): 28–37.

Subrayan, Carmen. "Mark Twain and the Black Challenge." In *Satire or Evasion? Black Perspectives on* Huckleberry Finn. Ed. James S. Leonard, et al. Durham: Duke University Press, 1992.

Sundquist, Eric J. "Mark Twain and Homer Plessy." In *Mark Twain: A Collection of Critical Essays*. Ed. Sundquist. Englewood Cliffs, N.J.: Prentice Hall, 1994. Also in *Mark Twain's* Pudd'nhead Wilson: *Race, Conflict, and Culture*. Ed. Susan Gillman and Forrest G. Robinson. Durham and London: Duke University Press, 1990.

Tabei, Koji. [Another American Tragedy: The Tragedy of *Pudd'nhead Wilson*.] *Seinan Gokuin Daigoku: Eigo Eibungoku Ronshu / Seinan Gokuin University: Studies in English Language and Literature* 30.1–2 (December 1989): 794–818.

Thomas, Brook. "Tragedies of Race, Training, Birth, and Communities of Competent Pudd'nheads." *American Literary History* 1.4 (Winter 1989): 39–55.

Toles, George E. "Mark Twain and *Pudd'nhead Wilson*: A House Divided." In *Mark Twain: An Anthology of Recent Criticism*. Ed. Profulla C. Kar. Delhi: Pencraft, 1992.

• Turner, Arlin. "Mark Twain and the South: An Affair of Love and Honor." *The Southern Review* 4, n.s. (April 1968): 493–519.

Wagenknecht, Edward. ["Development of Plot and Character in *Pudd'nhead Wilson*."] Introduction to *Pudd'nhead Wilson*. Avon, Conn.: The Limited Editions Club, 1974.

Wheelock, C. Webster. "The Point of Pudd'nhead's Half-a-Dog Joke." *American Notes and Queries* 8.10 (June 1970): 150–51.

Whitley, John S. *"Pudd'nhead Wilson*: Mark Twain and the Limits of Detection." *Journal of American Studies* 21.1 (April 1987): 55–70.

Wigger, Anne P. "The Composition of Mark Twain's *Pudd'nhead Wilson* and *Those Extraordinary Twins*: Chronology and Development." *Modern Philology* 55 (November 1957): 93–102.

Wiggins, Robert A. ["The Flawed Structure of *Pudd'nhead Wilson*."] In *Mark Twain: Jackleg Novelist*. Seattle: University of Washington Press, 1964.

Wonham, Henry B. "Getting to the Bottom of *Pudd'nhead Wilson*; Or, A Critical Vision Focused (Too Well?) for Irony." *Arizona Quarterly* 50.3 (Autumn 1994): 111–26.

———. "The Minstrel and the Detective: The Functions of Ethnic Caricature in Mark Twain's Writings of the 1890s." In *Constructing Mark Twain: New Directions in Scholarship*. Ed. Laura E. Skandera-Trombley and Michael J. Kiskis. Columbia: University of Missouri Press, 2001.

• Wood, Barry. "Narrative Action and Structural Symmetry in *Pudd'nhead Wilson*." In *Pudd'nhead Wilson and Those Extraordinary Twins*. Ed. Sidney Berger. 2nd ed. New York: Norton, 2005. 336–47.

Yim, Jin-hee. ["Mark Twain's *Pudd'nhead Wilson*: Fall of American Eden."] *The Journal of English Language and Literature* 39.3 (Fall 1993): 549–67.

ONLINE RESOURCES

As the preface to this edition indicates, thousands of sites on the World Wide Web include material on *Pudd'nhead Wilson* and *Those Extraordinary Twins*. The following, accessed in October 2004, is a good starting point for research. Several sites merely offer the complete texts of the works, drawn from early editions that lack the authority of the present version.

http://etext.lib.virginia.edu/railton/wilson/pwhompg.html

Links include "Sources and Pre-texts," "Twain & Twins," "Advertisement & Promotions," a Facsimile of the first American edition, a complete electronic text of the two stories, "Selected Illustrations," "Contemporary Reviews," *"Pudd'nhead* on Stage," and "Library Attributions."